AN OLIVER STONE FILM

JFK

THE BOOK OF THE FILM

The Story That Won't Go Away

SCREENPLAY BY
OLIVER STONE & ZACHARY SKLAR

Pages

P. 105 to 113 - Meeting in Washington Park - m.
X

P. 162 to — - Power of Sword in War.

P. 533 - — L B J - "get me elected and you can have your damn War."

Study the past...

Past is prologue...

Eternal vigilance is the price of liberty...

JFK
THE BOOK OF THE FILM

The Documented Screenplay

by OLIVER STONE and ZACHARY SKLAR

BASED ON

"ON THE TRAIL OF THE ASSASSINS" BY JIM GARRISON

"CROSSFIRE: THE PLOT THAT KILLED KENNEDY" BY JIM MARRS

PUBLIC SOURCES

OLIVER STONE'S RESEARCH NOTES
COMPILED BY JANE RUSCONI

APPLAUSE
BOOKS

211 WEST 71 STREET • NEW YORK NY • 10023

An Applause Original

JFK: The Book of the Film
A Documented Screenplay

Library of Congress Cataloging-in-Publication Data:

Stone, Oliver.
  JFK: the book of the film / Oliver Stone and Zachary Sklar:
  p. cm. — (The Applause screenplay series)
  ISBN: 1-55783-127-0 (paper)
  ISBN: 1-55783-128-9 (cloth)
  Based on "On the Trail of the Assassins" by Jim Garrison and
  "Crossfire: The Plot That Killed Kennedy" by Jim Marrs and on public
sources."
  Includes bibliographical references.
  1. Kennedy, John F. (John Fitzgerald), 1917-1963 —Assassination.
I. Sklar, Zachary, II. Garrison, Jim, 1921- On the Trail of the
Assassins. III. Marrs, Jim. Crossfire: The Plot That Killed Kennedy. IV.
Title. V. Series.
PN1997.J447 1992
791.43'72—dc20
                                        91-45606
                                        CIP

APPLAUSE BOOKS
211 West 71st Street
New York, NY 10023
Phone: 212-595-4735 Fax: 212-721-2856

First Applause Printing, 1992

The publisher wishes to commend Data Reproductions for their valiant service in the printing of this volume.

CONTENTS

I. JFK: The Documented Screenplay
Screenplay with historical annotations.

II. The JFK Debate
Reactions and Commentaries

III. Historical Documents

IV. Credits

RESEARCH NOTES:

Actual dialogue, testimony, facts and exhibits are used throughout the screenplay. This research is referenced to various documents as follows:
[WC 4H, p. 161.]
See abbreviations below.

More detailed notes are presented as follows:
■ David Ferrie fired from Eastern Airlines: [HSCA X. p. 108.] Milton E. Brener notes that many Eastern pilots refused to fly with Ferrie because he was "physically filthy,"[Brener, *The Garrison Case: A Study in the Abuse of Power* p.46; Philip H. Melanson, *Spy Saga: Lee Harvey Oswald and U.S. Intelligence*, (Praeger, 1990), p. 39].

ABBREVIATIONS:

WC: **Warren Commission Hearings and Exhibits**
November 23, 1964 - 26 Volumes [The 26 volumes are officially *Hearings Before the President's Commission on the Assassination of President Kennedy.*]

WC 6H, p. 20 - Citations from the *testimony* (Volumes 1-15) are referred to by volume and page

WC 16H CE 12, p. 20 - Citations from *exhibits* (Volumes 16-26) are referred to by volume, exhibit number and page number, if necessary

WR: **Warren Commission Report - September 24, 1964**
[The official name of the Warren Commission is *The President's Commission on the Assassination of President Kennedy.*]

CD: **Warren Commission Document**
The Commission Documents are Commission materials that, for no apparent reason, were not included in the Commission's 26 volumes. Instead, they were deposited at the National Archives and sealed for 75 years. Since 1964, all but two dozen of the CDs have been declassified.

HSCA Report : Report of the House Select Committee on Assassinations - March 29, 1979 - 12 Volumes

HSCA X. p. 20 - Citations from the hearings are referred to by volume and page number

Church Committee: We use the popular name—the Church Committee (named for chairman Sen. Frank Church)—for citations from the 1975 Interim Report of the Select Committee to Study Governmental Operations with Respect to Intelligence Activities, United States Senate —*Alleged Assassination Plots Against Foreign Leaders.*

The following film is based on the investigation of District Attorney Jim Garrison of New Orleans into the mystery of President Kennedy's murder. It includes information gathered from public sources and from the private investigations of the JFK research community. Deep thanks go to them for their unceasing public-minded efforts.

Most of the characters are real; a few are composites based on real people. Certain events are speculations on what might have happened. In some cases the names have been changed to protect both the innocent and the guilty.

The screenplay is the original source from which the filmmakers worked. It is not the final film. Certain scenes in this screen play have been cut and some have been transposed to other places in the film.

— O.S.

JFK

The Documented Screenplay

To sin by silence while others doth protest makes cowards out of men.
                                    --Ella Wheeler Wilcox

Credits run in counterpoint through a 7 to 10 minute sequence of documentary images setting the tone of John F. Kennedy's Presidency and the atmosphere of those tense times, 1960 through 1963. An omniscient narrator's voice marches us through in old-time Pathé newsreel fashion:

VOICE 1 January, 1961—President Dwight D. Eisenhower's Farewell Address to the Nation—

EISENHOWER ADDRESS

EISENHOWER ... The conjunction of an immense military establishment and a large arms industry is new in the American experience. The total influence—economic, political, even spiritual—is felt in every city, every statehouse, every office of the Federal Government ... In the councils of government we must guard against the acquisition of unwarranted influence, whether sought or unsought, by the military industrial complex. The potential for the disastrous rise of misplaced power exists and will persist ... We must never let the weight of this combination endanger our liberties or democratic processes. We should take nothing for granted ...

> ∎ Eisenhower's Farewell Address: January 17, 1961 [The Public Papers of President Dwight D. Eisenhower, 1960-61 (U.S. Government Printing Office).] The speech coins the phrase "military-industrial complex."

ELECTION IMAGERY

Schoolkids reciting the Pledge of Allegiance. WPA films of farmers harvesting the Texas plains. Rain, thunderheads, a dusty car coming from far away on a road moving towards Dallas. Cowboys round up the cattle. Young marrieds in a church. Hillsides of tract homes going up. The American breadbasket, the West. Over this we hear Eisenhower's address. As we move into the election campaign of 1960, we see the TV debates, Nixon vs. Kennedy, Mayor Daley, Kennedy victorious ...

Against this is juxtaposed other forces: segregation, J. Edgar Hoover, military advisors, Castro, Marilyn Monroe, Lumumba ... three frames of the Zapruder film counter-cut ... ending with the Kennedy inauguration and the irony of Earl Warren administering the oath as he will Kennedy's eulogy.

VOICE 2 November, 1960—Senator John F. Kennedy of Massachusetts wins one of the narrowest election victories in American history over the Vice-President Richard Nixon by a little more than 100,000 votes. Rumors abound that he *stole* the election in Illinois through the Democratic political machine of Mayor Daley ... (*inauguration shots*) At his inauguration, at a time when American males all wore hats, he let his hair blow free in the wind. Alongside his beautiful and elegant wife of French origin, Jacqueline Bouvier, J.F.K. is the symbol of the new freedom of the 1960s, signifying change and upheaval to the American public, scaring many and hated passionately by some. To win the election and to appease their fears, Kennedy at first takes a tough Cold War stance.

■ 1960 election: J.F.K.'s margin of victory: [David Wallechinsky and Irving Wallace, *The People's Almanac* (Doubleday, 1975), p. 313.]

■ Mayor Daley rumors: [George Michael Evica, *And We Are All Mortal* (University of Hartford, 1978), p. 155.]

BAY OF PIGS IMAGERY

The beach, the bombardment, the rounding up of prisoners, Kennedy's public apology, Allen Dulles standing next to J.F.K., both uncomfortable with the small talk ...

VOICE 3 He inherits a secret war against the Communist Castro dictatorship in Cuba, a war run by the CIA and angry Cuban exiles out of bases in the Southern United States, Panama, Nicaragua and Guatemala. Castro is a successful revolutionary frightening to American business interests in Latin America—companies like Cabot's United Fruit, Continental Can, and Rockefeller's Standard Oil. This war culminates in the disastrous Bay of Pigs invasion in April 1961 when Kennedy refuses to provide air cover for the exile brigade. Of the 1600 men who invade, 114 are killed, 1200 are captured. The Cuban exiles and the CIA are furious at Kennedy's irresolution ... Kennedy, taking public responsibility for the failure, privately claims the CIA lied to him and tried to manipulate him into ordering an all-out American invasion of Cuba. He vows to splinter the CIA into a thousand pieces and fires Director Allen Dulles, Deputies Charles Cabell and Richard Bissell, the top leadership of the Agency.

■ Secret war against Cuba: J.F.K. takes blame for Bay of Pigs, April 22, 1963. He reiterated that he bore sole responsibility in a White House Statement on the following Monday: "The President is strongly opposed to anyone within or without the administration attempting to shift the blame." [Arthur Schlesinger, *A Thousand Days* (Houghton Mifflin, 1965), p. 290.]

■ "splinter into a thousand pieces": [*The New York Times*, April 23, 1966.]

■ Kennedy fires Dulles, Cabell, Bissell: [Warren Hinckle and William W. Turner, *The Fish Is Red* (Harper & Row, 1981), p. 112.]

SECRET WAR IMAGERY

Cuban rallies, footage of training camps, espionage activities, boats, cases of weapons, Robert Kennedy ... John Roselli, Sam Giancana, Santos Trafficante, Richard Helms (the new CIA chief), Bill Harvey, head of ZR/RIFLE, Howard Hunt ...

VOICE 4 ... The CIA, however, continues its secret war on Castro with dozens of sabotage and assassination attempts under its ZR/RIFLE and MONGOOSE programs—The Agency collaborates with organized crime elements such as John Roselli, Sam Giancana, and Santos Trafficante of Tampa, whose casino operations in Cuba, worth more than a hundred million dollars a year in income, Castro has shut down.

■ ZR/RIFLE: [Church Committee, Alleged Assassination Plots Involving Foreign Leaders (U.S. Government Printing Office, 1975), p. 181-190.] ZR/RIFLE was formulated sometime in "early 1961," the date has never been determined, and was headed by CIA officer William Harvey. The program's objective was to establish an "executive action capability." [Also see David C. Martin, *A Wilderness of Mirrors* (Harper & Row, 1980), p. 120-124; Evica, *And We Are All ...*, p. 254-259.]

■ MONGOOSE: President Kennedy issued a memo announcing the MON-GOOSE program on November 30, 1961. Gen. Edward G. Lansdale functioned as Chief of Operations and within a few months, William Harvey took charge of the CIA's Task Force W, the CIA unit for Mongoose operations. In 1975-76 the Church Committee questioned all the principal players and found that the program was never explicitly sanctioned by the Kennedy White House. In fact several former Kennedy Administration officials flatly denied ever authorizing the program. [Church Committee, Alleged Assassination Plots ... , p. 134-179.]

■ CIA/Mafia collaboration: [Church Committee, Alleged Assassination Plots Against Foreign Leaders, p.71-89; Hinckle and Turner, *The Fish is Red*, p. 23-60; Charles Rappleye and Ed Becker, *American Mafioso: The Johnny Roselli Story* (Doubleday, 1991), p.175-227; John H. Davis, *Mafia Kingfish: Carlos Marcello and the Assassination of John F. Kennedy* (Signet, 1989), p. 96-99, 402-407; Robert Sam Anson, *They've Killed the President!* (Bantam, 1975), p. 305-331; Evica, *And We Are All ...*, p. 192-244; David Scheim, *Contract on America: The Mafia Murders of John and Robert Kennedy*, (Shapolsky, 1989).]

CUBAN MISSILE CRISIS

Khrushchev, Kennedy, Castro on television, meetings with Cabinet, Russian vessels in Caribbean, U.S. nuclear bases on alert, civilians going to underground safe areas ... the Russian ship turning around, the country smiling ...

VOICE 5 In October 1962, the world comes to the brink of nuclear war when Kennedy quarantines Cuba after announcing the presence of offensive Soviet nuclear missiles 90 miles off American shores. The Joint Chiefs of Staff and the CIA call for an invasion. Kennedy refuses. Soviet ships with more missiles sail towards the island, but at the last moment turn back. The world breathes with relief but backstage in Washington, rumors abound that J.F.K. has cut a secret deal with Russian Premier Khrushchev not to invade Cuba in return for a Russian withdrawal of missiles. Suspicions abound that Kennedy is "soft on Communism."

■ Cuban Missile Crisis: Joint Chiefs and CIA pressure to invade: [Robert F. Kennedy, *Thirteen Days: A Memoir of the Cuban Missile Crisis* (Norton, 1968).]

■ Secret deal not to invade Cuba: On November 20, 1962, J.F.K. delivered a statement on Cuba announcing the impending Soviet withdrawal of missiles from the island. In discussing the Accord reached with the Soviets, Kennedy said that once the missiles were definitively removed, we would "give assurances against invasion of Cuba." He went on to add that the US "shall neither initiate nor permit aggression in this hemisphere."

■ To appease the anger of the Cuban exile community, Kennedy promised to continue Washington's efforts against Castro: "We will not, of course, abandon the political, economic and other efforts of this Hemisphere to halt subversion from Cuba nor our purpose and hope that the Cuban people shall someday be truly free. But these policies are very different from any intent to launch a military invasion of the island."

NUCLEAR TEST BAN IMAGERY

Closing down Cuban Camps, McNamara speaking, Khrushchev and Kennedy, the "hot line" telephone system inaugurated, Kennedy with Jackie and children sailing off Cape Cod ... Vietnam introduction, early shots, Green Berets, counterinsurgency programs, Ed Lansdale, leading up to the Test Ban signings ... then J.F.K. at American University, June 10, 1963.

VOICE 6 ... In the ensuing months, Kennedy clamps down on Cuban exile activities, closing training camps, restricting covert operations, prohibiting shipment of weapons out of the country. The covert arm of the CIA nevertheless continues its plan to assassinate Castro ... In March '63, Kennedy announces drastic cuts in the defense budget. In November 1963, he orders the withdrawal by Christmas of the first 1,000 troops of the 16,000 stationed in Vietnam. He tells several of his intimates that he will withdraw all Vietnam troops after the '64 election, saying to the Assistant Secretary of State, Roger Hilsman, "The Bay of Pigs has taught me one, not to trust generals or the CIA, and two, that if the American people do not want to use American troops to remove a Communist regime 90 miles from our coast, how can I ask them to use troops to remove a Communist regime 9,000 miles away?" ... Finally, in August 1963, over the objections of the Joint Chiefs of Staff, the United States, Great Britain and the Soviet Union sign a treaty banning nuclear bomb tests in the atmosphere, underwater and in space ... Early that fateful summer, Kennedy speaks of his new vision at American University in Washington.

■ Clampdown on Cuban exile activities: [Hinckle and Turner, *The Fish Is Red*, p. 156-158; Martin, *Wilderness of Mirrors*, p. 141-145.] In the immediate fall-out of the Missile Crisis, William Harvey was dismissed from his post in charge of the CIA's anti-Castro operations. In anticipation of an invasion, Harvey had ordered ten exile commando teams to Cuban waters, ready with beacons and flares to act as a guide for the invading force. Purely by chance, Robert Kennedy learned of Harvey's "preparations" and was furious.

■ Defense budget cuts: On March 30, 1963 Secretary of Defense Robert S. McNamara announced a plan to close 52 domestic and 22 overseas bases over the next three years. [Marrs, *Crossfire*, p. 302.]

■ Withdrawal of 1,000 troops from Vietnam: National Security Action Memorandum 263, a top secret directive (see Appendix); implemented the first adviser withdrawal from Vietnam. [See John M. Newman, *J.F.K. and Vietnam* (Warner Books, 1991), p. 407-412.]

■ Kennedy tells several of his intimates: These "intimates" included Senators Mike Mansfield and Wayne Morse, Assistant Secretary of State Roger Hilsman, House Speaker Tip O'Neill and aide Kenny O'Donnell. [Kenny O'Donnell, *Johnny We Hardly Knew Ye*, (Pocket Books, 1973), p. 18; Tip O'Neill, *Man of the House* (Random House, 1987), p. 175-176; also see: Roger Hilsman, letter to *The New York Times*, January 20, 1992; Arthur Schlesinger, Jr., *R.F.K. and His Times*, Chapter 19, "The Vietnam Legacy" (Houghton Mifflin, 1973), p. 734-756)]

■ Nuclear Test Ban Treaty: [Schlesinger, *A Thousand Days*, p. 893-913.]

J.F.K. What kind of peace do we seek? Not a pax Americana enforced on the world by American weapons of war ... we must reexamine our own attitudes towards the Soviet Union ... If we cannot now end our differences at least we can help make the world safe for diversity. For, in the final analysis, our most basic link is that we all inhabit this small planet. We all breathe the same air. We all cherish our children's future. And we are all mortal ...

■ American University speech: June 10, 1963, full text printed in the Public Papers of President John F. Kennedy, 1963. Schlesinger notes J.F.K.'s disappointment in public reaction to the speech, which the President considered a "major statement on peace." In the week following the address, he received a total of 50,010 letters—but only 896 concerned with the American University speech. Of that total, only 25 were hostile. An impending freight rate bill provoked 28,232 letters in the same period. [Schlesinger, *A Thousand Days*, p. 910.]

CONCLUDING KENNEDY IMAGERY

Diplomats at the United Nations ... Adlai Stevenson, Castro ... Martin Luther King and the March on Washington (a snatch of his "I Have a Dream" speech) ... Bobby Kennedy and Jimmy Hoffa going at it ... U.S. Steel Chairman's remarks in the steel face-off, men going to courtrooms with briefcases, ... Teddy Kennedy, Rose, Joe, the Kennedy family, all teeth and good looks ... and of course John campaigning, always campaigning, shaking hands, smiling, that supremely warm smile and sense of grace and ability to convey to crowds their oneness with him ... forever ... culminating in the more specific Texas shots ... with Jackie in San Antonio, and Houston ... then at Fort Worth ... then at Love Field moving through the clouds toward the Dallas/Forth Worth plain which suddenly breaks into view as we descend ...

■ Robert Kennedy and Jimmy Hoffa: [Robert F. Kennedy, *The Enemy Within* (Harper & Row, 1960), p. 36-117; Walter Sheridan, *The Rise and Fall of Jimmy Hoffa* (Saturday Review Press, 1973); Evica, *And We Are All ...*, p. 219-236.]

■ U.S. Steel face-off: [Schlesinger, *A Thousand Days*, p. 634-40.]

LOUISIANA HIGHWAY - DAY (1963)

A moving car carrying two Cuban males disgorges a rumpled, screaming woman, Rose Cheramie, a whore in her thirties, lying there bleeding in the dirt. The car drives off.

■ Rose Cheramie: [HSCA X. p. 197-205; New Orleans District Attorney Records; Louisiana State Police Memo from Lt. Francis Fruge, 4/4/67.] Cheramie, a woman with a history of drug addiction and prostitution, also furnished useful drug trafficking information on several occasions for the FBI. Lt. Fruge, who picked up Cheramie on November 20, 1963 and later brought her to the hospital, told the HSCA that he called the Dallas police after the assassination to report the Cheramie story but was told that the police were not interested. While searching for leads in Louisiana, Jim Garrison came across the Cheramie incident and investigated it further.

HOSPITAL - DAY (1963)

We see Rose, badly cut but quite lucid, trying to reason with a policeman, Lt. Fruge, and a doctor—in a remote black-and-white documentary.

ROSE ... They're going up to Dallas ... to whack Kennedy. Friday the 22nd, that's when they're going to do it. In Dealey Plaza. They're gonna whack him! You gotta call somebody, these are serious fuckin' guys!

DOCTOR (*to the police officer*) Higher 'n a kite on something. Been like this since she came in.

> ▌Corroboration of Cheramie's story turns up in a Feb. 1, 1967 article in the Madison, WI, *Capital Times*. A doctor, Wayne Owen, reports having treated three men at a Louisiana hospital on Nov. 19, 1963 for injuries sustained in a car accident. During the course of their treatment, one man told Owen and 10 other interns that he knew about a "plot to kill Jack Kennedy" involving "Jack Rubenstein," among others. [HSCA X. p. 197-205; New Orleans District Attorney Records; Louisiana State Police Memo from Lt. Francis Fruge dated April 4, 1967.]

BACK TO DOCUMENTARY IMAGES

We see the last close-ups of Kennedy shaking hands on the tarmac at Love Field, smiling, into the motorcade ... the downtown streets of Dallas, people packing the sidewalks clear back to the buildings, hanging out of windows ten stories up, schoolgirls surging out into the street in front of the car. The President is wildly popular—except for the occasional posters calling for his arrest for treason ...

VOICE 7 More rumors emerge of J.F.K.'s backdoor efforts outside usual State Department and CIA channels to establish dialogue with Fidel Castro through contacts at the United Nations in New York. Kennedy is seeking change on all fronts. Bitter battles are fought with Southern segregationists to get James Meredith into the University of Mississippi. Three months after Kennedy submits a sweeping civil rights bill to Congress, Martin Luther King leads 250,000 in a march on Washington. Robert Kennedy, as Attorney General, for the first time ever vigorously prosecutes the Mafia in American life, bringing and winning a record number of cases—288 convictions of organized crime figures (only 35 were made in 1960) including 13 grand juries against Jimmy Hoffa and his Teamsters Union. The President also takes on Big Business, forcing back steel prices, winning 45 of 46 antitrust cases during 1963 and he wants to help everyday taxpayers by ending age-old business privileges like the oil depletion allowance and the fees paid to the Federal Reserve Bank for printing America's currency. Revolutionary changes are foreseen after J.F.K.'s assumed reelection in 1964. Foremost in the political consciousness of the country is the possibility of a Kennedy dynasty. Robert Kennedy in '68, Teddy Kennedy in '76. In November, 1963 John Kennedy travels to Texas, his popularity sagging to 59% largely due to his civil rights stand for which he is particularly hated in the South. Texas is a crucial state for him to carry in '64. With him is Vice-President, Texan Lyndon Johnson and Texas Governor John Connally. On

November 21, they visit Houston and San Antonio. On the morning of November 22, he speaks in Fort Worth, then flies 15 minutes to Love Field in Dallas, where he takes a motorcade through downtown Dallas on his way to speak at 12:30 at the International Trade Mart. Later, the motorcade takes him through Dealey Plaza at 12:30 ... *(a beat)*

▌Oil depletion allowance: [Marrs, *Crossfire*, p.277.] Jim Garrison saw Kennedy's oil policy as a possible motive for his murder. And as far as Texans are concerned, Kennedy left no doubt that he was headed directly for the 27 1/2% deduction that is something very dear to some people in Texas [quoted in Milton E. Brener, *The Garrison Case: A Study in the Abuse of Power*, (Potter, 1969), p. 222.]

▌Backdoor negotiations with Cuba [Church Committee, Alleged Assassination Plots..., p. 173-174.] Ambassador William Attwood told the Committee that in the fall of 1963, he had several meetings with the Cuban Ambassador to the United Nations to discuss the prospects for re-establishing U.S.-Cuba relations.

▌James Meredith: [Schlesinger, *A Thousand Days*, p. 940-947.]

▌Submits civil rights bill to Congress: June 19, 1963. [Schlesinger, *A Thousand Days*, p. 967, 968-973.]

▌R.F.K. vs. organized crime: [Robert F. Kennedy, *The Enemy Within*] recounts the McClellan Committee Hearings, for which Kennedy served as Chief Counsel from 1957-1959. Also see sources for CIA-Mafia plots (p.3) and R.F.K. vs. Jimmy Hoffa (p.5).

▌Takes on big business: [Marrs, p.275] On June 4, 1963, Kennedy signed Executive Order 11,110, which called for issuance of $4 billion in notes through the U.S. Treasury rather than through the Federal Reserve System.

▌J.F.K.'s trip to Texas: [Schlesinger, *A Thousand Days*, p. 1019-1023.]

DEALEY PLAZA - THAT DAY (NOV. 22, 1963)

We see a massive overhead shot of the Plaza as it lay then. Credits conclude under shot—and we have the subtitle "November 22, 1963."

A young epileptic screams and suddenly collapses near the fountains in front of the Texas School Book Depository. He has a violent epileptic fit that attracts surrounding attention. Dallas policemen run over to him. We hear the siren of an ambulance roaring up.

TIMECUT TO ambulance loading the epileptic man and taking off.

▌[Marrs, *Crossfire*, p. 42-44; Jerry Rose, "The Epileptic Seizure," *The Continuing Inquiry*, Penn Jones, Jr., ed. (The Midlothian Press), Feb. 22, 1984, p. 8-22.]

AMBULANCE VOICE We are en route to Parkland.

▌Peter Dale Scott notes in *The Dallas Conspiracy* [unpubl. manuscript, I, p. 8-10] that the Dallas Police radio transcript contains the instructions to "cut all traffic for the ambulance going to Parkland," [23H p. 841] effectively sealing off any possible exits out of Dealey Plaza save for the designated motorcade route to Stemmons Freeway. He also remarks that the seizure occurred at precisely the time the pilot car—containing an Army Intelligence Reserve officer and the local Army Reserve commander—reached the Houston Street fountain. Another witness to the seizure was Army Intelligence agent James W. Powell, in Dealey Plaza for still-unknown reasons [CD p. 206, 19-20]. Powell took at least one photograph of the Texas School Book Depository near the time of the shooting and minutes later was "trapped" inside the building when it was sealed off [CD p. 354].

▌Ambulance driver Aubrey Rike told us that his ambulance had been called to Dealey Plaza several times on false alarms in the weeks preceding the Presidential visit. The calls were all mid-day and asked for an ambulance "in front of the fountain," the site of the seizure. Rike says it later occurred to him that someone could have been timing their trip to Dealey.

BACK TO a montage of the shooting. We see Kennedy, in the last seconds, waving, turning the corner at Houston from Main ... We see TV footage and a piece of Zapruder film from before the shooting; fragmented images ...

CUT TO staged shots of crowd people looking on. The images are grainy to match the tone of the Zapruder film. People are on rooftops, hollering. The crowd is wild with enthusiasm. We pan past Jack Ruby and slam into him in black-and-white. The camera shows a Cuban man with a radio; a man with an umbrella; subliminals. Through open windows on the fifth floor of the Criminal Courts Building, convicts watch and holler from their jail cells. We see the sixth floor of the Texas Book Depository with open windows and a vague blur of a figure and a rifle. The clock on the Hertz sign reads 12:30.

VOICE We'll be there in about five minutes ...

A motorcycle officer paralleling the Kennedy car tries to use his radio. It's jammed. The sound of the jammed Dictabelt drives the rest of the sequence.

▌A copy of the Dictabelt fell into the hands of Dallas archivist Mary Ferrell. She presented the tape to the HSCA, resulting in the last-minute acoustics analysis that led to the conclusion that there was a 95% certainty of a Grassy Knoll shot and therefore, a second gunman. [HSCA Report, p. 65-93]

▌In 1981, the Justice Department announced that a panel of experts from the National Academy of Sciences ruled in a new analysis that the HSCA panel's findings of a fourth shot were incorrect. The NAS group found that Sheriff Bill Decker's voice could be heard on the Dictabelt, ordering his men into the railroad yard, at the same time as the sound impulses that the HSCA claimed were gunshots occurred. Thus, the NAS concluded, the sound impulses were not gunshots in Dealey Plaza after all.

However, the NAS findings are valid only if the Dictabelt recording they analyzed was the original and if the needle that recorded the acoustic information in the 1963 Dictabelt system did not jump back (as it often did) during the recording of these events. The NAS did not check for either of these criteria. Researcher Gary Mack did—and confirmed the presence of two "hum tones," which are produced in the dubbing process on the Dictabelt tape, indicating that it is, indeed, a duplicate rather than the original. [See Summers, *Conspiracy*, p. 474-475, and sources; conversation with Gary Mack, 1991.]

We see Zapruder, a short middle-aged man, shooting his 8 mm film from the Grassy Knoll, and then we see Jackie Kennedy—floating on film, her voice, high, soft:

JACKIE KENNEDY (*voice restaged*) And in the motorcade, you know I usually would be waving mostly to the left side and he was waving mostly to the right, which is one reason you're not looking at each other very much. And it was terribly hot. Just blinding all of us ... We could see a tunnel in front of us. Everything was really slow then. And I remember thinking it would be so cool under that tunnel ... [WC 5H p. 179.]

The camera rests on Jackie for a beat, and then we see the shot of the little schoolgirl skipping on the grass.

CUT TO the approaching overpass. J.F.K. waves ... Mrs. Connally turns to J.F.K.. The shot is crazy, fractured, surreal.

MRS. CONNALLY (*voice-over*) Mr. President, you can't say that Dallas doesn't love you. [WC 4H p. 179.]

JFK (*voice-over*) No, you certainly can't.

Then we hear the shots: the volley sounds like a motorcycle backfire. We catch a glimpse of a muzzle flash and smoke. We see a view from the street of the Texas School Book Depository—all in line with the "official" version of events. Pigeons by the hundreds suddenly shoot off the roof. Then the screen (our screen) goes gray as did CBS TV's first bulletins to the country.

CBS BULLETIN (*full screen*) ... We interrupt this program to bring you this flash bulletin. A burst of gunfire! Three bursts of gunfire, apparently from automatic weapons, were fired at President Kennedy's motorcade in downtown Dallas.

We hear voices under this from everywhere, colliding in confusion and horror:

VOICES OH NO! MY GOD THEY'RE GOING TO KILL US ALL! Be still. You're going to be all right. LET'S GET OUT OF HERE. WE'RE HIT! LAWSON, THIS IS KELLERMAN. WE ARE HIT. GET US TO THE HOSPITAL IMMEDIATELY. PULL OUT OF THE MOTORCADE. TAKE US TO THE NEAREST HOSPITAL.

    ▮ "They're going to kill us all!": John Connally. [WC 4H p. 133.]

    ▮ "We're hit! Lawson, this is Kellerman ... ": Secret Service Agent Roy Kellerman to Secret Service Agent Winston G. Lawson [WC 2H p. 73-74.]

JACKIE KENNEDY VOICE Oh, no, they've shot Jack ... I love you, Jack ... Jack ... they've killed my husband ...

CBS BULLETIN (*voice-over*) ... The first reports say that President Kennedy has been seriously wounded by the shooting. More details just arrived. United Press say the wounds to President Kennedy perhaps could be fatal. Repeating: President Kennedy has been shot by a would-be assassin in Dallas. Three bursts of gunfire, apparently from automatic weapons ...

VOICES (*blending under*) IT CAME FROM THERE. SECURE THAT AREA BEHIND THE FENCE. IT'S THAT BUILDING UP THERE.

▌ "Secure that area behind the fence": Dallas Sheriff Bill Decker [WC 19H, Decker Exhibit 5323, p.2.]; Dallas Police Chief Jesse Curry [WC 4H, p. 16.1.] Both local law enforcement groups—sheriffs and police—immediately sent their men to the Grassy Knoll area.

We hear sirens and screeching tires. The screen is still gray, randomly intercut with the end of the Nix film showing the car escaping. There are wildly tracking shots of the crowd running towards the Grassy Knoll. The camera pans up the little set of stairs. We see more faces. Someone in a suit stops our camera. Secret Service?

We see the briefest glimpse from the Zapruder film. The camera moves in on the open umbrella next, then to the freeway sign, then to Mrs. Kennedy out of the car reaching for help, then to the agent rushing onto the rear fender. The car finally speeds away. The people on the other side of the underpass wave at the oncoming hearse from hell. (These are fragmented, mystifying shots. The main effect is one of blackout—of not knowing; of being in the dark, as we all were back then.)

▌ Jackie climbing out of the car: Contrary to popular rumor (and a famous routine by comedian Lenny Bruce), Mrs. Kennedy was not trying to escape the crossfire, but apparently retrieving a fragment of bone and brain tissue on the trunk of the car. She turned the fragment over to Dr. Marion Jenkins at Parkland Hospital. [Conversation with Dr. Marion Jenkins, April 1991]

▌ Agent climbing onto car: Special Agent Clint Hill of the Secret Service was the only one in the follow-up car to react with speed. Riding to Parkland in the back seat of the limousine, Hill noticed that the "right rear portion of his (Kennedy's) head was missing." [CE1024]

CUT TO JIM GARRISON'S OFFICE - NEW ORLEANS - SAME DAY (1963)

Pause. The lovely old china clock on the wall reads 12:35. Somewhere a car backfires. We see a close-up of the clock moving to 12:36. We hear the sound of a pen on paper, scratching ... We see a shot of Jim Garrison as a young air pilot in World War II; hear the sound of airplanes. The camera moves to framed photos of Jim as a young, Lincolnesque lawyer ... we hear sounds of political rallies, cheering ... a shot of Jim's grandfather shaking hands with President William Taft. The sound of bulldozers carries us to a shot of Jim staring at piles of decaying corpses at Dachau ... a photo of Clarence Darrow ... a law degree and an appointment as District Attorney of the New Orleans Parish ... Mother Garrison with young Jim on the desk ... another family—his own. We look across the thick desk with the chess set, A Complete Works of William Shakespeare *and a Nazi helmet with a bullet hole in it ... to Jim himself writing—pen to paper. We sense the quiet intellect of the 43-year-old man. The clock ticks in the awful suspended silence. It's as if the air itself has been sucked from the silent room. This is the last moment of peace before the World will rush through the door in all its sound and fury—to change his life forever. The camera haywires into a close-up of Jim as he looks up ... and knows.*

Lou Ivon, Jim's chief investigator, is already standing there in the room. He is burly, in his 30s—his expression universal for that day.

> ■ Lou Ivon: Lou Ivon, Garrison's investigator, was not with the District Attorney's office in 1963. An assistant DA named Frank Klein originally told Garrison the news of the assassination [*Trail of the Assassins*, p. 3-4]. Because Klein resigned from the office over a personal dispute in early 1967 [*Trail of the Assassins*, p. 128-129] and because Ivon figures so strongly in the office's investigation of the assassination, we introduced Ivon in this scene.

JIM What's wrong, Lou?

LOU Boss, the President's been shot. In Dallas. Five minutes ago.

Jim is stunned. His look of horror and shock speaks the same language as on faces all across America that Black Friday.

JIM Oh no! ... How bad?

LOU No word yet. But they think it's in the head.

Jim gets up, heading rapidly for the door.

JIM Come on. Napoleon's has a TV set.

NAPOLEON'S RESTAURANT - THE QUARTER - DAY (1963)

The midday customers all stare solemnly at the TV set high in the corner of the café. The manager, ashen, serves drinks to Jim and Lou.

> ■ The real Jim Garrison and Frank Klein watched the news at Tortorich's, not Napoleon's, and, lest we misguide any visitors to New Orleans, Napoleon's does *not* have a television.

NEWSMAN 1... apparently three bullets were found. Governor Connally also appeared to be hit. The President was rushed by the Secret Service to Parkland Memorial Hospital four miles from Dealey Plaza. We are told a bullet entered the base of the throat and came out of the backside, but there is no confirmation, blood transfusions are being given, a priest has administered the last rites.

> ■ "entered the base of the throat": CBS News broadcast Nov. 22, 1963, reported by correspondent Dan Rather.

JIM There's still a chance, dammit! Come on, Jack—pull through.

MANAGER (*Italian, distracted*) I don't believe it. I don't believe it. Here, in this country.

They all look up, expectant, as Walter Cronkite interrupts on the TV:

WALTER CRONKITE From Dallas, Texas—the flash apparently official, President Kennedy died at 1 P.M. Central Standard Time, 2 o'clock Eastern Standard Time, some 38 minutes ago. (*choked pause*) Vice-President Johnson has left the hospital in Dallas, but we do not know to where he has proceeded. Presumably, he will be taking the oath of office shortly, and become the 36th President of the United States. [CBS News broadcast, 2:38 EST Nov. 22, 1963.]

There are sounds of shock, muttering, some sobbing in the restaurant. Lou gulps down his drink. Jim sits stunned.

JIM I didn't always agree with him—too liberal for my tastes—but I respected him. He had style ... God, I'm ashamed to be an American today.

He holds back the tears. The food comes. Lou waves it off. They just sit there.

EXTERIOR KATZENJAMMER'S BAR - CAMP STREET - SAME DAY (1963)

Katzenjammer's is an Irish working class bar across Canal St. in a seedy area near the Mississippi River, just off Lafayette Square.

INTERIOR KATZENJAMMER'S BAR - SAME DAY (1963)

A variety of loud Irish working men sit on stools watching the TV. There are a few formica tables with chairs against the walls, and an unused pool table.

NEWSMAN 2 Many arrests have been made here today. Anyone looking even remotely suspicious is being detained. Most of the crowd has gone home but there are still many stunned people wandering around in Dealey Plaza unable to comprehend what happened here earlier today.

> ▌At least a dozen people were arrested in Dealey Plaza immediately after the shooting (cf. notes p. 167).

On the TV, we see the scene at Dealey Plaza. The reporter has several men, women and children gathered around him. He puts his microphone in their faces.

BLACK WOMAN (*crying*) It's all so terrible. I jes' can't stop crying. He did so much for this country, for colored people. Why?

MAN (*Bill Newman, with wife and kids*) I grabbed my kids and wife and hit the ground. The bullets were coming over our heads—from that fence back on the knoll—I was just so shaken. I saw his face when it hit ... he just, his ear flew off, he turned just real white and then went stiff like a board and flopped over on his stomach, with his foot sticking out, he ... (*breaks down*) [WFAA-TV News footage Nov. 22, 1963.]

CUT TO the picket fence above the Grassy Knoll.

WOMAN 2 I thought ... it came from up there, that building.

CUT TO the Book Depository.

MAN 2 I heard shots from over there.

CUT TO the County Records Building.

NEWSMAN 2 How many shots?

WOMAN 3 About 3 to 4 ... I don't know ... (*crying*)

MAN 3 I never thought it could happen in America.

Back in the bar, the camera moves to two patrons seated at a table by themselves, far enough away not to be heard. Guy Banister is a sturdy, imposing ex-FBI agent in his 60s, steel gray hair, blue eyes, ruddy from heavy drinking. He wears a small rosebud in his lapel. Jack Martin is a thin, mousy man in his mid-50s, wearing a Dick Tracy hat. They're both drinking Wild Turkey heavily. The TV blares loudly across the room over their voices.

BANISTER All this blubbering over that sonofabitch! They're grieving like they knew the man. It makes me want to puke.

MARTIN God's sake, chief. The President was shot ...

BANISTER A bullshit President! I don't see any weeping for all the thousands of Cubans that bastard condemned to death and torture at the Bay of Pigs. Where are all the tears for the Russians and Hungarians and Chinese living like slaves in prison camps run by Kennedy's Communist buddies—All these damned peace treaties! I'm telling ya Jack, that's what happens when you let the niggers vote. They get together with the Jews and the Catholics and elect an Irish bleeding heart.

MARTIN Chief, maybe you had a little too much to drink.

BANISTER Bullshit! (*yells across the room*) Bartender, another round ... (*finishes his drink*) Here's to the New Frontier. Camelot in smithereens. I'll drink to that.

▮ Banister and Martin at Katzenjammer's Bar: [Police Report #K-12634-63 Nov. 25, 1963; Garrison, *Trail of the Assassins*, p. 29-32; HSCA X. p. 129-130.]

NAPOLEON'S RESTAURANT - DAY (1963)

Several hours have elapsed. The clientele has grown, drinking, watching the tube with the insatiable curiosity the event engendered. People stare in from the street ... There is a silence in the restaurant.

TELEVISION INSERT: image of a Dallas policeman hauling a Mannlicher-Carcano rifle with a sniperscope over the heads of the press gathered in the police station.

NEWSMAN 3 ... this is the rifle, it is a Mannlicher-Carcano Italian rifle, a powerful World War II military gun used by infantry and highly accurate at distances of 100 yards.

▮ Mannlicher-Carcano: The initial descriptions of the Carcano weren't entirely accurate. The rifle, a WWII-era Italian carbine, had earned the nickname "the humanitarian rifle" because it was never known to injure anyone on purpose. Oswald's weapon was in particularly bad shape, described to the Warren Commission by FBI experts as "a cheap, old weapon" [WC 4H p. 29] with "wear and rust" [CD 2974]. The expert shooters who test-fired the rifle for the Commission declined to practice with it out of "concern with breaking the firing pin." The FBI experts also found that the telescopic sight on Oswald's rifle was not mounted properly and had to adjust it before they were able to hit what they were aiming at [WR p. 182; Robert Sam Anson, *They've Killed the President!* (Bantam Books, 1975), p. 75-78; Meagher, *Acces-*

sories, p. 106-111; Evica, *And We Are All ...*, p. 1-62 for a thorough discussion of alleged murder weapon.].

We see images of the textbook boxes—the sniper's nest in the sixth story of the Book Depository—and then the view out the window looking down at Elm Street.

NEWSMAN 3 ... the assassin apparently fired from this perch ... but so far no word, much confusion and ...

CUT TO Newsman 2 at a different location or in studio.

NEWSMAN 4 A flash bulletin ... the Dallas Police have *just* announced they have a suspect in the killing of a Dallas police officer, J.D. Tippit, who was shot at 1:15 in Oak Cliff, a suburb of Dallas. Police are saying there could be a tie-in here to the murder of the President.

TELEVISION INSERT: Lee Harvey Oswald, a bruise over his right temple, is apprehended at the Texas Theatre.

NEWSMAN 4 The suspect, identified as Lee Harvey Oswald, was arrested by more than a dozen police officers after a short scuffle at the Texas movie theatre in Oak Cliff, several blocks from where Officer Tippit was killed, apparently with a .38 revolver found on Oswald. There is apparently at least one eyewitness.

TELEVISION INSERT: Oswald is booked at the station. A surly young man, 24, he claims to the press:

TV OSWALD No, I don't know what I'm charged with ... I don't know what dispatches you people have been given, but I emphatically deny these charges.

> ▌Note: All of Oswald's dialogue while in police custody comes verbatim from news footage of the assassination weekend.

VOICE FROM THE BAR They oughta just shoot the bastard.

The room bursts out with an accumulated fury at the young Oswald—a tremendous release of tension. On the TV we see the excitement in the newsmen's eyes; they all sense that this is the break they're looking for in the case.

Garrison and Ivon watch the TV, and then Garrison stands and pays the bill.

LOU One little guy with a cheap rifle—look what he can do.

JIM Let's get outta here, Lou. I saw too much stuff like this in the war.

As they leave, the camera holds on the image of Oswald.

MISSISSIPPI RIVER WATERFRONT- TWILIGHT (1963)

The sun is setting through thunderheads over the Mississippi River waterfront as Banister and Martin wobble out, drunk, down the street.

BANISTER Well, the kid musta gone nuts, right? (*Martin says nothing, looks troubled*) I said Oswald must've flipped. Just did this crazy thing before anyone could stop him, right?

MARTIN I think I'll cut out here, chief. I gotta get home.

BANISTER (*strong-arms Martin*) Get home my ass. We're going to the office, have another drink. I want some company tonight.

BANISTER'S OFFICE - NIGHT (1963)

Rain pours down outside 531 Lafayette Street as Banister opens several locks on the door and turns on the lights. The frosted glass on the door says "W. Guy Banister Associates, Inc., Investigators." It's a typical detective's office with spare desks, simple chairs, large filing cabinets and cubicles in the rear.

BANISTER (*repetitive*) Who'd ever thought that goofy Oswald kid would pull off a stunt like an assassination? (*Martin waits*) Just goes to show, you can never know about some people. Am I right, Jack? (*Martin, frightened now, doesn't reply*) Well, bless my soul. Your eyes are as red as two cherries, Jack. Don't tell me we have another bleeding heart here. Hell, all these years I thought you were on my side.

MARTIN Chief, sometimes I don't know whether you're kidding or not.

BANISTER I couldn't be more serious, Jack. Those big red eyes have me wondering about your loyalty.

Banister, going to a file cabinet to get a bottle out, notices one of the file drawers is slightly ajar. He flies into a rage.

BANISTER Who the hell opened my files! You've been looking through my private files, haven't you, you weasel?

MARTIN You may not like this, chief, but you're beginning to act paranoid. I mean, you really are.

BANISTER You found out about Dave Ferrie going to Texas today and you went through all my files to see what was going on. You're a goddamn spy.

MARTIN (*angry*) Goddammit chief, why would I ever need to look in your files? I saw enough here this summer to write a book.

BANISTER I always lock my files. And you were the only one here today ... (*stops as he hears Martin*) What do you mean, you son of a bitch?

MARTIN You know what I mean. I saw a lot of strange things going on in this office this summer. And a lotta strange people.

Enraged, Banister pulls a .357 Magnum from his holster, cursing as he suddenly slams it into Martin's temple. The smaller man crumples painfully to the ground. [New Orleans Police Report #K-12634-63, Nov. 22, 1963.]

BANISTER You didn't see a goddamn thing, you little weasel. Do you get it? You didn't see a goddamn thing.

JIM GARRISON'S HOME - THAT NIGHT (1963)

Jim and his wife, Liz, watch the television. She is in her early 30s, an attractive, quiet southern woman from Louisiana. They live in a spacious two-story wood house, suburban in feel.

TELEVISION IMAGE: Reporters are jammed in the Assembly Room of the Dallas Police Headquarters as Oswald is brought through the corridor, officers on either side of him.

NEWSMAN 5 (*over the din*) Did you shoot the President?

TV OSWALD I didn't shoot anybody, no sir. I'm just a patsy.

The camera moves onto Jim with Liz and the children—Jasper, the oldest at 4, holds his dad's hand. On Liz's lap, Snapper, the youngest, is asleep. Virginia, the 2-year-old, is pestering the Boxer dog ... and Mattie, the heavyset black housekeeper, 35, is in tears.

LIZ My god, he sure looks like a creep. What's he talkin' 'bout ... a patsy?

TELEVISION IMAGE: Oswald in front of the cameras, on a platform.

▌[Press conference, Nov. 23, 1963, 12:06 AM CST, at Dallas Police Station Assembly Room.]

TV OSWALD Well, I was questioned by a judge. However, I protested at the time that I was not allowed legal representation during that very short and sweet hearing. Uh, I really don't know what the situation is about. Nobody has told me anything except that I am accused of, uh, murdering a policeman. I know nothing more than that and I do request that someone come forward to give me, uh, legal assistance.

NEWSMAN 5 Did you kill the President?

TV OSWALD No. I have not been charged with that. In fact nobody has said that to me yet. The first thing I heard about it was when the newspaper reporters in the hall, uh, asked me that question.

NEWSMAN 6 You have been charged.

TV OSWALD Sir?

NEWSMAN 6 You have been charged.

Oswald seems shocked.

NEWSMAN 5 Were you ever in the Free Cuba Movement or whatever the ...

RUBY (*a voice at the back*) It was the Fair Play for Cuba Committee ...

Oswald looks over and spots Ruby in the back of the room, on a table. Recognition is in his eyes. The police start to move him out.

■ Ruby at Oswald press conference: [WR, p. 208; WFAA-TV News footage, Nov. 23, 1963.] Jack Ruby actually supplied the correct name of the Fair Play for Cuba Committee in a subsequent press conference with Dallas District Attorney Henry Wade. Wade told the reporters that Oswald was a member of the "Free Cuba movement or whatever" and Ruby corrected him. The Free Cuba Movement was a CIA-funded anti-Castro group and the FPCC was a pro-Castro group under investigation by the CIA. Apparently, Ruby knew the difference. NBC and WFAA-TV news footage shows Ruby in the audience. An uncredited still photo, most likely from the WFAA film, was published as CE 2424.

NEWSMAN 6 What did you do in Russia? What happened to your eye?

TV OSWALD A policeman hit me.

GARRISON He seems pretty cool to me for a man under pressure like that.

LIZ Icy, you mean. (*shudders*) He gives me the willies ... come on sugarplums, it's past your bedtimes ... (*to Jim*) Come on, let's go upstairs. (*rises*) Mattie—get a hold of yourself.

MATTIE Why, Mr. Jim? He was a great man, Mr. Jim, a great man ...

Jim is moved by her.

TV IMAGE: Texas D.A. Henry Wade addresses the journalists. [WFAA-TV Reel PKT 27 CE 2169 (transcript) 2.]

TV WADE There is no one else but him. He has been charged in the Supreme Court with murder with malice. We're gonna ask for the death penalty.

Jim moves to the phone as Liz starts the kids up the stairs. The TV cuts to stills of Oswald's life. Two newsmen sit in a studio, smoking, sharing information.

FRANK (NEWSMAN 7) ... so several hours after the assassination, a disturbed portrait is emerging of Lee Harvey Oswald. Described as shy and introverted, he spent much of his childhood in New Orleans, Louisiana and went to high school there. After a stint in the Marines, he apparently became fascinated by Communism and in 1959 defected to the Soviet Union.

BOB (NEWSMAN 8) He married a Russian woman there, Frank, had a child, and then returned to the United States after 30 months. But he is still believed to be a dedicated Marxist and a fanatical supporter of Fidel Castro and ultra left wing causes. He spent last summer in New Orleans and was arrested in a brawl with anti-Castro Cuban exiles.

FRANK (NEWSMAN 7) And apparently, Bob, Oswald had been passing out pro-Castro pamphlets for an organization called Fair Play for Cuba, a Communist front he reportedly belongs to.

BOB (NEWSMAN 8) And we have Marina Oswald, his Russian-born wife, who has identified the rifle found in the Book Depository as belonging to her husband. And we have ...

■ The details of Oswald's biography—the defection to Russia, the Marxist agitation—gave the public the lone nut, leftist drifter image of Oswald that the Warren Commission later endorsed. In the Feb. 21, 1964 issue of *Life*, this "official" biography was immortalized in an article titled "The Evolution of an Assassin." The cover bore the damning "backyard photo" of Oswald.

TELEVISION IMAGES of Kennedy's casket coming off the plane in Washington D.C. play under the newsman. ... Jackie stands there in her blood-spotted dress ... we cut to the photograph of L.B.J. taking the oath of office earlier that day ... and a still photo of Robert Kennedy's reaction ...

JIM (*on the phone*) Lou, I'm sorry to disturb you this late ... yeah, matter of routine but we better get on this New Orleans connection of Oswald's right away. Check out his record, find any friends or associates from last summer. Let's meet with the senior assistants and investigators day after tomorrow, Sunday, yeah, at 11 ... Thanks Lou ...

GARRISON CONFERENCE ROOM - 2 DAYS LATER - DAY (1963)

Jim is with his key players: Lou Ivon, chief investigator; Susie Cox, in her 30s, an efficient, attractive Assistant D.A.; Al Oser, Assistant. D.A. in his 40s, serious, spectacled; Bill Broussard, Assistant D.A., handsome, volatile, in his 30s; Numa Bertell, D.A. in his 30s, chubby and friendly, and several others. They sit around a conference table with a black-and-white portable TV on a side table showing the current Sunday, November 24 news from Dallas.

■ The actual District Attorney "Special Team" investigating the J.F.K. case consisted of Chief Investigator Louis Ivon, Assistant District Attorneys Andrew Sciambra, Al Oser, James Alcock, Charles Ward, D'Alton Williams and Numa Bertell, and a host of volunteer investigators and researchers. [Garrison, *Trail of the Assassins*, p. 275.]

MARINA OSWALD (ON TV) Lee good man ... he not shoot anyone ... [ABC News Footage, Nov. 23, 1963, Sherman Grindberg Library.]

Camera moves to Lou Ivon, looking at paperwork.

LOU As far as Oswald's associates, boss, the one name that keeps popping up is David Ferrie. Oswald was seen with him several times last summer.

JIM I know David—a strange character.

LOU He's been in trouble before. Used to be a hot shot pilot for Eastern Airlines, but he got canned after an alleged homosexual incident with a 14-year-old boy.

■ David Ferrie fired from Eastern Airlines: [HSCA X. p. 108] Milton E. Brener notes in *The Garrison Case: A Study in the Abuse of Power*, that many of Eastern's pilots refused to fly with Ferrie because he was "physically filthy," p. 46. [Philip H. Melanson, *Spy Saga: Lee Harvey Oswald and U.S. Intelligence*, (Praeger, 1990), p. 39.]

BILL (*on phone, excited*) ... get Kohlman ... he told somebody the Texas trip ... yesterday mentioned to somebody about Ferrie ... find it out.

On the TV we see the first image of the "backyard photos" of Lee Harvey Oswald hold-ing the rifle.

NEWSMAN 1 ... these backyard photos were found yesterday among Oswald's pos-sessions in the garage of Janet Williams' home in Irving, Texas, where Marina Oswald and her children are living. The picture apparently was taken earlier this year. Police say the rifle, a cheap World War II Italian-made Mannlicher-Carcano, was ordered from a Chicago mailing house and shipped to Oswald's alias A. Hidell at a post office box in March, 1963. This is the same rifle that was used to assassinate the President.

▌Janet Williams is based on characterizations of Ruth Paine, an Irving, Texas woman with whom Marina was living at the time of the assassination. After meeting the Oswalds through their mutual friend George de Mohrenschildt, Ruth Paine helped arrange for Oswald's job at the Book Depository, turned up lots of evidence in her garage linking Oswald to the crime, and kept a cal-endar and address book that showed her careful notations of the Oswalds' comings and goings. She turned it over to the Warren Commission. She gave the Commission a very negative image of Oswald. Also, on the day after the assassination, the FBI monitored a call between her line and her husband Michael's line at Bell Helicopter. The topic was the assassination. One party says: "We both know who's responsible." [Anthony Summers, *Conspiracy*, (McGraw-Hill, 1980) p. 580fn, 71, CD206 cited as source.]

▌Ruth Paine's testimony: [WC 2H p. 430-517, 3H p.1-140, 9H p. 331-425, 11H p. 153-155, p. 389-398.] (Note: Inexplicably, the HSCA did not contact Ruth Paine over the course of their investigation.)

▌photos of Oswald with rifle: [WC 16H CE 133A, 133B, 134; de Mohren-schildt print] Although the Dallas police, Irving police and FBI combed the Paine house for Oswald's effects in the hours after his arrest, the two "back-yard photos" did not turn up until the following afternoon when the Dallas police came back for a second search. There is some dispute over who found the photos and exactly what it was they found—while the Warren Commis-sion stated that one negative and two prints were found, police testimony clearly indicated that there was an additional negative found. [Meagher, *Accessories*, p. 205-209 and citations.]

A third print—a much clearer version—surfaced in 1967 in the possession of Oswald's mysterious friend George de Mohrenschildt. On the back of the print, someone had written, "Hunter of Fascists, ha ha!" in Cyrillic script. HSCA handwriting experts concluded that the writing was not Oswald's, nor was it Marina's or de Mohrenschildt's. According to the HSCA panel, the inscription had been written then rewritten in pencil, as though the writer was not familiar with Cyrillic script. [HSCA II. 386-388; Summers, *Conspiracy*, p. 211 and citations.]

In 1976, a fourth print—and a new pose entirely—came to light. The widow of Dallas policeman Roscoe White turned it over to the Senate Intelligence Committee [HSCA II. 321]. This "new" pose was identical to the stance used for the Dallas police re-enactment photo [CE748]. Several other Dallas policemen are known to have made copies of the Oswald photo (including this pose) over the assassination weekend to keep as souvenirs, but this does not begin to explain why the White print was not included in the Warren Commission's material.

[Note: In what appears to be nothing more than a publicity-seeking hoax, a Texas group that included White's son and widow presented "evidence" in 1990 that White was the real assassin behind the picket fence. Many of their claims have been debunked. (See David B. Perry, "Who Speaks for Roscoe White?," *The Third Decade*, November 1991.)]

The camera moves back to the staff, who watch, obviously influenced.

COX That ties it up ...

NUMA Another nut. Jesus, *anybody* can get a rifle in Texas.

BILL (*hangs up*) So it seems that Dave Ferrie drove off on Friday afternoon for Texas—a source told Kohlman he might have been a getaway pilot for Oswald.

Members of the team exchange looks of surprise and disbelief.

JIM Hold your horses. What kinda source?

BILL (*grins*) The anonymous kind, Chief.

OSER I think I remember this guy Ferrie speaking at a meeting of some veterans group. Ranting against Castro. Extreme stuff.

▌Ferrie spoke at a meeting of the New Orleans chapter of the Military Order of World Wars in July, 1961 and was asked to discontinue his ranting when he became "too critical of President Kennedy." [HSCA X. p. 107.] Members of the group clearly recalled—and reported to the FBI—Ferrie's boasting of his involvement with the CIA and recounting how he had trained pilots in Guatemala for the Bay of Pigs invasion. [Rosemary James and Jack Wardlaw, *Plot or Politics?* (Pelican, 1967), p. 46.] Oddly enough, the HSCA summary does not mention Ferrie's tales of his CIA exploits, even though they cited the same FBI Reports as their source for Ferrie's criticism of J.F.K. Despite having these reports, the Committee took the CIA at their word when told that Ferrie was not associated with the agency. [HSCA, X. p .105-122.]

NEWSMAN 1 We go back now to the basement of police headquarters where they're about to transfer Oswald to County Prison ...

TV IMAGE: The basement of the Dallas police headquarters—waiting. Men mill around as Oswald is led out of the basement by two deputies. Jack Ruby rushes forward out of the crowd—and into history—putting his sealing bullet into Oswald. Total chaos erupts ...

The camera is on the staff, looking. We hear gasps.

ANNOUNCER He's been shot! Oswald's been shot!

VARIOUS VOICES Goddamn! Look at that ... Look at that ... I don't believe this ... Right on TV! What is going on? Who is this guy ... oh Jesus. *(etc.)*

Jim is silent.

LOU Seventy cops in that basement. What the hell were they doing!

NEWSMAN 1 Jack Ruby ... Who is Jack Ruby? Oswald is hurt ...

We see images of Oswald being lifted onto the stretcher, into the ambulance, and the newscaster crouching, whispering. Everybody in the room is stunned still.

LOU Well, no trial now. Looks like somebody saved the Dallas D.A. a pile of work.

They look to Jim. There's a pause. He is deeply disturbed.

JIM (*quietly*) Well, let's get Ferrie in here anyway ...

GARRISON OFFICE - NEXT DAY - DAY (1963)

The portable television plays to Jim alone, sitting in his chair smoking a pipe. We see searing images of the funeral—crowds of mourners, the casket being driven through the streets, the honor guards, the horses, the dignitaries walking behind, Jackie veiled ... the faces of De Gaulle, MacMillan, Robert Kennedy. We intercut briefly to Lyndon Johnson sitting down earlier that day with the Joint Chiefs of Staff ... and then a future cut to Johnson in the Oval Office (staged). The shots are very tight, uncomfortable—noses, eyes, hands—very tight.

As the door opens following a knock, David Ferrie is brought into Jim's office by two police officers and Lou Ivon. Jim stands up, cordial.

> ▮ Ferrie/Garrison conversation: [Secret Service report Dec. 13, 1963, CO-2-34, 030; FBI Report Nov. 26, 1963, #89-68; Garrison, *Trail of the Assassins*, p. 7-8; Harold Weisberg, *Oswald in New Orleans: Case for Conspiracy with the CIA* (Canyon Books, 1967), p. 185-187.]

LOU Chief ... David Ferrie

Ferrie suffers from alopecia, a disease that has removed all his body hair, and he looks like a Halloween character—penciled eyebrows, one higher than the other, a scruffy reddish wig pasted on askew with glue, thrift store clothing, His eyes, however, are swift and cunning, his smile warm, inviting itself, his demeanor hungry to please.

JIM (*shakes hands*) Come in, Dave. Have a seat, make yourself comfortable. Coffee?

FERRIE Do you remember me, Mr. Garrison? I met you on Carondolet Street right after your election. I congratulated you, remember?

JIM How could I forget? You make quite a first impression. (*on intercom*) Sharon, could you please bring us some coffee? (*Ferrie laughs; pause*) I've heard over the years you're quite a first-rate pilot, Dave. Legend has it you can get in and out of any field, no matter how small ... (*Jim points to the pictures on his wall*) I'm a bit of a pilot myself, you know. Flew grasshoppers for the field artillery in the war.

Ferrie glimpses the low-volumed TV—and images of the funeral. He looks away, jittery, and takes out a cigarette. Sharon brings the coffee in.

FERRIE Do you mind if I smoke, Mr. Garrison?

JIM (*holds up his pipe*) How could I? Dave, as you know, President Kennedy was assassinated on Friday. A man named Lee Harvey Oswald was arrested as a suspect and then was murdered yesterday by a man named Jack Ruby. (*on each name, watching Ferrie's reaction*) We've heard reports that Oswald spent the summer in New Orleans and we've been advised you knew Oswald pretty well.

FERRIE That's not true. I never met anybody named Oswald. Anybody who told you that has to be crazy.

JIM But you are aware, he served in your Civil Air Patrol unit when he was a teenager.

> ∎ The Warren Commission seemed particularly anxious to determine if Oswald knew Ferrie through the CAP. [HSCA VIII. p. 103-115; WC 8H p. 14 (Voebel testimony) CE 3119 p. 19; Melanson, *Spy Saga*, p. 42-43.] Oswald's childhood friend Edward Voebel told the FBI and the Commission that he and Oswald were members of the CAP "with Capt. Dave Ferrie" [CE 1413 p. 825; HSCA X. p. 108], and he told the FBI that he thought Oswald had attended a party at Ferrie's house during this time [CE 1413 p. 826]. Despite their obvious worries, the Warren Commission Report makes no mention of Ferrie [HSCA X. p. 103-115]. Years later, the HSCA found six witnesses to confirm Oswald's membership in Ferrie's group and finally admitted, all things considered, they were "puzzled by Oswald's apparent association with Ferrie" [HSCA Report, p. 145.]

FERRIE No ... if he did, I don't remember him. There were lots of kids in and out ... y'know.

JIM (*hands him a current newspaper*) I'm sure you've seen this. Perhaps you knew this man under another name?

FERRIE No, I never saw him before in my life.

JIM Well that must've been mistaken information we got. Thanks for straightening it out for us. (*puffs on his pipe, Ferrie looks relieved; images of the funeral continue on the TV*) There is one other matter that's come up, Dave. We were told you took a trip to Texas shortly after the assassination on Friday.

FERRIE Yeah, now that's true. I drove to Houston.

JIM What was so appealing about Houston?

FERRIE I hadn't been there ice skating in many years, and I had a couple of young friends with me, and we decided we wanted to go ice skating.

JIM Dave, may I ask why the urge to go ice skating in Texas happened to strike you during one of the most violent thunderstorms in recent memory?

FERRIE Oh, it was just a spur of the moment thing ... the storm wasn't that bad.

JIM I see. And where did you drive?

FERRIE We went straight to Houston, and then Saturday night we drove to Galveston and stayed over there.

JIM Why Galveston?

FERRIE No particular reason. Just to go somewhere.

JIM And then Sunday?

FERRIE In the morning we went goose hunting. Then headed home, but I dropped the boys off to see some relatives and I stayed in Hammond.

JIM Did you bag any geese on this trip?

FERRIE I believe the boys got a couple.

JIM But the boys told us they didn't get any.

FERRIE *(fidgeting, lighting another cigarette)* Oh yes, well, come to think of it, they're right. We got to where the geese were and there were thousands of them. But you couldn't approach them. They were a wise bunch of birds.

JIM Your young friends also told us you had no weapons in the car. Dave, isn't it a bit difficult to hunt for geese without a shotgun?

FERRIE Yes, now I remember, Mr. Garrison. I'm sorry, I got confused. We got out there near the geese and it was only then we realized we'd forgotten our shotguns. Stupid, right? So of course we didn't get any geese.

> ■ Ferrie's trip to Texas: [FBI Report Nov. 26, 1963, #89-68; Secret Service Report Dec. 13, 1963, CO-2-34; Weisberg, *Oswald in New Orleans*, p. 185-187.]

JIM I see. *(stands up)* Dave, thank you for your time. I'm sorry this has to end inconveniently for you, but I'm going to have you detained for further questioning by the FBI.

FERRIE *(shaken)* Why? What's wrong?

JIM Dave, I find your story simply not believable.

Lou and the two cops escort Ferrie out of the office as Jim turns to the television image of Kennedy's final moments of rest. The bugler plays taps. John Jr., 3 years old, in an image which will become famous, salutes his Dad farewell. The riderless horse stands lonely against the Washington sky.

FBI OFFICE - NEW ORLEANS—NEXT DAY (1963)

At a small press conference, the FBI spokesman reads a statement.

> ■ FBI statement: [Garrison, *Trail of the Assassins*, p. 11.]

FBI SPOKESMAN Gentlemen, this afternoon the FBI released David W. Ferrie of New Orleans. After extensive questioning and a thorough background check, the Bureau found no evidence that ...

GARRISON'S OFFICE - SIMULTANEOUS WITH PREVIOUS SCENE

In Garrison's office see the same broadcast, on the portable television. Lou, Broussard, Numa and Jim watch.

FBI SPOKESMAN *(on TV)* ... Mr. Ferrie knew Lee Harvey Oswald or that he has had any connection with the assassination of President Kennedy. The Special Agent in Charge would like to make clear that Mr. Ferrie was brought in for questioning by the District Attorney of Orleans Parish, not by the Federal Bureau of Investigation. The Bureau regrets any trouble this may have caused Mr. Ferrie ...

NEWSMAN 9 ... in national news, President Johnson has announced the creation of a blue ribbon presidential commission to probe the events in Dallas.

Lou looks at Jim, angry.

LOU Correct me if I'm wrong. I thought we were on the same side. What the hell business is it of theirs to say that?

BILL Pretty fast, wasn't it. The way they let him go.

JIM They must know something we don't. *(dismisses it)* So, let's get on with our lives, gentlemen ... we got plenty of home grown crimes to prosecute ...

He reaches to turn off the TV and get back to work. The last image on the TV is:

NEWSMAN 9 The Commission will be headed by Chief Justice of the United States Supreme Court, Earl Warren, and is expected to head off several Congressional and Texas inquiries into the assassination. On the panel are Allen Dulles, ex-chief of the CIA, Representative Gerald Ford, John J. McCloy, former head of Chase Manhattan Bank ...

Jim's hand flicks the TV off as the overture ends.

▌Executive Order 11130 on Nov. 29, 1963 created a seven-man President's Commission on the Assassination of President Kennedy, popularly known as the Warren Commission after its chairman, Supreme Court Chief Justice Earl Warren. The other members were Representative Hale Boggs (D-LA), Senator John Sherman Cooper (R-KY), Representative Gerald R. Ford (R-MI), Senator Richard B. Russell (D-GA), businessman/former High Commissioner of Germany (and responsible for commuting most of the sentences handed down at Nuremberg) John J. McCloy, and ex-CIA Director Allen W. Dulles. It is incredible that Dulles was selected to investigate Kennedy's death. In 1961, after the Bay of Pigs fiasco, J.F.K. fired Dulles—along with his deputies Richard Bissell and General Charles Cabell—from his CIA post.

AERIAL SHOT - WASHINGTON, D.C. - DAY (1966)

We look down at the White House from the plane's point of view. A subtitle reads: "THREE YEARS LATER."

INTERIOR OF PLANE

SENATOR RUSSELL LONG (*looking out the window*) That's a mess down there, Jim. We've bitten off more "Vietnam" than we can possibly chew.

Jim, now 46, reads the front page of The Washington Post *which details the latest battle in Vietnam. He sits next to Senator Long from Louisiana, in his 50s, who's drinking a whiskey. They're on a crowded businessman's shuttle. We see a close-up of a newspaper article about the Vietnam war: "more troops asked by Westmoreland."*

> ▌Garrison/Long conversation: [Nov. 1966: James A. Autry, "The Garrison Investigation: How and Why It Began," *New Orleans*, April 1967, p. 8; Garrison, *Trail of the Assassins*, p. 13-14.]

LONG (*continuing*) Sad thing is the way it's screwing up *this* country, all these hippies running around on drugs, the way young people look you can't tell a boy from a girl anymore. I saw a girl the other day, she was pregnant—you could see her whole belly, and you know what she painted on it? "Love Child." It's fuckin' outa control. Values've gone to hell, Jim ... Course it figures when you got somebody like that polecat Johnson in the White House.

JIM I sometimes feel things've gone downhill since John Kennedy was killed, Senator.

LONG Don't get me started on that. Those Warren Commission fellows were pickin' gnat shit out of pepper. No one's gonna tell me that kid did the shooting job he did from that damned bookstore.

STEWARDESS Here you go, Senator Long.

The stewardess brings more drinks.

JIM (*surprised*) I thought the FBI test-fired the rifle to make sure it could be done?

LONG Sure, three experts and not *one* of them could do it! They're telling us Oswald got off three shots with world-class precision from a manual bolt action rifle in less than six seconds—and accordin' to his Marine buddies he got Maggie's drawers—he wasn't any good. Average man would be lucky to get two shots off, and I tell ya the first shot would *always* be the best. Here, the third shot's perfect. Don't make sense. And then they got that crazy bullet zigzagging all over the place so it hits Kennedy and Connally seven times. One "pristine" bullet? That dog don't hunt.

> ▌Rifle tests: One of the FBI experts succeeded in getting two hits in under 5.6 seconds but he was shooting from a tower half as high as the sixth-floor "sniper's perch" and at a stationary target. [Sylvia Meagher, *Accessories After the Fact*]
>
> ▌Fellow Marine Nelson Delgado said of Oswald's marksmanship: "It was a pretty big joke because he got a lot of Maggie's drawers, you know, a lot of misses, but he didn't give a darn." [WC 8H, p. 133]; Sylvia Meagher's discussion on pages 131-133 of *Accessories After the Fact* effectively destroys any notion of Oswald's competence with the rifle.

JIM You know, something always bothered me about that from day one, and I can't put my finger on it.

LONG If I were investigatin', I'd round up the 100 best riflemen in the world and find out which ones were in Dallas that day. You been duck hunting? I think Oswald was a good old-fashioned decoy. What'd he say? "I'm just a patsy." Out of the mouth of babes y'ask me.

JIM You think there were other men involved, Russell?

Russell looks at Jim quizzically and laughs.

LONG Hell, you're the District Attorney. You read the Warren Report—and then you tell me you're satisfied Lee Oswald shot the President all by his lonesome.

JIM Russell, honestly you sound like one of those kooky critics spreading paranoia like prairie fire. I just can't believe the Chief Justice of the United States would put his name on something that wasn't true.

> ▌ The "kooky critics" remark refers to the fact that by 1966, the Warren Commission was already being seriously questioned. Books by Mark Lane (*Rush to Judgment* [Holt, Rinehart & Winston, 1966]), Edward Jay Epstein (*Inquest: The Warren Commission and the Establishment of Truth* [Bantam Books, 1966]) and Harold Weisberg (the *Whitewash* series Vols. I-IV [Hyattstown, 1965, 1967] Vols. I-II [Dell, 1966, 1967]) sold well and presented compelling evidence of a conspiracy, or at the very least, of a less-than-thorough investigation by the Warren Commission. By 1966, Gallup and Harris polls showed that 66% of the American public did not believe that Oswald was the lone assassin [Edward Jay Epstein, *Counterplot*, (Viking, 1968), p. 148]. Even the *Life* magazine cover of Nov. 25, 1966 screamed for a new investigation, calling the Warren Commission conclusions a "matter of reasonable doubt."

LONG (*to the stewardess*) Honey, another one of these. This one's as weak as cricket pee-pee. Yessir, you mark my words, Jim, Vietnam's gonna cost Johnson '68 and it's gonna put that other varmint Nixon in—then watch your hide, 'cause there ain't no offramps on a freeway to Hell!

GARRISON'S STUDY - NIGHT (1966)

The study is lined with bookshelves up to the ceiling; we see photos of family, a chess set. Jim, smoking his pipe, reads in a red leather chair from one of the 26 thick Warren Commission volumes piled all over the place. Liz enters. Jasper, now 7, draws on a piece of paper on the floor at Jim's feet.

LIZ Jim, dinner's just about ready ... I've got a surprise for you ... tried something new ... Jim? Jim, dinner.

JIM (*lost in thought*) Mmmm ... sure smells good ... but Egghead, do you realize Oswald was interrogated for twelve hours after the assassination, with no lawyer present, and nobody recorded a word of it? I can't believe it. A police captain with 30 years experience and a crowd of Federal agents just had to

know that with no record anything that Oswald said would be inadmissable in court ...

■ Dallas police and federal agents questioned Oswald for over twelve hours during his stay at the station. Not one word of it was recorded, and Dallas Homicide Captain Will Fritz says he did not take any notes [WR, p. 180]. As Jim Garrison noted: "Even if we assume that the public offices in Dallas are unusually small and the stenographers unusually large, it does not explain why a compact tape recorder was not used." [Jim Garrison, *Heritage of Stone* (G.P. Putnam's Sons, 1970, Berkeley, 1972), p. 67.] The agents present during the questioning furnished statements to the Warren Commission which were collected in Appendix XI of the Report. Many researchers feel that this appendix is one of the few "honest" sections of the Report—in it we learn, among other things, that Oswald said he was eating lunch on the first floor when the motorcade passed by and that he said that the "backyard photos" of himself with the rifle were fakes.

LIZ Come on now, we'll talk about it at the table, dinner's getting cold. (*to Jasper*) What are you doing in here?

JASPER Daddy said it was all right if I was real quiet.

JIM (*rising to dinner*) Sure it is. Freckle Face, if I ever handled a minor felon like that, it'd be all over the papers. I'd catch hell. And this is the alleged murderer of the President?

GARRISON DINING ROOM - (1966)

Two-year-old Elizabeth watches "Crusader Rabbit" on TV as the new one-year-old sits in diapers with Liz at one end of the dinner table. Jim sits at the other end. There are five kids now, ages 7, 5, 4, 2 and 1 ... and Mattie, the housekeeper. Dinner's finished, they pass plates, the children horse around ... the boxer dog, Touchdown, begs for a piece of the action. Jim, not a big eater, feeds him ice cream.

JIM Again and again they ignore credible testimony, leads are never followed up, its conclusions are selective, there's no index, it's one of the sloppiest, most disorganized investigations I've ever seen. Dozens and dozens of witnesses in Dealey Plaza that day are saying they heard shots coming from the Grassy Knoll area in front of Kennedy and not the Book Depository behind him, but it's all broken down and spread around and you read it and the point gets lost ...

■ Warren Commission volumes: The Commission did not index the 11 volumes of Exhibits, nor were they compiled in any logical order. Researcher Sylvia Meagher published her own index in 1967, giving researchers a means of locating specific exhibits, subjects and names [Sylvia Meagher, *Master Index to the J.F.K. Assassination* (Scarecrow Press, 1966)].

■ Grassy Knoll witnesses: According to the Warren Commission Report, "no credible evidence" suggests that the shots were fired from anywhere other than the Book Depository. [WR p. 61] In 1965, researcher Harold Feldman went through the Commission volumes and found that out of 121 witnesses surveyed, 38 gave no opinion as to where the shots came from, 32 thought they came from the Book Depository and 51 felt the shots came from the

Grassy Knoll area [Harold Feldman, "Fifty-One Witnesses: The Grassy Knoll," *Minority of One*, March 1965].

MATTIE I never did believe it either!

LIZ (*politely listening*) Uh huh ... Mattie, I'll do the dishes, you take Eb up now. And Elizabeth, too, your bedtime, honey.

ELIZABETH JR. Nahhhh! I don't wanna go to bed!

LIZ Honey, that was three years ago—we all tried so hard to put that out of our minds, why are you digging it up again? You're the D.A. of New Orleans. Isn't the Kennedy assassination a bit outside your domain? I mean all those important people already studied it.

JIM I can't believe a man as intelligent as Earl Warren ever read what's in those volumes.

LIZ Well maybe you're right, Jim. I'll give you one hour to solve the case ... until the kids are in bed. (*rising, she puts her arms around him from behind and kisses his ear*) Then you're mine and Mr. Kennedy can wait 'til morning. Come on, everybody say goodnight to Daddy.

JASPER (*showing his drawing*) Dad, look what I drew.

JIM (*rising*) That's something, Jasper. What is it?

JASPER A rhinoceros. Can I stay up another hour?

Virginia and Snapper each get one of Jim's shoes as he dances with them, holding one with each hand.

JIM (*dancing*) Pickle and Snapper, my two favorite dancing partners.

As the children dance, they fall off Jim's feet, laughing and giggling. He throws each in the air and kisses them.

JIM Goodnight, my doodle bugs.

KIDS Goodnight, Daddy.

Liz comes over, smiling. Jim takes her in his arms.

LIZ One hour, y'hear? Some Saturday night date you are. (*sighs*) Mama warned me this would happen if I married such a serious man.

JIM Oh, she did, huh? When I come up I'll show you how Saturday night got invented.

GARRISON STUDY - LATER THAT NIGHT (1966)

The clock on mantelpiece reads 3 A.M. Jim is alone, smoking his pipe. In the stillness, his mind crawls all over the place. The camera closes on the thickly-worded pages of the Warren Report.

FLASHBACK TO the Warren Commission hearing room in Dallas, 1964. We hear thin, echoey sound as the attorneys question some of the witnesses. The overall effect is vague and confusing, as is much of the Warren Report. A Mr. Ball is questioning Lee

Bowers, the switchman in the railroad yard. Bowers, in his early 40s, has a trustworthy, working-man face and a crew cut.

❚ Bower's testimony: [WC 6H p. 284-9.]

BOWERS ... I sealed off the area, and I held off the trains until they could be examined, and there was some transients taken on at least one train.

ATTORNEY Mr. Bowers ... is there anything else you told me I haven't asked you about that you can think of?

BOWERS Nothing that I can recall.

ATTORNEY Witness is excused ...

Jim, upset, reads on ... Another witness, Sgt. D.V. Harkness of the Dallas Police responds to a second attorney:

❚ Harkness testimony: [WC 6H p. 312]

SGT. HARKNESS ... well we got a long freight that was in there, and we pulled some people off of there and took them to the station.

We see another FLASHBACK—to the Dallas rail yards on the day of the assassination. Three hoboes are being pulled off the freight by the Dallas policemen.

ATTORNEY (*voice-over*) You mean some transients?

SGT. HARKNESS (*voice-over*) Tramps and hoboes.

ATTORNEY (*voice-over*) Were all those questioned?

FLASHBACK TO Dealey Plaza, an hour or less after the assassination. The three hoboes are marched by shotgun-toting policemen to the Sheriff's office at Dealey Plaza. We note that they do not look much like hoboes.

SGT. HARKNESS (*voice-over*) Yes sir, they were taken to the station and questioned.

JIM (*astounded*) And? (*writes "incomplete"*)

ATTORNEY (*voice-over*) (*switching subjects*) I want to go back to this Amos Euins (*voices dribble off*)

❚ Amos Euins, a 15-year-old high school student, told Harkness shortly after the shooting that he saw a rifle and the shooter in the sixth floor window. He described the man in the window as definitely having a "bald spot on his head." He insisted he could not identify the man any further, not even to the point of saying if he was black or white. Oswald's hair was thinning on top but by no means did he have a bald spot [WC 2H p. 201-210].

BOWERS (*voice-over*) ... yes sir, traffic had been cut off into the area since about 10, but there were three cars came in during this time from around noon till the time of the shooting ... the cars circled the parking lot, and left like they were checking the area, one of the drivers seemed to have something he was holding to his mouth ... the last car came in about 7 to 10 minutes before the shooting, a white Chevrolet, 4-door Impala, muddy up to the windows.

> ▌Cars circling parking lot: [WC 6H p. 285-6]. Also see Lane and D'Antonio *Rush to Judgment* [film, 1966]. Bowers, in his only taped interview, describes the cars in greater detail, as well as the Warren Commission's lack of interest in his account.

The camera's point of view is now from the railroad tower near Dealey Plaza. We are fourteen feet off the ground, overlooking the parking lot behind the Grassy Knoll. The shot includes this last car circling in the lot.

BOWERS (*voice-over*) ... Towards the underpass, I saw two men standing behind a picket fence ... they were looking up towards Main and Houston and following the caravan as it came down. One of them was middle-aged, heavyset. The other man was younger, wearing a plaid shirt and jacket ...

Inside the railroad tower, Bowers glances out, busy with the main board, flashing lights, a train coming in.

BOWERS (*voice-over*) ... there were two other men on the eastern end of the parking lot. Each of 'em had uniforms ...

> ▌It is unclear what Bowers meant about these two men. He says "One of them was a parking lot attendant ... One or two. Each had uniforms similar to those custodians at the courthouse." The Warren Commission counsel, Joseph Ball, did not ask him to elaborate. [WC 6H p.287]

We see the parking lot from Bowers' point of view—at a distance, but we have a sense of the cars and see the men at a distance, two uniformed men. The parking lot is bumper-to-bumper with a sea of cars. Rain that morning has muddied the lot. These brief images are elaborated on later.

BOWERS (*voice-over*) ... at the time of the shooting there seemed to be some commotion ... I just am unable to describe—a flash of light or smoke or something which caused me to feel that something out of the ordinary had occurred there on the embankment ...

We feel a growing intensity: music, drums—but all blurred. We see a puff of smoke but no sound because of the window Bowers is glancing through. A motorcycle cop shoots up the Grassy Knoll incline. People run, blurring into a larger mosaic of confusion. Bowers is confused, seeing this.

> ▌Puff of smoke: At least eight witnesses, especially those standing on the Triple Underpass, reported seeing a puff of smoke rising in front of the trees behind the fence on the Grassy Knoll. [Austin Miller—WC 19H, CE5323, p. 485; Frank Reilly—WC 6H, p. 230; Nolan Potter—WC 22H, CE1418; James Simmons—WC 22H, CE1416; Clemon Johnson—WC 22H, CE1422; Richard Dodd—WC 22H, CE1420; Walter Winborn—WC 22H, CE1417; Thomas Murphy—WC 22H, CE 1421.]
> In addition, several others reported smelling gunpowder near the Knoll, including police officers Earle Brown [WC 6H, p. 233] and Joe Smith.[WC 7H, p. 535]

■ Patrolman Joe M. Smith threw his bike down and ran up the incline. He appears in many films and still photos of Dealey Plaza, running up the incline, gun drawn, towards the Triple Underpass.

INTERCUT with Jim's heart pounding as he reads.

Back in Dealey Plaza, S. M. Holland, an elderly signal supervisor, stands on the parapet of the railway.

■ S.M. Holland: [WC 6H p. 243, CE 2003, p. 212, Decker Exhibit 5323, p. 480, Josiah Thompson, *Six Seconds in Dallas: A Microstudy of the Kennedy Assassination*, (Bernard Geis Associates, 1967; [rev.] Berkeley, 1976), p. 120-124.]

HOLLAND (*voice-over*) Four shots ... a puff of smoke came from the trees ... behind that picket fence ... close to the little plaza—There's no doubt whatever in my mind.

We see the scene from Holland's point of view—the puff of smoke lingering under the trees along the picket fence after the shooting.

GARRISON BEDROOM - ANOTHER NIGHT (1966)

Jim is asleep, having a tortured dream.

DREAMSCAPE FLASHBACK: We see the Zapruder film, in slow-motion and J.F.K.'s face just before he goes behind Stemmons Freeway sign. Jim sits up suddenly.

JIM NO!

Liz stirs, shaken.

LIZ Honey, you all right? (*looks at watch*)

JIM It's incredible, honey—the whole thing. A Lieutenant Colonel testifies that Lee Oswald was given a Russian language exam as part of his Marine training only a few months before he defects to the Soviet Union. A Russian exam!

■ Lt. Col. Allison G. Folsom, USMC [WC 8H p. 307, WC 19, Folsom Exhibit p. 622]. Note: The Warren Commission Report claimed Oswald "studied the Russian language," presumably on his own using a Berlitz grammar book, while in the Marines. However, Russian is a difficult language to master for an American—it takes about 1100 hours of study to acquire fluency [Melanson, *Spy Saga*, p. 78-79]—and the self-study scenario seems unlikely-to-impossible in the face of his confirmed expertise. When Marina met him in Minsk, she did not realize at first that he was an American; she thought that he was from the Baltic states [WR p. 703]. The transcripts of the executive sessions of the Warren Commission, released in 1974, indicate that perhaps the Commission actually felt differently. Chief Counsel J. Lee Rankin tells the Commissioners: "...we are trying to run down, to find out what he studied at the Monterey School of the Army in the way of languages ..." [Executive Session, Jan. 27, 1964]. It is especially interesting that Rankin is trying to determine *what*, not *if*, he studied at the Monterey School (now called the Defense Language Institute).

LIZ (*sitting up, angered*) I cannot believe this. It's four-thirty, Jim Garrison. I have five children are gonna be awake in another hour and ...

JIM Honey, in all my years in the service I never knew a single man who was given a Russian test. Oswald was a radar operator. He'd have about as much use for Russian as a cat has for pajamas.

LIZ These books are getting to your mind, Mr. Garrison. I wish you'd stop readin' 'em!

JIM And then this Colonel tries to make it sound like nothing. Oswald did badly on the test, he says. "He only had two more Russian words right than wrong." Ha! That's like me saying Touchdown here (*points to the dog*) is not very intelligent because I beat him three games out of five the last time we played chess.

LIZ (*gives up*) Jim, what is going on, for heaven's sake! You going to stay up all night every night? For what? So you'll be the only man in America who read the entire 26 volumes of the Warren Report?

JIM Liz, do I have to spell it out for you? Lee Oswald was no ordinary soldier. That was no accident he was in Russia. He was probably in military intelligence. That's why he was trained in Russian.

LIZ (*with a quizzical look*) Honey, go back to sleep, please!

JIM Goddammit! I been sleeping for three years!

She takes him now, gently, and pulls him down on top of her and kisses him.

LIZ Will you stop rattling on about Kennedy for a few minutes, honey ... come on ...

LAFAYETTE SQUARE - NEW ORLEANS - MORNING (1966)

A Sunday, early. We see a statue of Ben Franklin in an empty square frequented by drunks who doze on benches in a little leafy park in the center of the Square. The camera moves to Jim by himself and then moves to a sedan, pulling up, which disgorges Lou Ivon and Bill Broussard.

JIM Morning, boys. Ready for a walking tour?

BILL At 7:30 Sunday morning? It's not exactly fresh blood we're sniffing here, boss.

JIM (*points*) Old stains, Bill, but just as telling.

TIME CUT TO Jim indicating 531 Lafayette Street, a seedy, faded, three-story building across the street from the square.

JIM Remember whose office this was back in '63? 531 Lafayette Street.

LOU Yeah, Guy Banister. Ex-FBI man. He died couple years ago.

> ▮ Banister died of a heart attack in June, 1964. [N.O. Police Department Records, F-3764-64 June 8, 1964.] His partner in the private detective agen-

cy, Hugh F. Ward, was killed the following year when the plane he was pilot-ing for former New Orleans mayor Delesseps Morrison crashed in Mexico. [See Flammonde, *The Kennedy Conspiracy*, 1967, p. 115.]

FLASHBACK TO the exterior of the Banister Office on a day in 1963. The door is now clearly labeled "W. GUY BANISTER, INC. INVESTIGATORS." It opens and Ban-ister comes out in slow motion, neatly dressed, rose in his lapel—the same office and same man we saw three years before when he pistol-whipped Jack Martin. Banister seems to be smiling right at us, greeting us.

JIM (*voice-over*) ... headed the Chicago office. When he retired he became a private eye here. I used to have lunch with him. John Birch Society, Minutemen, slightly to the right of Attila the Hun. Used to recruit college students to infil-trate radical organizations on campus. All out of this office. Now come around here, take a look at this ...

■ Guy Banister and 544 Camp Street: [Henry Hurt's *Reasonable Doubt* and Anthony Summers' *Conspiracy* have excellent chapters on Oswald and 544 Camp Street. Also see HSCA, X. p. 126-132; Hinckle and Turner, *The Fish Is Red*, p. 203-209.]

Back to the Lafayette Square of 1966. Jim walks Ivon and Bill to the corner, to anoth-er entrance to the same building—this one with a sign that says "544 Camp Street."

JIM 544 Camp Street. Same building as 531 Lafayette, right ... but different address and different entrances both going to the same place—the offices on the second and third floors.

Bill studies the present sign: "Crescent City Dental Laboratory," and gives Jim a puz-zled look.

JIM Guess who used this address?

Lou gets it and glances up. We FLASH BACK TO the exterior of 544 Camp Street in 1963. Lee Oswald comes out the door into a full close-up, now clearly seen by us, and heads out into the street as Guy Banister intercepts him on the sidewalk, holding a leaflet and pointing to "544 Camp Street" stamped on it. Guy seems miffed at Oswald, tells him something quickly, and then moves on.

■ The Warren Commission concluded that although the address was stamped on Oswald's literature, "extensive investigation was not able to connect Oswald with that address." [WR, p. 408] Considering that the FBI was con-ducting the investigation and that Guy Banister was a well-known former agent who once headed the second-largest field office (Chicago) in the coun-try, the fact that Banister was never questioned in regard to Oswald's FPCC—allegedly located in the same small building as Banister's private detective agency and the CIA-supported Cuban Revolutionary Council—the FBI investigation was obviously more cursory than extensive. During the Garrison investigation and in later years, Oswald's presence at 544 Camp was verified by a number of former Banister associates, among them his sec-retary Delphine Roberts and her daughter, Jack Martin, Daniel Campbell, and anti-Castro activist Ronnie Caire. [Summers, *Conspiracy*, p. 294-298] CIA operative William Gaudet claimed to have seen Oswald and Banister together. [Hurt, *Reasonable Doubt*, p. 291]

BANISTER (*under*) See this? What the hell is this doing on this piece of paper? ... (*he moves away*) Asshole.

LOU (*voice-over*) My God! Lee Harvey Oswald

JIM (*voice-over*) Bull's-eye. How do we know he was here? Cause this office address was stamped on the pro-Castro leaflets he was handing out in the summer of '63 down on Canal Street. They were the same leaflets that were found in his garage in Dallas.

FLASHBACK to Canal Street in New Orleans on a summer day in 1963. Oswald, in a thin tie and white short-sleeved shirt, and wearing a homemade placard reading "Hands Off Cuba"; "Viva Fidel!," is hawking leaflets to pedestrians with two young helpers.

▌Oswald actually worked by himself on Canal Street on Aug. 9, 1963. However, for his next agitation event—this time in front of the International Trade Mart on Aug. 16—Oswald was assisted by two young men, one of whom he hired at the local employment office and the other a Latin (said to be a Mexican) who turned up with Oswald on a number of occasions but whose identity remains unknown [Weisberg, *Oswald in New Orleans* p. 205-6; Summers, *Conspiracy*, p. 272-3].

A large white-haired businessman in a white suit, very distinguished, walks with a friend on Canal Street. Oswald glances at him and meets his eyes. The businessman enters an office building. This man is Clay Bertrand, later known as Clay Shaw.

▌A WDSU-TV newsfilm of Oswald leafletting in front of the International Trade Mart shows a white-haired man resembling Clay Shaw walking along the building towards Oswald. The man turns and enters the building through a side door. At this point Oswald disengages himself from his Marxist agitation and heads off down the street in the direction of "Shaw." Many people, including Jim Garrison, feel that it *is* Shaw—they say that he walks with Shaw's characteristic limp—but the man is far in the distance and the film does not make it conclusive.

Some Cubans, led by Carlos Bringuier, now appear. One of them, "the Bull," is heavyset with dark glasses. More of him will also be seen.

▌Carlos Bringuier and Cubans: Carlos Bringuier, a Cuban exile, was the New Orleans delegate to the Cuban Student Directorate (DRE), an anti-Castro group (CD 205 indicates that Oswald attended a DRE meeting in Dallas as well). A few days before the leafletting incident, Oswald approached Bringuier at his clothing store to volunteer his services in the anti-Castro crusade, lending Bringuier his Marine training manual as proof of his commitment to the cause. Bringuier was concerned that Oswald was trying to infiltrate his organization. [WC 10H, p. 32-59; Hinckle and Turner, *The Fish Is Red*, p. 170-173, 210-211; Evica, *And We Are All* ..., p. 283-289 and citations.]

JIM (*voice-over*) He was arrested that day for fighting with some anti-Castro Cubans ... but actually he had contacted them a few days earlier as an ex-Marine trying to join the anti-Castro crusade. When they heard he was now pro-Castro, they paid him a visit ...

CARLOS (*haranguing passersby*) He's a traitor, this man! Don't believe a word he tells you! (*to Oswald*) You sonofabitch, you liar, you're a Communist, go back to Moscow.

Carlos throws Oswald's leaflets in the air and pulls off his glasses, prepared to fight. Oswald only smiles, and puts his arms down in an X of passivity.

OSWALD Okay, Carlos, if you want to hit me, hit me.

There is no real fight, but the police, as if pre-alerted, arrive. Arrests are made. We see Oswald in a room in the police station, talking with FBI Agent John Quigley. A calendar on the wall shows that it's August, 1963.

▮ Oswald's arrest: [WC 22H CE 1413—New Orleans Police Report #H-4843-63; Melanson, *Spy Saga*, p. 30-31.]

▮ Although the Bringuier contingent was by all accounts the antagonist in the incident, Oswald pleaded guilty to disturbing the peace and was fined a token amount. The Cubans walked off scot-free. Oswald now had a police record in connection with his "pro-Communist" activities. New Orleans Police Lt. Francis Martello interviewed Oswald at the police station and felt that he "set them up, so to speak, to create an incident" [WC 6H, p. 61]. (Note: Curiously, two home movies of the event surfaced in later years, both taken by passersby. Neither is of good enough quality to discern exactly what happened, but it still doesn't excuse the FBI's lack of interest when, four days after the assassination, one of the filmmakers notified his local bureau. The FBI passed the message along to Washington but never looked at the film [Weisberg, *Oswald in New Orleans*, p. 175].)

JIM (*voice-over*) There was no real fight and the arresting Lieutenant later said he felt it was a staged incident. In jail, Oswald asked to talk to Special Agent John Quigley of the FBI who showed up immediately. They have a private session. Oswald is released and Quigley destroys his notes from the interview ...

▮ "It is the usual practice to destroy your notes after the completed work has been returned to you for proofing ... " [WC 4H p. 433; CE 826 (FBI Report dated 8-15-63)].

In a television studio in 1963, Oswald debates Carlos Bringuier with two moderators.

▮ Aug. 23, 1963: WDSU's William Stuckey hosted a weekly radio show called "Latin Listening Post." Intrigued by Oswald's arrest ("Leftists are as common in New Orleans as panthers are in Lapland" [James and Wardlaw, *Plot or Politics?*, p. 13]), Stuckey invited Oswald to appear on his program to debate Carlos Bringuier and Edward S. Butler, head of the staunchly anti-Communist (and Trade Mart tenant) Information Council of the Americas. Rather than focusing on the Cuban issue, the anti-Castro side confronted Oswald about his defection. There is some discrepancy in how Butler and Stuckey learned of Oswald's background. Stuckey claims that both the FBI and Butler called him before the debate to advise him that he had a former defector on his hands. Butler said he had confirmed Oswald's Soviet connections with "someone at the House Un-American Activities Committee." [Priscilla Johnson McMillan, *Marina and Lee*, (Harper & Row, 1978) p. 352; Summers, *Conspiracy*, p. 279.] On the other hand, Agent Quigley says in his FBI Report [CE 826] that Bill Stuckey advised the Bureau on Aug. 30 of Oswald's defection to Russia.

JIM (*voice-over*) ... but the arrest gets him a lot of publicity and as a result Oswald appears on a local TV debate that established his credentials as a Communist ...

BRINGUIER But you're a Communist, are you not, and you defected to Russia.

OSWALD No, I am not a Communist. But I am a Marxist-Leninist.

BRINGUIER What did you do when you were in Russia?

OSWALD (*defensive*) I worked while I was there. I was always under the protection of ... that is to say, I was not under the protection of the U.S. Government.

> ▌Oswald makes an intriguing slip during the debate. The Warren Commission published the transcript [Stuckey Exhibit 21H], and an audio tape is available from the National Archives. Researchers who obtained both were quick to realize an error in the transcript. In response to a question from Stuckey—How did you support yourself in Russia?—Oswald clearly says: "I worked in Russia. I was under the protection of the—that is to say, I was not under the protection of the American government." The Warren Commission transcribes it as: "I worked in Russia. I was *not* under the protection of the—that is to say, I was not under the protection of the American government ... " After the taping, Oswald popped into the WDSU-TV studio for a quick interview, admitting on film that he was a Marxist. [WDSU news footage, Aug. 23, 1963.]

Back in 1966, Jim walks with his two assistants.

BILL What the hell's a Communist like Lee Oswald doing working out of Banister's?

> ▌Delphine Roberts, Banister's secretary and confidant, told Garrison's investigators: "Mr. Banister was connected with people associated with both the conservative element as well as the Communist element or 'Left Wing.' He often told me being in the type of work he was—security—you rub shoulders with all kinds of characters in order to be able to get information from both sides." [New Orleans District Attorney Records, Statement of Delphine Roberts, 1/19/67.]

JIM Y'ever heard of a double agent, Bill? I'm beginning to doubt Oswald was ever a Communist ... after the arrest, 544 Camp Street never appeared on the pamphlets again. Now here's another one for you: What would you say if I told you Lee Oswald had been trained in the Russian language when he was a Marine?

LOU I'd say he was probably getting intelligence training.

JIM Lou, you were in the Marines. Who would be running that training?

LOU The Office of Naval Intelligence.

JIM Take a look across the street.

We see the Post Office building across the street.

LOU Post Office.

JIM Upstairs. In 1963 that was the Office of Naval Intelligence—And just by coincidence, Banister, before he was FBI, was ONI. What do they say?

LOU "Once ONI, always ONI"?

BILL Well, he likes to work near his old pals.

> ■ The Office of Naval Intelligence encompasses the intelligence division of the Marines. Banister served in Naval Intelligence in World War II [HSCA X. p. 123] and the program in which Oswald defected to the Soviet Union was most likely run by ONI given Oswald's status as a Marine.

Jim makes a gesture encompassing the whole Square.

JIM Bill, Lou, we're standing in the heart of the United States Government's intelligence community in New Orleans. That's the FBI there, the CIA, Secret Service, ONI. Doesn't this seem to you a rather strange place for a Communist to spend his spare time?

LOU What are you driving at, boss?

JIM We're going back into the case, Lou—the murder of the President. I want you to take some money from the Fees and Fines Account and go to Dallas—talk to some people. Bill, I want you to get Oser on the medical, the autopsy, Susan on Oswald and Ruby histories, tax records ...

BILL Lord, wake me, please. I must be dreaming.

JIM No, you're awake, Bill, and I'm dead serious. And we're going to start by tracking down your anonymous source from three years ago. How did you find out Dave Ferrie drove to Texas that day?

RACETRACK - DAY (1966)

A straggly group of people watch from the grandstands eating hotdogs and talking in small clusters. The horses are running early morning laps. Three men sit apart in the bleachers. A scared Jack Martin, three years older than when last seen, still wearing the Dick Tracy hat, sucks up coffee like a worm does moisture. He has the red puffy cheeks of an alcoholic and deeply circled, worried eyes. Bill and Jim wait.

> ■ Garrison Conversation with Martin: [Garrison, *Trail of the Assassins*, p. 29-32, 38-41. (For more on Martin, see HSCA X. p. 129-130; New Orleans District Attorney Records; 544 Camp Street sources).]

JIM You're not under cross-examination here, Jack. What I need is a little clarification about the night Guy Banister beat you over the head with his Magnum.

You called our office hopping mad from your hospital bed. Don't tell me you don't remember that?

Jack looks away and doesn't respond.

JIM Here's my problem, Jack. You told me you and Guy were good friends for a long time?

MARTIN More than ten years.

JIM And he never hit you before?

MARTIN Never touched me.

JIM Yet on November 22, 1963—the day of the President's murder—our police report says he *pistol-whipped* you with a .357 magnum. (*Martin's eyes are fixed on Jim*) But the police report says you had an argument over the *phone bill*. Here, take a look at it. (*Martin looks at the police report*) Now, does a simple argument over phone bills sound like a believable explanation to you?

SUDDEN FLASHBACK to the night of the pistol-whipping. The camera shows Banister laying Martin's head open; the beating; the humiliation.

MARTIN (*shaking his head slowly, dreamily*) No, it involved more than that.

Bill looks at Jim.

JIM How much more?

MARTIN (*waits*) I don't know if I should talk about this.

JIM Well, I'd ask Guy—we were friendly, you know—heart attack, wasn't it?

MARTIN If you buy what you read in the paper.

JIM You have other information?

MARTIN I didn't say that. All I know is he died suddenly just before the Warren Report came out.

JIM Why did Guy beat you, Jack?

MARTIN Well, I guess now that Guy's dead, it don't really matter ... it was about the people hanging around the office that summer. I wasn't really part of the operation, you know. I was handling the private-eye work for Guy when that came in—not much did—but that's why I was there ... it was a nuthouse. There were all these Cubans coming and going. They all looked alike to me ...

FLASHBACK to Banister's office in 1963. There are Cubans in battle fatigues and combat boots; duffle bags are lying around. David Ferrie, in fatigues, directs the Cubans as they carry crates of ammunition and weapons into a back room. Martin observes from another desk.

▌Ferrie, Banister and several anti-Castro activists were implicated in a late 1961 raid on a munitions bunker leased by Schlumberger Wells services in

Houma, Louisiana. [HSCA X. p. 127; Flammonde, *The Kennedy Conspiracy*, p. 118-9; *New Orleans States-Item*, Apr. 25, 1967; Brener, *The Garrison Case: A Study in Abuse of Power*, p. 48-49] Some of the material taken in the Houma raid resurfaced on August 1, 1963 when the FBI raided the arms cache at the Cuban exile training camp on Lake Pontchartrain.

Garrison alleged that the Houma raid was organized by the CIA to procure weapons for the local anti-Castro forces—making the Houma outing more of a simple "pick-up" than a "raid" (the HSCA maintained that the arms were "stolen," avoiding the issue of CIA involvement). There are strong indications that Garrison was right. New Orleans attorney Milton E. Brener represented some of the individuals implicated in the raid and writes: "it appears clear that the Schlumberger Wells bunker was serving that night as a transfer point for explosives with the acquiesence of its management and with officials of the United States Government, including, presumably, the Central Intelligence Agency." [Brener, *The Garrison Case: A Study in the Abuse of Power*, p. 48-49]. When reached by telephone, Brener said his information on the raid was subject to attorney-client privilege and would not discuss his sources.

MARTIN (*voice-over*) Dave Ferrie—you know about him?

JIM (*voice-over*) Was he there very often?

MARTIN (*voice-over*) Often? He practically lived there. It was real cloak and dagger stuff. They called it Operation Mongoose. The idea was to train all these Cuban exiles for another invasion of Cuba. Banister's office was part of a supply line that ran from Dallas, through New Orleans to Miami, stockpiling arms and explosives.

Still in 1963, we see the exterior of Banister's office. A dozen Cubans follow Ferrie downstairs into the street, and pile into several cars, duffles thrown in with them. Ferrie drives the lead car.

JIM (*voice-over*) All this right under the noses of the intelligence community in Lafayette Square?

We see the cars cross the long Lake Pontchartrain Bridge and enter a remote guerrilla training camp. Bayou and jungle are all around.

MARTIN (*voice-over*) Sure. Everybody knew everybody. It was a network. They were working for the CIA—pilots, black operations guys, civilians, military—everybody in those days was running guns somewhere ... Fort Jefferson, Bayou Buff, Morgan City ... McAllen, Texas was a big gun-running op.

■ [Hinckle and Turner, *The Fish Is Red*, p. 198-203; Flammonde, *The Kennedy Conspiracy*, p. 110-112.]

■ Lake Pontchartrain training camp: The training camp was located in Lacombe, across the lake from New Orleans. It was run by the Cuban exile MDC, the Christian Democratic Movement, and owned by the de la Barre famiy, and received considerable support from the Somoza family of Nicaragua. The camp was a highly-secret, elite affair—several Bay of Pigs veterans and Cuban exiles with intelligence ties trained there. A cache of weapons and explosives—some of which came from the 1961 raid on the Schlumberger arms bunker—was stored at a nearby cottage owned by Julius McLaney, brother of gambling syndicate organizer Mike McLaney. [Evica, *And We Are All ...*, p. 286-289; Hinckle and Turner, *The Fish Is Red*, p. 198-203; Flammonde, *The Kennedy Conspiracy*, p. 110-112; also see Jack Anderson's column of May 4, 1963 for more on Mike McLaney.]

At the guerrilla training camp at Lake Pontchartrain in 1963, we see scenes of basic training—shooting, obstacle courses, calisthenics—led by Ferrie and other trainers. Scattered among the Cubans are several white American mercenaries. We catch a glimpse of Oswald and glimpses of several other men we will see again, in sprinklings.

■ There is no evidence of Oswald's ever being at the camp, although there are several unconfirmed rumors of his visiting anti-Castro centers in Miami. [WC 10H, p. 84: Vance Blaylock testimony, conversation with Howard Davis] and Los Angeles [conversation with Gerry Patrick Hemming, Robert D. Morrow, *The Senator Must Die!*, (Henry Regnery Co., 1976), p. 282.]

JIM (*voice-over*) Where is Banister in all this?

MARTIN (*voice-over*) Banister was running his camp north of Lake Pontchartrain. Ferrie handled a lot of the training. There was a shooting range and a lot of tropical terrain like in Cuba. A few Americans got trained, too. Nazi types. Mercenaries. But Ferrie was the craziest.

It's night at the training camp. FBI agents race up in cars in the middle of the night, swarming over the camp, rounding up the trainees.

MARTIN (*continuing voice-over*) Anyway, late summer the party ended. Kennedy didn't want another Bay of Pigs mess, so he ordered the FBI to shut down the camps and confiscate the napalm and the C-4. There were a buncha Cubans and a couple Americans arrested, only you didn't read about it in the papers. Just the weapons got mentioned ... 'cause the first ones behind bars would've been Banister and Ferrie, but I think the G-men were just going through the motions for Washington. Their hearts were with their old FBI buddy Banister.

We see FBI agents loading dynamite, bomb casings, arms, 155 mm artillery shells, etc.

■ FBI raid on camp, Jul. 31, 1963: [*New Orleans Times-Picayune*, Aug 1, 1963, p. 1; Hinckle and Turner, *The Fish Is Red*, p. 198-200.] Researcher Peter Dale Scott notes that, of the many shut-downs of anti-Castro camps that year by Bobby Kennedy's Justice Department, the Lake Pontchartrain raid was the only one reported by the major wire services and *The New York Times* (Aug. 1, 1963, p. 6). According to Scott, this indicates that a highly-placed source, perhaps R.F.K. himself, asked for the publicity. Meanwhile, other anti-Castro groups continued to flourish, most notably the Chicago-based Junta del Gobierno de Cuba en el Exilio. [HSCA X. p. 95-99; Peter Dale Scott, *Beyond Conspiracy*, section of unpublished manuscript, 1979.] Apparently, these groups had the sanction of the brothers Kennedy. Among the arrestees was Richard Lauchli, a member of the right-wing extremist group the Minutemen. [New Orleans District Attorney's records]

Back at the racetrack in 1966, Jim listens.

MARTIN Like I said, a fuckin' nuthouse ...

JIM And Oswald?

Martin hesitates. We hear the rhythmic beating of the horse hooves and Martin sucking on the steaming cup of coffee.

MARTIN *(finally)* Yeah, he was there, too ... sometimes he'd be meeting with Banister with the door shut. Other times he'd be shooting the bull with Ferrie. But he was there all right.

JIM Anything more specific, Jack? It's important ...

FLASHBACK TO Banister's office in 1963. Banister and Martin shooting the breeze as the straight-laced middle-aged secretary, Delphine Roberts, hurries in.

MARTIN *(voice-over)* Yeah, one time the secretary got upset, I remember ...

SECRETARY I can't believe it, Mr. Banister. Lee Oswald is down on Canal Street giving out Communist leaflets supporting Castro!

Banister just looks at her and laughs.

BANISTER It's okay, Delphine, he's with us.

> ■ Delphine Roberts: [HSCA X. p. 129; Summers, *Conspiracy*, p. 295.] Another Banister employee, George Higgenbotham, says he was "kidding Banister about sharing a building with people passing out leaflets on the street" and Banister said, "Cool it ... one of them is mine." [New Orleans District Attorney's Records, memo dated Apr. 12-17, 1968.]

Back at the racetrack ...

JIM Anyone else involved at Banister's level?

MARTIN *(shrugs)* There was one guy, I don't know, big guy, business guy, white hair—I saw him come into the office once. He looked out of place, y'know—like a society guy. Can't remember his name. *(thinking)* Oswald was with him.

FLASHBACK to Banister's office on a day in 1963. Martin is snooping in Banister's files. Cut to Martin leaving the office as a big businessman with white hair briefly talks to Oswald and then goes into Banister's private office.

MARTIN *(voice-over)* He had something to do with money. I remember him cause Guy, who didn't kiss anybody's ass, sure kissed his.

Banister lets the man into his private office.

MARTIN *(voice-over)* Clay something, that was his name—Clay ...

JIM Bertrand. Clay Bertrand?

> ■ There is no official record of Clay Shaw/"Bertrand" visiting 544 Camp Street. However, Ferrie associate Thomas Beckham testified to a Shaw-Banister relationship to Garrison's office and the HSCA [New Orleans District Attorney Records; HSCA Record Group 233 J.F.K., Subject #014888] and

former CIA operative Robert Morrow claims in his book *Betrayal* (a book with intriguing but mostly unsubstantiated information that should be taken with extreme caution) that Banister and Shaw arranged for delivery of Carcano rifles for the assassination team. [Morrow, *Betrayal* (Henry Regnery, 1976), p. 114-115.]

MARTIN Yeah! That's it. (*pause, paranoid*) I don't know. Maybe it wasn't. I gotta go.

JIM (*to Bill*) Clay Bertrand. He's in the Warren Report. He tried to get Oswald a lawyer. [WC 11H p. 325-39 (Dean Andrews Testimony).]

JIM Was Kennedy ever discussed, Jack?

MARTIN Sure. 'Course they hated the sonofabitch, but ...

JIM ... the assassination, Jack?

MARTIN (*tightens*) Never. Not with me sir, never ... Listen, I think I'd better go. I said enough. I said all I'm going to say. (*rises suddenly*)

JIM Hold on, Jack. What's the problem?

MARTIN What's the problem? What's the problem? Do I need to spell it out, Mr. Garrison? ... I better go ...

JIM Nobody knows what we're talking about, Jack.

MARTIN You're so naive, mister.

Martin picks his way nervously down the bleacher benches.

CAR - FRENCH QUARTER - DAY (1966)

Jim drives, with Numa in the front and Bill in the back.

BILL Well, it's a terrific yarn, Chief, but the man's an obvious alcoholic with a reputation lower than crocodile piss.

JIM Does that bother you, Bill? I always wondered in court why it is because a woman is a prostitute, she has to have bad eyesight.

BILL He'll never sign a statement, boss, let alone get on a witness stand.

JIM When something's rotten in the land, Bill, it generally isn't just one fish, we'll get corroboration ... find this Clay Bertrand. If I were a betting man, I'd give you 10 to 1 it's an alias. Start checking around the Quarter.

BILL ... and the six of us, with almost no budget and in secret, are going to solve a case that the Warren Commission with dozens of support staff and millions of dollars couldn't solve. We can't keep up with the crimes in the Parish as it is, Chief.

JIM The murder of a President, Bill, is a crime in Orleans Parish too. I didn't pick you because of your legal skill, you know ...

BILL Gee, thanks boss.

Jim pulls the car over to park.

JIM … but because you're a fighter. I like a man who isn't scared of bad odds.

FRENCH QUARTER SIDEWALK - DAY (1966)

Jim and the others get out of the car and head towards Antoine's Restaurant. A black woman greets him.

BLACK WOMAN How ya doing, Mr. Garrison? Remember me—from the piano bar at the Royal Orleans?

JIM I surely do. We sang "You're the Cream in My Coffee."

She laughs. Others move in on him.

JIM (*to Numa*) Make sure we come back here, now.

ANTOINE'S RESTAURANT - DAY (1966)

They enter a busy lunchtime crowd in an elegant eatery. Lou Ivon and Al Oser are waiting for them as they're shown to their table by the Maitre d'.

MAITRE D' Mr. Garrison, we have not seen enough of you lately.

JIM Been too busy, Paul—an elected man can't have as much fun as he used to … (*seeing Lou and Al*) Welcome back, Lou. Find out anything on those hobos?

Lou's been waiting, excited. He gives Jim blowups of the five hobo photographs.

▌Tramp photos: About an hour after the assassination, the Dallas police pulled three men off of a railroad car in the train yard. The men, who appeared to be tramps, were marched across Dealey Plaza to the Sheriff's Office. Aside from photos taken by three news photographers, there was no official record of this event—no arrest records, no identifications, no explanation at all. Researcher Richard E. Sprague (who gave the photos to Garrison) found the pictures in Dallas in 1967 and they soon became the subject of speculation among the research community. Researchers contended that they weren't "real" tramps, noting that they had recent haircuts, shined shoes and clean clothes. Some believed that two of the tramps were Watergate burglars E. Howard Hunt and Frank Sturgis, a notion dispelled by the 1973 Rockefeller Commission, largely on the grounds that the "tramps" in question didn't look enough like Sturgis and Hunt—the Rockefeller panel did not have any hard, objective evidence that the men in question were not Sturgis and Hunt. [Rockefeller Commission Report, p. 255-257; Garrison, *Trail of the Assassins*, p. 207-210; Marrs, *Crossfire*, p. 332-333.]

Finally, in February 1992, there was a breakthrough in the mystery of the tramps. Their arrest records were found in the Dallas police files, made available to the public following the release of *JFK*. All evidence indicated that the men were, in fact, tramps. Identified as Gus W. Abrams, Harold Doyle and John Forrester Gedney, they were held by the police for four days and not released immediately, as previously believed.

The Dallas FBI office followed up on this new information and contacted Doyle and Gedney (Abrams is probably deceased). According to both men, they had spent the night of November 21 at a shelter where they showered, shaved and got clean clothes before attempting to hitch a ride on a train out of Dealey Plaza. [Ray LaFontaine and Mary LaFontaine, "First Look at Dallas' JFK Files," *The Houston Post*, February 2, 1992; George Lardner, Jr., "FBI Questions 'Tramps' at JFK Slaying Site," *The Washington Post*, March 4, 1992.]

LOU They took 'em to the Sheriff's office, *not* the police station, and they let 'em go. No record of them *ever* being questioned.

JIM I can't say that comes as a surprise anymore.

LOU A photographer from *The Dallas Times Herald* got some great shots of them, never published ...

The camera moves in on the photographs.

FLASHBACK TO the "hoboes" being escorted to the Sheriff's office—as per Sgt. Harkness' earlier description.

LOU (*voice-over*) ... take a good look, chief, do any of 'em look like hoboes you remember?

JIM Hoboes I knew of old used to sleep in their clothes—these two look pretty young.

LOU ... not a single frayed collar or cuff, new haircuts, fresh shaves, clean hands— new shoe leather. Look at the ear of the cop ... That's a wire. What's a cop wearing a headset for? I think they're actors, chief; they're not cops.

Susie Cox arrives.

JIM Who the hell are they, then! Hi, Susie, sit down. (*to Lou*) This could be it. Let's start looking for 'em. How 'bout that railroad man, Lee Bowers? Saw those men at the picket fence?

LOU Graveyard dead. August this year. (*Jim curses quietly*) A single car accident on an empty road in Midlothian, Texas. The doctor said he was in some kind of strange shock when he died. (*pause*)

> ▌ A one-car crash at 9:30 A.M. on a straight, dry road—this is often considered one of the suspicious deaths associated with the J.F.K. case. There are rumors of a witness who saw a black car drive Bowers into a bridge abutment. [Mark Lane, *A Citizen's Dissent*, (Dell, 1975) p. 203.]

JIM (*shares the look*) We need to find more witnesses, Lou.

LOU There was Rose Cheramie. A whore. Two Cubans threw her out of a car on the way to Dallas. She talked to a cop from a hospital bed two days before the assassination, said Kennedy would be hit that Friday. She said she was a dope runner for Jack Ruby and that Ruby knew Oswald for years ...

JIM Can we find her?

LOU Graveyard dead near Big Sandy, Texas in '65. Two in the morning on some highway. A hit and run.

> ▌ Rose Cheramie's death: [HSCA X. p. 204; Texas Department of Health Death Certificate 56985; Joe H. West and J. Gary Shaw, report of conversation with Jerry Don Moore, Jan. 30, 1990.] Moore, who allegedly struck Cheramie, swears he never hit her—she had tire tracks on her shoulder but Moore's tires were completely bald. He also noticed four suitcases lined up down the center stripe of the road and a red Chevrolet parked nearby that was not there a short time later.

FLASHBACK to Rose lying dead on an empty highway.

BILL Why not go right to the horse's mouth, chief? Jack Ruby's been rotting in a Dallas jail cell for three years. Maybe he's ready to crack?

JIM If we go to him our investigation'll hit the front pages by sunrise. Blow up right in our face. Ruby was just given a new trial. If he has something to say, it'll be there. Susie, what did you find out on Oswald?

> ▌ The Texas Criminal Court of Appeals overturned the conviction on Oct. 5, 1966. On Dec. 7, the trial was moved to Wichita Falls in northern Texas. According to Jim Marrs, there was "every likelihood that within another month or two, Ruby would walk free after his time in jail was counted against a probable short prison term for murder without malice. He certainly would have been allowed to post bond." Two days later, Ruby entered Parkland Hospital and was dead within a month. [Marrs, *Crossfire*, p. 431.]

SUSIE Negative on his tax records. Classified. First time I know a D.A. can't get a tax record. I put together a list of all the CIA files on Oswald that were part of the Warren Report and asked for them. There are about 1200 documents— (*gives it to Jim who reads*) Oswald in the USSR, in Mexico City, Oswald and the U2, a CIA 201 personnel file, a memo from the Director on Oswald, travel and activities—can't get *one* of them. All classified as secret on the grounds of national security. It's real strange.

> ▌ Since the time of the Garrison investigation, a few Oswald files, including the parts of the "201" file, have been released. By definition, a CIA 201 file is opened when a person is considered to be of "potential intelligence or counterintelligence significance." Oswald's 201 file was opened on Dec. 9, 1960, over a year after he arrived in the Soviet Union [HSCA Report, p. 200]. If the CIA did not want the Warren Commission to know about something, they simply did not give the Commission the file. We know the CIA did not disclose any information that would give away the CIA-Mafia plots against Castro—the Church Committee brought them to light ten years later. Remember also that Warren Commissioner and ex-CIA chief Allen Dulles knew full well about these plots and declined to tell the Commission.

> ▌ The CIA says they did make all of their Oswald material available to the HSCA. What happened next is entirely the fault of HSCA Chief Counsel G. Robert Blakey. An internal CIA memo released through a Freedom of Information Act suit says that the HSCA did not look at all the documents avail-

able to it. At that time the CIA acknowledged having 1196 documents on Oswald, mostly kept in the "201" file. Of these, 260 are still classified. The HSCA files are locked away in their entirety until 2029 without even an index of their records made available to the public.

BILL Maybe there's more to this, Susie. The CIA's keeping something from our enemies.

SUSIE Yes, but we're talking about a dead warehouse employee of no political significance. *Three years later* and he's still classified? They gave us his grammar school records, a study of his pubic hairs ... Put it in context, Bill, of what we know about Oswald. Lonely kid, no father, unstable childhood, high school dropout—wants to grow up and be a spy, joins the Marines at 17. He learns Russian, he acts overtly Marxist with two other Marines, but he's stationed at a top secret base in Japan where U2 spy flights over Russia originate. He's discharged from the Marines supposedly because his mother's sick. He stays home 3 days, then with a $1500 ticket from a $203 bank account, he goes to Moscow ...

▌Grammar school records: [WC 23H, CE1873.]

▌Study of pubic hairs: [WC 26H, CE3002.]

▌Marxist Marine: [Edward Jay Epstein, *Legend: The Secret World of Lee Harvey Oswald* (McGraw-Hill, 1978), p. 60-62; Melanson, *Spy Saga*, p. 10-11.]

▌Atsugi (Japanese base): According to the Warren Commission, Oswald was stationed at Atsugi from Sep. 12, 1957 to Nov. 2, 1958. [WR p. 683.] During that same time, Atsugi was the origin of the top-secret U-2 flights over the Soviet Union. In other words, Atsugi was no ordinary Marine Air Base and hardly the place to station a Marine who professed his love for all things Soviet. [Melanson, *Spy Saga*, p. 8-10 Epstein, *Legend*, p. 53-83].

▌Discharge: Oswald applied for a hardship discharge, normally tough to get, on the grounds that his mother was disabled. His mother's physicians, Rex J. Howard and Rex Z. Howard, sent the Marine Corps affidavits concerning Marguerite Oswald's disability. One, dated Sep. 3, 1959, says that Howard has been treating Mrs. Oswald since Sep. 5, 1959. [WC 19H p. 736-7, 19H p. 658.] Another is dated Sep. 4, 1959, the day after Oswald was transferred out of his Marine unit in preparation for his discharge. The discharge came through in a hurry, taking effect Sep. 4, 1959 [WR p. 689], one day before Rex Z. Howard began to treat Marguerite and the very day that Rex J. Howard first saw his disabled patient. [See discussion in Scott, *The Dallas Conspiracy*, II-8.]

▌$1,500 ticket from a $203 bank account: Passage to Moscow cost at least $1,500, many times more than the $203 in Oswald's bank account [WR p. 256]. Without borrowing money from friends or family, Oswald came up with the full amount. The Warren Commission decided that Oswald's habits indicated that "he could be extraordinarily frugal when he had reason to be." [WR p. 257.] Either that or he got help from somewhere.

FLASHBACK TO Moscow in 1959. We see shots of the city—strange and eerie black-and-white stills. Inside the U.S. Embassy Oswald slaps his passport on the table with a formal letter. Two consuls attend him.

■ Oswald embarked on Sep. 21, 1958, reaching the Soviet Union on a train from Helsinki on Oct. 15. [WR p. 690.] Questions remain as to how he got to Helsinki. The official story has him flying in from London; however, there was no commercial flight that would have brought him there from London on that day. [WC 26H CE 2676, p. 32; HSCA Report p. 211.] Neither the Warren Commission nor the HSCA could resolve this issue.

OSWALD (*voice stilted*) I want to renounce my citizenship and become a Soviet citizen. I'm going to make known to them all information I have concerning the Marine Corps and my specialty therein, radar operation ...

SUSIE (*voice-over*) One of the consuls, John McVickar, says Oswald's performance was not spontaneous—it seemed coached. Oswald gives an interview to a journalist.

■ John McVickar: "Oswald was tutored" [WC 8H p. 153]; Richard Snyder testimony [WC 8H]. The Snyder and McVickar accounts do not agree with each other. Snyder maintains that he was the only one in the room with Oswald, yet McVickar, by his own admission and his clear knowledge of the incident, was most definitely present. Researchers soon discovered that Snyder (unlike McVickar) was not your average State Department official. CIA Document #609-786 says that Snyder joined the CIA in 1949 but left in 1950 to work for the office of the High Commissioner of Germany (at that time headed by Warren Commissioner John J. McCloy). Perhaps he merely went under State Department cover—the HSCA discovered that his CIA file had been "red-flagged" and kept "segregated," based on a DCI (Director of Central Intelligence) statement and a "matter of cover" [HSCA Report, p. 215; Melanson, *Spy Saga*, p. 134.]

In November, 1991, Snyder appeared on ABC's *Nightline* and reiterated the familiar tale of Oswald the lonely, Marxist defector. Unfortunately, ABC correspondent Forrest Sawyer was unaware of the intriguing documents on Snyder's background and did not question his assessment of Oswald.

■ Just three days before Oswald showed up at the Embassy, Snyder wrote a letter to his higher-ups at the State Department in Washington asking for advice "as to how far the Embassy ought to go in 'defection' cases ... of persons like Webster." [WC 18H p. 110.] "Webster" refers to Robert E. Webster, another young American who defected two weeks before Oswald and returned to the U.S., also two weeks before Oswald. Even more intriguing, there are several references in the Warren Volumes to an Embassy Dispatch 224, dated Oct. 26, 1959, which dealt with *both* the Oswald and Webster cases. [CE 917, WC 18H p. 115; CE 914.] The date of the Dispatch raises questions—it is five days *before* Oswald first came to the Embassy on Oct. 31. [cited in Scott, *The Dallas Conspiracy*, II-12.]

Continuing the Moscow flashback, we see Oswald talking with a female journalist in his small room in the Hotel Metropole. Again he sounds robotic.

OSWALD I will never return to the United States for any reason. It is a capitalist country, an exploitive, racist country. I am a Marxist since I was 15. I've seen poor niggers and that was a real lesson. People hate because they're told to hate, like school kids. It's the fashion to hate people in the U.S.

■ After his arrival in Moscow, Oswald granted lengthy interviews to two American journalists, Priscilla Johnson of the North American Newspaper Alliance and Aline Mosby of United Press International. The interviews are virtually identical and neither was published nationally, although the Mosby account made the pages of newspapers in Fort Worth, Oswald's hometown. [WC 26H p. 90.] After the assassination, Johnson (now Priscilla Johnson McMillan) found more success with her Oswald piece. She made a few changes in her recollection of the interview—Oswald, originally "Joe College with a slight southern drawl" became "the stuff of which fanatics are made"—and it was published widely. Not long after, McMillan won the contract to write Marina Oswald's account of her marriage, a book that, despite a hefty advance, finally made it to the bookstores in 1977 after 13 years of delays. Researchers speculate as to McMillan's integrity and authenticity as a journalist. McMillan's name appears on a list of "State Department employees in contact with Oswald in Moscow" [CD 49 p. 24]. CIA Document #646-277 says Johnson "has been employed on a part-time basis within the U.S. Embassy." McMillan has gone on to become one of the Warren Report's staunchest defenders. As she noted at a public forum in 1975, "I've devoted a lot of time to Oswald's life so I have a vested interest in his having done it." [Quoted in Jerry Policoff, "The Second Dallas Casualty" in *Government by Gunplay: Assassination Conspiracy Theories from Dallas to Today*, Sid Blumenthal & Harvey Yazijian, eds. (Signet, 1976)]. For more on Priscilla Johnson McMillan and Oswald see Peter Whitney's excellent "Priscilla and Lee: Before and After the Assassination" in the May and Nov. 1991 issues of *The Third Decade*. (Contact Dr. Jerry Rose, *The Third Decade*, SUNY-Fredonia College, Fredonia, NY 14063.)

SUSIE (*voice-over*) The Russians are skeptical—want to send him back. Maybe they suspect he's a spy. He supposedly slashes his wrists in a suicide attempt so that they're forced to keep him, and he disappears for six weeks, presumably with the KGB.

■ Suicide attempt: [WC 26H CE 2778, WC 16H p. 94, 24H p. 333, 18H p. 450.]Oswald's autopsy report mentions a superficial transverse scar on his left wrist, certainly not severe enough for a suicide attempt.

We see photos of the city of Minsk, in Russia, Oswald with various friends and tourists, shots of Lee and Marina with a new baby.

SUSIE (*voice-over*) Finally they shuttle him to a radio factory in Minsk where he lives as high on the hog as he ever has—he's given 5,000 rubles, a roomy apartment with a balcony, has affairs with local girls.

JIM ... makes sense—he's a spokesman.

SUSIE But he never writes, speaks, or does any propaganda for the Russians. He meets Marina, whose uncle is a colonel in Soviet intelligence, at a trade union dance; she thinks he's Russian the way he speaks, six weeks later they marry, have a daughter.

■ According to the Warren Commission, Oswald met Marina at a trade union dance in Minsk [WC 16H p. 102, 22H p. 745]. But Marina was not so sure. Katya Ford, a friend of the Oswalds', said that Marina told her that Lee had defected to the Soviet Union after working at a trade show in Moscow [CD 5

p. 259]. What is striking is that the trade show story belongs to another 1959 defector, Robert Webster.

NUMA Didn't someone say he didn't speak good Russian?

JIM It's a contradiction, Numa, get used to them. The only explanation for the royal treatment is he did give them radar secrets. Or fake secrets.

We see documentary shots of the U2 on Russian soil … Francis Gary Powers … The Summit Conference canceled … Eisenhower and Khrushchev.

SUSIE *(voice-over)* I don't know if it's coincidence, but Oswald had a top security clearance and knew about the U2 program from his days at Atsugi Air Base in Japan. Six months after he arrives in Russia, Francis Gary Powers' U2 spy flight goes down in Russia. That plane was *untouchable*. Powers hinted that Oswald could've given the Russians enough data to hit it. As a *direct result*, the peace summit between Khrushchev and Eisenhower failed. I can't help thinking of that book *Seven Days in May*, maybe someone in our military didn't want the Peace Conference to happen, maybe Oswald was part of that. It gets weirder.

■ Powers blames Oswald: [Gary Powers with Curt Gentry, *Operation Overflight* (Holt, Rinehart & Winston, 1970), p. 358; Dwight D. Eisenhower, *Waging Peace*; Fletcher Knebel, *Seven Days in May*.]

BILL Susie, you're an assistant D.A., remember. Stick to what you can prove in court.

SUSIE You want facts, Bill? Okay. From 1945 to '59 only two U.S. soldiers defect to Russia. From '59 to '60, seven defect, six return, one of them another Marine a month before Oswald. All of them young men made to seem poor, disenchanted.

■ Summers quotes an interview with Victor Marchetti, former executive assistant to CIA Deputy Director Richard Helms:

"At the time, in 1959, the United States was having real difficulty in acquiring information out of the Soviet Union; the technical systems had, of course, not developed to the point that they are at today, and we were resorting to all sorts of activities. One of these activities was an ONI program which involved three dozen, maybe forty, young men who were made to appear disenchanted, poor American youths who had become turned off and wanted to see what communism was all about. They were sent into the Soviet Union, or into eastern Europe, with the specific intention that the Soviets would pick them up and "double" them if they suspected them of being U.S. agents, or recruit them as KGB agents. They were trained at various naval installations both here and abroad, but the operation was being run out of Nag's Head, NC." [Summers, *Conspiracy*, p. 145.]

JIM Don't get sidetracked! How does he get back to the States? That's the point. Does he have any problems?

SUSIE None! The State Department issues him a new passport in 48 hours and loans him the money to travel. He's never investigated or charged by the Navy for revealing classified information or, as far as we know, debriefed by the CIA.

> ∎New passport: [Melanson, *Spy Saga*, p. 19-22; Meagher, *Accessories After the Fact*, p. 336-339.]

> ∎No debriefing: [CIA Document #1004-400; Epstein, *Legend*, p. 312; HSCA Report, p. 207.] The Report notes that the CIA Domestics Contact Division debriefed an average of 25,000 tourists annually between 1959 and 1963 [p. 218.] It seems unlikely that they would ignore a defector. When Richard Helms testified before the Warren Commission in 1964, he assured them: " ... there is no material in the Central Intelligence Agency, either in the records or in the mind of any of the individuals, that there was any contact had or even contemplated with him." [WC 5H p. 121.] As noted earlier, the CIA opened the "201" file on Oswald in December, 1960. Helms also told the Commission that he checked "our file cards and personnel files and all our records." Either he made a grave error of oversight or he was lying under oath.

JIM This is a man whose secrets caused us to change our radar patterns in the Pacific! He should've been prosecuted as a traitor!

SUSIE The FBI finally gets around to talking to him in Dallas and runs a file on him as a miscreant Communist type.

> ∎Dallas FBI agent James Hosty's name, address, unlisted telephone number and car license plate number were all listed in Oswald's address book, all of which were left off the official FBI list of the contents of Oswald's book until the Warren Commission staff noticed the omission. The FBI and the Warren Report strove for an innocent explanation for Oswald's having this information, claiming the FBI address was readily available to the public and that Marina had noted Hosty's license number during one of his two "routine" visits to the Paine house. Meagher effectively debunks these notions [WR p. 327; Meagher, *Accessories After the Fact*, p. 210-219].

JIM But who meets him when he gets off the boat in New York in June '62?

The screen shows photos of New York: Empty docks ... a ship coming in ... Wall Street on a Sunday morning—Graphic Weegee-type black-and-white stills, then a photo of Spas T. Raikin.

> ∎Spas T. Raikin:[WR p. 173; Scott, *The Dallas Conspiracy*, Ch. 2, p. 23.] Raikin served as Secretary General of the American Friends of the Anti-Bolshevik Nations, a group affiliated with the FBI, U.S. military intelligence and the World Anti-Communist League. Raikin is hardly the sort one would expect to greet an avowed Marxist.

SUSIE (*voice-over*) Spas T. Raikin, a leading member of an *anti*-Communist group.

JIM (*voice-over*) And Marina? Does she have a problem getting out?

SUSIE (*voice-over*) None either. It's bizarre. It's next to impossible to get Russian sweethearts out. Nor does Lee have any problem getting a new passport when he wants to go to Cuba and Russia in '63. A man who has *defected* once already. It's crazy!

▮ After securing a new passport, Oswald went to the Mexican consulate in New Orleans to apply for a tourist card: [Meagher, *Accessories After the Fact*, p. 334; 336; Weisberg, *Whitewash*, p. 239-242.] In 1975, researchers discovered that the man who received his tourist card immediately before Oswald was a CIA employee named William Gaudet. [HSCA Report, p. 218; Summers, *Conspiracy*, p. 336-338.]

JIM Dammit, it doesn't add up! Ordinary people get blacklisted for leftist affiliations! The State Department did everything short of dispatching a destroyer to Minsk to insure Oswald's return. Only intelligence people can come and go like that.

FLASHBACK TO a Forth Worth map factory. We see Oswald at work on photo mattes with a Minox spy camera. The camera shows close-ups of maps and then flashes to a hand in the photographic solution. We see a close-up of Oswald's head in a photograph—the same headshot that will be superimposed on the Oswald photo—and a razor blade cutting mattes.

▮ Minox camera: [Earl Golz, "Oswald Camera Disappeared During FBI Investigation," *The Dallas Morning News*, Jun. 15, 1978; Earl Golz, "Oswald Pictures Released By FBI," *The Dallas Morning News*, Aug. 7, 1978.] The prints developed from the roll of film found among Oswald's possessions are mostly civilian scenes in Europe but five show "military scenes either in the Far East or Central America." According to a 1975 CBS program called "The American Assassins," Dallas Policeman Gus Rose related how New Orleans FBI Agent Warren De Brueys pressured him to remove the camera from the Dallas Police Inventory Sheet. [WC 24H, CE 2003 p. 296-300.]

▮ Backyard photos: The authenticity of the backyard photos has been the subject of ongoing controversy. Oswald himself told the Dallas police that the photos were faked, that it was his head transposed on somebody else's body. [WR p. 608-609.] Apparently, the Secret Service and Dallas police suspected he was telling the truth—they spent hours trying to recreate the photos in the backyard over the days following the assassination. Normally, we assume that photos are authentic and don't go about trying to recreate them unless there is clearly a problem—after all, the federal agencies did not re-enact other damning photos of Oswald, such as the ones of him handing out pro-Castro leaflets on the street in New Orleans.

But after a long and careful scientific analysis, the HSCA's photographic panel decided that the photos were authentic (see HSCA volume IV). However, not all researchers are satisfied with their verdict, and indeed, often for good reason. For instance, although Marina told the Warren Commission she took a photo of Oswald in that pose, she said she took only one photo, and then said she wasn't so sure how many she took when more shots surfaced. Recently, Marina told researchers she was standing "on the stairs" when she took the photo—but the stairs are in full view in the picture, making that impossible.

When the Dallas City Council voted to make the Dallas police files public following the release of *JFK*, researchers discovered interesting new evidence: a print of the backyard with a white silhouette in place of the Oswald figure. According to *The Houston Post*, the silhouette "appears to be an example of matting, a darkroom technique that can serve as an intermediate step in the combining of photographic images." ["First Look at Dallas' JFK Files," Ray LaFontaine and Mary LaFontaine, *The Houston Post*, February 2, 1992.] Matting is exactly what Oswald seemed to think created the image of him with the rifle—someone transposed his face on another body and, possibly in turn, transposed that figure on the Oswalds" backyard. At the present time, the origin of this new print is still uncertain. It could be an early re-enactment or comparison photo, a far more innocent explanation.

For a good overview of the problems associated with the backyard photos, see *Fake*, a videotape by Texas researcher Jim Marrs and Jack White (available through JFK video, Fort Worth, Texas).

SUSIE *(voice-over)* The next thing we know he's living in Dallas/Ft. Worth in October '62 working 6 months at Jaggars–Chiles–Stovall, a photographic firm that contracts to make maps for the U.S. Army ... He starts work only days before the government reveals Russian missiles in Cuba and the crisis explodes. Oswald may have had access to missile site footage obtained by the U2 planes and works alongside a young man who'd been in the Army Security Agency.

> ▌Jaggars-Chiles-Stovall: [Melanson, *Spy Saga*, p. 82-86; Hurt, *Reasonable Doubt*, p. 220-224.]

> ▌Young man: Dennis Ofstein was the same age as Oswald and had studied Russian while in the ASA. Oswald and Ofstein struck up a friendship of sorts with Oswald lending Ofstein Russian-language newspapers, explaining terms like "microdots"—a method of sending spy information—and describing to him patterns of Soviet military dispersements. [Melanson, *Spy Saga*, p. 82-88; Ofstein testimony, WC 10H p. 203.]

JIM ... sort of like Benedict Arnold coming back to George Washington's cabinet.

SUSIE ... equally incongruous is Oswald becoming chummy with the White Russian community of Dallas—all rabid *anti*-Communists.

FLASHBACK TO Fort Worth in 1963. In Oswald's cheap apartment, seven White Russians, including George de Mohrenschildt, a distinguished grey-haired man in his late fifties, are visiting Marina and Oswald, bringing old dresses, groceries, and toys and milk for the crying baby, whose cradle is two suitcases.

> ▌"White Russians" was a term given to Russians who opposed the Bolsheviks in the 1917-19 Revolution. After the Communists took control, many of these Russians—mostly educated and upper-class—left the Soviet Union for the U.S. Another flood of exiles arrived in the U.S. after World War II. [Marrs, *Crossfire*, p. 113-114; Scott, *The Dallas Conspiracy*, Chapter III.] (Note: While in the Marines, Oswald told fellow soldier Nelson Delgado that the Russian-language newspaper he read was "not Communist; it's a White Russian." [WC 8H p. 242.])

SUSIE *(voice-over)* His closest friend is an oilman named George de Mohrenschildt who's about 35 years older than Oswald, who's only 23 and supposedly broke. De Mohrenschildt is a member of the Dallas Petroleum Club, speaks five languages and was in French Vichy Intelligence during the War. Also rumored to have been a Nazi sympathizer and member of the "Solidarists," an international anti-Communist organization with many Eastern Europeans and ex-Nazis, many of them brought here by the CIA after the war, many of them involved in oil and munitions interests in Dallas and the Southwest. You figure it.

■ De Mohrenschildt biography: [Summers, *Conspiracy*, p. 192-200; Scott, *The Dallas Conspiracy*, p. 2, 1-5.]

■ Vichy Intelligence: [WC 9H p. 193-194.]

■ "Solidarists": *Nomenclature of An Assassination Cabal* by the pseudonymous William Torbitt (Texas attorney David Kopeland) (self-published, 1970) defines the Solidarists as a Czarist Russian, Eastern European and Middle East exile organization whose common link seemed to be in seeing their homelands fall to Communism [p. 19-20].

AL Where'd you get all this Nazi stuff?

SUSIE (*hands him a file*) Read it. They called it "Project Paperclip."

■ Project Paperclip: The pre-CIA Office of Strategic Services (OSS) mounted "Project Paperclip" as a means of bringing German scientists and other professionals—some of whom were guilty of war crimes, including running the Nazi slave-labor factories—into the U.S. The eminent Dr. Werner von Braun, longtime head of NASA's Space Program, and General Walter Dornberger, von Braun's superior and former administrator of Peenemunde rocketworks and the Dora concentration camp, both came to the U.S. through the auspices of Paperclip. [Clarence Lasby, *Project Paperclip* (Athenaeum, 1971); Tom Bower, *The Paperclip Conspiracy* (Little Brown, 1987); Linda Hunt, *Secret Agenda* (St. Martin's Press, 1991).]

JIM (*voice-over*) This is the guy that keeps turning up in colonial countries and each time something strange happens. Coup d'états, presidents overthrown. He shows up on a "walking tour" of Guatemala's Cuban invasion camps just before the Bay of Pigs invasion. If we don't *know* he's CIA, let's circle him *very probable*—Oswald's handler.

■ De Mohrenschildt's travels: Researcher Michael Levy obtained a CIA document from former CIA Deputy Director Richard Helms stating that de Mohrenschildt's trip to Yugoslavia furnished "foreign intelligence which was promptly disseminated to other federal agencies in 10 separate reports. Another stated that de Mohrenschildt provided similar reports after traveling in Mexico and Central America. [*Dallas Times-Herald*, "Oswald Friend Labeled CIA Informant in Memo," Jul. 27, 1978.]

We see Oswald and de Mohrenschildt talking with the others and a magazine cover with J.F.K. the subject of discussion.

OSWALD I think he's made some mistakes on Cuba, but he's doing a pretty good job. If he succeeds, in my opinion, he'll be a great President. And a really attractive one too—open features, great head of hair ... (*laughs*)

■ Oswald on J.F.K.: "I like President Kennedy." [WC 1H p. 233 (Marguerite Oswald).] *New Times*, Jun. 24, 1977 has George de Mohrenschildt quoting Oswald as saying "If he succeeds he will be the greatest President in the history of the country." [WR p. 267.] Secret Service Inspector Thomas J. Kelley reports Oswald telling him: "My wife and I like the President's family. They are interesting people. I have my own views on the President's national policy ... I am not a malcontent; nothing irritated me about the President." In 1988, Marina Oswald told a writer that Oswald "adored" J.F.K. ["Marina Oswald—Twenty-Five Years Later," *Ladies Home Journal,* Nov., 1988.]

SUSIE (*voice-over*) De Mohrenschildt draws a picture of Oswald as an intellectual, well read, speaks excellent Russian, a man who adored J.F.K.

JIM That's scenery. Don't get sidetracked. This is the man, bottom line, who nailed Oswald to the Warren Commission as a potentially violent man, and linked him to the rifle.

TIME CUT TO Oswald's apartment on a different day in 1963. George de Mohrenschildt points out a Mannlicher-Carcano rifle in the closet, turns to Lee.

▌De Mohrenschildt links Oswald to rifle: [WC 9H p. 249] De Mohrenschildt carefully makes it clear that he never actually saw the rifle; he only watched as his wife and Marina pointed to it. This visit was the last meeting of any kind between the Oswalds and the de Mohrenschildts [Marrs, *Crossfire,* p. 283].

GEORGE So, Lee, what are you taking a potshot at this week—rabbits or fascists?

Lee's look is sickly. He freezes up.

▌Shortly after an unknown gunman fired at retired Army Maj. Gen. Edwin Walker, a right-wing extremist and segregationist, at his Dallas home, George de Mohrenschildt asked Oswald "How is it that you missed General Walker?" [WR p. 724.] De Mohrenschildt's wife attributed the apparently spontaneous remark to her husband's "sense of humor."

Oswald's alleged reaction to the remark figured strongly in the Warren Commission's implication of Oswald in the Walker incident—a case that otherwise remains unsolved. De Mohrenschildt told the Warren Commission that Oswald "sort of shriveled" [WR p. 282]; Marina termed it "became almost speechless" [WC 22H p. 777]. Certainly, the Commission thought, Oswald was guilty.

Although the HSCA concluded that the evidence "suggested that Oswald attempted to murder General Walker," they acknowledged eyewitness accounts indicating more than one person was seen fleeing the Walker scene, and noted that the committee had only "conducted a limited investigation" before "no leads were developed, and this line of inquiry was abandoned." [HSCA Report, p. 61fn.] [For more on Gen. Walker, see Summers, *Conspiracy,* p. 205-210 and citations; Meagher, *Accessories,* p. 283-292.]

RESUME scene of White Russian gathering in Oswald's apartment.

SUSIE The only Russian that suspects Oswald of still being a Communist is Anna Meller. But her Russian friend tells her "he's checked" with the local FBI and was told Oswald is all right.

Anna Meller, one of the guests, glances at a copy of Das Kapital *in a pile of books, and talks to another Russian man about it ... Talking now to Lee and Marina are Janet and Bill Williams, a mid-American couple in their late twenties, freshly minted.*

▌Meller noticing *Das Kapital:* [WC 8H p. 382.]

  ▌Oswald "all right": CD 950, interview of Teofil Meller (Anna's husband) by Dallas police Feb. 17, 1964. Meller told Dallas police he had "checked with the FBI and they told him that Oswald was all right." Anna Meller told the Warren Commission that fellow Russian émigré George Bouhe told her that he "asked and they tell me he's checked." Checked, Meller assumed, with the FBI. [WC 8H p. 383.]

SUSIE *(voice-over)* ... the Oswalds are introduced by George de Mohrenschildt to Janet and Bill Williams. It's through Janet Williams in October '63 that Lee gets the warehouse job, right smack on Elm Street at the Book Depository, which is owned by another oilman with ties to defense and military intelligence.

JIM *(voice-over)* Presumably so he can now exercise his intellect stacking schooltexts at $1.25 an hour ...

  ▌At the time of the assassination, oilman D. H. Byrd owned the building. Byrd had strong business ties to Army Intelligence Reservist Jack Crichton, who later arranged for translators for Marina. [Scott, *The Dallas Conspiracy*, p. 3-31.]

We see Oswald and another man in the Texas School Book Depository in 1963. They are hauling and stacking school textbooks—an obviously lower-level job for Oswald after the map factory. We cut ahead to empty graphics of the sealed-off area, the window site, the cafeteria.

SUSIE *(voice-over)* All I can find out about the Williams' is their tax returns are classified and that Bill Williams, a descendant of the Cabots of Massachusetts, has links through his family and United Fruit to the CIA and does classified work for Bell Helicopter which requires a security clearance—so what is Oswald, a defector, doing visiting his wife in his house? Williams has a relationship at Bell with General Walter Dornberger, another one of the Nazis we brought in after the War for our missile program. He used slave labor to build the V-2 Rockets for Hitler before Bell needed him.

  ▌Bill and Janet Williams: Janet and Bill Williams are based on characterizations of Ruth and Michael Paine, Michael Paine was a Cabot through both parents and a second cousin of United Fruit Company/Gibraltar Steamship head Thomas Dudley Cabot. [Scott, *The Dallas Conspiracy*, IV, p. 2-3.]

  ▌Michael Paine at Bell Helicopter: [WC 2H p.385-386.]

  ▌Walter Dornberger at Bell Helicopter: For more on Dornberger's Nazi past and work at Bell see Richard Lewis, *Appointment on the Moon*, p. 21-22; Lasby, *Project Paperclip*, p. 30-37; Christopher Simpson, *Blowback* (Weidenfield and Nicholson, 1988), p. 22, 27-31.

JIM I wonder about the Williams'. Just where did the first description of Oswald come from at 12:44? No one knows. They claimed it was Brennan's, but his description came after 1 P.M. Who called? Somehow the FBI's been tapping the Williams' and picks up a call between Bell Helicopter and Janet's phone, an unidentified voice saying "We both know who's responsible." Who called? Why's the Bureau been tapping them?

> ■ Description of Oswald: The police radio alerted officers to look for a "slender white male about 30, 5 feet, 10 inches, 165 pounds, carrying what looked to be a 30.30 or some type of Winchester" [CE 1974, p. 24-25]. The Warren Report (p. 144) has witness Howard L. Brennan giving the description to Dallas police prior to the broadcast. However, by Brennan's own admission, he talked to Secret Service agent Forrest Sorrels who didn't return from Parkland until at least 12:55 P.M. [WC 3H p. 145-146].

> ■ Phone call from Bell Helicopter: CD 206, an FBI report, mentions an intercept of a phone call between Ruth Paine's home and Michael Paine's office on the afternoon of November 23. According to the document, "a male voice was heard to say he felt sure Lee Harvey Oswald had killed the president but did not feel Oswald was responsible, and further stated, 'We both know who is responsible.'"

We see the interior of the Williams' home in Irving on a day in 1963.

SUSIE (*voice-over*)... His wife, Janet Williams, studied Russian in college and her father worked for the Agency for International Development, which works hand in hand with the CIA. She suddenly becomes Marina's best friend. Marina fights often with Lee about many things—his secrecy, the lack of money. She says Lee is not sexually adequate. Lee hits her on several occasions. Bill Williams' convenient separation from Janet (he moves back after the assassination) allows Janet to invite Marina to move into her house in Irving. There Marina and Lee have a second daughter—while Lee, now 24, stores his belongings in Janet's garage and rents a small room in Dallas under an alias of "O.H. Lee."

> ■ Ruth Paine testimony: [WC 2H p. 430-517, 3H p. 1-140, 9H p. 331-425, 11H p. 398-404.] Inexplicably, the HSCA did not question the Paines.

We see Marina and Oswald in bed at night in the Williams' house, in a tender scene. Oswald says goodbye to his child.

TIME CUT TO Oswald living in a boarding house. It is at night, and he sits in his room alone. The housekeeper, Earlene Roberts, heavyset, white, in her 60s, comes in and asks him if he wants to watch some TV with her. He declines.

SUSIE (*voice-over*)... When he's arrested, Marina buries him with the public. Her description of him is that of a psychotic and violent man.

FLASHBACK TO Marina on TV, a different person from before.

MARINA I do not want to believe, but I have too much facts ... tell me that Lee shot Kennedy [News footage, Sherman Grindberg Archives].

JIM (*voice-over*) Yeah, after, they take her to Six Flags Inn in Arlington, prepare her for the interviews, teach her how she should answer—and after two months and 46 interviews, she has a nervous breakdown. (*flashback*) Oswald was no angel, that's clear, but who was he?

■ Marina and her children were taken to the Inn of the Six Flags outside of Fort Worth immediately after the assassination: [WC 1H p. 164, 1H p. 471-2.] The manager of the motel soon became Marina's business agent and brokered the sale of the "backyard photos" to the press. [Scott, *The Dallas Conspiracy*, III-20; see Chapter III for more details on the Inn's ownership and associations.]

BACK TO Antoine's Restaurant.

BILL I'm lost, boss. What are we saying here?

JIM We're saying that when Oswald went to Russia, he was not a real defector, that he was an intelligence agent on some kind of mission for our government and he remained one till the day he died, that's what we're saying.

BILL And therefore because Oswald pulled the trigger, the intelligence community murdered their own commander in chief. That's what you're saying!

JIM I'll go you one better! Maybe Oswald didn't even pull the trigger, Bill. The nitrate test indicates he didn't even fire a rifle on November 22nd. And on top of that, they didn't even bother to check if the rifle had been fired that day.

■ Oswald's nitrate test: Oswald tested positive for nitrates on both hands but negative on his cheek, which could have confirmed that he had fired a rifle. Nitrates are often found on the hands—from urine, bleach, kitchen matches and many other items—but not so often on the cheek. The Warren Commission found the results "inconclusive" and the test "unreliable"; at any rate, they don't aid the cause for Oswald's guilt. [WR p. 560-561.]

■ Rifle tested for recent firing: [Meagher, *Accessories After the Fact*, p. 120.] There is no record that indicates that the Mannlicher-Carcano was ever tested to verify that it had been fired that day. When asked by the Warren Commission if there was metal fouling in the rifle barrel (a sign of recent firing) when he examined it the morning after the shooting, FBI Expert Robert Frazier answered, "I did not examine it for that."[WC 3H p. 395.]

BILL He had his palm print on the weapon.

JIM It went to the goddamn FBI and they didn't find a goddamn thing. It comes back a week later and *one* guy in the Dallas police department suddenly finds a palm print which for all I know he could've taken off Oswald at the morgue. There's no chain of evidence, Bill. And what about the two guns actually *seen* in the Depository? One an Enfield photographed by a newsman and the other a Mauser, described by Deputy Weitzman ... Maybe, just maybe, Lee Oswald was exactly what he said he was Bill—"a patsy." Take it at face value. Lou, Susie, I'm going with my gut here. He's got an alias of Hidell to buy the rifle, "O.H. Lee" to rent the room, right? What's in a name, right? In intelligence, they're assumed to be fake. A name is sort of like a postbox number, a code—

several different people can use the same name, right? Then why can't somebody be using Oswald's name?

∎ Palm print: Initial FBI and Dallas police tests found only traces of two fingerprints, neither one identifiable. According to the Warren Report, Lt. Day of the Dallas police succeeded in lifting a partial palm print, identified as Oswald's, on the underside of the barrel shortly before sending the rifle off to Washington. Contrary to standard procedure, Day did not photograph the print before lifting it, and apparently lifted it so completely that not a trace of it remained on the rifle when it arrived at the FBI lab. Nor was there a trace of the print's having been lifted. The print laid low for a few days, officially surfacing in public from the FBI lab on Nov. 29, a full week after the assassination. [Meagher, *Accessories After the Fact*, p. 120-21; Marrs, *Crossfire*, p. 443-45; Anson, *They've Killed The President!*, p. 76-77.] Marrs suggests that the palm print came from Oswald—not from the rifle at all but after his death. The FBI dispatched a crew to Miller Funeral Home in Fort Worth armed with cameras, a crime lab kit and, oddly enough, the Mannlicher-Carcano. FBI Agent Richard Harrison confirmed to researcher Gary Mack in 1978 that it was his understanding that his fellow agent intended to put Oswald's palm print on the rifle for "comparison purposes." But the Dallas police had fingerprinted Oswald three times already [Marrs, *Crossfire*, p. 444-45].Whatever the circumstances, the government version cannot *disprove* this particular palm print scenario. The funeral home director told Jim Marrs: "I had a heck of a time getting the black fingerprint ink off of [Oswald's] hands." [Marrs, *Crossfire*, p. 444.] The Dallas police had fingerprinted Oswald three times over the weekend—they had all the "comparison prints" they needed.

In 1984, the FBI agent who transported the rifle from Dallas to the FBI lab in Washington on the night of the assassination told researcher Henry Hurt: "I just don't believe there ever was a print ... All I can figure is that it was some sort of cushion, because they were getting a lot of heat by Sunday night."

∎ Three guns in the Texas School Book Depository: Deputy Sheriff Seymour Weitzman first reported that the rifle found on the sixth floor was a Mauser, also confirmed by a CIA document (released Mar. 16, 1976, dated Nov. 28 1963). Later, he told the Warren Commission that he was mistaken, that in fact it was a Mannlicher-Carcano with a Mauser bolt action. In addition to the Mauser and the Carcano, a British Enfield appears in the Dallas Cinema Associates film of Dealey Plaza on Nov. 22, 1963. [Garrison, *Trail of the Assassins*, p. 98-99.]

∎ aliases: "O.H. Lee" [WC 6H p. 438, Earlene Roberts; Meagher, *Accessories*, p. 188-190, 196-197]; "Hidell." [WC 17H, CE 773.]

∎ Someone using Oswald's name: "Since there is a possibility that an imposter is using Oswald's birth certificate, any current information the Department of State may have concerning subject will be appreciated." [CD 294B, Hoover Memo to State Department Office of Security, Jun. 3, 1960.] Imagine that—J. Edgar Hoover is writing personal memos about Lee Harvey Oswald in 1960.

We see blank faces around the table.

BILL But why?

JIM To frame him, obviously. You got to get in your minds how the hell spooks *think*, Bill! They're not ordinary crooks.

LOU I never *could* figure out why this guy orders a traceable weapon to that post office box when you can go into any store in Texas, give a phoney name and walk out with a cheap rifle which can never be traced.

> ▮ Traceable weapon: Researcher Fred Newcomb came up with an intriguing explanation for why Oswald might have ordered his weapons through the mail. In January, 1963, Senator Thomas J. Dodd (D-CT) was gathering evidence for his subcommittee to bolster proposed gun-control legislation. The Dodd Committee was especially concerned with mail order which could be readily obtained by anyone without restrictions, including criminals, psychopaths and political subversives. Oswald's mailbox in Dallas seemed to be teeming with subversive activity, receiving all sorts of Communist literature and correspondence. Moreover, both of the mail-order houses from which he ordered his weapons (Klein's Sporting Goods and Seaport Traders) were specific targets of the Dodd Committee's investigation. [Hurt, *Reasonable Doubt*, p. 300-302: Melanson, *Spy Saga*, p. 59.] As Peter Dale Scott notes: "This apparent obsession with the ordering of weapons by interstate mail would be otherwise strange for someone who in this period was never once observed to be using them." [Scott, *Beyond Conspiracy*, p. 579.]

JIM Unless he or someone else wants him to get caught. Maybe he never ordered the weapon, Lou. Somebody else did. It was picked up at the post office early morning when Oswald's time sheet shows him clocked in at his job. Lou, come alive. These things are not adding up.

> ▮ Even if Oswald was clocked in at work when the rifle was allegedly picked up, timecards are not a good index of Oswald's whereabouts. While working for the Reily Coffee Company in New Orleans, Oswald often read magazines next door at the Crescent City Garage. [Meagher, *Accessories After the Fact*, p. 49-50; WC 10H p. 227.] According to Book Depository Records, Oswald was clocked in for a full 8-hour day on Nov. 22, 1963. [CE 1949, p.6, cited by Meagher, p. 270.]

BILL I still have to question what the legal basis is that supports this, boss. Susie's stuff is colorful, but ...

JIM Let's start making some assumptions about the man. Why would he leave a path as big as Lee Harvey Oswald's? This is not a thin trail, gentlemen, it is a very *wide* one. Who found the evidence? Who set him up? Lou, Bill, Susie, I want you to go back and check all the sightings of Oswald in Dallas, New Orleans and Mexico in the summer and fall of '63—see if it's the same guy.

AL Boss, Oswald impersonators? Sounds like James Bond now.

JIM Al, you can't tell a mink from a coonskin unless you see the fur up close. Goddamn, Sam! If we don't start reading between the lines here! Y'all gotta start thinking on a different level—like the CIA does. We're through the looking glass. Here white is black and black is white.

BILL What do you think, Lou?

LOU I'm just an investigator, Bill. I leave the theories to you lawyers.

BILL You, Numa?

NUMA A week ago I would've said this is nuts, but now ... (*shakes his head*) ... there's a lot of smoke there, but there's some fire.

BILL Now you guys, come on. You're talking about the United States Government here!

JIM We're talking about a crime, Bill. No one is above the law. Reduce it. A crime was committed. Let's get to work.

MEDICAL UNIT - JAIL - DAY (1966)

Jack Ruby, thick fudge of an angry face, flu-ridden, confronts a doctor and two guards in his cell.

RUBY Christ, what the hell kinda needle is that? I just got a cold for Chrissake. I don't want any shot!

DOCTOR Please relax, Mr. Ruby. This'll calm you down and clear this up.

RUBY Doc, I'm telling you, I don't need any shots.

DOCTOR Mr. Ruby, I don't want to involve the guards. It'll just take a few seconds.

Ruby looks over at the two guards, who eye him. The Doctor gives him the injection.

▮ Ruby was diagnosed and died within a month. For certain kinds of cancer—like pancreatic, which Ruby's physician said he had—this is not terribly unusual. What *is* unusual is that Ruby had just been granted a retrial. Ruby himself expressed concern for his life in his testimony to the Warren Commission, in letters from jail and in conversations with a deputy sheriff. He told the sheriff he had been injected with cancer cells under the guise of a cold treatment. [See Marrs, *Conspiracy*, p. 429-433, for a good discussion of Ruby's mysterious cancer.]

At the time of Ruby's death, the U.S. government was actively developing bacteriological weapons and toxins at the Army Chemical Corps research center at Fort Detrick. Via a program called MKNaomi set up in 1952, the CIA's Technical Services Staff worked with the Chemical Corps to obtain such weapons for the agency's use in the field. [Ranelagh, *The Agency*, p. 207; also see Joint Hearings, *Project MKUltra*, U.S. Government Printing Office, 1977; Philip H. Melanson, "High Tech Mysterious Deaths," *Critique*, Fall/Winter 1984-1985.]

The point here is that while allegations of injectable cancers, mysterious heart attacks and other convenient deaths may sound paranoid and far-fetched, the U.S. military and intelligence agencies did—in undisputed, documented fact—develop these capabilities.

FLASHBACK TO Ruby's jail cell in 1964. Ruby talks to men with their backs to us. Lawyers and police clutter the cell, making Ruby hyper-nervous. The chief official's white hair and avuncular voice are all we see and hear of him; his back is to us.

■ Ruby testimony to Warren Commission: [WC 5H p. 194-198.]

RUBY Then do you understand that I cannot tell the truth here? In Dallas. That there are people here who do not want me to tell the truth ... who do not want me to have a retrial?

OFFICIAL Mr. Ruby, I really can't see why you can't tell us now ...

Ruby catches the stern face of Sheriff Bill Decker from the corner of his eye, the Assistant D.A. next to him.

RUBY When are you going back to Washington, sir?

OFFICIAL (*looks at watch*) I am going back very shortly after we finish this hearing— I am going to have some lunch.

RUBY Can I make a statement? If you request me to go back to Washington with you right now, that is if you want to hear further testimony from me, can you do that? Can you take me with you?

OFFICIAL No, that could not be done, Mr. Ruby. There are a good many things involved in that.

RUBY What are they?

OFFICIAL Well, the public attention it would attract. And we have no place for you there to be safe, we're not law enforcement officials, and many things are at stake in this affair, Mr. Ruby ...

RUBY ... But if I am eliminated there won't be any way of knowing. Consequently a whole new form of government is going to take over our country, and I know I won't live to see you another time. My life is in danger here. Do I sound screwy?

OFFICIAL Well I don't know what can be done, Mr. Ruby, because I don't know what you anticipate we will encounter.

RUBY Then you don't stand a chance, Mr. Chief Justice, you have a lost cause. All I want is a lie-detector test, and you refuse to give it to me. Because as it stands now—and the truth serum—how do you pronounce it—Pentothal—whatever it is. They will not give it to me, because I want to tell the truth ... And then I want to leave this world.

The camera pauses on Ruby's face. The men rise and leave in the shadows.

PARKLAND MEMORIAL HOSPITAL - (1967)

Jack Ruby is escorted out of the infirmary, dead of cancer.

■ Ruby died at 10 A.M. on Jan. 3, 1967 of pancreatic cancer [Marrs, *Crossfire*, p. 431].

BROUSSARD'S RESTAURANT - NEW ORLEANS - (1967)

The puffy, smiling face of Dean Andrews, framed by huge black glasses, talks in a Louisiana hippie argot of the 50's. The restaurant has a fancy French decor, mirrored walls, marble—it serves the cream of Louisiana society.

> ■ We've tried to keep Dean Andrews' unique dialect as intact as possible in this screenplay. Andrews' testimony to the Warren Commission [WC 11H p. 325-339] is long on slang and short on legal language—the incredulous Warren Commission attorney repeatedly asks Andrews to clarify his terms. Garrison's recollection of this scene is found on pages 79-83 of *On the Trail of the Assassins.*
>
> When asked if he thought Oswald killed the president, Andrews, a former Navy ordnanceman who shot up to 40,000 rounds a day with a rifle for five years, answered, "I know good and well he did not. With that weapon, he couldn't have been capable of making three controlled shots in that short time." [WC 11H p. 330.]

ANDREWS Why you keep dancing on my head for, my man? We been thicker'n molasses pie since law school.

JIM Because you keep conning me, Dean. I read your testimony to the Warren Commission and ...

ANDREWS There you go. Grain of salt. Two sides to every coin ...

JIM You tell them the day after the assassination you were called on the phone by this "Clay Bertrand" and asked to fly to Dallas and be Lee Oswald's lawyer.

ANDREWS Right.

JIM Now that's pretty important, Dean. You also told the FBI when you met him, he was six foot two. Then you tell the Commission he was five foot eight. How the hell did the man shrink like that, Dean?

ANDREWS They put the heat on, my man, just like you're doing. I gave 'em anything that popped into my cabeza. Truth is, I never met the dude ...

Sudden FLASHBACK to Andrews' office on a day in 1963. Clay Bertrand sits, back to us, talking to Andrews. He has close-cropped white hair. He is the same patrician man we've seen earlier with Oswald on Canal Street and in Banister's office. Andrews is evidently lying.

ANDREWS (*voice-over*) I don't know what the cat looks like and furthermore I don't know where he's at. All I know is sometimes he sends me cases. So one day he's on the phone talkin' to me about going to Dallas and repping Oswald ... (*notices a woman, in present*) Hey, pipe the bimbo in red. What ever happened to that little gal you was dating in the Quarter—from Opelousas, y'know, elevator didn't go to the top floor but tits could smother gumbo with.

> ■ Andrews' contact with "Clay Bertrand": An FBI report dated Dec. 6, 1963, states that Andrews is now convinced that the call he received from "Clay Bertrand" was "a dream." Over the next few months, the dream apparently

becomes reality, or else Andrews wants to tell the truth; he goes before the Commission counsel on Jul. 21, 1964 and says that the call did take place but he still can't say for sure who Bertrand is. As for his statements to the FBI that Bertrand was a figment of his imagination, Andrews said, "That's what the Feebees [FBI] put on." [WC 11H p. 331-337; CE 1931, 2899, 2900, 2901, 3094, 3104; CE 2900.]

∎ Andrews testified that he told the FBI himself of Bertrand's call the very afternoon that it happened [WC 11H p. 332], making it unlikely that the call, or Bertrand, was a figment of his imagination or a dream.

Jim, in present, looking briefly—a pretty girl walking in.

JIM (*remembering*) Yeah, she was pretty, all right, but not half as cute as you, Deano. You shoulda tried a legitimate line of business.

ANDREWS (*chuckles*) You can't ever say crime don't pay in Louisiana, Jim—only not as good as it used to. Good chowder, ain't it?

JIM When did you first do business with this Bertrand?

ANDREWS (*bored*) Oh, I first heard these street cats jiving about him back in '56, '57 when I lived down in the Quarter.

JIM Street cats?

ANDREWS Swishes. They swish, y'know. Young fags, you know. They'd come into my bureau needing help, no bread, and I'd say, hey man, I ain't Rockefeller, who gonna back you up? These cornmuffins go to the phone and dial ...

FLASHBACK TO Andrews' office on another day in 1963. We catch a glimpse of a young swish sitting in Andrews' office talking on the phone. Andrews is also on the phone to Bertrand, unseen, on the other end.

∎ Shaw at Andrews' office: Andrews claimed that Shaw/Bertrand never came to his office [WC 11H p. 334-335]. However, according to Edward Whalen, a "professional criminal" who claimed Ferrie and Shaw asked him to kill Garrison, Andrews appeared at Shaw's house while Ferrie and Shaw tried to convince him to take the job. Whalen declined [Garrison, *Trail of the Assassins*, p. 122-125; New Orleans District Attorney Records (Statement of Whalen to James L. Alcock, Sept. 18, 1967)].

ANDREWS (*voice-over*) The dude on the other end says ...

CLAY BERTRAND I'm Clay Bertrand. Whatever they owe, I guarantee.

ANDREWS Hey, suits me, Daddy Warbucks—how do I get in touch with you?

CLAY BERTRAND I'm around.

ANDREWS (*voice-over*) And that's how I first heard of Clay Bertrand.

JIM (*in present*) What was his voice like?

ANDREWS You knew you weren't talking to some low life fag, you know. He had command of the king's English.

JIM Did he pay?

ANDREWS Always—like tits on a pig. I wish I had a million of those bimbettes.

JIM And Oswald?

ANDREWS (*just a slight hesitation*) Like I told to the Washington boys, Bertrand called that summer and asked me to help the kid upgrade his Marine discharge ...

JIM So you saw Oswald how many times?

ANDREWS Three, four. He came in with a few Cubano swishes one time I remember ...

FLASHBACK TO a third day at Andrews' office in 1963. Oswald is in the office with two young boys.

JIM (*voice-over*) Recall any names?

ANDREWS (*in present*) Mario, José—they wear names like you and I wear clothes. Today the name is Candy, tomorrow it's Butsie. I wish I could help you, Jim.

JIM Did you speak to Oswald in Dallas?

ANDREWS (*knee-jerk reaction*) Hell, no! I told this Bertrand cat right off, this isn't my scene, man. I deal with muni court, I'm a hack in nigger town, that kid needs a hot dog.

JIM Then how the hell did you get in the Warren Commission, Dean? Except through the phone records in the Dallas jail?

ANDREWS (*nervous moment*) There were no phone records.

JIM Of course there weren't. 'Cause they disappeared. And yet the Commission found you, Dean.

ANDREWS I don't know how they got to me. Maybe cause I repped him here. The Feebees run background checks. On my mama's breasts, man, that's all I got. (*pauses, adjusts*) There wasn't no conspiracy, Jim. If there were, why the hell didn't Bobby Kennedy prosecute it as Attorney General, he was his *brother* for Chrissake. How the fuck three people could keep a secret like that, I don't know. It was Oswald. He was a nut job. Faggot, y'know, hated this country.

> ▌Bobby Kennedy: Then-Attorney General Robert F. Kennedy was effectively cut out of any investigation of his brother's death when President Johnson convened the Warren Commission and took the case out of the Justice Department's hands. Kennedy remained in office for a scant five months after his brother's death before resigning to run for Senate.
>
> By all accounts, R.F.K. was in shock over his brother's death and troubled by the Warren Report. In 1966, he remarked to Arthur Schlesinger that he wondered "how long he could continue to avoid comment on the Report." According to Schlesinger, Kennedy "regarded it as a poor job but was

unwilling to criticize it and thereby re-open the whole tragic business."
[Arthur Schlesinger, Jr., "JFK: Truth and Fiction," *Wall St. Journal*, January 10, 1992.]

R.F.K.'s former press secretary, Frank Mankiewicz, says that, if elected president, Kennedy planned to re-investigate his brother's murder and said so publicly at a small college in southern California shortly before his death.

As Andrews resumes eating his crabmeat Louie with gusto, Jim reaches over and grabs the fork in mid-air.

JIM Dean, I think we're having a communication problem. I know you know who Clay Bertrand is. Now stop eating that damn crabmeat for a minute and listen. (*gets Dean's attention*) I'm aware of our long friendship, but I want you to know I'm going to call you in front of a grand jury. I took nine judges on, Deano, right here in New Orleans, and I beat 'em all. If you lie to the grand jury as you've been lying to me, I'm going to charge you with perjury. Now, am I communicating with you?

▌Garrison, outraged at the Criminal Court judges' refusal to grant him funds to investigate organized crime in New Orleans, criticized the judges publicly, charging that they were corrupt and lazy. The judges counterattacked and the matter was finally decided in the United States Supreme Court. In a landmark ruling, the Court ruled in Garrison's favor, saying "speech concerning public affairs is more than self-expression; it is the essence of self-government" [Flammonde, *The Kennedy Conspiracy*, p. 9].

Andrews puts down the fork, shaken, silent for a moment.

ANDREWS Is this off the record, Daddy-o? (*Jim nods*) In that case, let me sum it up for you real quick. If I answer that question you keep asking me, if I give you the name of the "Big Enchilada," y'know, then it's bon voyage, Deano—I mean like permanent. I mean like a bullet in my head. You dig? Does that help you see my problem a little better? You're a mouse fighting a gorilla. Kennedy's dead as that crab meat. The government's still breathing. You want to line up with a dead man?

At a nearby table, a waiter has just poured brandy on Crêpe Suzettes. A blue flame hovers in the air as Jim leans forward across the table, speaking deliberately.

JIM Read my lips, Deano. Either you dance into the Grand Jury with the real identity of Clay Bertrand or your fat behind is going to the slammer. Do you dig me?

Andrews stands suddenly.

ANDREWS You're just as crazy as your mama. Goes to show it's in the genes! Do you have any idea what you're getting into, my man? You think Jack Ruby just up and died of cancer in four weeks after he gets a retrial? That's some kinda new cancer—I'd say that's a "going out of business cancer." You got the right ta-ta, but the wrong ho-ho. The government's gonna jump all over your head, Jimbo, and go "cock-a-doodledoo!"

Andrews drops his pink napkin in the crabmeat and waddles out. Jim now feels closer to the truth than ever.

ANGOLA PRISON - LOUISIANA COUNTRYSIDE - (1967)

From the point of view of an approaching car, the prison looms over the swamp, dogs patrolling the wire.

VOICE (*voice-over*) District Attorney Garrison to see Prisoner 5388. Ward Block 237B.

GUARD'S VOICE (*voice-over*) Send him on in.

PRISON DORMITORY - (1967)

A chief guard walks Jim and Bill into a circus-like atmosphere. In Louisiana the prisoners can wear any outfit they choose, which makes this prison look like Mardi Gras. There are many transvestites.

GUARD (*with evident pride*) ... we don't need no gates out there, sir, we got the "swamp." Many of 'em gone in there but none come out ... Hey, Willie!

Willie O'Keefe, a handsome, muscled, young chickenhawk with an earring, bandana, colorful clothes, an aura of burned truth in his intense, staring brown eyes and thick country accent, sashays over.

GUARD You got some company, wants to talk wid you. You behave now, boy, y'hear?

▌ "Willie O'Keefe" is a composite character drawn from four of Garrison's witnesses: Perry Russo, David Logan, Raymond Broshears, and William Morris. Three of them met Shaw through Ferrie; the fourth, Morris, was introduced to Shaw, who called himself "Clay Bertrand," by a mutual friend. Like O'Keefe, Logan and Broshears met Shaw/Bertrand at French Quarter bars. Broshears, who also had intelligence connections, reported seeing Shaw and Ferrie together on several occasions, including a time when Shaw handed Ferrie an envelope filled with cash. Logan and Morris became more intimate with Shaw, frequenting Shaw's restored carriage house on Dauphine Street. Russo's story—that he met Shaw at a party at Ferrie's at which the assassination was discussed—made him one of Garrison's key witnesses. [Garrison, *Trail of the Assassins*, p. 86 (Morris), p. 119-121 (Broshears and Logan), p. 151-156 (Russo); New Orleans District Attorney Records.]

None of these witnesses was in prison at the time of Garrison's investigation. We chose to make O'Keefe a convict to illustrate the "quality" of Garrison's witnesses, which received lots of criticism. As Garrison said, "It's true, I would rather have a bank president or a successful lawyer or a successful businessman ... The question is, is he telling the truth or not. There are many attorneys who are brilliant liars and there are dope addicts who never learned to lie." [Flammonde, *The Kennedy Conspiracy*, p. 296.]

TIME CUT TO the prison work area, where Willie talks, leaning against a tree looking out on a mangrove swamp. It's lunch break and other prisoners move in the background, eating, socializing.

JIM I want to thank you, Mr. O'Keefe, for this time.

O'KEEFE Call me Willie. I ain't got nuthin' but time, Mr. Garrison. Minutes, hours, days, years of 'em. Time just stands still here like a snake sunnin' itself in the road ...

BILL Clay Bertrand, Willie?

O'KEEFE Yeah. Clay. I met him sometime in June of '62 at the Masquerade Bar. Dave Ferrie took me there, for the express reason to meet him.

JIM For sexual purposes?

O'KEEFE Well ... yeah.

FLASHBACK TO the Masquerade Bar in the French Quarter. It's nighttime and Ferrie, Bertrand and O'Keefe sit at a back booth. Bertrand, as seen earlier, is an imposing, white-haired patrician man, over six feet tall, heavily defined bones and eyelids, in his late 40s or early 50s.

BILL (*voice-over*) Did he pay you for this?

O'KEEFE (*voice-over*) Twenty dollars each time. Hell, it's no secret. That's what I'm here for.

They rise to leave. Bertrand with a slight limp.

JIM (*voice-over*) Anything else unusual about him you'd be able to describe in a court of law, Willie?

O'KEEFE (*voice-over*) I remember he had some kinda thing wrong with his left leg. He limped. Don't get me wrong, he's not one of those, you know, limp wrists. He's a butch John. You'd meet him on the street, you'd never snap. You could go fishing with him, play poker with him, you'd never snap in a million years. So one night we were over at Ferrie's place. Having a party. Sometime in the late summer of '63.

FLASHBACK TO Dave Ferrie's apartment on a night in 1963. The place is filled with messy bricabrac, including two dozen mouse cages for Ferrie's cancer experiments. Ferrie, Bertrand, O'Keefe, and four Cubans in battle fatigues are laughing and fooling around. Oswald is in a corner cleaning a .22 rifle with a scope on it. He looks different, unkempt, unshaven. A record player grinds out a speech in Spanish by Castro. Some other people are there as well—it's a beatnik scene: sandals, hanging out, only one woman. Ferrie is taking pictures throughout of the group horsing around, photographing Oswald.

▪ Ferrie's apartment: [Criminal District Court for the Parish of Orleans, Transcript of Preliminary hearing, No. M-703, Clay L. Shaw, Arrestee, testimony of Perry Raymond Russo, p. 51-68; Garrison, *Trail of the Assassins*, p. 151-156.]

O'KEEFE (*voice-over*) ... there were about nine or ten people, Cubans, friends of Dave doing some stuff in the bush with him. Place was a mess. Dave's mind is a mess, (*laughs*) y'know he had all those mice cages around cause he's working on this cure for cancer ... Dave's smart—real smart—speaks five languages, knows philosophy, medicine, military history, politics. He wanted to be a priest but they defrocked him 'cause he was queer ...

BILL (*voice-over*) And that's where you met Oswald for the first time?

O'KEEFE (*voice-over*) Yeah, strange guy. Dave introduced him as ...

FERRIE Willie, say hello to Leon Oswald.

> ▮ The name "Leon Oswald" pops up in a few places, most notably here and in the Sylvia Odio incident. There are also reports of "Harvey Lee Oswald" (in a destroyed Army Intelligence file), a "Harvey Oswald" (appearing at the Selective Service Bureau in Austin, Texas), "Lee Henry Oswald" (CD 631, a CIA document concerning the Mexico City trip) and finally, on Oswald's last paycheck at the TSBD, "Leslie Oswald," a name that appears nowhere on his payroll paperwork with the company or on his other paychecks [conversation with Peter Dale Scott, Sept., 1991]. On two unemployment applications, Oswald himself misrecorded his name as "Lee Harry Oswald" [WC 19H p. 229] and "Lee Havey Oswald" [WC 21H p. 282]. [See Peter Dale Scott, *Beyond Conspiracy*, unpubl. manus., p. 573-579.]

O'KEEFE (*over the racket*) How ya doing?

OSWALD (*sullen, to Ferrie*) What the fuck's he doing here?

O'KEEFE Fuck you, man.

Ferrie separates them. Oswald seems to resent an outsider being there.

FERRIE (*to O'Keefe*) Leon's in a bad mood, don't get excited, he's all right.

JIM (*voice-over*) Would you say this "Leon" was actually Lee Harvey Oswald?

O'KEEFE (*in present*) Fuck, yes. Hell, I'm already in jail. I got no reason to lie to you. I ain't no nigger.

BILL Go on, Willie.

O'KEEFE (*present merging to past*) ... well the party got crazier and crazier, one of those, y'know "beatnik" type things

FERRIE (*to O'Keefe*) We're having a little meeting here. (*indicates the second player*) That's Castro. Sounds like Hitler doesn't he? Sonofabitch is going to go. Real soon.

CUBANS *Muerte a Fidel! Muerte!*

BERTRAND (*irritated at the noise, to Ferrie*) Oh, stop it already! What are all these people doing here anyway? I can't bear all this infernal noise.

FERRIE Clara, don't be so sensitive.

BERTRAND I didn't come here for a pep rally. Get all this riffraff out of here.

FERRIE Okay, okay.

TIME CUT TO later that night, when only O'Keefe, Ferrie, Bertrand, Oswald and three Cubans are left.

O'KEEFE (*voice-over*) ... finally they got out of there and I found myself alone with Dave and this Leon, two of the Cubans, and this guy Bertrand. Dave pulled out his clippings which he was always carrying around. He'd been obsessed with Castro and Kennedy for months and he started in again ...

FERRIE (*waving a clipping, drunk*) Kennedy fucked us in '61, '62, and he's fuckin' us now! And that fuckin' zealot Bobby Kennedy is the fuckee! The nerve of that little asswipe closing the camps. Took all our C-4! Took 10,000 rounds, 3,000 pounds of gunpowder, all our weapons. Next we'll be living in a world where only the cocksucking Reds will have all the weapons and we'll be surrounded. If we want a free Cuba, we gotta whack out the fucking beard.

CUBAN That faggot Kennedy won't let us. Our hands are empty—how can we kill him?

BERTRAND (*moving with a drink, walks with a slight limp*) ... It's a real problem getting at him. Castro's got informers on every block.

FERRIE (*pointing to a map of Cuba on the wall*) Bullshit! There's all kinds of new stuff. I heard about rockets in an umbrella—they're tested at Fort Detrick? I can show you a dozen poisons. Stick it in his food, he'll die in three days, no trace. We can put something in his beard, make it fall out, he'll look fuckin' ridiculous without his beard.

> ▮ Rockets in an umbrella: In 1975, the Church Committee heard testimony from Charles Sensenay, a CIA weapons developer who worked at Fort Detrick. Sensenay described a dart gun disguised as an umbrella—when the "umbrella" was opened, a dart could be fired through the webbing. The CIA ordered fifty such dart guns, according to Sensenay, and they were available for use in 1963. In his testimony to the same committee, former CIA director William Colby called the gun a "nondiscernible microbioinoculator" and insisted it had never been used. [Church Committee Hearings, cited in Richard E. Sprague and Robert Cutler, "The Umbrella System: Prelude to an Assassination," *Gallery*, June, 1978.]
>
> In his book on Allen Dulles, Director of Central Intelligence from 1953-1961 and Warren Commissioner, Leonard Mosely noted Dulles's enthusiasm for these gadgets:
>
> "... now (in the early 60s) he was interested in mind-bending drugs, portable phials of lethal viruses and esoteric poisons that killed without a trace. Allen's sense of humor was touched when he learned that the unit working on these noxious enterprises was called the Health Alteration Committee and he added to his collection of CIA curios a noiseless gun which the Committee had produced for firing darts smeared with LSD, germs, or

venom at enemy agents or foreign personalities whose existence the CIA was finding embarrassing." [Mosely, *Dulles* (Dial Press, 1978), p. 459.]

▌ Fort Detrick, Maryland, housed the Army Chemical Corps biological warfare lab until 1969. The lab carried out the infamous MK-ULTRA program designed by the CIA to research "behavioral modification" [CIA Research in Behavior Modification, Senate Select Committee on Intelligence, Hearings Aug. 3, 1977; Ranelegh, *The Agency*, p. 777-778 fn.27; Marks, *The Case for the Manchurian Candidate*]. Fort Detrick's information number is 301-668-8000.

▌ Speaking of mind altering drugs, a fascinating *Rolling Stone* article by Martin A. Lee, Robert Ranftel and Jeff Cohen, "Did Lee Harvey Oswald Drop Acid?" (Mar. 3, 1983) explored CD 194 and an FBI Memo (SAC to File, Nov. 25, 1963 #NO 89-69-80) in which a New Orleans Asst. District Attorney tells the FBI that Oswald had stopped by his office that summer to talk about an LSD-like drug and Aldous Huxley's *Brave New World* (which Oswald had checked out of the library in Sept., 1963). The FBI did not follow up.

▌ Castro assassination attempts: ["Alleged Assassination Plots Involving Foreign Leaders," Interim Report of the Senate Intelligence Committee (commonly called the Church Committee), U.S. Government Printing Office, 1975. (Note: Hinckle & Turner, *The Fish Is Red*, is the best layman's book on U.S.-Cuban relations in the 1960s, but terribly difficult to find.)]

CUBAN (*drunk*) Why don't we just take care of the main problem? Which is that piece of shit Kennedy. He's doing all kinds of deals! Kissing Khrushchev's ass. I wouldn't even call him *President* Kennedy.

O'KEEFE (*voice-over*) ... then the Cubans left and the bullshitting was going on, Dave was drunk, really drunk and he starts in with Kennedy again.

FERRIE See, what Kennedy done, with him you should take a knife and stab and kill the fucker where he is now. I mean it. This is true. But I tell you something. I hope I get a week's notice. I'll kill. Right in the fuckin' White House. Somebody's got to get rid of this fucker.

Oswald looks up, listens quietly.

O'KEEFE Oh, c'mon, Dave, you're never gonna get *that* sonofabitch.

FERRIE No? It won't be long, mark my words. That fucker'll get what's comin' to him. And it can be blamed on Castro. Then the whole country'll want to invade Cuba. All we got to do is get Kennedy in the open.

Bertrand, with his arms around O'Keefe, laughs, tries to change the subject.

BERTRAND David, David, always some harebrained scheme or another ... Oh? What do I see here? Ooooh, let's have some more champagne, shall we!

O'KEEFE (*interested in Ferrie's proposal*) What about the Secret Service, the cops?

FERRIE (*pacing, hyper*) No problem if it's planned right. Look how close they got with de Gaulle. Eisenhower was always riding around in an open top. I know somebody who actually went up and touched Eisenhower once. We need to have three mechanics at three different locations. An office building with a high-powered rifle. Triangulation of crossfire is the key. You get a diversionary shot gets the Secret Service looking one way—Boom! You get the kill shot. The crucial thing is one man has to be sacrificed, then in the commotion of the crowd the job gets done and the others fly out of the country to someplace with no extradition. I could do that myself. I could fly to Mexico, and then Brazil.

> ∎ De Gaulle assassination attempts: Between 1958 and the mid-1960s, French leader de Gaulle was the target of some serious assassination attempts and countless others that never got off the ground. In 1975, a front-page story in *The Chicago Tribune* presented evidence that the CIA was involved in at least one of the attempts:
>
> "Sometime in the mid-1960s—probably in 1965 or 1966—dissidents in the de Gaulle government are said to have made contact with the CIA to seek help in a plot to murder the French leader ... According to the CIA briefing officer, discussions were held on how best to eliminate de Gaulle, who by then had become a thorn in the side of the Johnson Administration because of his ouster of military bases from French soil and his demands that United States forces be withdrawn from the Indochina War ... There is, however, no evidence the plot got beyond the talking stage." [*The Chicago Tribune*, June 15, 1975, cited in Blum, *The CIA: A Forgotten History* (Zed, 1986), p. 169-170.]
>
> Former CIA director William Colby confirmed that "foreigners" had sought the Agency's assistance with such a plot, although he insisted the CIA declined to participate. [*The Chicago Tribune*, June 20, 1975, cited in Blum, *The CIA ...*, p. 170.]
>
> *Oswald listens, playing with his rifle. Bertrand suddenly turns cold, flashing a look at Ferrie.*

BERTRAND Why don't we drop this subject ... it's one thing to engage in badinage with these youngsters, but this sort of thing could be so easily misunderstood. (*he squeezes Ferrie*)

FERRIE Ouch!

O'KEEFE (*voice-over*) I didn't think much about it at the time. Just bullshit, y'know, everybody likes to make themselves out to be something more than they are. Specially in the homosexual underworld. But then when they got him (*merging to the present*) I got real scared, y'know. Real scared. And that's when I got popped.

BACK TO the prison work area. Jim and O'Keefe continue talking.

JIM Willie, are you willing to repeat your statements under sodium pentothal? Under the supervision of a doctor?

O'KEEFE Fuck, yeah! I told you so. And you can tell 'em all I told you so.

JIM You realize the things you're saying, Willie, are going to be attacked by a lot of different people.

O'KEEFE Bring on all the motherfuckers! Bring their college degrees in here! I got nuthin' to hide. They can't buy me. You can't buy me. I don't even need this parole. This is about the truth coming out. You're a goddamn liberal, Mr. Garrison, you don't know shit, cause you never been fucked in the ass. Fascism is here now, fascism is ...

JIM No one's trying to buy you, Willie. It's important to know why you're telling us this.

O'KEEFE (*pauses*) You wanna know why? 'Cause that motherfucker Kennedy stole that fuckin' election, that's why! Nixon was gonna be one of the great Presidents 'til Kennedy wrecked this fuckin' country. Got niggers all over the fuckin' place asking for their rights, where do you think we got all this fuckin' crime now, 'cause Kennedy promised 'em too damned much. Revolution comin'. Fascism's coming back. I tell ya this—the day that Communist sumbitch died was a great day for this country. I jes' hate to think they're blaming it on some silly fuckin' Oswald who didn't know shit anyway. People should know why that sumbitch was killed. 'Cause he was a Communist. Put me on the stand, go ahead, I'll tell the same goddamn story, I'm proud of it, don't matter fuck all to me, things don't change.

As he talks, Jim shares a sickened look with Bill. Whatever truth he may be telling is necessarily compromised by an attitude that could be destroyed in court.

GARRISON HOME - NIGHT (1967)

Jim, Lou, Al, Susie, and Numa sit around the table having an after hours conference. The kids run in and out of the room, playing. Susie is doing the talking, showing new paperwork and photos.

SUSIE ... Your hunch was right, boss, but it's even spookier than we thought. Starting in September '63 on, two months before the assassination, there are sightings of Oswald all over Dallas, buying ammunition, getting a telescopic sight fixed, going to rifle ranges ... Early November, a Dallas downtown Lincoln-Mercury dealership where he tells the salesman Albert Bogard ...

▮ False Oswalds: [Summers, *Conspiracy*, p. 368-393; Anson, *They've Killed the President!*, p. 191-217; Melanson, *Spy Saga*, p. 105-115.]

FLASHBACK TO the Lincoln-Mercury dealership. Oswald is deliberately kept in half or three quarter shots—a mystery figure. He kicks the tires on a used red Mercury Comet, cocky.

▮ Downtown Lincoln-Mercury Dealership:[WC 10H p. 352-356 (Albert Bogard Testimony); Meagher, *Accessories after the Fact*, p. 351-356.]

"OSWALD" Let's take it out for a test drive.

The salesman, Bogard, is hesitant. "Oswald" doesn't look like he's got a dime to his name.

"OSWALD" (*sensing Bogard's hesitancy*) ... Hey, I got a lotta money coming in the next two weeks.

In the next scene we see the car, driven by "Oswald," zooming up the ramp and disappearing onto the freeway.

SUSIE (*voice-over*) ... despite the fact he has no license and from what Marina says, does not know how to drive, he hits the curves like Mario Andretti at the Indy 500. Bogard later told his boss he drove "like a madman."

Resume the scene at the dealership.

BOGARD Three hundred bucks down, Mr. Oswald, you can drive outta here with it.

"Oswald," unhappy, starts to leave.

"OSWALD" Who you kidding! For this heap? Forget it ... No honest working man can afford a car anymore in the goddamn country! Maybe I'll have to go back to Russia to buy a car ...

SUSIE (*voice-over*) ... really dumb dialogue like he's trying to draw attention to himself. A real moron. He walks out. The salesman remembers him as about 5'7", but we know from his draft card he was actually 5'11" ...

> ■ Oswald's height: Anson, *They've Killed the President!*, p. 209, charts Oswald's ever-varying height, weight and eye-color. What needs to be determined is on which of these occasions was Oswald *actually* measured/examined as opposed to *self-reporting* his statistics. After all, it is not unusual to stretch the truth about one's height or weight.

LOU ... several witnesses see him on several separate days at different firing ranges.

FLASHBACK TO a Dallas firing range in 1963.

> ■ [Meagher, *Accessories after the Fact*, p. 371-372; Summers, *Conspiracy*, p. 279-281.]

LOU (*voice-over*) ... one time, November 9, he decides he needs to practice on the target of the guy next to him. Says something really dumb to the guy, who says Oswald was a great shot.

> ■ [WC 10H p. 380 (testimony of Garland Slack).]

MAN Hey, watcha doing, boy ... that's my target.

"OSWALD" Hey, sorry, buddy. I just thought it was that sonofabitch Kennedy, y'know. I couldn't help myself. (*laughs*)

JIM (*in present*) ... about as subtle as a cockroach crawling across a white rug.

SUSIE I'll go you one better, Lou. He shows up at Silvia Odio's, a Cuban lady in Dallas working in the anti-Castro underground—remember that name, a solid witness. The two Cubans introduce him as "Leon Oswald."

> ■ Silvia Odio: [WR p. 321-324; HSCA Report, p. 137-139; Summers, *Conspiracy*, p. 386-393; Meagher, *Accessories After the Fact*, p. 376-387. Also see Gaeton Fonzi, "Who Killed J.F.K.?," *The Washingtonian*, November 1980.]

FLASHBACK TO the corridor of Silvia Odio's apartment in Dallas on a night in 1963. Oswald drags behind two Cubans—one is "the Bull," heavyset with a scar over his left eye, who we saw at the Canal Street incident, and the other, "the Indian," is quiet and cold. The men ring the doorbell and talk to a concerned Silvia as Oswald hangs back, watching, in the shadows. The men give her intimate information about her father, who is imprisoned in Cuba. The men chatter ad lib in Spanish.

SUSIE (*voice-over*) ... the Cubans want Silvia, whose parents are political prisoners in Cuba, to help them raise money to assassinate Castro. Something about the men bothers her. She tells them she doesn't want anything to do with violence ... about 48 hours later one of the Cubans calls her back ...

We see a shot of Silvia on the phone in her apartment intercut with a shot of "the Bull," in a gas station phone booth, on a night in 1963.

THE BULL (*on the phone, in Spanish*) This guy Leon Oswald's great, he's kinda nuts ... he told us we don't have any guts, us Cubans, cause Kennedy should've been whacked after the Bay of Pigs, and some Cubans should've done that, it's easy to do, he says—you know he's a Marine, an expert shooter ...

Silvia Odio is surprised to hear this information volunteered. "The Bull's" eyes are on "Oswaldo," outside the booth with "the Indian." They're hanging out, talking to a mystery man, an Anglo.

SUSIE (*voice-over*) ... It's like he's giving her information she doesn't even ask for. She's scared, doesn't see them again till she sees Oswald's picture in the paper. But the Warren Commission says she has bad eyesight because they have Oswald in Mexico at this time, trying to get back into Cuba. The Cubans think he's a double agent so they won't take him. The CIA has a camera outside the Cuban Embassy and says this is Oswald in Mexico. (*hands over a picture*) You figure it.

▌Mexico City photo: [WC 16H, CE237.]

Jim looks at the famous photo ... the camera closes in on a heavyset man who looks nothing like Oswald. Liz has come back in and overhears.

AL• If this is Oswald, it must be our third Oswald.

JIM The interesting thing is the extent to which the Warren Commission went to make him a Communist. They got almost 150 pages and 130 exhibits of the report on this Mexico trip and the picture doesn't even match. I'm beginning to think the point of the Mexican episode was to lay the blame at Castro's door. If Oswald, or someone purporting to be Oswald, had gotten into Cuba, come back, then killed the President, the American public once again would've screamed for a Cuban invasion ...

> ▌The HSCA Report manages two mentions of the Mexican trip, simply saying it weighed into their conclusion that the assassination was not the result of a Castro-related conspiracy [WC 16H CE 237; HSCA R p. 107; Summers, *Conspiracy*, p. 342-367]. (Note: An HSCA Staff Report on Oswald in

Mexico, prepared by staffer Edwin Lopez, remains classified with the HSCA material. Lopez contends that his report proved conclusively that Oswald was never in Mexico City [conversation with Lopez, Jan. 1991]. Why didn't the HSCA Report address this issue?)

At a public forum, former CIA officer David Atlee Phillips said "...when the record comes out, we will find that there was never a photograph taken of Lee Harvey Oswald in Mexico City. We will find out that Lee Harvey Oswald never visited..." [Mark Lane, *Plausible Denial* (Thunder's Mouth, 1991), p. 82.]

Susie picks up the famous Life *magazine cover shot of Oswald holding a rifle in his backyard.*

SUSIE I even have doubts about this photo, boss. It pretty much convicted Oswald in the public mind. Well, according to Captain Fritz, Oswald told him during his interrogation the photo was a fake.

FLASHBACK TO the Dallas Homicide Office in 1963. Oswald is being interrogated by Will Fritz, Dallas Homicide Chief, who shows him the original of the photo from the Williams garage.

▌Photo of Oswald: [WR p. 608-609.]

OSWALD ... That's not me.

FRITZ It came from Janet Williams' garage.

OSWALD Well, I never saw that picture. It is my face, but my face has been super-imposed—the rest of the picture is not me at all. I've done a lot of photographic work, and that picture was made by someone else.

FRITZ So who the hell are you? Alex Hidell or Oswald?

OSWALD Well, you're the policeman, you work it out.

▌[WR p. 608-609.] As Captain Fritz recounts the scene:
"He [Oswald] said the picture was not his, that the face was his face, but that this picture had been made by someone superimposing his face, the other part of the picture was not him at all and that he had never seen the picture before. When I told him that the picture was recovered from Mrs. Paine's garage, he said that the picture had never been in his possession ... He told me that he understood photography real well, and that in time, he would be able to show me that it was not his picture, that it had been made by some-one else."

Many of these apparent problems with the photos are examined in *Fake*, a videotape by Jack White and Jim Marrs, available through JFK Video, Fort Worth, Texas.

▌Alek J. Hidell ID card: [CE 795-796 (selective service card); WR p. 181-182; Meagher, *Accessories After the Fact*, p.181-199; HSCA Report, p. 221-224; Hurt, *Reasonable Doubt*, p. 236-239.] Oswald had a forged Selective Service card bearing his photo and the name "Alek J. Hidell" in his wallet when he was arrested. [WR p. 615.] He explained the alias to Capt. Fritz as a name he had "picked up in New Orleans while working in the Fair Play for Cuba organization." [WR p. 602.] As the interrogation wore on, Oswald told Fritz, "I've told you all I'm going to about that card ... You have the card. Now you know as much about it as I do." [WR p. 636.]

The "Hidell" name was used to order the Mannlicher-Carcano rifle as well as the alleged Tippit murder weapon.

SUSIE (*in the present*) Oswald, who worked for Jaggars-Chiles-Stovall, did know spy photography pretty well. I took this picture to two experts. Look at the way the shadows on the nose fall in a straight line like it's high noon. But the shadow here on the ground reads like late afternoon or early morning. It's not the same time. Also look at the crop marks across the chin. It seems like his head is pasted on somebody else's body implicating him with this rifle and gun.

We see a blowup of the photo—the shadows, the crop mark ...

SUSIE And of the two newspapers in his hands, one is Leninist, the other Trotskyite. Any genuine Socialist would know they hate each other's politics!

FRENCH QUARTER - SAME NIGHT (1967)

Broussard walks past a jazz wake leaving the cemetery—black flambeurs carry torches, people sing "When the Saints Go Marching In." Bill is with a local gambler type.

> ■ Garrison's search for "Bertrand": [Garrison, *Trail of the Assassins*, p. 85-87.] Garrison's investigators had more than one witness identify "Bertrand" as Clay Shaw. Several people in the French Quarter made the identification, as did several other New Orleans witnesses.

MOBSTER Clay Bertrand? Sure I know him. He comes around the Quarter.

BILL Who is he, Joe? I've been to every bar, no one wants to talk.

MOBSTER I told your uncle I never met a lawman who wasn't a punk. You too, Bill, even if you're family. He's a big shot businessman. I seen him on the TV news a lot with all the other big shots. A fag, you know. Goes by another name down here.

BILL (*excited*) What's the other name?

MOBSTER Shaw. Clay Shaw.

BILL (*stunned*) Clay Bertrand is Clay Shaw? The guy who used to run the International Trade Mart?

MOBSTER Yeah, what's the big mystery? Everybody down here knows the guy.

BILL So why does he call himself Bertrand?

MOBSTER Who gives a shit what he calls himself?

BACK AT GARRISON'S HOME - (1967)

SUSIE ... now it gets positively spooky. In January, *1961*—in New Orleans, at the Bolton Ford Dealership—when the Oswald we know is in Russia—there is a man using the name "Oswald" to buy trucks for the Friends of Democratic Cuba. The salesman never saw him again, but guess who's on the articles of incorporation of the Friends of Democratic Cuba? *Guy Banister. (reactions from the others)* Banister has someone using the name "Oswald" to buy the trucks. Hoover, at the FBI, writes a memo dated June, 1960, that there could be someone using Oswald's passport and identity.

> ∎ Hoover memo: On June 3, 1960, Hoover sent a memo to the office of security of the State Department. "Since there is a possibility that an impostor is using Oswald's birth certificate, any current information the Department of State may have concerning the subject will be appreciated," Hoover wrote. [CD294B]

JIM   Goddamn! They put Oswald together from Day One! Like some dummy corporation in the Bahamas—you just move him around a board. Sent him to Russia, in and out, no passport problems. You got the word "microdots" in his notebook, you got the Minox camera and the electronic devices they find in his possessions, the sealed CIA 201 personnel file. For all we know, there could be a dozen Oswalds in different cities, countries—all of them leaving a trail of incriminating evidence that could easily be traced to a scapegoat after the assassination. Does the real Oswald know he's been put together? Who knows. It doesn't matter, does it? He's a low level spy, he doesn't know who he really works for ... *(pause)* Let's call it a night. *(to Lou)* Anything new on Ruby?

> ∎ Oswald's electronic devices: In addition to the Minox camera, Oswald had 3 other cameras, 2 pairs of binoculars, a compass and a 15-power telescope. None of his associates ever mentioned him using any of this expensive equipment [Summers, *Conspiracy*, p. 202-203].

The staff members, anxious to go home, have all risen ... and now sigh.

LOU   Mobbed up all the way. Tight with the Dallas cops. I'm digging, chief. I just need 10 more men and some more dollars.

JIM   I know you do, Lou. I'm doing three more lectures this month. You're all doing an incredible job, Sue, Al, Numa. But this is one where if you don't nail the other guy, you're dead. *(he pulls a book from the bookcase for Lou)* How did Jack Ruby die so quick? Of what? Cancer, right? A history of Nazi Germany, Lou. They were studying viral cancers as a weapon in the 30s. We learned a lot more than you think from the Nazis. Read this. Our biological warfare lab is in Fort Detrick, Maryland. Close to where the National Cancer Institute is located. Think about it. Think the unthinkable—question everything.

> ∎ U.S. recruitment of Nazis for biological warfare research: One of the more glaring beneficiaries of this program was Dr. Kurt Blome. In 1945, Blome admitted his leading role in Nazi bio-warfare research, including running experiments on concentration camp prisoners. After winning an acquittal at the Nuremberg medical trials, Blome found employment with the U.S. Army Chemical Corps, working once again in biological weapons research. [Linda Hunt, "US Cover-Up of Nazi Scientists," *Bulletin of the Atomic Scientists*, April, 1985, cited in Simpson, *Blowback*, p. xiii.]

Ruby died of cancer - US biological warfare viral cancer.

NUMA Even my own wife, chief, (*looking at his watch*) who's wondering where I am?

JIM (*looking at Liz*) Even your own wife, Numa. Any of you want to quit, do me a favor ... put us out of our misery.

They all raise their hands as Bill walks in, excited.

BILL I found Clay Bertrand.

They all stop, look.

SUSIE Who?

BILL Grab your socks and pull ... Clay Bertrand is Clay Shaw ...

SUSIE (*stunned*) No! ... Shaw! Director of The Trade Mart? This is incredible.

NUMA Pillar of the community by day, gay bars at night.

Liz Garrison is the most shaken, as she pours a fresh pot of coffee.

JIM Can you get some sworn statements?

BILL That's gonna be tough. Nobody's talking.

JIM I think we should have him in for a little talk.

LIZ Do you have any evidence against him, Jim? Clay Shaw's done so much for the city with all that restoration in the Quarter. He's well connected, all his friends, the money, people, be careful, Jim.

JIM It'll be off the record, honey. I'll bring him in on a Sunday. A quiet little chat between gentlemen.

Liz walks out of the room silent. There is a tense pause.

GARRISON'S LIVING ROOM - EASTER SUNDAY (1967)

The TV is on to the latest Vietnam Reports—combat footage.

NEWSMAN 10 (ANNOUNCER) In heavy fighting in Vietnam today, seven more American soldiers died and 23 were wounded. The body count for this week now stands at 67 Americans and 626 enemy soldiers killed in action.

Liz plays with the kids looking for Easter eggs. The dog is barking—it's a scene of commotion. Jim is getting ready to go out.

LIZ Jim, come on, honey, get down on your hands and knees and hunt for Jasper's Easter egg.

JIM You know I don't like these tribal rituals, Freckle Face. I'm interviewing Clay Shaw this morning.

NEWSMAN 10 (ANNOUNCER) (*as TV cuts to President Johnson*) President Johnson, meanwhile at an informal press conference, said he regretted that there is no end in sight to the war in Vietnam, where 500,000 American troops are now

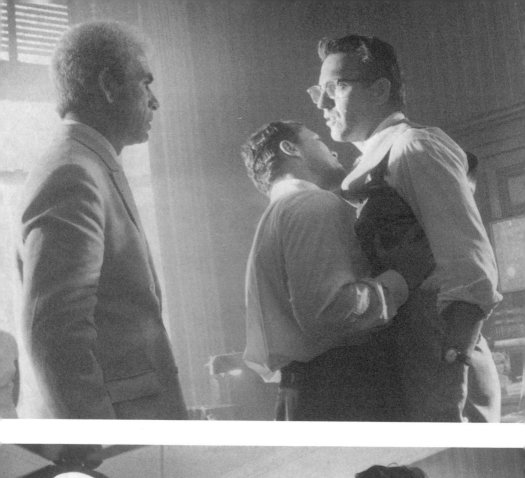

fighting. "We face more cost, more loss, and more agony." In his proposal to raise taxes, Johnson ...

▌[State of the Union Address, Jan. 10, 1967.]

LIZ *(surprised)* But Jim, we're going to Antoine's with the kids—like we do every year.

JIM No. I told you I was going to talk to Shaw.

LIZ But why in the Lord's name would you do it in the middle of Easter Sunday when you knew we were ...

JIM *(annoyed with her look)* Because when I scheduled it I didn't realize it was a holiday. You were there, why didn't you say something?

LIZ Look at the calendar, for Christ's sake. You said a Sunday, not Easter Sunday.

JIM I'm sorry, but it's important. Clay Shaw is important. I'm sorry.

LIZ You're missing most of your life, Jim, and you don't even know it. The kids are missing out too. *(harder)* It's not just *you* making the sacrifice here, honey.

Her words stop him. One of the kids watches them.

JIM Look, I'll rush and be there by two, I promise. Go ahead without me.

As he leaves, the camera holds on Liz.

GARRISON OFFICE - (1967)

Clay Shaw ("Bertrand"), in an elegant white summer suit, is shown in. Indeed, there is a slight limp to his gait which Jim notices right away. He shares a look with Bill. Susie is also in the room. Shaw's rich bassoon voice drips with dialect. Imperiously smoking a Gaulois, Shaw has about him an air of authority matched only by Jim's.

▌[Garrison, *Trail of the Assassins*, p. 144.]

CLAY SHAW Mr. Garrison—what can I do for you on Easter Sunday?

JIM I'm sorry, Mr. Shaw, to interrupt this holiday, but I feel this is a conversation we might better have out of the everyday bustle in this office ...

SHAW *(sitting)* I'm not sure I understand.

JIM *(bringing some papers forward)* Well ... in an investigation we're conducting your name has come up a number of times.

SHAW I wouldn't imagine where.

JIM We recently talked to a number of men who claim to know you. Are you acquainted with a David Logan?

SHAW No. Never heard of him.

JIM A Perry Russo?

SHAW No.

JIM A Willie O'Keefe?

SHAW No, I don't believe I know anyone by that name.

JIM Mr. O'Keefe told us he met you at the Masquerade Bar down in the Quarter and several evenings later you had him over for dinner at your apartment on Dauphine Street. Do you recall that?

> ▌Masquerade Bar/dinner at Shaw's: This scene is based on two separate incidents. A young man named William Morris had been introduced to Shaw/"Bertrand" at the Masquerade Bar and subsequently visited Shaw at his house. Another man, David Logan, gave Garrison his account of dinner at Shaw's carriage house. [Garrison, *Trail of the Assassins*, p. 86, 119.]

FLASHBACK TO Clay's Dauphine Street residence, in the Quarter, at night in 1962. The butler opens the door and O'Keefe is admitted to the townhouse. Shaw appears behind the butler.

SHAW (*voice-over, in present*) Of course not. I don't know this man. Obviously then, I wouldn't have him to dinner. Incidentally, I do not live in an apartment. It's an 1860s house built by Gallier. I've restored it faithfully. You know I am quite an advocate of restoration.

At Shaw's house, dinner is served at a long table by the black butler. The table is decorated by a sumptuous setting of silver and candelabra. Shaw uses a bell to summon the butler.

JIM (*voice-over*) Perhaps a few more details about the evening will refresh your memory. Mr. O'Keefe told us dinner was served by a uniformed waiter—a colored man. He particularly remembers that you sat at one end and he at the other—which he found rather unusual because the table was so long. Does that bring back memories of Willie O'Keefe?

SHAW (*in present*) Not at all. But on the other hand, I do have a lovely Chippendale dining table and I often have a friend over sitting at one end while I sit at the other. That is precisely the point of a long dining table. The splendor of the meal adds to the enjoyment of it.

JIM I would imagine a uniformed waiter helps.

SHAW It adds a taste of elegance for which I must confess a weakness now and then. I call him Smedley. His real name is Frankie Jenkins—but I could hardly imagine anything more uncouth during dinner than my turning toward the kitchen and hollering, "Frankie!" ... Where is this leading to, Mr. Garrison?

Willie O'Keefe and Clay Shaw leave the dining table.

JIM (*voice-over*) After dinner you paid him to have sex with you.

SHAW (*voice-over, laughing*) Pffft! Absolute nonsense. The Quarter is filled with vivid imaginations, my dear Mr. Garrison—grimy young hoodlums who'll say and do anything. As you well know.

JIM (*voice-over*) ... in the course of that night, Mr. O' Keefe said a man named David Ferrie stopped by the house ... along with another young man ... .

At Shaw's townhouse, we see Ferrie coming in, with another young chicken.

SHAW (*voice-over*) Who?

JIM (*voice-over*) ... David Ferrie ...

SHAW (*voice-over*) No. I have never known anyone by that name. Of course never having met Mr. O'Keefe I could hardly have met Mr. Ferrie ...

JIM (*voice-over*) ... and that the four of you partied early into the morning hours ...

We see the four men in drag, smiling for the flash camera, champagne bottles in hand. Ferrie sniffs some poppers, then shoves a popper in Shaw's face.

FERRIE You're mine, Mary. Go get the fucking tools out, bitch. *Now!* I want some ass.

Ferrie forces more poppers on Shaw. The camera moves to Shaw's bedroom, where Ferrie scatters a drawer full of leather tools.

FERRIE (*to Shaw*) Come here, bitch. (*Ferrie grabs Shaw by the hair*) You want this? The only way you get this is do what I say. (*Ferrie whacks Shaw*) I'm the man. Don't ever forget it. (*Shaw begs and whines*) You want it? *You want it?* (*Ferrie spits on Shaw*) Fuck you and your rich friends. You're nothing but a rich whore! You're my woman! Get the cat! (*to young man*) Strip! Now, woman. I want to see skin.

    ▌A 1954 FBI memo noted that Clay Shaw was "given to sadism and masochism in his homosexual activities" [cited in Hurt, *Reasonable Doubt*, p. 281]. New Orleans District Attorney's office photos show Shaw's collections of whips and chains and also hooks in a beam in the ceiling of Shaw's bedroom.

BACK TO Garrison's office.

JIM (*in present*) Let me show you his picture. (*he hands Shaw a general photo of Ferrie*)

SHAW (*in present*) No. I'm sure I've never met anyone of such a bizarre appearance.

    ▌Two photos of Shaw and Ferrie together at a party were published in the May 12, 1967 issue of *The Councilor*, a Shreveport (LA) publication. Researcher Edgar Tatro first saw the photos in the parking lot outside the Criminal Courts Building during a recess in the Shaw trial. "We all assumed Garrison had seen them too," recalls Tatro. Unfortunately, he hadn't, and lacked hard evidence of a Shaw-Ferrie relationship.

    The right-wing *Councilor's* objective in printing the photos and aiding Garrison's case was to "make America safe from political assassination and that

Hale Boggs and other left-wing imposters on the Warren Commission can be exposed as the liars they are."

JIM Does the name Clay Bertrand mean anything to you?

SHAW Clay Bertrand? Clay Bertrand? I believe there was a man with a name similar to that who worked at the Chamber of Commerce. Is that the man you had in mind?

JIM No, it was not. Do you know an attorney by the name of Dean Andrews?

SHAW One meets so many attorneys in my business. No, I don't believe I know Dean Andrews.

Jim is getting incredibly irritated. He feels Shaw is lying.

CUT TO Antoine's Restaurant, where Liz and all five kids look at menus.

SNAPPER I'm hungry! When're we gonna eat!

LIZ We're going to start without him and he'll be here for dessert. Snapper, you put that back!

VIRGINIA I want a Shirley Temple!

SNAPPER Me, too.

JASPER (*disappointed*) When's Daddy coming, Mama?

LIZ Soon. He's real sorry he can't start with us but he's promised to be here ...

BACK TO Garrison's office later that day. Everyone looks tired as the questioning goes on. Shaw sucks on endless Gauloises.

JIM (*handing a photo to Shaw*) Mr. Shaw, can you identify this man?

SHAW Naturally. (*he looks up*) Are you claiming, Mr. Garrison, that Mr. Oswald also had dinner with me?

JIM (*humorless*) Mr. Shaw, did you ever meet Lee Harvey Oswald?

SHAW You really have me consorting with a cast of sordid characters, don't you, Mr. Garrison.

JIM Please answer the question.

SHAW Of course not! Such a pity, that assassination. In fact, I admired President Kennedy. A man with true panache, and a wife with impeccable taste.

Jim shows Shaw a newspaper clipping.

JIM Mr. Shaw, this is an Italian newspaper article saying you were a member of the Board of Centro Mondo Commerciale in Italy, that this company was a creature of the CIA for the transfer of funds in Italy for illegal political-espionage activities. It says that this company was expelled from Italy for those activities.

■ *Paese Sera* article, Mar. 4, 1967: Rome-based Centro Mondo Commerciale and its Swiss affiliate Permindex were ostensibly trade organizations whose purpose was to "aid in the establishing of a permanent exposition and generally assist in terms involving trade." [Flammonde, *The Kennedy Conspiracy*, p. 215.] In 1962, Charles de Gaulle drew attention to Permindex, publicly accusing it of raising funds for the Secret Army Organization (OAS) that tried on several occasions to assassinate him. [Marrs, *Crossfire*, p. 499; see also *Le Devoir*, Mar. 16, 1967; Torbitt, *Nomenclature of an Assassination Cabal*, p. 17-21; and "Permindex: Britain's International Assassination Bureau," *Executive Intelligence Review*, Nov. 14, 1981.]

SHAW I'm well aware of this *asinine* article. And I am thinking very seriously of suing this rag of a newspaper.

JIM It says that this company has heavily Fascist ties to the French secret army organization that tried to assassinate de Gaulle in 1960.

SHAW Nonsense. What next?

JIM ... and that this company is linked to the Schlumberger tool company here in Houma, Louisiana—which is where their arms may have come from to David Ferrie and his Cubans ...

■ Schlumberger raid: [New Orleans District Attorney's Office Records; *New Orleans States-Item*, "Mounting Evidence Links CIA to 'Plot' Probe," Apr. 25, 1967, p. 1; Brener, *The Garrison Case*, p. 48-50.]

SHAW Mr. Garrison, you're reaching. I am an international businessman. The Trade Mart which I founded is America's commercial pipeline to Latin America. I trade everywhere. I am accused, as are all businessmen, of all things. I somehow go about my business, make money, help society the best I can and try to promote free trade in this world.

■ According to *New Orleans States-Item* reporters Rosemary James and Jack Wardlaw, the Trade Mart, organized in 1947, is "a non-profit organization designed to promote world trade, particularly with Latin America, and to increase foreign commerce through the Port of New Orleans."

JIM Mr. Shaw, have you ever been a contract agent with the Central Intelligence Agency?

Shaw glares at him. Silence.

SHAW (*with powerful contempt*) And if I was, Mr. Garrison ... do you think I would be here today ... talking to somebody like you?

JIM No, people like you don't have to, I guess—people like you walk between the raindrops.

SHAW (*rising*) May I go? Regardless of what you may think of me, Mr. Garrison, I am a patriot first and foremost.

JIM I've spent half my life in the United States military serving and defending this great country, Mr. Shaw, and you're the first person I ever met who considered it an act of patriotism to kill his own president.

SHAW Now just a minute, sir! You're way out of line!

Susie and Bill quiet Jim down.

BILL Come on, chief. (*as he shows Shaw to the door*) I'm sorry, Mr. Shaw, it's getting late. That's all the questions we have. Thank you for your honesty and for coming in today.

SHAW I enjoyed meeting with you, gentlemen, and you, Miss Cox. It was most pleasant. I wish to extend to each of you—and to each of your families—my best wishes for a happy Easter. (*he exits*)

JIM (*beat, excited*) "One may smile and smile and be a villain." Goddammit! We got one of 'em!

GARRISON'S HOME THAT NIGHT (1967)

Jim walks in, contrite. Liz is shutting down the house. Some of the kids are still up.

JASPER Daddy! Where you been?

JIM (*kisses Liz*) Hi, Freckle Face.

LIZ (*seething*) Hi.

JIM Tough day.

LIZ My sympathies.

JIM Liz, I'm really sorry. The meeting went much longer than expected.

LIZ We waited for you ... hours, Jim. You could have telephoned, for God's sake. It's Easter! You promised, Jim.

JIM I don't know what to say except I'm sorry. I just don't have rabbits on my mind.

LIZ I think you care more about John Kennedy than your family! All day long the kids are asking, "Where's Daddy?" What am I supposed to tell your kids, Jim!

JIM I don't know what to tell them. How 'bout the truth—I'm doing my job to make sure they can grow up in a country where justice won't be an arcane, vanished idea they read about in history books, like the dinosaurs or the lost continent of Atlantis.

LIZ That sounds dandy, but it sure doesn't replace a father and a husband on Easter Day.

JIM (*angry, turns away*) It's going to get worse, honey.

GARRISON'S OFFICE HALLWAY - MORNING (1967)

Jim, is coming down the corridor with Broussard, is confronted by some 20 local journalists and TV crew members. We hear a hubbub of fierce questioning—ad libs but Jim, puzzled, brushes by, seeking refuge in his office. Lou, Al, Numa and Susie are all waiting for him. The regular staff—some 30 people—are looking, wondering. Lou presents him with the front page of the New Orleans States-Item.

▮ [*New Orleans States-Item*, Feb. 17, 1967.]

LOU Congratulations, Boss—you're page one!

We see a close-up of the headline: "D.A. LAUNCHES FULL J.F.K. DEATH PLOT PROBE—Mysterious Trips Cost Large Sums."

INSIDE GARRISON'S OFFICE

JIM (*striding into his office reading the paper*) Goddamn Sam!

LOU And it ain't pretty (*reading the copy*) ... "the DA has spent more than $8,000 on unexplained travel and investigative expenses since November, 1966."

NUMA ... they went to the public records and got the vouchers we requested for withdrawals.

SUSIE Shaw must've gotten them on our tail.

AL ... could be Ferrie, Martin, Andrews, any of 'em.

BILL We didn't talk to Ruby 'cause of them and they're on our asses for a measly $8,000!

Jim, at his desk, finishes reading the article. A huge picture of him is on the front page. He puts down the paper, reaching for a long, gold pen that is part of the desk set.

JIM They hunted down the news, it's their business. Getting angry doesn't accomplish a damned thing, but this changes everything. We either pull out now or we go through some heavy flack together.

They look at each other.

JIM Bear in mind, each of you, this may affect the rest of your careers, your lives ... (*pause*) if any one of you pull out, I assure you I will bear no ill feelings towards that person and will reassign you to regular duties ...

No takers.

JIM There is it then. Thank you. It means very much to me. I'm giving this office $6,000 from my National Guard savings so we can continue. I will make speeches where I can to pick up additional money. Some local businessmen are putting together a fund for us and ...

SHARON (*coming in*) Mr. Garrison, what shall I tell them? They're piling up outside the door. They want a statement, the phones are going crazier than bugs on a cake.

Everyone waits. Jim stands, repacks his briefcase with papers and reference books and heads for the back door elevator.

JIM Neither confirm, deny, nor discuss, Sharon. Goodbye, ladies, gentlemen, I'm going home where I can get a decent day's work done.

LOU IVON'S APARTMENT - NEW ORLEANS - (1967)

Lou drinks a beer in front of the TV news in his small bachelor apartment. A fan is blowing.

NEWSMAN 11 (*editorial*) … Mr. Garrison's own silence on the subject has raised some interesting questions. With taxpayer money has he uncovered some valuable new evidence or is he merely saving the information which will gain for him exposure on a national level? Mr. Garrison it seems, should have some explanation.

The phone rings and Ivon picks it up.

■ [Garrison, *Trail of the Assassins*, p. 138.]

LOU Yeah?

DAVE FERRIE'S VOICE (*very agitated*) Did your office plant that garbage in the fucking paper?

LOU Who is this?

FERRIE (*voice-over*) You know damn well who it is.

LOU Dave?

FERRIE (*voice-over*) Yeah, you got it. Since you're the only straight shooter in that fuckin' office, I'd like an answer from you. Did you plant it?

LOU Dave, do you think we're out of our minds? The whole building's been a zoo since that broke. We can't get a thing done. Reporters crawling everywhere. You think we want that?

We see Ferrie in a phone booth on the street outside his apartment house in the French Quarter. He's a nervous wreck, watching the reporters and TV cameras surrounding his place, waiting for him.

FERRIE (*yelling*) *Somebody* planted that fucking story! And *somebody* tipped off the press I'm one of Garrison's fucking suspects. I can't go home. I'm out on the street. The maggots are *everywhere*! Do you know what you've done to me? It's all over the national news now. You know what you've done to me?

LOU Calm down, Dave, what?

FERRIE I'm a dead man! From here on, believe me, I'm a dead man.

LOU What are you talking about, Dave? You weren't mentioned in the story. Don't jump to conclusions.

FERRIE You think your investigation's been all that secret? You know, when you talk to people, they talk to other people.

LOU What did they ...

FERRIE You still questioning any Cubans?

LOU Dave, you know that's where this road leads.

FERRIE It leads farther than that.

LOU Dave, just calm down. Meet me in the lobby of the Fontainbleau in 20 minutes. I'll have a suite reserved for you under an assumed name.

FERRIE (*unsure*) The Fontainbleau? 20 minutes?

LOU (*hopeful*) Yeah. Come on, Dave, come on our side. I guarantee you the boss'll protect you ... (*there's a long silence as Ferrie, torn, agonizes*) Dave?

FERRIE (*dreamy*) ... give me protection?

LOU Yeah! He'd kill for you Dave. He likes you. Your mind.

FERRIE I got no place to sleep. I'll meet you in 20 minutes.

Ferrie hangs up. Pause. At his end, Lou Ivon hangs up, excited.

GARRISON'S HOME - NIGHT (1967)

The phone rings. Liz picks it up. Jim is watching the TV news: Martin Luther King is delivering a speech against the Vietnam War.

KING (ON TV) President Kennedy said on one occasion, "Mankind must put an end to war, or war will put an end to mankind." I pray God that America will hear this before it's too late, because today we're fighting a war I'm convinced is one of the most unjust wars that has ever been fought in the history of the world. [Martin Luther King, March on Washington, April 1967.]

LIZ (*on the phone meanwhile, testy*) No, he's not here now. And he would not take calls here if he were! So please call the office number. Thank you (*hangs up*). Two of them even had the gall to come to the door this afternoon, one all the way from England.

JIM Did they live ... ?

LIZ It's not funny, Jim, I'm scared ...

JIM Don't be. Nothing to be scared about, honey, I been through four years of war—this is nothing.

The phone rings again.

KING (ON TV) ... sending them 8,000 miles away to guarantee liberties in Southeast Asia which they have not found in Southwest Georgia or East Harlem. So we have been repeatedly faced with the cruel irony of watching Negro and white boys on TV screens as they kill and die for a nation that has been unable to seat them together in the same school.

LIZ I haven't, Jim.

JIM Nothing is gonna happen to you. I won't let it.

LIZ Leave us ALONE for God's sake! (*recognizes the voice*) ... Oh, it's Lou.

FONTAINBLEAU HOTEL SUITE - THAT NIGHT

Jim and Lou watch as Ferrie paces wildly, speeding.

> ▌Ferrie at Fountainbleau: This scene is based on an actual conversation at the Fountainbleau between Ferrie and Lou Ivon shortly before Ferrie's death. Garrison's book does not go into detail, mentioning the incident only in passing (see page 139). What is included in this scene comes from Ivon's recollections, various Garrison memos on Ferrie, and remarks from Ferrie's lengthy ideological paper trail. At times, however, we had to put words in Ferrie's mouth to write this scene and used our best judgment based on Ferrie's biography. The idea is that Ferrie was nervous, talky and frantic. In Lou Ivon's words, he was "about to break." Keep in mind that Ferrie was known for his far-flung ideas and opinions and said all kinds of outlandish things, including that President Kennedy "oughta be shot" shortly after the failed Bay of Pigs invasion. The FBI decided that, in this case, such a remark was a "colloquial expression" [see Weisberg, *Oswald in New Orleans*, p.184]. [For more on Ferrie see HSCA X. p.105-122; Flammonde, *The Kennedy Conspiracy*, p. 18-43; Weisberg, *Oswald in New Orleans*, p. 163-206; Melanson, *Spy Saga*, p. 39-53.]

FERRIE I'm caught in the middle. They're after me. It's almost over.

LOU Listen, Dave, why don't we order some room service, have a bite, relax. I'll stay as long as you want.

FERRIE I don't know who to trust anymore. Yeah, sure I could use a pot of hot coffee and a few packs of Camels. You got anything new in the investigation?

As Lou picks up the phone and orders room service, Jim answers.

JIM You mean about the Cubans getting trained north of the lake?

FERRIE (*incoherent*) Oh, you got that? Banister's pet project. Getting paid by the government to work against the government. Beautiful. What a mind he had, what a guy, Guy. He had all those files.

> ▌Banister's files: According to people who worked in Banister's office, Banister had extensive files on various public figures and political groups, mostly "subversive" left-wing organizations. What happened to them after Banister died remains something of a mystery.

When Banister died, his professional and personal life were a shambles. He was evicted from 544 Camp, owing several months back rent. He and his wife were estranged, due to his ongoing affair with his secretary, Delphine Roberts, who shared Banister's anti-communist venom. The day before he died, Banister and Roberts were in the process of moving Banister's files and library to Roberts' house.

According to New Orleans District Attorneys affidavits, most of Banister's material was seized by his creditors. Roberts admitted to taking a "few sensitive things" and turning them over to G. Wray Gill, Ferrie's employer and attorney for the powerful Marcello crime family. Mary Banister accused Roberts of stealing the files; Roberts charged that the widow burned them. What we do know is that in late 1964 Mary Banister sold a five-drawer file to the Louisiana State Police, gave other files to Aaron Kohn (head of the New Orleans Crime Commission), and split his library between Banister's friend, Kent Courtney, and the Louisiana State University Library. The Louisiana State Police "routinely destroyed" the Banister files but they did keep part of the index to the files. Among the titles:

American Central Intelligence Agency
Ammunition and Arms
Anti-Soviet Underground
B-70 Manned Bomber Force
Civil Rights Program of J.F.K.
Dismantling of Ballistic Missile System
Dismantling of Defenses, U.S.
Fair Play for Cuba Committee
International Trade Mart
"Lee Harvey Oswald" was one of the sub-headings for the FPCC file. [Garrison, *Trail of the Assassins*, p. 37-38; New Orleans District Attorney Records, statement of Delphine Roberts (1/19/67), Emile Stopper (12/30/66) and interview with Guy Johnson (8/24/67); HSCA X. p. 130-131.]

In *On the Trail of the Assassins*, Garrison claims Mary Banister told his investigators that "federal agents" carted off filing cabinets "within an hour or two" of Banister's death. Garrison cites from memory (his records "were stolen") an interview with Mrs. Banister as his source. Although she talked to the HSCA, there is no indication in the summary of her testimony that she repeated this allegation.

JIM Who was paying you, Dave?

FERRIE You think I was a getaway pilot for the assassination, don't you?

JIM I don't know. Were you? (*Dave laughs*) Who you scared of, Dave?

FERRIE Everybody! The Agency. The Mob. The Cubans. Yeah, follow the Cubans. Check them out. Here, in Dallas, Miami. Check out a guy named Eladio del Valle. My paymaster when I flew missions into Cuba—he's somewhere in Miami. You're on the right track.

■ Flammonde reports that Ferrie told Garrison he was paid $1,500 per mission by Del Valle [Flammonde, *The Kennedy Conspiracy*, p. 119].

Lou writes it down. Seeing him writing makes Ferrie even more paranoid.

FERRIE Hold it! Hold it! I'm not cooperating with anyone. There's a death warrant for me, don't you get it! Wait a minute. You're not bugged, are you?

He feels Lou for bugs, but out of a sense of hierarchy, ignores Jim. He checks around the room—the phone, behind paintings, flower vase, light fixtures—as the batty conversation continues:

LOU Dave, I always play square. No bugs. I'd love you to go on the record, but I'm in no hurry. Whenever you're ready.

FERRIE (*checking the room*) I don't have much time. They don't even need bugs anymore. They got these fuckin' satellite waves. They put a bug in a friend of mine when he was born, right up his nostrils, subcutaneous, between his eyes. He was one of those products of a crossbreeding experiment. A Nazi rocket scientist father and a Commie spy mother. You'd never believe half the shit the Agency does. (*holding his neck*) I'm so fuckin' tired. Haven't slept since that shit article came out. Why'd you guys have to go and get me involved with this?

LOU Did we involve you, Dave, or did Clay Shaw?

FERRIE That cocksuckin' faggot! He's got me by the balls.

LOU What do you mean?

FERRIE Photographs—compromising stuff. And he'll use 'em. The Agency plays for keeps … (*still checking the room for bugs*) I knew Oswald. He was in my Civil Air Patrol unit. I taught him everything. A "wanna be," y'know, nobody really liked him cause he was a snitch. I treated him good. He'd talk about his kid, y'know, really wanted her to grow up with a chance, but … He got a raw deal. The Agency fucked him. Just like they're gonna fuck me.

JIM Let me get this straight, now. Clay Shaw is blackmailing you?

FERRIE Fuckin' A. How do you think the Agency gets people to do their bullshit? Fuck knows what they got on Oswald!

Room service knocks, and Ferrie jumps and rushes to the bathroom.

FERRIE Who is it?

BELLHOP (*voice-over*) Room service.

Jim whispers something and Lou goes to the door, takes the service table without letting the bellhop in. Jim, excited but trying to stay even, continues with Ferrie.

JIM Was it the same Oswald, Dave, that was in Dallas, or was it an impersonator?

FERRIE Same one. I didn't know no impersonator.

FLASHBACK TO Ferrie at the party with Oswald (obscured) per Willie O'Keefe's witness. Jim, in the present, doesn't feel right about it.

JIM Did you take a good look at the TV when they had Oswald?

FERRIE (*shrugs, can't be bothered*) Black, black—just give it to me. (*takes the fresh coffee from Lou, lights a Camel*) Shit. I'm so exhausted. My neck is killing me. I've got cancer. Had it for years. I been working with mice, y'know, trying to come up with a cure.

JIM Dave, can I just ask you this directly? Did you ever work for the CIA?

FERRIE (*laughs*) You make it sound like some remote fuckin' experience in ancient history. Man, you never leave the Agency. Once they got you, you're in for life.

> ▌The CIA continues to deny Ferrie's association with them. Yet Ferrie himself boasted of the relationship and Victor Marchetti, former executive Assistant to CIA Deputy Director Richard Helms, told journalist Anthony Summers that a CIA colleague told him "Ferrie had been a contract agent to the Agency in the early sixties and had been involved in some of the Cuban activities" [Summers, *Conspiracy*, p. 300].

JIM And Shaw?

FERRIE Shaw's an "untouchable," man—highest clearance. Shaw, Oswald, the Cubans—all Agency.

JIM What about Ruby?

FERRIE Jack? Jack was a pimp. A bagman in Dallas for the Mob. He used to run guns to Castro when he was still on our side. Check out Jack Youngblood. Shit—we almost had Castro. Then we tried to whack him. Everybody's flipping sides all the time. It's fun 'n' games, man, fun 'n' games.

> ▌Jack Youngblood: a fictitious name.

> ▌Ruby's ties to organized crime: After examining Ruby's 30-year relationship with known (some of them very well-known) organized crime figures, the HSCA concluded that, although he was not a "member" of organized crime, he associated with these types [HSCA Report 149]. Ruby himself admitted to running guns to Cuba in a letter smuggled out of jail. ["In the Shadow of Dallas," *Ramparts*, 1967, p. 56.]

> ▌Ruby and organized crime: The Warren Commission deliberately altered documents referring to Ruby's mob ties. David Scheim's *Contract on America* makes the point with two Commission documents, CD 84 and CE 1536, which are two versions of the same story. CD 84 was not published in the Commission volumes. It runs two pages and mentions a man who is heavily connected to Ruby via organized crime. The published version, CE 1536, is only two paragraphs long. All references to organized crime have been excised and what remains is no more than a benign statement by a man who knew Ruby casually [Scheim, *Contract on America*, p. 174-175]. No member of the Commission or its staff has ever explained this curious act of censorship.

LOU What about the mob, Dave? How do they figure in this?

FERRIE They're Agency, too. Don't you get it? CIA and Mafia together. Trying to whack out the Beard. Mutual interests. They been doing it for years. There's more to this than you dream. FBI fucking hates the CIA. Navy Intelligence got something to do with it too. Check out "Alan Pope" in Miami. Jack Young-blood. Bill Harvey. Colonel Roselli. The shooter, I hear, was a Dallas cop—the bagman at Ruby's club. I heard he shot his own partner. Got that? Check out the rich fucks in Dallas. H.L. Hunt. He's dirty. Check out the Minutemen. They're tied in somehow. General Walker. He's dirty. That's all I know. But the Agency always runs the show. Check out something called "Mongoose," Operation Mongoose. Government, Pentagon stuff, they're in charge, but who the fuck pulls whose chain who the fuck knows, fun 'n' games man—check out Southeast Asia—that's the next big number—the heroin trail. "Oh, what a deadly web we weave when we practice to deceive."

∎ Alan Pope: American pilot of a CIA B-26 shot down and captured over Indonesia in 1958. [John Ranelagh, *The Agency: The Rise and Decline of the CIA* (Simon & Schuster, 1986), p. 334.]

∎ Bill Harvey: Legendary CIA man who ran the Berlin Tunnel Project and the infamous ZR/RIFLE "Executive Action" program. [Church Committee Interim Report, Alleged Assassination Plots Against Foreign Leaders, p. 180-190 (ZR/RIFLE); Martin, *Wilderness of Mirrors*.] [For more on Harvey, see David C. Martin, *Wilderness of Mirrors*; Evica, *And We Are All* ...., p. 254-259.]

∎ Colonel Roselli: Army officer Bradley Earl Ayers knew famed mobster Johnny Roselli as "Colonel Roselli" when he worked at the JM/WAVE station in Miami. He writes that Roselli "worked out of the CIA headquarters in Washington" and "was one of the few Americans actually authorized to go on commando missions into Cuba." [Earl Bradley Ayers, *The War That Never Was* (Bobbs-Merrill, 1976), p. 38.]

Roselli testified about the CIA-Mafia plots in a secret appearance before the Church Committee in April, 1976. There was to be no further questioning of Roselli. On July 28, 1976, his dismembered body was found in an oil drum floating off the Florida coast. [For more on Roselli's death, see Rappleye and Becker, *All American Mafioso*, p. 3-5, 320-321; Evica, *And We Are All...*, p. 259-269.]

∎ "Shooter was a Dallas cop": In a transcript of a meeting between Garrison and researchers Bernard Fensterwald, William Turner and Richard E. Sprague, Garrison says that Ferrie claimed that "[Officer] Tippit was one of the guns on the roof" [Transcript of meeting, Sept. 21, 1968, p. 130].

∎ H.L Hunt: Hunt backs anti-Castro Cubans [Hinckle and Turner, *The Fish Is Red*, p. 202]. Hunt voices his concerns about the threat of a Kennedy dynasty in a July 11, 1963 letter to Senator Harry Byrd: "The stake is the entire future of the nation" [Letter to Senator Byrd, Box 270, Byrd Papers, University of Virginia Library]. Hunt is trying to persuade Southern Democrats to switch affiliation to the Republican Party.

∎ Minutemen and Garrison Investigation: [William W. Turner, "The Inquest," *Ramparts*, Jun. 1967. For more on Minutemen see James Coates, *Armed and Dangerous*.] At least one member of the Minutemen was arrested at the anti-Castro training camp at Lake Pontchartrain.

∎ General Walker: [Meagher, *Accessories After the Fact*, p. 283-292; Marrs, *Crossfire*, p. 255-265; Summers, *Conspiracy*, p. 205-210, 214-217.] The Warren Commission decided that Oswald fired a shot at General Edwin Walker, well-known for his segregationist, extremist right-wing views, on Apr. 12, 1963. They based their conclusions on several photographs found among Oswald's belongings and a note he allegedly left for Marina with instructions on what to do should he get caught. Eyewitness testimony indicated that it was probably not Oswald. The HSCA "abandoned" their inquiry into the Walker affair but admitted it was likely the work of more than one person [HSCA Report, p. 61n, 98n].

▮ Operation Mongoose: [Church Committee Report, p. 139-190; Turner and Hinckle, *The Fish Is Red*, p.111-126; John Prados, *President's Secret Wars: CIA and Pentagon Covert Operations from WWII to Iranscam* (Quill, 1986), p. 211-214; Ranelegh, *The Agency*, p. 383-390.]

▮ Heroin trail—Southeast Asia: [The best source on this is Alfred M. McCoy's *The Politics of Heroin: CIA Complicity in the Global Drug Trade* (Lawrence Hill, 1991), which updates his classic *The Politics of Heroin Trafficking in Southeast Asia* (Harper & Row, 1972). Also see Chapter 14 of Henrik Kruger's *The Great Heroin Coup* (South End Press, 1980).]

JIM Then who killed the President?

FERRIE Oh man, why don't you stop. This is too fuckin' big for you! Who did Kennedy? It's a mystery wrapped in a riddle inside an enigma. *Even the shooters don't fuckin' know!* Don't you get it yet? I can't be talking like this. They're gonna kill me. I'm gonna die! (*he sits down, cracking, sobbing*) I don't know what happened. All I wanted in the world was to be a Catholic priest—live in a monastery, study ancient Latin manuscripts, pray, serve God. But I had this one terrible, fatal weakness. They defrocked me. And then I started to lose everything.

He bows his head, holding it in his hands, and his wig starts to come off in his hands.

FERRIE Shit! Forgot to glue this fuckin' rug today. You know, at one time I even had a full head of hair like everyone else. And then I lost that. That fuckin' Clay Shaw. I hate the bastard. All I got left is in his rotten, bloody hands. He tipped the newspapers—I know it. That's how the Agency works. They use people, chew them up, spit 'em out. Now it's my turn.

JIM (*empathetic*) Dave, it's going to be okay. Just talk to us on the record and we'll protect you. I guarantee it.

There's a long silence. Ferrie, spent, stares at Jim. He's about to crack, but ...

FERRIE They'll get to you, too—they'll destroy you ... They're untouchable, man ... (*then*) I'm so fucking exhausted I can't see straight.

JIM Get some rest, Dave, and you'll feel better in the morning. We'll talk then.

FERRIE Yeah, yeah. But leave me alone for awhile. I got to make some calls.

His eyes are going again. Deals ... intrigue—thru the tears.

LOU Whatever you say, Dave. I'll be home. Okay—

Lou and Jim share a look.

■ Garrison describes how they got Ferrie a room at the Fountainbleau but he did not stay there [Garrison, *Trail of the Assassins*, p. 139].

CORRIDOR OF GARRISON'S OFFICE - A FEW DAYS LATER (1967)

A mob scene. Press from the U.S. and all over the world are filling the corridor. A French reporter tries to get past the receptionist as Numa passes him with a stack of mail. Also in the hall are many individual citizens who have come to give tips and theories. One of them is dressed as Satan in a red jump suit with mask, horns, tail and a pitchfork.

■ [Conversations with Garrison, Ivon, Bertel, 1991.]

FRENCH REPORTER *(waving credentials)* *Paris Match*. We are the largest magazine in all of France.

SOVIET REPORTER My name is Bulgarinov. I am with *Literaturnaya Gazeta* of Moscow.

AMERICAN REPORTER Bill Turner. *Ramparts*.

■ William W. Turner chronicled the Garrison investigation for the San Francisco-based *Ramparts*. Turner's reporting is perhaps the best account of the case as it progressed: ["The Inquest, June, 1967; "The Press vs. Garrison," Sept., 1967; "The Garrison Commission on the Assassination of President Kennedy," Jan., 1968; "Epstein's Garrison," Sep., 1968.]

A mailman, black, comes through lugging three sacks of mail.

MAILMAN Coming through, out of the way.

RECEPTIONIST You know who killed the President? Mr. Garrison is busy but his assistant …

A camera moves by into the interior offices.

MONTAGE OF OFFICE SHOTS:

BILL BROUSSARD'S OFFICE

A man with the demeanor of Julius Caesar walks into Bill's office.

■ Julius Caesar: Among the many oddballs who came to offer Garrison information was a Californian named Howard Rice Knight. He claimed to be a reincarnation of Julius Caesar and as proof, wore a toga. He claimed to have been offered $10,000 by Jack Ruby to lend a hand to Shaw, Ferrie and Oswald in planning the assassination. The allegations never amounted to anything. [Brener, *The Garrison Case*, p. 196.]

CAESAR *(raising arm)* Hail! Et tu, Brutus?

BILL And you, too, my friend …

Bill escorts him out before he gets the chance to sit down, and then heads for Jim's office.

JIM GARRISON'S OFFICE

Numa joins Jim with a stack of new mail.

NUMA Love a duck! It takes twenty minutes to get into this office these days. Are we famous or what?

Jim is reading Newsweek, *deeply hurt. There are newspapers all over his desk.*

JIM Notorious is more like it. "Jim Garrison is right. There has been a conspiracy in New Orleans—but it's a plot of Garrison's own making" ... and this—"one of the D.A.'s investigators offered an unwilling witness $3,000 if only he would fill in the facts of the alleged meeting to plot the death of the President" ... How can they write that? Where did they come up with this? ... (*sorting through others*). "A charlatan," "power-mad," a "hulking D.A." (*New York Post*), "Morbid Frolic in New Orleans."

> ∎ *Newsweek*: "The J.F.K. 'Conspiracy,'" May 15, 1967. The article bears the byline of Hugh Aynesworth, a reporter with a dubious history in the J.F.K. case.
>
> At the L.B.J. Library, Texas researcher Gary Mack found a teletype to L.B.J. press secretary George Christian. Aynesworth enclosed a copy of the *Newsweek* story asking Christian to pass it on to the President. Aynesworth writes: "My interest in informing governmental officials of each step along the way is because of my intimate knowledge of what Jim Garrison is planning ... I intend to make a complete report of my knowledge available to the FBI as I have done in the past." (Teletype reprinted in *Coverups!*, Gary Mack (ed.), Nov., 1982.)

Bill has come in during this, completely frazzled.

BILL The crazies have taken over the asylum! It's a zoo out there.

NUMA Sensational garbage sells newspapers, Jim. What else is new? Look at the thousands of letters you're getting. That's where the heart of the country is. (*reads from one*) "Dear Mr. Garrison, God bless you for having the courage to go after the murderers of President Kennedy. Please don't stop till they're behind bars. I am a beautician here in Hannibal, Missouri, and my husband is a janitor in the local high school. We have four kids and not an extra lot of money but we enclose a contribution to help with your work. We are praying for you. God bless, Judith Hardy, Hannibal, Missouri."

Numa pulls a dollar bill from the envelope.

NUMA That's what it's about, boss. For every lousy article in the press there's a hundred of these.

Jim is moved. Bill is not.

BILL That's fine, Numa, but what about all the people who aren't writing letters. They're sitting home reading all these lies. I just heard NBC crew's in town to do a "White Paper"—not on the Kennedy killing, but on us. One of their top guys, Harry Stoner, is talking to everybody he can find about you, boss ...

JIM Oh Jesus. Stoner! ... Why doesn't he call me?

NUMA (*to Bill*) What do you want to do, Bill—fold up and close the store? You sure sound like it.

BILL Look, this is bigger than all of us. We can't try a case in this atmosphere.

Sharon has come in during this, signalling to Jim.

SHARON Mr. Miller's been waiting.

JIM (*remembering*) Oh! Send him in. (*to Numa*) Denver oilman wants to support the investigation. (*specifically to Bill*). Bill, I know what you're thinking, but sometimes when it makes no sense that's exactly when you just gotta stick to it, head down.

Sharon shows in Mr. Miller, the Denver oilman. He's a self-assured, impressive man in his 50's with a western accent, cowboy boots and hat, and a well-cut gabardine suit.

JIM Welcome, Mr. Miller. Jim Garrison. Would you care for some coffee?

MILLER Yes, thank you, Mr. Garrison. Your coffee's almost Turkish down here but I could get used to it.

Numa leaves. Bill indicates he'd like to sit in. Jim nods okay. Miller pays no attention to Bill.

MILLER I'm glad you could find time to see me. I flew down from Denver this morning on my private jet.

JIM Yes, your letter indicated you were in the oil business up there.

MILLER I've done quite well in Denver, Mr. Garrison, but I have to admire someone like you—and I have the means to back up what I say.

JIM We can use all the support we can get. I think these might interest you.

Jim has gathered together a group of photos of the shooting. Sharon bringing the coffee.

JIM They've been enlarged and show a lot of detail ...

MILLER Splendid, love to see them.

He glances at the photo but continues on across the room, looking at the pictures on the walls.

MILLER Where were you? Europe, Pacific?

JIM Germany.

MILLER You were lucky. I spent three years in the Pacific. (*he looks out the blinds at Tulane Avenue*) I've never seen an avenue with such a profusion of bail-bonding companies. Why is that?

JIM (*nettled by Miller's moving around*) I imagine because this is the Criminal District Court Building (*showing a photo*). This is an enlargement of a potential shooter standing behind the picket fence. We ...

We see a blurry blowup of something behind the picket fence. Miller takes the photo, glances at it and sits down.

> ∎ Blowup: Garrison is referring to the Polaroid of the motorcade and the Grassy Knoll taken by Mary Moorman a fraction of a second before the fatal headshot (cf. notes p. 122).

MILLER I know about that shot. A terrible tragedy. (*Puts the picture back on the desk*) How much do you have for carrying on your investigation?

JIM If you must know, virtually nothing.

MILLER How many men are working with you on this?

JIM Less than you would guess. Most days two to three assistant D.A.s. A handful of police investigators.

MILLER That's all you've had all this time?

JIM That's it.

Jim expectant of some help. A pause. Then:

MILLER I admire you, Mr. Garrison. How did you manage to make your way into Guy Banister's operation?

The clock is ticking. Jim shares a look with Bill. The cards are on the table.

JIM That was never in the newspapers, Mr. Miller.

Miller smiles, stands, paces the room. He continues to ignore Bill completely.

MILLER I'm going to be very frank with you. You've done a great job, an astounding job considering the limited resources available to you. But the best you can ever hope for is to stir up a lot of confusion. You're not going to do this country any good, and you're not going to do yourself any good. (*he sits back down and looks directly at Jim*) You don't belong here. On this Mickey Mouse street with that cheap strip of bail bond shops.

JIM The job manages to keep me pretty busy.

MILLER Nonsense. You should be in a job where you can make decisions that have impact, affect the world. Here you're trying to climb up the steep side of Mount Everest.

He leans forward across Jim's desk, tapping his manicured index finger on the desk. Clearly visible to Jim and to us (in a close-up) is Miller's Annapolis ring tapping.

MILLER I propose you accept an appointment to the bench in Federal District Court and move into a job worthy of your talent. (*he leans back and pauses*) Do you have any idea, do you have any *conception* of how easily such an appointment can be arranged?

JIM And what would I have to do?

MILLER Stop your investigation ... it was a magnificent effort but it's over and done with. The press is already on your behind and that's only the beginning, my boy, only the beginning ...

JIM How long do you think it would take me to be appointed?

Jim's eyes go to Bill. He could be wrong, but it's almost as if Bill were going along with the idea now.

MILLER (*smiling, thinking Jim is hooked*) Well, ordinarily these things take a long time. But in your case, with your record it can be expedited—easily. I *guarantee* it.

Jim leans back, puts his feet up on the corner of the desk, waving them like fans. Bill waits.

JIM *Who are you*, Mr. Miller? (*no answer—just the sound of the overhead fan*) You see that helmet over there? (*the Nazi helmet with a bullet hole on his desk*) I picked that up at the Dachau concentration camp when we liberated it in 1945. It was the most horrifying sight I've ever seen, Mr. Miller. Pyramids of decaying, stinking bones and skin one on top of the other. I don't enjoy looking at that swastika every day, Mr. Miller, but I keep it there to remind me of what can happen when a country turns from free democratic principles to Fascism, when a few madmen turn human beings into digits and millions sit in silence and do nothing about it.

Miller waits. Bill waits. Jim comes forward with his reply.

JIM Mr. Miller, you and I have met under a great misunderstanding. I haven't the remotest interest in becoming a Federal Judge. And nothing is going to keep me from going ahead with my investigation of John Kennedy's murder.

Miller's entire demeanor tightens into a corkscrew of anger and danger.

JIM Bill, Mr. Miller and I have finished our conversation. Would you show him out?

Bill has a strange reaction—a sudden exhalation of breath as if an entire house of cards were collapsing. He rises, but Miller goes first, leaving silently. Once he's gone, Bill turns wearily to Jim.

JIM Those bastards! That's proof enough right there of what we're up against. The whole goddamn Federal Government, Bill!

BILL Well, they offered you the carrot and you turned it down ... you know what's coming next, don't you, boss?

■ Mr. Miller: [Garrison, *Trail of Assassins*, p. 132-6.] Researcher Gus Russo has established that "Mr. Miller" is really John J. King, a Denver oilman with a strange history in the J.F.K. case. His real name is found in Sybil Leek and Bert Sugar's book, *The Assassination Chain*, (Corwin Books, 1976) p. 311. Russo found an FBI teletype dated Nov. 27, 1963, stating that Jack Ruby " ... was a close friend of John J. King, prosperous Dallas businessman. King visited Carousel Club numerous times" [FBI Teletype to Director and SAC, Dallas from SAC, New Orleans, Re: Background of Ruby, Nov. 27. 1963]. In the July 9, 1970, *Dallas Morning News*, reporter Earl Golz wrote that, in 1969, "Denver oilman John J. King ... had spent $11,350 to try to acquire the (assassination) rifle and the .38-caliber pistol allegedly used by Oswald to shoot J.D. Tippit." Most recently Russo has contacted King's son (King is deceased), who confirms his father's actions.

GARRISON'S CONFERENCE ROOM - ANOTHER DAY (1967)

The staff is assembled. We see the headline in the Times-Picayune, *which says: "FERRIE CALLS GARRISON PROBE A WITCH HUNT."*

LOU Boss, I tell you something or somebody is putting tremendous heat on David Ferrie. If we sit on our behinds any longer, I don't think the guy's going to hold on.

SUSIE *(raps the newspaper)* Look at this bullshit! He keeps changing what he says. We can't possibly call him to a Grand Jury.

JIM Susie, watch the language, would you please.

AL My instinct is that Ferrie is going to keep on deteriorating, and we'll end up getting more out of him when he finally cracks. If we call him now, he might freeze up and we could lose the best shot we've ever had.

LOU You don't get it, guys—he can't go down any further. We got to protect him full time.

JIM *(rises, looks at his watch)* I have a plane to catch ... going to Washington. An interesting lead, says he's closely connected to these events, but he won't come down here ... I know what you're going through with Ferrie, Lou. We'll talk tomorrow.

LOU I'm onto Ferrie's Cuban paymaster, Eladio del Valle, in Miami. I gotta get him in, boss. I need more men—I can't even pull the teams to watch Ferrie ... This is our case!

Numa rushes in with a young investigator, Williams—displaying a miniature microphone.

NUMA HOLD IT, CHIEF ... .

JIM *(to Lou)* You just need some sleep, Lou. It won't look so bad when ...

Numa makes violent signals to shut up—not to talk—sticking the microphone in front of Jim. Williams searches the walls for the bug. Numa signals everyone outside.

■ Bugging Garrison's office: [Garrison, *Trail of the Assassins*, p. 220 fn.] Several years after the Shaw trial, documents released through the Freedom of Information Act suits showed that both the FBI and CIA had monitored Garrison's every move during the years of his investigations—and it didn't stop there.

Take, for example, CIA document 1127-987, dated 19 July 1968. Addressed to "certain" station chiefs, the document is a cover sheet for Edward J. Epstein's negative article on Garrison published in *The New Yorker* (13 July 1968):

"If the Garrison investigation should be cited in your area in the context of renewed anti-U.S. attacks, you may use the article to brief interested contacts, especially government and other political leaders, and to demonstrate to assets (which you may assign to counter such attacks) that there is no hard evidence of any such conspiracy."

A year earlier, in April, 1967, the CIA had issued document 1035-960, (see Section III) titled "Countering Critics of the Warren Report." This document aimed to stem the increasing dissatisfaction with the Warren Report. "We do not recommend that discussion of the assassination question be initiated where it is not already taking place. Where discussion is active, however, addresses are requested."
The CIA's recommended course of action is, perhaps, most sinister of all:

"To employ propaganda assets to refute the attacks of the critics. Book reviews and feature articles are particularly appropriate for this purpose."

By 1968, it was clear that Clay Shaw would have to stand trial on conspiracy charges. The FBI stepped in to help the Shaw defense team. In addition to running extensive background checks on all twelve jurors, the FBI passed on information about Garrison's prospective witnesses to Shaw's attorneys. Even the document notes that this is an unusual service for the Bureau:

"Though the current inquirer, Attorney Wegmann (Shaw's counsel) is in no sense a Federal Government agency, his inquiry had been transmitted to us through a Federal agency, because of this and because of the unique nature of the case, it is felt that we should furnish information similar in scope to what we gave the CIA and the National Security Agency."

Many of the released documents are blacked out virtually in their entirety. [Documents available through Assassination Archives and Research Center, Washington, D.C.]

■ While working as an investigator for the HSCA, journalist Gaeton Fonzi uncovered documents that showed that 11 intelligence operatives had been infiltrated into the Garrison investigation. Unfortunately, these documents remain classified along with the rest of the HSCA's material. On February 5th, 1992, the television program *Inside Edition* aired a segment that announced these findings but, according to anchor Bill O'Reilly, no major newspaper would even assign a writer to look into the story. (Robert Hennelly and Jerry Policoff, "JFK: How the Media Assassinated the Real Story," *Village Voice*, March 31, 1992.)

GARRISON'S MAIN OFFICE

The staff comes out into the office with Jim, disturbed.

JIM What the hell is … .

NUMA Williams found this in your office … We think the conference room is also bugged. And maybe the phones. The whole place needs debugging.

The whole staff from the conference room reacts. Jim looks stunned.

JIM I don't believe it!

SUSIE Bugging the District Attorney's office of New Orleans! It's outrageous!

Sharon has been standing there trying to get Lou's attention.

SHARON It's urgent for you, Mr. Ivon … .

Lou goes to the phone.

NUMA Well, believe what you want, boss, but we got to be more careful. All these new volunteers, any one of them could be …

JIM Okay, you handle it, Numa. I don't have time for this nonsense. (*to the hidden mikes loudly*) We've obviously got the bastards worried now. I'm going to Washington.

Everyone laughs, but the camera goes to the look of shock on Lou's face as he holds the receiver. They all look over at him; feeling the bad news before they hear it.

LOU Dave Ferrie's dead. The body was found at his apartment two hours ago.

Jim's look says "There goes the case."

OUTSIDE FERRIE'S APARTMENT - FRENCH QUARTER - (1967)

Jim and his staff storm into the area, which is cordoned off by police. Members of the press are all over, yelling questions at Jim.

JIM (*to chief police officer*) This case is in our jurisdiction. I don't want anyone from a Federal agency in here without an explicit Federal court order. You got that, Hank? (*Hank looks at him weirdly*)

NEWSMAN 10 Was Ferrie murdered, Mr. Garrison? Do you have any leads?

INSIDE FERRIE'S APARTMENT

The apartment is filthy and sinister. Hundreds of mice squeal in their cages, upset by the invasion of men and light. Nothing seems to have been washed in years. There is an accumulation of furniture, college pennants, photos of young boys in training, books everywhere, ammunition, guns, a piano, maps, fake college degrees on the walls. Ferrie's naked body lies on the couch with a sheet over it. He is unwigged, his eyebrows unpainted, false teeth next to him. Jim studies the corpse as the coroner comes alongside.

▮David Ferrie found dead: [*New Orleans States-Item*, "Key J.F.K. Probe Figure Ferrie Found Dead Here," Feb. 22, 1967, p. 1; Garrison, *Trail of the Assassins*, p. 140-143; *Washington Post*, "Key Suspect in J.F.K. Plot Found Dead," George Lardner, Jr., Feb. 22, 1967.] The coroner ruled that Ferrie died of natural causes—a massive brain hemorrhage—and, based on the condition of the body, said Ferrie had died "sometime [the previous] evening." However, *Washington Post* reporter George Lardner Jr. claimed to have been at Ferrie's apartment until 4 A.M. On learning that Lardner was with Ferrie until that time, he said "I can't rule out the possibility he might have died as late as 4 A.M.," but he insisted that was "absolutely the latest possible time of death" [*New Orleans States-Item*, Feb. 23, 1967]. The young man who found the body told police he "didn't know Ferrie" and "just happened to wander in" [*New Orleans Times-Picayune*, Feb. 22, 1967]. Ferrie lived on the second floor.

▎The coroner's photos of the death scene are quite revealing and certainly don't indicate natural causes. About 15 prescription bottles sit empty in the living room and Ferrie has contusions on the inside of his mouth. Both current New Orleans Coroner Dr. Frank Minyard and noted forensic pathologist Dr. Cyril Wecht maintain that these contusions indicate foul play—as if someone was applying heavy pressure to keep Ferrie's mouth closed.

JIM What's it look like, Nick?

CORONER I don't see any violence, Jim. Heart attack, maybe an aneurysm. Looks like natural causes.

Jim picks up several empty, capless medicine bottles on a table next to the sofa and looks at them. Lou and Bill come over with a typed suicide note.

▎Suicide notes: [Flammonde, *The Kennedy Conspiracy*, p. 34-36 (text of both suicide notes).]

BILL It's addressed to no one and no signature. "To leave this life is, for me, a sweet prospect. I find nothing in it that is desirable and on the other hand, everything that is loathsome." ...

LOU Pretty flowery for Dave Ferrie.

The words from the note hang there weirdly, as Jim paces on into the apartment, one of the medicine bottles in his hand. The music grows, and a sinister feel of danger and death pervades the atmosphere. Then the sounds drop away.

FERRIE'S BATHROOM

Along both sides of the mirror Jim finds globs of purplish glue alongside Ferrie's wig. He looks up into the mirror. He imagines sounds of struggle, thrashing, pleading— Ferrie's ghostly voice. Jim looks down at the medicine in his hand and moves into Ferrie's bedroom.

FERRIE'S BEDROOM

Jim hands Lou the medicine bottle.

LOU Proloid?

JIM I took it once for a low thyroid condition ... (*he walks away*) It raises the metabolism, Lou. (*pause*) Did David Ferrie strike you as the kind of person who had a low metabolism ... ?

LOU I'd say the opposite—hypertension.

■ Proloid: [Garrison, *Trail of the Assassins*, p. 142-143.]

CLOSET IN FERRIE'S APARTMENT

Jim runs an eye through Dave's closet, cluttered with shabby jackets. His eye falls on a neat but faded lace and satin, some sort of garment of priestly origin, he takes it in his hand.

JIM Ferrie was the only one to express some kind of remorse about this whole thing. I think it got him killed.

Susie Cox walks in, a new message written on her face.

SUSIE Boss, we just got bad news from Miami. They found Ferrie's Cuban friend— Eladio del Valle—this morning, hacked to death with a machete in his car. He was tortured, shot in the heart at point-blank range and his skull was split open with an axe ...

LOU Jesus—if that ain't the Devil's piss! Those bastards!

■ Death of Eladio del Valle: [Turner & Hinckle, *The Fish Is Red*, p. 269; Flammonde, *The Kennedy Conspiracy*, p. 19; James and Wardlaw, *Plot of Politics*, p. 46. They cite as their source Diego Gonzales Tendedera, the Miami correspondent for *El Tiempo*.]

Jim's mood darkens, and he heads back into the living room as Ferrie's corpse is being trundled out the door. The sickness is everywhere; an oppressive mood. Bill comes up.

BILL Found another note, same thing, no name, no signature. "When you receive this, I will be quite dead, so no answer will be possible. I offered you love. All I got in return in the end was a kick in the teeth."

JIM Jesus, they must've been hard pressed to come up with *that* one.

Jim, feeling ill, wanting to leave, stops the coroner before he exits ...

JIM (*gives the coroner the empty bottle*) Nick, what would happen if a man suffering from hypertension were to take an entire bottle of Proloid?

CORONER He'd die pretty quick, either a heart storm or a ruptured blood vessel in the brain.

JIM Can you ascertain if there's Proloid in his system?

CORONER Not in a routine autopsy, but if we looked at the spinal fluid, there might be a high level of iodine, but it's difficult to know. Whatcha thinkin', Jim?

JIM Well, it doesn't make sense, Nick—he was afraid of dying, then he kills himself in a way that leaves no trace, but he leaves two unsigned suicide notes.

CORONER (*shrugs, skeptical*) If it's a suicide. I seen weirder, Jim. (*exits*)

BILL The fact is he's gone, chief, and so's our case.

LOU Not unless we go for Shaw *now*.

BILL With whose testimony? Willie O'Keefe? A male prostitute. Jack Martin? A drunk? Vernon Bundy? A dope fiend. Shaw's got respect, the newspaper editors, the American Bar Association—they're not ...

> ■ Vernon Bundy: [Transcript of Preliminary Hearing, No. M-703, Clay L. Shaw, Arrestee, Mar. 14-17, 1967; *New Orleans States-Item*, Feb. 8, 1969. p. 2; Garrison, *Trail of the Assassins*, p. 156-159.] Bundy, a 29-year-old admitted heroin addict, told Garrison's office that he had seen Oswald and Shaw together near the sea wall at Lake Pontchartrain. As Bundy prepared a heroin injection for himself, he watched a young man and a "tall, white-haired" man talk for about 15 minutes. The older man, whom Bundy identified as Shaw, gave the younger man, whom he identified as Oswald, a roll of money. The younger man dropped some yellow leaflets on the ground, one of which Bundy used to wrap the rest of his dope in. He testified at both the grand jury hearing and the Shaw trial.

SUSIE I'm afraid I'm with Bill on this one. We haven't got the goods yet.

LOU We wait, Shaw's gonna get whacked. Oswald, Ruby, Ferrie, del Valle, Banister, Bowers ... how many corpses you lawyers gotta see to figure out what's going on?

JIM All right, all right. Break it up.

BILL Where you going, boss?

JIM I don't know, Bill, I just don't know.

OUTSIDE FERRIE'S APARTMENT THAT SAME NIGHT

As Jim, questioned by reporters, gets in his car and leaves, Bill waves goodbye to Lou and walks toward his own car, dejected. The area is cordoned off and humming with activity. Frank, an FBI man who knows Bill from previous cases, approaches him out of the crowd. He wears a hat, suit, and tie.

FRANK Bill.

BILL Hey, where y'at, Frank? You're wasting your time here. Big Jim gave strict orders. No FBI allowed.

FRANK It's you I want to talk to, Bill.

BILL (*laughs*) Boss would fry me in hog fat if he knew ... (*motions to car*)

FRANK (*getting in the car*) Your boss got a serious problem, Bill. Real serious. We know what's been going on at your office.

BILL (*smiles*) Yeah, I guess you do.

FRANK You've got nothin', Bill. I'm talking as a friend now. You're riding on the Titanic. Time to jump off before you get destroyed along with Garrison ...

BILL Frank, I don't want to hear it.

FRANK Senator Long set your boss up, my friend ...

This gets Bill's attention.

FRANK Who do you think fed him that information? Garrison's going down. We're talking about your career here, Bill, your life. You're a young guy ... we know you're working that Castro thing.

BILL No, I'm not ...

FRANK Yes, you are. Look we know Oswald didn't pull that trigger. Castro did. But if that comes out, there's gonna be a war, boy—millions of people are gonna die. That's a hell of a lot more important than Jim Garrison. (*suddenly*) Goddammit, look at me when I talk to you! You're too goddamn self-opinionated, now *shut up*. If you got a brain in that thick skull of yours, listen to me. Listen real hard.

Bill, taken aback, listens.

WASHINGTON D.C. - PARK - (1967) *Meeting in Washington*

Jim walks down from the Lincoln Memorial, where he is met unobtrusively by a military man in his 50s in casual civilian clothing, hat on his head, an erect posture. They walk towards the Mall, with the Capitol building looming in the background.

> ▎X scene: This scene purports to illustrate the problems Garrison—and indeed, anyone investigating the Kennedy assassination —had with the FBI. Garrison's staff remember a total lack of cooperation from the Bureau. Some of the key New Orleans witnesses reported being intimidated by agents.
>
> In the 1967 CBS documentary *The Warren Report*, Cuban exile Orest Peña told how New Orleans FBI agent Warren DeBrueys (to whom Peña served as an informant) threatened him with physical harm if he told the Warren Commission that he had seen Oswald and DeBrueys on several occasions. DeBrueys denied Peña's allegations. (HSCA Report, p. 192-193). Dean Andrews also claimed the FBI was bothering him. He told the Warren Commission: "You can tell when the steam is on. They are on you like the plague. They never leave. They are like cancer. Eternal." (WC 11H, p. 334.)
>
> Add to these allegations the documented fact that 11 government agents had infiltrated the Garrison investigation and one starts to get a good picture of what the Garrison office was up against.
>
> "X" is loosely based on Col. L. Fletcher Prouty USAF (Ret.) who served as Chief of Special Operations with the Joint Chiefs of Staff during the Kennedy years. While the authors met with Prouty, Jim Garrison did not meet him until several years after the Clay Shaw trial. However, over the course of his investigation Garrison came to believe that the root causes of the assassination loomed much larger than the plot in New Orleans. As Garrison told James Kirkwood days after the Shaw trial ended:

"I have found that the assassination was much more complex than anyone believed and that a corner of it—I've never pretended it was more—existed in New Orleans ... John Kennedy was killed because he was against the war in Vietnam. There is no doubt of that. [James Kirkwood, *American Grotesque* (Simon & Schuster, 1970), p. 572-573.]

X Jim Garrison?

JIM Yes.

X (*shakes hands*) I'm glad you came. I'm sorry about the precautions.

JIM Well, I just hope it was worth my while, Mr ... .

The man doesn't answer. Jim, after his meeting with Miller and loss of Ferrie, is testy and suspicious.

X I could give you a false name, but I won't. Just call me X.

JIM I've already been warned by the Agency, Mr. Whoever. If this is another type of threat, I don't ...

X I'm not with the Agency, Mr. Garrison, and I assume if you've come this far, what I have to say interests you. But I'm not going to name names, or tell you who or what I represent. Except to say—you're close, you're closer than you think ...

Something about his manner speaks of authority, knowledge, and above all, old-fashioned honesty—the eyes looking you straight on. He indicates a bench.

X Everything I'm going to tell you is classified top secret ... (*significant look*) I was a soldier, Mr. Garrison. Two wars. I was one of those secret guys in the Pentagon that supplies the military hardware—the planes, bullets, rifles—for what we call "black operations"—"black ops," assassinations, coup d'états, rigging elections, propaganda, psych warfare and so forth. World War II—Rumania, Greece, Yugoslavia, I helped take the Nazi intelligence apparatus out to help us fight the Communists. Italy '48 stealing elections, France '49 breaking strikes—we overthrew Quirino in the Philippines, Arbenz in Guatemala, Mossadegh in Iran. Vietnam in '54, Indonesia '58, Tibet '59 we got the Dalai Lama out—we were good, very good. Then we got into the Cuban thing. Not so good. Set up all the bases for the invasion supposed to take place in October '62. Khrushchev sent the missiles to resist the invasion, Kennedy refused to invade and we were standing out there with our dicks in the wind. Lot of pissed-off people, Mr. Garrison, you understand? I'll come to that later ... I spent much of September '63 working on the Kennedy plan for getting all U.S. personnel out of Vietnam by the end of '65. This plan was one of the strongest and most important papers issued from the Kennedy White House. Our first 1,000 troops were ordered home for Christmas. Tensions were high. In November '63, one week after the murder of Vietnamese President Diem in Saigon, and two weeks before the assassination of our President ...

■ In *On the Trail of the Assassins,* Garrison recounts a meeting he had with sometime intelligence operative Richard Case Nagell. Nagell's story—that in mid-1963 he discovered a plot to kill the President and tried to alert the government—still needs to be fully examined. [Garrison, *On the Trail of the Assassins,* p. 182-186; Hinckle and Turner, *The Fish Is Red,* p. 226-228; Nagell also appears in Robert Morrow's *Betrayal* as "Richard Carson Filmore."]

■ For a good overview of covert operations in the post-World War II era, see L. Fletcher Prouty, *The Secret Team* (Prentice Hall, 1973); Ranelagh, *The Agency*; William Blum, *The CIA: A Forgotten History* (Zed, 1986); Prados, *Presidents' Secret Wars: CIA and Pentagon Covert Operations from WWII Through Iranscam.* For Vietnam pre-war and war history, see John M. Newman, *J.F.K. & Vietnam: Deception, Intrigue and the Struggle for Power* (Warner Books, 1992); Stanley Karnow, *Vietnam: A History* (Viking, 1983); McCoy, *The Politics of Heroin* (Lawrence Hills, 1991).

■ For Kennedy administration policy on Vietnam and early Vietnam war history, see John M. Newman, *J.F.K. and Vietnam: Deception, Intrigue and the Struggle for Power*; Arthur Schlesinger, Jr., *Robert Kennedy and His Times* (Houghton Mifflin, 1978), p. 734-757; Peter Dale Scott, *The War Conspiracy: The Secret Road to the Second Indochina War* (Bobbs-Merrill, 1972); Alfred McCoy, *The Politics of Heroin.*

FLASHBACK TO the Pentagon offices in 1963. X strides down a busy hall and into the offices of one of his superiors, Major General Y, a lean, cold warrior, battlefield handsome, civilian clothes, and several advisors. There's a U.S. flag on the wall. The status of Y is only clear by the sign on the desk, the name blocked by a passing figure.

X (*voice-over*) ... a strange thing happened. I was sent by my superior officer, call him Y, to the South Pole as the military escort for a group of international VIPs. This trip had nothing to do with my nine years of work in Special Operations. It was sort of a "paid vacation."

We hear vague ad-lib mutterings on the soundtrack indicating a friendly atmosphere, and we see stock footage of a C-130 transport flying to Antarctica and ice floes on the surface of the sea.

Then, at a New Zealand airport, we see X, in a uniform, at a newsstand reading of Kennedy's assassination. The banner headline of an "Extra" edition of The Christchurch Star *screams out "KENNEDY SHOT DEAD."* [Nov. 23, 1963 Special edition]

■ *The Christchurch Star,* November 23, 1963, Special Edition: [See discussions by L. Fletcher Prouty in "Setting the Stage for the Death of J.F.K., " *Freedom,* Feb-March 1987, p. 36 and in "Visions of a Kennedy Dynasty," *Freedom,* April-May 1987, reprinted by Prevailing Winds Research, p.14.]

X (*voice-over*) It wasn't until I was on my way back in New Zealand that I read of the President's murder. Now, Oswald was charged at 7 P.M. Dallas time with Tippit's murder. That was 2 in the afternoon the next day New Zealand time, but already the papers had the entire history of an unknown 24-year-old man, Oswald—a studio picture, detailed biographical date, Russian information— and were pretty sure of the fact he'd killed the President alone, although it took them four more hours to *charge* him with the murder in Texas. It felt as if, well, a cover story was being put out like we would in a black op.

Back at the Pentagon offices, we see X returning and meeting Y. The atmosphere is cordial, but Y is slightly different from before—more harried, more nervous. He turns away to light a cigarette; he doesn't want the usual conversation.

X (*voice-over*) Anyway, after I came back I asked myself why was I, the chief of special ops, selected to travel to the South Pole at that time to do a job that any number of others could have done? One of my routine duties if I had been in Washington would've been to arrange for additional security in Texas. The Secret Service is relatively small, and by custom the military will augment them. I checked it out when I got back and sure enough, I found out someone had told the 112th Military Intelligence Group at 4th Army Headquarters at Fort Sam Houston to "stand down" that day, over the protests of the unit Commander, a Colonel Reich ...

> ▌In 1963, the 112th was based at Fort Sam Houston in San Antonio. They
> also had an office in New Orleans. Col. Prouty kept his original notes on this
> telephone call. [Scott, *The Dallas Conspiracy*, p. 1-10.]

We see an outdoor shot of the Texas Army Headquarters on a day in 1963. Inside, on the same day, Col. Reich is on the phone, puzzled.

X (*voice-over*) Now this is significant, because it is standard operating procedure, especially in a known hostile city like Dallas, to supplement the Secret Service. Even if we had not allowed the bubbletop to be removed from the limousine, we'd've put at least 100 to 200 agents on the sidewalks, *without question!* There'd already been several attempts on de Gaulle's life in France. Only a month before in Dallas UN Ambassador Adlai Stevenson had been spit on and hit. We'd have arrived days ahead of time, studied the route, checked all the buildings ... We never would've allowed all those wide-open empty windows overlooking Dealey ... *never* ... We would have had our own snipers covering the area. The moment a window went up they'd have been on the radio. We would've been watching the crowds—packages, rolled up newspapers, a coat over an arm, never would have let a man open an umbrella along the way— Never would've allowed that limousine to slow down to 10 miles per hour, much less take that unusual curve at Houston and Elm. You would have *felt* an Army presence in the streets that day, but none of this happened. It was a violation of the *most basic* protection codes we have. And it's the best indication of a massive plot in Dallas. Who could have best done that? People in my business, Mr. Garrison. People like my superior officer could've told Col. Reich, "Look—we have another unit coming from so and so providing security. You'll stand down." That day, in fact, there were some individual Army Intelligence people in Dallas and I'm still trying to figure out who and why. But they weren't protecting the client. One of them, by the way, was caught in the Book Depository *after* police sealed it off.

In Dealey Plaza, 1963, we see an Army intelligence man taking a shot with a Minolta camera.

■ Army Intelligence in Dealey Plaza: As previously mentioned (see p. 8 fn), James Powell of Army Intelligence was in Dealey Plaza taking photographs. Powell himself appears in the Bond and Willis photos of the president's car, snapping away with his Minolta, proving that he must have taken quite a few pictures in Dealey Plaza. Inexplicably, only one photo, showing the upper floors of the Book Depository, taken by Powell has surfaced. The HSCA, who apparently discovered and released the photo, determined that it was taken about 30 seconds after the shooting [HSCA Report, p. 85-86]. The question remains: exactly what was Powell doing in Dealey Plaza?

X (*voice-over*) Army Intell had a "Harvey Lee Oswald" on file, but all those files have been destroyed. Many strange things were happening that day, and Lee Harvey Oswald had nothing to do with them. We had the entire Cabinet on a trip to the Far East. We had a third of a combat division returning from Germany in the air above the United States at the time of the shooting, and at 12:34 P.M., the entire telephone system went dead in Washington for a solid hour, and on the plane back to Washington, word was radioed from the White House Situation Room to Lyndon Johnson that one individual performed the assassination. Does that sound like a bunch of coincidences to you, Mr.Garrison? Not for one moment. The cabinet was out of the country to get their perception out of the way. The troops were in the air for possible riot control. The phones didn't work to keep the wrong stories from spreading if anything went wrong with the plan. *Nothing* was left to chance. I bet you there were even backup teams and cars on the other side of the underpass in the event that Kennedy got through wounded. They would have moved in with vehicles like they did with de Gaulle. He could not be allowed to escape *alive*.

■ "Harvey Lee Oswald" file: Army Intelligence maintained a file on Oswald until 1973, when it was destroyed, a "routine" procedure. Although the HSCA found the file was under "Lee Harvey Oswald," early reports from the Fourth Army's 112th Intelligence Group indicated that they referred to a "Harvey Lee Oswald" [HSCA Report, p. 221-4; Scott, *The Dallas Conspiracy*; Melanson, *Spy Saga*, p. 124-125].

■ Cabinet in Tokyo: [William Manchester, *Death of a President: November 20-25, 1963* (Harper & Row, 1967; Popular Library, 1968), p. 193; Prouty, "Setting the Stage for the Death of J.F.K.," *Freedom*, Feb./Mar., 1967.]

■ Telephone system out in Washington: Manchester describes Ted Kennedy running door-to-door in Washington about an hour after the assassination in search of a working telephone [Manchester, *Death of a President*, p. 198-199]. ABC newsman Sam Donaldson challenged this point on the program *Primetime Live*, saying that he had been in Washington and was able to make calls. It seems to be more of a case of sporadic "brown-outs" than a total "blackout." According to Manchester, "Lines would go dead, return to normal when a sufficient number of people had hung up and go dead again and return to life, over and over." (*Death of a President*, p. 206.)

telephone system in washington went out   109

■ One-third of a combat division returning from Germany: Members of the 49th Armored Division was airborne en route to the U.S. as part of Operation Big Lift at the time of the assassination. [*Facts on File*, November, 1963]

■ Call from situation room: [Manchester, *Death of a President*, p. 224.]

[Handwritten left margin: I knew W.C. Nott was fiction]

The camera is on Jim, listening. This information is much greater than he ever envisioned, and he is stunned. X pauses.

X ... I never thought things were the same after that. Vietnam started for real. There was an air of, I don't know, make-believe in the Pentagon and CIA. Those of us who'd been in secret ops since the beginning knew the Warren Commission was fiction, but there was something ... deeper, uglier. And I knew Allen Dulles very well. I briefed him many a time in his house. He was also General Y's benefactor. But for the life of me I still can't figure out why Dulles was appointed to investigate Kennedy's death. The man who had fired him. I got out in '64. I retired from the U.S. Air Force.

[Handwritten left margin: Dulles put on W.C.]

JIM I never realized Kennedy was so dangerous to the establishment. Is that why?

[Handwritten left margin: describes what JFK wanted to bring about!]

X (*chuckles*) That's the real question, isn't it—"Why?"—the "how" is just "scenery" for the suckers ... Oswald, Ruby, Cuba, Mafia, it keeps people guessing like a parlor game, but it prevents them from asking the most important question— Why? *Why was Kennedy killed? Who benefitted? Who has the power to cover it up?* ... You know in '61 right after the Bay of Pigs—very few people know about this—I participated in drawing up National Security Action Memos 55, 56 and 57. These are crucial documents, classified top secret, but basically in them Kennedy instructs General Lemnitzer, Chairman of the Joint Chiefs, that from here on forward ...

■ NSAMs (National Security Action Memos): [Prouty, *The Secret Team*, p. 114-116; Newman, *J.F.K. and Vietnam*, p. 98-99, (see Appendix).] Copies of all declassified NSAMs are available through the National Security Archive, a non-profit group based in Washington, D.C. (Contact the National Security Archive at 1755 Massachusetts Avenue NW, #500, Washington, DC 20036, phone 202-797-0882.)

FLASHBACK TO the Pentagon offices on a day in 1961. A document is moved by hand into Lemnitzer's office where we see a set of hands holding it while it's read. There's a look of surprise on Lemnitzer's face.

[Handwritten left margin: firing Allen Dulles, Richard Bissell, Gen. Charles Cabell]

X (*voice-over*) ... the Joint Chiefs of Staff would be wholly responsible for all covert paramilitary action in peacetime. This basically ended the reign of the CIA— "splintered it," as J.F.K. promised he would, into a "thousand pieces,"—and now was ordering the military to *help*. This was *unprecedented*. I can't tell you the shock waves this sent along the corridors of power in Washington. This and, of course, firing Allen Dulles, Richard Bissell, and General Charles Cabell, all of them sacred cows of Intell since World War II. You got some very upset people here.

110

■ J.F.K.'s promise to "splinter the CIA into 1000 pieces": [*The New York Times,* April 23, 1966.]

DOCUMENTARY IMAGES flash on the screen—Allen Dulles, sweet-faced, smiling, at the Warren Commission Hearing and visiting Dealey Plaza; General Charles Cabell and Richard Russell ...

X (*voice-over*) Kennedy's directives were never really implemented, because of bureaucratic resistance, but one of the results was that the Cuban operation was turned over to my department as "Operation Mongoose," which meant that people like my superior officer, General Y, took over the Cuban personnel that were being trained to invade Cuba—and the bases like the training camp at Pontchartrain in your home state that were closed down by Kennedy ... and that's how the "black ops" people, people like General Y, ended up taking the rules of covert warfare they'd used abroad and brought 'em into this country. Now they had the people, the equipment, bases and the motivation ... check out an old CIA man, Bill Harvey—ran something called "Executive Action," which carried out foreign assassinations. Harvey was also involved with the fake defection program that got Oswald into Russia. Check out the Cabell brothers. Interesting links to this case.

■ During the MONGOOSE era the CIA's JM/WAVE headquarters on the University of Miami's South Dade Campus, under the dummy name "Zenith Technological Services," became their largest station in the world, employing over 600 American personnel and burning up a $500 million budget from Feb. 1962 through Jan. 1963. [Hinckle and Turner, *The Fish Is Red,* p.113-135.] (For a first-hand account of JM/WAVE operations, see Ayers, *The War That Never Was.*)

■ Cabell brothers: In 1963, Earle Cabell was the mayor of Dallas. His brother, General Charles Cabell, was Deputy Director of the CIA until he was fired in the aftermath of the Bay of Pigs fiasco. Shortly after the failed invasion, General Cabell addressed the Foreign Policy Association in New Orleans. Clay Shaw, program chairman of the group, introduced Cabell at the function. [Hurt, *Reasonable Doubt,* p. 282-283.]

At Arlington Cemetery on the same day, Jim visits the grave of President Kennedy. We see the eternal flame. Jim thinks about what he should do now. The size of it stuns him. He is lost, reeling back to the past in his mind.

DISSOLVE TO DOCUMENTARY FOOTAGE of Dachau concentration camp: thousands of bodies are piled and bulldozed ... And then back to Jim at Arlington Cemetery reliving it ... only the enormity of past evil can prepare him to confront present evil. In a strange way, it reassures him.

X (*voice-over*) ... don't underestimate the budget cuts Kennedy called for in March of '63 either—close to 52 military installations in 25 states, 21 overseas bases, you're talking big money. You know how many helicopters have been lost in Vietnam? About three thousand *so far.* Who makes them? Bell Helicopter. Who owns Bell? Bell was near bankruptcy when the First National Bank of Boston approached the CIA about developing the helicopter for Indochina

111

usage. How 'bout the F-111 fighters? General Dynamics in Fort Worth. Who owns that? Find out the defense budget since the war began. $75 going on a *hundred* billion ... $200 billion'll be spent there before it ends. In 1950 it was $13 billion. No war, no money. Sometimes I think the organizing principle of any society is for war. The authority of the state over its people resides in its war powers. Even Eisenhower—military hero of WWII—warned us about it: "beware the military-industrial complex," he said. Kennedy wanted to end the Cold War in his second term. He wanted to call off the moon race in favor of cooperation with the Soviets. He signed a treaty with the Soviets to ban nuclear testing, he refused to invade Cuba in '62, and he set out to withdraw from Vietnam. But that all ended on November 22, 1963.

∎ Defense budget cuts, Mar. 1963: [Marrs, *Crossfire*, p. 305; Schlesinger, *A Thousand Days*, p. 312-319.]

∎ Bell Helicopter: In the early 1960's, 1st National Bank of Boston had the Textron company as a major client. The bank advised Textron to take over a near-bankrupt company, recommending Bell because the helicopter market was bound to benefit from the developments in Southeast Asia [Prouty, "Visions of a Kennedy Dynasty," *Freedom*, April-May 1987].

∎ Defense budgets (with inflation adjustments): 1950—$13 billion ($83.9 billion); 1961—$49.6 billion ($195.2 billion); 1965—$49.5 billion ($256.5 billion); 1966—$64.5 billion ($301 billion) [*National Defense Budget Estimates, Fiscal Year 1992*, Department of Defense. Courtesy of the Center for Defense Information, 1500 Massachusetts Avenue NW, Washington, DC 20005].

∎ Nuclear test ban: [Schlesinger, *A Thousand Days*, p. 893-917.]

FLASHBACK TO the White House, 1963. Lyndon Johnson is with Henry Cabot Lodge. We see them as shadowy figures from a distance across the wide room, or near a veranda with a porch and plenty of light. Johnson, his back to us, talks in a loud, thick Texas drawl (mostly muted) and signs a document.

X *(voice-over)* Only four days after J.F.K. was shot, Lyndon Johnson signed National Security Memo 273, which essentially reversed Kennedy's new withdrawal policy and gave the green light to the covert operations against North Vietnam that provoked the Gulf of Tonkin incident. In that document lay the Vietnam War ...

∎ Signed on Nov. 26, 1963, NSAM 273 (see Appendix) effectively changed the White House policy toward the Vietnam war, cancelling Kennedy's plans for withdrawal by 1965 and containing escalatory language that paved the way for increased military involvement in Southeast Asia. [Newman, *J.F.K. & Vietnam: Deception, Intrigue and the Struggle for Power*, Ch. 23; Scott, "Vietnamization and the Drama of the Pentagon Papers," Chomsky and Zinn, eds., *The Pentagon Papers*, Gravel Edition, p. 211-247.]

In the park with X, Jim is staggered by all this information. X ceases walking and looks at Jim.

112

National Security agency Memorandum 273

"Politics is Power" nothing more.   *FBI - Abraham Bolden - Black agent*   *J•F•K*

JIM I don't ... I can't believe it. They killed him because he wanted to change things. In our time—in our country?

X (*shrugging*) Kings are killed, Mr. Garrison. Politics is power, nothing more. But don't believe me. Don't trust me. Do your own work, your own thinking.

JIM The size of this is ... beyond me. Testify?

X No chance in hell, Mr. Garrison. I'd be arrested and gagged, declared insane and hospitalized ... maybe worse. You, too. I can only give you background, you got to find the foreground, the little things ... Keep digging. Y'know you're the only person ever to bring a trial in the murder of John Kennedy. That's important—it's historic.

> ▌ Declared insane and hospitalized: This actually did happen to a few federal agents associated with the JFK case. Richard Case Nagell (cf. notes on p.107) spent years in a federal psychiatric institution following his attempt to warn the government of the assassination plot. CIA agent Gary Underhill claimed to have a knowledge of an Agency plan to kill J.F.K. and was found shot dead in 1964. His death was ruled a suicide, although it appears as though the normally right-handed Underhill shot himself with his left hand (Torbitt, *Nomenclature...*, p.193). Secret Service man, Abraham Bolden, the first African American to serve on the White House detail, was denied an opportunity to testify to the Warren Commission about lapses of Secret Service protection in Dallas, and then was convicted and imprisoned on dubious charges of trying to sell government files (Anson, *"They've Killed the President!"*, p. 57-59; Mark Lane, *A Citizen's Dissent*, p. 193).

JIM I haven't yet. I don't have much of a case.

X (*rising to leave*) But you don't have a choice anymore. You've become a significant threat to the national security structure. They would've killed you already, but you got a lot of light on you. Instead, they're gonna destroy your credibility; they already have in many circles in this town. You're some kinda ego-crazed southern caricature to many folks. Be honest—the best chance you got is come up with a case, something, anything, make arrests, stir the shitstorm. You gotta hope to reach a point of critical mass where other people will come forward and the government will crack. Remember, fundamentally people are suckers for the truth, and the truth is on your side, 'bubba. I hope you get a break ...

Jim watches this mystery man walking away. The figure vanishes in the Washington breeze. Flags flap over some distant memorial to some distant history of the Republic. Jim rises, a decision made.

EXTERIOR OF CLAY SHAW'S HOUSE - NEW ORLEANS - (1967)

Jim, Lou, Bill, Al, Numa and several policemen stand at the door as Clay Shaw comes to it.

> ▌ Shaw arrest: [Flammonde, *The Kennedy Conspiracy*, p. 70-79; *New Orleans States-Item*, March 2, 1967; *New Orleans Times-Picayune*, March 2, 1967.]

LOU Mr. Shaw, you're under arrest, charged with conspiracy and entering into an agreement with other persons for the specific purpose of committing the crime of murder of President John F. Kennedy in violation of ... *The voice dropping away as the devastated look on Shaw's face spreads, sickly, undone, his arrogant public composure gone, face now filled with terror, disbelief.*

LOU ... we have a warrant to search the premises ...

The policemen take Shaw while the D.A. staff moves into the carriage house past the butler, Frankie Jenkins.

INSIDE SHAW'S HOUSE

In the bedroom, Numa points out to Jim the hooks screwed into the ceiling. Al pulls out five whips, several lengths of chain, a black hood and matching black cape. Dried blood is on one whip.

NUMA It's either a Mardi Gras outfit, or we got the Marquis de Sade here, chief.

JIM I don't care if he was doing it with the giraffes in the zoo, Numa, it's none of our business. Let's keep this side of it quiet, shall we ...

AL When you're in a war, boss, you use every weapon you got.

JIM Not *one* word. That's an order.

> ▌Shaw's possession of whips and leather gear: [*New Orleans States-Item,* Mar. 2, 1967; Hurt, *Reasonable Doubt,* p. 281.] A 1954 FBI memo noted that Shaw was "given to sadism and masochism in his homosexual activities." Although Garrison's critics accused him of exploiting Shaw's homosexuality, Garrison did not bring it up at the trial—as he writes in *On the Trail of the Assassins:* "These accoutrements hardly were inculpatory in themselves. Different people have different hobbies" (p. 147).

NEW ORLEANS POLICE STATION

Shaw is being fingerprinted. He seems rattled. Police officers try to get the press under control.

OFFICER Name? First, middle, last.

SHAW Clay Lavergne Shaw.

OFFICER HABIGHORST Address?

SHAW 1313 Dauphine, New Orleans.

HABIGHORST Ever use any aliases?

SHAW Clay Bertrand.

> ▌Shaw admits alias to Habighorst: [*New Orleans Times-Picayune,* "Records Allegedly Linking Shaw, Bertrand Released," Jul. 20, 1968; State of Louisiana vs. Clay L. Shaw, court transcripts, Feb. 19, 1969, p. 52-75 (Habighorst testimony).]

Habighorst notes it as routinely as Shaw seems to have said it, without thinking, possibly preoccupied by thoughts of press people pushing in.

HABIGHORST Next of kin?

NEWSMAN 12 Mr. Shaw—What do you have to say?

MONTAGE - NEWSREEL MUSIC

We see a shot of the exterior of the Justice Department in 1967.

JUSTICE DEPARTMENT CONFERENCE ROOM

The acting Attorney General speaks to the press.

ATTORNEY GENERAL ... Yes, Mr. Shaw was included in our investigation and there was no connection found at all between Shaw and the President's assassination.

■ Immediately following Shaw's arrest, acting Attorney General Ramsey Clark told reporters that Shaw had been investigated in November and December 1963. He did not offer any explanation as to why the Justice Department felt it necessary to investigate Shaw in the first place. [*New York Post*, March 2, 1967: *New Orleans States-Item*, March 2, 1967.].

On March 3, a story in *The Washington Post* noted that Clark's remarks affirmed Garrison's suspicion that Shaw and Clay Bertrand were one and the same. A Justice Department spokesman reiterated this for reporter George Lardner, Jr.: "It's the same guy."

A few months later, the Justice Department issued an official "clarification," following a request from Shaw's attorneys:

"The Attorney General has since determined that this was erroneous. Nothing arose indicating a need to investigate Mr. Shaw" [*New York Times*, June 3, 1967; *Washington Post*, "Justice Admits Error in Shaw-Bertrand Tie," June 3, 1967; see discussion in Weisberg, *Oswald in New Orleans*, p. 212-213, 222-226; Flammonde, *The Kennedy Conspiracy*, p. 70-71].

GARRISON'S OFFICE - CONFERENCE ROOM - (1967)

Jim confronts a packed room. Bill is with him.

JIM If Mr. Shaw had no connection to the assassination, why did the FBI investigate him? And why, if they did, is his name not mentioned once in the entire 26 volumes of the Warren Report, even if it is to *clear* his name? I doubt this Attorney General would qualify for my staff.

We see a shot of the Supreme Court building in Washington, D.C. and then a corridor inside the building. A Chief Justice, looking gray and wise like Earl Warren, moves along the corridor in his black robe delivering his verdict to the press.

CHIEF JUSTICE No, I don't think so. Mr. Garrison has presented absolutely nothing publicly to contradict our findings. As yet I have not heard one fact to refute the Commission determination that Lee Oswald was the lone killer ...

■ Warren made the statement from Peru, invoking the language he always used to uphold the Warren Commission findings: "I have not heard anything which would change the Report in any way, shape or form" [*New Orleans States-Item*, Mar. 4, 1967].

In his own office, Jim responds to Justice Warren:

JIM I congratulate Mr. Shaw. Most witnesses have to wait for trial before they're allowed to produce sacred cows like the Chief Justice of the land as a character witness, who is of course not under oath and free from the laws of perjury.

NEWSMAN 13 Mr. Garrison, if what you say is even partly true in this case, you realize you are damaging the credibility of our government, possibly destroying it?

JIM ... Let me ask you ... is a government worth preserving when it lies to the people? It has become a dangerous country, sir, when you can't trust anyone anymore, when you can't tell the truth. I say let justice be done, though the heavens fall.

■ Garrison made this remark in an interview published in the May 22, 1967 issue of *Der Spiegel*. As declassified CIA documents show, the Agency was perplexed by Jim's comment and sent a memo about it to J. Edgar Hoover (CIA Memorandum for Director, FBI, dated June 19, 1967).

It doesn't play with the press. They shuffle off, quiet, whispering.

GARRISON'S HOUSE - (1967)

Liz and Jim watch, silently devastated, as the NBC "WHITE PAPER" unfolds attacking Jim. They can do nothing. Liz leaves the room, upset.

■ White Paper: "NBC's WHITE PAPER-The J.F.K. Conspiracy: The Case of Jim Garrison" aired nationally on June 19, 1967. It gave a very negative picture of both Garrison and the New Orleans investigation.

Declassified CIA documents indicate that the CIA knew about the slant of the NBC show several weeks before the program aired. CIA Memorandum 3, Garrison and the Kennedy Assassination, June 1, 1967 notes that Gordon Novel, a potential Garrison witness, is in contact with NBC's "special correspondent" Walter Sheridan:

"(Novel's) ties to Walter Sheridan suggest a possibility that NBC is coaching Novel to get maximum publicity before picturing him on a TV program intended to destroy Garrison's act."

The same memo goes on to say that the attorney of another Garrison witness went to see Sheridan in Washington, offering to sell him a tape purporting to contain a conversation in which a Garrison assistant offered a bribe to the witness. The attorney's asking price was $5,000; he "rejected" Sheridan's offer of $500. NBC went on to report charges of bribery against Garrison's office; however, the CIA documents indicate the only bribery going on was done by NBC's investigator, Walter Sheridan.

Following the broadcast, Garrison immediately appealed to the FCC for equal time and was granted a half-hour of uninterrupted primetime on the NBC network on July 15, 1967 [tape available from NBC Archive; see partial transcript in Flammonde, *The Kennedy Conspiracy*, p. 320-321].

HOTEL SUITE - NEW ORLEANS - (1967)

Julia Ann Mercer, 28, looks at Jim with sincere eyes. Her husband, a prosperous Republican businessman, watches from the corner. Jim—along with Al—has her testimony in front of him.

JIM ... in the sheriff's report, Mrs. Mercer, it says you were at Dealey Plaza two hours before the assassination but that ...

MERCER Yes, it was about 11 in the morning. I was driving west on Elm Street, toward the Triple Underpass, in a rented car—a blue Valiant. I'll never forget that day.

FLASHBACK TO Dealey Plaza in 1963. It's a normal scene—cars, traffic, people starting to arrive for Kennedy's appearance. We catch a glimpse of Julia Ann Mercer, 23, driving, then stopping in traffic.

MERCER (*voice-over*) ... there was quite a bit of traffic and I was stopped alongside a green pickup truck. It was very noticeable because it was blocking traffic and it was parked with two wheels up on the curb. When I saw the gun, I thought— the Secret Service is not very secret.

> ▌Pickup truck: Mercer was not the only one who reported seeing the pickup. A police officer in the area saw the truck and believed it had broken down [WC 24H p. 522].
>
> Mercer has kept a low profile since the assassination. The last researcher to locate and talk to her was Henry Hurt in 1983. She told Hurt the same story she told Garrison and seemed to be a very credible witness. Unfortunately, as Hurt writes, "at this late date, it seems highly unlikely that the complete truth will ever be known about the experience of Julia Ann Mercer."
>
> The HSCA claimed it had been unable to locate Ms. Mercer. It does not seem that they tried very hard. Jim Garrison sent his material on Mercer to the Committee and offered to give them her married name and present address if their investigators wanted to speak to her. He never received a reply, but noticed that the Committee did acknowledge receipt of the Mercer materials he sent. [Garrison, *On the Trail of the Assassins*, p. 219, HSCA X11 p. 369-370.]

She glances over at the man in the driver's seat. It's Jack Ruby, wearing a green jacket. Then she sees a young white man in his mid-20s, in gray jacket, brown pants, plaid shirt and wool stocking hat, getting out of the passenger side, going to the rear of the van, opening a tool compartment and removing a package that looks like a rifle wrapped in paper. He walks up the embankment in the direction of the picket fence. Ruby looks over and stares at Julia Ann, who turns away and notices three police officers standing near a motorcycle on the overpass bridge. Her eyes lock with Ruby's a second time and as the traffic moves, she drives on.

MERCER (*voice-over*) The next morning, Saturday, I went to the FBI office and the agents showed me photographs ...

In the Dallas FBI office, Mercer sits at a table looking at photos. Two FBI agents stand near her showing her photos. She shakes her head "no" several times, until they put a shot of Jack Ruby in front of her. She holds it up.

MERCER (*voice-over*) I picked out three pictures that looked generally like the driver of the truck and then ...

MERCER That's the man.

FBI AGENT (*to Second Agent*) Jack Ruby.

SECOND AGENT What about these others? You said they might be him.

MERCER They look a little like him. But no, (*holding up the Ruby photo*) I'm sure this is the man.

Back in the present, Jim continues to question Mercer.

JIM You mean you identified him on Saturday, the day before Ruby shot Oswald?

MERCER That's right. When I saw him on TV, I was shocked. I said to my family, "that was the man I saw in the truck."

JIM (*skeptical*) ... but you didn't seem nearly so sure in your statement to the Warren Commission.

MERCER That's what bothers me, Mr. Garrison. You see, they've been altered. My statements ...

Jim is silent. Mercer picks up the report and finds the pertinent paragraphs:

MERCER This says "Mercer could not identify any of the photographs as being identical with the person she had observed slouched over the wheel of a green Ford pickup truck." That's not true. I recognized him and I told them so ... They also said it was a dark green air conditioning truck, which it was not. And here ... (*she goes to another report*) ... on the Dallas Sheriff's report. This is really strange. See that notarized signature on the bottom of each page? That's not my signature. And there never was any notary present during any of my questioning. (*she hands the papers back to Jim*) I guess that's all ...

JIM Mrs. Mercer, as a former FBI man, it's difficult to accept this.

MERCER I know, but Mr. Garrison, the FBI is just not doing their job.

HUSBAND I'm a Republican, Mr. Garrison, and I don't go in for this kind of government bashing, but I must tell you something's not right when they don't even bother to call Julia in front of the Warren Commission.

JIM They didn't call a lot of people, Mr. Mercer. I think it's now safe to say the Warren Report is a work of fiction.

▌Julia Ann Mercer: [WC CE 2003 p. 40; Garrison, *Trail of the Assassins*, p. 216-219; Hurt, *Reasonable Doubt*, p.114-116.]

INT. DALLAS CLUB - NIGHT - (1967)

BEVERLY, a woman of ample proportions and a big, cute Texas face, ex-club singer, meets with JIM and LOU IVON in a nightclub not unlike Ruby's Carousel.

IVON Beverly, tell Mr. Garrison about the Carousel club.

▮ Dallas night club: This scene is partially based on the recollections of Beverly Oliver, a Texas woman who claims to be the "Babushka Lady" filming the motorcade in Dealey Plaza. Oliver worked at the Colony Club, across the street from the Carousel, and knew Ruby and many of his employees. Oliver is not alone in reporting a Ruby-Oswald-Ferrie connection via the Carousel Club. Numerous others—including Rose Cheramie, several Ruby employees, Dallas constables and a Texas attorney—reported that Oswald and Ruby knew each other [Marrs, *Crossfire*, p. 402-412; Evica, *And We Are All...*, p. 97-98, 110-113].

David Ferrie comes into the Carousel Club scene a more mysterious way. Beverly Oliver claimed to have seen Ferrie at the club. A Dallas cab driver, Raymond Cummings, told Garrison's investigators that he had driven Ferrie and Oswald to the Carousel in early 1963. But the most intriguing and credible account of all comes from a document buried deep in the Warren Commission volumes. CE2038 is an interview of NBC cameraman Gene Barnes by two FBI agents:

Barnes said Bob Mulholland, NBC News, Chicago, talked in Dallas to one Fairy (sic), a narcotics addict now out on bail on a sodomy charge in Dallas. Fairy said that Oswald had been under hypnosis from a man doing a mind reading act at Ruby's "Carousel." Fairy was said to be a private detective and the owner of an airplane who took young boys on flights "just for kicks"...

"Fairy" is clearly meant to be the man we know as Ferrie—the details of his life are simply too similar.

Mulholland, who went on to become president of NBC News, later told journalist Peter Noyes that he had been quoted incorrectly. According to Noyes:

"(Mulholland) said that shortly after the assassination he heard FBI agents mention Ferrie's name and a possible link to Oswald and he relayed that information to his reporters..."

Whatever the situation, if FBI agents, and perhaps newsmen as well, were mentioning Ferrie's name in Dallas the weekend of the assassination—along with very unique, specific details about Ferrie (that he was a pilot, that he liked young boys, that he had a history of sodomy charges and narcotics use) and about an Oswald-Ruby connection—there is something to all this that has yet to be explained.

We know that Ferrie was not in Dallas (he was in Houston) the weekend of the assassination; thus, it was not the real Ferrie talking to NBC or the FBI. The most logical explanation is that someone or some group (the FBI, in this case) was deliberately trying to link Ferrie to a Ruby-Oswald-Carousel Club connection that very weekend. But why?

The Warren Commission "found no evidence" that Ruby and Oswald knew each other but acknowledged "possible but tenuous third-party links" [WR

p. 650]. The HSCA handled the Ruby-Oswald situation in typically ambiguous fashion, leaving the question unresolved:

"...the Committee's investigation of Oswald and Ruby showed a variety of relationships that may have matured into an assassination conspiracy. Neither Oswald nor Ruby turned out to be "loners," as they had been painted in the 1964 investigation." [HSCA Report, p. 148]

BEVERLY (*voice-over*) Oh yes, I used to go over there a lot to see Jack and especially my friend Jada who danced there. It was the real swinging spot in town. Everybody came. Businessmen, politicians from Austin, Lyndon Johnson's friends ... Dallas was a slow town back then. You chewed toothpicks, played dominos, spit and dated policemen. But Jack's was exciting. There were always cops there. Jack liked 'em around, but he used to throw the drunks out himself, 'cause he was kinda a violent-tempered man ... it seemed everybody in those days knew Jack was with the Mob. The cops were "bad" back then—they'd shake you down for the money in your pocket. They put a lotta people in the cemetery, especially colored people ...

LOU Beverly, what about Lee?

Jada and Beverly sit down at the table with Ferrie, Oswald, and Jack, with Jack doing the buying. It's too loud to hear anything.

BEVERLY (*voice-over*) Oh, yeah. One time I came in, Jack introduces me to these two guys. He said, "Beverly, this is my friend Lee ... " and I didn't catch the other guy's name. He was a weird-looking guy with those funny little eyebrows. The other guy, Lee, didn't make much of an impression either. He wasn't good-looking or nuthin', he didn't look like he had any money, and he was in a bad mood, so I didn't pay him much mind. Well, I might not remember a name, but I always remember a face. When I saw him two weeks later on the television, I screamed, "Oh, my God—that's him! That's Jack's friend!" I knew right then it had something to do with the Mafia ... Well, about a week later, after she told the newspapers she'd met this guy Lee with Jack, Jada disappears off the face of the Earth ... (*the camera moves in on Jada*) never knew what happened to her till Herman offered to sell me her wardrobe. I said, "but Jada's coming back," and I remember the way he smiled ... and I knew she was never coming back.

▌Jada: (real name Janet Adams Conforto) was the featured dancer at the Carousel club in 1963. After the assassination, she told Dallas newsmen that she had seen Oswald at the Carousel Club (Marrs, *Conspiracy*, p. 406). Investigators for Nigel Turner's documentary, *The Men Who Killed Kennedy* (presented in the U.S. on the Arts and Entertainment cable network as part of the Kurtis Investigative Reports Series), found evidence that Jada had died in a motorcycle accident in 1971. Her legendary performance has survived, however, on a 1963 soft-core film titled *Mondo Exotic* (available through JFK Assassination Information Center, Dallas, TX).

BACK TO the 1967 scene.

JIM Will you testify, Beverly?

BEVERLY I don't think so, sir.

LOU I thought when we came here, we had an agreement.

BEVERLY I just don't want to become another statistic like her. If they can kill the President, do you think they're gonna think twice about a two-bit showgirl like me?

LOU We could call you in, Beverly.

JIM I know the pressure you're under, Beverly. Don't think I don't. (*as he exits:*) I understand.

DISSOLVE TO DEALEY PLAZA - (1967)

Our view is from the roof of the building on the extreme south side of the Plaza. J.C. Price, the building engineer, in hat and overalls, points for Jim and Lou.

> ▌J.C. Price: [WC CE 2003, p. 222; Decker Exhibit 5323, p. 492; Lane, *Rush to Judgment*, p. 24-25; also see interview in "Rush to Judgment" film (Mark Lane & Emile D'Antonio).]

PRICE ... yes, sir, right here on this spot. The shots came from near that wooden fence over there, near the overpass.

The camera tightens on the picket fence.

PRICE (*voice-over*) I saw a man run from the fence and go behind the Book Depository—30 minutes later I gave this information to the Sheriff.

On the overpass near Dealey Plaza, S.M. Holland, a tan, elderly, leather-faced signal supervisor, points to the picket fence for Jim and Lou. His accent is thick and rural. We saw him before, briefly, when Jim was reading the Warren Report.

> ▌S.M. Holland: [WC CE 2003, p. 222; Decker Exhibit 5325, p. 480; Holland Exhibits; Mark Lane and Emile D'Antonio, "Rush to Judgment" (filmed interview).]

HOLLAND I made it very clear to the Warren people one of the shots came from behind that picket fence. I heard the report and saw the smoke come out about 6 or 8 feet above the ground, right out from under those trees. There is no doubt whatsoever in my mind ...

FLASHBACK TO the restaged shooting. The smoke hangs under the trees.

CUT TO Richard Dodd on the overpass. He's a cowboy type with a hat and an even thicker accent than Holland.

> ▌Richard Dodd: [Lane, *A Citizen's Dissent*, p. 158, 194, 212, Mark Lane and Emile D'Antonio, "Rush to Judgment" (filmed interview).]

DODD (*pointing*) ... we, all four of us, all railroad men, standing here, seen about the same thing. The smoke came from behind the hedge—and a motorcycle policeman dropped his cycle in the street and run up the embankment ...

FLASHBACK to the motorcycle ...

BACK TO 1967. Jim and Lou walk with Dodd and Holland near the picket fence. We feel the emptiness of the area now and see the normal amount of traffic driving by.

HOLLAND ... we came around here to look for tracks. It rained that morning and we found a bunch. Cigarette butts. Someone'd been standing about here ...

The camera shows the "spot" and Lou sighting.

LOU This is a good spot, chief, for the head shot.

Jim looks, reliving the moment.

Later Jim and Lou stand on the south side of Elm Street in Dealey Plaza talking to Jean Hill, an attractive, 30-ish teacher. Her demeanor has a rock-solid Texas back-country conviction to it; she's a woman not easily frightened.

> ■ Jean Hill: [WC 6H p. 205-223 (testimony); CE 2003, p. 212; Decker Exhibit 5323, p. 480; Marrs, *Crossfire*, p. 322-324 (sees Ruby); author's conversations with Jean Hill, Mar. 1991.]

JEAN HILL ... I was standing here next to my friend Mary Moorman, who took the photograph when he was killed ...

We see a flash of the Moorman photograph—a blurry Polaroid with the President in the foreground and the picket fence in background. We will return to this photograph in more detail later.

> ■ Mary Moorman's famous Polaroid shows the grassy knoll and the President's limousine just before the fatal head shot. The Warren Commission did not examine or print the photo in the Volumes but it was published widely by UPI. Researchers poured over blowups of the photo, hoping to find evidence of a Grassy Knoll gunman, often called "The Badgeman" because an image thought to be a shooter seems to be wearing a dark shirt with a badge, like a police uniform. The HSCA found the photo of poor quality but recommended it be studied in light of the acoustics evidence indicating a gunman on the Knoll. In the fall of 1991, a foreign group agreed to undertake a project to see if state-of-the-art scientific analysis could reveal new information in the photo [Marrs, *Crossfire*, p. 81; conversations with researcher Gary Mack].

JEAN HILL I jumped out in the street and yelled, "Hey Mr. President, look over here, we wanna take your picture." He looked up and then shots rang out. Mary fell to the ground right away, shouting, "Get down, they're shooting, get down, they're shooting." I knew it but I was moving to get closer to him. The driver had stopped—I don't know what was wrong with that driver. And then, out of the corner of my eye, I saw this flash of light, in the bushes and that last shot ... just ripped his head off, I mean, blood, brains, just blew everything ...

FLASHBACK TO the day of the shooting. We hear the sound of shots and see the Grassy Knoll from Jean's point of view.

HILL (*voice-over*) I looked up and saw smoke from the Knoll. And everything was frozen—seemed like people wasn't even breathing, like you're looking at a picture—except this one guy. I saw this one guy running from the Book Depository towards the railroad tracks. And that was the same man I saw on TV two days later shooting Oswald. That was Jack Ruby. No question about it.

Blurry image—we're not at all sure what or who or if ... but a seed is planted. We see smoke—the same smoke Bowers saw ... then Jack Ruby in a brown coat running from the Book Depository toward the railroad tracks. Then we see Jean's view as she runs toward the Knoll along with others. There are yells, shouts, and general confusion.

HILL (*voice-over*) It was him I was chasing up the Grassy Knoll, thinking our guys had shot back and maybe we got one of them. I don't know what I would have done if I had caught him, but I knew something terrible had happened and somebody had to do something.

At the picket fence, we see blurry images of police officers, railroad workers, cigarette butts, muddy footprints, confusion ...

HILL (*voice-over*) I never did catch him. All I saw in that parking area were railroad workers and Dallas' finest.

Two Secret Service types approach her suddenly, and one of them puts an arm on her shoulder.

FIRST AGENT Secret Service, ma'am. You're coming with us.

HILL Oh no, I'm not. I don't know you. We gotta catch this shooter—don't you realize?

SECOND AGENT (*grabbing her other shoulder*) I said you're coming with us. I want the pictures in your pocket.

HILL (*voice-over*) ... he put a hurt on me but good.

HILL I don't have any pictures! I have to go back and find my friend Mary. Lemme alone!

The two agents hustle her away.

FIRST AGENT Hush! Just smile and keep walking.

▮ Secret Service agents on Grassy Knoll:[WR p. 52.] Regarding the Secret Service: "None stayed at the scene of the shooting and none entered the Texas School Book Depository at or immediately after the shooting." [WC 7H, p. 535 (Smith);WC 6H, p. 196. (Fischer); Dallas *Morning News*, "SS imposters spotted by J.F.K. witnesses," Earl Golz, Aug. 27, 1978].

▮ FBI Agent James Hosty told the HSCA that Patrolman Smith may have encountered a Treasury agent named Frank Ellsworth. Ellsworth denied the allegation [Marrs, *Crossfire*, p. 324].

Oddly enough, Secret Service Inspector Thomas J. Kelley's report of
Oswald's interrogation at the police station shows that Oswald himself may
have encountered a "false" Secret Service Agent. Oswald told Kelley that as
he was leaving the Book Depository, "a young crew-cut man rushed up to
him and said he was from the Secret Service, showed a book of identification
and asked him where the phone was" [WR p. 629]. Some people feel Oswald
may have encountered a reporter but the man has never been identified.

*Hill, 32 years old that day, is shown into a third floor office of the County Courts
Building—which has a view of the assassination area. Other Secret Service agents are
there. Some 18 people are detained there.*

■ The 18 people detained at the County Courts Building for the afternoon of
the assassination were most of the witnesses in front of the Grassy Knoll and
on the Triple Underpass bridge-area witnesses. Only some of them were
called to testify to the Warren Commission [WC CE 2003 p. 409-410].

TIME CUT TO two men interrogating Hill.

HILL (*voice-over*) These new people never identified themselves. They musta been
watching the whole thing 'cause they knew everything Mary and me had been
doing that day. I guess I wasn't too hard to find—wearing that red raincoat ...

MAN 1 How many shots you say you heard?

HILL Four to six.

MAN 1 That's impossible. You heard echoes ... echoes. We have three bullets and
three shots which came from the Book Depository and that's all we're willing
to say.

HILL (*voice-over*) ... which is strange 'cause this is less than 20 minutes after the
assassination.

HILL No, I saw a guy shooting from over there. He was behind that fence. What
are you going to do about it?

MAN 1 We have that taken care of. You only heard three shots and you are not to
talk to anyone about this. No one, you hear?

HILL (*voice-over*) I was scared. It was all kinda queer, but it sure felt like two and two
was coming up three ... and then they took Mary's five snapshots from me, sent
them to Washington, and when they returned them weeks later, two of them
had the backgrounds mutilated [Marrs, *Crossfire*, p. 324]... The only one we saved
was in Mary's camera. I didn't want to go to Washington when the Warren
Commission subpoenaed me ... so the lawyer come down here and interviewed
me at Parkland Hospital.

*In a Parkland Hospital office in 1964, a lawyer interviews Jean Hill. A female stenog-
rapher takes notes.*

■ [WC 6H 205-223; conversations with Jean Hill, 1991.]

HILL (*voice-over*) He asked me why I thought I was in danger and I said:

HILL Well if they can kill the President, they can certainly get me.

LAWYER That doesn't make sense, Mrs. Hill. We have the man that killed the President.

HILL No, you don't!

HILL (*voice-over*) He kept trying to get me to change my story about the shots. He was getting hot under the collar, and telling the woman not to write when he wanted.

HILL Look, do you want the truth, or just what you want me to say?

LAWYER I want the truth.

HILL The truth is that I heard between four and six shots. I'm not going to lie for you.

LAWYER ... you heard echoes.

HILL No. I had guns all my life. I used to go turtle shooting.

LAWYER I realize you're under a great deal of stress ... it's clouded your judgment ...

HILL (*voice-over*) So off the record, he starts talking about my family, and even mentioned my marriage was in trouble like I didn't know it or something. He got angrier and angrier and then:

LAWYER Look, we can put you in a mental institution. We can make you look crazier'n Marguerite Oswald, and everybody knows how crazy she is.

HILL (*voice-over*) I knew something was crooked as a dog's hind leg, 'cause no one who is just taking a deposition gets that involved and angry ... sure enough, when I finally read my testimony as published by the Warren Commission, it was a fabrication from start to finish.

JIM Are you willing to testify, Mrs. Hill?

Back at the Knoll.

HILL (*without hesitation*) Damned right I would. Somebody's got to tell the truth around here 'cause the Government sure ain't doing it.

> ▋Jean Hill: Garrison did not meet Jean Hill, although he tried to contact her. Like several assassination witnessess (among them Arnold and Barbara Rowland, Johnny Calvin Brewer), Hill did not talk to researchers or investigators about the case after testifying to the Warren Commission. Hill (like the Rowlands) felt they had been subject to undue harrassment by the FBI and avoided getting dragged back into the assassination controversy (author's interviews with Garrison, Hill, Brewer; interview of Arnold and Barbara Rowland by Robert J. Groden, 1990).

DISSOLVE TO a scene inside the Texas School Book Depository in 1967. Jim and

Lou walk the floor and look out the windows. Lou has a Mannlicher-Carcano in his hand, with a sight and clip. We see Oswald's supposed view of the limousine as he pulls the trigger. Now, innocuous traffic goes by, but the iris of the camera tightens into a sniper's scope.

LOU The Zapruder film establishes 3 shots in 5.6 seconds. Here. I'm Oswald. Time me.

> ∎ The Zapruder Film: The basis for judging the time span of the shots is Abraham Zapruder's Bell & Howell 8mm camera which ran at 18.3 frames per second [WR p. 97], the basis for judging the time span of the shots. Oswald's rifle had a recycling time of 2.3 seconds—"recycling" meaning only time to work the bolt and fire again, and not time to aim [WR p. 97]. The Warren Commission decided that the shooting happened in no less than 4.8 seconds and in no more than 7.9 seconds [WR p. 117], depending on which of the three shots missed the car entirely. When taking into account the constraints of the Warren Commission—that JFK could not have been hit before frame 210 because of the tree in front of the building—a close visual analysis of the Zapruder film indicates that the shooting sequence, beginning with frame 210 and ending with the fatal head shot of frame 313, runs 103 frames, or 5.62 seconds. (Robert J. Groden, *A New Look at the Zapruder Film, Government by Gunplay*, p. 3-9; Evica, *And We Are All...*, p. 65-73 and citations.)

Lou cocks the Mannlicher for the first shot. Jim looks at this watch. Lou assumes the Oswald pose, crouched at the window aiming out.

JIM Go!

Lou pulls, quickly recharges the bolt, fires, recycles, fires.

LOU Time?

JIM Between six and seven seconds.

LOU The key is the second and third shots came right on top of each other, and it takes a minimum 2.3 seconds to recycle this thing (*he recycles the bolt for firing*), The other problem is there was a tree right there (*he points*) blocking the first two shots at the time they occur in the Zapruder film.

JIM Didn't Hoover say something about that? The leaves had fallen off in November?

LOU It was a Texas Live Oak, boss. (*he shakes his head*) It sheds its leaves the first week of March. You try to hit a moving target at 88 yards through heavy foliage with this cheap 13-dollar sucker, the world's worst shoulder weapon. No way. The FBI tried two sets of tests and *not one* of their sharpshooters could match Oswald's performance. Not one. And Oswald was at *best* a medium shot. The scope was defective on it, too. I mean this is the whole essence of the case to me. The guy couldn't *do* the shooting. Nobody could. And they sold this lemon to the American public.

> ∎ FBI rifle tests: [Meagher, *Accessories After the Fact*, p. 106-110.] Rifle tests: As Meagher notes, the expert riflemen retained by the FBI did not equal

Oswald's shooting feat. Only one rifleman scored two out of three hits in less than 5.6 seconds, and this was under much easier conditions than Oswald would have faced in Dealey Plaza. The FBI targets were stationary, the tower from which the experts shot was only half as high as the sixth floor window and the gunmen could take as much time as they wanted to aim their first shot. The FBI had also taken pains to adjust the scope on Oswald's rifle so that it could be properly aimed. Had Oswald used the scope in its misaligned November 22 condition, he would never have hit what he was aiming at.

In 1967, CBS decided to do some rifle tests of their own for a multi-part special called "The Warren Commission." They built an elaborate shooting range and used a moving target. The rifle they used was somewhat faster than Oswald's. After discarding an astounding 17 of the 37 trials due to "trouble with the rifle," the CBS marksmen average 1.2 hits over 5.6 seconds. Those figures do not give much credence to Oswald's ability to get 2 hits in 5.6 seconds with a much slower weapon. Walter Cronkite, however, had a different interpretation:

"It seems reasonable to say that an expert could fire that rifle in five seconds. It seems equally reasonable to say that Oswald, under normal circumstances would take longer. But these were not normal circumstances. Oswald was shooting at a president. So our answer is: probably fast enough." [Thompson, *Six Seconds in Dallas*; Appendix F, p. 292-295, Robert Hennelly and Jerry Policoff, "J.F.K.: How the Media Assassinated the Real Story," *Village Voice*, March 31, 1992.]

JIM   The Zapruder film is the proof they didn't count on, Lou. We gotta get our hands on it.

LOU   That means we gotta subpoena *Time-Life* on it.

▮ Garrison's office successfully subpoenaed *Time-Life* and held the first public screening of the Zapruder film at the Clay Shaw trial (see p. 151). Although former Time, Inc. executives—most notably Richard B. Stolley (*The Greatest Home Movie Ever Made*, *Esquire*, November 1973; *Shots Seen Around The World*, *Entertainment Weekly*, January 17, 1992)—still insist that the publishing giant did not suppress the film. The fact of the matter is, *Time-Life* turned down many lucrative offers for film and TV use and never once used it in any way except for publishing select frames. And their publication of the individual frames was often misleading (to put it mildly).

In the December 12, 1963 issue of *Life*, a *Life* journalist claimed the Zapruder film showed how Oswald, firing from behind the limousine, could hit J.F.K. in the front of the throat. This film, he said, showed Kennedy turning around to wave at the crowd. This is utter nonsense, according to even the most cursory look at the film. For the October 2, 1964 issue, *Life* printed three different versions of a feature on the Zapruder frames, changing the photos and captions *twice* after the original version already hit the newsstands. The third and final version, presumably the one that best satisfied *Life's* editors, printed, in a caption accompanying frame 313 (the fatal head shot), that the president's head exploded "forward" (Jerry Policoff, *The Second Dallas Casualty*, *Government by Gunplay*, p. 216).

As Members of Fairness and Accuracy in Reporting (FAIR) noted in an open letter to Stolley, "One need not believe in a conspiracy of any kind to

observe that *Time-Life* actions regarding the Zapruder film were journalisti-
cally indefensible." (*Why Did Time-Life Bury the Zapruder Film?* Version of
Time Inc.'s Editorial Director *Doesn't Stand Up, Extra!* April/May 1992.)

JIM (*looks out the window*) Why not just shoot Kennedy coming up Houston?
There's plenty of time—he's out in the open—a frontal shot?

> ❚ Shooting J.F.K. on Houston: Weisberg notes that J. Edgar Hoover himself
> raised this point [Weisberg, *Whitewash*, p. 110]:
>
> "Why didn't he shoot the President as the car came toward the storehouse
> where he was working?...there were some trees between his window on the
> sixth floor and the cars." [WC 5H p. 105]
>
> Anyone who has ever been to Dealey Plaza knows this is not true. The tree
> does not block the view on to the Elm-Houston corner-but it does impede
> the line of sight down Elm Street where the shooting occurred.

*Jim points the Carcano south, right up Houston Street, following a car that happens to
be passing by—a convertible with an unknown woman driving.*

LOU I asked myself the same thing. Common sense. Even if you miss the first shot,
if he accelerates you still got him for a second shot. No ... the only reason for
waiting to get him on Elm is you got him in a triangulated crossfire. You got
him on a flat low trajectory from the front at the fence there.

*The camera swings to the Grassy Knoll and the picket fence as seen from the sixth floor
of the Depository.*

LOU ... you put a third team there—in that building, on a low floor.

The camera swings to the Daltex Building across the street.

LOU (*voice-over*) When Kennedy gets to the kill zone, it's a turkey shoot.

JIM (*aiming*) How many men?

LOU One shooter. One spotter on a radio. Maybe three teams. I'd say these were
professional riflemen, chief, serious people. Hunters ... patient. It takes skill to
kill with a rifle, that's why there's been no execution of an executive with one in
200 years ..." 3-2-1 ... green!" (*he taps Jim on the shoulder*) Or else "Abort!
Abort!"

Jim pulls the dead trigger, reliving the moment through the scope on a passing car.

LOU (*voice-over*) Main Street's over there—the original parade route on the way to
the Trade Mart. Too far right? Impossible shot ...

Jim swings the scope up to confront Main Street. Another car is in his sight. Too far.

LOU (*voice-over*) So they changed the route to bring it this way. Moving at a normal
25 mph, they knew the motorcade would have to slow to about 10 miles per
hour to make this turn. That's where you get him.

The camera swings to the Houston and Main intersection.

JIM Who do you think changed the parade route?

LOU Beats me. City officials. Secret Service. Dallas police. They did a dry run with Chief Curry a few days before. But they didn't bother running through Dealey. They stopped right there, said something like, "and afterwards there's only the freeway," and went home.

> ▌ The motorcade route was printed in the Dallas papers throughout the week before the Presidential visit. The actual planning of the route is as follows: Meetings took place on Nov. 13-15 to decide the President's motorcade route from Love Field to the Trade Mart. Present at the meetings were Dallas Police Chief Jesse Curry, Assistant Chief Charles Batchelor, White House Secret Service agent Winston Lawson, Forrest Sorrels and a Captain Gannaway, head of the Dallas Police's Special Services Bureau (and like many in the SSB—and Lawson—a member of the Army Intelligence Reserve). According to Curry, Lawson was the "central figure and primary planner" of security arrangements [Robert J. Groden & Harrison Edward Livingstone, *High Treason* (The Conservatory Press, 1989), p. 155]. Lawson reduced the number of motorcycles flanking the limousine from 8 to 4 [Groden & Livingstone, *High Treason*, p. 152], and then moved them to the rear of the car rather than at the sides [Scott, *The Dallas Conspiracy*, II, p. 1-12]. According to the pseudonymous James Hepburn's *Farewell America* (Frontiers Publishing Co., 1968), Curry, Lawson and Sorrels drove a shortened version of the route on Nov. 18. They went as far as the intersection of Main and Houston in Dealey Plaza. Curry pointed down toward the Triple Underpass, saying, "And afterwards, there's only the freeway." [Hepburn, *Farewell America*, p. 352.] The many open windows, tall buildings and open spaces on the motorcade route seem inconceivable today. Keep in mind, however, that America's notion of the dangers public figures face comes directly from the J.F.K. assassination and the subsequent assassinations of the '60's.

JIM You know who the mayor was?

LOU No.

JIM Earle Cabell. And guess who his brother is?

LOU Who?

JIM General Charles Cabell. Deputy Director of the CIA. Fired by Kennedy in '61 because of the Bay of Pigs fiasco, he moved back to the Pentagon, called Kennedy a "traitor." When he came to New Orleans to address the Foreign Policy Association, you know who introduced him? Our friend Clay Shaw.

> ▌ Shaw introduces Gen. Charles Cabell in New Orleans: [Hurt, *Reasonable Doubt*, p. 282-283; CIA Memo #1326-1042 "Garrison Investigation," 28 September, 1967.]

LOU The Warren Commission call him?

JIM (*shaking his head*) His boss was the one on the Warren Commission who handled all the leads to the intelligence community.

LOU Allen Dulles?

JIM (*he nods*) Head of the CIA since '53. Kennedy fired them both. Cabell was his deputy for nine years. (*sickened*) Talk about the fox investigating the chicken coop. Now we'll have to subpoena them, Lou.

LOU They're gonna love you, chief.

Lou walks to another window in the empty Book Depository where Oswald supposedly did his dirty deed and looks out over the Plaza, with all its ghosts. Jim and Lou are two men—with only two men's power. A terrible aloneness pervades their minds.

JIM Maybe we should just call it a day, Lou. Go home. While we're still a little behind. We got two people killed, maybe more we never thought about.

LOU You never got anyone killed, boss. Their actions killed them years before. If we stopped now, it'd be even more wrong.

FLASHBACK TO 1963—the sixth floor of the Texas School Book Depository—the same place Jim and Lou are now. Jim looks around and sees one shooter and one spotter with a lunchbox radio, in repairman clothes. Jim is watching. Neither of these men is Oswald. We hear the sounds of the motorcade below. The shooter pulls the trigger on the Carcano. A loud frightening sound snaps Jim back to the present.

JIM (*in present*) Subpoena them, Lou—Dulles, the Cabells, *Time-Life* ... the whole damned lot of 'em!

GARRISON'S OFFICE - 9 MONTHS LATER - 1968

We see another smoke-filled conference of assistants. Paperwork is stacked in the corners almost to the ceiling; there are coffee cups and doughnuts on desks. The disorganization and lack of resources are apparent. The staff working on this project now numbers some eleven people, and there are some new investigators and assistants. We sense that the trial is drawing closer.

AL The U.S. Attorney in Washington "declines" to serve our subpoena on Allen Dulles, Charles Cabell, CIA Director Richard Helms, or any FBI agent we named.

> ▌ U.S. Attorney declines to serve subpoenas: [New Orleans District Attorney Records; *New Orleans States-Item*, May 22, 1968; Garrison, *Trail of the Assassins*, p. 182; Flammonde, *The Kennedy Conspiracy*, p. 242-243.] Clay Shaw also had problems in calling certain witnesses. After filing a suit in federal court to block Garrison's prosecution, the Shaw defense team sought U.S. Attorney General Ramsey Clark as a defendant. Shaw's attorney's attempted to get a judgment declaring the Warren Report valid and binding by all courts and claimed it was the Attorney General's responsibility—not Shaw's—to defend the Report. U.S. Attorney Louis LaCour's office successfully fought the motion, and the government avoided a potentially embarrassing ruling on the Warren Commission. [*New Orleans Times-Picayune*, "Clark called in Shaw Case," June 14, 1968; *New Orleans States-Item*, "US Fighting Shaw Move to Involve Clark," June 17, 1968.]

JIM Well, what do you expect from a pig but a grunt.

AL Without them, it's going to be near impossible, chief, to prove Shaw's connection to the CIA. We got the same problem with the governors. All of them. Reagan in California won't give us Brading, Ohio refuses Orville Townsend, Texas on Arcacha, and Nebraska on Sandra Moffet.

BILL What the hell is going on? Never before has an extradition request from this office been refused.

> ■ Extradition requests refused: [Garrison, *Trail of the Assassins*, p. 181-182; Flammonde, *The Kennedy Conspiracy*, p. 200-202, 204.]

AL We haven't tried to get Julia Anne Mercer in?

JIM No, she could get hurt. If you believe what's happening to these other people.

NUMA She's the best damn witness we have!

JIM I just don't want to do it. What else?

Numa is opening another stack of letters. The dollar bills keep coming. He points to two giant stacks of mail.

NUMA Hate mail here. Fan mail here. The bad news is the IRS has just requested an audit on your income from this office.

JIM (*he snorts*) I expected that two months ago, and they're wasting their time ... The bad news is the National Guard has just asked me to resign after 18 years. (*we see his hurt*) Well, maybe that's good news—it was never as good as combat, but this is. Bill, any more on Oswald and Shaw?

> ■ Garrison in National Guard: Jim Garrison actually resigned from the National Guard due to ideological differences. As he told James Kirkwood in 1969: "I became so disgusted over Vietnam that I quit the National Guard." [Kirkwood, *American Grotesque*, p. 572.]

BILL Yeah. They were seen together in Clinton in early September. The Civil Rights Movement was running a voter registration drive.

> ■ Clinton: [HSCA Report, p. 142-145; State of Louisiana vs. Clay L. Shaw, court transcripts, Feb. 6, 1969 (witnesses Corrie Collins, Henry E. Palmer, John Manchester, Reeves Morgan, Willie Dunn).]

BILL (*voice-over*) ... rumor is Shaw, a local boy, was working on some arms deal to discredit the civil rights movement. No one really knows what they were doing there, but everyone sure saw 'em. They stood out like cottonballs. I got whites and blacks saw 'em, but last time I checked there was nothing illegal with registering to vote. We still got the Negro junkie, Vernon Bundy, saw 'em talkin' at the seawall near Lake Pontchartrain. But it's tough, boss—no one wants to talk about Shaw. He's ...

LOU (*back to present*) You know you keep saying that.

BILL Keep saying what?

LOU You're not digging.

JIM I think Clinton is a breakthrough. Shaw denies he knows Ferrie or Oswald. Is that right? It proves he's a liar. Keep on it, Bill. (*a look from Lou*)

SUSIE This is interesting—are you ready for this? Oswald went to see the FBI two weeks before the assassination. It seems Special Agent Hosty made three routine visits to his house, supposedly to keep an eye on Marina Oswald ...

> ■ Oswald at Dallas FBI Office: [HSCA Report, p. 195; Summers, *Conspiracy*, p. 370-372; Hurt, *Reasonable Doubt*, p. 252-255; Evica, *And We Are All...*, p. 319-327.]

FLASHBACK TO Dallas FBI office in 1963. Oswald is at the counter addressing the female receptionist.

OSWALD I want to see Special Agent Hosty.

RECEPTIONIST I'm sorry, he's not in. Can someone else help you?

OSWALD Can I use a pen?

SUSIE (*voice-over*) He left a note. Hosty told a Dallas newspaperman it was a warning to him to stop questioning Marina at their home when Oswald was not present. She was not a citizen, so possibly he was threatening to deport her back to Russia.

TIME CUT TO FBI Agent James Hosty confronting his agitated superior, FBI Agent Shanklin in one of the cubicles.

SUSIE (*voice-over*) But what the note really said no one knows because his boss Shanklin told Hosty ...

SHANKLIN (*reading the note*) Oswald's dead now. There's no trial. Get rid of it. I don't even want this in the office. Get rid of it, Hosty. (*he gives it back to Hosty*)

SUSIE (*voice-over*) Hosty tore it up and flushed it down the toilet. Waggoner Carr, the Attorney General of Texas, says he had evidence from the Dallas Sheriff's office that Oswald had been employed as an undercover informant for the FBI at a salary of $200 a month, beginning more than a year before the murder.

> ■ Oswald as FBI informant: [Warren Commission Executive Session Transcripts, Jan. 22, 1964 and Jan. 27, 1964; Gerald R. Ford with John R. Stiles, *Portrait of the Assassin*, p. 13-25; Epstein, *Inquest*, p. 47-54.] Texas Attorney General Waggoner Carr called Warren Commission Chief Counsel J. Lee Rankin in Jan., 1964 to advise that he had information that Oswald had been a paid informant for the FBI since Sept. 1962. Oswald's informant number, he said, was S-179. His source was impressive: Dallas District Attorney and former FBI man Henry Wade. The Commission received the same information from another agency—the Secret Service—who named as their source Dallas Deputy Sheriff Allan Sweatt. In the secret Executive Sessions, former CIA chief Allen Dulles noted there was no way to disprove that Oswald was an informant—not even the man who recruited him would tell under oath. In fact, he said, "he ought not tell it under oath." The esteemed Commission-

ers dealt with the issue by not dealing with it. On Feb. 6, 1964, J. Edgar Hoover sent them an affidavit assuring them that Oswald was never a Bureau informant [WC 17H p. 815-818]. The Commission was satisfied. "Never has a crime been so thoroughly investigated," Gerald Ford wrote in *Portrait of the Assassin*, p. 25. We also know that Ford informed the FBI on the activities of the Warren Commission. In a memo to J. Edgar Hoover, aide Cartha DeLoach noted that he had met with Ford, who indicated he would keep DeLoach "advised as to the activities of the Commission" [internal FBI memo, December 12, 1963].

JIM (*in present*) This is just speculation, people, but what if the note was describing the assassination attempt on J.F.K.? (*the staff members seem surprised by the thought*) Come on guys, think—that's the only reason to destroy it, because if it was any kind of threat, like Hosty said, they would've kept it 'cause it makes their case against the "angry lone nut" stronger! Remember the New Orleans meeting with Agent Quigley the day he got busted?

FLASHBACK TO Oswald, under arrest, meeting with Quigley. [WC 4H p. 331-340; WC 17H, CE 826, p. 758-762.]

JIM ... there again Quigley destroyed the notes of the meeting. I think we can raise the possibility that Oswald not only was an informant but that he may well have been the original source for the telex we have dated November 17 warning of the Kennedy assassination in Dallas on November 22.

Holds up the telex. We see a close-up: "URGENT TO ALL SACS FROM DIRECTOR."

JIM William Walter, the night clerk on duty here in the FBI office, gave me a copy of this. It went all over the country. Nothing was done, and the motorcade went ahead on schedule—and this wasn't even *mentioned* in the Warren Report! Read it, Al.

AL (*voice-over*) "Threat to assassinate President Kennedy in Dallas, Texas, November 22 - 23. Information received by the Bureau has determined that a militant revolutionary group may attempt to assassinate President Kennedy on his proposed trip to Dallas, Texas, etc, etc ... "

FLASHBACK TO New Orleans FBI office in 1963. Walter, the night clerk, receives the teletype, reads it, and runs it.

JIM (*voice-over*) ... shortly after the assassination, Walter says, the telex was removed from all the files in all cities, as an obvious embarrassment to the Bureau. I believe Oswald was sending information through Hosty ...

▮ William Walter telex: [HSCA Report, p. 191; *The Los Angeles Free Press Special Report*, 1978, p. 10; Garrison, *Trail of the Assassins*, p. 220-221; Hurt, *Reasonable Doubt*, p. 306fn.] As Garrison notes in his book, he met Walter and obtained a copy of the teletype through researcher Mark Lane. The HSCA spoke to Walter several times and, in the end, rejected his story, mainly because they could not corroborate it. Henry Hurt concurred, based on his own contacts with Walter. We feel that the Walter allegations, like virtually every other aspect of the J.F.K. case, warrant further investigaton.

FLASHBACK TO a Dallas safe house in 1963. Oswald, Ruby, and several Cubans including the Bull and the Indian are talking.

> ▌Dallas Safe House: [Torbitt, *Nomenclature of an Assassination Cabal*, p. 20.] Although Torbitt says the house was at 3126 Harlandale Ave., a report from Deputy Sheriff Buddy Walther in the Dallas Sheriff's Supplemental Report says Secret Service man Forrest Sorrels told him of a house at 3128 Harlandale where Oswald had been meeting with some Cubans. Researcher George Michael Evica notes that 3126 is the correct number [Evica, *And We Are All Mortal*, p. 100]. Recently, two men who claimed to know Oswald in Dallas and in New Orleans have told researchers independently that the safe house was directly behind Oswald's boardinghouse. Researcher Gus Russo called the landlady (the daughter of Oswald's landlady) to ask who lived in the back house. She answered that they were "Latins or Cubans."

JIM (*voice-over*) ... I have a hunch that from the get go, Oswald had infiltrated this group, probably Cubans or right-wing extremists. He was at the Book Depository that day, told to be there by their handlers, either to prevent the assassination or to take part in it. They coulda told him anything, either 1) they were going to close down the plotters that day, or 2) they were going to fake an attack on Kennedy to whip up public opinion against Russia or Cuba and reverse his policies—it doesn't really matter what they told him, 'cause he was *under orders*, he was a foot soldier.

> ▌Oswald infiltrated a group: Oswald cultivated contacts on both ends of the political spectrum, from the leftist Fair Play for Cuba Committee and the Soviet Embassy, to Carlos Bringuier's DRE and the Banister Organization. Obviously, he had some purpose in mind—and it clearly wasn't a case of ideology. His antics aroused suspicion on both sides: the FPCC saw his letter-writing campaign as a possible infiltration attempt by an intelligence agency and, likewise, Bringuier felt Oswald was trying to infiltrate his anti-Castro organization, possibly as part of the crackdown on exile activities. (WC 10H p. 35.)
>
> It was a valid hypothesis, and it was not lost on the two Warren Commission attorneys charged with examining the question of a foreign conspiracy (the Commission did not even entertain the idea of a domestic plot). Counsels David Slauson and William Coleman posed the idea in an internal memorandum: The Slauson-Coleman memorandum was not included in the Commission's volumes or documents (CDs) and is still heavily blacked out, despite its "declassified" status. But one thing is clear: Although Coleman and Slauson said the facts were "sufficient to warrant additional investigation," nobody—including the two memo-writers—followed up.

Underneath the voice-over we hear and see Oswald, with a floor plan of the Book Depository, at the center of the group. Jack Ruby, Bull, and the Indian, two or three young Cubans and a young white shooter—the man in the plaid shirt described by Julia Ann Mercer—are also there.

OSWALD (*to the two young Cubans*) I can get you in and up there. This is a shot out the southeast window of the sixth floor. That floor will be unoccupied between noon and 12:30.

BULL What about the elevator?

OSWALD I can close it off. The only access is a stairwell.

BULL ... We get them in as an air-conditioning unit.

RUBY No. A floor refurbishing group. Got the van, the uniforms ... .

> ■ Floor refurbishing: At the time of the assassination, a group of Book Depository employees were installing plywood on the upper floors of the building. On November 22, 1963, the floor-laying crew was working on the sixth floor [WC3H p. 163-164 (Bonnie Ray Williams)].
>
> We know from eyewitness testimony—Arnold Rowland, Ruby Henderson, Carolyn Walther, Norman Similas (for sources see notes p. 163) that there were probably *two* people (one of whom had a rifle) on the sixth floor at the time of the shooting. There is strong evidence that Oswald was where he said he was: down on the first floor eating lunch (see notes p. 167).
>
> Thus, whoever was on the sixth floor at 12:30 P.M., got up into the building without being noticed by TSBD employees (unless TSBD employees were involved in the plot, a scenario lacking evidence). A person in a workman's uniform would stand a good chance of getting to the top of the building without being stopped. ...

OSWALD (*his back to the screen*) ... if we can get the motorcade to turn from Main onto Houston, that'll do the trick, 'cause it'll slow down to make the turn here. You can't miss. (*to the two young Cubans*) He's a dead duck.

Ruby shares a look with Bull unbeknownst to Oswald, and then we see the looks on the faces of Jim's team.

BILL I don't buy it, chief—why would the FBI cover it up? You're talking the whole FBI here. A telex that disappears from every single FBI office in the country?

JIM There's a word—orders.

Back in Garrison's office in 1968 ...

SUSIE ... or a cover-up! Jesus, Bill, don't you have enough proof of the FBI's complicity now?

BILL (*to Susie*) Maybe I have a little more respect for this country's institutions than you do, Susie. You tell me how the hell you can keep a conspiracy going between the Mob, the CIA, FBI, and Army Intelligence and who knows what else, when you know you can't even keep a secret in this room between 12 people! We got leaks everywhere! We're going to trial here! What the hell do we really got? Oswald, Ruby, Banister, Ferrie are dead. Shaw—maybe he's an agent, I don't know, but as a covert operator in my book he's wide open for blackmail 'cause of his homosexuality.

JIM Shaw's our toehold, Bill. I don't know exactly what he is, where he fits, and I don't care. I do know he's lying through his teeth and I'm not gonna let go of him!

BILL So for those reasons, you're going to trial against Clay Shaw, chief? Well, you're gonna lose! We should be investigating all our Mafia leads here in New Orleans—Carlos Marcello, Santos Trafficante—I can buy that a hell of a lot easier than the Government. Ruby's all Mob, knows Oswald, sets him up. Hoffa—Trafficante—Marcello, they hire some guns and they do Kennedy and maybe the Government doesn't want to open up a whole can o' worms there because it used the Mob to get Castro. Y'know, Castro being assassinated sounds pretty wild to John Q. Citizen. So they close the book on J.F.K. It makes sense to me.

JIM I don't doubt their involvement, Bill, but at a low level. Could the Mob change the parade route, Bill, or eliminate the protection for the President? Could the Mob send Oswald to Russia and get him back? Could the Mob get the FBI, the CIA, and the Dallas Police to make a mess of the investigation? Could the Mob appoint the Warren Commission to cover it up? Could the Mob wreck the autopsy? Could the Mob influence the national media to go to sleep? And since when has the Mob used anything but .38's for hits, up close. The Mob wouldn't have the guts or the power for something of this magnitude. Assassins need payrolls, orders, times, schedules. This was a military-style ambush from start to finish ... a coup d'état with Lyndon Johnson waiting in the wings.

BILL Oh, now you're saying Lyndon Johnson was involved? The President of the United States?

His voice is challenging. There's a pause. The men exchange looks and wait.

JIM I know this, Bill—Lyndon Johnson got $1 billion for his Texas friends, Brown and Root, to dredge Cam Ranh Bay for the military in Vietnam. That's just for openers.

▌Cam Ranh Bay: [Marrs, *Crossfire*, p. 299; Robert Caro, *Path to Power*, p. 458-475.]

BILL Boss, are you calling the President a murderer?

JIM If I'm so far from the truth, why is the FBI bugging our offices? Why are our witnesses being bought off and murdered? Why are Federal agencies blocking our extraditions and subpoenas when we were never blocked before?

BILL Maybe 'cause there's some rogue element in the Government!

The others in the room groan at the reasoning. Bill feels embittered, cornered.

JIM With a full-blown conspiracy to cover it up? Y'ever read your Shakespeare, Bill?

BILL Yeah.

JIM Julius Caesar: "Brutus and Cassius, they too are honorable men." Who killed Caesar? Twenty, twenty-five Senators. All it takes is one Judas, Bill—a few people, on the inside, Pentagon, CIA ...

BILL (*he gets up*) This is Louisiana, chief. How the hell do you know who your daddy is? 'Cause your mama *told* you so ... You're way out there taking a crap in the wind, boss, and I for one ain't going along on this one. (*he exits*)

Jim sighs, saddened. Bill was one of his best men.

LOU Chief, I've had my doubts about Bill for a long time. He's fighting everything.

JIM We need him back.

AL Bill wasted a goddamn month trying to prove that mob boys like Brading and Jack Ruby played ball in right field with Hunt Oil ...

> ■ Mafia Theories: While there is some credible evidence that organized crime played a part in the assassination, the-Mob-did-it theories cannot account for the unending chain of falsified and withheld government documents (the CIA's Mexico City caper, the FBI's sanitized version of Oswald's address book, and military intelligence's refusal to turn over the files) or the federal government's apparent disinterest in solving the case.
>
> Not that organized crime isn't well-versed in the business of assassination. The CIA hired them as the operative partner for the plots against Castro and also recruited selected foreign hitmen to carry out other foreign assassination plots (Church Committee, *Alleged Assassination Plots...*, p. 43-48, 74-89). In all of these documented cases, however, it was the CIA calling the shots, the mobsters were simply mechanics.

LOU I don't trust the guy.

JIM (*standing*) Gentlemen, I will not hear this. I value Bill as much as anyone here. (*Lou reacts angrily*) We all need to make room for someone else's ideas, Lou, especially me. Maybe Oswald is what everyone says he is and I'm just plain dumb wrong.

AL I've seen him copying files, leaving here late at night.

LOU I just plain don't trust him anymore.

JIM (*angry*) Maybe you didn't hear what I said. I will not tolerate this infighting among the staff. I warn you that ...

LOU (*suddenly*) Boss, then I'm afraid I can't continue working with Bill.

Tension, silence.

JIM (*pause, then quietly:*) Are you giving me an ultimatum, Lou?

LOU What?

JIM (*pause, then quietly:*) Are you giving me an ultimatum, Lou?

LOU Well, if that's what you want to call it. I didn't ever think it would come to this. I guess I am, boss.

JIM I will not have any damned ultimatums put to me, Lou. I'll accept your resignation.

LOU You sure got it. You're one stubborn and stupid sonofabitch D.A. and you're making one hell of a mistake!

He storms out.

> ∎ The real-life Lou Ivon did not quit Garrison's J.F.K. investigation team.

SUSIE Aren't you being a little hard?

JIM No, I don't think I am, Susie. Anyone else?

Silence. Jim exits.

GARRISON'S LIVING ROOM - (1968)

It's after dinner and toys scattered around the living room. Snapper is chasing his sister Elizabeth around. Virginia, 6, runs to the ringing phone in the living room, as her mother and Mattie, stunned, watch the news of Martin Luther King's death on TV.

MATTIE My God! My God! What have they done! *(angrily)* It's lynchin' time!

VIRGINIA I'll get it. *(into phone)* Hello.

MALE VOICE Hello. Is this Jim Garrison's daughter?

VIRGINIA Yes?

MALE VOICE Virginia or Elizabeth?

VIRGINIA Virginia.

MALE VOICE Virginia, you're a lucky little girl. Your daddy has entered you in a beauty contest. Would you like to be in a beauty contest?

VIRGINIA That sounds fun.

MALE VOICE I need some information from you then. How old are you?

VIRGINIA Six.

MALE VOICE And how tall are you?

CUT TO Jim's study, where Jim also watches the news in horror. We see TV images of Martin Luther King on the motel balcony, dead.

CRONKITE-TYPE (NEWSMAN 9) To repeat—39-year-old Martin Luther King, who preached non-violence and won the Nobel Peace Prize, was cut down earlier today by a sniper's bullets while standing on the porch of the Lorraine Motel in Memphis, Tennessee. He was surrounded by his closest aides. The police say they have no suspects at this time. Mr. King—

Jim, visibly shaken, slams his book down on the desk in frustration.

BACK TO the male voice on the phone.

MALE VOICE And you get off from school at 3 every day?

VIRGINIA Yes.

MALE VOICE Do you walk home?

VIRGINIA Uh huh.

Liz comes to the phone, a wary look on her face.

LIZ (*taking the phone*) Who you talking to?

MALE VOICE Okay, Virginia, that's all I need to know. I'll call you again when it's time for the beauty contest.

LIZ Who's this? ... Hello? ... Hello?

After a pause, the man hangs up.

VIRGINIA (*excited*) Mama, I'm going to be in a beauty contest!

LIZ What did he ask you?

VIRGINIA Well, he asked me everything. He asked me ...

Liz freaks out. She marches into Jim's study.

LIZ Did you enter Virginia into a beauty contest?

JIM (*absorbed in the TV*) What?

LIZ (*hysterical*) A man just called. He asked her everything! Her height, her weight, when she came home from school.

JIM (*distracted*) Honey, some crackpot. Martin Luther King was killed in Memphis today!

LIZ (*screaming*) Your daughter's life was just threatened!

JIM Just a crank making phone calls. Happens a dozen times a day at the office.

LIZ Our home, Jim! A kidnapper, a murderer, who knows!

JIM Only cowards make crank calls, sweetheart, nothing is going to happen.

LIZ How do you know? How do you even know what goes on in this house anymore! You're too busy making speeches, stirring up every crazed Klansman in Louisiana after us!

JIM Get a hold of yourself.

LIZ I'm leaving. I'm taking the kids and I'm leaving! I won't stand it anymore ...

The kids, hearing the shouting, come to watch from the door of the study.

JIM Honey, come on. The government wants you to be scared. They want everybody to be scared to speak out. They count on it. But there's nothing to be scared of.

LIZ You and your government! What's the matter with you? Don't you have any feelings? Your daughter! What kind of man are you!

Jim controls himself, shoos the kids out, closes the door.

JIM I'll take them up to my mother's if it'll make you feel better. Spend a week. I'll change the locks, the phone lines, I'll even get a bodyguard, all right? Elizabeth, get a hold of yourself.

LIZ Jim, before this Kennedy thing, nothing mattered to you in this life more than your children. The other night Jasper tried to show you a drawing. You didn't even notice he was there. He came to me bawling his little eyes out. Jim, he's sensitive—he needs more from you.

JIM I promise I'll make more time for Jasper.

LIZ Is it such a chore? I don't understand you.

JIM Damn it, if I say I'll spend more time with him, I'll spend more time with him. I can't fight you and the world too, Liz ...

LIZ I'm not fighting you, Jim, I'm just trying to reach you. You've changed.

JIM Of course I've changed! My eyes have opened, and once they're open, believe me, what used to look normal seems insane! And now King. Don't you think this has something to do with that? Can't you see?

LIZ (*she explodes*) I don't want to see, goddammit! I'm tired. I've had enough! They say you don't have anything anyway! Everybody in town's talking. You're ruining this man Shaw's life! You're attacking him because he's homosexual! Going ahead with this stupid "trial"! Did you ever once stop and consider what he's going through?

JIM (*astounded*) That's not why I'm attacking him! You don't believe me—all this time you never believed me.

LIZ Oh, I don't know anymore! I believe there was a conspiracy, but not the government. I just want to raise our children and live a normal life! I want my life back!

The children press in at the door. Mattie, ignoring them, is enraged as she watches King's eulogy on TV. Riots are already breaking out.

JIM Well so do I, goddammit! So do I! I had a life too, y'know—I had a life, too. But you just can't bury your head in the sand like some ostrich, goddammit, Elizabeth! It's not just about you—and your well-being and your two cars and your kitchen and your TV and "I'm jes' fine honey." While our kids grow up into a shithole of lies! Well, I'm not "fine" about that, I'm angry. My life is fucked, Liz! And yours is, too ! And if you don't want to support me I can understand that but don't you go start making threats of taking the children away.

LIZ You never talked to me this way before, Jim Garrison. I'm not making any threats. I'm leaving you. I'm taking the kids to my mother's. I am—I am ...

She runs out, past the stunned kids, sobbing as she goes up the stairs. Jim pursues her like an angry spirit, yelling up the stairs at her.

JIM Go on then, get out! Go hide someplace. Join the rest of 'em! They'll tell you I'm crazy. You got plenty of people'll tell you Jim Garrison's crazy. You won't have a problem filing your divorce papers on me ... *somebody's* got to try, goddammit, somebody!

The kids move away, fearful. Quaking with rage and hurt, Jim stands there at the bottom of the stairs, strangled with pain. He takes a law dictionary in his hand and throws it across the room. Jasper and Virginia come over to him.

JASPER Are we going away, Daddy?

JIM Well, it looks like it, Jasper.

JASPER Because of Kennedy? (*a beat. Jim doesn't answer*) Are the same people gonna kill us, Daddy?

JIM No, Jasper, nobody's gonna kill us.

VIRGINIA Do you love us?

JIM Yes, of course I do, honey.

VIRGINIA No. I mean like mommy loves us. She really loves us.

JASPER I'm scared.

JIM (*bending down*) There's nothing wrong with feeling a little scared, Jasper, Virginia. Telling the truth can be a scary thing. It scared President Kennedy, but he was a brave man. If you let yourself be too scared, then you let the bad guys take over the country, don't you—and then everybody gets scared.

JASPER/VIRGINIA Stay with Mom, Daddy ... please.

JERRY JOHNSON SHOW - (1968)

The band strikes up "When The Saints Go Marching In" introducing Jim, who strides in from the wings to shake hands with Jerry Johnson, the friendly-looking host.

▮ "Jerry Johnson Show": Jim Garrison appeared on the Tonight Show on January 31, 1968. He had a full 45 minutes with Johnny Carson—the only other guest on the show was the folksinger Melanie. Although no footage of the show survived, an audio tape can be found through the J.F.K. research community and Jim Garrison describes his experiences on pages 207-215 of *On the Trail of the Assassins*

We really did shoot this scene but it ended up on the cutting room floor due to time constraints. *Washington Post* reporter Michael Isikoff, in a tongue-in-cheek Op-Ed piece, saw something sinister in this omission from the "real" Garrison story ["H-e-e-e-r-e's Conspiracy!" *Washington Post*, December 29, 1991]. Perhaps including the scene here will set the record straight.

SIDEKICK And now, Jerry, here's Big Jim Garrison, District Attorney of New Orleans, Louisiana.

The audience is enthusiastic. Jim smiles and waves, then sits down next to Johnson.

JOHNSON Welcome, District Attorney Garrison. May I call you Jim?

JIM I've been called everything under the sun, Jerry. Call me whatever you like.

He reads from a script on the desk.

JOHNSON First we had your charge that the Cuban exiles killed the President, then the Mob, then you said the oil billionaires did it, then you said the Minutemen and the Ku Klux Klan collaborated to do it, now your latest theory seems to be that the CIA and the FBI and the Pentagon and the White House all combined in some elaborate conspiracy to kill John Kennedy. Let me ask you, is there anyone besides Lee Harvey Oswald who you think did not conspire to kill the President?

He fixes his eyes on Jim, waiting for a reply. A weariness has set in on Jim. Once more into the slaughter.

JIM How many hours do I have to answer that one? Well let's just say this, Jerry— I've stopped beating my wife. (*the audience laughs*) ... Or maybe you should ask Lyndon Johnson. We know he has some answers.

The audience, loving it, cheers. Johnson looks at Jim blankly, and reads the next question on his list.

JOHNSON There have been a number of reports in reputable news media—*Time, Newsweek*, our own NBC—that you have gone way beyond the legal means available to a prosecutor, that you've intimidated and drugged witnesses, bribed them, urged them to commit perjury. What is your response?

JIM Your faith in the veracity of the major media is touching, Jerry. It indicates that the Age of Innocence is not yet over. But seriously, Jerry, people aren't interested in Jim Garrison—they want the hard evidence! They want to know why he was killed and what forces were opposed to ...

JOHNSON (*interrupting*) Some people would say you're paranoid.

JIM (*laughing*) Well, if I am, why is the Government concealing evidence?

JOHNSON *Are* they? Why would they?

JIM (*pulling out his briefcase*) That's exactly my question, Jerry. Maybe I'd better show you some pictures so you can begin to understand what I am talking about.

He pulls out a large blowup of the Allen photo of the three hoboes and starts to hold it up in front of the camera.

JIM These arrests were photographed minutes after the assassination, and were never shown to the American public. They show ...

It takes Johnson a few moments to realize what's happening. When he does, he lunges like a cobra for the photographs, pulling Jim's arm down so the pictures are out of the camera's view.

JOHNSON *(sharply)* Pictures like this don't show up on television!

JIM *(holding the picture up again)* Sure they do. The camera can pick this up.

JOHNSON *(yanking his arm down)* No, it can't!

Jim swings the picture up a third time, but the stage director gives a "cut" signal—finger across the throat—and the red light on the camera blinks off. The monitor shows another camera panning the audience.

JIM *(quickly realizing he's about to be cut off)* Those men you just saw were arrested in Dallas minutes after the assassination. They were never seen again. No record of arrest, no fingerprint, no mugshot, nothing. They all got away.

The director frantically gives Johnson the "cut" sign.

JOHNSON We'll be back after these messages.

The audience cheers as the commercial comes on.

GARRISON'S HOME - (1968)

Jim comes home. His wife and two of the children are waiting in the doorway. They kiss. Al Oser interrupts.

AL Jim, bad news. Bill's turned, boss. I think he's given everything we've got to the Feds.

> ▌Broussard's defection: Broussard is a composite character based on several Garrison aides and investigators that, for a variety of reasons, became disillusioned with the investigation and turned files over to the press and, even worse, the Shaw defense team.

NUMA We studied the memos—there was nothing there, chief, nothing! When we went to confront him, the landlady said that sonofabitch just took off, left everything.

SUSIE I'm sorry.

JIM I know.

LIZ *(to Jim)* I'm sorry.

NUMA Something sure scared him.

JIM Bill doesn't scare that easy. Somebody got to his thinking. He was never that good a thinker.

On the TV, the news is on.

NEWSMAN 9 Much is at stake tonight in California. Public opinion polls show Senator Robert Kennedy of New York leading Senator Eugene McCarthy of Minnesota. Their anti-Vietnam War message is obviously striking a chord with the voters, and whoever wins tonight will certainly emerge as the favorite over Vice-President Humphrey to win the nomination in Chicago in August. That man now seems to be Senator Kennedy.

We see a shot of Robert Kennedy in Los Angeles with his supporters.

NUMA Sure sounds like he's winning.

JIM He'll never make it. If he wins, they'll kill him. He wants to avenge his brother. He'll stop that war. No, they'll kill him before they let him become President.

> ■ CNN talk show host Larry King interviewed Garrison for his syndicated radio show shortly before the 1968 California primary. During a post-interview conversation, Garrison told King that if Bobby Kennedy got the Democratic nomination, he would be killed. (*Larry King Live*, CNN, December 20, 1968.)

Liz shares a look with Al and Numa.

AL Boss, with Broussard they have everything. All our witnesses, our strategy for the trial. We'd have to doublecheck all his work, there could be false leads ... we gotta rethink this trial. We don't have a choice.

JIM I don't think so, Al. You remember the Hemingway story, "The Old Man and the Sea"? (*Al nods*) The old fisherman manages to catch this great fish—a fish so huge he has to tie it to the side of the boat to get it back in. But by the time he reached shore, the fish had long since been picked apart by sharks and nothing was left but the skeleton.

NUMA Then what are we going through all this trouble for?

JIM It's a means to an end. This war has two fronts—in the court of law, we hope, against the odds, to nail Clay Shaw on a conspiracy charge. In the court of public opinion, it could take another 25 or 30 years for the truth to come out, but at least we're going to strike the first blow.

LIZ And if you're wrong?

JIM (*rising*) I never doubted for a second that I was. (*softly:*) Will you come to the trial, Elizabeth?

LIZ I don't think so, Jim ...

She walks out.

We see the outside of Jim's house and hear crickets chirping—the purr of the suburb. Inside, the TV election results are still on.

NEWSMAN 1 With 53% of the precincts reporting, Senator Kennedy continues to hold a lead of 48% to 41% over Senator McCarthy. CBS News has projected Senator Robert Kennedy the winner of the crucial California primary.

Jim is in the kitchen fixing himself a sandwich. There's a strange feeling in the house. We hear the wind—a shutter sighing. Jim suddenly doesn't feel alone in the kitchen.

ROBERT KENNEDY (*voice-over on TV*) ... and that is what has been going on within the United States over the last three years—the division, the violence, the disenchantment, whether it's between blacks and whites, between poor and the more affluent, or between age groups or the war in Vietnam—we can start to work together. We are a great country, an unselfish country and a compassionate country. I intend to make that my basis for running.

He waves and leaves the podium, going back through the kitchen of the hotel. Jim is frozen in his spot, shaken. The ghost of Jack Kennedy—as he was before the killing—stares at him through the kitchen, as if encased in a hologram. The hooded eyes watch Jim without expression. They're communicating, in some strange subliminal way. Suddenly shots ring out from the television and there's pandemonium.

NEWSMAN 1 (*shaken*) SENATOR KENNEDY HAS BEEN SHOT! WE DO NOT KNOW HOW SERIOUS IT IS YET. SENATOR KENNEDY HAS BEEN SHOT.

The television shows a scene of confusion. Jim walks out, looking at the TV, struck down with his foreknowledge and his inability to do anything about it.

In their bedroom upstairs that night, Jim gently wakes Liz and holds her.

JIM They killed him, honey.

LIZ (*groggily*) Huh?

JIM (*strangled*) He won ... and they killed Robert Kennedy. They shot him down ...

LIZ (*realizing, with terror*) Oh no! No! I can't believe it. I can't believe it. Both of them, both brothers, oh my God! ...

She clings to him, horrified. He caresses her hair. They look in each other's eyes.

LIZ You're right, it hasn't ended, has it? ...

He kisses her gently—They start to make love, numbed, needing each other, needing their love in an increasingly terrifying world.

JIM (*awkward*) I wish I could've loved you more ... I feel sometimes like I didn't ever ... love you or the children enough ... I'm sorry.

▋ Many critics of *J.F.K.*—most notably *Nightline* host Ted Koppel—have pointed to this scene as an example of our "dishonesty." We condensed the timeframe of the R.F.K. assassination to show what we felt was important:

the effect of the second Kennedy murder on Jim Garrison. Sen. Robert Kennedy was shot after 11 P.M. Pacific time, which would have been after 1 A.M. in New Orleans. Although Kennedy's final speech and the shooting weren't broadcast live, it was showing on the networks within hours. Right away it was clear from the severity of the head wound that Kennedy would not live. He died some 28 hours later. In our scene, Jim (who is, as usual, working into the early morning hours) sees footage of the chaos at the Ambassador Hotel, hears the announcer saying "Senator Kennedy has been shot" (we never claim the footage is live) and he goes upstairs to tell his wife that "they killed Robert Kennedy." We do not feel that we compromised the "truth" of the incident.

OUTSIDE THE COURTS BUILDING - NEW ORLEANS - (JAN. 1969)

The scene is a like a circus. Armed, uniformed guards with walkie-talkies are every-where. Guards with rifles are on the rooftop. There are crowds of reporters from around the world and many onlookers. Everyone going into the courtroom is frisked by electronic metal detectors.

INSIDE THE COURTROOM

Jim, accompanied by Mattie, the maid, but not his wife, forges his way through a tightly packed crowd to the prosecution table, joining Al, Susie, Numa, and others from his team. Young law students have come to watch. The crowd is noisy to the point of unruliness. Suddenly there's a hush as everyone cranes their necks to see Clay Shaw and his attorneys, Irvin Dymond and two others, enter the court. Shaw, impeccably dressed, his high handsome cheekbones sucking on an ever-present cigarette in a porce-lain filter (smoking in court was allowed then), smiles to those who greet him as if they were not really there and limps past Jim with a stoney indifference.

The clerk starts pounding the gavel to call the court to order as Judge Edward Aloysius Haggerty sweeps in and takes the bench. He's a stocky little Jimmy Cagney look alike with fierce blue eyes under bushy brows. The jurors—nine white men and three black men—all dressed in suits and ties, look on.

CUT TO Willie O'Keefe pointing out Clay Shaw.

▌ Trial: State of Louisiana vs. Clay Shaw, Criminal District Court, Parish of Orleans, #198-059 1425(30) Session "C," ran from February 1, 1969 through March 1, 1969. The court reporters, Dietrich & Bendix Inc., retained the transcripts after the trial ended in an acquittal (the court keeps only records of convictions) and made them available to us for this project. Garrison did not conduct the bulk of the trial. Assistant D.A.s James Alcock and Alvin Oser did most of the questioning and cross-examination. Both New Orleans newspapers, the now-defunct *States-Item* and the *Times-Picayune*, covered the trial very thoroughly. Another good source for the actual court proceedings is James Kirkwood's *American Grotesque*, an extensive, if terribly biased (Kirkwood is a confidant of Shaw's and knows little about the J.F.K. case), account of the trial.

O'KEEFE That's Clay Bertrand. That's the man I saw at David Ferrie's.

Irvin Dymond cross-examines O'Keefe.

DYMOND (*words wafting*) That's who you *say* you saw ... a confessed homosexual, convicted of solicitation, pandering ... a man who has lied about most everything, who ...

▌ "...a man who has lied": Perry Russo—one of the real life characters that make up Willie O'Keefe—failed a polygraph test administered by Garrison's staff (Brener, *The Garrison Case*, p. 109; Edward J. Epstein, *Garrison's Case*, *The New Yorker*, July 13, 1968). The District Attorney's office lacked corroboration for Russo's testimony about the party at which "Bertrand," Ferrie and "Leon Oswald" discussed the assassination. Garrison subpoenaed several individuals that Russo named as also present at the party, but the extradition requests were refused (see notes, p. 131). By putting Russo on the stand, Garrison ran the risk of seeing Russo's story—which the District Attorney honestly believed—fall apart under cross-examination.

Polygraph results are rarely admissible in court because they are not considered reliable.

TIME CUT TO Vernon Bundy, a poor black man, who points at Shaw.

BUNDY It was that man there, yessir. He was at the Pontchartrain wall with the man who shot the President. I remember him cause o' his limp there ...

DYMOND ... a heroin addict, injecting himself at the wall, barely conscious ...

▌ Vernon Bundy: [*New Orleans States-Item*, Feb. 8, 1969, p. 2; Kirkwood, *American Grotesque*, p. 225-230.] According to court reporter Helen R. Dietrich, Bundy's testimony was taken by hand and never transcribed because the case ended in an acquittal. However, Bundy testified at the Grand Jury hearing and that transcript is available (Criminal District Court for the Parish of New Orleans, No. M-703, Clay L. Shaw, Arrestee, March 14-17, 1967).

TIME CUT TO Jim looking over at a strange man, Matthews, a kind of lawyer, making notes and conferring with Shaw and Dymond. Matthews seems to have some authority over both men.

Corrie Collins, a black woman who is one of the CORE workers from Clinton, is on the stand.

COLLINS (*pointing at Shaw*) ... that was the man there. He dropped Oswald off on the voter line. I remember 'cause they were the only white strangers around that morning. That big, black Cadillac of his made me think they might be FBI.

TIME CUT TO the Town Marshall on the stand.

TOWN MARSHALL (*looking at Shaw*) ... said he was a representative of one International Trade Mart in New Orleans.

DYMOND ... more than five years ago, for two minutes. It's fair to say you could be mistaken, isn't it?

▌ Clinton witnesses: [State of Louisiana vs. Clay L. Shaw, testimony given February 6-7, 1969 by Corrie Collins, Willie Dunn, Henry E. Palmer, John Manchester.] The HSCA interviewed the Clinton witnesses and decided they were "telling the truth as they knew it...If these witnesses were not only truthful but accurate as well in their accounts, they established an association of an undisclosed nature between Ferrie, Shaw and Oswald less than three months before the assassination." [HSCA Report, p. 142-143.] While many researchers feel that the "Shaw" figure could have been Banister, Registrar of Voters Henry E. Palmer testified that he knew Guy Banister (they served in the Navy together) and claimed he would have recognized him.

TIME CUT TO Dymond cross-examining Dean Andrews, shaking his head.

ANDREWS ... figment of my imagination ... The cat's stewing me, the oyster's shucking me I told him, you got the right ta-ta but the wrong ho-ho ... Bertrand is not Shaw, scout's honor and you can tell him I said so ...

SUSIE (*counter-arguing*) Objection, your Honor. This office has won a conviction of perjury against Dean Andrews on this matter

> ∎ Perjury charge - Dean Andrews: Garrison's office won a conviction of perjury against Andrews on the grounds that he was lying when he said that he did not know who "Clay Bertrand" was. Garrison eventually dismissed the charges, due in part to Andrews' fear that he would not live through a six-month sentence because of his serious heart condition. Andrews died in 1970 of heart disease. [Garrison, *On the Trail of the Assassins*, p. 243 fn.]

DYMOND Exception taken. That case is on appeal!

Arguments follow.

TIME CUT TO Charles Goldberg, a mild-looking New York accountant, on the stand with Dymond cross-examining.

DYMOND (*relishing this*) Mr. Goldberg, you claim you met David Ferrie and Clay Shaw while on a vacation here from your accounting business in New York, you had drinks and, under the influence discussed killing Kennedy, is that not so?

GOLDBERG I did.

DYMOND (*consulting his paperwork*) Is it not also true that you fingerprinted your daughter when she left New York to go to Louisiana State University?

GOLDBERG Yes, I did ... .

Jim stunned, looks at Susie and Al, who are equally puzzled. A sinking feeling pervades them.

DYMOND Is it not also true that you fingerprinted her when she returned at the end of the semester?

GOLDBERG I did.

DYMOND Why?

GOLDBERG Well, I wanted to make sure she's the same girl I sent.

DYMOND I see ... and why are you experiencing this paranoia?

GOLDBERG (*launching into his explanation*) Well, you see, I've been subject to hypnosis and psychological warfare ever since 1948, when I was in Korea ...

We see the faces of people in the courtroom ... the judge's face ... obviously Goldberg is disturbed (or maybe he is telling the truth, but it doesn't play well) ... Jim looks at Al sickly.

AL He was one of Broussard's witnesses, chief. I'm sorry. He was totally sane when we took his affidavit.

SUSIE But how does Dymond know what to ask? FUCK! We're dead.

GOLDBERG ... when someone tries to get your attention—catch your eye—that's a clue right off.

> ■ Charles Goldberg: (real name - Charles Spiesel) [*New Orleans States-Item*, February 8-9, 1969. James Kirkwood, *American Grotesque* (Simon & Schuster, 1968) p. 231-248.] Kirkwood relates how the defense was tipped off to Spiesel by reporter Hugh Aynesworth (cf. note page 95). Aynesworth said the idea that Spiesel was a nut came to him "as he awakened from a dream" and he called the Shaw defense team to offer the names of some investigators in New York to contact about getting information on Spiesel (p.248). A very timely—and very suspect—dream.
>
> At first, Shaw attorney Irvin Dymond felt that Spiesel was a credible and damaging witness. In a speech to the Chicago Executives Club, Dymond called Spiesel "one of the most impressive, apparently truth-telling witnesses I have ever seen in my life." The defense received the file on Spiesel from the investigator recommended by Aynesworth just minutes before the cross-examination began. (Irvin Dymond, "Clay Shaw's Defense Attorney Relives Events Connected with Trial," Executives Club Newsletter, Chicago, IL, May 9, 1969, p. 4.) There is a good chance that Spiesel was telling the truth about meeting Shaw and Ferrie at a party. When asked to show the jury where the gathering he claimed to have attended took place, he led them to two identical buildings on Esplanade St. and said he was sure it was one of two. As it turned out, Shaw used to own one of the buildings, and at one time had an apartment in the back. [Kirkwood, *American Grotesque*, p. 634.]

TIME CUT TO Jim calling Officer Habighorst to testify.

GARRISON Your Honor, I call police officer Aloysius Habighorst to the stand.

Habighorst, the clean-cut police officer who booked Clay Shaw on the day of his arrest, starts forward.

JUDGE HAGGERTY I'm going to have to ask the jury to leave the courtroom.

JIM What!

This is an ugly surprise for Jim. We see him at the bench arguing loudly with the judge. Susie, Dymond and Al are also there.

JUDGE HAGGERTY I'm sorry, Jim, but the defendant did not have his lawyer present when asked.

FLASHBACK TO 1967, in the New Orleans police station. Shaw is being booked. The press is there and Habighorst is questioning him.

HABIGHORST Any aliases?

SHAW Clay Bertrand.

We see a close-up on Habighorst typing this in.

JIM (*voice-over*) Jesus, Ed, from time immemorial it's been standard booking procedure to ask an alias. You know that. There's no constitutional requirement that says a lawyer has to be present for routine questions.

JUDGE I call 'em as I see 'em, Jim. I'm ruling it inadmissable.

JIM That's our case!

JUDGE If that's your case, you didn't have a case. I wouldn't believe whatever Habighorst said, anyway.

JIM I can't believe you're saying this in the courtroom.

JUDGE (*feistier*) Well, I *am* saying it. Bring in the jury.

AL We're filing for a writ to the appellate court.

JUDGE You do that.

■ Habighorst proceedings: booking card inadmissable [State of Louisiana v. Clay L. Shaw, Habighorst testimony, February 19, 1969. Kirkwood, *American Grotesque*, p. 354-355. Garrison, *Trail of the Assassins*, p. 236-237]. The Habighorst proceedings were a crucial point in the trial. The three booking cards filled out at the police station on the night of Shaw's arrest had "Clay Bertrand" typed in the space marked "Alias." Officer Habighorst claimed that Shaw freely offered the information. The defense, however, charged that Shaw's attorney had not been present at the time of the questioning— not required for routine questioning and in any case, the attorney was standing about 20 feet away. Shaw denied ever giving an alias to Habighorst, and Judge Haggerty simply said he didn't believe the policeman. Garrison was not liked by the police, making it doubtful that they did him a favor by typing in "Bertrand." Furthermore, when Garrison's assistants questioned Shaw on the matter, he admitted that he could see Habighorst's typewriter and that Habighorst typed on the forms only in direct response to Shaw's answers to his questions—Habighorst did not add the alias on his own.

Dymond goes back to Shaw, very pleased. Shaw smokes, icy. Jim, devastated, sits, feeling it's over.

CUT TO Clay Shaw on the stand. Dymond cross-examines him.

DYMOND ... Oswald?

SHAW No, I did not.

DYMOND ... ever called Dean Andrews?

SHAW No, I did not.

DYMOND ... and have you ever met David Ferrie?

SHAW (*with a smirk of amusement*) No, I would not even know what he looked like except for the pictures I've been shown.

DYMOND ... did you ever use the alias Clay Bertrand?

SHAW No, I did not.

DYMOND Thank you ... Mr. Shaw.

> ▌Shaw testimony: State of Louisiana vs. Clay L. Shaw, testimony of Clay Shaw, February 27, 1969. [Kirkwood, *American Grotesque*, p. 403-411.]

Jim rises slowly out of his chair.

JIM Well, a very great actor has just given us a great performance, Your Honor, but we are nowhere closer to the truth. Let it be noted, my office is charging Clay Shaw with outright perjury on the fifteen answers he has given, not one word of this ...

> ▌Shaw perjury charges: [Garrison, *On the Trail of the Assassins*, p. 252-253.] On March 3, 1969, Garrison filed perjury charges against Shaw, specifically "with having testified under oath that he never met David Ferrie...We had more witnesses to prove this flagrant case of perjury than I had ever encountered as a district attorney." (Garrison, p. 252.) A federal court blocked the proceedings and Garrison lost on subsequent appeals. In the end, however, it seems that Garrison was right. There is ample evidence available now that proves that Shaw lied on the stand about his association with the CIA (see notes p. 184) and his relationship with David Ferrie (see notes p. 81).

JUDGE You're out of order, Jim Boy, now sit down. Strike those remarks!!

CUT TO later in the trial. A movie screen has been installed for the jury. Jim paces dramatically, as if waiting, casting looks at the door. Members of the press pack the hot room, and a fan turns overhead.

JIM To prove there was a conspiracy involving Clay Shaw we must prove there was more than one man involved in the assassination. To do that, we must look at the Zapruder film, which my office has subpoenaed. The American public has not seen that film because it has been kept locked in a vault in the Time-Life Building in New York City for the last five years. There is a reason for that. Watch.

> ▌Zapruder film locked in a vault: *Time-Life* bought the worldwide, all-media rights to the Zapruder film for the princely sum of $150,000. Originally, they just bought the print rights, a sensible decision seeing as they only published magazines, but when *Life* publisher C.D. Jackson saw the film, he found it so disturbing that he asked the company to snap up all rights and withhold it from public viewing "at least until emotions had calmed" (Richard Stolley, "The Greatest Home Movie Ever Made," *Esquire*, November 1973).

C.D. Jackson, then the publisher of *Life*, had a very interesting background. In a 1977 *Rolling Stone* article, reporter Carl Bernstein called Jackson "Henry Luce's personal emissary to the CIA." Jackson had served as Eisenhower's Cold War propaganda adviser, providing CIA employees with *Time-Life* credentials as cover. [Carl Bernstein, "The CIA and the Media," *Rolling Stone*, October 20, 1977, p. 63; see Peter Dale Scott, *Crime and Cover-Up*, for more on Jackson.]

Garrison's subpoena resulted in the first public showing of the film. *Time-Life* handed over the film reluctantly, and at the end of the trial, put it back in its vault, perhaps still waiting for emotions to subside.

In 1975, researcher Robert Groden and newsman Geraldo Rivera gave the film its first network television showing. It was a huge success, moving many people—including congressmen—to fight for a new investigation. In 1975 *Time-Life* (having never used the film except for stills) quietly sold their huge investment back to the Zapruder family for $1. [Anson, *They've Killed the President!*, p. 82-85; Groden, "A New Look At the Zapruder Film," *Government by Gunplay*, p. 3-9.]

The Zapruder film (8mm) now rolls. We have seen pieces of it before in the opening of the film, but now we see it whole. It is crucial that this piece of film be repeated several times during the trial to drive home a point that is easily lost on casual viewing. The first viewing is silent except for the sound of the clanky projector. It lasts about 25 seconds, and then the lights come on. The jury is shaken. The judge is shaken. The people in the courtroom murmur. Even Clay Shaw is surprised at what he has seen. Jim says nothing, letting the truth of it sink in. Then:

JIM A picture speaks a thousand words. Yet sometimes the truth is too simple for some ... The Warren Commission thought they had an open and shut case: three bullets, one assassin—but two things happened that made it virtually impossible: 1) the Zapruder film which you just saw, and 2) the third wounded man, Jim Tague, who was nicked by a fragment down by the Triple Underpass. The time frame of 5.6 seconds established by the Zapruder film left no possibility of a fourth shot from Oswald's rifle, but the shot or fragment that left a superficial wound on Tague's cheek had to come from a bullet that missed the car entirely. Now they had two bullets that hit, and we know one of them was the fatal head shot. So a single bullet remained to account for all seven wounds in Kennedy and Connally. But rather than admit to a conspiracy or investigate further, the Commissioners chose to endorse the theory put forth by an ambitious junior counselor, Arlen Specter. One of the grossest lies ever forced on the American people, we've come to know it as the "magic bullet" theory.

CUT TO a drawing which has been put on a chair for the Jury. Jim has also moved Al, acting as J.F.K., into a chair directly behind the larger Numa, acting as Governor Connally. He demonstrates with a pointer.

JIM ... the magic bullet enters the President's back, headed downward at an angle of 17 degrees. It then moves upward in order to leave Kennedy's body from the front of his neck—his neck wound number two—where it waits 1.6 seconds, turns right and continues into Connally's body at the rear of his right armpit—wound number three. Then, the bullet heads downward at an angle of 27 degrees, shattering Connally's fifth rib and leaving from the right side of his chest—wounds four and five. The bullet continues downward and then enters Connally's right wrist—wound number six—shattering the radius bone. It then enters his left thigh—wound number seven—from which it later falls out and is found in almost "pristine" condition on a stretcher in a corridor of Parkland Hospital. (*he shows a mock-up of the "pristine" bullet*) That's some bullet. Anyone who's been in combat can tell you never in the history of gunfire has there been a bullet like this (*the court laughs*). The Army Wound Ballistics experts at Edgewood Arsenal fired some comparison bullets and not one of them looked anything like this one. (*he shows mock-ups of comparison bullets*). Take a look at CE 856, an identical bullet fired through the wrist of a human cadaver—just one of the bones smashed by the magic bullet. Yet the government says it can prove this with some fancy physics in a nuclear laboratory. Of course they can. Theoretical physics can prove an elephant can hang from a cliff with its tail tied to a daisy, but use your eyes—your common sense—(*he holds the bullet*) seven wounds, skin, bone. This single bullet explanation is the *foundation* of the Warren Commission's claim of a lone assassin. And once you conclude the magic bullet could not create all seven of those wounds, you have to *conclude there was a fourth shot and a second rifleman*. And if there was a second rifleman, there had to be a conspiracy, which we believe involved the accused Clay Shaw. Fifty-one witnesses, gentlemen of the jury, thought they heard shots coming from the Grassy Knoll, which is to the right and front of the President ...

▌Tague shot had to miss car entirely [Epstein, *Inquest*, p. 84-86; Marrs, *Crossfire*, p. 60-64.]: The Warren Commission could not decide which shot missed and laid out a scenario for each bullet missing the car entirely in their Report [WR p. 111-117]. Tague himself said that he thought it was the second shot that struck the curb in front of him [WC 7H, p. 555]. The HSCA concluded that the first shot missed [HSCA Report, p. 41].

Tague was standing on Main Street at the Triple Underpass when he was nicked on the face by an apparent bullet fragment or by a fragment of the curb. Although Tague reported the incident to a Dallas deputy sheriff [WC 7H p. 546] and to the Dallas police [WC 7H p. 556], there is no mention of Tague in CE 2003, the police report on the assassination. Two newsmen photographed the damaged curb a few days later, were questioned by the FBI and were later called to testify to the Warren Commission. They were asked no questions about the curb. The FBI summary report of December 9, 1963 maintains that there were three shots and all three bullets hit the car.

Tague did not appear before the Commission until July 23, 1964. In the Report, the Commission admitted: "the mark on the south curb of Main Street cannot be identified conclusively with any of the three shots fired" [WR p. 117]. It is quite obvious that neither the Commission nor its investigative agencies properly entertained the possibility that Tague was injured by a fourth shot.

▌Arlen Specter & the magic bullet: [Epstein, *Inquest*, p. 116-125; Thompson, *Six Seconds in Dallas*, p. 201-212.]

■ Bullet/wound trajectories: [Thompson, *Six Seconds in Dallas*, p. 115-140; HSCA II p. 161-191.]

■ "Pristine" bullet: Only 2.4 grains (1.5 percent of the total intact weight) are missing from WC, CE 399 [Thompson, *Six Seconds in Dallas*, p. 201-209] The ammunition test-fired for comparison by the Warren Commission was not so pristine (see below).

Supporters of the Warren Commission and the HSCA's confirmation of the single bullet theory like to assert that the government panels proved via neutron activation analysis (usually abbreviated NAA and regarded as a highly precise method of identifying metal fragments) that the bullet fragments removed from Governor Connally's wrist came from CE 399. However, this is a false claim.

The Warren Commission did not acknowledge having done any NAA tests in their volumes. In 1973, a declassified memo to the Commission from J. Edgar Hoover dated July 8, 1964, stated that the bullet fragments had undergone NAA. Hoover's convoluted wording does its best to obscure the important non-conclusion reached by these tests. He admits that there were "minor variations in composition" that prevented "positively determining" which bullet the fragment came from. In other words, the tests did not prove that the wrist fragments matched CE 399. Subsequent FOIA suits for the actual test data were unsuccessful—this information is important because NAA does not tolerate much in the way of "minor variations": it measures the concentration of elements to less than a billionth of a gram [Anson, *They've Killed the President!*, p. 91-92; Dr. Cyril Wecht, "J.F.K. Assassination: A Prolonged and Willful Coverup," *Modern Medicine*, October 28, 1974].

The HSCA performed NAA tests on the wrist fragments and reached a verdict of "highly likely," not "definite," for a good reason: the HSCA had no proof that the fragments tested actually came from Connally's wrist. The Committee retained Dr. Vincent P. Guinn who had performed the tests for the Warren Commission. Dr. Guinn noted in his report to the Committee that the fragments the FBI had given him for testing were definitely not the same fragments he tested in 1964 (they differed in weight). The National Archives assured Guinn and the FBI that these were the only fragments they had—they had no ideas what happened to the original set [HSCA I. p. 562].

On the way out of the HSCA hearing room, Dr. Guinn told a researcher a hypothetical scenario for the origin of the fragments:

"Possibly (the FBI) would take a bullet, take out a few little pieces and say, 'This is what came out of Connally's wrist.' And naturally, if you compare it with CE 399, it will look alike... I have no control over these things" [taped interview with David Lifton, September 9, 1978, cited by Hurt, *Reasonable Doubt*, p. 83].

Most recently, former HSCA Chief Counsel G. Robert Blakey told *New York Newsday* reporter Robert Greene that the "bullet and slivers checked by his experts are identical to those examined by the Warren Commission" and that researcher's claims to the contrary are "nonsense" [*Newsday*, March 29, 1992]. Clearly, as evidenced above, this is not true, at least according to the HSCA's own published material.

To sum up, the HSCA's NAA tests did not settle any doubts about CE 399 but instead raised new ones about the honesty of the FBI, the credibility of G. Robert Blakey and the safekeeping abilities of the National Archives. Twenty-eight years after the assassination, there is still no evidence that CE 399 hit either Connally or Kennedy. The bullet was never tracked through Kennedy's back or throat (see testimony of Dr. Pierre Finck, p. 158) and therefore, no bullet fragments were removed. Nor was any blood or tissue from either man found on the bullet. [WC 3H p. 428-429.]

▪ Edgewood arsenal comparisons: [Meagher, *Accessories*, p. 106-110 WC, CE 853 (fired through goat carcass); WC, CE 856 (fired through human wrist bone); Thompson, *Six Seconds in Dallas*, p. 151-152.]

▪ Fifty-one Grassy Knoll witnesses [Harold Feldman, "51 Witnesses: The Grassy Knoll," *Minority of One*, March 1965.]

Jim walks to a drawing of an overhead view of Dealey Plaza. On it are dots representing locations of the witnesses. He points to each portion. He pauses and looks out into the courtroom—Liz has entered accompanied by Jasper. Quietly she takes a seat. Jim is unbelieving at first, then very moved. He takes a beat, then:

JIM Key witnesses that day—Charles Brehm, a combat vet, right behind Jean Hill and Mary Moorman, S.M. Holland and Richard Dodd on the overpass, J.C. Price overlooking the whole Plaza, Richard Randolph Carr, a steelworker, who served in the Rangers in North Africa, William Newman, father of two children who hit the deck on the north side of Elm, Abraham Zapruder, James Simmons—each of these key witnesses has *no doubt whatsoever one or more shots* came from *behind* the picket fence! Twenty-six trained medical personnel at Parkland Hospital saw with their own eyes the back of the President's head blasted out.

▪ A good map of eyewitnesses in Dealy Plaza is found in Josiah Thompson's *Six Seconds in Dallas*, p. 252-271.

▪ Charles Brehm: [WC, CE 1425; CE 1003, p. 250; Decker Exhibit 5323, p. 526.]

▪ Richard Randolph Carr: [State of Louisiana vs. Clay L. Shaw, February 19, 1969 (Carr testimony); Thompson, *Six Seconds in Dallas*, p. 241-2, 244.]

▪ James Simmons: [Marrs, *Crossfire*, p. 58-59; Thompson, *Six Seconds in Dallas*, p. 121; WC 22H p. 833.]

CUT TO Dr. Peters on the stand.

PETERS (*describing the wound*) ... a large 7 cm opening in the right occipitoparietal area, a considerable portion of the brain was missing there. (*he gestures to his head*)

▪ Dr. Peters statement: [David Lifton, *Best Evidence: Disguise and Deception in the Assassination of John F. Kennedy*, (Macmillan, 1980) p. 323-325.]

CUT TO Dr. McClelland on the stand.

MCCLELLAND ... almost a fifth or perhaps a quarter of the back of the head—this area here (*he indicates his head*)—had been blasted out along with the brain tissue there. The exit hole in the rear of his head was about 120 mm. across. There was also a large piece of skull attached to a flap of scalp in the right temporal area.

> ■ Dr. McClelland statement: [WC 6H p. 33.] "I was in such a position that I could clearly examine the head wound. I noted the right posterior portion of the skull had been blasted." Interview of McClelland by Robert Groden, 1991 [Josiah Thompson, *Six Seconds in Dallas*, p. 107.]

FLASHBACK TO Parkland Hospital Emergency Room on that day in 1963. The doctors work on the President. The wounds on the back of his head are evident but will change later in the autopsy. He is placed into a bronze casket.

JIM (*voice-over*) Not one of the civilian doctors who examined the President at Parkland Hospital regarded his throat wound as anything but a wound of entry. The doctors found no wounds of entry in the back of the head. But the body was then illegally moved to Washington for the autopsy.

> ■ Parkland doctors—throat wound, no entry in back of head: [Thompson, *Six Seconds in Dallas*, p. 51-54 Meagher, *Accessories After the Fact*, p. 149-169.]

CUT TO the Secret Service team preparing to wheel the casket out. The Dallas Medical Examiner, Dr. Rose, backed by a justice of the peace, bars the way. A furious wrestling match ensues.

MEDICAL EXAMINER ... Texas Law, sir, requires the autopsy be done here. You're not taking him with you!

KENNY O'DONNELL Sonofabitch, you're not telling me what to do! Get the hell outta the way!

> ■ Removing body from Parkland: [WC 3H p. 96-97 (testimony of Roy H. Kellerman, Secret Service); Lifton, *Best Evidence*, p. 389-390; Manchester, *Death of a President.*]

The Secret Service agents put the doctor and judge up against the wall at gunpoint and sweep out of the hospital.

JIM (*voice-over*) ... because when a coup d'état has occurred there's a big difference between an autopsy performed by civilian doctors and one by military doctors working for the government.

FLASHBACK TO Love Field the same day. We see Air Force One taking off and a photo of L.B.J. being sworn in.

JIM (*voice-over*) The departure of Air Force One from Love Field that Friday afternoon was not so much a takeoff as it was a getaway with the newly sworn in President ...

DYMOND (*voice-over*) Objection, your honor.

JUDGE Sustained.

JIM (*voice-over*) On the plane, of course, Lee Harvey Oswald's guilt was announced. by the White House Situation Room to the passengers before any kind of investigation had started. The "lone nut" solution is in place.

DYMOND (*voice-over*) Objection! Your Honor!

JUDGE Sustained. Mr. Garrison, would you please ... bottle the acid.

FLASHBACK TO the Bethesda autopsy room in 1963. The room is crammed with military officers, Secret Service men and, at the center, three intimidated doctors. Pictures are being taken as they remove bullet fragments.

JIM The three Bethesda Naval Hospital doctors picked by the Military left something to be desired inasmuch as none of them had experience with combat gunfire wounds. Through their autopsy we have been able to justify eight wounds—three to Kennedy, five to Connally—from just 2 bullets, one of these bullets the "magic bullet."

▌Situation Room: [Manchester, *The Death of a President*, p. 224.] Bethesda Naval Hospital Autopsy:

CD7, known as the "Sibert-O'Neill Report," is a report on the autopsy by two FBI agents in attendance. The five-page document contains a list of those present at the autopsy as well as critical information about the autopsy procedures. From the Sibert-O'Neill Report, researchers learned (1) exactly how many and what type of x-rays and photographs were taken, (2) that the back wound was really located "below the shoulders and two inches to the right of the spinal column" not in the "back of the neck" as the official autopsy report claimed, (3) that autopsy pathologist Commander James J. Humes probed the President's back wound with his finger, found that the hole was about two inches deep and said that the bullet did not exit at all and must have worked its way out during cardiac massage in Dallas.

The third point is crucial: if the bullet that hit Kennedy's back did not exit, there is no single bullet theory. A second set of FBI documents, the Gemberling documents, confirm the Sibert-O'Neill claim that the bullet did not exit. One of the documents, an FBI teletype, concerns a Dallas newspaper report on the as-yet-unreleased autopsy findings. The Dallas paper said the bullet entered the back and exited the throat (the single bullet scenario); the FBI found this in conflict with agent Robert Gemberling's report that the bullet only penetrated two inches into the back.

Commission counsel Arlen Specter must have realized that the Sibert-O'Neill Report could negate his single bullet theory. He questioned the two agents on March 12, 1964. Both Sibert and O'Neill reinforced their claim, telling Specter that Dr. Humes and Dr. Finck felt that the bullet did not exit. [Administrative Records, J. Lee Rankin: December, 1963-March 1964, cited in Thompson, *Six Seconds in Dallas*, p. 45fn.] Somehow, Specter stuck with his magic bullet.

In April, 1964, the commission rounded up the three autopsy doctors, the Edgewood Arsenal ballistics experts, and several Commission counsels, including Mr. Specter, in order to clarify the lingering questions about the shooting sequence. The idea was to watch the Zapruder film and determine at which frames the first and second shots struck.

Counsel Melvin Eisenberg reported the "consensus": (1) No one believed that the bullet recovered from the stretcher could have penetrated Connally's wrist. (2) They felt if Connally was struck by the first bullet (the one they said hit Kennedy in the back), he was "probably also hit by the second bullet." (3) They expressed doubt that Connally was "ever in a position such that one bullet could have caused the five wounds he sustained." Mr. Specter noted his dissent from the majority opinion in this last point. [Memo from Eisenberg to Warren Commission, April 22, 1964.]

A final note on the location of the back wound. Although the Warren Report stated that the President was struck in the back of the neck, the Commissioners knew it wasn't true. In the minutes of the Executive Session of January 27, 1964, J. Lee Rankin broaches the troubling matter of the back wound:

"... since we have the picture of where the bullet entered in the back, that the bullet entered below the shoulder blade to the right of the backbone, which is below the place where the bullet came out in the neckband of the shirt in front ..."

Faced with the extreme improbability of a shot entering the back at a downward trajectory and exiting at a point more than six inches higher with an upward trajectory, the Commission chose to "relocate" the back wound to the back of the neck, a straight line through to the frontal neck wound [see drawing CE 385]. The Commission officially claimed not to have seen the autopsy photos; we know that at the very least, Chief Council Rankin took a look at them.

CUT TO Jim in court with a series of drawings indicating with arrows entry and exit wounds to Kennedy's neck and head. Dr. Finck is on the stand, erect, very precise, and irritated.

▌Dr. Pierre Finck: Dr. Finck was a lieutenant colonel in the U.S. Army, the head of the Wound Ballistics Section of the Armed Forces Institute of Pathology and, unlike Drs. James J. Humes and J. Thornton Boswell, a member of the American Academy of Forensic Sciences. Dr. Humes called him in to observe and assist after the autopsy was already underway. Although Finck was more experienced in forensic pathology than the others, his role in the proceedings was severely restricted. As he testified in New Orleans, "there were admirals [present], and when you are a lieutenant colonel in the Army you just follow orders." [See State of Louisiana vs. Clay L. Shaw, testimony of Dr. Pierre Finck, February 24-25, 1969; WC 2H p. 377-384 (Finck testimony); Garrison, *Trail of the Assassins*, p. 243-249; Finck appears in the London Weekend Television production "The Trial of Lee Harvey Oswald."]

JIM Colonel Finck, are you saying someone told you not to dissect the neck?

FINCK I was told that the family wanted examination of the head.

JIM As a pathologist it was your obligation to explore all possible causes of death, was it not?

FINCK I *had* the cause of death.

JIM Your Honor, I would ask you to direct the witness to answer my question. Why did Colonel Finck not dissect the track of the bullet wound in the neck?

FINCK Well I heard Dr. Humes stating that—he said ...

FLASHBACK TO Bethesda autopsy room.

HUMES Who's in charge here?

ARMY GENERAL I am.

FINCK (*voice-over*) I don't remember his name. You must understand it was quite crowded, and when you are called in circumstances like that to look at the wound of the President who is dead, you don't look around too much to ask people for their names and who they are.

JIM (*voice-over*) But you were a qualified pathologist. Was this Army general a qualified pathologist?

FINCK (*voice-over*) No.

JIM (*voice-over*) But you took his orders. He was directing the autopsy.

FINCK (*voice-over*) No, because there were others. There were admirals.

JIM (*voice-over*) There were admirals.

FINCK (*voice-over*) Oh yes, there were admirals—and when you are a lieutenant colonel in the Army you just follow orders, and at the end of the autopsy we were specifically told—as I recall it was Admiral Kenney, the Surgeon General of the Navy—we were specifically told not to discuss the case.

KENNEY (*in Bethesda scene*) Gentlemen, what you've seen in this room is intensely private to the Kennedy family and it is not our business to ...

Jim turns away from the jury. His point is made. Finck is no longer on the stand.

JIM In addition to which, 1) the chief pathologist, Commander Humes, by his own admission voluntarily burned his autopsy notes, 2) never released the autopsy photos to the public, 3) President Johnson ordered the blood-soaked limousine filled with bullet holes and clues to be immediately washed and rebuilt, 4) sent John Connally's bloody suit right to the cleaners, and 5) when my office finally got a court order to examine President Kennedy's brain in the National Archives in the hopes of finding from what direction the bullets came, we were told by the government the President's brain had *disappeared*!

▌ Commander Humes burns notes: [WC 3H p. 373.]

▌ Autopsy photos: [Hurt, *Reasonable Doubt*, p. 35-60, has a very good analysis of the medical and autopsy evidence.] In 1966, the Kennedy family placed the autopsy materials in the National Archives on the condition it not be made available to qualified researchers for five years. Garrison filed subpoenas to get the photos, x-rays and slides for the Shaw trial (in order to make his case against the single-gunman theory), but his request was denied [*New Orleans Times-Picayune*, "Court to Rule on DA Subpoena," January 16, 1969].

Shortly before Garrison's hearing on the autopsy material, Attorney General Ramsey Clark convened a super-secret panel of forensic pathologists to examine the photographs and x-rays. Although the panel did their work in February, 1968, their report was suppressed by Clark for nearly a year, an apparent attempt to block Garrison's move to obtain the medical evidence. [For more on the Clark Panel, see reprint in Weisberg, *Post-Mortem*; Evica, *And We Are All Mortal*, p. 91-92; Lifton, *Best Evidence*, p. 427-429.]

The Clark Panel confirmed the "official" findings—that J.F.K. was struck twice from behind—as did the Rockefeller Commission a few years later. Neither panel was being entirely honest. The Clark Panel maintained that Kennedy was shot in the back of the neck and the Rockefeller Panel confirmed the Warren Commission autopsy report while noting that the wound was really in the back, as indicated by the photos. They agreed wholeheartedly with the Warren Commission on the location of the head wound.

When the HSCA's medical panel looked at the same photos and x-rays in 1977, they too confirmed that "all shots were fired from behind." They did not, however, confirm the Warren Commission version of the wounds. The head wound had found a new location, or so it seemed, four inches higher up on the head, not at the base of the skull as in the Warren report [HSCA Report, p. 43]. When shown the autopsy photos and x-rays, all three Bethesda doctors insisted the purported entry wound near the crown was not what they observed in Bethesda. "I just don't know what it is but it is certainly not any wound of entrance." Dr. Humes said [HSCA VII p. 254.]

The HSCA should have cleared up this problem but didn't. The Committee did not show the photos and x-rays to the Dallas doctors who treated Kennedy at Parkland although they heard testimony from them, and incredibly, declined to question the Bethesda doctors because they "had come voluntarily" [HSCA VII, p. 243], an odd bit of behavior from an investigative body. The only doctor to have seen the body at both hospitals, White House physician Admiral George Burkely, was not questioned by either the HSCA or the Warren Commission.

As it stands now, neither the Dallas doctors nor the Bethesda doctors agree with the official HSCA location of the head wound. Put another way: no doctor who ever saw the president's body reported seeing an entry wound at the top rear of the head. The repeated failings of government panels to resolve even the most basic questions about the J.F.K. case—in this case, where the bullet wounds were—simply proves that a political body is not the proper forum for a homicide investigation.

▌Limo dismantled: The saga of the Kennedy limousine cast a few more doubts on the quality of the evidence in the J.F.K. case. The limo was left unattended outside the emergency room at Parkland. News footage—and later, photos published in *Life*'s November 1983 issue—showed a bucket of water beside the car. According to the caption, the car was being cleaned. Later that night, the car was shipped back to Washington where the FBI discovered two tiny bullet fragments (but failed to notice a dent on the inside trim of the windshield was cracked, ostensibly by a fragment). The frag-

ments were never marked for identification, so there is no way to be sure that the fragments admitted as evidence in the Commission Exhibits are really the fragments found in the car. [Hurt, *Reasonable Doubt*, p. 84 and citations; Weisberg, *Whitewash*, p. 297.]

A few days after the assassination, President Johnson requested bulletproof plating and glass for the car [WC 2H p. 65 (Kellerman testimony)]. Despite the renovations, Johnson never used the car during his term in office.

▌Connally suit sent to cleaners: [WC 5H p. 63-66, CD 827.]

▌Brain/material missing from archives: [*New York Times*, August 27, 1972.] Dr. Cyril Wecht, the first non-governmental forensic pathologist to view the autopsy materials at the National Archives, notified *New York Times* reporter Fred Graham about the apparently missing brain and slides. The evidence was last accounted for in 1966. Although other government-affiliated scientists, most notably the Clark Panel, had reviewed the medical evidence, they did not make public the disappearance of some of the most crucial materials. [Dr. Cyril Wecht, "Pathologist's View of the J.F.K. Autopsy: An Unsolved Case," *Modern Medicine*, November 27, 1972.]

There's a pause, and then a murmur from the court. Jim is on a roll and knows it. The faces in the courtroom are with him, absorbed, horrified. The law students are still there; they have been since day one. But it is Liz's interest that touches him the most.

JIM So what *really* happened that day? Let's just for a moment speculate, shall we? We have the epileptic seizure around 12:15 P.M. ... distracting the police, making it easier for the shooters to move into their places. The epileptic later vanished, never checking into the hospital. The A Team gets on the 6th floor of the Book Depository ...

▌Shooting scenario: Garrison lays out his own take on the events in Dealey Plaza on pages 280-284 of *Trail of the Assassins*. We draw from a wide range of other cited sources in our analysis.

▌Epileptic doesn't check into hospital: [CD 1245, FBI interview with ambulance driver Aubrey Rike; see notes p. 8.]

▌Sixth floor shooting team: Based on acoustics evidence, the HSCA concluded that three out of four total shots were fired from the vicinity of the southeast corner window of the Texas School Book Depository [HSCA Report, p. 51]. Scientists felt further tests might indicate some of these shots came from the nearby Dal-Tex building (cf. note below). Josiah Thompson's analysis indicated two shots were fired from the window [Thompson, *Six Seconds in Dallas*, p. 133-137]. Four witnesses told the Warren Commission that two men were in the sixth floor windows (cf. note p. 138) and numerous others reported seeing a rifle barrel sticking out from the infamous "sniper's perch" [Thompson, *Six Seconds in Dallas*, p. 135-135]. No witness descriptions of the men on the sixth floor implicated Oswald as the shooter.

FLASHBACK TO the Book Depository, 1963. A shooter and a two spotters dressed as working men move into the Oswald spot. One spotter produces the Mannlicher-Carcano.

JIM (*voice-over*) … They were refurbishing the floors in the Depository that week, which allowed unknown workmen in and out of the building. The men move quickly into position just minutes before the shooting.

The camera takes the shooter's point of view: we see down the street through a scope. His spotter wears a radio earpiece. The second spotter is working out of the southeast window.

JIM (*voice-over*) The second spotter is probably calling all the shots on a radio to the two other teams. He has the best overall view—"the God spot."

Inside the Dal-Tex Building, a shooter and a spotter dressed as air-conditioning men move into a small second-story textile storage room.

JIM (*voice-over*) B team—one rifleman and one spotter with a headset, with access to the building—moves into a low floor of the Dal-Tex Building.

  ▌Shooter in Dal-Tex building: This is based on the trajectory of the shot that hit Governor Connally. Thompson notes that several witnesses named the Dal-Tex building as the source of the shots and also that a young man was arrested by police in the Dal-Tex building minutes after the shooting [Thompson, *Six Seconds in Dallas*, p. 132]. The police and sheriffs who questioned the man did not make note of his name [WC 20H p. 49; WC 19H p. 526-527]. Even the HSCA's acoustics analysis couldn't rule out the Dal-Tex building as a firing point. The "Oswald" window is so close to the edge of the building that scientists noted that all shots but the third originated from the vicinity of the sixth floor "perch," but further testing might show the shots came from the Dal-Tex building just across Houston Street [Summers, *Conspiracy*, p. 21, citing HSCA VIII p. 5].

  ▌Grassy Knoll shooter: The HSCA's acoustics panel confirmed a 95% probability that the third shot came from behind the picket fence on the Grassy Knoll, to the right front of the President's car [HSCA Report, p.74] but that the shot fired from a distance of about 35 yards missed its target. The visual evidence from the Zapruder, Nix and Muchmore films says otherwise; the President's head snaps back as if shot from the right front.

  ▌Lee Bowers—2 men in railyard: [WC VI, p. 286-287; also Mark Lane and Emile D'Antonio, "Rush to Judgment."]

  ▌SS men on Knoll: [cf. notes p. 123.]

At the picket fence a shooter in a Dallas Police uniform moves into place, aiming up Elm Street. His spotter has a radio to his ear. Another man in a Secret Service suit moves further down the fence.

JIM (*voice-over*) The third team, the C team, moves in behind the picket fence above the Grassy Knoll, where the shooter and the spotter are first seen by the late Lee Bowers in the watchtower of the railyard. They have the best position of all. Kennedy is close and on a flat low trajectory. Part of this team is a coordinator who's flashed security credentials at several people, chasing them out of the parking lot area.

An "agent" in tie and suit moves on the underpass, keeping an eye out. In the crowd on

Elm Street, we catch brief glimpses of the umbrella man and the Cuban, neither of them watching Kennedy, both looking around to their teams. There is a third man, heavyset, in a construction helmet.

JIM *(voice-over)* ... Probably two to three more men are down in the crowd on Elm ... Ten to twelve men ... three teams, three shooters. The triangulation of fire Clay Shaw and David Ferrie discussed two months before. They've walked the Plaza, they know every inch. They've calibrated their sights, practiced on moving targets. They're ready. It's going to be a turkey shoot. Kennedy's motorcade makes the turn from Main onto Houston.

J.F.K. waves and turns in slow motion.

JIM *(voice-over)* ... six witnesses see two gunmen on the sixth floor of the Depository moving around. Some of them think they're policemen with rifles.

From Houston Street we look up at the sixth floor of the Book Depository and see the shooter moving around. Arnold Rowland points him out to his wife.

ARNOLD *(under)* ... probably a security agent.

> ▌Six witnesses see two men in sixth floor windows: [Arnold Rowland; WC 2H p. 175; Barbara Rowland, corroborated her husband's story, WC 6H, p. 181-183; Ruby Henderson: WC 24H p. 524; Carolyn Walther: WC 24H p. 522; Johnny Powell, Summers, *Conspiracy*, p. 43-44; interview with Earl Golz, *The Dallas Morning News*, December 19, 1978. Norman Similias: Harold Weisberg, *Photographic Whitewash*, p. 223-235; HSCA Report, p. 7; Hurt, *Reasonable Doubt*, p. 94; Summers, *Conspiracy*, p. 44-45.] A crucial piece of evidence in determining how many individuals were in the sixth floor windows at the time of the shooting is the home movie made by Charles Bronson. The Bronson film, taken shortly before the shooting, shows what might be human movement in the windows. The HSCA recommended that the Justice Department carry out a more thorough analysis of the film but to date, nothing has been done.That, however, could change. Following a recent KXAS-TV news segment on the Bronson film, the Dallas office of the FBI is setting up guidelines for an independently-verified scientific examination of the film to be done as soon as possible. Let's hope their interest is for real (author's conversation with researcher Gary Mack, April, 1992).

In the Dallas County Jail, Johnny Powell is one of many convicts housed on the sixth floor—the same height as the men in the Book Depository. We look across to the Depository through cell bars. Johnny and various cell mates are watching two men in the sixth floor of the Depository.

JIM *(voice-over)* John Powell, a prisoner on the sixth floor of the Dallas County Jail, sees them.

POWELL *(under)* ... quite a few of us saw them. Everybody was hollering and yelling and all that. We thought it was security guys ...

JIM *(voice-over)* ... they don't shoot him coming up Houston, which is the easiest shot for a single shooter in the Book Depository, but they wait till he gets to the killing zone between three rifles. Kennedy makes the final turn from Houston onto Elm, slowing down to some 11 miles per hour.

> ▮ Powell and Similas were never questioned by the Commission. Powell, in jail for three days on minor charges, said that many of his fellow inmates saw the two men. The Warren Commission was aware of the jail witnesses; a memo specifically reminded officials that the prisoners had an excellent view of the sixth floor at noon. No action was taken. [Golz, *Dallas Morning News*, December 19, 1978.] Similas, a Canadian, took photos in Dealey Plaza. He claims a negative that would have shown the two men in the windows was "lost" when he turned his photos over to a Toronto newspaper [Marrs, *Crossfire*, p. 22-23].

All the shooters tighten, taking aim. It's a tense moment.

JIM (*voice-over, dramatic*) ... the shooters across Dealey Plaza tighten, taking their aim across their sights ... waiting for the radio to say "Green Green!" or "Abort, Abort!"

The camera is on Kennedy waving. A MONTAGE follows—all the faces in the square that we've introduced in the movie now appear one after the other, watching—the killers, the man with the umbrella, the Newman family, Mary Moorman photographing, Jean Hill, Abraham Zapruder filming it, S. M. Holland, Patrolman Harkness ... INTERCUT with the Zapruder and Nix films on J.F.K. in the final seconds coming abreast of the Stemmons Freeway sign.

JIM (*voice-over*) The first shot rings out.

CUT TO the Dal-Tex shooter firing. We see the back of Kennedy's head through his gun sight. Kennedy (stand-in) reacts in the Zapruder film.

JIM (*voice-over*) Sounding like a backfire, it misses completely ... Frame 161, Kennedy stops waving as he hears something. Connally turns his head slightly to the right.

Everything goes off very fast now. Repeating intercuts are slowed down with shots of Kennedy reacting in the Zapruder film.

JIM (*voice-over*) Frame 193—the second shot hits Kennedy in the throat from the front. Frame 225—the President emerging from the road sign. He obviously has been hit, raising his arms to his throat.

CUT TO the picket fence shooter hitting him from the fence. We see Kennedy (stand-in) from the point of view of his telescopic sight. In the Zapruder film, we see Kennedy clutch his throat.

JIM Frame 232, the third shot—the President has been hit in the back, drawing him downward and forward. Connally, you will notice, shows no signs at all of being hit. He is visibly holding his Stetson which is impossible if his wrist has been shattered.

CUT TO the Dal-Tex shooter. We see Kennedy from his point of view, and the Zapruder film in slow motion.

JIM Connally's turning now here. Frame 238 ... the fourth shot misses Kennedy and takes Connally in the back. This is the key shot that proves two rifles from the rear. This is 1.6 seconds after the third shot, and we know no manual bolt-action rifle can be recycled in that time. Connally is hit, his mouth drops, he yells out, "My God, they're going to kill us all" ... Here ...

> ■ Recycling time of Oswald's rifle: The Warren Report (p. 97) sets the "recycling" time needed to work the bolt of Oswald's Carcano at a minimum of "at least 2.3 seconds." This does not include time to aim and it is also the figure established for shooting at a stationary target. When asked how the firing time would be affected by a moving target, FBI expert Frazier replied, "It would have slowed down the shooting." [WC 3H p. 407; see discussion in Evica, *And We Are All Mortal*, p. 67-69.]

CUT TO the sixth floor shooter firing rapidly and missing Kennedy but hitting Connally (stand-in).

JIM ... the umbrella man is signalling "He's not dead. Keep shooting." James Tague down at the underpass is hit sometime now by another shot that misses.

CUT TO the umbrella man pumping his umbrella. The Cuban is looking off. The man on the curb in the construction helmet is looking not at J.F.K. but up at the Book Depository.

> ■ Umbrella Man pumps umbrella: [HSCA IV p. 432-33; Marrs, *Crossfire*, p. 29-33.] The HSCA determined that the umbrella man was a Dallas citizen named Louis Steven Witt. Witt came forward in August 1978 after the HSCA publicly urged anyone with knowledge of the umbrella man or his companion to contact them. Witt testified in a public hearing that he waved the umbrella to irritate Kennedy. Witt said a friend told him this would annoy the president; the HSCA decided it had something to do with Joe Kennedy's pro-German sympathies while serving as ambassador to Britain just prior to WWII—British premier Neville Chamberlain always carried an umbrella. Many researchers remain skeptical, citing the implausibility of the motive as well as numerous inconsistencies in Witt's account of his actions in Dealy Plaza and his known actions as seen in the photographs and films.

JIM The car brakes. The fifth and fatal shot—frame 313—takes Kennedy in the head from the front ...

CUT TO the picket fence shooter. We see J.F.K. from his point of view. He fires, and then we see Kennedy in the Zapruder film flying backwards and to his left in a ferocious, conclusive spray of blood and brain tissue. We repeat the shot.

JIM This is the key shot. Watch it again. The President going back to his left. Shot from the front and right. Totally inconsistent with the shot from the Depository. Again—*(repeats)* ... back and to the left. *(he repeats it like a mantra)* ... back and to the left ... back and to the left.

Kennedy's car speeds off. Jackie is like a crawling animal in a pillbox hat on the back of the car. The people on the other side of the underpass wave innocently as the car speeds through with its horrifying contents. Pigeons fly off the rooftop of the Book Depository.

■ Pigeons: Police Officer Marrion L. Baker, riding back near the press cars in the motorcade, saw a flock of pigeons suddenly fly up off the roof of the Book Depository, leading him to believe that the shooter was on the roof of the building [WC 3H p. 246].

JIM What happens then? Pandemonium. The shooters quickly disassemble their various weapons, all except the Oswald rifle.

CUT TO sixth floor spotter dumping the Mannlicher-Carcano in a corner as he leaves ... and then to the Dal-Tex spotter and shooter, who break down the gun and move out ... and then to the spotter with the fence shooter, who quickly breaks down the weapon, throwing it in the trunk of a car parked at the fence. He walks away. The fence shooter, dressed as a policeman, blends with the crowd.

CUT TO the umbrella man and the Cuban sitting quietly together on the north side of the curb of Elm Street.

CUT TO stunned, confused, people in the crowd—some lying on the ground, some running for the Grassy Knoll.

Back in the courtroom, patrolman Joe Smith is on the stand.

■ FBI agent James Hosty told the HSCA that patrolman Smith may have encountered a Treasury agent named Frank Ellsworth. Ellsworth denied the allegation (HCSA Report, p.184) but admitted to intriguing connections with the Oswald case.

In 1976, Ellsworth told *Village Voice* reporter Dick Russell that he had first-hand knowledge of an "Oswald double," a man named John Thomas Masen who looked like Oswald, and was questioned by federal agents immediately after the assassination. It was Masen, Ellsworth said, who was mistaken for Oswald around Dallas, most notably at the rifle range. Masen was tied to the right-wing paramilitary group, the Minutemen, the Hunt oil family, and was a frequent traveler to and from Mexico. George Michael Evica presents strong evidence that Masen was also the "Oswald" at the Carousel club (Evica, *And We Are All Mortal*, p. 98-113).

JIM (*voice-over*) Patrolman Joe Smith rushed into the parking lot behind the fence. He smelled gunpowder.

FLASHBACK TO the picket fence area where, with his gun drawn, Smith rushes across to a man standing by a car who reacts quickly, producing credentials. He is one of the hoboes. There's a strange moment when the camera moves from Smith's eyes to the man's fingernails.

SMITH (*voice-over*) ... the character produces credentials from his pocket which showed him to be Secret Service. So I accepted that and let him go and continued our search. But I regretted it, 'cause this guy looked like an auto mechanic. He had on a sports shirt and pants, but he had dirty fingernails. Afterwards it didn't ring true, but at the time we were so pressed for time.

JIM (*voice-over*) Yet all Secret Servicemen in Dallas that day are accounted for. None were on foot in Dealey Plaza before or after the shooting, till Dallas Secret Service Chief Forrest Sorrels returned at 12:55.

▌ Patrolman Joe Smith: [WC 7H, p. 535; HSCA Report, p. 183-184; Summers, *Conspiracy*, p. 50; Marrs, *Crossfire*, p. 74-75, 319-320.]

▌ Forrest Sorrels returns to Dealey Plaza: [WC 7H p. 347-8.]

Back in the courtroom, Liz is totally absorbed. Jim exchanges looks with her. The camera moves in for a close-up of Jim.

JIM (*pausing for effect*) What else was going on in Dealey Plaza that day? At least 12 other individuals were taken into custody by Dallas police. No records of their arrests. Men acting like hoboes were being pulled off trains, marched through Dealey Plaza, photographed, and yet there is no records of their arrests.

▌ Twelve other arrests in Dealey: [Marrs, *Crossfire*, p. 336-340.]

FLASHBACK TO the three hoboes being arrested ... marching across Dealey Plaza. The hoboes look familiar now.

JIM Men identifying themselves as Secret Service Agents were all over the place. But who was impersonating them?

FLASHBACK TO men in suits, ties, and hats moving people out of the parking lot area ... turning a policeman back.

FLASHBACK TO the Cuban, putting away a radio, and the umbrella man, who now rise and leave the area in opposite directions.

JIM (*voice-over*) And where was Lee Oswald? Probably in the second floor snack room. Eddie Piper and William Shelly saw Oswald eating lunch in the first floor lunchroom around twelve. Around 12:15, on her way out of the building to see the motorcade, secretary Carolyn Arnold saw Oswald in the second floor snack room, where he said he went for a Coke ...

▌ Oswald on 1st floor: [WR p. 548.]

▌ Eddie Piper: [WC, Vol.VI, p.383.]

▌ William Shelly: [WC, Vol.VII, p. 390.]

▌ Carolyn Arnold: [Summers, *Conspiracy*, p. 77-78; Interview with Earl Golz, *Dallas Morning News*, November 26, 1978.]

In the second floor lunchroom of the Book Depository we see Carolyn Arnold, a pregnant secretary, crossing past Oswald, who is in a booth.

CAROLYN ARNOLD (*voice-over*) He was sitting in one of the booths on the right hand side of the room. He was alone as usual and appeared to be having lunch. I did not speak to him but I recognized him clearly. I remember it was 12:15 or later. It coulda been 12:25, five minutes before the assassination, I don't exactly remember. I was pregnant and I had a craving for a glass of water.

On the sixth floor of the depository, Bonnie Ray Williams is eating a chicken lunch, alone.

JIM (*voice-over*) At the same time, Bonnie Ray Williams is supposedly eating his chicken lunch on the sixth floor, at least until 12:15, maybe 12:20 ... he sees nobody.

> ▮ Bonnie Ray Williams: [WC 3H p. 168-169.]

On the street, Arnold Rowland and his wife look up at the sixth floor windows and we see, from their point of view, two shadowy figures ...

JIM (*voice-over*) Down on the street, Arnold Rowland was seeing two men in the sixth floor windows ... presumably after Bonnie Ray Williams finished his lunch and left.

> ▮ Arnold Rowland: Rowland reported seeing the men in the windows at 12:15, a time corroborated by his recollections of a broadcast that came over the radio of a police motorcycle parked nearby [WC 2H p. 169]. Williams said he left the sixth floor at 12:15, but felt it may have been as late as 12:20 [WC 3H p. 69]. In any case, Rowland's description of the men did not fit Williams.

We see footage of J.F.K. coming up Houston—waving.

Oswald walks into the second floor lunchroom as policeman Marrion Baker runs in, gun at his side. He is about 30 feet from Oswald. Roy Truly, the superintendent, runs in a moment later.

JIM (*voice-over*) ... Kennedy was running five minutes late for his appointment with death. He was due at 12:25. If Oswald was the assassin, he was certainly pretty nonchalant about getting himself into position. Later he told Dallas police he was standing in the second floor snackroom. Probably told to wait there for a phone call by his handler. The phones were in the adjacent and empty second floor offices, but the call never came. A maximum *90 seconds* after Kennedy is shot, patrolman Marrion Baker runs into Oswald in that second story lunchroom.

BAKER Hey you! (*to Truly*). Do you know this man? Is he an employee?

TRULY Yes he is. (*as Baker moves on*). The President's been shot!

Oswald reacts as if hearing it for the first time. Truly and Baker continue running up the stairs. Oswald proceeds to get a Coke and continues out of the room.

> ▮ Marrion Baker: [WC 3H p. 246; WC, CE 1381 (p. 2-3).] Baker, riding further back in the motorcade, was on Houston Street near the Courts building when he heard the shots. When he saw a flock of pigeons fly up off the roof of the Book Depository, he surmised that the shooter was firing from the roof. He did not suspect the sixth floor, or any other floor for that matter. After briefly encountering Oswald on the second floor, he ran up to the roof, saw no one there and ran back down to join other law enforcement officials

and witnesses in the railroad yards [Conversation with Marrion L. Baker, March 1991].

CUT TO the sixth floor, where we see Oswald as the shooter. After firing, he runs full speed for the stairs, stashing the rifle on the other side of the loft. Our camera follows him roughly down stairs—we hear the loud sound of his shoes banging on the hollow wood—to the lunchroom, where Patrolman Baker and Superintendent Truly run in. Then they start to repeat the same action as seen in the previous scene.

JIM (*voice-over*) ... but what the Warren Report would have us believe is that after firing 3 bolt action shots in 5.6 seconds, Oswald then leaves three cartridges neatly side by side in the firing nest, wipes the rifle clear of fingerprints, stashes the rifle on the other side of the loft, sprints down five flights of stairs, past witnesses Victoria Adams and Sandra Styles who never see him, and then shows up cool and calm on the second floor in front of patrolman Baker—all this within a *maximum* 90 seconds of the shooting. Is he out of breath? According to Baker, absolutely not.

▌Sandra Styles: [WC, CE 1381 (p. 90-91).]

▌Victoria Adams: [WC 6H, p. 392.]

CUT TO the second floor. Oswald ambles past Mrs Reid, a secretary in the second floor office, on his way out, Coke bottle in hand and wearing his usual dreamy look ... there's a lingering close-up on his face.

JIM (*voice-over*) Assuming he is the sole assassin, Oswald is now free to escape from the building. The longer he delays, the more chance the building will be sealed by police. Is he guilty? Does he walk out the nearest staircase? No, he buys a Coke and at a slow pace, spotted by Mrs. Reid in the second floor office, he strolls out the more distant front exit, where the cops start to gather ...

▌Mrs. Reid: [WC 3H p. 274.]

Outside, we see Oswald stroll out the door of the Book Depository into the crowd. He heads for the bus stop to the east.

JIM (*voice-over*) Oddly, considering three shots are supposed to have come from there, nobody seals the Depository for ten more minutes. Oswald slips out, as do several other employees. Of course, when he realized something had gone wrong and the President really *had* been shot, he knew there was a problem. He may even have known he was the patsy. An intuition maybe—the President killed in spite of his warning. The phone call that never came. Perhaps fear now came to Lee Oswald. He wasn't going to stand around for roll call.

▌Oswald leaves Book Depository: [WR p. 619, report of FBI agent James Bookhout]. Oswald said he left work because "based on remarks by [foreman] Bill Shelley, he did not believe that there was going to be any more work that day."

▌Oswald leaves Depository: Typically, the Warren Commission did not ask Shelley about his reported conversation with Oswald [WC 6H p. 327-334 and 7H p. 390-393 (Shelley Testimony)]. If Shelley really did tell Oswald to go home for the day, it gives even less credence to the Commission's contention that Oswald was fleeing the Depository.

Moreover, Oswald was not the only Depository employee who left work early that day. In the confusion following the assassination at least a dozen of the Depository's 50 employees were unaccounted for. Depository manager Roy Truly told the FBI that he noticed that Oswald was missing "about 15 minutes" after the encounter with Baker and notified the police. As Philip Melanson notes in *Spy Saga*, Truly had, in a sense, accounted for Oswald on the second floor and accordingly, Oswald "would not be at the very top of Truly's suspect list" [Melanson, *Spy Saga*, p. 122-124 and citations].

▌ Roy Truly knew Oswald by the name "Lee Oswald" (no middle name). The name at the top of the Dallas Police's list of employees missing from the building was "Harvey Lee Oswald" [CE 2003 p. 127]. Where did this version of the name come from?

Back in the courtroom, Jim continues speaking:

JIM The story gets pretty confusing now—more twists in it than a watersnake. Richard Carr says he saw four men take off from the Book Depository in a Rambler that possibly belongs to Janet Williams. Deputy Roger Craig says two men picked up Oswald in the same Rambler a few minutes later. Other people say Oswald took a bus out of there, and then because he was stuck in traffic, he hopped a cab to his rooming house in Oak Cliff ...

▌ Rambler station wagon: Richard Randolph Carr sees men get in car [CD 385]. Minutes after the assassination, steelworker Richard Randolph Carr saw two men run from either behind or inside the Book Depository and jump into a Nash Rambler station wagon on Houston Street by the east side of the building. Two other men were waiting in the car which drove off in a hurry with one door still open [CD 385, Marrs, *Crossfire*, p. 318].

▌ Roger Craig: [WC, Vol. XIX, p. 524 (Decker Exhibit No. 5323); Marrs, *Crossfire*, p. 328-333.] A short time later, Deputy Sheriff Roger Craig saw a "white man running down the hill from the direction of the Book Depository Building and I saw what I think was a light colored Rambler station wagon with a luggage rack on top pull over to the curb." The man climbed into the car and it drove away. Craig reported the incident to a "secret service officer" (who has never been identified) and he later went to the police station and identified Oswald as the man he had seen getting into the car [WC 19H p. 524]. CD 5, an FBI report from witness Marvin C. Robinson, corroborates Craig's story of a man going down the hill near the Depository and into a "light-colored" Nash station wagon. [See discussion in Marrs, *Crossfire*, p. 328-332.]

Craig told the Warren Commission in April, 1964 his account of his visit to Captain Fritz's office the afternoon of the assassination:

"...Captain Fritz asked me was this the man I saw and I said 'Yes, it was'...Captain Fritz then asked him..., 'What about this station wagon?' And [Oswald] interrupted him and said, 'That station wagon belongs to Mrs. Paine ... Don't try to tie her into this. She had nothing to do with it.'" [WC 6H p. 270.]

The Warren Report decided it "could not accept important elements of Craig's testimony" and, based on Fritz's flat-out denial of Craig's being in his office that afternoon (he claimed Craig was taken to a different office for questioning), decided that Craig apparently imagined the encounter with Oswald (p. 160-161). However, when Dallas Police Chief Jesse Curry published his book, *The J.F.K. Assassination File* (American Poster and Publishing Co., 1969), Craig was somewhat vindicated—one of the photographs showed Craig in Fritz's office during the interrogation of Oswald.

FLASHBACK TO Oswald's boarding house. Oswald enters his room, passing Earlene Roberts, the heavyset white housekeeper.

JIM (*voice-over*) ... we must assume he wanted to get back in touch with his intell team, probably at a safehouse or at the Texas Theatre, but how could he be sure? He didn't know who to trust anymore ...

ROBERTS (*watching TV*) My God, did you see that, Mr. Lee? A man shot the President.

▐ Oswald at boardinghouse: [WC 6H p. 434-444 (testimony of Earlene Roberts).] Oswald registered at the boardinghouse with the name "O.H. Lee," a name that pops up in an FBI report from a Dallas insurance salesman named Ed Brand. According to Brand, a young man whom he had seen several times at the nearby bus stop came into his office (across the street from Oswald's rooming house) in early November, 1963 to inquire about insurance for a car he was thinking of buying. The man, who never came back to the office, produced a driver's license with the name O.H. Lee [Hurt, *Reasonable Doubt*, p. 397-398 and citations].

The camera closes in on Oswald's perplexed face. Earlene peeks out the shades as she hears two short honks on a horn.

Outside is a black police car driven by Tippit. Also in the car is the fence shooter, dressed as a Dallas policeman. The car drives by, honks twice, waits, then moves away. During this visual, we see the fence shooter changing from his uniform into civilian clothes.

JIM (*voice-over*) Oswald returns to this rooming house around 1 P.M., half hour after the assassination, puts on his jacket, grabs his .38 revolver, leaves at 1:04 ... Earlene Roberts, the housekeeper, says she heard two beeps on a car horn and two uniformed cops pulled up to the house while Oswald was in his room, like it was a signal or something ... Officer Tippit is shot between 1:10 and 1:15 about a mile away. Though no one actually saw him walking or jogging, the Government says Oswald covered that distance. Incidentally, that walk, if he did it, is in a straight line toward Jack Ruby's house. Giving the government the benefit of the doubt, Oswald would have had to jog a mile in six to eleven minutes and commit the murder, then reverse direction and walk 3/5 of a mile to the Texas Theatre and arrive sometime before 1:30. That's some walking.

▐ Police car in front of boardinghouse: [WC 6H p. 443-444.]

▐ Time of Tippit killing: The citizen's report over the radio of the Tippit shooting was at 1:16 P.M. and the Commission claimed the incident occurred at 1:15 [WR p. 165]. Several witnesses set the time of the actual shooting at as many as five minutes earlier. Helen Markham was walking to catch a 1:12 bus—and wasn't late or in a hurry [WC 3H p. 306; CE 2003 p. 37]. She claimed the time was 1:06 or 1:07. T.F. Bowley (who called in the murder on the radio) stopped his car when he saw Tippit's body and looked at his watch, which said 1:10 P.M. [CE 2003 p. 110.] Four others put the time at about 1:00; three others said 1:20 or 1:30 [see discussion in Meagher, *Accessories after the Fact*, p. 254-255].

If we assume Oswald left his rooming house at 1:04 or 1:05, the Commission's version gives him a maximum of ten minutes to walk the nine-tenths of a mile to the Tippit scene near the intersection of 10th and Patton. And remember, there were no witnesses to Oswald's route from the boarding house to Tippit. Could he have done it? Warren Commission counsel David Belin, armed with a stopwatch, re-enacted the walk for the official record. It took him 17 minutes [WC 6H p. 434]. This did not prevent the Report from concluding:

"If Oswald left his rooming house shortly after 1 P.M. and walked at a brisk pace, he would have reached 10th and Patton shortly after 1:15 P.M." [WR p. 165].

On a street, Oswald walks alone, fast. A police car pulls up alongside him on 10th Street. Oswald leans on the passenger side of the window. Officer Tippit, suspicious, gets out to question him. Oswald pulls his .38 revolver and shoots him down in the street with 5 shots.

JIM (*voice-over*) It's also a useful conclusion. After all, why else would Oswald kill Officer Tippit, unless he just shot the President and feared arrest? Not one credible witness could identify Oswald as Tippit's killer.

Domingo Benavides, hidden in his truck only a few yards away, watches as another unidentified man (not seen before) shoots and walks away.

JIM (*voice-over*) Domingo Benavides, the closest witness to the shooting, refused to identify Oswald as the killer and was never taken to a lineup.

> ❚ Domingo Benavides: [WC, Vol. VI, p. 444-454.] Although Benavides was the closest witness to the shooting (about 15 feet away) he refused to go down to the police lineup to identify Oswald.

We see Acquilla Clemons, a black woman, looking on. She watches as two men kill Tippit. One of them resembles the fence shooter. The other one is a mystery figure, seen before in the fringes. The men walk off quickly in opposite directions. We notice a policeman's uniform hanging in the back seat of Tippit's car.

JIM (*voice-over*) Acquilla Clemons saw the killer with another man and says they went off in separate directions. Mrs. Clemons was never taken to lineup or to the Warren Commission. Mr. Frank Wright, who saw the killer run away, stated flatly that the killer was not Lee Oswald. Oswald is found with a .38 revolver. Tippit is killed with a .38 automatic. At the scene of the crime Officer J.M. Poe marks the shells with his initials to record the chain of evidence.

■ Acquilla Clemons: [Mark Lane and Emile D'Antonio "Rush to Judgment," 1967 (filmed interview).] Researchers have never located Clemons since.

■ Frank Wright: [Interview with George and Patricia Nash, *New Leader*, October 12, 1964.]

■ Tippit killed with automatic: The first reports from the scene of the crime said that the suspect was armed with a ".32, dark finish, automatic pistol" [WC 1H p. 36; WC 23H p. 868] and minutes later changed to an "automatic .38 rather than a pistol" [WC 1H p. 40; WC 23H p. 870].

■ Officer J.M. Poe: can't identify cases [WC 7H p. 69].

CUT TO Policeman Poe marking the bullets.

JIM (*voice-over*) Those initials are *not* on the three cartridge cases which the Warren Commission presents to him.

On a Dallas avenue near the Texas Theatre, Oswald moves along, spooked. Police cars roar by with sirens blaring. Johnny Brewer, in a shoestore, spots him and follows him.

JIM (*voice-over*) Oswald is next seen by shoe salesman Johnny Brewer lurking along Jefferson Avenue. Oswald is scared. He begins to realize the full implications of this thing. He goes into the Texas Theatre, possibly his prearranged meeting point, but though he has $14 in his pocket, he does not buy the 75-cent ticket. Brewer has the cashier call the police.

■ Johnny Brewer sees Oswald: [WC 7H p. 1-8; author's interview with Johnny Brewer, March 1991.]

*Outside the Texas Theatre Oswald walks past the cashier, who is out on the sidewalk watching the police cars go by. A double feature is playing—*Cry of Battle *with Van Heflin and* War Is Hell. *He goes in.*

CUT TO 30 officers arriving at the theatre in a fleet of patrol cars.

JIM (*voice-over*) ... in response to the cashier's call, at least thirty officers in a fleet of patrol cars descend on the movie theatre. This has to be the most remarkable example of police intuition since the Reichstag fire. I don't buy it. They knew—someone knew—Oswald was going to be there. In fact, as early as 12:44, only 14 minutes after the assassination, the police radio put out a description matching Oswald's size and build. Brewer says the man was wearing a jacket, but the police say the man who shot Tippit left his jacket behind. Butch Burroughs, theatre manager, says Oswald bought some popcorn from him at the time of the Tippit slaying. Burroughs and witness Bernard Haire also said there was an Oswald look-alike taken from the theatre. Perhaps it was he who sneaked into the theatre just after 1:30.

■ Oswald's jacket: When we talked to Brewer, he insisted that Oswald was wearing a jacket outside the shoe store. In his testimony to the Commission, Brewer is asked twice by counsel David Belin if the man he saw wore a jacket and he answers, "No." [WC 7H p. 7.] Brewer, who had never seen his published testimony before, felt certain that Oswald was wearing a "light brown zipper jacket." Earlene Roberts claimed Oswald was zipping up his jacket as he left the house [WC 7H p. 115-117]. The suspect fleeing the Tippit scene, according to the Dallas Police, apparently took off his jacket, where it was found presumably by policeman W.R. Westbrook [WC 7H p. 115-117]. Despite a lack of evidence linking the jacket to Oswald, the Commission decided it belonged to the lonely Marxist assassin [Meagher, *Accessories After the Fact*, p. 274-280].

▮ Oswald arrest at Texas Theatre: [WR p. 176-179; Marrs, *Crossfire*, p. 350-358.]

▮ Bernie Haire: [Marrs, *Crossfire*, p. 354.]

Inside the theatre, Cry of Battle *is on the screen. Twelve to fourteen spectators sit scattered between the balcony and ground floor. Brewer leads the officers onto the stage and the lights come on. He points to Oswald.*

JIM (*voice-over*) In any case, Brewer helpfully leads the cops into the theatre and from the stage points Oswald out ...

The cops advance on Oswald, who jumps up, as if expecting to be shot.

OSWALD This is it!

POLICEMAN Kill the President, will you?

▮ "Kill the President, will you?": [WC 7H p. 6 (Brewer testimony); WR p. 179.] The Report notes that "it is unlikely that any of the police officers referred to Oswald as a suspect in the assassination." When we talked to Brewer, he said he was shocked that the Warren Report decided that he was mistaken. He insisted he heard someone, he wasn't sure if it was a uniformed or plainclothes officer, yell this in the theater.

Scared, Oswald takes a swing at a policeman. He pulls out his gun. The officers close in on him from the rear and front. A wrestling and shoving match ensues. One officer gets a chokehold on Oswald and another one hits him.

JIM (*voice-over*) The cops have their man! It has already been decided—in Washington.

Outside the theatre, Oswald, his eye blackened, is led out by the phalanx of officers. They are surrounded by an angry crowd.

CROWD Kill him! Kill him!

JIM (*voice-over*) Dr. Best, Himmler's right hand man in the Gestapo, once said "as long as the police carries out the will of the leadership, it is acting legally." That mindset allowed for 400 political murders in the Weimar Republic of 1923-32, where the courts were controlled and the guilty acquitted. Oswald must've felt like Josef K in Kafka's "The Trial." He was never told the reason of his arrest, he does not know the unseen forces ranging against him, he cries out his outrage in the police lineup just like Josef K excoriates the judge for not being told the charges against him. But the state is deaf. The quarry is caught. By the time he is brought from the theatre, a large crowd is waiting to scream at him. By the time he reaches police headquarters, he is booked for murdering Tippit ...

At the Dallas police station, Dallas Police Captain Will Fritz takes a call from a high official in Washington. In the background we notice Lee Oswald continuing to be questioned by federal agents. We hear Johnson's distinctive Texas drawl but we never see him.

JIM (*voice-over*) No legal counsel is provided. No record made of the long questioning.

HIGH OFFICIAL VOICE Howdy there, Cap'n. Thanks for taking care of us down in Dallas. Lady Bird and I will always be grateful.

FRITZ Thank you, Mr. President. We're doing our best.

HIGH OFFICIAL VOICE Cap'n, I know you're working like a hound dog down there to get this mess wrapped up, but I gotta tell you there's too much confusion coming out of Dallas now. The TVs and the papers are full of rumor 'bout conspiracies. Two gunmen, two rifles, the Russkies done it, the Cubans done it, that kinda loose talk, it's scarin' the shit outta people, bubba'. This thing could lead us into a war that could cost 40 million lives. We got to show 'em we got this thing under control. No question, no doubts, for the good of our country ... you hear me?

FRITZ Yes, sir.

HIGH OFFICIAL VOICE Capn', you got your man, the investigation's over, that's what people want to hear.

> ▌Call to Capt. Fritz: Dallas Police Chief Jesse Curry told the Warren Commission: "...nobody would tell me exactly who it was that was insisting 'just say I got a call from Washington and they wanted this evidence up there," insinuated it was someone in high authority that was requesting this.' [WC 4H, p. 195]. [Marrs, *Crossfire*, p. 357; Penn Jones, Jr., *Forgive My Grief* III, p. 101.] KXAS reporter Bob Sirkin claims to have discussed this episode with Captain Fritz himself. Shortly before Fritz's death, Sirkin asked him to go public with the story but Fritz declined.

The camera closes in on Oswald in background. He turns to an unseen Deputy, sad.

OSWALD Now everyone will know who I am.

> ▌Oswald: [WC 6H, p. 270 (Roger Craig testimony)]

JIM (*voice-over*) By the time the sun rose the next morning, he is booked for murdering the President. The whole country—fueled by the media—assumes he's guilty.

In an underground police garage, we see Jack Ruby being allowed in via an interior staircase by his police contact. He moves towards the outer edge of reporters, nervous.

> ▌Ruby enters basement: [Marrs, p. 414-429.] HSCA Report, p.157, notes: "Ruby probably did not come down the ramp [as the Warren Report

claimed], and that his most likely route was an alleyway located next to the Dallas Municipal Building and a stairway leading to the basement garage of police headquarters."

Oswald comes out with his two guards. We see a repeat of the assassination in stop time ... Ruby's eyes, Oswald's ... do they recognize each other?

JIM (*voice-over*) Under the guise of a patriotic nightclub owner out to spare Jackie Kennedy from having to testify at a trial, Jack Ruby is shown into the underground garage by one of his inside men on the Dallas Police Force, and when he's ready Oswald is brought out like a sacrificial lamb and nicely disposed of as an enemy of the people. By early Sunday afternoon, the autopsy has been completed on him. Who grieves for Lee Harvey Oswald? Buried in a cheap grave under the name "Oswald"? No one.

We see Oswald dying on the floor of the police station. A paramedic pushes in and starts administering artificial respiration, which only aggravates the internal hemorrhaging.

At a Texas cemetery, Oswald's mother weeps. Oswald is buried with a few people present, but there are no details, no dates. We see Marina whisked out by agents.

CUT TO Kennedy's funeral, which, in contrast, attracts thousands of mourners.

JIM (*voice-over*) Within minutes false statements and press leaks about Lee Oswald circulate the globe.

FLASHBACK TO X reading about it in the New Zealand Airport, and then back to the courtroom in 1969.

■ Garrison's closing argument: Garrison delivered the final argument for the state in the Shaw trial. The Assistant D.A.s who did much of the actual trial work, James Alcock and Alvin Oser, also gave summaries.
The full text of Garrison's summation is reprinted in the Appendix. It was also published in James Kirkwood's *American Grotesque* and is contained in the court transcripts. We've drawn from other sources here as well, most notably from Garrison's interview in the July 1967 issue of *Playboy*; *Heritage of Stone* (Garrison's first book); and the text of some of Garrison's speeches and lectures.

JIM The Official Legend is created and the media takes it from there. The glitter of official lies and the epic splendor of the thought-numbing funeral of J.F.K. confuse the eye and confound the understanding. Hitler always said "the bigger the lie, the more people will believe it." Lee Oswald—a crazed, lonely man who wanted attention and got it by killing a President, was only the first in a long line of patsies. In later years Bobby Kennedy and Martin Luther King, men whose commitment to change and to peace would make them dangerous to men who are committed to war, would follow, also killed by such "lonely, crazed men," who remove our guilt by making murder a meaningless act of a loner. We have all become Hamlets in our country—children of a slain father-leader whose killers still possess the throne. The ghost of John F. Kennedy confronts us with the secret murder at the heart of the American dream. He

forces on us the appalling questions: Of what is our Constitution made? What is our citizenship, and more, our lives worth? What is the future of a democracy where a President can be assassinated under conspicuously suspicious circumstances while the machinery of legal action scarcely trembles? How many political murders, disguised as heart attacks, cancer, suicides, airplane and car crashes, drug overdoses will occur before they are exposed for what they are?

Liz, watches, moved. Susie, Al and Numa are also there for the summation. Even Lou Ivon has come back to support his friend.

JIM "Treason doth never prosper," wrote an English poet, "What's the reason? For if it prosper, none dare call it treason." The generals who sent Dreyfus to Devils Island were among the most honorable men in France, the men who killed Caesar were among the most honorable men in Rome. And the men who killed Kennedy, no doubt, were honorable men. I believe we have reached a time in our country, similar to what life must've been like under Hitler in the 30's, except we don't realize it because Fascism in our country takes the benign disguise of liberal democracy. There won't be such familiar signs as swastikas. We won't build Dachaus and Auschwitzes. We're not going to wake up one morning and suddenly find ourselves in gray uniforms goose-stepping off to work ... "Facism will come," Huey Long once said. "in the name of anti-fascism"—it will come in the name of your security—they call it "National Security," it will come with the mass media manipulating a clever concentration camp of the mind. The super state will provide you tranquility above the truth, the superstate will make you believe you are living in the best of all possible worlds, and in order to do so will rewrite history as it sees fit. George Orwell's *Ministry of Truth* warned us, "Who controls the past, controls the future." The American people have yet to see the Zapruder film. Why? The American people have yet to see the real photographs and X-rays of the autopsy. Why? There are hundreds of documents that could help prove this conspiracy. Why have they been withheld or burned by the Government? Each time my office or you the people have asked those questions, demanded crucial evidence, the answer from on high has been "national security." What kind of "national security" do we have when we have been robbed of our leaders? Who determines our "national security"? What "national security" permits the removal of fundamental power from the hands of the American people and validates the ascendancy of invisible government in the United States? *That* kind of "national security," gentlemen of the jury, is when it smells like it, feels like it, and looks like it, you call it what it is—*it's Fascism!* I submit to you that what took place on November 22, 1963 was a coup d'état. Its most direct and tragic result was a reversal of President Kennedy's commitment to withdraw from Vietnam. War is the biggest business in America worth $80 billion a year. The President was murdered by a conspiracy planned in advance at the highest levels of the United States government and carried out by fanatical and disciplined Cold Warriors in the Pentagon and CIA's covert operations apparatus—among them Clay Shaw here before you. It was a public execution and it was covered up by like-minded individuals in the Dallas Police Department, the Secret Service, the FBI, and the White House—all the way up to and including J. Edgar Hoover and Lyndon Johnson, whom I consider accomplices after the fact.

The camera holds on onlookers shuffling and murmuring. Clay Shaw smirks, smoking his cigarette. The very grandiosity of the charge works in his favor. Jim is falling apart from built-up strain and fatigue. He looks over at Liz, gathering his spirit.

JIM (*his voice cracking*) There is a very simple way to determine if I am being paranoid here. (*laughter*) Let's ask the two men who have profited the most from the assassination—your former President Lyndon Baines Johnson and your new President, Richard Nixon—to release 51 CIA documents pertaining to Lee Oswald and Jack Ruby, or the secret CIA memo on Oswald's activities in Russia that was "destroyed" while being photocopied. All these documents are *yours*—the people's property—you pay for it, but because the government considers you children who might be too disturbed to face this reality, because you might lynch those involved, you cannot see these documents for another 75 years. I'm in my 40's, so I'll have shuffled off this mortal coil by then, but I'm already telling my 8-year-old son to keep himself physically fit so that one glorious September morning in 2038 he can walk into the National Archives and find out what the CIA and FBI knew. They may even push it back then. It may become a generational affair, with questions passed down from father to son, mother to daughter, in the manner of the ancient runic bards. Someday, somewhere, someone might find out the damned Truth. Or we might just build ourselves a new Government like the Declaration of Independence says we should do when the old one ain't working—maybe a little farther out West.

He approaches the jury.

JIM An American naturalist wrote, "a patriot must always be ready to defend his country against its government." Well, I'd hate to be in your shoes today. You have a lot to think about. Going back to when we were children, I think most of us in this courtroom thought that justice came into being automatically, that virtue was its own reward, that good would triumph over evil. But as we get older we know that this just isn't true. "The frontier is where a man faces a fact." Individual human beings have to create justice and this is not easy because truth often presents a threat to power and we have to fight power often at great risk to ourselves. People like Julia Ann Mercer, S.M. Holland, Lee Bowers, Jean Hill, and Willie O'Keefe have come forward and taken that risk. (*he produces a stack of letters*) I have here some $8,000 in these letters sent to my office from all over the country—quarters, dimes, dollar bills from housewives, plumbers, car salesmen, teachers, invalids ... These are people who cannot afford to send money but do, these are the ones who drive the cabs, who nurse in the hospitals, who see their kids go to Vietnam. Why? Because they *care*, because they want to know the truth—because they want their country back, because it belongs to us the people as long as the people got the guts to fight for what they believe in! The truth is the most important value we have because if the truth does not endure, if the Government murders truth, if you cannot respect the hearts of these people (*shaking the letters*), then this is no longer the country in which we were born in and this is not the country I want to die in ... And this was never more true than for John F. Kennedy whose murder was probably the most terrible moment in the history of our country. You the people, you the jury system, in sitting in judgment on Clay Shaw, represent the hope of humanity against Government power. In discharging your duty, in bringing the first conviction in this house of cards against Clay Shaw, "Ask not what your country can do for you, but what you can do for your country." Do not forget your young President who forfeited his life. Show the world this is still a government *of* the people, *for* the people, and *by* the people. Nothing as long as you live will ever be more important. (*he stares into the camera*) It's up to you.

He returns to the table and sits. The courtroom is still.

CUT TO later in the same courtroom. The jury files in, having reached a verdict. Jim, prepared, sits with his staff and Liz. The jury foreman enters the courtroom.

JURY FOREMAN   We find Clay Shaw ... not guilty on all counts.

> ■ Verdict: [March 1, 1969. *New Orleans States-Item*, "Not Guilty: Verdict is Unanimous," March 1, 1969. *New Orleans Times-Picayune*; "Shaw Found Not Guilty of Plotting to Kill J.F.K.," March 1, 1969.]

There's jubilation and commotion in the Court. Shaw stands, happily shaking hands all over ... Members of the press run for the phones. In the corridor outside the courtroom, the press interviews the jury foreman.

FOREMAN   We believe there was a conspiracy, but whether Clay Shaw was a part of it is another kettle of fish.

> ■ Jury foreman: [Garrison, *Trail of the Assassins*, p. 250-251.]

The camera moves to Jim, who walks out past the banks of reporters. TV lights are in his face. Liz is by his side.

ENGLISH REPORTER   Mr. Garrison, the American media is reporting this as a full vindication of the Warren Commission, do you ...

JIM   I think all it proves is you cannot run a trial even questioning the intelligence operations of the government in the light of day.

NEWSMAN 13   We understand that *The Times-Picayune* will call for your resignation—unfit to hold office. You've ruined Clay Shaw's reputation—are you going to resign?

JIM   Hell, no. I'm gonna run again. And I'm gonna win. Thank you very much. If it takes me 30 years to nail every one of the assassins, then I will continue this investigation for 30 years. I owe that not only to Jack Kennedy, but to my country.

He and Liz squeeze hands as they walk on.

DISSOLVE TO WASHINGTON, D.C. - (1970)

Jim waits on the same park bench as earlier in the film, overlooking the Mall or the Lincoln Monument ... as X walks up, a little grayer, a little more stooped, wearing ill-fitting civilian clothes.

JIM Well, thanks for coming.

X You didn't get that break you needed, but you went as far as any man could, bubba. (*he sits next to Jim*) What can I do for you?

JIM Just speculating, I guess. How do you think it started?

X I think it started in the wind. Money—arms, big oil, Pentagon people, contractors, bankers, politicians like L.B.J. were committed to a war in Southeast Asia. As early as '61 they knew Kennedy was going to change things ... He was not going to war in Southeast Asia. Who knows? Probably some boardroom or lunchroom somewhere—Houston, New York—hell, maybe Bonn, Germany ... who knows, it's international now.

> ▌1961- J.F.K. threatens to withdraw from Vietnam: [NSAM 111 dated Nov. 15, 1961, allowed for more advisors in Vietnam but did not allow for deployment of the combat troops the Joint Chiefs requested (Newman, *JFK and Vietnam*, p.136-139 and citations).]

CUT TO a New York City lunch club or executive dining room. From the window we have a towering view of the City. Four men in their 50s to 70s—old men, rich men, talk at a quiet table. Their figures are shadowy and we overhear their conversation obliquely, across faces flared out by sun bouncing off the skyscraper window.

X (*voice-over*) One worried sonofabitch with a few million bucks turns to the others ... with a few million bucks ... and says something pretty direct like ...

RICH MAN 1 The sonofabitch is gonna get re-elected by a bigger vote than ever in '64. It's gonna be worse than Roosevelt. The country won't survive as we know it.

RICH MAN 2 (*pause*) I agree, Bob, it can't go on. (*he looks to Man 3*)

RICH MAN 3 ... and Bobby in '68? Something's got to be done.

Looks pass among them. There's a pause, and then ...

RICH MAN 1 He's gotta go, Lou. The election's gotta be stopped.

There is a breathless moment with the thought in the air.

RICH MAN 1 I talk to a lot of people. I know I'm not the only one thinking this.

RICH MAN 2 What's the feeling in Washington, Jack?

FLASHBACK TO the Pentagon in 1962.

X (*voice-over*) ... so calls are made. Down to Washington. All over the world. They start talking about it. A few people here, there. Just conversations, nothing more ...

We see a general meeting with another general. They talk.

X (*voice-over*) Generals, Admirals, CIA people, and probably some people on the inside of Kennedy's staff—young, brilliant Judases, ready to go to war in Southeast Asia ...

FLASHBACK TO the White House, 1962. A general talks to one of Kennedy's staff—a bespectacled, bright young Harvard type.

X (*voice-over*) ... and maybe a Vice-President getting separate memos from Vietnam, eager to get his backers the billions of dollars in contracts for Southeast Asia ...

> ■ L.B.J. gets separate memos: On May 11, 1962, L.B.J. was on his way to visit South Vietnamese leader Diem. En route, he received a memo from the JCS to the Commander in Chief in the Pacific (CINCPAC) which stated: "President Diem should be encouraged to request that the U.S. fulfill its SEATO obligation...by the immediate deployment of appropriate U.S. forces to South Vietnam" (JCS 995614, 5/11/62). This memo did not go to the President, nor did it reflect his policy. [Newman, *J.F.K. & Vietnam*, p. 225-229.]

In a White House office, Lyndon Johnson meets with a cabinet member, a contractor, and two military men.

X (*voice-over*) Kennedy, like Caesar, is surrounded with enemies. Something is underway but it has no face. Yet everybody in the loop knows ...

The camera shows Washington, D.C. buildings from strange angles. The feeling is still, weird, angled, alien. The buildings are twisted.

X (*voice-over*) Money is at stake. Big money. A hundred billion. The Kennedy brothers target voting districts for defense dollars. They give TFX fighter contracts only to the counties that are going to make a difference in '64. These people fight back. Their way. One day another call is made ...

> ■ TFX fighter contracts: [L. Fletcher Prouty, "Visions of a Kennedy Dynasty," *Freedom*, April-May 1987, p. 8.]
>
> ■ NSAM 111: see Appendix.

In a Pentagon office, a man in civilian clothing is on the phone, his back to the screen. This is Mr. Y, X's superior officer. Shadows pervade the room. An unshuttered window overlooks the Potomac River and the White House.

X (*voice-over*) ... maybe to somebody like my superior who's been running the "Mongoose" program out of Florida and who has no love for Kennedy.

VOICE ON PHONE Bill, we're going. We need your help.

X (*voice-over*) Everything's cellularized. No one has said "he must die," there's been no vote, there's nothing on paper, there's no one to blame. It's as old as the Crucifixion: the Mafia firing squad, one blank, no one's guilty because everyone in the Power Structure who knows anything has a plausible deniability. There are no compromising connections except at the most secret point. But what's paramount is that it must succeed. No matter how many die, how much it costs, the perpetrators must be on the winning side and never subject to prosecution for anything by anyone. *That* is a coup d'état.

Y (*into phone*) When?

VOICE ON PHONE In the fall. Probably in the south. We want you to come up with a plan ...

X (*voice-over*) He's done it before. Other countries. Lumumba in the Congo, Trujillo, the Dominican Republic, he's working on Castro. No big deal. In September, Kennedy announces the Texas trip. At that moment, second Oswalds start popping up all over Dallas where they have the mayor and the cops in their pocket. Y flies in the assassins, maybe from the special camp we keep outside Athens, Greece—pros, maybe some locals, Cubans, Mafia hire, separate teams. Does it really matter who shot from what rooftop? Part of the scenery. The assassins by now are dead or well paid and long gone ...

JIM Any chance of one of them confessing someday?

X ... don't think so. When they start to drool, they get rid of 'em. These guys are *proud* of what they did. They did Dealey Plaza! They took out the President of the United States! That's entertainment! *And* they served their country doing it.

JIM (*in present*) ... and your General?

X ... got promoted to two stars, but he was never military, you know, always CIA. Went to Vietnam, lost his credibility when we got beat over there, retired, lives in Virginia. I say hello to him when I see him at the supermarket ...

JIM Ever ask him?

X You never ask a spook a question. No point. He'll never give you a straight answer. General Y still thinks of himself as the handsome young warrior who loved this country but loved the concept of war more.

JIM His name?

X Does it matter? Another technician. But an interesting thing—he was there that day in Dealey Plaza. You know how I know? (*Jim shakes his head*) That picture of yours. The hoboes ... You never looked deep enough ...

> ∎ General Y in photo: The idea for this scene has its roots in a story Col. Prouty has told many times that his former colleague, celebrated CIA man General Edward G. Lansdale, is seen from the back in one of the "hobo"

photos. We decided to check on Lansdale's movements in November, 1963. What we found among Lansdale's papers at the Hoover Institute piqued our curiosity even more.

Lansdale was "retired" from the Air Force in October 1963. He then went to visit his son in Arizona, driving by way of Texas. He wrote to a friend in San Antonio, saying he'd stop by on the way; by November 14, he still hadn't arrived at the friend's house. Among his papers from this period was a claim check from the Hotel Texas in Fort Worth, the hotel that the presidential entourage stayed at the night before the assassination. There was no identifying mark on the claim check and we could not track down the guest records of the hotel (which has had many different owners since 1963). Lansdale was furious with J.F.K. for two reasons: (1) he did not get the hoped-for ambassadorship to Vietnam and was subsequently taken off the Vietnam project to work on Operation Mongoose and (2) his good friend, South Vietnamese Ngo Dinh Diem, had been killed in a CIA-sanctioned coup in early October. He had masterminded assassination plots for the CIA, could he have done it in Dallas? Of course, we don't know, but it is fascinating to find he was in Texas that very week.

FLASHBACK TO one of the hobo pictures. Next to the freight entrance of the Book Depository, Y, in a dark suit, is nonchalantly walking past the hoboes, his back to us. The camera closes in on Y.

X (*voice-over*) I knew the man 20 years. That's him. The way he walked ... arms at his side, military, the stoop, the haircut, the twisted left hand, the large class ring. What was he doing there? If anyone had asked him, he'd probably say "protection," but I'll tell you I think he was giving some kind of "okay" signal to those hoboes—they're about to get booked and he's telling 'em it's gonna be okay, they're covered. And in fact they were—you never heard of them again.

JIM ... some story ... the whole thing. It's like it never happened.

X It never did. (*he smiles tartly*)

JIM Just think ... just think. What happened to our country ... to the world ... because of that murder ... Vietnam, racial conflict, breakdown of law, drugs, thought control, guilt, assassinations, secret government fear of the frontier ...

X I keep thinking of that day, Tuesday the 26th, the day after they buried Kennedy, L.B.J. was signing the memorandum on Vietnam with Ambassador Lodge.

FLASHBACK TO the White House, 1963. Johnson sits across the shadowed room with Lodge and others. His Texas drawl rises and falls. He signs something unseen.

JOHNSON Gentlemen, I want you to know I'm not going to let Vietnam go the way China did. I'm personally committed. I'm not going to take one soldier out of there 'til they know we mean business in Asia ... (*he pauses*) You just get me elected, and I'll give you your damned war.

■ "Just get me elected": [Stanley Karnow, *Vietnam: A History*, p. 326.] Karnow reports Johnson as saying "Just get me elected and then you can have your war." The setting is different–a Christmas cocktail party–and it was, Karnow notes, an example of Johnson's "assuaging the brass and the braid with promises he may never have intended to keep."

Johnson met with the Joint Chiefs on the morning of J.F.K.'s funeral to discuss Vietnam. On Tuesday, the 26th, NSAM 273 was signed.

X (*voice-over*) ... and that was the day Vietnam started.

CUT TO Documentary footage of—U.S. Marines arriving in full force on the beaches of Danang, March 8, 1965 ... as another era begins and our movie ends.

On a black screen we read:

•• In 1975, VICTOR MARCHETTI, former executive assistant to the CIA's deputy director, stated that during high-level CIA meetings during Shaw's trial in 1969, CIA director RICHARD HELMS disclosed that CLAY SHAW and DAVID FERRIE had worked for the Agency, and asked his assistants to make sure Mr. Shaw received Agency help at his trial.

> ▌Victor Marchetti: [*True*, April, 1975]

•• In 1979, RICHARD HELMS, director of covert operations in 1963, admitted under oath that CLAY SHAW had Agency connections.

> ▌Richard Helms: [Hunt vs. Weberman, S.D.Fla., 1979; Hunt vs. Liberty Lobby, S.D. Fla., No. 80-1121-Civ.-JWK, deposition of Richard McGarrah Helms, June 1, 1984, p. 37.]

•• It is now known that in 1963, U.S. military intelligence controlled more agents than the CIA and had almost as much money to spend. It surfaced in the 1970's that the Army had long been conducting surveillance and keeping files on thousands of private citizens in the name of national security. The prime targets were dissident-left-wingers of the kind Oswald appeared to be.

•• CLAY SHAW died in 1974 of supposed lung cancer. No autopsy was allowed.

•• WILLIAM SULLIVAN, Assistant Director of the FBI, died in the early morning hours of November 9, 1977 when he was mistaken for a deer in an open field in New Hampshire. Shortly before his death, Sullivan had a preliminary hearing with the HSCA. (Evica, *And We Are All....*, p.324-326; Jeff Goldberg and Harvey Yazijian, "The Death of Crazy Billy Sullivan," *The New Times*, July 24, 1978.)

•• GEORGE DE MOHRENSCHILDT committed suicide just hours afer HSCA investigator Gaeton Fonzi located him. (Fonzi, *The Last Investigation, The Washingtonian*, November 1980.)

•• In November, 1969 JIM GARRISON was re-elected to a third term as District Attorney of Orleans Parish. In June of 1971, he was arrested by Federal Agents on charges of allowing payoffs on pinball gambling by organized crime. In September of 1973, after defending himself in Federal Court, he was quickly found not guilty of charges that appear to have been framed against him. Less

than six weeks later, he was narrowly defeated for a fourth term as District Attorney.

•• In 1978, Garrison was elected Judge of the Louisiana State Court of Appeal in New Orleans. He was re-elected in 1988. To this date, he has brought the only public prosecution in the Kennedy killing.

•• ELIZABETH and Jim were divorced in 1978. He now lives in the same house he lived in with Elizabeth. She lives a block away. Their five children are grown.

•• SOUTHEAST ASIA: 58,000 American lives, 2 million Asian lives, $220 billion spent, 10 million Americans air-lifted there by commercial aircraft, more than 5,000 helicopters lost, 6½ million tons of bombs dropped.

•• A Congressional Investigation from 1976-1979 found a "probable conspiracy" in the assassination of John F. Kennedy and recommended the Justice Department investigate further. As of 1991, the Justice Department has done nothing. The files of the House Select Committee on Assassinations are locked away until the year 2029.

The camera moves onto the mottoes chiseled in the walls of the National Archives in Washington, D.C.:

"STUDY THE PAST"

"PAST IS PROLOGUE"

"ETERNAL VIGILANCE IS THE PRICE OF LIBERTY"

DEDICATED TO THE YOUNG,
IN WHOSE SPIRIT THE SEARCH FOR TRUTH
MARCHES ON.

THE END

The JFK Debate:

Reactions and Commentaries

Certain authors whose work was sought to form the following cross section of reaction declined to be included. The editors especially regret the absence of George Will, Arlen Specter and Anthony Summers from our selection.

ABOUT THE DEBATE

Frank Mankiewicz

The most significant thing about *JFK*—apart from the script which is so amply developed in this volume—is the reaction of the mainstream media not just to the movie itself, but even to the *idea* of the movie. As you read the pages which follow, try to ask what accounts for the extraordinary ferocity of the attacks on the film by the mainstream, political media, almost without exception by older journalists active at the time of the Kennedy assassination?

What emerges from this summary is a conclusion that *The New York Times* and its allies in the major commercial media set out—and nearly succeeded—not just to discredit or to attack Oliver Stone and his film, but to destroy it. The effort was enormous, and so, luckily, was its failure. *JFK* was a great box office success, seen by millions of Americans and many millions more abroad, and recent public opinion samplings indicate it will be the most sought-after home video in many years.

But why the venom? Why, for example, would *The New York Times*, ordinarily the grayest and calmest of newspapers, devote nearly thirty articles, op-eds, letters, notes, addenda, editorials and columns to the most savage attacks on the film? Why would journalists who had never since 1963 cast a questioning eye or a story or any research on the questions concerning the assassination of President Kennedy—men like Tom Wicker and George Will—devote so much destructive energy to the task of turning Americans against this film? *The New York Times* editorialized against the film and then carried notes to its editorial columns attacking the film on specific grounds, carried op-eds and letters to the editor attacking *JFK*—and endlessly delayed favorable responses—and it even carried "news" stories from its correspondent in Hollywood wondering editorially why Warner Bros. permitted the movie to go ahead and suggesting the studio censor it. Finally, the *Times* carried a blast at the movie by Warren Commission consultant David Belin, whose complaints about the film had already appeared many, many times, conveniently just in time to be reprinted in *Variety* to coincide with the final days of voting on the Academy Awards by motion picture industry members who were its readers.

The major attacks on *JFK* came not just from the likes of David Belin and Richard Mosk, whose frenzied interest in protecting the Warren Commission was understandable since they had helped create its disbelieved report; nor did the attacks come only from understandable sources like Joseph Califano and Jack Valenti, loyal Johnson men who rise predictably to defend against any suggestion that LBJ was other than that parfit gentle knight they wish he had been. Those attacks, as well as those like Alexander Cockburn's, from the hard left, are understandable. Cockburn's distress with *JFK*, of course, comes from its central notion that a democratically-elected president, under our system of government, could have accomplished good things and that he was killed from outside the system precisely because he wanted to accomplish those things. In Cockburn's demonology, nothing produced by the American political system is worth defending, and therefore not worth murdering either.

But what of the mainstream journalists? Men like George Will, for example, who almost certainly did not see the film (because he describes it as setting forth a theory of a vast conspiracy when in fact the film posits a very narrow and precise one), Anthony Lewis, George Lardner, and others who were directly involved in reporting the events of November 22, 1963, in Dallas, but who—except for an occasional sneer by Lardner at assassination historians—hardly gave the event a backward glance for nearly thirty years thereafter.

As self-appointed guardians of that particular history and the comforting "lone crazed gunman" theory of the assassination, Wicker, Lardner, Will, et al., could watch amusedly as what they and their colleagues called "kooks and cranks" began to question the preposterous Warren Commission verdict. Within a few years, an overwhelming majority of Americans had put on the record their strong disbelief in the Warren Commission's finding—that the lone gunman Oswald had killed President Kennedy (for no discernible motive) and that he had then been killed by another lone gunman, Jack Ruby, also apparently acting on a vagrant impulse. It would not wash. A flood of books, articles, speeches and even the odd documentary movie came along, but all under-financed and many vulnerable to the charge that here was merely another questioning of Dallas by a "conspiracy buff." And so long as the criticism was left to those easily criticized by the mainstream press, the Crime of the Century remained below the surface of American mainstream consciousness.

But underground, the American preoccupation with the murder of our President remained unsatisfied. How was President Kennedy killed, and by whom? More important, *why* was he killed? How could the famous "single bullet" have performed so many changes of course and erratic deviations and even a one-second pause in its flight through the bodies and limbs of President Kennedy and Governor Connally? Why did Lee Harvey Oswald deny the crime, when every prior assassin had proudly proclaimed his guilt and his motive? Why was Jack Ruby, a small-time hoodlum with clear organized crime connections, allowed into the Dallas police station—armed—at the very moment the alleged perpetrator of the Crime of the Century was being moved? For that matter, why was Lee Harvey Oswald, the defector and renouncer of U.S. citizenship to spy on the U.S. and give the information to the Soviets, allowed on a few days' notice to return to the United States unwatched and unmonitored, except for a quick association with CIA-connected people in Dallas? Why was Oswald roaming around New Orleans in the summer of 1963 distributing obviously bogus pro-Castro literature, while maintaining a headquarters in the same building as notorious anti-Castro right-wing zealots? Those who maintained these were unimportant questions that need not be answered were the true distorters of history, and the American public, by an overwhelming majority, knew it all the time.

Suddenly, bursting on the scene came Oliver Stone, an award-winning film director and writer with an all-star cast, backed by a $40 million budget and a studio (Warner Bros.) of great courage and determination. The film could not be stopped, so it had to be disparaged. Stone could not be discredited as a film maker, so he must be mocked and reviled as a historian. But the younger journalists were not convinced, nor were the film critics, nor were the more than 15 million Americans who flocked to see JFK. Read what the guardians of the Warren Commission official verdict have to say, to be sure, but then read Tom Oliphant of *The Boston Globe* Roger Ebert of *The Chicago Sun Times* and other film critics, read Robert Hennelley and Jerry Policoff of *The Village Voice*, and Gaeton Fonzi of the House Committee on Assassinations staff. Read Profs. Peter Dale Scott and Todd Gitlin, and chuckle at Gary Trudeau's exposure of the media "conspiracy" against Oliver Stone. With the demolition of the single bullet theory, the lone gunman theory collapses as well. And with a serious look at the Establishment journalists who attacked the film so frenziedly, a new generation of defenders of American history and American ideals has come to the fore. Perhaps that is the highest achievement of *JFK*.

MAY 14, 1991

DALLAS MORNING NEWS

JFK MOVIE AND BOOK ATTEMPT TO REWRITE HISTORY

Jon Margolis

Whether or not it is a gift, artistic talent conveys a responsibility. Those who can sway emotions ought to know what they are talking about, lest emotions be swayed toward foolishness.

Unhappily, there is no law of nature that ordains that talent will be accompanied by knowledge, much less by wisdom, and the uninformed poet, painter, musician or novelist is commonplace in our time.

Most do little harm because art, even popular entertainment, has far less impact than either its practitioners or its critics like to think. People are smarter than artists and critics, and know better than to confuse novels, movies or plays with reality. *The Right Stuff*, a good movie, did John Glenn's presidential campaign no good; and *Missing*, a bad one, had no discernible impact on public attitudes toward Latin America.

Still, some insults to intelligence and decency rise (sink?) far enough to warrant objection. Such an insult now looms. It is *JFK*, Oliver Stone's film based largely on a book called *On The Trail of the Assassins*, by Jim Garrison.

For those who have forgotten or are too young to remember, Garrison was the bizarre New Orleans district attorney who, in 1969, claimed that the assassination of President John Kennedy was a conspiracy by some officials of the Central Intelligence Agency.

Garrison even managed to put one hapless fellow on trial for his role in this alleged conspiracy. Having no case, Garrison lost in court. Nothing if not tenacious, he expanded his arguments for the book, published in 1988.

A very clever woman once said of another writer that her only believable words were "and" and "but." With Garrison, one can't be sure even of those conjunctions. One example among many: Garrison writes that the less-than-conclusive testimony of one waitress "constituted the totality of the witness testimony identifying Lee Oswald" as the man who killed a Dallas patrolman after shooting the president. There were in fact six witnesses who either saw the patrolman get shot or saw the armed gunman running from the scene. All six identified Oswald.

And lest you think that only movie directors and bizarre district attorneys have no shame, consider this: Warner Books, a division of Time-Warner, the largest publishing-entertainment conglomerate in human history, is paying Garrison $137,500 to re-issue the book when the movie comes out.

Speaking of conspiracy theories, what are the odds that this transaction will influence Time magazine's review of the book or the movie, considering that Warner Bros. is distributing the film, which after its theater run could appear on HBO and Cinemax, also owned by Time-Warner?

But, wait, it gets worse. According to people who have seen the script, Stone takes Garrison's fantasies one step farther. In the movie, it is not just the C.I.A., but Vice President Lyndon Johnson himself behind the plot to kill the president.

To remember Lyndon Johnson is not to love him. But the suggestion that Johnson would stoop to murder, stupidly plotting with men he knew enough to distrust, is even less credible than was Johnson at his worst.

Then there is the matter of evidence. Not a scintilla of it links Johnson to Kennedy's assassination. Not that there's much to link anyone at all to it other than Lee Harvey Oswald. Stone has said that "nobody" believes Oswald alone killed Kennedy. Actually, many of us do, not because anyone can be certain that there was no conspiracy, but because all conspiracies that have been alleged are unsupported by credible data and require far more suspension of disbelief than does acceptance of the prosaic likelihood that poor Oswald did it by himself, because he was mad.

But Stone is one of those who sees conspiracies everywhere. "We have a fascist security state running this country," he told a Los Angeles Times interviewer. "Orwell did happen. But it's so subtle that no one noticed."

How fortunate is he to be so much more observant than everyone else, to see this reality hidden from us mere mortals. But then, we're all pretty fortunate, living in the world's first fascist security state that freely allows dissent of its war policies throughout a war.

There is a point at which intellectual myopia becomes morally repugnant. Stone's new movie proves that he has passed that point. But then, so has Time-Warner, and so will anyone who pays American money to see the film.

MAY 19, 1991

THE WASHINGTON POST

ON THE SET: DALLAS IN WONDERLAND

How Oliver Stone's Version of the Kennedy Assassination
Exploits the Edge of Paranoia

George Lardner Jr.

The presidential motorcade is revving up on Main Street. The crowd outside the Texas School Book Depository gets ready for another round of cheering until the gunshots ring out. John F. Kennedy is about to be killed in Dealey Plaza again, and again, and again.

The director's instructions bark out over the walkie-talkies, making sure his sharpshooters get the message.

"I said, 'all five shots.' All right. Everybody in position now. Ready to fire."

Five shots? Is this the Kennedy assassination or the Charge of the Light Brigade?

Film maker Oliver Stone seems unperturbed. The controversial, Oscar-winning chronicler of the 1960s and the war in Vietnam (*Platoon, Born on the Fourth of July*) is in the midst of a $35- to $40- million production about the murder, tentatively titled *JFK*. His hero: former New Orleans District Attorney Jim Garrison whose zany investigation of the assassination in the late 1960s has almost faded from memory. Garrison, now 69, has pronounced himself well-pleased with the script, written by Stone and Zachary Sklar, who was editor of *On the Trail of the Assassins*, Garrison's 1988 book. He should be more pleased with the casting. Kevin Costner plays him.

The script is a movieland equivalent of Top Secret, and at Stone's Camelot Productions, everyone hired has to sign a confidentiality agreement about "the Project." Though Garrison, too, was sworn to secrecy, he told the *New Orleans Times-Picayune* that it was "a magnificent job." And he allowed that it "closely follows" his book.

What that means is that Oliver Stone is chasing fiction. Garrison's investigation was a fraud.

Stone has said that he considers himself a "cinematic historian" and has called

191

the assassination "the seminal event of my generation." But Harold Weisberg, a longtime critic of the F.B.I. and Warren Commission investigations of the assassination—and who has little patience for many of the conspiracy theories that keep popping up—protests: "To do a mishmash like this out of love for the victim and respect for history? I think people who sell sex have more principle."

"An interview with Oliver Stone?" his chief publicist, Andrea Jaffe, said. "What kind of story are you writing? ... A news story?" she said with a touch of caution, if not distaste. Two days later, the word came back: Stone wasn't talking.

A copy of the original script was obtained by Weisberg and made available to *The Washington Post*. And while there isn't space to list all the errors and absurdities, large and small, some are deserving of special mention.

THE MAN IN THE RED WIG

For this reporter, one of the most interesting flights of fancy involves the death of David Ferrie, one of Garrison's prime targets. I was probably the last person to see him alive.

In reality, in the wake of J.F.K.'s murder, authorities began receiving a wild batch of second-hand reports about Ferrie, a vain, nervous flight school instructor based in New Orleans: that he knew Lee Harvey Oswald and might have hypnotized him, that he might have gone to Dallas as a "getaway pilot" for a presidential assassin. Dismissed from Eastern Airlines in March 1963 because of a record of homosexual arrests, Ferrie had been interrogated shortly after the assassination by Garrison's men, the Secret Service and the F.B.I. (which found nothing). But Ferrie became a Garrison target when the DA decided in the fall of 1966 that the "truth" about the assassination remained untold by the Warren Commission, but was still within his grasp.

Ferrie denied knowing Oswald. In any case, he had an alibi. Employed as a private investigator for attorneys of reputed Mafia kingpin Carlos Marcello, Ferrie had been sitting outside a federal courtroom in New Orleans waiting for the verdict in a case against Marcello (not guilty) until several hours after Kennedy was killed. Then he went to Texas for a weekend trip with two of his ever-present, always-changing young companions. But they went to Houston and Galveston, not Dallas.

On Feb. 22, 1967, five days after the *New Orleans States-Item* disclosed Garrison's probe, Ferrie was found dead in his apartment. Garrison promptly pronounced him "one of history's important individuals" and claimed that he had been about to "arrest" Ferrie on unspecified charges. "There's no question about the fact that it's a suicide," the DA said.

The coroner, Dr. Nicholas Chetta, held flatly that Ferrie, 49, died of natural causes despite several undated notes found in his apartment that suggested suicide and unrequited love for a man named "Al". Chetta said death was due to a cerebral hemorrhage. Ferrie, he declared, could only have killed himself by worrying himself to death under the "stress and strain" of Garrison's investigation.

Stone gives Ferrie's demise a different spin, at least in the script he started with.

In a scene labelled the "NIGHT BEFORE," Ferrie runs into the toilet, looking terrified, chased by two Cubans known as "Bull" and "the Indian." They catch Ferrie at the sink, "yank him back by the hair," and start forcing medicine down his throat. Moments later, they are busy typing a note, perhaps trying to force Ferrie to sign it as "he convulses, dies."

Strange. I used that same bathroom a few hours later, in the course of a four-hour conversation with Ferrie (he said he was convinced Garrison's investigation would turn out to be a "witch hunt"). Ferrie was very much alive when we walked downstairs at around 4 a.m. I didn't see any Cubans—or anyone else.

As for Ferrie's hair, there was none to yank him back by. The grotesque-looking wretch wore a red wig that, which seemed to be cut from a rug, and penciled-in eyebrows. He didn't have a hair on his head or anywhere else, as reporters later confirmed on visits to the morgue. And there wasn't a mark on his body to suggest rough handling by any "Bull" or "Indian."

Two days after Ferrie's death, with the international press snapped to attention, Garrison announced that he had solved the assassination "beyond any shadow of a doubt." Not a conspirator would escape, Garrison declared. "The only way they can get away from us is by killing themselves."

THE HYPNOTIZED WITNESS

It was only after these surreal pronouncements that Garrison stumbled across his star witness, a 25-year-old salesman named Perry Russo. Russo knew Ferrie and, after prodding under hypnosis, claimed to have been at a party in September 1963 that wound up with Ferrie, Oswald and a New Orleans businessman named Clay Shaw discussing an assassination plot. The name "Clay" was first mentioned to the hypnotized Russo by the hypnotist.

On this flimsy pretext, Shaw was arrested on a charge of conspiring to kill Kennedy and, 22 grueling months later, brought to trial. It lasted 34 days and contained numerous embarrassments for the prosecution. Chief among them was Charles I. Spiesel, a New York accountant presented by Garrison's men as a surprise witness. He told of a June 1963 party in the French Quarter where, he said, Ferrie and Shaw talked freely about why Kennedy should be killed and how it could be done.

On cross-examination, it turned out that Spiesel, a short balding man in his fifties, had filed civil suits demanding millions of dollars from New York police, the Pinkerton detective agency, a psychiatrist and others, for conspiring to keep him under hypnosis and torture him until confidential information had been extracted. He estimated that 50 to 60 enemies had hypnotized him in the past few years, planting wild ideas in his head. It took jurors less than an hour to find Shaw not guilty.

How does Oliver Stone explain this and still make it a heroic Garrisonian struggle against the feds? Well, for one thing, the script eliminates Perry Russo; he doesn't exist. That is certainly a convenient device. I can remember conversations with Russo in June 1967. He invited me to bribe him to disclose "weaknesses" in his testimony.

"If you say anything about this," Russo added, "I'm going to have to call you a liar." I wrote a story about it anyway. Garrison showed no interest in it, at least none that I know about. But some two weeks later, he accused Walter Sheridan of NBC of "public bribery" for what appears to have been a similar set of conversations with Russo. Of course, nothing ever came of the charges.

For Stone, the dilemma is clear. The Shaw trial was a disaster, so the movie needed a villain to explain it away, a double agent on the DA's staff. Get ready to meet Bill Boxley, a very strange case indeed. He's also conveniently dead. He can't sue.

DEAD MAN ON THE GRASSY KNOLL

In Oliver Stone's script, Bill Boxley is depicted as an insidious insider who keeps scoffing at the idea of a conspiracy on the part of the intelligence community. At one point, Boxley tells Garrison he could buy the idea that the Mafia did it "a hell of a lot easier," then walks out when Garrison insists that "this was a military-style ambush from start to finish ... a coup d'état with Lyndon waiting in the wings."

"You're losing your marbles, chief," screenwriter Stone has the faithless Boxley saying.

Boxley's real name was William C. Wood, a gun-toting former CIA officer who was forced to leave the agency in 1953 because of alcoholism. A sometime journalist, salesman and private detective, he became interested in the investigation as an editor of a Texas weekly and was eagerly signed up by Garrison in May 1967 as a special investigator. Garrison gave him the alias of Boxley "to keep it quiet that we had a former agency man aboard." He saw in Wood/Boxley a chance to understand the "mentality of the agency."

The two grew quite close, but about 18 months later, Garrison fired him. The DA attributed Boxley's abrupt dismissal in a press release to "evidence recently developed by the District Attorney's staff [that] indicated current activity by him as an operative of the Central Intelligence Agency."

What Garrison didn't say then, or in his book, was that he was, with Boxley's help, about to indict for Kennedy's November 1963 murder a man who had committed suicide in August 1962.

That's right. Garrison, in his Alice-in-Wonderland world was convinced that a construction worker named Robert L. Perrin was the "man on the grassy knoll" who really shot J.F.K. He just wouldn't believe that Perrin was dead, even though a Louisiana state police employee who knew Perrin identified his arsenic laden corpse. The dutiful Boxley dredged up some downstairs neighbors who had never had a close look at Perrin to say they didn't recognize the morgue photo.

From there, the plot thickened. Neighbors identified one of the men in the celebrated "tramp photo" as someone who lived right across the hall from the man who was—or wasn't—Perrin!

Every student of the assassination knows about the three "tramps", probably local winos. They may have been guilty of mopery, but they had nothing to do with the assassination. They were found in a boxcar three blocks away, still hanging around 90 minutes after Kennedy was killed, and then were marched by police across the tracks in front of the Book Depository. They have been suspects ever since—"positively" identified as anyone and everyone from Watergate conspirator E. Howard Hunt to L.B.J.'s farm manager. "You have no idea of what's happened to those three poor men," says author Harold Weisberg.

According to Weisberg, who worked closely with Garrison and his staff until he became disgusted with the inquiry, Garrison was bent on indicting Perrin and the "tramps" on Nov. 22, 1968, to commemorate the fifth anniversary of the assassination. The DA's regular staff, alarmed that their boss was about to blow himself out of the water, tried to talk him out of it but all they could do was win a delay and appeal to Weisberg for help.

"Almost all of Boxley's nuttiness was feedback," Weisberg says. "He'd go out and make up the evidence to suit Garrison's theories."

Weisberg flew to New Orleans, holed himself up in the DA's office and wrote a lengthy report demolishing Boxley's claims. He also brought with him Philadelphia lawyer Vincent Salandria, an assasination critic full of far-out theories whom Garrison regarded highly. While Weisberg worked, Salandria met with Garrison to convince him that Boxley was "sent in by the CIA to destroy Garrison."

"I would see anybody trying to destroy Garrison as a CIA agent," Salandria recalled in a recent telephone interview. "In fact, I saw CIA when Oswald was killed by [Jack] Ruby. Even before. That weekend, I said if a Jew comes in and kills Oswald—and I'm not being anti-semitic, I'm married to a Jew—but if a Jew comes in and kills Oswald, then its CIA."

"I never met Boxley," Salandria told me. "I based my conclusions on standard operating procedure for intelligence agencies."

In the script, Garrison gets the news about Boxley from one of his prosecutors with the Shaw trial about to begin: "He [Boxley]'s working for the federal government," the aide tells Garrison. "It means they have everything, Jim. All our witnesses, our strategy for the trial." This serves as the excuse for the disastrous testimony of Charles Spiesel. "He was one of Boxley's witnesses, Chief," the Stone script quotes one of Garrison's prosecutors as saying. "I'm sorry. He was totally sane when we talked."

In fact, Boxley had nothing to do with Spiesel or his comeuppance. And there is no evidence that Boxley was working for the feds. But for Garrison, facts were irrelevant once he seized on an idea, as he demonstrated for his staff the day after Boxley was fired.

"It was a bizarre scene," Weisberg recalls. "Salandria was making a speech about how Leon Trotsky was killed. Garrison had a blackboard. He drew a map of the United States on it and gave a geographical dissertation on the 'seats of the conspiracy.' Up in the Pacific Northwest, he had a mark for the Boeing Co. Then there was Dallas for [oilman] H.L.Hunt. In New Orleans, there was the Michoud plant [Chrysler Aerospace]. Then there was Marietta, Georgia, for Lockheed."

THEY ALL KILLED J.F.K.

So who killed Jack Kennedy according to Oliver Stone? And why?

The script mentions a variety of scenarios, but the one given the most weight turns on a crossfire of five or more shots from the Book Depository, the rooftop of the County Records Building, sometimes the Dal-Tex Building, and, of course, "the grassy knoll."

The fatal shot is the fifth one, fired not by Lee Harvey Oswald, but from the knoll by a uniformed Dallas policeman, standing behind a picket fence. "Badgeman".

"Possibly, 'Badgeman's' been infiltrated from military intelligence into the Dallas Police Department," the screenplay for Kevin "Garrison" Costner says at one point. "Or maybe he was just a fake cop, who knows?"

Oswald doesn't pull a trigger. He's putzing around at the Coke machine in the second floor lunchroom of the Book Depository.

So who's upstairs in the sixth-floor sniper's lair? Some Cubans, it seems. "One of them is Bull," seen earlier muscling some medicine down Ferrie's throat. "Indian," the other figment of the Ferrie attack is on the rooftop of the County Records Building. Then there are the "grassy knoll shooters," setting up a triangle of fire.

In some takes, there are as many as seven shots tossed in as Costner-Garrison intones, "it's possible even a sixth shot takes the president in the rear of the head … a seventh shot hits Connally again."

The plethora of bullets comes as a surprise to the acoustics experts who studied a police recording of the noises in Dealey Plaza for the House Assassinations Committee in 1978. In findings that were later disputed by the F.B.I., the Dallas police and a panel of the National Academy of Sciences—but that still seem more plausible than any of the criticisms—the experts concluded that there was indeed a fourth shot from "the grassy knoll." Trajectory and other tests indicated strongly that it missed the presidential limousine.

"There is absolutely no [acoustical] evidence of a fifth shot," says Mark Weiss, one of the acoustics experts.

"The likelihood of there being five shots was so small that I didn't count it," said James Barger, another House committee expert.

The idea of a police officer firing from the knoll, hit or miss, stems from a picture taken on the other side of Elm street by a bystander, Mary Moorman, just as the fatal bullet blew the president's head apart.

In the background, behind the picket fence, the picture fades into foliage that looks like an ink blot. But if you look closely at blowups developed by two assassination researchers, Gary Mack and Jack White, and stare long enough, you can make out what could be a face, a light spot that could be a puff of smoke, and even what could be—keep staring—part of a shoulder patch.

The trouble is, this spot is too far away from the point at which the House acoustics tests place the "grassy knoll" shot.

In Stone's script, however, nothing succeeds like excess. He not only has

"Badgeman" killing Kennedy, he has him handing off his rifle to someone else who hands it off to someone else who—gasp!—"looks like one of the hobos" who puts it in a tool box.

Key advisers to Stone in the making of the movie are three founding directors of a for-profit assassination museum in Dallas. They seem never to have met a conspiracy theory they didn't like. It was the center that, about a year ago, unveiled the preposterous story of Ricky White, a 29-year-old salesman who claimed that his father, a former Dallas police officer, shot the president from the grassy knoll on orders from the CIA. White said that in a diary his father kept—later pilfered by the F.B.I., of course—his father said it was he, and not Lee Harvey Oswald, who killed Dallas police officer J.D. Tippit.

Oliver Stone met with Ricky White last year. Publicist Jaffe insists the story was rejected, but the movie script offers a scene showing Oswald, Tippit and "Badgeman" riding together in a patrol car. They argue. "Badgeman shoots Tippit. Oswald gets away," the script has Garrison intoning as the scene shifts to the Shaw trial. "I admit it's just a theory, but it gets to the source of some of the confusion here."

Since this is Oliver Stone, the "why" of the assassination should come as no surprise. It's Vietnam, of course. In a peroration that might have been written by Garrison himself, DA Costner assails the murder as "a coup d'état"—hold your breath—ordered up by "a shadow government consisting of corrupt men at the highest levels of the Pentagon, the intelligence establishment and the giant multinational corporations," carried out by elements of the intelligence community and covered up "by like-minded individuals in the Dallas Police Department, the Secret Service, the F.B.I. and the White House—all the way up to an including J. Edgar Hoover and Lyndon Johnson whom I consider accomplices after the fact."

The screenplay ends the Sunday Oswald was killed with a White House scene of Johnson meeting with his Vietnam advisors. "He signs something unseen" and tells them: "Gentlemen, I want you to know I'm personally committed to Vietnam. I'm not going to take one soldier out of there till they know we mean business in Asia."

That is nonsense. In a memo L.B.J. signed after that Sunday meeting, he explicitly stated that the 1,000 troop withdrawal would be carried out. And it was. There was no abrupt change in Vietnam policy after J.F.K.'s death.

LUNCH WITH KEVIN COSTNER

The tab was on Oliver Stone, so Pershing Gervais ordered the most expensive items on the menu. It was late March and Gervais, once Jim Garrison's chief investigator, had agreed to come to New Orleans for a chat with Stone and Kevin Costner.

Gervais says he tried to give Costner some friendly advice. "I told him, 'You look like a nice fella. You got a reputation for being a real good actor. But you're going to have to be superb to play an [expletive] like Garrison.'"

Costner just shrugged. "Costner said, 'Nobody in America believes Oswald did it,'" Gervais recalled. "I said, 'I'll show how dumb I am. I think it was him. The first time I saw Oswald's smirking face on television, after he was arrested, I knew it was him.'"

Gervais is in the minority, however, and has been for years. A *Washington Post* poll this month showed that 56 percent of the American public thinks the assassination was the result of a conspiracy (down from 66 percent at the height of the Garrison investigation). Only 19 percent think Oswald was acting on his own, as the Warren Commission concluded years ago. Of those who thought there was a conspiracy, 36 percent said Oswald fired the shots, while 49 percent said he was set up by others and did not fire any shots at all.

Stone , who is reportedly revising the script as he goes along, will begin filming in New Orleans shortly, taking his star-studded cast with him. It includes Sissy Spacek, John Candy, Walter Matthau and Jack Lemmon.

All the hoopla, of course, will obscure the absurdities, and palpable untruths in Garrison's book and Stone's rendition of it.

"I keep remembering, Stone said to me, 'I'm in this to make a buck,'" Gervais declared. "I thought, 'That sounds like an apology.'"

Longtime Dallas DA Henry Wade, now in private practice, said he thought the Republic would survive in any case. The last movie he saw in a real theater was Mark Lane's muddled stew of fact and fiction about the assassination, *Executive Action*, in 1973.

"It was wild as far as the facts were concerned," he said, "and it didn't win any Oscars ... I've always thought that the public, whether young or old, are smarter than they get credit for."

JUNE 2,1991

THE WASHINGTON POST
OUTLOOK

STONE'S *JFK*: A HIGHER TRUTH?
The Post, *George Lardner and My Version of the J.F.K. Assassination*

Oliver Stone

The following statement by Oliver Stone was originally submitted to The Washington Post *as a letter to the editor.* Outlook *has made minor deletions with the agreement of the author. Stone is aware that George Lardner has prepared the accompanying response.*

On May 19, *Outlook* ran a lengthy diatribe by George Lardner directed at *JFK*, my forthcoming film about the assassination of John F. Kennedy. Let me explain why we are making this movie and what it is about.

The murder of President Kennedy was a seminal event for me and for millions of Americans. It changed the course of history. It was a crushing blow to our country and to millions of people around the world. It put an abrupt end to a period of innocence and great idealism.

Today, nearly 30 years later, profound doubts persist about how President Kennedy was killed and why. The Warren Commission's conclusion that Lee Harvey Oswald acted alone is not believed by most people. The House Select Committee on Assassinations (HSCA) concluded in 1979 that President Kennedy "probably was assassinated as a result of a conspiracy" and that "government agencies performed inadequately" in investigating the assassination. Our movie is a metaphor for all those doubts, suspicions and unanswered questions.

The movie is not, as Lardner suggested, the "Jim Garrison story." It does use the Garrison investigation as the vehicle to explore the various credible assassination theories, and incorporates everything that has been discovered in the 20 years since Garrison's efforts.

It does not purport to "solve" this murder mystery. What I hope this film will do, when it is finished, is remind people how much our nation and our world lost when President Kennedy died, and to ask anew what might have happened and why. In the words of Thomas Jefferson, "Eternal vigilance is the price of Liberty."

In sticking by the Warren Commission report, *The Washington Post* has always supported and held to an account of the assassination more fictional than I could ever imagine.

The Warren Commission concluded that: 1) Oswald acting alone killed President Kennedy and Dallas police officer J.D. Tippit; 2) Jack Ruby acting alone killed Oswald; 3) there was no credible evidence of a conspiracy; 4) only three shots were fired.

Even today, our film is having to rely on bits and pieces of information because the Warren Commission urged that its material be sealed and kept from the public until the year 2039. Even then, the CIA has the option of continuing this censorship until the year 2118. Are the interests of the American public served by waiting this long?

I don't know if I'm more shocked or amused over the fact that a *Washington Post* reporter of the stature of George Lardner, who for years has covered government intelligence activities, would find our movie so important that he would admit in his article to obtaining a confidential first draft of our script through unofficial channels and then proceed to quote from it out of context (the draft has significantly changed as we are now on the sixth draft). Aside from the issue of whether a newspaper can print copyrighted material (including the end of a movie) and consequently seek to damage the commercial prospects of a private enterprise (a film company is not a government office; our documents are not public property), it is accepted practice in the theatrical sector 1) to wait for the movie to be made and review that (not the script) and 2) to not tell the audience what they are going to see. This is a standard The Post seems dedicated to changing.

Filmmakers and book publishers stay in business because they entertain and educate the public. Movies like *The Alamo, Patton, Dances with Wolves* and *The Battle of Algiers* have to sift through volumes of documentation, much of which contradicts itself.

Contradictions are the nature of reality. Both Congress and Harold Weisberg, whom Lardner quoted in the story, believe that the F.B.I. and CIA withheld evidence that might have resulted in different findings by the Warren Commission.

The Washington Post, and Lardner in particular, have stood by in silence while the CIA and F.B.I. have allowed evidence of a crime and historical documents significant to our history to be stolen or destroyed. It is as hard for me to understand The Post's silence as it is to understand Lardner's attack on an entertainment project.

Lardner takes a curious position on the assassination. He ridicules Garrison for thinking that the Warren Commission didn't tell the "truth" (his quotes) about the assassination and never bothers to say that the federal government wasn't convinced either—why else did the House Select Committee on Assassination exist? He even makes Weisberg—supposedly his ally—out to be anti-conspiracy despite the fact that Weisberg has done more damage to the Warren Commission than any other researcher through his persistent Freedom of Information Act suits.

The Post criticized Garrison for not having found the truth. Instead, we at Camelot Productions see Garrison as one of the few men of that time who had the courage to stand up to the establishment and seek the truth. He symbolizes the American public's nagging sense of doubt about the pat conclusions of the Warren Commission. And in him we have found a protagonist of merit.

Jim Garrison didn't want to see the flame of life that was John F. Kennedy extinguished without bringing his killer—or killers—to justice. Is the sad part that he failed, or that he was one of the few persons in America willing to try?

Concerning Lardner's presentation of the "facts":

◆ David Ferrie's death: Lardner is the last man we know of to see Ferrie alive. He claims he left Ferrie alive. He claims he left Ferrie's apartment at 4 a.m., but the coroner (Dr. Chetta) claimed that from Ferrie's state of rigor mortis, he had been dead since before 4 a.m. Also, the presence of two suicide notes and 15 bottles of pills (some empty) should indicate something more than natural causes. Additionally, the HSCA heard testimony that Ferrie worked for the CIA and confirmed that he was deeply involved with CIA-funded Cuban exile terrorists.

◆ The Clay Shaw verdict: Yes, the jury returned a verdict of not guilty on Clay Shaw, but Lardner does not point out the larger accomplishment of the trial. In interviews after the trial, most of the jurors indicated that they were now certain that there had been a conspiracy to kill the president, but whether Clay Shaw was part of it hadn't been proven beyond a reasonable doubt. Lardner ignores the fact that former CIA director Richard Helms admitted under oath that Shaw was a contact for the agency and that the agency had failed to acknowledge this. Lardner also ignores that Shaw was director of a company expelled from Italy for illegal espionage activities. Additionally, Lardner implies that Perry Russo was the only witness to link Shaw, Ferrie and Oswald, when in fact there were more than half a dozen witnesses who linked this trio. The HSCA in 1979 established "an association of an undetermined nature between Ferrie, Shaw and Oswald."

◆ The hobo photos: He says, "They may have been guilty of mopery, but they had nothing to do with the assassination." I'd love to know the source of this, especially as these men have never been identified. The Warren Commission testimony of Dallas police Sgt. D.V. Harkness places the hobos' arrest about 25-30 minutes after the shooting—not 90 as Lardner claimed—and they were taken off a train behind the Book Depository, not from the other side of Dealey Plaza, as Lardner asserted.

Bona fide hobos or imposters—either way, there's no justification for Dallas law enforcement officials' negligence in taking their names at such a critical time.

◆ Acoustics evidence: On page 71 of the HSCA Report, it says there were six impulse patterns on the Dictabelt, two of which did not come from either the Texas School Book Depository or the grassy knoll (the only locations tested). All six of these impulses exhibited the traditional S-curve of high-powered rifle fire in Dealey Plaza (that is, they could not have been anything else). Lardner claims that there is no evidence of a fifth shot, but what he should be saying is that the fifth shot—and the sixth—did not come from either firing point tested by the HSCA but from a third location.

◆ Vietnam policy: Lardner has misinterpreted National Security Action Memo 273, concerning an early withdrawal of troops from Vietnam, either wittingly or unwittingly, asserting that it "explicitly stated the 1,000-troop withdrawal would be carried out." Not true at all. It did not say that, and the withdrawal never happened. What we have here is deliberate attempt to disguise the policy reversal in the wake of Kennedy's death. After November 1963, no actual reduction of U.S. military men in Vietnam ever occurred. As we all know, the opposite happened. Kennedy is quoted several times by associates as intending to withdraw from Vietnam after the 1964 campaign. According to William Gibbons's *The Government and the Vietnam War*, the withdrawal of 1,000 troops was achieved on paper only, by "juggling the figures to make it look like there were 1,000 fewer men."

◆ Pershing Gervais: Lardner should not rely on someone like Pershing Gervais for insight into Garrison's character. As Garrison demonstrates in his book, *On the Trail of the Assassins*, Gervais tried to set Jim up for criminal prosecution.

◆ Oswald's alibi: Several witnesses, including Carolyn Arnold, Roy Truly, Mrs. Robert A. Reid and Officer Marion Baker all saw Oswald on the second floor of the Texas School Book Depository Building immediately before or after the shooting. Carolyn Arnold's insistence that she saw Oswald in the second floor lunchroom between 12:15 and 12:25 p.m. is mysteriously absent from her F.B.I. statement, probably because it proves that Oswald was definitely not the gunman seen by witness Arnold Rowland in the sixth-floor window at 12:15. Not a single witness can place Oswald on the sixth floor at the time of the shooting at all, let alone with a gun in his hand.

◆ The fourth shot: Lardner comes close to making history here as he admits "experts conclude there was indeed a fourth shot from the 'grassy knoll.'" This is the first time The Post has printed that there were four shots. Of course this destroys the Warren Commission. Or does Lardner think there were two lone assassins, each trying to kill Kennedy at the same time?

Why is Lardner so worried about our movie? Why is he so concerned that the investigation not be reopened? Lardner admits to a conspiracy, so why is he so afraid people might see it? If I am the buffoon he and Outlook's demonizing cartoon make me out to be, no one will really believe my film. I can't but feel there is another agenda here. Does *The Washington Post* object to our right to make a movie our way, or does it just object to our disagreeing with its views that the Warren Commission was right?

I suppose I shouldn't be surprised by a newspaper trying to kill the making of a movie. That has happened in Hollywood ever since the Hearst papers and its reporters attacked *Citizen Kane*. Should we be so surprised by history repeating itself so long after *Citizen Kane*? Not really.

But then one purpose of our movie is to see that in at least one instance history does not repeat itself. We can only hope the free thinkers in the world, those with no agenda, will recognize our movie as an emotional experience that speaks a higher truth than the Lardners of the world will ever know.

Reprinted by permission of the author.

JUNE 2, 1991

THE WASHINGTON POST
OUTLOOK

OR JUST A SLOPPY MESS?
Facts Speak for Themselves but Stone Doesn't Seem to Know Them

George Lardner Jr.

The best thing that can be said about Oliver Stone's letter is that he is not a careful reader of *The Washington Post*. He accuses us of still believing the Warren

Commission down the line, of standing by "in silence" while agencies we cover for the public "allowed evidence of a crime and historical documents ... to be stolen or destroyed." Since Stone offers no particulars, it is impossible to tell what he means. The only incident that comes to mind is the time a CIA officer rifled through files of the House assassinations committee. But I disclosed that episode in *The Post* in 1979.

Stone complains that his film has to rely on "bits and pieces of information" because so much is locked up. This is silly. Warren Commission records began to be made public in the mid-'60s. Hundreds of thousands of pages have been released since then. These included records that, *The Post* reported in 1977, showed the F.B.I. to be "more interested in investigating the motives and affiliations of its critics than in pursuing contradictions offered by the evidence at the scene of the crime."

After noting darkly that I have "covered government intelligence activities" for *The Post*, Stone says I "admit" in the *Outlook* article "to obtaining a confidential first draft of the script." The script is about as confidential as a press release. My copy, as I wrote, came from Harold Weisberg, a longtime critic of the Warren Commission. As Stone should know, many copies are floating about. One reporter told me he got a copy from a New York literary agent.

Let me take his other points one at a time:

◆ David Ferrie's death: Ferrie, a target of former New Orleans DA Jim Garrison's investigation, was found dead in his apartment on Feb. 22, 1967 around 11 a.m. I was probably the last man to see Ferrie alive. Is Stone suggesting that I interviewed a dead man? In fact, the coroner originally said Ferrie died around midnight, then redid that aspect of the autopsy after I told him he was wrong. "This man died a natural death," the coroner, Dr. Nicholas Chetta, declared several times in concluding Ferrie, who suffered from hypertension, died from a cerebral hemorrhage.

It is, of course, true that the House assassinations committee may have "heard testimony" about Ferrie and the CIA. It may also have "heard" that Kennedy was killed from a UFO. Ferrie was involved in anti-Castro activities, a fact widely reported at the time, but there is no proof that he worked for the CIA.

◆ The Shaw Verdict: Stone maintains that "the larger accomplishment" of the Clay Shaw travesty was that the jurors were convinced there had been a conspiracy to kill the president. Who needed a trial for that? A Harris poll almost two years earlier showed that two of three Americans believed the same thing. As for Shaw's "associations" with the CIA, he was a widely traveled businessman who had occasional contacts with the CIA's Domestic Contact Service. Does that make him an assassin?

I never suggested that Perry Russo was "the only witness to link Shaw, Ferrie and [Lee Harvey] Oswald." I said he was Garrison's key witness for a conspiratorial discussion the trio allegedly had and that Russo dragged Shaw into it after prompting by a hypnotist. Stone's script, at least the one he started with, eliminates Perry Russo. I'm not surprised.

◆ The hobo photos: As for the so-called "tramps," Weisberg points out that two independent investigations, undertaken in 1968 to establish the facts of the tramps' apprehension, showed that they had taken refuge in the boxcar to get drunk and that the only reason they were photographed in front of the Book Depository was that it was the only way for the police to walk them out of the yard without heisting them up to a loading dock behind the Central Annex Post Office. Stone's account of Sgt. D.V. Harkness's testimony is wrong; Harkness told the Warren Commission nothing about when and where in the railroad yard the "tramps" were picked up. Stone sees "no justification" for the failure of the Dallas police to get the men's names. But even if they had, conspiracy theorists would just insist the men had lied about who they were.

◆ Vietnam policy: Stone, in his script, has Lyndon Johnson meeting with his Vietnam advisers two days after the assassination, countermanding J.F.K.'s order to withdraw 1,000 military personnel from Vietnam by the end of 1963. I called the scene "nonsense" and said the L.B.J. memo after the meeting ordered the withdrawal to be carried out. Let me quote from NSAM No. 273: "The objectives of the United States with respect to the withdrawal of U.S. military personnel remain as stated in the White House statement of Oct. 2, 1963 [approving among other things 'plans to withdraw 1,000 military personnel by the end of 1963.']" Historian Gibbons told me the withdrawal did take place and was offset in succeeding months.

"Kennedy, if he had carried it out, would have done it just as Johnson did it," Gibbons said. He added that the withdrawal "was never more than a device ... a way of putting pressure on the [South] Vietnamese" to take up more of the burden. "Any thought that it had anything to do with getting out, withdrawing entirely," Gibbons said, "is absurd."

◆ Pershing Gervais: Garrison's book "demonstrates" nothing but a facility for gothic fiction. Gervais, incidentally, says he would be "delighted" to take a polygraph test on whether he tried to frame Garrison—and on any other points in dispute.

◆ Where Oswald was: Stone did change his response on this after I pointed out errors in his original reply, but he still misinterprets a descriptive paragraph in my May 19 article as an assertion as to where Oswald was, or wasn't, at the time of the shooting.

◆ Acoustics evidence: Acoustics experts for the House assassinations committee found six impulse patterns that *could* have been rifle shots because they passed "preliminary screening tests." Stone transforms this into proof positive. "Certainly, nothing I ever did or said would have supported his [Stone's] certainty," one of the experts, James Barger, told me. The experts concluded that there were four shots:

three from the Book Depository and one from the "grassy knoll."

It is typical of Stone's confusion that at one point he accuses us of adhering to the Warren Commission and later says my Outlook article was "the first time *The Post* has printed that there were four shots." I reported on that finding in several front-page stories in 1978; it was subsequently the subject of numerous stories in *The Post*, including articles highlighting the committee's finding that Kennedy was "probably assassinated as the result of a conspiracy."

On a more personal note: My acknowledgement that a probable conspiracy took place is not an acknowledgement that Garrison's investigation was anything but a fraud. And no amount of screenwriting can change that fact. Stone claims an interest in history. Why is he so sloppy with it?

JUNE 10, 1991

TIME

MORE SHOTS IN DEALEY PLAZA
Oliver Stone returns to the '60s once again with a strange,
widely disputed take on the Kennedy assassination

Richard Zoglin

Did Lee Harvey Oswald act alone? Were three shots fired in Dealey Plaza on that awful afternoon in November, or were there more? Was there a large scale, sinister conspiracy behind the assassination of John F. Kennedy, or just one troubled little man with communist sympathies and a Mannlicher-Carcano rifle?

Unanswered questions about the Kennedy assassination have nagged the nation for nearly 28 years, rousing emotions, inciting speculation, provoking arguments. It was probably inevitable that Hollywood would step into this minefield sooner or later—and probably inevitable that the man leading the charge would be Oliver Stone, filmdom's most flamboyant interpreter of the 1960s (*Platoon, The Doors, Born on the Fourth of July*).

Stone is only halfway through shooting his movie about the assassination, for which he has staged an elaborate re-creation of the event in Dallas. But already the film (at least an early draft of the script, which Stone has tried to keep secret) has come under vigorous assault. *The Washington Post* attacked the movie's "errors and absurdities." Experts on the assassination have voiced outrage at Stone's version of events. Stone has responded with dark hints of a conspiracy to discredit his movie. And who said the '60s were over?

The hero of Stone's film, scheduled for release in December by Warner Bros., is former New Orleans district attorney Jim Garrison, a wide-eyed conspiracy buff who in 1969 put New Orleans businessman Clay Shaw on trial for complicity in

Kennedy's murder. (The case ended in a quick acquittal.) Stone's script, a version of which was obtained by *Time*, is based largely on Garrison's 1988 book, *On the Trail of the Assassins*. Garrison is considered somewhere near the far-out fringe of conspiracy theorists, but Stone appears to have bought his version virtually whole-sale. One need look no further than the actor who will play Garrison: Hollywood's reigning all-American hero Kevin Costner.

In the early draft of Stone's script (co-written with Zachary Sklar, who edited Garrison's book), we learn that Oswald was just a pawn in an elaborate plot that ranged from seedy gay bars in the French Quarter to the corridors of power in Washington. We meet bizarre characters like David Ferrie, a homosexual ex-air-line pilot with a homemade wig and greasepaint eyebrows who claimed involve-ment in the conspiracy but died before he could testify. We witness shadowy meetings between Oswald and Jack Ruby before the assassination. We are told that as many as seven shots may have been fired at Kennedy from three different direc-tions—none of them by Oswald.

The killing was planned, Garrison discovers in the film, by a coalition that included the Mafia, the C.I.A. and other protectors of the military-industrial com-plex. In a key scene, the crusading D.A. has a rendezvous in Washington with a mysterious unnamed figure who describes how security for the President's visit to Dallas was slackened. It was all part of a plot, he tells Garrison, to eliminate Kennedy and put Lyndon Johnson in office so that the Vietnam War could be escalated. "This was a military-style ambush from start to finish." Garrison tells his staff later, "a coup d'état with Lyndon waiting in the wings."

David Belin, former counsel to the Warren Commission and author of two books on the assassination, calls the script "a bunch of hokum." By ignoring key pieces of evidence and misrepresenting others. Belin says, Stone casts doubt even on issues that are relatively clear-cut, like Oswald's murder of Dallas police officer J.D. Tippit. (Oswald was identified as the gunman at the scene by at least six eye-witnesses.) "It is a shame that a man as talented as Stone has had to go to such lengths to deceive the American public," says Belin.

In his article for *The Post*, George Lardner Jr., who covered the Shaw trial and now specializes in national-security issues, called Garrison's investigation "a fraud" and attacked the script for such dubious scenes as one in which Ferrie is murdered by two mysterious figures who force medicine down his throat. (The New Orleans coroner ruled that Ferrie died of natural causes, though two apparent suicide notes were found.) Lardner also ridiculed the film's attempt to explain away Garrison's botched prosecution of Shaw by inventing a Garrison aide who turns out to be a mole for the Feds aiming to sabotage the case.

Even critics of the Warren Commission find fault with Stone's version of events. Harold Weisberg, author of *Whitewash*, one of the earliest attacks on the Warren Report, calls Stone's script "a travesty" that dredges up bogus theories and unfounded speculation. Among them, the suggestion that three hobos arrested near the assassination site were involved (they were vagrants who had nothing to do with the assassination, says Weisberg), and Garrison's "discovery" that the route of Kennedy's motorcade had been changed at the last minute (a phony charge, says Weisberg, that was based on conflicting descriptions of the parade route in *The Dallas Morning News*).

Stone, with some justification, has objected to his film's being dissected even before it is finished. The criticisms, he says, are based on the first draft of a script that has been substantially revised. (The Ferrie murder scene, for example, has been eliminated.) Stone compares the *Post's* attack on his film to the Hearst newspapers' efforts to suppress *Citizen Kane* five decades ago. "This is a repeat performance," says Stone. "But nothing is going to stop me from finishing this movie." The director insists, moreover, on his right to make a movie that expresses his view of a critical historical event. "William Shakespeare made Richard III into a bad guy. Now the historians say he was wrong. Does that mean Shakespeare shouldn't have written *Richard III* ?"

Stone appears to have less tolerance for others who want to do the same thing. According to Hollywood sources, the director has worked hard to block a movie based on Don DeLillo's 1988 book, *Libra*, a fictionalized account of the assassination. "Stone has a right to make his film, but he doesn't have a right to try and stop everyone else from making their films," says Dale Pollock, president of A&M Films, which has been trying to make the DeLillo movie.

Stone maintains that the controversy is not something he has courted. "I'm not making this film for money," the director says of his lavishly publicized epic starring Hollywood's leading man. "I want to pay homage to J.F.K., the godfather of my generation." But if his film turns out to distort history, he may wind up doing more harm than homage to the memory of the fallen President.

—With reporting by Hays Gorey/Washington and Martha Smilgis/Los Angeles

JULY 1, 1991

TIME
LETTER

OLIVER STONE'S JFK

Oliver Stone

Your suggestion that I tried to stop the making of the movie *Libra*, a fictionalized account of the J.F.K. assassination, is outrageous [CINEMA, June 10]. No one I know in the film business—not even competing studio heads—has the power to stop any movie. The dollar rules. Your mistake is in keeping with the obvious discreditation of our movie. Former New Orleans district attorney Jim Garrison is called, without any justification, a "wide-eyed conspiracy buff" and "far out." Who are your "experts"? You review an unauthorized and outdated draft of the script, which amazes me since TIME usually reviews finished movies. After 25 years, don't our movie, *JFK*, and Garrison deserve a serious and fresh hearing, not old attitudes?

Reprinted by permission of the author.

NOVEMBER 1991

ESQUIRE

THE SHOOTING OF JFK

In his controversial new film, Oliver Stone solves the most traumatic mystery of our era. Is he right? Does he care? Or is history just another Oliver Stone movie?

Robert Sam Anson

"What is history? Some people say it's a bunch of gossip made up by soldiers who passed it around a campfire. They say such and such happened. They create, they make it bigger, they make it better. I knew guys in combat who made up shit. I'm sure the cowboys did the same. The nature of human beings is that they exaggerate. So, what is history? Who the fuck knows?"
—Oliver Stone

In the bar of the Westin hotel in downtown New Orleans, just blocks from where the plot to kill the thirty-fifth president of the United States may or may not have been hatched, Oliver Stone is a little upset. Actually, more than a little upset. He is in the midst of a colossal rant, biting back at "the Doberman pinschers of the establishment," otherwise known as those members of the national press intent on "destroying" his still-aborning film, *JFK.*

"You should be fucking ashamed of yourself!" he shouts, face flushed, neck cords popping. "You call yourselves journalists? You're caricatures of journalism!" Drained and sweaty from a tense day in the editing room, Stone is sucking on limes, throwing back shots of tequila. "It's not journalism you are doing! It's fucking *propaganda.* You are working for the Ministry of Information!" he went on, fortifying himself with a slug. "You have become Winston Smith! You have become George Orwell's creation! You could be a Russian working for Stalin in Pravda in 1935! You are liars! You just invent history! You should go back to school and learn honesty! That's where it starts! *Honesty!*"

Around the bar, drinks are frozen mid-sip. Everyone is staring at the bleary-eyed figure in blue jeans hurling abuse at tormentors none can see. Stone feels their gaze. He stops, flashes a gap-toothed grin, then does something that three-time Oscar-winners seldom do. He laughs at himself.

The moment is as rare as it is appealing. As his performance that jangly July afternoon demonstrated, being noisily raw-edged is Oliver Stone's trademark. He likes making incendiary statements (suggesting George Bush shoot himself, for a recent example), just as he likes making movies (*Salvador, Platoon, Born on the Fourth of July, The Doors*) that are not so much entertainments as meat-axes to the cerebellum. "I have truth in the eyeball," the director who's been called the Wagner of Hollywood has said of his style. "If you guys don't see it because you have to be further back because it's punching you in the face, it's your problem. I can't change the way I see the world."

These, though, have been especially trying days, so unsettling that with only weeks until the scheduled December debut of arguably his most important film, Oliver Stone is more than normally on edge. He is about to offer up a solution to the most vexing mystery of modern times: the assassination of John Fitzgerald Kennedy. Solve that riddle, Stone suggests, and you will discover why America plunged so irrevocably into Vietnam. It is a work no one has dared before and probably only Stone would. And without seeing a single frame of his movie, people have been saying the most terrible things.

He's been accused of distorting history and sullying the memory of a martyred president; of recklessness and irresponsibility, mendacity and McCarthyism, paranoia and dementia—even of treason. His lengthening list of opponents, which unites foes who've been fighting over the Kennedy assassination for decades, have characterized him as a liar, a hypocrite, a megalomaniac, and a charlatan. It's been written that his morals are "repugnant," that there is nothing "too obscene, too indecent, too unethical" that he would not do to "exploit and commercialize a great national tragedy." He has been charged by otherwise-sober folk with defamation of character, poisoning young minds, and undermining confidence in American institutions. Some have ridiculed his film (*Dances with Facts*); others have recommended that it be boycotted.

This has not stopped Oliver Stone. Giving as good as he's gotten, he's branded one critic a CIA agent, accused another of theft, and ventured the view that a vast, powerful plot is working hammer and tongs against him. He's cited Aristotle, Pontius Pilate, and Allen Dulles in defending his film, and likened himself to figures ranging from Orson Welles to William Shakespeare. Along the way, he has also charged past and present elements of his own government with conspiracy, murder, obstruction of justice, and aiding and abetting a felony before and after the fact—not to mention maintaining a laboratory in suburban Maryland where ex-Nazi scientists devise lethal cancer serums to silence bothersome opponents. Mostly, though, Oliver Stone has been plain angry.

"There's an agenda here," he says of those who challenge him. "They're controlled in certain ways ... Let's not be naive ... This controversy is meant to kill off the film, precensor it and maximize negative advance impact ... What this indicates is that they are scared. When it comes to President Kennedy's murder, they don't want to open the doors. They don't want the first inch of inquiry to go on."

SIX SECONDS IN DALLAS

To begin to understand this contention requires a primer, not in the ways of Hollywood, but in the murder of John Kennedy. The few, undisputed facts are these:

On November 22, 1963, at approximately 12:30 P.M., a convertible limousine bearing the president of the United States and his party entered an area in Dallas, Texas, known as Dealey Plaza. Riding in the front seat were two secret-service agents; immediately behind them, in jump seats, were Texas governor John Connally and his wife, Nellie. The limo's rearmost seat was occupied by thirty-six-year-old John Kennedy and his wife, Jacqueline.

At the base of a seven-story red-brick building called the Texas School Book Depository, the limousine made a hard, oblique left and began heading toward the shelter of a railway overpass two hundred yards distant. Several seconds later, just as the car entered the viewfinder of an 8-mm-home movie camera owned by a dress manufacturer named Abraham Zapruder, there was the sound of rifle fire.

An initial shot struck Kennedy, nicked his tie knot and caused him to lean forward and bring his hands up to his throat. Then Connally was hit, a bullet smashing into his back and through his chest and wrist before embedding itself in his left thigh. Another round went wide of the mark, striking the roadway and sending a shard of concrete into the cheek of a bystander. Then, with the still slowly moving limousine only yards from the base of a verdant rise topped by a six-foot picket fence, the president was hit again with explosive force by a round that blasted away the right side of his head and hurled him violently backward at a rate later calculated at one hundred feet per second.

Within moments of the shooting, police fanned out over the area. Most ran up the rise, which came to be called "the grassy knoll." Others entered the Book Depository, where in the second floor lunchroom, an officer came upon a newly hired stock boy drinking a Coke. A twenty-four-year-old ex-Marine who had once defected to the Soviet Union and had spent that summer in New Orleans, propagandizing on behalf of Fidel Castro, his name was Lee Harvey Oswald. The cop stuck his revolver in Oswald's stomach, then when told he was an employee, continued up to the sixth floor, where witnesses had reported seeing a rifleman in one of the windows. Concealed behind some boxes of textbooks, a World War II-vintage Italian army rifle was found. Whoever had been firing it had vanished.

At 1:15 P.M., fifteen minutes after the president was pronounced dead at Parkland Hospital, J.D. Tippit, a Dallas police officer, was shot to death on a sidewalk several miles from Dealey Plaza. Details of his killing were still coming in when a caller informed police that a man had rushed into a movie theater without paying, eight blocks from the Tippit murder. Teams of police and F.B.I. agents immediately converged on the scene. There, after a brief struggle and a shout from one of the officers—"Kill the President, will you?!"—Lee Harvey Oswald was arrested.

During twenty-three hours of interrogation, Oswald never wavered in his protestations of innocence. "I'm just a patsy," he told reporters. "I didn't shoot anybody, no sir." Whether the state could prove the contrary was never determined. Two days after the assassination, as Oswald was being transferred to the county jail, he was shot to death before a national television audience in the basement of the Dallas police department. His assailant was Jack Ruby, a local strip-joint operator.

Such were the bare-bone facts of the assassination and its aftermath. To flesh them out and quell rumors that his predecessor had been the victim of a conspiracy, Lyndon Johnson appointed a blue-ribbon investigation panel headed by Supreme Court Chief Justice Earl Warren. Following ten months of hearings and what was said to be the most exhaustive investigation in F.B.I. history, the Warren Commission issued its central finding: Acting alone, Lee Harvey Oswald had, indeed, slain the president of the United States, as well as Officer Tippit. The accused assassin's apparent motive: a deranged desire to make a name for himself.

The Warren Report was barely in print before a mixed bag of scholars, skeptics, and special-pleaders-assassination buffs, they were tagged—began to dismantle its contentions one by one. The buffs cast doubt on nearly everything, from Oswald's marksmanship (as a Marine, he'd barely qualified for the lowest level of competency) to the accuracy of his supposed weapon (bought for $21.45 through mail order, the rifle was misfitted with a telescopic sight and used ammunition last manufactured in 1944) to the direction from which the fatal head shot had been fired (two thirds of the witnesses placed it as coming from the grassy knoll—in front of Kennedy—while the Commission insisted it had come from the Book Depository to the rear, a claim seemingly contradicted by the Zapruder film and Newtonian laws of motion).

The buffs' most withering scorn, though, was for the Commission's finding that Kennedy and Connally had both been wounded by the first shot fired. The claim was crucial to the single-assassin thesis, for in the hands of an expert marksman working the bolt-action rifle without aiming, the Mannlicher-Carcano could be fired no faster than once every 2.3 seconds. The Zapruder film showed Connally reacting to being wounded no later than 1.6 seconds after Kennedy. That the Texas governor was hit so quickly after the first shot suggested a second shot, hence a second gunman.

To solve this conundrum, the Commission developed what came to be called the Magic Bullet Theory. Named after a round that had been recovered from a stretcher at Parkland, this bullet, according to the Commission, struck the president in the back, exited his throat, and went on from there to wound Connally five times, shattering two of his bones in the process. There were numerous problems with the theory, none more grievous than the condition of the Magic Bullet itself. Virtually pristine, it had lost but .65 percent of its original weight-about what could be expected after being fired through water. When the F.B.I. attempted to duplicate the results by firing identical rounds into both human and goat cadavers, all the test bullets were left grossly deformed.

The more the critics probed, the more holes they found. All that was missing, according to polls showing the overwhelming majority of Americans still disbelieving the explanation provided by their government, were the answers to two questions: Who? and Why?

THE SEDUCTION OF OLIVER STONE

The coming of Oliver Stone to the movie that would purport to answer those queries was slow and reluctant.

As a seventeen-year-old prep-school senior, he'd been shocked by the killing ("The world stopped; it stunned me that a young, handsome president could be killed like that"), but his reaction was no greater than that of most Americans. With his mind on other things—a brief try at Yale, a romantic voyage to Southeast Asia, enlistment in the Army—he was likewise only vaguely aware of the fire storm that followed the Warren Report's release. Not that knowledge at that point would have made much difference. He was a conservatively raised "Goldwater-Republican boy," inclined to accept what his government told him. Thus, Stone had no interest when, in late February 1967, a man who would one day play a major role in his life and in his art stepped before a bank of microphones to make a startling announcement. He had found the answers. He had solved the case.

The man was Jim Garrison, then the district attorney of New Orleans, and the only official, before or since, to bring criminal charges in the murder of John Kennedy. The move won him adoration by many, and, when his case ended in shambles two years later, vilification by many more. Stone had no opinion one way or the other. At the time, he had more immediate worries, like staying alive in Vietnam. He survived, but as a different person. "I said, 'Let's get some fucking rifles and go up on the rooftops. Let's go for Nixon,'" Stone would recount of his return home in 1968 as a twice-wounded, deeply radicalized vet. "Going to the the dark side, you really see the underside of life. Like Lee Harvey Oswald. I was in that world. I know that world. I know those people."

The rage accompanied him to film school, where Stone learned his craft under Martin Scorsese, who would later embark on a film about a fictional assassin, *Taxi Driver*. To some, Stone seemed as intimidating as his mentor's Travis Bickle. "You had the sense that he was obsessed about getting to what he thought was the truth of things," says a friend from those days. "He gave you the impression that he would do anything—take drugs, commit murder, *anything*—in order to get to the truth."

One of those truths, Stone decided by the time he was writing his Oscar-winning script for *Midnight Express*, was that the Kennedy assassination had turned the American universe upside down. Before the killing, he believed, all had been right; after it, all wrong. But for Stone, the most profound and personal consequence of Kennedy's death was the war in which he'd served. "If Kennedy had been in office," Stone says flatly, "Vietnam would not have happened." Till recently, though, Stone had no interest in how the killing itself had come about. "I thought that people like Mark Lane were crazy," he says. "I thought Lee Oswald had shot the president."

What changed his mind was a book that was sent to him in the summer of 1988, when he was filming portions of *Born on the Fourth of July*. The book was *On the Trail of the Assassins*; its author was Jim Garrison, the D.A. whose announcement had stunned the nation twenty-one years before. Three readings and a meeting with the author later, Stone was hooked. "Jim Garrison," he said, "opened my eyes."

Garrison often had that effect on people. A six-foot-six war hero of musical voice and boundless charm, he was hard to resist and the book he'd written hard to put down. In gripping prose, it laid out the story of his most famous criminal case, the prosecution of a retired businessman, Clay Shaw, for conspiracy in the murder of John Kennedy. The tale, as Garrison related it, was of a lonely but determined crusader battling overwhelming odds in the interest of truth and the American way—a narrative not unlike a typical Oliver Stone film. But where Stone's enemies numbered stingy studios and critics such as Pauline Kael, Garrison's included the CIA, the "brainwashing establishment media," assorted state governors, Cuban hitmen, the Department of Justice, the Kennedy family, and Lyndon Baines Johnson. All had conspired to frustrate a probe that had its beginnings in a drunken, assassination-night brawl between a dipsomaniacal private detective, Jack Martin, and his sometime employer, Guy Banister, an ex-F.B.I. man, extreme rightist, and suspected acquaintance of Lee Harvey Oswald. From there, the trail had led to a flamboyantly eccentric pilot, homosexual, and Banister associate named David Ferrie whose character (self-taught cancer researcher, self-ordained bishop, self-proclaimed killer of Cuban communists) and appearance (totally hairless, he penciled in eyebrow with greasepaint and wore a toupee so bad that it literally looked like a rug) made him impossible to forget. He, too, was a well-known Kennedy hater and rumored Oswald friend, and perhaps also, Garrison had been tipped, the get-away pilot for the cabal. But before the net could close, both Banister and Ferrie died, leaving sheaves of Oswald's pro-Cuba leaflets in his desk, the latter under most suspicious circumstances. Heedless of threats, Garrison had pressed on and at last found the conspiracy's mastermind: a widely beloved aesthete who, under what the D.A. deduced was CIA cover, was then engaged in nothing more shadowy than writing a play about New Orleans's first Spanish governor. At that point Garrison's enemies stepped in, so undermining the investigation that, in the end, Shaw went free and the truth was lost.

Such was the plot of *On the Trail of the Assassins*, and Oliver Stone was captivated. "It read like a Dashiell Hammett whodunit," he said later. "It starts out as a bit of a seedy crime with small traces, and then the gumshoe district attorney follows the trail, and the trail widens and widens, and before you know it, it's no longer a small-town affair. That seemed to me the kernel of a very powerful movie."

He was no less attracted to Garrison as the pivot on which the film would turn. The D.A., Stone said, was "somewhat like a Jimmy Stewart character in an old Capra movie—someone who undertakes to investigate something that has been covered up. He makes many mistakes. He has many frustrations. He has few successes. He is reviled, ridiculed, and the case he brings to trial crashes."

Later, director Stone would discover that there were certain facts that author Garrison had left out. His separation from the Army, for instance, which had come about following diagnosis that he was in need of long-term psychotherapy. Or his close association with organized crime, whose soldiers and capos he rarely prosecuted, and who returned the favor by picking up his Las Vegas expenses and selling him a house cut-rate. Or the bribery and income-tax-evasion trials in which he was exonerated. There were many such omissions in Jim Garrison's book, not least how his pursuit of Clay Shaw was, in many minds, one of the most grotesque chapters in American legal history.

The books and articles Oliver Stone would eventually read chronicled this grotesquerie, macabre incident by macabre incident. They told of testimony gained via truth serum and hypnosis; of "witnesses" who came forward following bribery, promise, and threat; of evidence manufactured, facts twisted, suspects—including one identified as a CIA man because he worked in a hotel a few miles from the agency's headquarters—snatched from the prosecutor's imagination. Mostly, though, these pages that Oliver Stone would later absorb told of Jim Garrison, who proclaimed, "There is no truth, there is only what the jury decides"; who hypothesized fourteen different groups of separately motivated plotters—homosexuals, White Russians, Dallas police, Cuban exiles, "the invisible Nazi substructure," before settling on the CIA and the military-industrial complex; who saw gunmen everywhere in Dealey Plaza, including in the sewers. In damning detail, they described the innocents he destroyed (including Shaw, who was left shattered by the experience and died soon after); the boasts he made of knowing the assassins, each and every one. They related as well the conclusion of his paranoid charade: a verdict of not guilty by a jury out less than an hour.

All this would in time be revealed to Oliver Stone; it did not shift his opinion. "I feel I gotta go back to those movies I believe in," he said in a speech a few months before paying Garrison $250,000 for the right to his book, "where my hero is facing certain extinction, surrounded on all sides by enemy swordsmen, but, by some shining light of inner force and greater love, turns the tables of fate and triumphs over all odds."

Oliver Stone had found that hero. Now all he had to do was make the movie.

STARTS, FITS, AND CON JOBS

Stone's habit was to never finish one job before starting another. So it was with *JFK*. With *Born on the Fourth of July* still filming, he began immersing himself in the assassination, paying particular attention to works arguing that Oswald, far from being the unbalanced loner of the Warren Report, enjoyed extensive ties to U.S. intelligence. The spook proponents made a persuasive case. From his service in the Marine Corps (which assigned him to a secret CIA air base as a radar operator) to his 1959 "defection" to the Soviet Union (where he threatened to commit espionage and married the niece of a colonel in the Soviet MVD) to his return to

Texas in 1962 (unquestioned by the CIA, which at the time was grilling tourists coming home from Yugoslavia) to the summer he spent in New Orleans before the assassination (promoting Castro one day, offering to train his enemies in guerrilla warfare the next), there were dozens of strange occurrences in Oswald's life that appeared to bear some intelligence agency's fingerprints.

According to declassified transcripts of their deliberations, the members of the Warren Commission had also been deeply suspicious of Oswald's background—his odd travels, his inexplicable financing, his facility in speaking Russian, his ability to elude surveillance devices, his ownership of a Minox camera, on and on—and suspicious as well (correctly, as it turned out) that both the CIA and F.B.I. were concealing vital evidence. But nothing had come of their worries. Instead, they had trusted in the assurances of their fellow Commission member, Allen Dulles, who'd been fired as CIA director by John Kennedy.

More by intuition than investigation, Garrison too had contended that spies were mixed up in the Kennedy killing, and since the Shaw trial, information had emerged suggesting that he was right. Declassified CIA documents confirm that Shaw had, in fact, been an informant for the agency's "domestic contact service," while the Church Committee and the Rockefeller Commission had revealed that assassination, of only if foreign leaders, had been a recurring topic of executive-suite chitchat at Langley. Despite Shaw's sworn denials, there also seemed to be reasonably good evidence that he had known Ferrie, possibly even Oswald. That, at any rate, was the hedged conclusion in 1979 of the House Select Committee on Assassinations. Relying on a subsequently disputed dictabelt recording of four shots in Dealey Plaza, the last coming from the grassy knoll, the Committee also concluded that there was a "95 percent probability" that the president had been a victim of a conspiracy—just as Jim Garrison had claimed.

Seasoned assassination buffs had known these things for years, but the knowledge had not ameliorated their low regard for now-Appellate Judge Garrison. Lacking their experience, Stone was like a conspiracy Rip Van Winkle awakening to a nightmare. His discoveries left him more convinced than ever of Garrison's rightness, but also convinced that, as a dramatic character, Garrison was badly in need of freshening. For Stone's contemplated film to be credibly up-to-date, Garrison had to be transformed from an historic individual to an artistic metaphor, a metaphor that would be shown in *JFK* uncovering facts that diligent others had only discovered a decade or two down the road. It required optioning a more current book and engaging as a screenwriting partner someone with knowledge not only of Garrison's case but of later conspiracy developments as well. Stone's selections were, respectively Texas journalist Jim Marrs's *Crossfire*, a Baedeker's guide to assassination theories, and Garrison's literary editor, New Yorker Zachary Sklar.

With the preliminary housekeeping out of the way, Stone commenced work on yet another movie, *The Doors*. But, per usual, he continued thinking of his next project, deciding that the time had arrived to find financing for *JFK*; with the elaborate, star-studded movie he envisioned, he would need millions more in financing than he had ever required before. The need led him to Warner Bros., which, ignoring Stone's recent public description of the studio as one of the industry's "cocksucker vampires," had been trying to lure him to do a picture about Howard Hughes. "If you're really serious about doing something about corruption," Stone said to Warners president Terry Semel during a meeting that put the Hughes idea to rest, "the biggest corruption of all is the Kennedy murder."

Semel's eyes widened as Stone sketched his idea. *JFK*, he said, would tell not one tale but three: Garrison's, Oswald's, and the real story of America's entrance into Vietnam. "I'm not interested in pinning the murder on specific individuals," he said. "I'm interested in the whydunit as opposed to the whodunit. I think if you understand the why, then you begin to understand the who, and the who is much larger than we think." cinematically, he would get that theme across by making of *JFK* what Kurosawa had made of *Rashomon*: a kaleidoscope of possible realities, with the audience left to select which among them was the actual truth. "If the movie is cut the way I think it is going to be cut," Stone said, "I think you will leave the theater ready to think about things and, I hope, rethink them, and begin to wonder about some of the givens, some of the sacred cows, some of the official story. Because that's what I think the Warren Commission is. It is America's official story." Wowed, Semel committed Warners for $40 million.

In New York, meanwhile, Sklar continued to work on the script. He'd write a few scenes and send them to California, where Stone would make corrections and additions and send them back. They argued a few times, reportedly over the demeaning shrift Stone gave female characters (an old complaint with the director) and his lurid handling of Shaw's homosexuality. In life, Shaw had been the soul of refined dignity, with exquisite tastes in literature, music, and Restoration-style architecture. In Stone's depiction, he grabbed obscenely after boys in a residence done up in early dungeon. As he had in his other "fact-based" films, *Born on the Fourth of July* and *The Doors*, Stone, who publicly condemned other directors for "distorting reality," was also transposing scenes, inventing characters, and creating situations, invariably strengthening the case for conspiracy. One such instance showed Ferrie being murdered by two assailants who stuffed pills down his throat; and indeed, contusions suggesting just that were found in Ferrie's mouth. According to the coroner however he'd died of a cerebral hemorrhage. According to Garrison, whose men had found two unsigned suicide notes at the scene, he'd killed himself. In Stone's script, Jack Ruby, who died of pancreatic cancer in 1967, suffered an even grislier demise. Shown begging Earl Warren to be taken back to Washington so that he might fully testify (true), and expressing fears for his life if he remained in Dallas (also true), Ruby, according to Stone's script, was finally shut up via lethal injection (not true at all).

Later, after the press began pillorying him for such scenes, Stone would defend himself by saying that even though *JFK* was "not a true story per se," all of its points had been researched and documented. He'd also cite the *Rashomon* analogy, telling a reporter he was "exploring all possible scenarios of who killed Kennedy and why." To alert the audience to the more fanciful of those explorations, he would sepia-tone the scene. "I feel I've behaved responsibly," he'd say. "I've done all my homework."

Stone had done his homework, at least up to a point. But because he'd come to the Kennedy case so late, he was uninformed about the bitter rivalries that had grown among the buffs, an ignorance that on more than one occasion alienated researchers who might have helped him. Those he did talk to found him inquisitive and open-minded, except on the subject of Garrison. "I looked Jim straight in the eye and asked him about it," he told a reporter who inquired about Garrison's links to New Orleans mob boss Carlos Marcello, who had made specific threats on Kennedy's life. "And Jim told me he'd only met him two brief times on social occasions. I believe him."

Whom else he believed was problematic for the script, as Stone seemed highly susceptible to sources serious scholars had dismissed years before. A leading case in point was Beverly Oliver, a nightclub singer turned born-again Christian and assassination buff. Among Oliver's many claims—which she had waited seven years after November 22, 1963, to make—was that she had seen Ferrie in Ruby's nightclub; been at Dealey Plaza during the assassination; taken crucial footage of the killing; had that film confiscated by the F.B.I. and CIA; and with her mobster husband met in a Miami hotel room with Richard Nixon. So many and so startling were her supposed involvements that one leading Commission critic dubbed her "an assassination buff's wet dream." Stone, though, found her story quite believable and included a Beverly Oliver character in the script.

He had less patience with those who equivocated, such as Gus Russo, a well-regarded researcher who'd been pursuing the case for two decades. Invited to brief Stone, Russo was told that if he "impressed" him, a lucrative consulting contract might be in the offing. The meeting did not go well. Remembers Russo: "I said to him, 'We don't have all the answers. We only have half of them. Here's what we know, here's what we don't know. But even if you go with the half we do know, it'll still make for a helluva movie.' Well, Oliver didn't like that one bit. He said, "I don't want half stories. I want the answers and I'm gonna get them." So I said to him, 'Good luck. If you can brainstorm in six months what a hundred of us have not been able to get in twenty years, I'll be the first to shake your hand.'"

Russo was just out the door when a fax arrived, promising everything Stone had been seeking—not only the identity of the assassin, but sixteen other items, from what was described as "the actual rifle that inflicted the fatal head shot" to the identity of "the person who eliminated key witnesses" to "the code names of the other gunmen involved" to "a picture of the assassin's wife and Jack Ruby together." The last item was the capper: "A letter to the assassin congratulating him on a job well done from a former president of the United States."

The source of this cornucopia was Larry Howard, a former Texas contractor who'd founded the JFK Assassination Information Center, in Dallas. Termed the P.T. Barnum of the conspiracy by one buff, Howard liked to boast that he'd never read a book on the Kennedy killing, and other buffs say that he'd become involved in assassinology strictly for the money. The conclusion of his fax to Stone was just as unvarnished. "We have uncovered the real truth behind the assassination," Howard proclaimed. "JFK was murdered by the real people who control the power base in the U.S. In their minds, he was a threat to national security and had to be eliminated."

By the time Howard's message arrived, virtually all his claims had been, or were about to be, demolished. Undaunted—or, as one buff speculated, "in way over his head and desperate for a story"—Stone nonetheless paid Howard's research center $80,000.

Following the purchase, a number of the more respected buffs found it hard to get through to Stone. "Once Oliver met Howard, the rest of us were cut off," said one who had briefly dealt with Stone and was suddenly frozen out. "Oliver had his story. He thought he had nailed it. He's so sure of himself, so arrogant and cocky. But that happens, I guess, after you win a few Oscars."

Stone, though, did not lack for companionship. Besides Howard, who was constantly at his elbow in Dallas, he was being besieged by promoters offering unique solutions to the case (photographs supposedly showing Kennedy being shot by his driver), novel interpretations of intended victims (Jackie, not Jack, had been the actual target), and, in the person of one ex-CIA man who invited him to invest in a Mideast gun-running deal, opportunities to quintuple *JFK*'s budget. There were more serious visitors too, including autopsy and ballistics experts, photographic analysts, theorists of every ideological shade and description. The one Stone heard out most intently was a former Air Force colonel named L. Fletcher Prouty.

An aide to the Joint Chiefs of Staff during the Kennedy years, Prouty since his retirement had become a quirky critic of the CIA, sometimes in books (*The Secret Team: The CIA and Its Allies in Control of the United States and the World*), more often in the pages of *Gallery*, one of the raunchier porno magazines. It was the colonel's theorizing about the assassination, however, that made him indispensable to Stone.

According to Prouty, Kennedy had been the victim of a military-industrial-complex plot triggered by his plan to withdraw from Vietnam. The intention had long been bruited by Kennedy partisans, but Prouty had come up with a number of declassified documents to buttress the claim. The most important was a top-secret National security Action Memorandum (NSAM 263) drafted only six weeks before the assassination. In it, Kennedy formally endorsed a recommendation that one thousand U.S. advisers be pulled out by the end of 1963, with a complete withdrawal of advisers to follow no later than the conclusion of 1965. Once NSAM 263 was signed, said Prouty, Kennedy was, for all intents, a dead man. As Prouty put it: "You could see changes in the civilians who came [into the Pentagon] from the companies and the officers who work in the companies. You never heard people talking about 'President Kennedy' anymore. It was 'that goddamn Kennedy.' Vietnam for them represented the potential of tens of billions of dollars. They could see what he was doing and that he was going to get away with it. This is what caused him to be murdered."

To cinch his case, Prouty produced another top-secret NSAM, approved by

Lyndon Johnson four days after Kennedy's murder. Missing from this document was any mention of withdrawal of U.S. military personnel. Instead, it presented a forthright plan for escalation, including preparations for attacking North Vietnam (bombing would indeed follow seven moths later) and employing U.S. combat troops to invade Laos up to a distance of fifty kilometers. "I think Johnson was scared to death," said Prouty, explaining the policy reversal. "When you put a guy like Lyndon Johnson in a car behind the president and shoot the bullets right over his head, there's only one thing old Lyndon thinks about, and that's *The bastards are shooting at me*. From that time, Lyndon was in the bag."

Prouty was not the first to argue the Vietnam-as-motive scenario (Garrison, among others, had subscribed to it, following the Shaw trial), but his résumé, which according to the colonel included clandestine skulduggery stretching from Romania to Indonesia, lent his hypothesis a sheen of extra credibility. Prouty, however, was not without fault. Like Stone, he had a tendency to see the CIA's dark hand everywhere. "If you had a thought in the shower," said a Stone associate, with only mild exaggeration, "Fletcher would say the CIA was responsible." Another liability was Prouty's fondness for putting himself at the center of great events, such as the 1961 Bay of Pigs invasion, where he claimed to have personally seen ships christened *Barbara* (as in future first lady Barbara) and *Houston* (after the future President's adopted hometown).

The more cautious buffs were leery of Prouty, whose role with the joint chiefs changed from by-line to by-line, and warier still of some of his claims, such as his suggestion that he'd been dispatched on a mission to the South Pole in November 1963, so that last minute plotting might go on without his detection. Stone, however, embraced him without reservation. Delighted to discover a beribboned source with views he'd come to only by instinct, he signed Prouty on as a technical adviser and rejiggered the script to include a Prouty-like character (Mr. X) who reveals to Garrison the full dimensions of the conspiracy. "It was a military-style ambush from start to finish," Stone's script had Garrison telling his staff following his first meeting with Mr. X, "a coup d'etat with Lyndon Johnson waiting in the wings."

FILMING AND FIRE STORM

As the fall of 1990 approached, Oliver Stone was behaving more and more like a spook himself. At Stone's Camelot Productions, where *JFK* was referred to only as *Project X*, employees were required to sign a secrecy agreement, and numbered drafts of the script were kept under lock and key. Lest more serious snoops discover what he was up to, Stone also had the premises swept for bugs. Then he engaged in some machinations of his own.

The target was Don DeLillo's *Libra*, critically acclaimed, best-selling novel about Oswald that had been optioned by A&M Films. With Phil Joanou (*State of Grace*) signed to direct a far simpler script than Stone's, it seemed likely that *Libra* would be in the theaters long before *JFK*. But all at once, odd things began happening. Actors who'd seemed ready to sign with *Libra* suddenly changed their minds, reportedly after receiving calls from Stone's agency, Mike Ovitz's powerful Creative Artists Agency, cautioning about questionable career moves. Joanou himself bailed out, after getting the same message, along with, sources say, a call from Stone, who told him, "My film's more cinematic than yours." Desperate to salvage the project, the producer's of *Libra* temporarily shelved plans for theatrical release and began negotiating with Time-Warner-owned HBO to release the movie on first-run cable. That too was scuttled.

Stone disclaimed any involvement in *Libra*'s problems, but not everyone in Hollywood believed him. "You don't get any more powerful in this town as a filmmaker than he is," said a screenwriter friend of Stone's. "When he says, 'I am not going to be happy about a competing project,' well, he doesn't have to say anything more."

Finding the right lead to play Garrison, however, proved trickier. Stone's first choice was Harrison Ford, but he was taking an extended vacation. His next nominee was Mel Gibson, but after a strained dinner meeting, Gibson passed as well. Finally, Stone sent the script to Kevin Costner, fresh from his triumph in *Dances with Wolves*. He seemed a weird choice. Where Garrison was the raucously outsized embodiment of the Big Easy's *le bon temps roulet*, the monotoned, monoranged Costner was a slight, tight goody-two-shoes. Stone, however, liked what he termed Costner's Americanness, a quality he deemed perfect for a story that would be "Capraesque." Without troubling to check the accuracy of the lines he'd be speaking ("Kevin's not particularly interested in history or politics," explained a friend), Costner assented, and a deal was struck: $7 million, plus a percentage of receipts.

Warners, which had wanted star power to enhance *JFK*'s allure, regarded Costner's fee a bargain. However, the studio was deeply worried about Stone's script. It was bogglingly complex, with 212 speaking parts, more than 1,000 camera setups, 95 scenes, 15 separate film stocks, and endless intercuts and flashbacks—"everything but footnotes," Stone joked. More alarming to Warners, the story at its initial length threatened to surpass four hours in screen time. "It'll shrink on camera," Stone promised Semel, who was pressing for the elimination of a number of scenes. When Semel seemed skeptical, Stone shrugged, "Maybe you should get Robert Towne to come in and rewrite this, because I don't know what to take out." "Aw, fuck," Semel groaned at the mention of the notoriously slow-working Oscar winner. "That'll take two years." The men laughed, and the scenes stayed. Warners, though, took one precaution. To test the marketability of the movie, it hired the Gallup organization to conduct a poll. When asked whether they had "positive interest" in seeing an Oliver Stone film on the assassination, nearly 70 percent of the respondents between the ages of eighteen and fifty-four answered yes. When the same question was put to those fifty-five and older, nearly half said no.

The curtain of secrecy that had shrouded *JFK* finally lifted—if only for a peek—late last February. In an interview with the industry trade paper *Variety*, Stone confirmed growing rumors that he was about to commence shooting a film on the assassination and declared that *JFK* would "prove" that Lee Harvey Oswald had not killed John Fitzgerald Kennedy. Vague on how he'd go about that, as well as the precise story his movie would tell, Stone said that in the interest of entertainment, he was taking some creative liberties, but not many. "I can't take too much," said Stone, "because the material is very important and sacred to the public." He then added solemnly: "John Kennedy was the godfather of my generation ... Like Hamlet, we have to try and look back and correct the inaccuracies."

Six weeks later, shooting began in Dealey Plaza, where after a prolonged battle and the payment of $50,000, Stone had secured rights to film on the Book Depository's famous sixth floor. The preparations to restore the building to its condition on November 22, 1963, had been elaborate: A wing that had been removed since was rebuilt, window frames repainted their original color, a floor restocked with three thousand identical book cartons, the trees outside trimmed to their height twenty-eight years before.

At last, there was a cry of "action!" As some of the eleven thousand who had turned out for Stone's extras call began to cheer and applaud, a black convertible Lincoln limousine bearing a stand-in president of the United States and his party began gliding to another appointment in Dallas. And, once again, there was the sound of rifle fire. "Cut!" someone yelled. "There's not enough smoke coming from the grassy knoll."

It was not all make-believe death in Dallas. There was also time for interviews ("I consider myself a person who's taking history and shaping it in a certain way," Stone told a reporter. "Like Shakespeare shaped *Henry V*"); firsthand investigation ("Impossible shot," judged the director after trying to crawl into Garrison's storm sewers); hijinks (a birthday party for the production's research coordinator where the guests wore David Ferrie masks); last-minute research (a chat with L.B.J. mistress Madeleine Brown, who reportedly quoted her lover as saying on November 21, "After tomorrow, I won't have to worry about those Kennedy boys anymore"); embarrassments (watching an enfeebled Garrison, playing the part of Earl Warren, go through seventeen takes); even visits with Oswald's widow, Marina, who said of Stone, "When he leaves, he takes the air in the room with him."

The goings-on did not amuse everyone. Particularly unhappy were the buffs, who, having had their credibility battered once by Garrison, were nervous that it would be clobbered again by what one critic called "this $40 million gorilla." None were more vociferous on the subject than seventy-eight-year-old Harold Weisberg, the dean of the assassination researchers. "You have every right to play Mack Sennett in a Keystone Kops Pink Panther," he wrote Stone, "but as an investigator, Jim Garrison could not find a pubic hair in a whorehouse at rush hour."

When no satisfactory response was forthcoming, Weisberg secured an early draft of the *JFK* script ("theft," Stone called it), and dispatched it to George Lardner, who had covered the Garrison investigation for *The Washington Post*. The result that greeted the production when it reached New Orleans was a lengthy feature article headlined DALLAS IN WONDERLAND: OLIVER STONE'S VERSION OF THE KENNEDY ASSASSINATION EXPLOITS THE EDGE

OF PARANOIA. Accompanied by a cartoon showing a grinning Stone leering into a limousine where Kennedy was having makeup applied, Lardner's story eviscerated both Garrison's investigation ("a farce" and "a fraud") and the ongoing production ("Is this the Kennedy assassination or the 'Charge of the Light Brigade'?"). But the most barbed bon mot came from Weisberg, who said of Stone, "I think people who sell sex have more principle."

Like the first rock in a landslide, Lardner's brickbat unleashed a cascade of press invective. In the *Chicago Tribune*, columnist Jon Margolis opined that by making a movie centered on Garrison, Stone was beyond morally repugnant. Unconcerned that one corporate sibling, Warner Bros., was bankrolling Stone, and that another, Warner Books, was paying Garrison $137,500 for his paperback rights, *Time* chimed in with a critique of its own. By attaching himself to "the far-out fringe of conspiracy theorists," the weekly newsmagazine intoned, "filmdom's most flamboyant interpreter of the 1960s ... may wind up doing more harm than homage to the memory of the fallen president."

Furious, Stone fired off stiff rejoinders to *Time* and the *Post*. Then, after getting into a shouting match with Ben Bradlee ("Jason Robards played that guy?" said Stone of the newspaper's executive editor. "It should have been Rod Steiger"), he let loose in an interview with the New Orleans Times-Picayune, lambasting the press for being "fucking asleep for twenty-eight years" and labeling Lardner "a CIA agent-journalist." Lardner considered suing for libel, but settled for a complete retraction. In the future, the reporter advised, "the little scumbag" should "shut up."

Stone, however, had been right about one thing: Save for a handful of inconsequential exceptions, the press had, indeed, been dozing since November 22, 1963.

There were good, nonconspiratorial reasons for the media's long slumber, not least of them the Garrison trial, which featured the indictment of several reporters on charges ranging from bribery to obstruction of justice. The facts of the Kennedy murder were also numbingly complex, with the Warren Commission alone generating nearly a million pages of testimony, exhibits, and evidence. Few news organizations had the resources to wade through that morass, and fewer still the willingness to contend with frequently Byzantine claims of often-bizarre buffs. "The people who believe in conspiracy theories are the quickest to become extremely vituperative," investigative reporter Seymour Hersh had told an interviewer, explaining his aversion to looking into the assassination. "One of these people calls you with a conspiracy theory and you say, 'I don't buy it.' And they say, 'Sure you don't buy it. It's because you are part of the conspiracy.' It's a gestalt I don't like."

Hersh conveyed the same sentiments to Stone during the Post fight. But Stone, who'd been collecting a catalogue of the press's numerous assassination errors, didn't seem to listen. Instead, he was far more impressed with a 1977 Carl Bernstein article quoting CIA officials as saying that the agency maintained four hundred reporters on its payroll (among them journalists at Time and the Post) and a 1967 CIA memo detailing stratagems for countering critics of the Warren

Commission. "Discuss the publicity problem with ... friendly elite contacts, especially ... editors," the agency had ordered its stations. "Employ propaganda assets to answer and refute the attacks of the critics ... reviews and feature articles are particularly appropriate for this purpose." The words were all Stone required to believe that forces most malevolent were out to get him.

"I'm sure he believes that Luce was part of the illuminati or some crazy thing," said a Stone friend, after listening to the director claim that "the Nazi way of thinking is very deeply embedded" in the media. "But that's Oliver: He needs his enemies to do good work."

Enemies Stone was gathering, and in copious supply. Some were galvanized by his cavalier regard for Shaw (as "a joke," Stone has filmed a not-to-be-used scene showing Shaw's jury bringing in a guilty verdict), others by his stubborn defense of Garrison, who himself was now apologizing to some of those he'd indicted. True, Stone conceded, the D.A. had suffered from hubris and had made serious mistakes, but that, he said, "only makes him like King Lear." Besides, Stone went on, "Garrison was trying to force a break in the case. If he could do that, it was worth the sacrifice of one man. When they went onto the shores of Omaha Beach, they said, 'We're going to lose five, ten, fifteen thousand people to reach our objective.' I think Jim was in that kind of situation."

Stone was still explaining that comment when difficulties of a different sort arose, caused not by his enemies but by his ally, Fletcher Prouty.

THE PROBLEM AND THE ANSWER

It was a small thing that started the trouble, so small it had almost gone unnoticed. Paging through a tiny, left-wing New York weekly, Stone's researchers had chanced upon an article identifying the colonel as a cause célèbre in the virulently anti-Semitic, racist Liberty Lobby. According to the story, Prouty the previous fall had been a featured speaker at the Lobby's annual convention; he contributed to its national radio program and newsletter (which featured such articles as "The Diary of Anne Frank Is a Fraud" and "White Race Becoming an Endangered Species"); and along with a grab bag of rightist crackpots, he'd been recently named to the national policy advisory board of the Lobby's Populist Action Committee.

At Camelot Productions, where Prouty was regarded as a genial, grandfatherly figure, the initial reaction was disbelief. It quickly turned to horror as more information poured in. The Lobby, it turned out, had been founded by one Willis Carto—an ex-John Birch Society functionary who, in addition to expressing admiration for Hitler, believed that Jews were, as he put it, "public enemy number one." He is "a very sincere and well-educated man," Prouty said. "I want to be for the things he's for."

That Prouty should be associated, even remotely, with Carto's views, was a public-relations time bomb. The bad news, though, did not end there. Garrison, Stone's staff discovered, had also appeared on the Lobby's radio program; and Prouty had sold the reprint rights to his book to the Lobby's Noontide Press, whose other offerings included numerous works arguing that the Holocaust was "a Jew-sponsored hoax."

When questioned, Prouty, the intelligence expert, pleaded ignorance. He had not known of Carto's Nazi leanings, he insisted; nor had he been aware that one of his fellow advisory-board members had been the leader of the Mississippi Ku Klux Klan, nor that the Committee itself was the successor to a Lobby-sponsored political party that in 1988 had nominated former KKK chieftain David Duke its presidential candidate. "I'm on [their] board," said Prouty, "but I don't know anything about it." As for his publisher's assertion that the holocaust was a lie, Prouty, who claims to have spoken at a National Holocaust Museum ceremony, would say only, "I'm no authority in that area." "My God," moaned a Stone assistant after listening to the rationalizations. "If this gets out, Oliver is going to look like the biggest dope of all time."

Stone—whose father is Jewish, as it happens—seemed unconcerned. After being assured by Prouty that he was neither a racist nor an anti-Semite ("I never met a Jew I didn't like," said Prouty) but merely a writer in need of a platform, he rejected advice to drop the colonel as a technical adviser and to rewrite Mr. X so that Prouty could not be identified. "I'm doing a film on the assassination of John Kennedy," said Stone, "not the life of Fletcher Prouty."

The bullheadedness had an element of calculation, because by then, Stone had recruited a Vietnam adviser with far more heft than Prouty, an active-duty U.S. Army major named John Newman.

Meticulous, low-key, methodical—everything, in sum, Prouty was not—Newman had been quietly working with Stone since the spring of 1991. He'd first learned of the film from a publishing friend who informed him that Stone had an assassination movie in the works, in which Vietnam would figure prominently. Stone's thesis, the friend had said, was that Kennedy, had he lived, would have withdrawn from Vietnam—precisely the subject that Newman, a highly experienced intelligence specialist, had been privately researching for his Ph.D. thesis for nearly a decade. During that time, he had ferreted out fifteen thousand pages of documents—three times the total of the Pentagon Papers—and interviewed scores of top-ranking sources. The data, checked and rechecked, had led him, bit by bit, doubt by doubt, to an explosive conclusion: Not only had Kennedy put in motion the withdrawal just weeks before his death, but an intricate secret operation, involving the U.S. Saigon command and certain U.S.-based foreign-policy officials, had been systematically deceiving the White House about the disastrous course of the war.

The extent of the scheme had been staggering. Body counts, pacification rates, captured-weapons totals, defectors—"the start-to-finish works," as Newman put it—all had been deliberately inflated, even as estimates of enemy strength had been deliberately slashed by nearly two thirds. The purpose of the fakery, which dwarfed any of the war's subsequent falsehoods, had been two-fold: to discourage thoughts of quick withdrawal and, at the same time, encourage the infusion of U.S. matériel and men. In design, it was meant to put the first light at the end of the

Vietnam tunnel.

Not everyone, though, had been misled. Even as Kennedy and his statistics-minded defense secretary, Robert McNamara, were being consistently lied to, a small number of administration hawks were being provided the truth by means of a secret back channel. Among that select circle, Newman found, had been the next in line in presidential succession, Lyndon Johnson.

Newman's painstakingly documented research established the vice-president's back-channel role conclusively—just as it did when the actual facts of the war were ultimately disclosed. That revelation had come in Honolulu, during a conference attended by senior members of the cabinet and the U.S. Saigon command. Later cited as proof that J.F.K.'s goals in Vietnam had continued after the assassination undisturbed, the meeting had been highlighted by a call by the military for a massive American buildup—a recommendation Kennedy had, in fact, repeatedly rejected. Change, though, was in the wind. It was November 20, 1963, when the conferees sat down in Honolulu. In two days, there would be a new president; in six, a new policy in Vietnam.

Characteristically cautious, Newman had made no public claim that either the deception plan or the timing of the Honolulu conference was linked to the assassination. All the same, the implications of his discoveries were obvious, as was their potential worth to Stone, who was still basing his Vietnam theories on Prouty's less-than-definitive NSAMs. Initially, Newman had been reluctant to become involved. Beyond worries about the reaction of his military superiors (who had twice denied Stone help on other films), he was dubious about Stone, whom, he'd been warned, was pursuing conspiracy will-o'-the-wisps. "If you get attached to that movie," a buff friend advised, "you'll be a limousine following a garbage truck." The ramrod-straight Newman was torn: repelled by what he'd been told about Garrison, and Stone's belief in him; drawn by an old-fashioned sense of duty. "I had a choice," Newman said later. "I could either sit back and wring my hands that Oliver Stone was some kind of bad guy, or I could try to do something with him for the sake of history." Finally, after several weeks of agonizing, Newman sent Stone a fifty-word telegram summarizing who he was and what he had found. The invitation to come to California arrived the next morning.

Since then, Newman had become a key but—at his own insistence—covert cog in the production. From his home in Virginia, where he was racing to finish a book for a publisher Stone had found for him, he talked frequently to the director by phone, and, on his own time, visited him a number of times in California and Dallas. Stone relied heavily on his advice, and despite continuing attacks from the media, which had now zeroed in on *JFK*'s Vietnam hypothesis (libel and nonsense, Lardner had called it in the *Post*), had upheld a pledge that he would in no way use Newman's intelligence credentials to promote the film. Grateful and increasingly impressed by Stone, Newman had steadily taken on more duties, including writing several key scenes in the movie and screening conspiracy updates that continued to come in from the ever-voluble Prouty. The latter was a crucial chore, for by the time the production reached Washington in late July, the colonel was causing troubles Stone could no longer ignore.

The new difficulty had its origins in Prouty's ongoing association with Harrison Livingstone, a contentious Baltimore author who'd won notoriety some years before by offering to sell a set of the Kennedy autopsy photos. The circumstances under which Livingstone had obtained the pictures were murky; what was certain was that Livingstone had a propensity for seeing people plotting against him, among them a Stone consultant, whom Livingstone publicly accused of being a CIA agent. Livingstone was also suspected of sending Stone an anonymous fax warning that a rival buff (another supposed CIA agent) was sabotaging *JFK* through a convoluted plan dubbed Operation Bad Boy. When Stone failed to hire him as a consultant, Livingstone turned on Stone himself, charging in a letter to Warren Commission critics that the director had pirated his work, nearly ruined him financially, and, in the bargain, committed sedition, which Livingstone defined as "communication ... which has as its objective the stirring up of treason."

It was such behavior that prompted many experts to give Livingstone a wide and wary berth. A notable exception was Prouty, who'd been assisting him in writing a book that would, Livingstone claimed, unravel the plot. Who the culprits were, Livingstone wouldn't say until publication. Not so discreet, Prouty was hinting that one of the plotters—the Ring, he called them—was none other than former Harvard dean, Kennedy national security adviser, and Ford Foundation president McGeorge Bundy. The preposterousness of the suggestion shook Stone. He was rattled even more to be informed by Newman that the colonel's Vietnam expertise was not all that had been assumed.

Newman's alarm sprang from a fax that Prouty had written after reading a declassified draft of NSAM 273. Composed on November 21, the draft had taken a substantially tougher line than October's NSAM 263, in which Kennedy had laid out his withdrawal plans. Nonetheless, the draft stopped well short of repudiating the president's goals. But that was not how Prouty read it. "That signature [on NSAM 273] puts him [Bundy] in a real nutcracker," he wrote to Stone. "To me, it appears that this strange Bundy move was some sort of a signal."

There was no signal, sinister or otherwise. Not only did the draft NSAM represent no real change in Kennedy policy, but Bundy's signature did not appear on it.

Bluntly, Newman tried to set Stone straight. "Oliver," he cautioned in a confidential fax, "I must tell you that if in your movie or on a talk show you say that McGeorge Bundy signed a document November 21 that suggests he was in on the murder, you will be made a laughing stock, and even buffoons like Lardner will have a field day." Then, in a sign of how well Newman was coming to know Stone, he added, "Be careful of oversimplifying things, Oliver. It will get you into trouble."

Newman's warning came at a particularly low moment for Stone. Former L.B.J. aide and Motion Picture Association of America president Jack Valenti had just gone on record criticizing the movie, and Robert Blakey, who had led the House probe of the assassination, had told a reporter, "I think the whole thing should be interred in Arlington Cemetery." Stories were also circulating that Warners was displeased as well. The studio, it was said, was especially unsettled by the seventh and latest version of the script, which had Johnson telling his advisers, "You just get me reelected and you can have your goddamn war." The fact that such a scene had actually occurred and been previously reported did little to assuage Warner's alleged anxiety.

Despite Stone's employment of Robert Kennedy press secretary Frank Mankiewicz as the production's senior public-relations adviser, the media also continued hammering at *JFK*, and more critical articles were in the works. "Oliver's had bad press before," shuddered Robert Spiegelman, a mass-communications professor serving as a Stone consultant, "but this is going to be the shit storm of his life."

The shoot too seemed to be taking its toll. After more than a year of seven-day weeks, researching, writing, filming, and editing, Stone was "a real bear," as one of his closest associates put it. His humor was not helped any by how he was treating his body. Evenings out with Costner, he was sometimes drinking, he admitted, more than he should, and what moments he did have for rest were often taken up composing responses to his enemies in the press. "Christ," Stone groused after one such late-night session. "I feel like a presidential candidate going through all this. Why do I have to defend my movie? I'm not running for office and I'm not asking for a reopening of the investigation. I'm making a movie that will come and go." With only days remaining until wrap, the problem was not Stone's condition, however; it was Fletcher Prouty, who was still saying of the draft NSAM: "There is a terrific story in those papers. They make it clear that someone was preparing the White House for the murder of JFK ... This is what the death of JFK is all about." Finally, on the second-to-last day of filming, Stone decided to act.

The showdown took place in an Interior Department office that had been made over to appear like the Pentagon lair of the chairman of the Joint Chiefs of Staff. While technicians set lights for the next scene, Stone summoned Prouty and Newman and came right to the point. Prouty's association with Livingstone must immediately end. No more information was to be provided to him, and Prouty was to do his utmost to ensure that he would not publish anything that would discredit the film. Then Stone turned to Prouty's misreading of the critical NSAM. "What's the story, Fletch?" he asked.

Prouty began by saying that he had confused the four-page draft NSAM 273 with the one-paragraph NSAM 263. When Stone, who had seen both documents, appeared dubious, Prouty switched tactics, claiming that the draft NSAM was a forgery and that the source from which it had come—namely, the Kennedy Library—had been "infiltrated." At that, Newman tore into him. Prouty was wrong, he said: about Bundy, about "infiltration," about the NSAMs, about the entire case. Unaccustomed to being dressed down by a junior officer, Prouty erupted. "Fletcher really went into orbit," recalled a witness to the meeting. "He jumped up and went into this long tirade about his forty years and how he had done everything and written everything and briefed everybody and if that wasn't good enough for Oliver, he was quitting."

At length, Stone managed to pacify Prouty and the session ended in edgy détente. The incident, though, seemed to mark a turning point for Stone, not only in his unquestioning regard for Prouty, from whom he gently began to distance himself, but in his attitude about the assassination and his film. Never again would he wax quite so rhapsodic about Garrison, whose appalling blunders he had belatedly begun to appreciate. Among his staff, which had long been trying to wean him from the D.A., there was hope that, in editing, Stone would loop in a line or two, making his new skepticism clear. Under the growing influence of more of the serious buffs, he was now even willing to admit doubt, not that there had been a conspiracy, or that Vietnam had been its ghastly consequence, but doubt in the certainty that he knew everything. For someone who claimed to have "truth in the eyeball," it was a seismic concession. How far it would extend, and with what results for *JFK*, was impossible to predict until prints were struck. But already Stone was sounding different. "When you make a movie like this," he reflected after another long editing session, "and you get attacked from all sides, sometimes you don't win. Sometimes you fail. But it is well worth it if you lost in an honorable cause. Pancho Villa, I always think of what he said: 'The defeats are also battles.'"

CLOSING CREDITS

The last of seventy-nine days of filming was in early August, at a spot on the Capitol Mall just a rifle shot from the Vietnam Veterans Memorial. After nearly a week of rain in Washington, the skies were cloudless and sunny, and a large crowd had gathered, most of them to see Costner, who, after a round of golf the day before with George Bush, had brought along one of the President's daughters-in-law to witness his performance. She was very pretty and very rapt.

Leaning against a nearby tree, head in his hand, Donald Sutherland, who had flown in from Paris to play Mr. X, was using the Stanislavsky method, California-style, to ready himself. He asked for quiet and that no one smoke within a hundred yards of him. Also present was a battery of flacks, among them a witness to another Kennedy assassination, Frank Mankiewicz, who, as he came up the greensward where the cameras were set smiled to a friend, "You know, I think this is the prettiest grassy knoll I have ever seen."

As was his custom, the director went through everything over and over again, insuring that each dialogue fragment and facial tic was precisely right. He was taking special care with this scene; coming at the movie's final moments, Mr. X would reveal to Garrison why John Fitzgerald Kennedy had died. The answer was etched in the black marble listing 58,000 names.

While Stone worked, his crew mingled restlessly, eager to be done and attend a blowout wrap party that had been scheduled for that evening. "What's Ed Asner playing?" a spectator with memories of Lou Grant called over. Costner's double cracked back: "The Texas School Book Depository."

A ripple of laughter snaked through the set. Stone grinned, but just barely. He appeared exhausted, yet unwilling to let go of what had been his obsession for the last year. "It's funny," he told a friend as the cameras were repositioned a last time. "Here I am, looking at these monuments"—he stopped and gestured at the Capitol and the obelisk to Washington in the distance—"these monuments I used to come and see as a kid. God, I was so impressed by the government then." He stopped and turned back to the slash in the earth where middle-aged men in ill-fitting combat fatigues were laying flowers. "And now," he resumed, "there's this. This … "

Before he could say more his assistant director cut in. The light was fading and preparations for the final retake were finished. The action this time went flawlessly. As Costner walked off, burdened by what Mr. X has told him about the assassination and Vietnam, two pig-tailed black girls took their cue and, impossibly happy, began dancing over the knoll. And then, Oliver Stone, who'd been observing from beneath a tent that resembled nothing so much as a GI's hutch, did something that was both crazy and wonderful: He leaped up, and, as the cameras rolled, joined in.

As he played, all-at-once young again, it seemed a different era, a time when John Kennedy was alive and the country itself seemed young. In Oliver Stone's smile was a memory of what America had been, before "the bad guys," as he called them, had stolen its hopes. By making a movie, he'd searched for those villains, and found in his work the beginnings of an answer. Perhaps to the mystery of a crime. Perhaps to the puzzle of himself.

DECEMBER 1991

ESQUIRE
LETTER

STONE SHOOTS BACK

Oliver Stone

Robert Sam Anson's article ("The Shooting of *JFK*," November) is filled with numerous errors, omissions, out-of-context quotes, and misunderstandings. Some cases in point: 1. *The character assassination of Jim Garrison.* Anson accepts the old disinformation rumors that Garrison is tied to the mafia, that he bribed and hypnotized his witnesses, and that he destroyed an innocent man, Clay Shaw. Not one hard shred of evidence is presented. One could, with more evidence, assert that it was the government and members of the press that bribed and otherwise obstructed Garrison's witnesses and falsely brought Garrison to trial on charges that seemed to be part of a frame-up; and that Shaw as a contact agent of the CIA and a perjurer on the stand was *far* from innocent. Anson accuses me of sensationalizing Shaw's homosexuality when he fully understands that it was that milieu that led to at least three crucial identifications of Shaw knowing Ferrie and to the discovery of Shaw's mysterious alter ego, Clay Bertrand. 2. *The character assassination of Colonel Fletcher Prouty.* Anson fails to mention the patriotic service Colonel Prouty has devoted to this country as a covert military operator linked to the CIA. More than an "aide," Prouty was, at the end, chief of Special Operations, working for the Joint Chiefs of Staff, and a key player. Through other sources I know he often briefed Dulles, Landsdale, Bissel, et cetera. His revelations and his book *The Secret Team* have not been discredited in any intelligent way. I regret his involvement with Liberty Lobby, but what does that have to do with the Kennedy/Vietnam issue? The truth does not always come from lawyers in three-piece suits. In cases like this it more often comes from street types, criminals, and people with "histories" who talk. "Cautious buffs," Anson calls Prouty's detractors, as if they had some special dignity. Men, I call them, who have never been behind closed doors with Dulles and Cabell. 3. *The character assassination of Oliver Stone.* Aside from having two thirds of my quotations out of context ("truth in the eyeball" was a quote about cinematic style in reference to *Born on the Fourth of July*—here transposed as if I had the truth in the JFK killing, which I never had or claimed to have), Anson resorts to the tired cliché of a Hollywood megalomaniacal director, blinded by his Oscars, thinking only he can solve the mystery, only to be defeated in the process by "cautious buffs". Anson gives full credence to the *Libra* rumor. As if there is anyone in this business who can stop a competing financial entity. It doesn't happen that way. The *Libra* script was written and made many rounds long before *JFK*—and was rejected on the basis of its quality, or lack thereof. *Ruby*, a film of a similar nature, was made simultaneously, and it hounded us all over Dallas. 4. I never offered the role of Jim Garrison to Mel Gibson, so he never turned it down.

5. Kevin Costner *did* read the script several times and stretched me at several meetings to make improvements before he would commit. At the pinnacle of his career, it was brave of him to take on such a politically difficult project. 6. Madeleine Brown never said the idiocy to me that is ascribed to her. 7. Larry Howard may be a "P.T. Barnum" to Anson, but his exhibit in Dallas is a valuable educational tool for many thousands of visitors who would otherwise be limited to viewing the official sixth-floor exhibit. 8. Last, I have not, nor do I intend, to "distance" myself in any way from Garrison's or Colonel Prouty's long efforts in this case. They may have made mistakes, but they fought battles that Anson could never *dream* of.

In making *JFK*, my point was not to indict individuals, but to understand history. Garrison's investigation is part of this history but hardly the focus. Jim Garrison was not perfect. He did not string up the assassins and solve the case. The Clay Shaw trial is over, but the larger questions—who killed Kennedy and why?—persist.

Reprinted by permission of the author.

LOS ANGELES TIMES

OPINION
THE POLITICAL RORSCHACH TEST

What Americans think about the Kennedy assassination reveals what they think about their government

Jefferson Morley

How we make sense of the assassination of John F. Kennedy is directly related to how we make sense of American public life. To explain how the President of the United States came to have his head blown off in broad daylight, we must choose among the millions of available facts. The choices we make—to accept the credibility of the Warren Commission, which concluded a lone gunman was to blame, or to believe eyewitnesses who heard gunshots coming from the grassy knoll, and so decide more people were involved—are shaped, consciously and unconsciously, by our premises about the U.S. government and the way power is exercised in America.

The events of Nov. 22, 1963, have thus become a kind of national Rorschach test of the American political psyche. Those six seconds of gunfire in Dallas' Dealey Plaza serve as an enigmatic ink blot into which we read our political concerns.

The history of the Kennedy assassination in the American imagination is a chronicle of shifting hopes and fears. In Kennedy's death, Americans have seen a cathartic test of national resilience or a paranoid nightmare of triumphant corruption. The controversy over *JFK*, Oliver Stone's coming feature film, is only the latest chapter in this story.

The central issue is conspiracy. The notion that unknown conspirators murdered Kennedy took root quickly. In the spring of 1964, one-third of Americans believed Lee Harvey Oswald acted in concert with others. Within two years the figure had doubled. Every poll taken over the last quarter century has shown between 60% to 80% of the public favoring a conspiratorial explanation. Director Stone only exaggerated slightly when he told Washington reporters recently, "More people have claimed to see a live Elvis than claim to believe in the Warren Commission."

The fear of conspiracy is a long-running theme in American life. In the 1830s and 1840s, there was a pervasive mistrust of secret societies, such as the Masons. In 1919, and again in the late 1940s and early 1950s, there were popular fears of communist conspiracy. The conspiracy theories of the Kennedy assassination that emerged in the mid-1960s are part of this tradition. Unaccountable forces are seen lurking behind the facade of democratic government. The official explanation of public events is considered incomplete, if not deceptive. The conspiracy theories of Kennedy's death, however improbable, reveal the tradition of mistrust of the established order.

That's no small part of the reason why Stone and conspiracy theorists are criticized so fiercely today. Those who believe Oswald acted alone are not only defending the anti-conspiratorial theory advanced by the Warren Commission. They are also defending the credibility of senior U.S. government officials, the integrity of U.S. law enforcement and intelligence agencies and the capabilities of the national media. (If there was a conspiracy, the media has thus far failed to uncover it.) The lone-gunman theory of Kennedy's death, in its own way no less implausible than some of the conspiracy theories, depends on confidence in the legitimacy of national political authority.

For 25 years, the imaginative recreation of the Kennedy assassination has been a way to explore the twin issues of confidence and conspiracy in U.S. history. At first, confidence seemed to hold the upper hand. In the aftermath of the assassination, there was a string of bestselling novels, including *Night of Camp David* and *The President's Plane is Missing*, which turned on mortal peril to the President. In these optimistic narratives, the President (or his successor) was an attractive, pragmatic liberal in the Kennedy mold. Dangerous forces—racism, insanity, the nuclear arms race—conspired against him, and the country was plunged into a crisis of confidence. But the fictional President prevailed and national well-being was restored.

Official organs, no less than novelists, sought to reassure the public about the assassination. The National Commission on the Causes and Prevention of Violence, appointed by President Lyndon B. Johnson after the assassinations of Martin Luther King Jr. and Robert F. Kennedy, presented a psychological profile of assassins emphasizing their alienation and sexual dysfunction. The report stressed the "critical importance" of maintaining an "overwhelming sense of the legitimacy of our government and institutions." It suggested that doubts about the lone gunmen were "a product of the primal anxieties created by the archetypal crime of parricide—not the inadequacy of the evidence of the lone assassin."

Then in the early '70s came revelations about John Kennedy's mistresses and Mafia connections, about Watergate conspirators and machinations of the Central Intelligence Agency. The idea that criminal associations, murderous plots and orchestrated deceit might characterize the highest levels of U.S. government was shown to be plausible, if not realistic. Fear of conspiracy was legitimized. The Kennedy assassination became the inspiration for a darker vision of U.S. public life, especially in Hollywood.

Alan Pakula's paranoid thriller *The Parallax View* (1975) reworked the Kennedy assassination into liberal myth. Joseph Frady, a newspaper reporter played by Warren Beatty, stumbles onto the mysterious corporation that has assassinated a promising Kennedy-style politician. Frady's boss is poisoned, a friend's houseboat is firebombed. When Frady figures out where the next assassination will take place, he tries to intervene, only to be killed and posthumously framed as the assassin himself. The movie closes with a Warren Commission-style tribunal ruling that Frady was "confused," and any speculation that he did not act alone is conspiracy mongering. "Parallax View" was a model of liberal paranoia—a corporate monolith dedicated to murdering progressive hope and pinning the blame on the lone man who knew the truth.

Taxi Driver (1976), directed by Martin Scorcese, was also essentially about the Kennedy assassination. The title character, Travis Bickel is, like Lee Harvey Oswald, an ex-Marine. Superficially, he fits the profile of an assassin as developed by the National Commission on Violence—a misfit driven to kill by resentment, envy and mental instability. But, Bickel, as played by Robert DeNiro, is a man recoiling from the degradation of a permissive society. When he tries to help a young prostitute get off the streets, she spouts cliches of liberation. When he develops a crush on a pretty campaign worker, he discovers that she believes in her candidate, a handsome Kennedy-like fraud who does little more than intone meaningless slogans. Travis stalks the candidate but is thwarted by the Secret Service. He then turns on the young prostitute's pimp and customers and, after a bloody rampage, winds up a hero in the tabloids. In *Taxi Driver*, a decadent America gets the assassin it deserves.

In 1977, the House of Representatives responded to the pervasive mood of cynicism about government by reopening the investigation of the Kennedy assassination. In 1979, the House Special Committee on Assassinations concluded that unknown conspirators were responsible—a finding that only compounded the cynicism. "Next thing you know," gibed Johnny Carson, "they'll be blaming World War II on Hitler."

With the Reagan era came a new mood of confidence—at least among Washington's political elite. In 1983, one former aide to Robert Kennedy declared "We are done with debunking." Yet the public remained skeptical as ever about the assassination. A 1983 *Washington Post*/ABC News poll found 80% of Americans believed more than one person was responsible for Kennedy's murder.

But Kennedy's masculine style and aggressive foreign policy were back into vogue. Critical examination of the underside of his presidency was increasingly viewed as another passe form of liberal self-flagellation. The Times re-examined the Warren Commission and pronounced the lone gunman theory persuasive. The commemoration of the 20th anniversary of the assassination, unlike the 10th or 15th, was heavy on nostalgia about Kennedy's Camelot, light on speculation about the assassination.

However, by 1988, the 25th anniversary, the conspiracy theme was reasserting itself. The Iran-Contra affair revealed an oddly familiar extra-legal conspiracy featuring assassination manuals and anti-Castro Cubans, as well as a presidential commission of inquiry that did its best to avoid the unseemly truth. Don DeLillo's best-selling novel, *Libra*, portrayed Oswald as the witting and unwitting tool of anti-communist conspirators enraged by Kennedy's betrayal at the Bay of Pigs.

"What has become unravelled since Dallas," DeLillo wrote in 1988, "is not the plot, of course, not the dense mass of character and events, but the sense of a coherent reality."

The imaginative recreation of the Kennedy assassination from the pot-boiler novels of the '60s to Stone's *JFK* is a ceaseless quest to restore that sense of coherent reality to the American story. The crime of the century remains unresolved less because we don't know who fired the fatal shots than because there is no agreement whether the story of the Kennedy assassination should be invested with confidence in our national institutions or with fears of conspiratorial power.

Jefferson Morley is a former associate editor of the New Republic and former Washington editor of The Nation.

Reprinted by permission of the author.

DECEMBER 15, 1991

THE TIMES-PICAYUNE

THE GARRISON PROBE: THE STORY HOLLYWOOD WON'T TELL
(alternately subtitled: The Trial of Clay Shaw)

James O'Byrne

In 1967, New Orleans District Attorney Jim Garrison declared flatly that he had solved the 1963 assassination of John F. Kennedy, which he claimed was a conspiracy hatched in an apartment on Louisiana Avenue Parkway.

"I wouldn't say this if we didn't have the evidence beyond a shadow of a doubt," Garrison said.

He vowed he would shatter the government's conclusion that Lee Harvey Oswald acted alone, killing Kennedy with a rifle shot to the brain as the president's limousine rolled through Dallas Nov. 22, 1963.

Within days, an army of newspaper and television reporters from around the world descended on New Orleans, trying to uncover Garrison's smoking gun.

What Garrison delivered shocked the world. On March 1, 1967, Clay Shaw, 54, was marched handcuffed up the steps of the Criminal Court Building before a national television audience, charged with conspiring to murder Kennedy. The gentlemanly, well-respected businessman, playwright, opera lover and French Quarter preservationist cut a highly unlikely figure for an assassination conspirator.

Two years to the day after his arrest, Shaw was acquitted. A jury that heard 34 days of testimony unanimously rejected the charge in less than an hour, a stunning rebuke to Garrison.

The Shaw case is about to achieve national notoriety again. Garrison's probe is the focus of the Oliver Stone movie *JFK*, opening Friday.

Kevin Costner plays the district attorney, through whom Stone advances theories that there was a far-flung conspiracy involving the CIA and other federal agencies, and possibly even Kennedy's successor, President Lyndon Johnson.

What has disquieted many involved in the real case is that Stone makes Garrison's pursuit and trial of Shaw a noble endeavor and thereby rehabilitates Garrison's national image a quarter century after Shaw's arrest.

Many, including some of Garrison's assistants at the time, believe Shaw never should have been arrested, much less tried. The reason: There was never credible evidence to indicate Shaw was guilty of anything more sinister than being the object of the district attorney's single-minded obsession with the assassination.

The case against Shaw was far from ironclad.

The key witnesses who tried to link Shaw to the assassination plot included:

◆ Perry Raymond Russo, a 25-year-old publicity-seeking insurance salesman from Baton Rouge who was shown pictures of Shaw, drugged once with sodium pentothal, or "truth serum," hypnotized twice by Garrison's office and asked a series of leading questions in an effort to refresh his memory.

Russo was central to the case because he was the only witness who testified that Shaw discussed killing Kennedy. His original story was that he attended a party at which Shaw, Oswald and David Ferrie, a pilot and self-styled detective, talked about killing the president. That straight-forward assertion disintegrated during the trial.

◆ Charles I. Spiesel, an articulate New York accountant who calmly testified that he went to a party in New Orleans and saw Shaw and Ferrie together talking about Kennedy.

Spiesel just as calmly testified under cross-examination that he had been followed and hypnotized dozens of times by the New York Police Department and private detectives; that he had been rendered impotent and incapable of doing his accounting work by the frequent involuntary hypnosis; and that he regularly fingerprinted his daughter when she went off to college, and again when she returned, to make sure the government hadn't kidnapped her and replaced her with an exact replica.

◆ Vernon Bundy, a heroin addict in Orleans Parish Prison at the time the district attorney's office brought him forward to testify that he saw Shaw and Oswald together at the Lakefront one day while Bundy was shooting heroin.

Garrison, now 70, retired in November from his judgeship on the state 4th Circuit Court of Appeal. He is in poor health and a spokeswoman said he is not well enough to be interviewed. Before he became ill, he said he was pleased with Stone's script.

CULTURALLY ACTIVE

Shaw was not famous in New Orleans, but he was widely known and beloved in the city's cultural and trade communities. A decorated major in World War II, Shaw from 1946 to 1965 worked for the International Trade Mart, which promoted trade between New Orleans and countries around the world. He was a voracious reader and spoke several languages ... He attended and supported the symphony, the opera and the theater.

Shaw also was an avid preservationist of French Quarter architecture. He is widely regarded as being among the first to recognize the importance of saving old buildings in the Quarter by converting them into homes and apartments. He bought, restored and sold dozens of buildings, and is believed to have built the Quarter's first swimming pool.

Shaw retired early from the Trade Mart. At 52, he had saved enough money to live comfortably while fulfilling his dream to write plays and travel.

But two years later, he was indicted in the crime of the century. By the time he was acquitted, his savings were gone, wiped out by legal and investigators' fees. Five years after the trial, he was dead of cancer.

"It ruined his life," said Rosemary James, who owns a local public relations company, and was then a reporter for The States-Item and a close friend of Shaw's. "All his savings went to defend himself. After the trial, he had to go back to work, and shortly thereafter he got sick."

Shaw was known by his close friends to be a homosexual. Garrison would later seize on that as one piece in the fanciful case he built against Shaw.

STORY STARTS WITH LAWYER

The bizarre tale that ended with Shaw's acquittal began much earlier, in the mind of New Orleans lawyer Dean Andrews.

Andrews appeared before the Warren Commission—the official panel that conducted a 10-month investigation of the assassination and concluded that Oswald acted alone. Andrews testified that a man he knew as Clay Bertrand called him the day of the assassination and asked him to go to Dallas to represent Lee Harvey Oswald. Andrews said he assumed Bertrand was homosexual, because he often asked Andrews to represent homosexual clients.

Commission investigators couldn't find Clay Bertrand and concluded he did not exist. Andrews would testify five years later, at Shaw's trial, that he had invented Bertrand.

But Garrison believed Bertrand existed, and was in fact Clay Shaw. He believed this despite the fact that Andrews had described the man he later admitted was a figment of his imagination as 5-foot-8, with sandy hair and blue eyes and about 170 pounds.

Shaw was an imposing figure. He stood nearly 6 feet 6 inches tall, weighed 220 pounds and had a shock of white hair.

Author David Chandler, who covered the Shaw case for Life magazine, remembers vividly when Garrison met him and a senior Life editor to tell them how he had concluded that Clay Bertrand was Clay Shaw.

"He proceeded to spell out what I call the silly syllogism of who Clay Bertrand was," Chandler recalled. "He said, 'First, they're both named Clay. Second, they're both homosexuals. They both speak Spanish. Thus, Bertrand is Clay Shaw.'"

Chandler said he was stunned that Garrison seriously advanced the Shaw theory. But Garrison said at the time that Shaw was not the target of the probe. The real target, Garrison said, was David Ferrie.

FERRIE'S INVOLVEMENT

Ferrie was a bizarre character. An accomplished pilot, he lost his job with Eastern Airlines when he was arrested in Jefferson Parish on charges of fondling a juvenile boy. The charges later were dropped.

Ferrie was completely hairless, and he painted on oversized eyebrows with a grease pencil and wore a crudely made red wig. He mostly made his living teaching people to fly, and picking up detective work here and there. He was interested in fostering a Cuban revolution to oust Fidel Castro, and befriended Cubans intent on doing the same.

On the day of Kennedy's assassination, Ferrie drove to Houston and Galveston, Texas. He said he and two friends had decided to take a break and get out of town, to visit an ice-skating rink in Houston. He was detained and interviewed by the F.B.I. and the Secret Service in 1963 shortly after Kennedy's death, and cleared of any involvement.

But Garrison considered the F.B.I. to be part of the assassination plot. When he began his probe, he tagged Ferrie as the getaway pilot for the assassins.

Ferrie alerted the press to Garrison's probe early in 1967.

Whether Ferrie would have been charged is anyone's guess. On Feb. 22, 1967, Ferrie died in his apartment. Trash, empty coffee cups, cigarette butts and a veritable drugstore of prescription medication were strewn about the room.

Garrison immediately proclaimed Ferrie "one of history's most important individuals." Garrison claimed he was just about to arrest Ferrie when he died, and suggested Ferrie had killed himself.

But the coroner said a ruptured blood vessel at the base of Ferrie's brain had burst. The coroner said high blood pressure could have forced the vessel to rupture, and Ferrie had high blood pressure—even before Garrison began investigating him.

GARRISON'S TRANSFORMATION

By the time of Ferrie's death, some of Garrison's assistants had become concerned that the probe was spinning out of control.

Leads that Garrison was convinced were critical turned out to be dead ends. The pressure from the press was mounting to deliver something—anything—to support the bold contention that the assassination had been solved.

And Garrison's theories seemed to be changing daily.

Life magazine's Chandler remembers Garrison changed dramatically as the investigation proceeded.

Garrison had been a good friend of Chandler's since 1961. Chandler said Garrison was the best man at his wedding in 1965. But when Chandler began asking pointed questions about the investigation, Garrison threatened to indict him for perjury—a tactic Garrison would use repeatedly to quiet his critics.

"He had changed from a liberal, crusading, dedicated public officer to a megalomaniac," Chandler said. "Once he became fixed on the Kennedy probe, he became absolutely ruthless in his pursuit of it."

But with Ferrie's death, some of his assistants saw a way out.

"A few of us quite frankly were relieved," said John Volz, the former U.S. attorney for the eastern district of Louisiana who was then an assistant to Garrison. "We were hoping this was the opportunity we had been waiting for to shut it down, say the key to the case had died and get out. Unfortunately, Garrison's reaction was just the opposite."

Volz had been heavily involved in the investigation in its early stages, but drew Garrison's ire when he was sent to Dallas to check out Garrison's belief that a bar near the Dealey Plaza assassination site was somehow key to understanding the conspiracy.

When Volz came back, he told Garrison, "There's nothing to it, chief."

Volz recalls that Garrison was incredulous. He offered Volz the lowest insult in his arsenal: "You have the imagination of an F.B.I. agent." In a move Volz now considers fortuitous, he was taken off the case.

LOYALTY TO DA WANES

Garrison desperately needed the loyalty of his assistants. As the investigation continued, he felt it slipping away.

He suffered a major setback with the arrest of Shaw eight days after Ferrie's death.

William Gurvich, one of Garrison's chief investigators, had seen enough. Gurvich resigned, called a press conference and declared the investigation a hoax. He flew to Washington and told Robert Kennedy that Garrison's probe would never shed light on his brother's death. Then he went to work for Shaw's defense team.

There were other defections. Tom Bethell, today an editor for the American Spectator magazine in Washington, D.C., was a researcher for Garrison, culling information on the Warren Commission probe from the National Archives. Later, Bethell came to New Orleans to supervise the investigation files.

Bethell became disillusioned after learning that Garrison planned to put Spiesel on the stand.

"A couple of assistants went off to interview Spiesel and came back and said, 'Well, he'd make a good witness, but he's crazy,'" Bethell said. "Then I realized they were planning to use him anyway."

Bethell not only quit, he turned over a copy of the witness list to F. Irvin Dymond, Shaw's attorney. At that time, prosecutors were not required by law to provide such lists to the defense. Bethell was subsequently indicted on charges of illegally removing files from the office, but was told he wouldn't be prosecuted as long as he kept his mouth shut.

As it turned out, Bethell's defection was pivotal. An investigation of Spiesel, which cost Shaw $4,000, turned up the incriminating information about his hypnosis claims and his fear that the government might replace his daughter with a replica.

Like a Perry Mason episode, the files on Spiesel arrived by plane in New Orleans after Dymond had begun cross-examining Spiesel. He rushed an assistant out to the airport.

"That guy was outwardly a very, very credible witness—an accountant, well-spoken, well-dressed," Dymond recalled. "He would have been devastating if we had not been able to discredit him."

In his 1988 book "On the Trail of the Assassins," Garrison says he knew nothing about Spiesel's background. Garrison blamed the slipup on the assistant who prosecuted the case, James Alcock. He also suggested that the government had planted Spiesel to sabotage his case. Alcock, now a lawyer in Houma, declined to be interviewed.

RUSSO AS WITNESS

Shaw's trial began Jan. 21, 1969, nearly two years after his arrest. In the intervening time, the district attorney's office had scrambled to buttress the case, but still had only one witness to testify that Shaw met with Ferrie and Oswald and talked about killing Kennedy—Perry Raymond Russo.

At a preliminary hearing shortly after Shaw's arrest, Russo had testified adamantly and persuasively that Shaw was at Ferrie's apartment when an assassination was discussed.

But by the trial, Russo's story had changed in many respects.

For example:

◆ Before the trial, Russo had met with a police sergeant to discuss the case. Russo testified he told the sergeant he couldn't say for sure if Shaw was the man at the party, and if forced to say yes or no, he'd say no.

◆ When Dymond asked Russo why he had so confidently identified Shaw at a preliminary hearing in 1967, Russo said Dymond had made him angry by asking him if he believed in God.

◆ At the trial, Russo admitted that, while he heard Ferrie discuss killing the president, he did not hear Shaw mention the possibility at all.

FROM BAD TO WORSE

But as bad a witness as Russo proved to be, Spiesel was worse.

A handsome, nattily dressed man who arrived at court every day wearing a hat and smoking a cigar, Spiesel was a frightening witness for the defense.

His testimony for the prosecution was that he had come to New Orleans in May

1963, where he had met Ferrie and been invited to a party at an apartment at Dauphine Street and Esplanade Avenue. Once there, Spiesel said he identified Shaw as among 10 or 11 people present.

"Someone brought up the name of President Kennedy and just about everyone began to criticize him," Spiesel testified. "Then someone said, 'Somebody ought to kill that son of a bitch.'"

Under cross-examination by Dymond, Spiesel acknowledged that he was suing New York City for $16 million for repeatedly letting police hypnotize him and harass him out of business. He suggested it might be part of a communist plot.

Spiesel calculated that he had been hypnotized by 50 or 60 people. "How can you tell?" Dymond asked.

"After all this time I am an expert," Spiesel said.

SHAW'S SECOND ARREST

Two days after Shaw was acquitted of conspiring to kill Kennedy, Garrison had him arrested again and charged with perjury. Garrison said he planned to prosecute Shaw for his testimony in his own defense that he knew neither Oswald nor Ferrie.

Those charges hung over Shaw for two years, until a federal judge in 1971 prevented Garrison from pursuing the charges, blasting the district attorney for harassing Shaw.

Shaw eventually filed a federal damage suit against Garrison, but he died before the case came to trial.

Garrison has remained convinced of a widespread conspiracy to assassinate Kennedy. In 1989, he told an Associated Press reporter that he believed about 18 people were involved in the assassination, including at least three riflemen, two radiomen, two spotters, six members of the Dallas Police Department Homicide Division and three or four others for training, on-site planning and logistics.

For Shaw's closest friends, *JFK* puts a cruel twist on history by suggesting that Garrison, rather than Shaw, was victimized by the investigation.

"Clay Shaw could have lived a tasteful, quiet, lovely life for 25 or 30 years on what he had saved," close friend James said. "Instead, his life was wrecked to advance Garrison's agenda.

"The cynicism was appalling."

Reprinted by permission of The Times-Picayune ©1991 Publishing Co.

THE NEW YORK TIMES

DOES *JFK* CONSPIRE AGAINST REASON?

Oliver Stone transforms a discredited theory into the sole explanation for the assassination

Tom Wicker

More than halfway into *JFK*, Oliver Stone's three-hour movie about the assassination of President Kennedy, New Orleans District Attorney Jim Garrison and his wife, Liz, are seen watching a television documentary about Mr. Garrison's investigation of the events of Nov. 22, 1963, in Dallas.

The documentary's anchorman is heard charging that the District Attorney used improper methods to get witnesses to support his case against New Orleans businessman Clay Shaw for his part in a supposed conspiracy surrounding the murder of President Kennedy. Kevin Costner, portraying Mr. Garrison, suggests by facial expression and dialogue that the charge is unfair and rigged to destroy his credibility—thus attacking the credibility of the documentary.

Frequently in *JFK*, the District Attorney alleges that the media are engaged in a coverup of a monstrous conspiracy, which Mr. Stone confidently depicts as having resulted in the assassination of a President, the war in Vietnam, the later killing of Robert Kennedy, perhaps even the murder of the Rev. Martin Luther King Jr.

It is a measure of Mr. Stone's heavily weighted storytelling that he gives only a fleeting glimpse of that one-hour documentary which was broadcast by NBC on June 19, 1967. Its evidence—the script is available—establishes without doubt that Mr. Garrison and his aides threatened and bribed witnesses, who then lied in court, and that they concealed the results of a polygraph test that showed one witness, Vernon Bundy, to be lying.

So much for the advertising for the Stone film, which proclaims of Mr. Garrison: "He will risk his life, the lives of his family, everything he holds dear for the one thing he holds sacred—the truth."

In fact, of all the numerous conspiracy theorists and zealous investigators who for nearly 30 years have been peering at and probing the assassination of John F. Kennedy, Mr. Garrison may be the most thoroughly discredited—and not just by the NBC documentary. His ballyhooed investigation ended ignominiously when his chosen villain, Clay Shaw, was acquitted; and the whole Garrison affair is now regarded, even by other conspiracy believers, as having been a travesty of legal process.

Despite all this, Jim Garrison is clearly the film's hero. He is played by Mr. Costner, one of Hollywood's hottest box-office attractions, fresh from his triumph in "Dances With Wolves." Sissy Spacek plays his wife, and in an arrogant bit of casting against type, the real-life Mr. Garrison makes a cameo appearance as Chief

Justice Earl Warren.

JFK which opens on Friday, stirred controversy last summer when a draft of Mr. Stone and Zachary Sklar's screenplay found its way to the press. Based chiefly on Mr. Garrison's 1988 book, *On the Trail of the Assassins*, it adopts his argument that Lee Harvey Oswald—the lone Presidential assassin, according to the Warren Commission—was merely a patsy put forward to shield the actions of an immense body of conspirators involved in the murder and coverup.

The controversy arose over fears that the film would develop a web of speculation and fiction around a tragic event of major historic significance. And indeed, it does treat matters that are wholly speculative as fact and truth, in effect rewriting history.

Mr. Stone built into his movie an all-encompassing defense. As in the scene of the television documentary, the film's Jim Garrison repeatedly says that any critics of his thesis are either part of the great conspiracy he has conceived or are helping to cover it up. The only one of his assistants who argues and disagrees with him is shown to have been coerced by the F.B.I., a primary participant in Mr. Garrison's sprawling conspiracy.

Of course, any article critical of the movie—this one included—can be dismissed in the same way, as part of the alleged conspiracy and its continuing coverup. Mr. Stone has already called himself, in U.S.A. Today, a target for "a thousand and one vultures out there, crouched on their rocks." These were not just "the usual Hollywood vultures," he said, but " a lot of these paid-off journalist hacks that are working on the East Coast with their recopied [sic] political theories ..."

But there's a gaping hole in the movie's advance counterattack: If a conspiracy as vast and consequential as the one claimed could have been carried out and covered up for three decades, why did the conspirators or their heirs allow Mr. Stone to make this movie? Why not murder him, as they supposedly murdered others? Why, for that matter, didn't they knock off Mr. Garrison himself when—as Mr. Stone tells it with so much assurance—the New Orleans district attorney began so fearlessly to follow their trail?

PIECING TOGETHER A GREAT CONSPIRACY

JFK begins with real footage of President Eisenhower's farewell address, in which he eloquently warned of the dangers of the "military-industrial complex." This sets up Mr. Stone's contention—borrowed, or swallowed whole, from Mr. Garrison—that generals, admirals and war profiteers so strongly wanted the war in Vietnam to be fought and the United States to stand tall and tough against the Soviets that when President Kennedy seemed to question these goals, he had to be killed so Vice President Johnson could take office. Mr. Stone clearly implies that this was done with Johnson's connivance.

"Who benefited?" asks Donald Sutherland in one of the film's frequent star turns in minor parts (Jack Lemmon, Walter Matthau, and Ed Asner provide others.) Mr. Sutherland, playing an unnamed former military officer who sounds like any of a number of hawkish fanatics hanging around Washington, specifically names such beneficiaries as Johnson and the Bell Corporation, which supplied helicopters for Vietnam.

President Kennedy, historian Stone asserts, was considered "soft on communism" after the test-ban treaty with the Soviet Union and a conciliatory speech at American University, both in 1963. No doubt some in the military and the John Birch Society held that paranoid view; but to anyone active in Washington at that time it's ridiculous to suggest that such an opinion was widely shared.

Mr. Stone's film nevertheless insists that Mr. Kennedy had so enraged the nation's hawks that the military-industrial complex, with the help of the Central Intelligence Agency and the Federal Bureau of Investigation, actually planned and carried out the assassination, then covered it up through the Warren Commission (ostensibly set up to investigate the assasination and headed by Chief Justice Warren), with the aid of the Dallas police and the nation's press and television.

Mr. Stone may be on firmer ground when he claims that the assassination prevented President Kennedy from carrying out a planned withdrawal from Vietnam. That Kennedy might not have expanded the war as President Johnson did in 1964 is a plausible, if not conclusive, argument; I made it myself in 1968, in a speculative passage of my book *J.F.K. and L.B.J.* It seems less likely that Kennedy had already decided, at the time of his death, to extricate the nation from the quagmire of Vietnam after his expected re-election. Still, it's arguable that he had so decided, or soon would have.

Mr. Stone not only depicts these debatable possibilities as facts; his film claims that for these reasons Mr. Kennedy was killed—though I know of no reputable historian who has documented Kennedy's intentions, much less found them the motive for his murder. It's true that this motive, among numerous others, has been speculated upon before, in more or less responsible terms, depending on who was doing the speculating.

But this movie presents itself as more than speculation; it claims truth for itself. And among the many Americans likely to see it, particularly those who never accepted the Warren Commission's theory of a single assassin, even more particularly those too young to remember November 22, 1963, *JFK* is all too likely to be taken as the final, unquestioned explanation.

Flashily put together under Mr. Stone's famous imprimatur and using much film footage of actual events and real people, starring the Hollywood idol Kevin Costner, and confident of its own rightness and righteousness, *JFK* may prove persuasive to audiences with little knowledge of the events presented. Asserting that the future of justice in America depends on the exposure of Mr. Stone's nightmarish visions of conspiracy, as discovered through the depicted heroism of Jim Garrison, the film is also presented—especially in a long and weepy courtroom summation by Jim Garrison—as a call to courage and idealism, which may appeal to a people apparently hungry for both.

But if *JFK* and its wild assertions are to be taken at face value, Americans will have to accept the idea that most of the nation's major institutions, private as well as governmental, along with one of its Presidents, conspired together and carried out Kennedy's murder to pursue the war in Vietnam and the Cold War, then covered up the conspiracy until Mr. Garrison and Mr. Stone unearthed and exposed it.

EVIDENCE PRESENTED FROM A STACKED DECK

In an era when mistrust of government and loss of confidence in institutions (the press not least) are widespread and virulent, such a suggestion seems a dubious public service, particularly since these dark allegations are only unproven speculations, and the "evidence" presented is often a stacked deck.

President Kennedy, for instance, is pictured in real footage, being interviewed by Walter Cronkite on the first 30-minute broadcast of evening news by CBS, a few weeks before the assassination. The President's remarks indicated that he was becoming disillusioned with the war in Vietnam, thus seeming to support Mr. Stone's insistent thesis.

But the film does not even mention Mr. Kennedy's interview with David Brinkley a week later, when NBC began its 30-minute news program. Then, the President confirmed his belief in the "domino theory"—which suggested that the fall of Vietnam to Communism would precipitate collapses in the surrounding countries in Southeast Asia—and added: "China is so large, looms so high ... that if South Vietnam went, it would not only give them an improved geographic position for a guerrilla assault on Malaya but would also give the impression that the wave of the future in Southeast Asia was China and the Communists."

There's no suggestion of withdrawal in that later interview; and even if Mr. Kennedy may have been balancing his earlier remarks owing to protests from Saigon and from American Hawks, it is misleading for Mr. Stone to cite only one of two equally verifiable texts, the one favorable to his case.

Again, when Jim Garrison watches the shooting of Robert Kennedy (in 1968) on television, he tells his wife that now he's "really scared." Liz Garrison, who has been doubtful of her husband's case, suddenly believes in him. This turnaround leaves the extraordinary impression that Robert Kennedy's murder somehow proved that Mr. Garrison was right about John Kennedy's murder and the great conspiracy. Just what this "proof" consists of, the film does not attempt to explain.

The depiction of the Robert Kennedy assassination, though using real news footage, includes two bits of trickery. Adroit cutting makes it appear as though he were shot while concluding his speech to an applauding audience on the night of his victory in the California primary; actually, he had left the stage and was departing through a hotel kitchen when he was cut down. Mr. Garrison not only sees the shooting on television; he immediately tells his wife that Robert Kennedy has been killed—when, in fact, Kennedy lived until the following night.

An alert listener also will pick up, in many of the speeches by Jim Garrison and his dedicated aides, a number of phrases like "has something to do with," "what if," "a possibility," "may well have been," "possibly." Such hedges make it clear that even Mr. Stone cannot be sure that all the "facts" he throws out relentlessly are facts.

THE WARREN COMMISSION: PART OF THE PROBLEM?

Through frequent, detailed discussions of their investigation by Jim Garrison and his assistants, Mr. Stone is merciless in his assault on the Warren Commission—not merely the report's errors of omission and commission but the group's alleged complicity in the conspiracy and coverup.

At one point in the film, Jim Garrison refers to Arlen Specter, who as a member of the commission staff had devised its controversial "single-bullet" theory, as one of the "grossest liars" in the nation. Some who watched Mr. Specter, now a Republican Senator from Pennsylvania, during the Clarence Thomas hearings may be tempted to agree; but the reference is another attempt to picture the commission report as a deliberate falsehood and part of a widespread coverup.

The Warren Commission was under time pressure; its report was hurried out, and it contains errors, omissions and debatable interpretations. Its conclusion that Oswald, acting alone, killed John Kennedy, is widely disbelieved. The commission is a fair target for criticism of its procedures and findings; but you have to be paranoid indeed to believe that the Chief Justice and his colleagues deliberately framed Oswald for a crime he didn't commit, while covering the tracks of the many who were actually responsible.

When the Warren Commission report began to be widely questioned, I discussed it—sometime in the late '60s—with Edward Bennett Williams, the renowned criminal lawyer. He defended the report in the following manner:

In every crime to which there are no credible eyewitnesses, the prosecution (in this case the Warren Commission) examines available evidence and presents a theory of what may have happened. The defense presents an opposing theory. Neither theory is likely to be airtight, without flaws or questionable assertions; even physical evidence, let alone circumstantial, is not likely to be that indisputable. But in the end, a jury usually believes one theory or the other, and convicts or acquits on that basis.

The commission report, Williams said, was a prosecution theory and, as such, did have holes and deficiencies. But he believed a jury would accept it in preference to *any other theory* that at the time had been presented. Considered by itself, the commission report might be picked apart by its critics; but what, Williams asks, did they present in its place? Was any other theory of what happened in Dallas as plausible? Until a more believable theory was brought forward, the commission report seemed to him the most reasonable explanation of what happened.

I agree with that, though my opinion is not held dogmatically. I'm willing to believe that Oswald did not act alone, or that he was innocent of the killing, or that there was a conspiracy, or that the mob did it in response to Robert Kennedy's actions as Attorney General, or that Fidel Castro was or was not involved as a result of the Bay of Pigs fiasco and the Cuban Missile Crisis, or any combination of the above. I'm willing, *but only if someone presents an explanation of what happened that's believable and reasonable*—not paranoid and fantastic.

After many years of consideration, I doubt that the truth about the Kennedy assassination has yet been told. It may never be. So to question what happened, to doubt the Warren Commission's or anybody's version, is legitimate, perhaps even necessary, but in my opinion not conclusive.

My dissent from Mr. Stone's film is not that he believes that Oswald was a patsy, or that there was a conspiracy or even that he depicts the conspiracy as fascist, a corruption of Constitutional government so far-reaching as to threaten the end of the democratic system in America. He has a right to believe those things, even to believe against the evidence that Mr. Garrison's shabby investigation was a noble and selfless search for truth.

But I and other Americans have an equal right not to believe such things, a right to our own beliefs. Mr. Stone insists on one true faith about Nov. 22, 1963—as though only he and Mr. Garrison could discern the truth, among the many theories of what happened that terrible day. Moreover, he implies that anyone who doesn't share his one true faith is either an active part of a coverup or passively acquiescent in it.

Finally, he uses the powerful instrument of a motion picture, and relies on stars of the entertainment world, to propagate the one true faith—even though that faith, if widely accepted, would be contemptuous of the very Constitutional government Mr. Stone's film purports to uphold.

DECEMBER 22, 1991

NEW YORK TIMES
LETTER

VIA THE DIRECTOR'S VIEWFINDER

Oliver Stone

To the Editor:

I am sorry that Tom Wicker, whom I respect as a journalist—and who wrote so insightfully on President John F. Kennedy and so movingly about his death—chose to attack my film *JFK* ["Does 'J.F.K.' Conspire Against Reason?" Dec. 15].

I only wish that Mr. Wicker and other journalists who have so strongly criticized my film would have applied over the years the same passionate intensity of effort into trying to find out who really killed President Kennedy and why.

In endorsing the vitriolic NBC documentary "discrediting" Jim Garrison, he fails to note the program was so one-sided that Mr. Garrison successfully petitioned the Federal Communications Commission for rebuttal time.

A declassified C.I.A. memo dated June 1, 1967, says that then NBC correspondent Walter Sheridan was "coaching [witness] Gordon Novel to get maximum publicity before picturing him on a TV program intended to destroy Garrison's act." The show did not air until several weeks later—how did the C.I.A. know its point of view? So much for Mr. Wicker's "truth."

In casting me as "paranoid" regarding the media, Mr. Wicker is cynical when he must know a first draft of the script of *JFK* was stolen and criticized in such publications as *The Washington Post* and Time magazine. Never has an unfinished movie been so prejudged and precensored. Even paranoids have enemies. But on Mr. Wicker's playing field, the press is allowed to dish it out, but woe if the victim tries to defend himself.

Let me further suggest that the media itself is part of the problem and seems to resent it when an artist tries to interpret a history that newsmen have failed to explain. From day 1, the American media (in contrast to most foreign media) never looked for an honest motive in President Kennedy's killing and accepted the cover story of Lee Harvey Oswald as lone assassin put out by Government officials and reinforced by the appointed Warren Commission, which allowed the intelligence agencies to disclose files and investigate leads at their discretion.

In dismissing my rationale of President Kennedy's being "soft on Communism" as a possible motive, Mr. Wicker is disingenuous when he denies that the military and intelligence communities were apoplectic about J.F.K.'s policies, from the Bay of Pigs (where he refused to supply air support) to the Cuban missile crisis (where he refused to bomb Cuba and where he made a deal with Premier Nikita Khrushchev), from the nuclear test-ban treaty to his October 1963 National Security memorandum ordering the withdrawal of the first 1,000 troops from Vietnam by Christmas. Several participants in books and oral histories have attested to a high degree of tension between Kennedy and the military.

Nor does Mr. Wicker pay attention to the size and illegitimacy of Operation Mongoose, or the back-channel negotiations with Fidel Castro because of C.I.A. opposition, the impending closure of military bases at home and abroad and major defense cuts. He ignores the fractious history of conflict with the Joint Chiefs over Laos and Vietnam (as far back as 1961), which is described in a new book by Maj. John Newman, *J.F.K. and Vietnam*, and which was sent by my associates to Mr. Wicker in the hopes he would accept a fresh perspective.

But, of course, artists are not allowed to invade the territory of "experts" like Mr. Wicker, who in this case seems to be part of the problem, not the solution. That is why, in my opinion, the best work on the Kennedy assassination has come wholly from concerned private citizens.

Mr. Wicker accuses me of brain-washing the public with "the powerful instrument of a motion picture." If nothing else, people's capacity to resist brainwashing is shown by the fact that after 28 years of being pounded by the Oswald-did-it-alone mantra, the majority still do not believe it, and that after years of Kennedy-bashing, John F. Kennedy is still a figure of hope and idealism to the American People.

In accusing me of subverting the Constitution and rewriting history in some sort of artistic fascist takeover, I can only answer that I see it as a troubled history in desperate need of full disclosure. If *JFK* is a small first step in making that happen, then I know I've succeeded. There is absolutely no excuse whatsoever for the American public to wait until 2029 for the House Select Committee on Assassinations records to be released, nor to have the C.I.A., F.B.I. and military intelligence files withheld for all eternity.

Has Mr. Wicker in his cynicism totally given up on what de Tocqueville most admired about America: its capacity for self-correction? If I am subverting faith in our institutions at a critical time, I must wonder along with Jim Garrison: "Is a government worth preserving when it lies to the people, when it is no longer accountable to the people? It has become a dangerous country, sir. I say, let justice be done though the heavens fall!"

Mr. Wicker replies: The director of JFK is not, as he claims, an artist. He is a polemicist.

Reprinted by permission of the author.

JANUARY 5, 1992

THE NEW YORK TIMES
LETTER

AN ADVISER SPEAKS OUT

L. Fletcher Prouty

Tom Wicker castigates the former District Attorney of New Orleans, Jim Garrison, for trying to do what Texas law officers and courts have studiously avoided. Mr. Garrison attempted to the best of his ability to prove what men like Lyndon B. Johnson had come to believe: that the assassination in Dallas had been part of a conspiracy.

Because Mr. Garrison's account of that trial provides Oliver Stone with a complete panoply of "assassination lore," it gives him an excellent foundation for that part of his broad drama. From that base Mr. Stone goes on to present a full spectrum of facts, such as President Kennedy's documented plan to withdraw all Americans from Vietnam by the end of 1965 and to bring 1,000 of those men home by Christmas 1963. That Presidential directive created enormous pressures within the United States political and industrial complex.

Tom Wicker writes: "I know of no reputable historian who has documented Mr. Kennedy's intentions." He could quite easily have acquired this information from "Vol. IV, 1961-1963, Foreign Relations of the United States," published by the United States Government Printing Office in 1991. Rather, Mr. Wicker blames this "speculation" on an "unnamed former military officer who sounds like any number of hawkish fanatics hanging around Washington."

I happen to be that "fanatic" whom Oliver Stone asked to serve as an adviser to him and his screenwriters, for the simple reason that I had lived through that era and had been working for the Joint Chiefs of Staff when President Kennedy ordered the publication of National Security Action Memorandum No. 263 of October 1963 saying precisely those things that I have written above.

Col. L. Fletcher Prouty, United States Air Force (Retired), was an adviser to Oliver Stone during the filming of JFK.

Reprinted by permission of the author.

DECEMBER 17, 1991

UNIVERSAL PRESS SYNDICATE

INTERVIEW WITH OLIVER STONE

Roger Ebert

Oliver Stone talks rapidly and yet with a certain weariness, as if he knows the answers but fears he will not be listened to. He defends his new film, *JFK*, with a rush of dates and references and facts, and then when he is asked about the film's detractors, he reveals an underlying bitterness:

"This has been a distressing experience," he says. "It was disturbing to have this film attacked so early. Never before in the history of movies has a film been attacked in first-draft screenplay form. All the established media seem to be terrified of my movie, as if it's somehow going to destroy their lives. I'm amazed at their fear. What stake do they have in it?"

This was a week before *JFK* opened on Dec. 20. Dan Rather had attacked the film on CBS, *The Washington Post* had printed and criticized some of the screenplay, political pundit Tom Wicker had written a negative cover story in *The New York Times* entertainment section, and Newsweek had splashed across its cover: "Why Oliver Stone's new movie can't be trusted."

Their criticisms all boiled down to a couple of key points: They felt Stone's movie was based on unsupportable speculation, and they believed his film's hero, former New Orleans District Attorney Jim Garrison, was an unscrupulous publicity-seeker who drummed up his celebrated case against Clay Shaw out of thin air.

These points are no doubt well taken. I believe they are irrelevant to the film, which is not a documentary, not a historical study and not a courtroom presentation, but a movie that weaves a myth around the Kennedy assassination—a myth in which the slain leader was the victim of a monstrous conspiracy. The pollsters tell us that most Americans believe this anyway. Even Tom Wicker, down deep in his piece, says he does not believe the Warren Commission's finding that Lee Harvey Oswald acted alone. Well, who does? And yet the image of Oswald as the lone killer has been the official establishment myth for 28 years. Is it such a terrible thing Stone has done, to weave a counter-myth?

Here on the movie beat, I always sort of quail when anybody makes a film that ventures out of pure Hollywood fantasy and into the real lives of the experts in the front section of the newspaper. I'm sure to be treated to many analytical studies of the factual accuracy of the film, in which the writers may be sound in their knowledge of history, but seem to have little idea why they or anyone else in the audience really goes to see a movie. People will not buy tickets to *JFK* because they think Oliver Stone knows who killed Kennedy. And when *Babe* comes out this summer and inspires all sorts of disillusioned analysis on the sports page, that movie's factual accuracy will have nothing to do with the tickets IT sells, either.

People go to the movies to be told a story. If it is a good story, they will believe it for as long as the movie lasts. If it is a very good story, it may linger in their memory somewhat longer. In the case of *JFK*, which I think is a terrific example of storytelling, what they will remember is not the countless facts and conjectures that the movie's hero spins in his lonely campaign to solve the assassination. What they will remember (or, if they are young enough, what they will learn) is how we all felt on Nov. 22, 1963, and why for all the years afterward a lie has seemed to lodge in the national throat—the lie that we know the truth about who murdered Kennedy.

There are many facts, factoids, fictions and distortions in *JFK*, all used in the service of the story. To dissect the movie like a documentary is pointless. Tom Wicker in the Times, for example, complains that when Stone shows the assassination of Robert Kennedy, the movie makes it look as if Bobby were shot at the end of his California victory speech, rather than shortly after. Does Wicker think Stone was trying to deceive us on this point? Hasn't everyone seen the footage of Sirhan in the hotel kitchen? All through *JFK* Stone uses the technique of the jump-cut, the flash-forward, the impatient edit to the next event. He is using it here. Literate filmgoers know that.

Newsweek, in its warning against the pitfalls of the docudrama form, notes with concern, "Only the alert viewer will be able to distinguish real documentary footage from reconstructed scenes," which is true enough, but then the magazine cites with alarm such scenes as when "a police officer brings the murder rifle to Oswald's corpse and presses his palm print into the barrel." Give us a break. Is there ANYONE dumb enough to believe a cop would allow himself to be photographed while faking evidence?

Oliver Stone is bitter about Wicker and Rather and his other detractors, but he doesn't use his best argument: that this is a movie. He counterattacks on a personal level, essentially saying that *JFK* is disliked by old-guard journalists who have a personal stake in the lone assassin theory because, by their inaction, they have allowed it to stand for all of these years.

"A lot of people who are attacking my credibility," Stone says, "are older journalists who were there then and obviously endorsed the Warren Commission. Tom Wicker was there and says Garrison has no case and points to an NBC documentary that is so one-sided that when it was aired, Garrison went to the FCC and successfully got rebuttal time on NBC. If it was shown now, it would be an embarrassment to NBC.

"And Dan Rather made his career out of being at Dealey Plaza. He was one of the few journalists allowed to see the Zapruder film at the time, and he came out of it saying the force of the shot drove the president forward in his seat. That is an outright lie; either that or he's blind. He certainly has a stake in the assassination because of his reporting of it. He bought the Oswald theory, and here I am, this punk from Hollywood who apparently knows nothing about history or politics, and who am I to come in with my artistic interpretation of those events?"

Here Stone does have the visible evidence on his side. Few people, Rather included, are going to be able to come out of *JFK* arguing that the final bullet drove Kennedy forward. In the movie, the Zapruder film of the assassination is played over and over, blown up to 35mm, as the Garrison character (Kevin Costner) chants, like a mantra: "Back ... and to the side. Back ... and to the side." And yes, it does seem that the final bullet must have come from in front of Kennedy, even though that fact, all by itself, destroys the theory that Oswald did all of the shooting from behind the motorcade.

Has Rather seen your film?

"No."

Are you going to show it to him?

"No. Let him go to the theater to pay for it; he's gotten enough free rides and he's abused his power, as far as I can see. He hasn't even seen the movie, but he says that MY theories are half-baked?"

Stone is angry now, but then Stone is Hollywood's angriest director, a man who in the screenplay for *Midnight Express* and in his own films *Salvador*, *Platoon*, *Wall Street*, *Born on the Fourth of July* and *The Doors*, and now more than ever in *JFK*, seems to be saying that he was lied to back in the 1960s, and now he wants to set the record straight.

"I hate conventional thought," he says. "I always did. I think I went through a period of being institutionalized myself—in boarding schools, army, merchant marine and college—in the 1960s. I've seen conventional thinking and I'm always rebelling against it. I see conventional thinking in most of the histories of the period. I think historians are finally starting to address the issue of what Kennedy was really doing from '61 to '63."

What he was doing, according to *JFK*, was proposing to emasculate the military-industrial complex Eisenhower warned against in his farewell speech in 1960. Stated bluntly, Stone believes Kennedy was killed because his policies were bad for the arms business.

"There was a civil war in this country," Stone says. "Kennedy provoked such hostility and hatred. His death was cheered in the South because of his support for Martin Luther King. He was moving to change things on all fronts. He was starting to end the Cold War. He made a deal with Khrushchev and Russia in 1962 to end the missile crisis, and he furthered the deal when he signed the Nuclear Test Ban Treaty in 1963. He installed the Hot Line. He made the American University speech where he described the Soviets for the first time in American history as mortals, like us, who care about their children. He seemed to have an expanding vision of the world, much like Gorbachev did in Russia in the '80s.

"Kennedy himself said, in 1962 after he read the novel *Seven Days in May,* which is about a military coup in the United States, that if he had another Bay of Pigs, that could happen to him. Well, he did have another Bay of Pigs; he had several. He had the missile crisis. They wanted him to invade Cuba; he didn't. They wanted him to send combat troops to Vietnam and Laos; he didn't. I think Kennedy prophesied his own death with those words."

Stone is famous for the pressure he puts himself under while making his films, which almost always involve daunting logistical problems, like staging infantry combat or re-creating rock concerts with thousands of fans. After *JFK,* he said, he feels utterly drained: "I think it was the most distressing film I've had to make. I knew I'd have eyes on the back of my head while I was directing this film. It was very difficult not to be rattled by the attacks saying this film was a monstrosity. Any piece of work like this is an act of love and trust and a leap of faith. You need to nurture something like this. To be attacked and stabbed in the back was not easy."

What he has achieved is, among other things, one of the most complicated films I have ever seen. By that I do not mean it is hard to follow; the main thrust is always there, and the audience always knows what it needs to know. But Stone's screenplay uses countless sound and image bites, it jumps around freely in time, it shows the same events in different ways from different points of view, and even in Garrison's long summation to the jury, the movie jumps back and forth from testimony to flashbacks to conjecture to possibility. At the end Stone deliberately makes it impossible for us to know exactly what he thinks happened on Nov. 22, 1963. The movie is more urgently about what he believes did NOT happen.

Do you, I asked him, have a personal theory about the assassination? Do you think you know the names of the guilty?

"I do. My own conclusions go harder and further than the film. I think I pulled back to some degree because I didn't have the proof necessary to name names and I can only make a hypothesis, and that's a very heavy thing to lay on somebody—to accuse them of killing the president. After the film is out there and the public has had a chance to see it and react to it, I think the discussion could be furthered."

One way that could happen, he says, is if the locked CIA, F.B.I. and Senate files on the assassination were to be made public.

"I think we should follow the example of today's Russia, Romania and East Germany. I think we should invade the CIA and the F.B.I. and get these files out. Get the military intelligence files out on Lee Harvey Oswald; get the military intelligence files on Jack Kennedy that day in Dallas—why the security precautions were what they were. There's so much that they never gave to the Warren Commission. We should get the House Select Committee to release their files that are embargoed till 2029. They could just take a vote now and release all those files. It only takes one congressman."

From his tone of voice, Stone made it obvious that he did not think the Congress contained such a man.

"People in power are afraid to ask the obvious questions. From day one they accepted the cover story that Oswald did it alone. Oswald said he was the patsy. A lot of people believed him, but not the establishment. Since that day the media has chanted the mantra that Oswald did it alone. But the American public, which has been brainwashed with that for 28 years, has never accepted it. They smell a rat."

DECEMBER 17, 1991

THE WASHINGTON POST

KENNEDY ASSASSINATION: HOW ABOUT THE TRUTH?

Gerald R. Ford and David W. Belin

The media treatment of the Kennedy assassination tragedy and the Warren Commission Report is a microcosm of one of the central problems facing our democratic society: False sensationalist claims are given wide dissemination, the truth is submerged, and the responsible press usually does not undertake sufficient effort to expose the fraud that is being perpetrated. Two vivid examples are the recent series of five one-hour A&E television programs about the Kennedy assassination called "The Men Who Killed Kennedy" and the new Oliver Stone-Kevin Costner film, *JFK*.

The common denominator of these commercial productions is the big lie—the assertion that the top echelons of our government were conspiratorially involved in the assassination and that Lee Harvey Oswald was not the lone gunman who killed President Kennedy and Dallas Police Officer J.D. Tippit.

In *JFK*, the big lie is disseminated through Kevin Costner, who portrays New Orleans District Attorney Jim Garrison. Repeatedly, he asserts the assassination was a coup d'etat—a "public execution" with a cover-up "all the way" to the top, including Lyndon Johnson, whom he calls an accessory after the fact. In the A&E series, the big lie is disseminated through key interviewees who are portrayed as purported experts, such as Col. Fletcher Prouty (a consultant to Oliver Stone in the production of *JFK*), who asserts: "You see, you're dealing with a very high echelon of power ... otherwise, how could you have gotten people like the chief justice of the Supreme Court to participate in the cover-up?"

False charges of this kind are a desecration to the memory of President Kennedy, a desecration to the memory of Earl Warren and a fraudulent misrepresentation of the truth to the American public.

The basic format underlying the dissemination of lies is to cover up the overwhelming weight of the evidence and instead paste together scraps of testimony to form a case for conspiracy and an attempt to cover up the guilt of Lee Harvey Oswald. For instance, approximately 20 doctors have examined the autopsy photographs and X-rays of President Kennedy as members of formal panels. Nineteen of these experts have concluded that all of the shots that struck President Kennedy came from the rear. The 20th asserts that there was supposedly a simultaneous fourth shot that struck President Kennedy in the head and disintegrated, leaving no physical evidence of the bullet. This odd-man-out appeared repeatedly on the A&E network in a number of the sequences.

Nowhere does any one of the overwhelming majority of 19 experts appear in the telecast or in *JFK*. Nowhere is there any mention of the fact that they concluded that all of the shots came from the rear and that this conclusion is confirmed by the unequivocal ballistic evidence which shows that the bullet that passed through President Kennedy's neck and struck Gov. Connally were fired from Oswald's rifle found at the Texas School Book Depository Building. Instead *JFK* and the television production emphasize the backward movement of President Kennedy's head when he was struck, without telling the audience that wound ballistic experts unequivocally testified that the movement was not caused by the impact of the bullet but was rather caused by a massive neuromuscular reaction that occurs when there is major damage inflicted to nerve centers of the brain.

The A&E network is owned one-third by NBC and one-third by Capital Cities/ABC. When Michael Millardi, president of the broadcast group of Capital Cities/ABC, Inc., was asked about the A&E network's misrepresentations, he sidestepped the issue and instead replied that "it is our judgment that the extreme interest in the subject matter" and "the international perspective ... all warranted A&E's decision to telecast the program."

Robert Wright, president of NBC, when contacted about the misrepresentations in the A&E program, chose to have Brooke Bailey Johnson, an A&E executive, reply. Johnson refused to comment about why none of the majority of 19 medical experts was ever shown on A&E. Instead, Johnson wrote, "We elected to purchase and telecast these programs for a number of reasons. The ongoing interest in the subject matter was a factor, as was a belief that the multi-channel environment in which we operate is a highly appropriate one for the debate of controversial issues."

But so far as the public is concerned, there is no debate because the other side—which happens to be the truth—is almost never shown to the public. Certainly it is not shown in the Oliver Stone-Kevin Costner film, reputedly produced at a cost approaching $40 million.

Like the A&E series, *JFK*, alleges a conspiracy supposedly including elements of the CIA, with the ultimate proof of the conspiracy supposedly being the killing of Oswald by Jack Ruby on Nov. 24, 1963. Oliver Stone's fantasy involves what Garrison calls "triangulation"—three separate gunmen firing a total of six shots, with Oswald as the "patsy" who is killed by the conspirators' hit man, Jack Ruby. But nowhere in the movie do viewers see anything about the overwhelming evidence that disproves the conspiracy claims, including central witnesses to these events such as Postal Inspector Harry Holmes.

On Sunday morning, Nov. 24, 1963, Holmes was on his way to church with his wife. At the last minute, he decided instead to go to the Dallas police station to see if he could help his friend, Capt. Fritz. Holmes had been assisting Fritz in the investigation of the murder of President Kennedy and the murder of Officer Tippit, the Dallas policeman who was killed by Oswald about 45 minutes after the Kennedy assassination and whose murder is really the Rosetta Stone to understanding the truth about the assassination. Holmes entered Capt. Fritz's office, where Oswald was being interrogated by Fritz and representatives of the Secret Service and the F.B.I.. After they finished their interrogation, Fritz turned to Holmes and gave him the opportunity to ask questions, and the session was extended for approximately another half-hour.

Jack Ruby meanwhile had come downtown to the Western Union office to send a money order to one of his employees. The time stamp on the money order showed that he was at the Western Union office at 11:17 a.m. Jack Ruby went from the Western Union office to the basement of the nearby police station, where he joined a group of newspersons awaiting the transfer of Oswald to the county jail. Oswald was killed at 11:21 a.m. If Harry Holmes had just continued on to church that morning, the interrogation session would have ended a half hour earlier, and Oswald would have been transferred long before Jack Ruby ever got to the Western Union office. Obviously, if Jack Ruby were part of a conspiracy, he would have been downtown at least a half hour earlier. Of course, common sense would also dictate that a would-be conspiratorial "hit man" would not kill his target in the middle of a police station, where he would be certain to be apprehended for murder.

But nowhere do the movie audiences seeing *JFK* or A&E's television audience ever learn about Postal Inspector Holmes, whose testimony is one of many elements showing that Jack Ruby was not conspiratorially involved. Nor does *JFK* or A&E include any portion of the testimony of Rabbi Hillel Silverman, who saw Jack Ruby many times in Ruby's cell and who is convinced that Ruby was truthful when he said that he was not conspiratorially involved. Nor do viewers of the movie or the A&E television series learn about Jack Ruby's request for a lie detector test and the results of that test, which although not 100 percent accurate, confirmed that Jack Ruby was not part of any conspiracy.

Nowhere does the A&E telecast of the movie show the vivid testimony of the single most important witness to the assassination—Howard Brennan, who actually saw the gunman fire from the south-east corner window of the Texas School Book Depository Building—the window where cartridge cases were found, which ballistically were shown to have come from Oswald's rifles. It was Brennan who notified the police of the source of the shots and who described the assassin as slender, about 5 feet, 10 inches, 150 to 160 pounds, white—a description remarkably close to Oswald.

Nowhere do the viewers learn that the most probable time span of Oswald's three shots was around 10 seconds, in light of the fact that one of Oswald's shots missed—most likely the first or the last. Instead, Garrison speaks only of three shots being fired within 5.6 seconds, when most likely the 5.6-second time span was between the two shots that struck the president.

Nowhere in *JFK* (or in the A&E television script) does the viewer ever learn that six eye-witnesses, including cabdriver William Scoggins, who saw Oswald from as close a range as 12 feet, saw Oswald at the Tippit murder scene or running away from the Tippit murder scene with gun in hand, and positively identified Oswald as the gunman. Oswald was apprehended in the Texas Theater because an alert Dallas citizen, Johnny Calvin Brewer, became suspicious when he saw Oswald duck into Brewer's shoe store as police sirens were heard coming down the street. Brewer trailed Oswald to the Texas Theater and had the cashier call the police. When they approached Oswald, he pulled out his revolver, and ballistic evidence proved that this was the Tippit murder weapon.

The viewers of *JFK* and "The Men Who Killed Kennedy" never learn about these facts, nor do they ever learn about all of the other massive body of evidence which conclusively proves beyond a reasonable doubt that Oswald was the lone gunman who killed President Kennedy and Officer Tippit and that there was no cover-up by Earl Warren or by the Warren Commission.

When will Hollywood produce a movie that tells the truth? When will the A&E network—when will NBC and Capital Cities/ABC—produce five hours of commercial television that presents the truth? When will the responsible leaders of our free press, who owe so much to Earl Warren, stand up for the truth, expose the techniques that have been used to disseminate the big lie and fully defend Earl Warren's name from the slanderous charges that have been made against him and the Warren Commission?

There are some who assert in the face of this conspiracy barrage by the mass media, particularly movies and television, that we will never know the truth. That simply is not accurate. The truth is known: Lee Harvey Oswald was the lone gunman who killed President Kennedy and Dallas Police Officer J.D. Tippit. Those of us who served on the Warren Commission and those lawyers on the staff who examined the evidence in depth know that to be the truth—beyond a reasonable doubt. And if the press were ever to approach this with the kind of diligence and with the kind of fairness that the American people have the right to expect, then the overwhelming majority of Americans will not only eventually understand the truth but will also understand the techniques of the perpetration of the big lie so that the kind of deceptive techniques used by the producer of *JFK* and the A&E series "The Men Who Killed Kennedy" will be exposed for all to see. The press owes that obligation to the memory of President Kennedy, to the memory of Earl Warren and, indeed, to the American people.

Former President Gerald R. Ford was a member of the Warren Commission. David W. Belin was counsel to the Commission.

DECEMBER 24, 1991

THE WASHINGTON POST

THE JFK ASSASSINATION—WHAT ABOUT THE EVIDENCE?
Response letter to the editor

Oliver Stone

One day after prominently displaying a "news" story in which David Belin—the ultimate frustrated losing prosecutor as almost the lone defender of the Warren Commissions's version of the assassination of President Kennedy—called me a "prostitute" and my unreleased film, *JFK*, a lie worthy of Adolf Hitler, *The Washington Post* saw fit last Tuesday to give him nearly half its op-ed page to continue his intemperate assault.

Belin and former president Gerald Ford are the last of a dying breed: Warren Commission apologists. Today, not even the government itself contends the Warren Commission investigation into the assassination of President Kennedy was an adequate one. The 1976-79 House Select Committee on Assassinations (HSCA) concluded that the CIA, the F.B.I. and military intelligence withheld information from the Warren Commission, and these agencies and the commission never thoroughly investigated even the possibility of conspiracy.

Belin and Ford make their case by using a combination of ignorance of new evidence and a selective presentation of Warren Commission material. As the reader will see from this presentation of their bald assertions versus the evidence, it is not a very good case.

BELIN AND FORD: Nineteen medical experts have examined the autopsy photographs and x-rays of President Kennedy and concluded that all the shots struck Kennedy from the rear.

EVIDENCE: While the "official" autopsy photos and x-rays do show that all shots came from the rear, the 26 trained medical personnel—doctors, nurses, technicians—who treated the president at Parkland Hospital testified to the Warren Commission that they saw an exit-type wound in the back of the head, a wound that is inconsistent with the photos and x-rays. Neither the Warren Commission nor the HSCA showed the photos and x-rays to the Dallas doctors. Until this happens, the medical evidence proves absolutely nothing.

BELIN AND FORD: Unequivocal ballistics evidence show that the bullet that struck the president in the head and the bullet that passed through President Kennedy's neck and struck Gov. Connally were fired from Oswald's rifle.

EVIDENCE: The evidence is far from unequivocal. The Warren Commission tests reported "minor variations" in the various bullet fragments, making the results at best inconclusive. More sophisticated analysis by the HSCA came to the same non-conclusion—that it was "highly likely" but not certain that the fragments matched each other in composition.

Belin still believes (as of his 1988 book, "Final Disclosure") that Kennedy was shot in the back of the neck. The autopsy photographs show that the wound was in his *upper back*, making it even more unlikely that the "magic bullet" exited through his throat and struck Gov. Connally. Moreover, Belin and Ford are obviously unaware of the declassified F.B.I. document stating the bullet in the back penetrated only about two inches and did not exit—proving that the "single bullet" scenario could not have happened at all.

TAKING EXCEPTION

BELIN AND FORD: A "massive neuromuscular reaction" caused the president's head to move backward when struck from the rear by a bullet.

EVIDENCE: A "massive neuromuscular reaction," according to Messrs. Ford and Belin, occurs when there is "massive damage inflicted to nerve centers of the brain." The nerve centers of the brain are the pons, the medulla, the cerebellum—all located in the rear of the brain. According to the Warren Commission and the HSCA, the head shot damaged the right cerebral hemisphere of Kennedy's brain—not a nerve coordination center, not capable of causing a "massive neuromuscular reaction."

BELIN AND FORD: Postal Inspector Holmes delayed Oswald's transfer, thus proving Ruby was not part of any conspiracy.

EVIDENCE: If Ruby was part of a conspiracy and Ruby was allowed into the police station by a contact there, then the Holmes excuse is nonsense. The conspirators would make sure Ruby was there for the transfer. Ford and Belin argue that no would-be hit man would kill his target in a police station. No, of course not, unless he had help.

BELIN AND FORD: Rabbi Hillel Silverman said he is convinced Ruby was telling him the truth when he says he wasn't conspiratorially involved.

EVIDENCE: Ruby told the Warren Commission he couldn't tell the truth on Dallas and begged to be taken to Washington. He also gave press conferences in 1966 saying he would like to tell the truth. By then Ruby was no longer in contact with Silverman. The rabbi left the Dallas area in 1965. Why Belin thinks we should take Silverman's word over Ruby's is unclear.

BELIN AND FORD: Jack Ruby's lie detector test results—although not 100 percent accurate, confirmed that Ruby was not part of any conspiracy.

EVIDENCE: While the polygraph results show Ruby was not lying when he said he acted alone, Belin and Ford conveniently leave out J. Edgar Hoover's comment in Appendix XVII of the Warren Report that, based on a psychiatrist's diagnosis of Ruby as a "psychotic depressive," the polygraph results should be considered "non-conclusive."

BELIN AND FORD: Witness Howard Brennan saw the gunman fire out the sixth-floor window and gave his description to the police.

EVIDENCE: Warren Commission counsel Joseph A. Ball questioned Brennan and found several reasons to doubt his credibility:

◆ Brennan's account had several glaring inaccuracies with respect to the gun-man's clothing and his shooting position.

◆ Brennan could not identify Oswald as the gunman when he first viewed the police lineup. Two months later, Brennan repeated to the F.B.I. that he wasn't able to identify Oswald at the lineup. But in March 1964 Brennan told the Warren Commission that he could have identified Oswald as the gunman but *he lied to protect himself and his family*.

BELIN AND FORD: The most probable time span of Oswald's three shots was around 10 seconds.

EVIDENCE: *Nowhere* is there evidence of 10 seconds. The Warren Commissioner concluded the time frame was from 4.8 to 7.9 seconds, depending on which of the three shots missed the car completely. The HSCA set a *maximum* time span of 8.3 seconds—but based on four shots and two gunmen. Most serious research agrees on the 5.6 seconds indicated by the Zapruder film.

BELIN AND FORD: Cabdriver William Scoggins saw Tippit's killer from within 12 feet and identified his as Oswald.

EVIDENCE: Although Scoggins did identify Oswald as the culprit, we know the lineups Scoggins viewed were heavily biased. Fellow cabbie William Whaley saw the lineups at the same time as Scoggins and told the Warren Commission:

> " ... you could have picked Oswald without identifying him just by listening to them because he was bawling out the policemen, telling them it wasn't right to put him in with these teenagers ... he told them they were trying to railroad him and he wanted his lawyer ... "

Scoggins saw the lineup on Saturday, long after Oswald's name and occupation had been broadcast widely. Unlike the other men in the lineups, Oswald gave his correct name and place of work.

What Belin and Ford never mention is that Scoggins (as well as another credible witness) reported that Tippit's killer was walking *west* on 10th street—the wrong direction for Oswald to be walking.

BELIN AND FORD: Ballistics evidence proved that Oswald's revolver was the Tippit murder weapon.

EVIDENCE: There is no chain of evidence for the four cartridge cases found at the scene. Both policemen who handled them marked them with their initials, but neither could identify the cases as the ones they turned in when they testified to the Warren Commission—they couldn't find their initials. *Furthermore, the cartridge cases—two Western-Winchester and two Remington Peters—don't match the bullets—three Western-Winchester, one Remington-Peters—recovered from Tippit's body.*

BELIN AND FORD: Those of us who served on the Warren Commission and its staff know it to be the truth—beyond a reasonable doubt—that Lee Harvey Oswald was the lone gunman who killed President Kennedy and Officer Tippit.

EVIDENCE: Apparently Ford and Belin didn't keep in touch with their colleagues. Commissioners Hale Boggs, Richard Russell and John Sherman Cooper had grave doubts from the start about the "single bullet" theory. In later years they went public with their dissatisfaction with the commission's finding. "I had strong doubts," Boggs said. Cooper was "unconvinced" by the single-bullet theory. In a 1970 *Washington Post* article, Russell said he believed President Kennedy was killed as the result of a criminal conspiracy and joined forces with researcher Harold Weisberg in an effort to declassify commission transcripts.

Conveniently, Ford and Belin wrap up their presentation by referring to the "other massive body of evidence which conclusively proves beyond a reasonable doubt that Oswald was the lone gunman." They decline to present this massive body of evidence to the readers. Should we take these men at their word? Probably not.

Former president Ford's actions have been called into question more than once in the JFK case. For example, Ford seems to have reported on the Warren Commission to the F.B.I. A Dec. 12, 1963, internal F.B.I. memo from Hoover aide Cartha DeLoach noted:

"Ford indicated he would keep me thoroughly advised as to the activities of the commission. He stated this would have to be done on a confidential basis, however, he thought it had to be done. He also asked if he could call me from time to time and straighten out questions in his mind concerning our investigation."

With regard to Belin, there is overwhelming evidence that he was less than truthful in taking Charles Givens's testimony for the Warren Commission. Givens, a co-worker of Oswald's at the Book Depository, originally told Dallas police he saw Oswald on the *first* floor shortly before noon on the day of the assassinations. Later, he told the Warren Commission he had seen Oswald all alone on the *sixth* floor at that same time. In a memo written before he spoke to Givens, Belin made note of the first statement, yet he did not mention it when Givens told him the new "sixth floor" version.

An F.B.I. document found at the National Archives—available to the commission—put Given's credibility in doubt. The document quoted Dallas policeman Jack Revill as saying Givens "would probably change his testimony for money." In his books and articles, Belin champions Givens as the man who placed Oswald on the sixth floor shortly before the shooting. Researchers have asked Belin about this on many occasions; he has yet to provide an answer.

In earlier tandem performance, Belin appeared as Ford's counsel when the former president testified before the HSCA. During a break in a hearing, Ford, obviously thinking the microphones were turned off, leaned over to Belin and asked, "Have I compromised anything yet?"—a rather curious statement under the circumstances.

All of Ford and Belin's "evidence" comes from the commission volumes and report—they ignore all of the Commission Documents (not published within the volumes), all of the evidence turned up by the Jim Garrison investigation, the 1975 Senate Intelligence (Church) Committee hearings, the House Select Committee on Assassinations investigation and all of the evidence brought to light over the years by private researchers and scholars through Freedom of Information Act suits and rigorous document analysis. The reason is simple: None of this evidence strengthens their dog-eared conclusions. Most of it contradicts them.

The Ford/Belin piece is tired, obsolete, highly selective information, printed many times before over the past 28 years, not believed by 75 percent of the American people or even supported by the conservative findings of the HSCA that JFK was killed as the result of a "probable" conspiracy.

It is disappointing that prominent men like Belin and Ford are so narrow and vindictive in their rendering of history and their ugly condemnation of me and my film. It is more disappointing *The Washington Post* gives them a forum for their discredited views.

Reprinted by permission of the author.

THE WASHINGTON POST
LETTERS

FREE FOR ALL

CREDIT L.B.J.

L. Fletcher Prouty

Gerald R. Ford and David W. Belin report that I participated in the A&E series "The Men Who Killed Kennedy" and was a consultant to Oliver Stone for his movie *JFK*. They allege that I disseminated a "big lie" and "a fraudulent misrepresentation of the truth to the American people." Nothing could be further from the truth, and neither writer had the courtesy or guts to check their hatchet job with me beforehand.

Let's look at the record. They credit me with this quotation: "You see, you're dealing with a very high echelon of power ... otherwise, how could you have gotten people like the chief justice of the Supreme Court to participate in the coverup?"

In his own book, "The Vantage Point" (1971), former president Lyndon B. Johnson wrote:

"The idea of a national commission was first mentioned to me by Eugene Rostow of Yale Law School ... Dean Rusk and columnist Joseph Alsop ... "

He went on to say:

"I knew it was not a good precedent to involve the Supreme Court in such an investigation, Chief Justice Warren knew this too and was vigorously opposed to it ... He opposed serving on constitutional grounds. He said that if asked, he would refuse."

Then Johnson said:

"There was no doubt in my mind that the Chief Justice had to be convinced."

Those words of Lyndon Johnson's, along with my knowledge of his well-known powers of persuasion, are among the things I had in mind when I made the above statement.

In the *Atlantic Monthly* of July 1973 Leo Janos, an old friend of L.B.J.'s, wrote, not long before Johnson died:

"Johnson expressed his belief that the assassination in Dallas had been part of a conspiracy [saying,] 'I never believed that Oswald acted alone' ... and [his belief that] 'we had been operating a damned Murder Inc. in the Caribbean.'"

This is no place to elaborate on the above, but those statements, written and spoken, by the most concerned man in the presidential procession in Dallas on Nov. 22, 1963, ought to be enough to convince anyone that the words attributed to me were neither a "big lie" nor "fraudulent misrepresentations."

The writer was chief of special operations for the Joint Chiefs of Staff from 1955-64

Reprinted by permission of the author.

WELCOME SKEPTICISM

Roger Kosson

I'm no expert on the JFK assassination, but it seems to me that Oliver Stone has done us all a valuable service and does not deserve the pillorying he has received in the media. What George Will ["'JFK': Paranoid History," op-ed, Dec. 26] and other critics fail to appreciate is that Stone has reminded us of what our Founding Fathers knew 200 years ago when they set out a Bill of Rights: that we should be vigilant in seeing that government does not become too powerful. A sure way for government to gain such power is if its citizens do not question its actions and pronouncements.

Why, then, has Stone been so roundly criticized for challenging the "official" version of the Kennedy assassination? The truth of Stone's version of history is not the issue. Rather, Stone's point is that we should not take at face value the official assertions that Lee Harvey Oswald acted as a crazed lone gunman in assassinating President Kennedy. I believe that stone would agree that *his* version of history should not be swallowed as incontrovertible fact as well.

Stone's contribution is in reminding us that complacency is a threat to democracy just as much as, if not more than, we thought communism was. The Pentagon Papers, the Gulf of Tonkin Resolution, Watergate and Iran-contra should be proof enough that we need no reminder. But apparently our blind acceptance of the invasion of Grenada and lack of outrage at Pentagon censorship throughout the gulf war indicate that we have not fully learned our lesson. Stone should be applauded for continuing what has been, and should continue to be, one of our wisest traditions: raising a healthy dose of skepticism at the words and deeds of our government.

Reprinted by permission of the author.

Donald Squires

With his vitriolic diatribe against Oliver Stone, George Will joins the avalanche of Stone-bashing that seems all the rage and all out of proportion to the release of what is, after all, just a movie. Like others, Will seems to deliberately ignore the fact that Garrison's and Stone's theory about a conspiracy to kill Kennedy is just that—a theory. It is a theory that attempts to explain some of the more troubling aspects of the assassination that point to at least some element of participation by some person or persons working within the government.

But just as Clay Shaw's not-guilty verdict neither proved his innocence nor validated the Warren Commission Report, the various "flaws" in Stone's movie similarly do not somehow eliminate the hundreds of as yet unexplained pieces of evidence and testimony that contradict the lone-assassin theory. One does not have to agree with Stone's conclusion to believe that a conspiracy existed. Moreover, even if Stone's theory is wrong, that does not make the movie, as Will put it, "an act of execrable history and contemptible citizenship."

It is ironic that the movie *JFK*, which Stone has never claimed to be the conclusive answer to this mystery, is being subjected to much more nitpicking scrutiny by the mainstream press than the Warren Commission Report ever has been. I would have more confidence in Will's and others' objectivity if, along with their criticism of Stone, they also supported the opening of evidence sealed by the Warren Commission and House Select Committee on Assassinations. Or would asking for that evidence also be an act of "contemptible citizenship?"

Reprinted by permission of the author.

Jaime Aparisi

As a 24-year-old second-year law student at Catholic University I have just recently entertained the notion that John F. Kennedy was assassinated through a conspiracy perpetrated by the CIA or other government officials. I and friends of my age owe much gratitude to Oliver Stone for his eye-opening motion picture, *JFK*. After seeing the movie I was not content to limit my exposure to the subject and so I have read some of the leading literature on the matter.

Recently your paper had published columns concerning *JFK* by David Belin and Gerald Ford, George Will, Stephen S. Rosenfeld and Stone himself. Stone's movie is attacked on the basis that it is unpatriotic, fallacious and stirs up unwarranted and harmful sentiment against the government for something that occurred 28 years ago and should be left alone. As someone who was born after Nov. 22, 1963, I find the attacks on *JFK* exhibit the obvious biases and protection of the vested interests in Washington circles at best, and a misunderstanding of the value of truth in the democratic process at worst.

The days are over when Walter Cronkite can tell the nation that it is in its best interest to believe the "official" version of a national disaster because it will promote national security. Watergate and Iran-contra have dispelled any myths about the credibility of the CIA or other government actors.

The answer to who shot John F. Kennedy is important because our government should be held accountable for its actions. But more important, the answer carries much value in framing the mood and manner in which the American people will scrutinize future actions by their government.

As someone of the post-Kennedy generation with no illusions about government excesses, I believe I speak for most when I say that an objective analysis of the weight of the evidence on both sides clearly shows that *JFK* is an accurate representation of history. No more convincing evidence of this can be asked than Lyndon Johnson's statement that he never believed that Oswald acted alone and the House Select Committee on Assassinations' determination that a conspiracy was "probable" in the murder of John F. Kennedy.

Reprinted by permission of the author.

I'M THE 'ODD MAN OUT'

Cyril H. Wecht

In their op-ed article, "Kennedy Assassination: How about the Truth?" (December 17th), Gerald R. Ford and David W. Belin bemoan the fact that neither the five-part series, "The Men Who Killed Kennedy," shown in October-November on the A&E television network, nor Oliver Stone's recently released movie, *JFK*, includes an appearance by any of the physicians who have examined President Kennedy's autopsy photographs and x-rays. These doctors support the findings of the Warren Commission, namely, that Oswald, a sole assassin, fired three shots, one of which produced seven wounds in Kennedy and Governor John Connally, and emerged in near-pristine condition with only 1.5% loss of its original weight after some incredible mid-air vertical and horizontal gyrations in the course of its momentous journey. The writers are extremely unhappy about the fact that the one physician who reviewed these autopsy materials and disagreed with the WC "appeared repeatedly on the A&E network in a number of the sequences." So painful is this fact to Ford and Belin that they can only bring themselves to refer to this person as "odd man out." Evidently, the same *Washington Post* ombudsman who found nothing wrong with George Lardner's vicious diatribe against Oliver Stone and his movie, *JFK*, in a scathing op-ed piece several weeks ago, saw nothing unethical or unfair about such a cowardly, anonymous reference in this December 17th article by two of the people who should have a lot of explaining to do to the American public about how and why the official governmental investigation of a President's murder was handled in such an inept, biased, and limited fashion.

The "odd man out" has a name and identity—the undersigned. I am a Board-certified anatomic, clinical, and forensic pathologist, who has performed approximately 11,000 autopsies and reviewed more than 25,000 others. I am a past President of the American Academy of Forensic Sciences and the American College of Legal Medicine; member of six graduate school faculties; author of 300 published scientific articles; editor or co-editor of 30 published professional books; and a member of the editorial boards of 20 national and international medicolegal and forensic scientific journals. I have lectured in more than 60 foreign countries (several times on the JFK assassination), and have been qualified as an expert in forensic pathology for trial testimony in approximately 30 states. While none of these credentials automatically makes my analysis of the Kennedy assassination correct, I would suggest they do qualify me to render a competent, professional opinion regarding this highly controversial murder.

Any time that the former President and Iowa attorney, any of their old WC colleagues, or any physicians who support the WCR, would like to debate this subject on national television, I am available. Such an opportunity would be most welcome and highly pleasurable.

In August, 1972, when I examined all the JFK materials at the National Archives, I "discovered" that the President's brain, microscopic tissue slides, and kodachromes of the internal chest wounds were missing, after having been specifically identified in an inventory dated April 26, 1965. More than one-half of the WCR physician-supporters, whom Ford and Belin would have *Washington Post* readers believe are such credible, unbiased experts, were aware before my public disclosure in 1972 that these critical pieces of physical evidence had been illegally and surreptitiously removed from the National Archives (by a yet unidentified person). Apparently, they never felt ethically or morally compelled to refer this important finding to the news media. Even today, almost 20 years later, the silence of all these physicians regarding the missing medical evidence is deafening.

I fully expect continuing critiques by *The Washington Post*, editorially and indirectly through its op-ed page, on anyone who dares to challenge the validity of the WCR. Obviously, that is your First Amendment right and publishing authority. I can only hope that your newspaper has enough sense of journalistic fairness and ethics to also publish at least an occasional response from the individuals who are attacked in an ad hominem manner. As for myself, kindly have the grace and courage to refer to me by name the next time an attempt is made to demean me professionally. If some self-appointed WCR sycophant, snide columnist, or envious colleague wishes to challenge my findings and criticize me personally on your op-ed page, I trust hereafter you will have the decency to insist that the writer refer to me by name. Perhaps, *The Washington Post* would provide a forum for a face-to-face confrontation via a public debate. Let the public be the judge.

The writer is a Forensic Pathologist and Former President, American Academy of Forensic Sciences.

Reprinted by permission of the author.

LONELY MAN IN THE MIDDLE

Harold Weisberg

It took 27 years, but David Belin, writing with Gerald R. Ford, has finally said one thing with which I agree: Nigel Turner's A&E network series "The Men Who Killed Kennedy" and Oliver Stone's current commercialization and exploitation of that great tragedy are both very, very bad ["Kennedy Assassination: How About the Truth?" op-ed, Dec. 19].

I am responsible for what Stone has converted into a nonexisting "establishment" press-CIA conspiracy to destroy him and his movie. I gave reporter George Lardner Oliver Stone's script, which is based on former New Orleans district attorney Jim Garrison's fantasy of self-justification, his book "On the Trail of the Assassins."

Belin, as he has in the past and with the same cliches, insists that he and the Warren Commission were right solely because they say they were right.

Like other defenders of the Warren report, Belin demanded, "Where is the new evidence?" As I showed in my first book of 26 years ago, *Whitewash: The Report on the Warren Report*, no new evidence was needed because the evidence the commission had disproves its conclusions.

It is not easy, but Belin is being unfair to Jim Garrison. To do this he had to contradict the most basic conclusion of the Warren Report that he insists is the truth, the sequence of and time permitted for the three shots that in all official "solutions" Lee Harvey Oswald fired.

Belin writes that "Garrison speaks only of three shots being fired within 5 to 5.6 seconds." Garrison did not write that. The commission itself did—without any Belin dissent. Now that Belin can no longer pretend not to know that the world's best shots, including the "masters" used by the commission, could not duplicate the shooting attributed to Oswald within the commission's 5.6 seconds, he conjectures—in open contradiction of the report he insists was accurate—that "the most probable time span of Oswald's three shots was around 10 seconds."

As in the past Belin repeats what is not true, not even possible, that there is "unequivocal ballistics evidence which shows that ... the bullet that passed through President Kennedy's neck and struck Gov. Connally" was fired by Oswald from the rear.

There is no such evidence, ballistic or otherwise. This is the theory invented by now Sen. Arlen Specter, known as the "single-bullet theory" featuring "the magic bullet."

Belin refers to all the supposed experts who confirmed this official fiction. He is careful not to refer to the actual findings of a Department of Justice panel of the most preeminent forensic pathologists. I published every word of what they filed in facsimile in my *Post Mortem* in 1975. Belin had it and was reading it that November when we debated at Vanderbilt University.

The report on the examination of the JFK autopsy pictures and x-rays by this panel of experts proves the commission was wrong in locating the fatal wound in the president's head; it was four inches higher than the commission said.

That magic and unscarred bullet that Belin says inflicted seven nonfatal wounds on both victims, smashing one of Connally's ribs and his wrist, and did not strike bone that would have deflected it as it transited the president's neck, actually deposited five bone fragments in that area.

It was already a physical impossibility for this magic bullet to have the imagined career indispensable to the lone-assassin "solution." But if any bullet had entered Kennedy's back, the commission knowingly mislocated the hole it left. That hole is four or more inches lower than the commission said and in the back, not the neck. This is verified in some of the "new" evidence, which I published and Belin had—

the official certificate of death.

The rest of the official career of this magical bullet, and there is nothing like this career in science or mythology, is that in transiting the president's neck from back to front it went through the president's shirt collar and the knot of his tie. It did not, and some of the commission and its staff, including Belin, knew it.

Specter questioned Charles Carrico, the only doctor who saw the president before any emergency procedure in Parkland Hospital and before any of his clothing was removed. Specter did not ask Carrico where the anterior neck wound was located. Former CIA director and commission member Allan Dulles then did ask this question.

Carrico pointed to above his collar!

Those 19 Humpty-Dumptys Belin refers to as experts cannot alter this truth, which destroys the commission's conclusions. With the bullet hole "above" the shirt collar, it could not have caused the damage to the collar and tie.

If the commission had done its job, it would have gotten what I did via the Freedom of Information Act, a clear picture of the damage to the president's shirt collar.

With the button and the button hole exactly in line and with the pattern at each end of the collar also coinciding exactly, the damages to the ends of the collar that overlapped when buttoned as it was do not coincide, as they would have if caused by a bullet.

The damage to each side is a slit, not a hole made by a bullet. Both slits are frayed. On the president's right, as worn, the slit begins below the neckband and extends downward. It is only about half the length of the slit in the left side as worn. This larger slit extends upward well onto the neckband, to where, if caused by a bullet, it would have struck the button.

The button is unscathed.

The damage to the shirt was not caused by any bullet.

It was caused, as the commission's transcript indicates, in emergency procedures. Carrico demonstrated this for me by grasping his own tie with his left hand and making cutting motions upward and downward with his right hand. He told me what he was not asked by the commission, that two nurses under his supervision cut the tie off with a scalpel. There was no time to untie the knot. It was the scalpel that made the slits in the shirt collar.

Fewer pontifications from Belin would make less appropriated when applied to him his castigation of Stone and Turner, who deserve it also: "False charges ... are a desecration to the memory of President Kennedy."

The Stones of one extreme and the Belins of the other confuse, mislead and deceive the people.

What gets lost in all this controversy is that there is a middle ground. I confess loneliness in my occupancy of it. It is the ground that finds the commission failed us and proves this with fact and official documentation. It also finds that the proliferating conspiracy theories mislead and confuse as much as or more than the faulted official conclusions.

Reprinted by permission of the author.

SAN FRANCISCO WEEKLY

JFK: TRAGEDY INTO FARCE
Death in Dallas, Jackie's dress and the decline of America

Andrew O'Hehir

Historians talk about the American Century, but it barely lasted 20 years. If the sound of Zeros at dawn over Pearl Harbor awoke the clumsy American colossus to its new role as world leader, the sound of rifle fire in Dealey Plaza signaled the beginning of its irreversible decline.

Centuries from now they will write that America, born in the bloodshed of genocide, began to die with one solitary blood sacrifice. The mid-century social consensus, the shared faith in progress that had been passed from F.D.R. to Truman to Ike, was exploded in an instant, all its trapped internal contradictions rising to the surface like noxious gases pouring from an erupting volcano.

Anyone who studies the photographic record of November 22, 1963, is haunted by one image above others: the dazed Jacqueline Kennedy, wearing a blank stare and a pink suit still smeared with her husband's blood, standing alongside Lyndon Johnson in Air Force One as he takes the oath of office. Three hours earlier she was a society wife, playing the role of loyal helpmate to her vain, philandering, patrician, social-democrat husband. But at that fateful moment she was America, transfixed by history, too numb to try to wash away the bloodstains. It was a moment of truth, a hole in the fabric of time, when we caught a glimpse of our nation's real and terrible legacy before looking away again.

No living human knows precisely what strange scenario reached its climax in that crucial six seconds in Dallas. Three or more shots were fired by one or more assailants; a man died. Beyond that, impenetrable layers of lies, death, idiocy, incompetence and psychosis have made the "truth" about John Fitzgerald Kennedy's death literally unknowable. But there are further truths. On another level, we all know exactly what happened: Things went "wrong," Planet America rolled off its axis, mere anarchy was loosed upon the world. Another truth is that we don't need or want to know who killed Kennedy: we need the J.F.K. assassination as a nightmarish religious vision, a dark shrine for self-flagellating worship, a negative miracle as mysterious as the Holy Ghost or the doctrine of transubstantiation.

All this has little to do with Kennedy the man, however we judge his presidential record or the hilarious and alarming accomplishments of his private life. J.F.K.'s Camelot was a shared illusion, a structure of belief; if the gunfire in Dallas hadn't shattered it, something else would have. Our national fixation on the assassination relates to John Kennedy's life in the same way that the apocalyptic fervor of Christian fundamentalism reflects the life of Yeshua, the Jewish carpenter from Nazareth.

J.F.K. is an American obsession as deep as baseball, a field of bad dreams littered with esoteric terminology, statistical minutiae and strange symbols, an intellectual morass as complex and frustrating as the interpretation of scripture. The devil, in this case, is definitely in the admittedly seductive details:

Why is a man standing under an open umbrella on that sunny Dallas day? What are the enigmatic shapes on the "grassy knoll"? (If you seek a superabundance of answers to this question, there is actually a bimonthly publication called the Grassy Knoll Gazette.) What about the pristine "magic bullet" found on John Connally's stretcher that supposedly went through Kennedy's throat, then changed direction and wounded the Texas governor? Was Lee Harvey Oswald a CIA stooge, a KGB plant or a Mafia hireling? (Oswald's corpse was exhumed in 1981 at the behest of especially ghoulish assassination buffs; disappointingly, he turned out to be himself after all.) Did the "three tramps" briefly detained near Dealey Plaza include convicted hitman Charles V. Harrelson (father of Woody on Cheers) and/or future Watergate burglar E. Howard Hunt? Was the presidential casket that left Parkland Memorial Hospital that afternoon the same one that came off the plane at Andrews Air Force Base in the evening? Where is Kennedy's brain?

That way lies madness, to be sure. But when it's this exciting, who needs sanity? Those who are enraged at Oliver Stone's film *JFK* for its heavily fictionalized blending of various assassination theories are missing the point. As Stone has apparently grasped in his blockhead populist way, the J.F.K. killing has been fiction for a long time. It's the creation myth we use to understand the discords of contemporary America: the tale of the fall from grace, for which we keep vainly seeking redemption. If it hadn't happened, we would have had to invent it.

Our lovable lout of a nation arrived late to the modern age, like a hayseed soldier putting his boots on the table at a distingué Parisian nightclub. But we made up for lost time at Hiroshima and Nagasaki. The Bomb not only vaporized and mutilated thousands of human beings, it unwittingly launched the era of international cultural dislocation that came to be called postmodernism.

This had far-reaching consequences, to be sure, although they weren't obvious right away. Our cavity-free, milk-fed children, their bodies made strong in 12 ways by Wonder Bread, thenceforward slept in the darkening shadow of the mushroom cloud. From generals to artists, we all grew up addicted to the nuclear threat. Years later we would realize that our bombs had conceived a new Japan in our own image, a Japan dedicated to taking over and surpassing our once-triumphant idealogical blend of narcissism and capital.

But it was on that autumn day in Dallas that postmodernism came home to roost. Dallas seemed like a magic trick, or the culmination of some elaborate practical joke; it traumatized us because we couldn't figure out how it worked. We still feel sure that if we go through it one more time we'll see the concealed wires leading to the book depository window, spot the clown on the grassy knoll, decode the umbrella man's secret message. But its still the same stale pie in our face, all over again.

The Kennedy killing was obviously more than an "ordinary" political assassination. It was also more than a metaphorical loss of innocence, which is how it appears in countless movies and TV commercials. Metaphor is a cold construction of Hellenic logic, while what happened November 22, 1963, in Dallas was a ritual event of the most profound order, a reshaping of our national paradigm.

Many Americans, even those too young to remember the event, see the Kennedy assassination as the trigger that released all the perceived disorder of the last three decades. Vietnam; the race riots and white flight; Bobby, Martin and Malcolm; the '68 Democratic convention; the Panthers; People's Park; Kent State; Attica; Nixon and Watergate; Jonestown; Moscone and Milk; the Tehran embassy; the Beirut Marine barracks; crack; AIDS; homelessness; Iran-Contra; the Persian Gulf.

If we could run the Zapruder film in reverse, patch up the President's gruesome head wound, send the bullets flying back to the chambers whence they came, return the assassins to their sinister underworld, and back up the Lincoln convertible so that Jack and Jackie are once again waving to the crowds in the Texas sunshine, then we could also walk backwards through the last 30 years, becoming younger and more hopeful, forgetting tragedies one after another, arriving finally at a point of innocent stasis where we can stand forever watching the American sunrise with immortal delight. But we can't.

Our Puritan legacy has left us a people with a taste for absolute doctrine, be it religious or secular, from the right or the left. We prefer a pure visionary flame, an illumination of history as a mystically unified field, to an acceptance of life as a complex of vagaries, accidents and random cross-currents. All good assassination theories seem to interlink, with jesuitical precision, as much recent historical turmoil as possible. Psychologically, the reasons for this are clear. If the central villainous conspiracy of our time—headed up, let's say, by Bush, Nixon, L.B.J., Bill Casey and J. Edgar Hoover—has had its dark tentacles everywhere for 30 years, then the disastrous condition of America today is *not our fault*.

Oliver Stone has largely accepted the thesis advanced by former New Orleans District Attorney Jim Garrison, who argues that the J.F.K. killing was essentially a right-wing coup d'état staged by the CIA and the military. This is certainly the intuitive belief of many Americans; it might even contain elements of the truth. But our pursuit of the answers is so fervid, so pathological, that no truth will ever be complete enough to satisfy us.

Garrison, a noted mob confidant who was diagnosed as mentally unbalanced while in the Army, is one short step away from people who've been abducted by aliens, or who see an immense network of Satanic covens beneath suburbia. His CIA plot is plausible, but as Robert Sam Anson catalogued in his excellent *Esquire* cover story, it was one of 14 different hypothetical conspiracies Garrison had worked out, some of which featured the gay underground, the Dallas Police

Department and Czarist Russians. He also believes there were nine gunmen in Dealey Plaza, including some firing from the sewer drains. (The umbrella man was shooting poisoned darts.) Once you develop a theory, there are no philosophical limits to its growth.

Fourteen plots and nine assassins obviously present a more fertile imaginative field than the bleak, rocky landscape of Lee Harvey Oswald's paranoid psychology (which strongly resembles the maladjusted stereotype of the conspiracy theorist). And the point is no longer to solve J.F.K.'s murder, if indeed it ever was. The point is to interpret the assassination to fit our particular dysfunctional world view; to prove to ourselves that there is order to the universe and that we understand it, even if others refuse to.

Stone speaks of himself in interviews as Hamlet trying to solve the mystery of his father's death, or as Shakespeare altering the outlines of English history to fit *Henry V.* As pompous as these analogies are, they underline the grotesque appropriateness of his project. America *does* imagine itself, like Hamlet, the damaged heir to a noble legacy; if we can make J.F.K. conform to the dimensions of tragedy rather than of cruel and amoral farce, we will be avenged, and our angst relieved.

Even more importantly, we need to be able to read history as a *story*. Shakespeare's *Henry V* has a clear conflict, a dramatic resolution and a moral, along with ethnic jokes and a romantic subplot (whereas the historical Henry's French campaign was a bitter and pointless massacre, inspired by competing interpretations of an arcane treaty). Like the other main conspiracy theories, Garrison's has a strong narrative element: good guys (Jack and his innermost circle, except Lyndon) tricked by omnipotent and ruthlessly efficient bad guys (too numerous to mention); the hapless nation, left victimized and fatherless, destroying itself in paroxysms of grief; the intrepid investigator (Garrison, now played by Kevin Costner) who will lay bare the truth, and achieve mystical reunion between father and child.

Oliver Stone readily admits that he's trying to find out why he got so fucked up in Vietnam, his contention being that had Kennedy lived, the war would not have continued long. That issue itself is problematic, but never mind. The real point is that we have *all* been fucked up by post-1963 life in declining America. We are searching our collective past for that one traumatic event in the same way that therapist and neurotic patient scour the rocks of memory for the childhood horror that can explain everything.

America's trauma is real enough. But it doesn't stem from some dramatic cataclysm, from shadowy figures with guns arrayed among the storm drains and shade trees of Dealey Plaza. Its source is the untheatrical, non-narrative slow grind of history. There's nothing intoxicating about this trauma: it just hangs around us like fetid gas in the air.

If you like morals, late 20th-century American life certainly offers them. You can say that the bad karma from our national sins—the slaughter of the Indians, the arrival of the slave ships, imperialism, international corporate capitalism—has been visited upon us. Or that the loss of faith, either in meaningful spirituality or in science, has driven us insane; as the empire crumbles, we cling to our pantheon of martyred deities: Bogart, Marilyn, James Dean, Elvis, the Kennedys. Our republic's unresolved tensions, long held in check by a combination of forcible oppression and the unfulfilled but still-exciting promise of liberty for all, have emerged as gaping fissures that now threaten to tear the continent apart. In some ways, it's miraculous they took so long.

The Kennedy assassination was a moment when we caught a glimpse of our republic's demise. Ironically, it also brought Americans together to grieve as no other event has before or since. History suggests that an earlier and far different nation went through a crucial period of self-examination when Grant and Lee met at Appomattox Court House, when Lincoln spoke at Gettysburg, when John Wilkes Booth entered the presidential box at Ford's Theater. That troubled republic reassessed itself and went forward; but the psychological and physical violence that has ravaged America over the past three decades makes the Civil War of the 1860's look refreshingly straightforward.

We'll never know who killed John Kennedy. But we know enough. We know that our myth-making zealotry has made every theory valid and every preposterous scenario true. We know that Kennedy's death was overdetermined; we have concocted a thousand reasons why it happened. But we haven't faced the chill reality of Jackie's bloodstained suit, her shocked gaze meeting the eyes of posterity. Her husband's blood was our only way of witnessing, and lamenting, the blood of the Algonquin, of the African, of the Iraqi children not yet born. We are all conspirators in those deaths, and without the sickness they engendered, we would have had neither Kennedy's assassination nor our demented fascination with it.

We can no longer use J.F.K. as a crutch, if our democracy is to survive. We created J.F.K., and killed him, to evade responsibility for the worsening calamity of America, and the calamities America has inflicted on the world. To survive, we need to walk away from the quagmire of Dallas. To walk away, we first need to stand still for a few moments, staring at ourselves in the camera lens, and feel the blood soak through our clothes.

DECEMBER 19, 1991

THE WALL STREET JOURNAL

A BETTER CONSPIRACY THEORY THAN OLIVER STONE'S

Jonathan Kwitny

What distresses me about Oliver Stone's new movie *JFK* is not that I think it will persuade the country of Mr. Stone's thesis, that the rest of the government killed Kennedy. Rather, I think the movie, with its many distortions, will reinforce the more widely held view—already expressed in early criticism of the film—that the assassination is a morass, not understood and maybe not understandable. This thesis, while less noxious than Mr. Stone's, also ignores the evidence.

Because of the intellectual dishonesty in the work of early Warren Commission critics like Jim Garrison, the hero of the film and author of a book on which it is based, I tended for years to accept the commission's "lone nut" theory. While flawed, it was the most satisfying around. Then, in 1978, some lawmen I had long respected, who had joined the staff of the House Select Committee on Assassinations, invited me to Washington. In a day, they laid out previously unassembled evidence that changed my mind.

Amid much corroborative detail, the key fact was this: In the months before the assassination, Lee Harvey Oswald and Jack Ruby—the two men everyone agrees committed crimes that week-end—were both working with intimates of Carlos Marcello, the Mafia boss of the South. And Marcello, an experienced murder-plotter, had the strongest motive for murdering President Kennedy: The president's death saved Marcello and his empire from ruin; probably nothing else could have.

Now, that alone doesn't prove anybody killed anybody (although with additional evidence it makes a helluva case). But it does prove, at least to me, that anyone honestly seeking truth about the assassination has to go over the Marcello mountain before taking the road further.

You can't write it out of your script as Messrs. Garrison and Stone—and some of their critics—have done. The movie dwells on two men Oswald worked with in 1963, Guy Banister and David Ferrie, who are depicted as intelligence agents arming Cubans for a new Bay-of-Pigs-type invasion called Operation Mongoose, which we're told Kennedy cancelled. Not so.

What Messrs. Banister and Ferrie, private investigators, were mainly doing in those months was helping Marcello defend a second deportation proceeding the Kennedy's brought against him, to be tried—maybe not so coincidentally—Nov. 22. Mr. Ferrie was Marcello's private pilot, meeting with him often. Messrs. Ferrie, Banister and Marcello all hated Fidel Castro and actively encouraged his

Cuban opposition. But considering that the stakes were Marcello's vast gambling, dope and kickback empire (Ruby helped run the Dallas end), and that Marcello was almost killed when the Kennedy's forcibly deported him to the Guatemalan jungle in 1961, is it really likely that anti-communism is what moved this group to undertake something so dangerous as killing a president?

The film says former C.I.A. director Richard Helms testified that Ferrie's friend Clay Shaw "worked for" the C.I.A.; in fact, Mr. Helms said only that Mr. Shaw, like many businessmen travelling abroad, sometimes told inquiring agents in the U.S. what he'd seen.

Consider also that on Nov. 22—as Marcello went to trial, Mr. Ferrie went mysteriously to Texas and Kennedy went to his death—C.I.A. officer Desmond Fitzgerald, calling himself "the personal representative of Robert Kennedy," delivered yet another weapon (a booby-trapped pen) to yet another Cuban exile to try to kill Castro.

Messrs. Garrison and Stone would have you believe the Kennedy's had suddenly turned into flower children, bent on breaking up the C.I.A. and embracing Khrushchev, and that this was the motivation for the assassination. But just weeks before the murder, President Kennedy had staged a coup installing a military government in Vietnam. *JFK* makes the coup sound like a surprise to Kennedy. Kennedy's foreign policy team, and brother Robert, continued to support the war for years. Operation Mongoose was never an invasion plot, but a campaign of sabotage against Castro nurtured by the Kennedys.

Messrs. Garrison and Stone bring up Marcello only to accuse the assassination conspirators of trying to stop Mr. Garrison with public smears linking him to Marcello. Mr. Garrison says in his 1988 book, *On the Trail of the Assassins*, that in 12 years as New Orleans district attorney he never met Marcello (not something I'd think a DA would want to boast of).

What the movie doesn't say is that the corruption charges against Mr. Garrison were largely compiled by Walter Sheridan, then with NBC News. Mr. Sheridan had been the Kennedys' chief aid on rackets investigations since the 1950s and was so close to the family he took a job with Teddy after Bobby died. Mr. Sheridan obviously wasn't on the assassination team. Marcello, on the other hand, was a comrade in crime of Kennedy nemesis Jimmy Hoffa, and Mr. Sheridan exposed that, which is what led him to Mr. Garrison.

Yes, a lot remains unanswered about the assassination: How many guns were there? (It's unlikely Oswald fired alone, but not impossible.) Why did Mr. Ferrie go to Texas? (To fly some killers out? To help kill Oswald?) Was Oswald supposed to have been killed earlier, and was the job botched? (I suspect so.)

But the basics were becoming clear. This movie, supposedly about truth, has sadly muddied the waters.

Mr. Kwitny, a former Journal reporter, wrote and presented a PBS documentary on the Kennedy assassination.

THE NEW YORK TIMES
OP-ED

WHO IS REWRITING HISTORY?

Oliver Stone

Members of the media establishment gets upset when art gets *political*, especially when they disagree with the politics and fear the viewpoint. When this priesthood is challenged as the sole or privileged interpreters of *our* history, they bludgeon newcomers, wielding heavy clubs like "objectivity" and charging high crimes like "rewriting history."

The leading detractors of my film *JFK* have been political journalists like Tom Wicker of *The New York Times*, George Lardner of *The Washington Post*, Dan Rather of *CBS News* and Kenneth Auchincloss at *Newsweek*, all of whom covered events of that period.

I think what is clear from their efforts to destroy my film's credibility is that history may be too important to leave to newsmen. And that artists certainly have the right—and possibly the obligation—to step in and reinterpret the history of our times. Was it not Dan Rather who, upon viewing Abraham Zapruder's film of the assassination, reported that the fatal shot to the head drove President Kennedy "violently forward." Years later, when the film was finally shown to the American people, it was clear that Kennedy's head was going backward.

My critics are outraged that I pose the view that Kennedy's desire to wind down the cold war and the Vietnam War is a possible motive for the murder. When a leader of a any country is assassinated, the media normally ask: "What political forces were opposed to this leader and would benefit from his assassination?"

It seems a little strange to me, 28 years later, that such a question was rarely asked once it was established that Lee Harvey Oswald was not simply mentally ill. And that in its stead, the dramatic cover story, with Lee Harvey Oswald as sole assassin and Jack Ruby as earnest vigilante, was immediately substituted and accepted by almost the entire American media (in sharp contrast to the foreign media). A great John Wayne movie, but why? Why was the possibility of a political motive rarely discussed (or only vaguely attributed to diversionary theories involving pro-Castro forces or the Mafia) after it was clear that there was evidence that undercut the Warren Report?

Whether or not there was a fundamental difference between Kennedy's and Johnson's Vietnam policies deserves more debate. For years most historians assumed there was no basic difference. But people such as John Newman, an Army major in intelligence who has written a book on the subject, Fletcher Prouty, a former Air Force colonel who served as director of special operations at the Pentagon in the early '60s, and Peter Dale Scott, a professor at the University of California at Berkeley, should have their day in court.

A basic chronology underlies their view. In June 1963 in a speech at American University, Kennedy envisions a world without the cold war and arms race. He sets the stage for détente, defying the "military-industrial complex," a phrase coined by Eisenhower. Kennedy and Khrushchev have already negotiated the first step: a modus vivendi on the Cuban problem (no Soviet missiles, no U.S. invasion). In July 1963 they install the nuclear hotline and in August sign the first-ever nuclear test-ban treaty.

Later in August, Gen. Charles de Gaulle of France proposes a reunited, neutral Vietnam and plans to visit Kennedy in February to talk about it.

In September, Kennedy states the war is Vietnam's, not ours, to decide and then he approves secret negotiations with Fidel Castro outside the State Department-CIA channels. In October, the White House forecasts that 1,000 men would be withdrawn from Vietnam by the end of 1963 and that the U.S. military mission would be over by the end of 1965. That same month Kennedy authorizes the pull-out in a national security action memo—NSAM 263. The Government projects major Pentagon cuts.

Kennedy is killed on Nov. 22. Two days later, Lyndon Johnson meets with Henry Cabot Lodge and the Joint Chiefs of Staff about the Vietnam "crisis." Four days after the assassination, Johnson overrides NSAM 263 with NSAM 273—step one in reversing Kennedy's direction. A "withdrawal" occurs on paper—1,000 men are rotated home—but more are sent back to Vietnam by February. Johnson's NSAM 273 opens the way for air attacks on North Vietnam and increased covert warfare. Finally, in August 1964, Johnson uses the bogus Tonkin Gulf incident to start the air war and win a Congressional mandate to do as he sees fit in Vietnam.

By March 1965, 15 months after Kennedy's death, the first combat troops are sent, something Kennedy refused to do. No difference between Kennedy and Johnson on Vietnam? With the nexus of interest—military, business, political—standing to profit from the hundred-billion-dollar war, there's ample reason to believe that therein lies the motive.

Jim Garrison, though some have tried to discredit him, sought that motive and in suggesting the possibility of a nightmare unacceptable to our official historians, he has been vilified through time. The failure of his case against Clay Shaw cannot be equated with a full vindication of the Warren Report. To bring a case against the covert apparatus of this country was nigh impossible then, as it is now with Lawrence Walsh's failure to find the light of day against Oliver North and the Iran-Contra plotters.

The issue of our times—as the media keep repeating—is democracy. Real democracy is not some illusion and must be based on truth told to the people. We applauded the Soviets when, in the name of democracy, they finally told their people the horrible truth of Stalin's murders, yet we ignore the murder of our President. Do our people deserve any less? If Kennedy was killed by a political conspiracy of his opponents and it has been covered up, then our so-called democratic system has betrayed us.

The real issue is trusting the people with their real history. The real issue is opening all the files of the House Select Committee on Assassinations, embargoed until 2029, *today*. The real issue is opening all C.I.A., F.B.I. and military intelligence files, held for all eternity, on Oswald, Ruby, Kennedy and Dallas 1963. All of them—without the crucial parts blacked out. Only then can we start to have a real democracy. *JFK* strikes a blow for that open debate.

DECEMBER 20, 1991

THE NEW YORK TIMES

OLIVER STONE'S PATSY: *JFK* FILM REVIVES A MALICIOUS PROSECUTION

John P. MacKenzie

In an unworthy attempt to showcase his personal theories about the murder of John F. Kennedy, a self-promoter named Jim Garrison, the New Orleans District Attorney in 1967, concocted conspiracy charges against a retired local businessman named Clay Shaw. Mr. Garrison alleged that the crime in Dallas had been hatched in New Orleans by Mr. Shaw, Lee Harvey Oswald and another man.

Two years later a jury, after a monthlong trial and a closing oration from Mr. Garrison, took only 50 minutes to acquit. The jurors concluded that, whatever doubts they might have had about the Warren Commission's finding that Lee Harvey Oswald acted alone, Mr. Garrison had utterly failed to link Mr. Shaw to any crime.

A day later the unchastened D.A. filed a perjury case, charging Shaw with lying when he denied meeting with or knowing his alleged co-conspirators. A Federal judge took the rare step of finding "bad faith" on Mr. Garrison's part and enjoined the second prosecution.

Mr. Shaw died in 1974, thus ending his own suit charging a malicious Garrison prosecution and a gross violation of his constitutional rights. He had a strong case of fabricated evidence, perjured testimony and abuse of power over the local legal machinery. In fact Mr. Garrison's sins were worse than that: He had appropriated another human being to make a self-serving political statement.

Oliver Stone's new movie *JFK* not only fails to concede this evil but perpetuates it. About the only suggestion of a moral problem for the prosecutor, played by Kevin Costner, is expressed by his alienated wife, played by Sissy Spacek. She accuses her husband of picking on Mr. Shaw because he's gay and supposedly vulnerable. But by the end of 3 hours and 20 minutes on the screen, she too accepts the "value" of his mission.

Mr. Stone is as careless with truth as is his hero. He depicts the prosecutor's fabrications as actual events, and adds fabrications of his own. Like the D.A., Mr. Stone is indifferent to the rights of the accused and cynical in denying Clay Shaw his humanity. The movie is ostensibly dedicated to truth; instead it revives a malicious prosecution and, like the prosecutor, uses Clay Shaw to promote a theory of grand conspiracy.

Allegations of conspiratorial meetings with Mr. Oswald and others, which would have convicted Mr. Shaw if the jury had believed them, are portrayed on the screen as actually happening. The movie also depicts as true a policeman's contention that Shaw, after his arrest, admitted using the alias "Clay Bertrand."

Since the shadowy Bertrand was a prime Garrison suspect, Mr. Shaw would hardly have given that incriminating answer. Indeed, the officer's testimony was so preposterous that Judge Edward Haggerty ruled it inadmissible partly because it was unbelievable. That was an astonishing act of incredulity almost unheard of on that particular local bench. Yet the film portrays the judge's action as finicky obstructionism.

These inventions exceed even the questionable liberties enjoyed by television "docudrama." In docudrama, some scenes and even some characters may be created for dramatic reasons or to tell a real-life story more clearly. But it is dismaying to see entire episodes that have been virtually laughed out of court.

Mr. Stone glosses quickly over the jury's ringing "not guilty," strikes up triumphal music and ends the film with a written epilogue. It says that in 1979 Richard Helms, who was Director of Central Intelligence at the time of the Shaw prosecution, admitted that contrary to the defendant's testimony, Mr. Shaw had "worked for" the C.I.A., one of Garrison's perceived conspirators. But all Mr. Helms said was that Shaw was a C.I.A. "contact," like many businessmen and academics who are sometimes debriefed on returning from abroad.

Lee Harvey Oswald is accurately quoted as contending before he was shot that he was a "patsy" in the Kennedy case, a victim of a frame-up. Prosecutors and historians will long debate whether he was indeed the fall guy arrested to divert attention from a monstrous global conspiracy. What they are not morally free to do is make a patsy out of someone like Clay Shaw to advance those theories and schemes.

CHICAGO TRIBUNE

JFK: IS HISTORY THAT WHICH GETS BROADCAST THE LOUDEST?

Bob Katz

The assassination of President Kennedy occupies a singular role in American history not merely for its monumental political impact: It garnered the highest Nielsen TV ratings of any event ever, Super Bowls included. The tragedy has always straddled twin peaks: national significance and popular intrigue. The fact that the murder was never satisfactorily solved has been a large part of its allure. Anyone—butcher, baker, reporter, film director—has been free to conjure the fatal scenario.

So why are the media so angry about the new movie *JFK*? Interviewers attack director Oliver Stone for tampering with history. Months before release, the film was assailed in Time magazine and *The Washington Post* for inaccuracies. A big-budget movie caught fiddling with the facts? That seems like a small affront for such loud complaints. Hollywood has never been the land of footnotes.

Outcries against the veracity of *JFK* are, in fact, misplaced frustration at the movie's more fundamental heresy: "Historical truth" can now be molded, edited, air-brushed. But we should feign no shock.

Having witnessed the extensive crimes of the Nixon administration reduced to the legalistic "what did the president know and when did he know it," having watched the nearly treasonous subterfuge of Iran-contra recast as but a nit-picking allegation of disobeying congressional mandates, it should come as no surprise that truth is up for grabs, and history has become that which gets broadcast the loudest.

Who but an ivory-tower pedant still believes in the primacy of "facts"? The so-called facts are as susceptible to the sleek techniques of promotion and spin control as the new Infiniti or candidate Dan Quayle. Our Age of Innocence with respect to the truth is over; history will be whatever the majority of people—and our proxy, the viewing public—chooses to believe. Lacking all faith in our ability to discover truth, we raise our hands in abject surrender to await the polling results.

I spent nearly 10 years in the 1970s working on the J.F.K. assassination, as a researcher, lobbyist and lecturer. I believed that the Kennedy case could be officially solved. Witnesses and culprits were alive. There were photographs and films to be analyzed. Footprints and fingerprints were, if not fresh, at least theoretically retrievable. "Facts" were the dot pattern emerging on the screen; collect enough of them and more people might see the picture.

In 1978, Congress, feeling the report of the Warren Commission to be inadequate, launched its own investigation. After two years, a House committee issued a sort of minimalist conclusion: likelihood of more than one gunman; probable influence by members of organized crime.

Officially, that is where the case rests. There will be no more congressional probes, no more indictments, no trials. If someone comes forward to confess, 28 years later, who's going to believe it? Scriptwriters? A few conspiracy buffs? Dots will be added to the image, while some will be subtracted.

The prospect that an issue deep and dear will be adjudicated by the carnival barkers of Tinseltown is indeed troubling. Certainly there are better ways for a country to reach a consensus on who killed its president. Jack Ruby, killer of Lee Harvey Oswald, should have been brave enough to let the chips fall where they may. The press should have been more independent and vigorous.

If, however, we do turn to Hollywood for the last word on the awful darkness of Nov. 22, 1963, it is not because we lacked other means of obtaining the "big picture." The Kennedy assassination is not one of those stories, like the savings and loan scandal, that suffers from neglect. Dozens of credible books have been written. Excellent journalistic accounts have appeared in prestigious publications and on mainstream television shows. Source material is available in libraries to anyone willing to dig.

Having once believed that the Kennedy assassination, to paraphrase one of the Warren commission attorneys, was the Rosetta stone of American politics, I now sit helplessly back and sigh. The issue has passed on to a higher authority. Would I be so sanguine if I disagreed with Oliver Stone's central premise of conspiracy? If another director filled the screen with a hackneyed portrait of a demented Oswald (Robert DeNiro, say, directed by Martin Scorsese) venting his private psychosis across Dallas' Dealy Plaza, would I not sputter and fume? I certainly would.

But I'd know better than to complain that long-lamented, ill-served truth was at stake. The truth in this case lies buried forever. The Unsolved Murder of the Century has entered the realm of myth. As myth it will be internalized, digested, maybe even understood. If a majority embraces Stone's *JFK*, that's because it represents the version of popular choice, interpreted by our medium of preference. History as defined by box-office returns may strike many as a deplorable development, but we have been heading in that direction a long, long time.

Reprinted by permission of the author.

THE BOSTON GLOBE

THE POLITICS OF *JFK*

Thomas Oliphant

Before you see the film *JFK* (which, if you've any sense, you will), you should know something about the city that lurks and hovers menacingly throughout Oliver Stone's riveting tale of murder and deceit—this one.

It's important because of an ironic twist to the politics of Stone's latest work, which, as art, is simply magnificent; as historical drama, is honest on a level few here will understand, and, as polemic, is devastatingly effective.

This is the city whose best and brightest failed to solve the assassination of a president to the public's satisfaction, and to the minimum standards of thoroughness and logic, despite nearly a decade of all-out support for its official investigation from the journalistic and political establishments.

And yet, after nearly two decades of continual pummelling of the still-official version in the world of print (suffered nearly in silence), much of the town is aghast at the appearance of this film and has taken after Stone with a vengeance.

The irony is multiple and ludicrous. The town whose main industry has been failing with monotonous regularity since the day John Kennedy was murdered dares to condemn a dramatization of one of its most despicable failures. The town whose paralyzed government is the deserved butt of national humor doesn't even understand that its media mobilization against Stone can only backfire spectacularly. The town whose remaining defenders of the One-Lone-Nut-Murdered-By-One-Lone-Nut version of the crime (including, by the way, presidents and Congresses who routinely refuse to reopen the case) insist that the rest of us believe them and also refuse to help make public the reams of evidence in the case that will otherwise remain locked up until the year 2029.

As ever undeterred by its ridiculous position, Washington's attack upon Stone consists of two major points:

◆ He alleges a conspiracy so vast (military, intelligence, industrial, right-wing fruitcake, Cuban exiles, the F.B.I., Texas authorities, even Lyndon Johnson) as to be ridiculous.

Stone does no such thing to my eyes. In his spellbinding blend of drama, documentary, and even dramatized documentary, he suggests possibilities through his characters and then illustrates them. His point of view is clearly that President Kennedy's murder originated in military intelligence opposition to post-Cuban-missile-crisis changes in policy away from the Cold War, against a second invasion of Castro's Cuba, and, above all, against Vietnam.

However, Stone leaves one free to accept all or none of his suggestions; only elitist Washington would assume a mass audience of zombies, incapable of viewing a political film carefully and critically.

◆ He has built his story around a fabricated hero—Jim Garrison, the former New Orleans district attorney—who was an incompetent buffoon who slandered a local businessman in the pursuit 24 years ago of an imagined network of assassination conspirators in the city's low-life community.

Not so. *JFK* Garrison has visible, and large, warts, and is well within the boundaries of dramatic license as portrayed by Kevin Costner. The passage of time, moreover, has strengthened the real Garrison's basic case. The businessman (the late Clay Shaw) lied in denying ties to the C.I.A., and witnesses insist to this day they saw him with Lee Harvey Oswald and the bizarre character Garrison believed drove to Texas in time for the assassination to be the real killers' getaway pilot (the late David Ferrie).

History is not always what is left when falsehoods and rumors are professionally discarded; history can also be the product of political power's warping tools. The Warren Commission's 28-year-old report is at least in part that; it failed in its declared purpose long ago.

In conversations here and in California, Stone told me he sees J.F.K. as myth in the classical sense of the term, meaning allegory that points to an inner truth.

As such, it is credible; it is honest. Stone asks us to consider the possibility that John Kennedy's murder was, in effect or in fact, a coup d'etat. We don't have to, but it is interesting that Washington's attack on him does not include any hint of a willingness to let us see that long-suppressed evidence.

Reprinted courtesy of The Boston Globe.

DECEMBER 22, 1991

THE WASHINGTON TIMES

THE SUM OF ALL FEARS
How six seconds in Dallas define our faith in America

David Klinghoffer

The debate over the death of John F. Kennedy, renewed this weekend with the release of Oliver Stone's *JFK*, long ago took on the contours of certain medieval religious disputes. The logic of the debate is right out of Spain and France of the 13th and 15th centuries.

In that age, Christian kings hauled up rabbis to argue with priests about the validity of Jewish theological concepts. This proved an impossible challenge, however, since argument can proceed only when the disputants share basic relevant premises.

Unfortunately for the rabbis, the Christian debaters held to what were, as the rabbis saw it, incomprehensible presuppositions about the nature of God, divine law, sin and salvation. Inevitably, the rabbis were declared heretics, and their books were burned.

Starting this weekend, the famous leftist director Oliver Stone in effect hauls up members of the Warren Commission, first convened to investigate the assassination in December 1963. The charge: By claiming President Kennedy died at the hand of a lone gunman, they committed a deliberate deception.

Like Jim Garrison, the former New Orleans district attorney whose book *On the Trail of the Assassins* is the basis of Mr. Stone's *JFK*, the director sees the president's death as a group effort.

Other conspiracy enthusiasts have picked the Soviets, the Cubans, the mob or Texas oilmen as their own evil masterminds. Following Mr. Garrison (played by Kevin Costner in the movie), Mr. Stone prefers that all-around team of no-goodnicks, the C.I.A..

Unfortunately for Earl Warren, Gerald Ford, Allen Dulles and the rest of the often-derided Warren Commission, Mr. Stone holds to assumptions about the nature of power in this country that, one suspects, they would find every bit as incomprehensible as those French and Spanish rabbis found the assumption of medieval Christianity.

These assumptions, on the order of a religious faith, make it all but impossible to argue with conspiracy theorists.

Mr. Stone has called America a "fascist security state." He seems to mean it. In his best known films—*Platoon, Born on the Fourth of July, Wall Street,* even *The Doors* he has devoted himself to an angry cataloging of our national sins.

In his consuming distrust of American institutions, Mr. Stone is, among fellow theorists, not alone.

Reasons still exist to remain tentatively skeptical of the Warren Commission report and its neat, one-man conclusion. But read a few of the other well-known books purporting to solve the same mystery, and one thing above all becomes clear. From virtually the moment it happened, the Kennedy assassination has served for believers and skeptics alike, as what you might call an index of citizen faith.

Are we a democracy or a dictatorship? Does the rule of law hold sway over our lives, for the most part, or do the powers of lawlessness? As a rule, proponents of conspiracy have committed themselves to the darker view.

MATTER OF FAITH

In his account, Mr. Garrison (who appears in the movie as a bulge-eyed Earl Warren) presents the assassination as a "coup d'état."

"I believe," he wrote in 1988, " that what happened in Dealey Plaza in Dallas ... was instigated and planned long in advance by fanatical anti-communists in the United States intelligence community, that it was carried out, most likely without official approval, by individuals in the C.I.A.'s covert operations apparatus and other extra-governmental collaborators, and covered up by like-minded individuals in the F.B.I., the Secret Service, the Dallas police department and the military, and that its purpose was to stop Kennedy from seeking détente with the Soviet Union and Cuba and ending the Cold War."

What is interesting about the Stone-Garrison thesis is *not* that it might be true.

Even months before the release of *JFK*, journalists without any previous grudge against Mr. Stone had concluded that no movie based on Mr. Garrison's 1967 investigation and unsuccessful prosecution of New Orleans businessman Clay Shaw could be worth much as history.

The journalists merely were repeating humiliating criticisms made at the time of the original Garrison investigation—or fraud, as it commonly has been designated. Witnesses supposedly had been bribed, threatened, drugged. Jim Garrison himself was accused of consorting with the mob.

"On the Set: Dallas in Wonderland" was the title of George Lardner's attack in *The Washington Post* this summer, based on a purloined script for Mr. Stone's film. Newsweek has called the film "propaganda." Tom Wicker of *The New York Times* asked, "Does 'JFK' Conspire Against Reason?" (Yes, Mr. Wicker thinks.)

The rest of the national press was just then picking up on a fact reported by Diana West in *The Washington Times* after the release of Mr. Stone's second Vietnam movie, the highly imaginative "true life" story *Born on the Fourth of July*. As a historical dramatist, Miss West documented, Mr. Stone feels free to slight history in favor of drama.

But even if the director had made a straightforward documentary, admitting the alleged holes and inconsistencies in Mr. Garrison's case, there would remain this: Like Oliver Stone, Jim Garrison has come to accept, as a matter of faith, the doctrine that the United States is an essentially corrupted nation.

Once a self-described "old-fashioned patriot," Mr. Garrison now believes a deceptive "secret government" rules the land. This is a government in which the C.I.A., in cahoots with the military, may freely assassinate political leaders not to its liking.

In the sense that the Kennedy assassination was a "coup d'état," we therefore live today under an illegal, unacknowledged, coup-enforced regime.

PARANOIA

In *JFK*, Kevin Costner, as Mr. Garrison, drops the word "fascism." Well, what can you call it *but* a dictatorship, with George Bush in the fuehrer's chair? Or is he the puppet fuehrer?

Certainly, if you believe Mr. Garrison, any guarantee of the democratic transfer of power has been abolished.

"When I tried to bring some of these disturbing connections to light, the United States government and the major media came down hard on me," Mr. Garrison wrote. "As a result of my investigation of the Kennedy assassination and my experiences afterward, my life and my consciousness were forever changed."

That has to be putting it mildly.

In a self-defense published in *Premiere* magazine, Mr. Stone acknowledges being influenced by a book called *The CIA and Its Allies in Control of the U.S. and the World*, by L. Fletcher Prouty.

About the paranoia of a filmmaker, what more needs to be said?

SUSPICION

There is no dissuading either Oliver Stone or Jim Garrison. For this faith has the effect of neutralizing any counter argument you can think of.

Any evidence contrary to the assumption of conspiracy—such as the gruesome autopsy photos showing a re-entry bullet wound in the president's head consistent with the type of wound made by a gun fired from Lee Oswald's supposed rest in the Texas School Book Depository—may be dismissed as evidence of conspiracy. Somebody manufactured them.

In this view, the very opposition of the press and the federal government to the idea of conspiracy is itself part of conspiracy.

There is similarly no winning with conspiracy theorist Jim Marrs. His book *Crossfire: The Plot That Killed Kennedy*, was optioned by Mr. Stone along with Mr. Garrison's *On the Trail of the Assassins*.

Mr. Marrs writes of the "American business-banking-politics-military-crime power structure."

Whew!

Jack Kennedy, the poor naive soul, Mr. Marrs wrote, "really believed he was president and he set out to shake up the status quo of Big Banking, Big Oil, Big Military-Industrial Complex with its powerful Intelligence Community, and Big Organized Crime."

Once "the nation's top business-crime-military leadership" realized what Kennedy was up to, "the assassination conspiracy went into action."

It's from this author that Mr. Stone derives the virtual crowds of suspicious onlookers present along the Dallas parade route on Nov. 22, 1963. They read like a paranoiac's nightmare. "Umbrella man." "Badge man." A tall blond man. An "elderly Negro." Jack Ruby, later the assassin of Lee Oswald. The three hobos. A man supposedly suffering a seizure of some sort, perhaps as a diversion to distract the Dallas cops.

You wonder where all the innocent bystanders found room to innocently stand by.

William F. Buckley, Jr. has written that "the general skepticism on the question of who killed J.F.K. is really in the nature of a cognate question: Who really ordered Watergate? Who really was guilty of aggression at the Tonkin Gulf? Who really started the Cold War? What were the motives of the Founding Fathers?"

Ask a person, that is, what he thinks about those six seconds in Dealey Plaza and you have asked him for a capsule summary of his faith in America.

MOBBED

What kind of nation are we? What is our major problem? Observers with varying opinions tend to reach opposing conclusions about the Kennedy assassination.

On Nov. 22, 1963, G. Robert Blakey, now the leading proponent of a divergent conspiracy theory, was an enthusiastic young prosecutor under Attorney General Robert Kennedy. Mr. Blakey, then 27, assisted in the harassment of reported Mafia leaders Carlos Marcello and Santo Trafficante, Jr.

Now a law professor at Notre Dame, Mr. Blakey surely remembers that time as among the most exciting chapters in his lawyer's life. Fifteen years later, he would serve as chief counsel to the House Select Committee on Assassinations.

Employing acoustical evidence that a fourth shot had been fired at the president by a rifle other than Oswald's, the committee declared that there indeed had been a conspiracy. But that evidence later was discredited when a crucial audiotape was demonstrated to have been recorded a minute or more after the shooting.

In 1981, Mr. Blakey co-wrote a book called *The Plot to Kill the President*. The subtitle: *Organized Crime Assassinated JFK*. The villains: Mr. Blakey's old nemeses, among others, Carlos Marcello and Santo Trafficante, Jr., feeling betrayed by John Kennedy, for whom they procured the sexy brunette Judith Campbell, and mad as hell at Robert Kennedy's aggressive crusade against them.

Neither in 1963 nor in 1978, when the House committee reported its findings, did everyone accept the concept of the mob as monolithic crime organization—rational, ever lucid, almost passionless and capable of mobilizing its forces to perform even so enormous a task as the murder of a U.S. president.

For Mr. Blakey, on the other hand, adhering to a pre-*GoodFellas* viewpoint, it was natural to seek the president's killers among the mob.

ON THE RIGHT

But the iconic power of the Kennedy assassination extends beyond leftists and career anti-mobsters. Until the demise of Soviet influence in the world, the political right has seen international communism as a threat powerful enough to define the purposes of American public life.

The government, the argument goes, exists to protect us from international communism. The communists know this. To weaken our defenses, they might very well make an attempt on the life of our chief political leader.

For some on the right—such as Revilo Oliver, a professor at the University of Illinois—it became obvious right away that the Cubans and the Soviets had a hand in Dealey Plaza.

But conservatism also implies a basic trust in national institutions. Excluding the participation of foreign governments, when there happens a thing as terrible of the assassination of a president, it could *only* be an aberration, a freak, the work of a lone nut.

Robert Belin, once counsel to the Warren commission, now a lawyer in Des Moines, Iowa, leads the lonely fight against all the conspiracy theories, foreign and domestic. Reading his book, "Final Disclosure: The Full Truth About the Assassination of

President Kennedy," you wouldn't necessarily guess he and Oliver Stone shared the same native land.

Mr. Belin is no blind admirer of the C.I.A.. But when he writes about, for instance, the Iran-Contra scandal, he sees only "abuses."

"On the whole," he judges, the agency's "people are as good as, or perhaps even better than, the people of virtually every other government department or bureau."

DOUBTING

Of course, Mr. Belin makes arresting points.

In fingering the C.I.A. and the mob, the conspiracists often refer us to the many mysterious friendships cultivated by Jack Ruby over the years. In killing Oswald, was he, as some say, acting out a suicide mission for the Mafia?

Mr. Belin introduces a certain postal inspector, Harry Holmes, whose unexpected presence at the Dallas City Jail delayed the moment when Oswald would be led down an open ramp to his death. Unexpectedly showing up that Sunday morning, Mr. Holmes got a chance to interview Oswald after other officials had tried it themselves.

At the moment Oswald should have been on that ramp, were it not for Harry Holmes, Jack Ruby would have missed meeting him and his police escort. At the originally scheduled moment, Ruby was down the street at a Western Union office. A time stamp proves it.

Had there been a conspiracy to silence Oswald by killing him, Ruby certainly would have arrived on time.

But who's to say that the time stamp wasn't itself manufactured—still further evidence of the conspiracy spied by Oliver Stone?

Once a mind has started down that road, doubting evidence for the very reason that it appears evidential, apocalyptic conclusions follow closely behind.

To the extent you accept the notion that we live in a basically just, if imperfect, society—a notion seemingly obvious, though not to persons like Oliver Stone—it is difficult to accept one of the numerous conspiracy theories hatched in the past 28 years. To the extent you don't, it becomes a hell of a lot easier.

Fascist security state—to use Mr. Stone's phrase—here we come.

Reprinted with permission of The Washington Times.

NEWSWEEK

TWISTED HISTORY

Oliver Stone's JFK is not just an entertainment, it's a piece of propaganda for a huge conspiracy theory of the Kennedy murder

Kenneth Auchincloss, Ginny Carroll, Maggie Malone

Here we go again. The school book depository. The sixth floor window. The grassy knoll. The umbrella man. The fourth shot. The pristine bullet. The eternal flame.

Re-create Dallas as it was on Nov. 22, 1963. Prune trees so they are the same length they were that day. Send an identical open limousine into the tight turn onto Elm Street, headed for the triple underpass. Roll the cameras on an event that stunned America and seared its heart. Follow the script:

Then the SHOTS: A volley sounding like a motorcycle backfire. A GLIMPSE of a MUZZLE FLASH … smoke.

Looking up from the TEXAS SCHOOL BOOK DEPOSITORY—all in line with the "official" version of events … PIGEONS by the hundreds suddenly shoot off the roof. But the SCREEN (our screen) GOES GRAY as did the CBS-TV first bulletins to the country.

CBS BULLETIN (FULL SCREEN)

… we interrupt this program to bring you this flash bulletin. A burst of gunfire! Three bursts of gunfire, apparently from automatic weapons, were fired at President Kennedy's motorcade in downtown Dallas …

But this is definitely not the "official" version of events. This is the movie *JFK* as brought to you by Oliver Stone, director of *Platoon*, *Wall Street* and *The Doors*. In this version, Lee Harvey Oswald certainly does not act alone, may never even have fired a shot. The assassination, as seen through the eyes of Stone and his protagonist Jim Garrison, at the time the real-life New Orleans district attorney, was a grand conspiracy involving the C.I.A., the F.B.I., the Army and Navy, anti-Castro Cubans, New Orleans lowlifes and the Dallas police force. The motive: to thwart the dovish tendencies of John F. Kennedy who, if he had lived, would have pulled all American troops out of Vietnam, settled the cold war with the Soviet Union and patched up relations with Castro's Cuba. The shooting was, as Garrison (played by Kevin Costner) keeps insisting, a coup d'état that continues to gnaw at the American body politic. Stone makes plain his hope that the film will cause the investigation to be reopened. It ends with this message on the screen: DEDICATED TO THE YOUNG, IN WHOSE SPIRIT THE SEARCH FOR TRUTH MARCHES ON. The producers are preparing a "study guide" to the movie for use in schools.

In effect, Stone is inviting America to adopt an alternative version of history. His film categorically rejects the report of the Warren Commission, the imperfect but painstaking government investigation that concluded that Oswald murdered Kennedy acting on his own. That conclusion has never satisfied a great part of the American public: a *Washington Post* survey last May indicated that 56 percent believe there was some sort of conspiracy to kill J.F.K., and only 19 percent agree with the Warren Commission findings. And a vast network of conspiracy buffs has flourished ever since the assassination, tracing tangled lines of connection between obscure figures and erecting baroque palaces of supposition (page 52). This movie draws on many of these old notions—and will doubtless stir up a new wave of them.

It has also stirred up a torrent of outrage. Well before its release, the film had already set off a barrage of articles and even cover stories (*Life, Esquire, Texas Monthly*), mostly denouncing Stone for twisting the facts. Stone in turn has been stung into angry suggestions that the establishment media are simply subscribing to the Great Warren Commission Cover-up. Garrison, who was much ridiculed in the press for his handling of the case, thought journalists had turned into coconspirators, witting or unwitting, in an official scheme to conceal the dark truths of Nov. 22, 1963. This is beyond-the-looking-glass stuff: anyone entering the assassination debate is instantly transported into a frenzied fantasy world, in which the same evidence can be used to bolster either side (Oswald was the killer, Oswald was framed) and analysts are assumed to be agents with secret motives of their own.

The problem with *JFK*—writ very large because it's a big movie with big stars about a big event—is the problem of the docu-drama. A movie or a television show that re-creates history inevitably distorts history. It has to compress things into a short span; it has to extract clarity out of the essential messiness of life; it has to abide by certain dramatic conventions: major scenes, major characters, major speeches. All this makes for exaggeration. "It's like writing history with lightning," exclaimed Woodrow Wilson when he saw the first docu-drama, *Birth of a Nation*, in 1915.

In *JFK* all these problems are compounded by taking a highly speculative version of events—the Garrison/Stone conspiracy theory—and grafting it onto real events. Only the alert viewer will be able to distinguish real documentary footage from reconstructed scenes, shot in black and white, that often represent Garrison's suppositions about what might have happened. In presenting Kennedy's autopsy, for example, what appear to be genuine still photographs are intercut with dramatized footage. And these black-and-white re-creations abound. A police officer brings the murder rifle to Oswald's corpse and presses the palmprint onto the barrel. A mysterious figure deposits the "pristine bullet" (the one supposed to have wounded both Kennedy and John Connally) on what seems to be Connally's gurney in Parkland hospital. A second "Oswald" appears at a rifle range in Dallas, assassins gather behind the fence on the grassy knoll. This is a film in which the real and the imagined, fact and fiction, keep shading into one another. As Leonard Garment wrote after seeing *The Final Days*, the TV film on Nixon's fall, "A viewer watching a well done docudrama will find it near impossible to keep in mind the difference between its factual basis and the dramatic embellishments. It is all there, right before his very eyes, occupying the same level of reality." That's particularly true of young audiences who weren't alive in 1963. "We live in a media age, " says film critic Leonard Maltin. "If a television or theatrical movie can paint a vivid enough picture for young people, they'll believe that's the way it was."

That's clearly what Oliver Stone is hoping will happen. *JFK* is not just an entertainment, it's a work of propaganda. In some some prerelease screenings, Stone has personally asked those who write about the film not to discuss its thesis, so that audiences can make up their minds for themselves. That request is out of bounds. Of course people should make up their own minds about the Kennedy assassination. But in doing so they should be aware of some information that *JFK* leaves out and some dubious material that it includes. What was the evidence that Oswald acted alone? Is it true that Kennedy was planning a pullout from Vietnam? Was Jim Garrison a brave and lonely battler for truth?

THE EVIDENCE AGAINST OSWALD

The Oswald of *JFK* is even more bizarre than the the angry loner portrayed by the Warren commission: an anti-Castro activist who distributed pro-Castro literature as a cover, a hanger-on in a seedy New Orleans set of homosexuals and anti-Castroites who talk wildly of killing Kennedy. He may have known enough about the plot to try to warn the feds about it in advance but seems to take no part in the shooting. When he realizes J.F.K. has been shot from the building where he works, it suddenly dawns on him that he's the "patsy," set up to take the rap. So he leaves the building, goes home to get a gun, maybe (or maybe not) kills Officer Jay D. Tippit, then winds up in a movie theatre, where the police have been tipped off to find him.

Some findings of the Warren Commission that do not appear in the movie:

♦ He was the owner of the Mannlicher-Carcano 6.5-mm rifle found on the sixth floor of the Depository building. Ballistics tests show that the bullets that struck Kennedy and Connally came from that rifle.

♦ The morning of the assassination, Oswald carried to work a long, thin paper parcel—"curtain rods," he said. Paper wrapping consistent with that seen on the parcel was found on the sixth floor, along with the parcel.

♦ The autopsy on Kennedy's body produced the unanimous medical finding that all the shots that struck him came from the rear. A House Select Committee on Assassinations investigated further in the late seventies, calling in a wound ballistics expert to evaluate the sudden backward movement of the president's head which some take as proof that the final shot came from in front. The committee determined that the rearward movement of the head could have come from nerve damage, and was not "fundamentally inconsistent with a bullet striking from the rear."

◆ A number of eye witnesses identified Oswald as the man who shot Officer Tippit. The shell casings that the gunman tossed away at the scene were identified as having come from Oswald's revolver which he had when he was arrested at the movie theater.

And if there was a conspiracy—particularly the massive conspiracy posited in this movie—is it imaginable that not a single member of it has cracked? The tug of conscience, the lust for notoriety, even greed for money (for such a story would be worth many thousands of dollars as well as immunity) would surely have brought someone forward in the past 28 years.

IF KENNEDY HAD LIVED.

It's an essential part of Stone's thesis that Kennedy was planning to pull out of Vietnam once he was re-elected. Not only that, but he would have healed relations with America's communist rivals. That's why the conspiracy was hatched: the military-industrial complex wanted their war, and Kennedy was going to take it away from them. Vice President Lyndon Johnson was much more their kind of guy.

Does that notion seem plausible? Stone's interpretation draws heavily on the work of a young Army major named John Newman, who will soon publish (with a boost from Stone) a book called *JFK & Vietnam*, based on his Ph.D. thesis. He is persuaded that by the Spring of 1963, Kennedy had decided to get all American troops out of Vietnam, even if it meant losing the war, but to wait until after the 1964 election for fear that the withdrawal would hurt him politically. Newman's evidence: two anti-war senators, Mike Mansfield and Wayne Morse, remember Kennedy telling them as much and so does his friend and assistant Kenneth O'Donnell. ALso, shortly before he died he ordered that 1,000 U.S. advisers (out of a total of more than 16,000) be withdrawn from Vietnam by the end of the year.

This really does not seem terribly compelling. J.F.K.'s statements to the senators even if not colored by wishful memories, could have been tinged with politics. And the 1,000-man withdrawal, around 6 percent of the total, was just a token that might never have been repeated. McGeorge Bundy, who was Kennedy's special assistant for national security affairs, doesn't believe it signified any shift of policy, nor does he know of any evidence that Kennedy had a private plan for pulling out of Vietnam. "I don't think we know what he would have done if he'd lived," Bundy said last week." I don't know, and I don't know anyone who does know." What's more, he added, "Kennedy didn't hide his views: his public statements were what he believed." And his public statements were about bearing the burden and staying the course. In the speech he was scheduled to deliver at the Dallas Trade Mart just minutes after he was killed, he was going to say: "Our assistance to these nations can be painful, risky and costly, as is true in Southeast Asia today. But we dare not weary of the task … We in this country, in this generation, are—by destiny rather than by choice—the watchmen on the walls of freedom." Newman argues that all this was just politically motivated deception.

If there was no clear sign that Kennedy was going to pull out of Vietnam, there was no clear motive for Stone's grand conspiracy to kill him.

THE REAL JIM GARRISON

In the movie, Jim Garrison is an all-American hero—how could he not be with Kevin Costner in the part? Beset by doubters on all sides, stymied by the F.B.I., ridiculed by the press, he pushes on regardless, a lonely seeker after truth, justice and the American way. In New Orleans, they regard Garrison a little differently.

Rosemary James covered his investigation for the now defunct New Orleans States-Item. "He went from a highly intelligent eccentric to a lunatic in the period of one year," she said last week. "Every time press interest in the case would start to wane, he would propound a new theory. One week it would be 14 Cubans shooting from storm drains. The next week, it would be H.L. Hunt and the far right in Dallas. This was no Robin Hood—no Untouchable either."

Charles Ward, now a judge on the state court of appeals, was one of Garrison's assistants in the case. "Most of the time you marshal the facts, then deduce your theories," he told The Times-Picayune in 1983. "But Garrison deduced a theory then marshalled the facts. And if the facts didn't fit, he'd say they had been altered by the C.I.A.."

Some of his staff became alarmed about his behavior. He would call meetings, then disappear into the men's room for a while, emerge with a new theory and send aides to try to prove it. Former investigator William Gurvich, who defected to Shaw's defense team, told of him spreading out a road map on his desk and drawing circles around places where Oswald or some of his friends had lived in New Orleans. Then he'd order background checks on people who lived in the same neighborhoods.

The climax of *JFK* is Garrison's long, impassioned closing argument in the Clay Shaw trial. In fact, Garrison did not deliver the main closing argument in the case; Assistant D.A. James Alcock did. And Garrison did not even stick around for the verdict—not guilty, after less than an hour's deliberation by the jury.

Fact and fiction—the Kennedy assassination is an inexhaustible mine of both. Oliver Stone would have us believe that the truth is still elusive, that there are sources still untapped, leads unpursued, villains on the loose. It's not impossible. But it's also fair to say that this may be the most exhaustively investigated event in history—which paradoxically accounts for many of the loose ends still dangling at its edges. Officially and unofficially, professionally and amateurishly, the occurrences of Nov. 22, 1963 have been sifted and resifted and doubtless will be sifted again. So much so that this is no longer just an episode in American history—it's a cult. The movie *JFK* is not history; it's an act of devotion, a declaration of faith.

NEWSWEEK

WHAT DOES OLIVER STONE OWE HISTORY?

David Ansen

As Oliver Stone was putting the finishing touches on his epic *JFK* last week, he sat down with Newsweek's David Ansen to defend the highly controversial perspective of the film. Some highlights from the interview:

ANSEN: What's your responsibility to history? What if you're wrong?

STONE: I would live with that. I think the artist's obligations are to interpret history and reinterpret it as he sees fit. If I did my homework, I don't feel I have a responsibility to Clay Shaw [the New Orleans businessman tried by zealous prosecutor Jim Garrison for conspiracy to kill J.F.K.] because he was proven innocent in court. Clarence Darrow lost the Scopes trial, but that doesn't make what he did any less right.

Filmmakers make myths. They take the true meanings of events and shape them. D.W. Griffith did it in *Birth of a Nation*. In *Reds*, Warren Beatty probably made John Reed better than he was [but] was truthful in a mythic sense. I made Garrison larger than he is for a larger purpose.

Is Clay Shaw violated by my work? Is he going to come haunt me at night, drive me to the edge of madness? I have to live with my conscience and if I have done wrong, it's going to come back on me. John Kennedy might be in my dreams too, saying, "Do it, go out there, find my assassins, bring them to justice."

ANSEN: You've said that it's a mistake to idealize Kennedy. Yet the movie does just that.

STONE: Again, it was a question of do I have time in this three-hour scenario to really get into Kennedy stealing the election in '60? Or that he said one thing to the public and did another behind their backs? Those are valid points and I stand faulted on both Garrison and Kennedy. But my defense would be that there is a larger issue at stake. Ultimately, they were good guys.

ANSEN: Are you hoping that this film will reopen the case?

STONE: No, I don't think it will because most of the participants are dead. But the American public should demand access to the files of the House Select Committee [sealed until 2029]. And a public inquiry should get underway about the C.I.A.. They should be reined in. They were supposed to gather intelligence, originally, not practice covert operations and destabilize governments. As an intelligence-gathering apparatus, they have been sorely remiss recently on the Soviet

Union as well as in Iraq and Iran. Maybe the movie can contribute to a climate for reform.

ANSEN: And you truly believe that if Kennedy had lived this world would have been a very different world?

STONE: Totally. It would have been a much healthier place. The massacre in Southeast Asia would not have occurred. The cycles of poverty and recession were fueled by the war economy by Johnson. Inflation resulted on a massive scale. The whole economic world shifted as a result of the Vietnam war.

And it wasn't like we went over there and just lost 58,000 lives—we killed 2 million people. The C.I.A. practiced what they had been doing in the '50s on a much larger level in Vietnam. The covert mentality continued right into the '90s. You go from Vietnam into Watergate and into the '80s with Irangate.

The forces that killed Kennedy did not operate in a vacuum. That parallel covert government has existed through the last 28 years. Lawrence Walsh couldn't bring Oliver North and that bunch to justice. It's a mentality that won't go away. One hopes the movie would make people want to strip away the lies and covert operations.

A couple of lunatics like Jim Garrison keep saying, hey, wake up, something happened. People like me, sons of Jim Garrison, promulgate the theory. I think people are more on my side than the government's. If they don't believe me this go-round, they'll believe me when another shocking thing happens.

DECEMBER 23, 1991

NEWSWEEK

A TROUBLEMAKER FOR OUR TIMES
Oliver Stone's heretical history is a stunner

David Ansen

"It's only a movie," Alfred Hitchcock once said, calming the concerns of Kim Novak and putting his scarifying visions into tidy perspective. Hitch was right, of course, and wrong. No movie is only a movie, and least of all Oliver Stone's *JFK*, which is destined to become fodder for every op-ed writer in the country. Stone's movie puts the critic—and the audience—in a strange, indeed absurd, position: we are asked not only to pass judgment on its virtues as an entertainment but to hand down a judgment on history, which in this case means rendering a verdict on the C.I.A., the F.B.I., military intelligence, anti-Castro Cubans, Lee Harvey Oswald,

Clay Shaw, L.B.J. and everyone else who is in one way or another implicated in the conspiracy that, Stone argues, resulted in the murder of our 35th president in Dealey Plaza.

My advice is: don't trust anyone who claims the movie is hogwash. And don't trust Stone either. Movies are, almost by definition, a demagogic art form: they can emotionally persuade you of just about anything, which is precisely why Stone's movie will be dissected with vehemence. An entire generation of filmgoers is hereafter going to look at these events through Stone's prism. If history is a battlefield, *JFK* has to be seen as a bold attempt to seize the turf for future debate.

It is also "just" a movie, and one that for three hours and eight minutes of dense, almost dizzying detail, is capable of holding the audience rapt in its grip. If Stone was just a clumsy hack *JFK* could be as easily dismissed as Hollywood's first, long forgotten conspiracy movie, *Executive Action* (1973). But Stone's work is, on many levels, stunning. Using as a base Jim Garrison's *On the Trail of the Assassins* and Jim Marrs's *Crossfire*, Stone and coscenarist Zachary Sklar structure their film as a thriller, with New Orleans D.A. Garrison (Kevin Costner) as the beleaguered investigator who stumbles upon links between Oswald (Gary Oldman) and local right-wing, anti-Castro zealots that implicate those in the highest corridors of power. It is, quite deliberately, a *Mr. Smith Goes to the Assassination*, complete with a climactic courtroom peroration that is a 90-proof Capraesque barn raiser, down to the Jimmy Stewart catch in Costner's throat.

A TRUE BELIEVER

At this, a lot of people are going to cry foul. By turning Jim Garrison—a troubling, shoot-from-the-hip prosecutor whose credibility has been seriously questioned—into a mild-mannered, four-square Mr. Clean, Stone is asking for trouble. *JFK* Garrison is perhaps best viewed more as a movie convention than as a real man. Stone has always required a hero to worship, and he turns the D.A. into his own alter ego, a true believer tenaciously seeking higher truth. He equally idealizes Kennedy, seen as a shining symbol of hope and change, dedicated to pulling out of Vietnam and to ending the cold war.

But it is possible to remain skeptical of *JFK*'s Edenic notions of its heroes and still find this movie a remarkable, necessary provocation. Real political discourse has all but vanished from Hollywood filmmaking; above and beyond whether Stone's take on the assassination is right his film is a powerful, radical vision of America's drift toward covert government. What other filmmaker is even thinking about the uses and abuses of power? The first footage we see is Eisenhower's farewell address in 1961, in which he presciently warned the nation to guard against the growing threat of the military-industrial complex, and everything that follows is an illustration of that thesis. That *JFK* comes out in the reign of our first ex-C.I.A. president is an irony that hangs unstated over the movie.

Anyone who's ever dipped into the contradictions of the assassination knows what a spellbinding, crazy-making story it is—and Stone does it justice. He manages to pack in an astonishing amount of information while maintaining suspense and narrative clarity. Quasi documentary in style, *JFK* shifts between color and black and white, fact and speculation, newsreel and staged re-creation, so that you can't always tell what's real footage and what's not, never mind what's true and what's not.

Charged as Stone's style is, he mercifully discards the strong-arm tactics of "Born on the Fourth of July." Costner's understated integrity gives the film a steady anchor. He's playing an icon and he plays him with unfussy grace. The flamboyant roles go to the villains, a fascinating gallery of shady characters, none more bizarre than Joe Pesci's David Ferrie, the hairless, chain-smoking mercenary pilot whose untimely death crippled Garrison's case. Tommy Lee Jones is a powerful, if too overtly sinister, presence as Clay Shaw, and Kevin Bacon shines as the fascist hustler/convict (a composite character) who claimed to be privy to Shaw and Ferrie's plotting. (That all three are homosexual has made the gay community understandably nervous, but the film itself shouldn't be charged with homophobia.)

The cast, studded with star cameos (Garrison himself pops up, ironically, as Earl Warren), is too huge to single out. But mention must be made of Oldman's creepy Oswald, and Donald Sutherland's mesmerizing turn as the mysterious X (based on L. Fletcher Prouty, former aide to the Joint Chiefs of Staff and an adviser on the film) who serves as the film's Deep Throat.

What X tells us may be more than many people can, or want, to swallow. No one should take *JFK* at face value: it's a compellingly argued case, but not to be confused with proof. But my hat is off to the filmmaker—and Warner Bros.—for the reckless chutzpah of the attempt. Make no mistake: this is one very incendiary Hollywood entertainment. Two cheers for Mr. Stone, a troublemaker for our times.

TIME

PLUNGING INTO THE LABYRINTH

Feisty filmmaker Oliver Stone counters criticisms of the conspiracy theory and cover-up scenario in his "tsunami wave" of a movie, JFK

Lance Morrow & Martha Smilgis

Q: In *JFK* you commingle real news footage with re-created historical scenes. Do you consider the film a docudrama, a work of fact or fiction?

A: Am I a zebra? Am I a giraffe? What color are my spots? These are categorizations, and I tend to resist them. During the trial Jim Garrison says, let's speculate for a moment what happened that day. He goes on to speculate as to the events as they might have happened with more than one shooter. So I'm giving you a detailed outlaw history or counter-myth. A myth represents the true inner spiritual meaning of an event. I think the Warren Commission was a myth, and I think the movie, hopefully, if its accepted by the public, will at least move people away from the Warren Commission and consider the possibility that there was a coup d'état that removed President Kennedy.

Q: Do you feel you as a filmmaker have a responsibility to historical fact?

A: Whenever you start to dictate to an artist his "social responsibility" you get into an area of censorship. I think the artist has the right to interpret and reinterpret history and the events of his time. It's up to the artist himself to determine his own ethics by his own conscience.

Q: Are you comfortable with this film in your own conscience?

A: Totally. I dispute the "objective" version of events in Dealey Plaza as stated by the Warren Commission. The entire Warren Commission Report, 26 volumes, is a rat's nest of confusing facts, and that's been pointed out not just by me but by many critics before me.

Q: Is it accurate to say that you think the assassinations of John Kennedy, Martin Luther King and Bobby Kennedy are linked?

A: I think the removal of the three most progressive leaders of the '60s during a time of bitterness and dissension and civil war in this country is very much tied into the assassination. I use the term civil war in its full implications, going back to the 1960s, where we were divided between hawks and doves, hippies and straights. These three leaders were pulling out of the war in Vietnam and shaking up the country. Civil rights, the cold war itself, everything was in question. There's no doubt that these three killings are linked, and it worked. That's what's amazing. They pulled it off.

Q: Who's "they"? Who do you think has profited from the Kennedy and King assassinations?

A: As shown in the movie, the money that was involved was enormous by any standard. Cold war money. It's not just Vietnam money. It's military-industrial money. It's nuclear money. It's the American war economy that Eisenhower warned us about, that came into being in this country in the 1940s, after World War II. It's also the continuation of the covert state, the invisible government that operates in this country and seems to be an unelected parallel government to our legitimate government. The C.I.A. and military intelligence all got out of hand somewhere in the 1960s. It suddenly reached another level, where the concept of assassination—the wet affair, liquidation—became the vogue.

Q: When you say a parallel government, do you mean a specific arm of the Executive Branch, like "special ops"?

A: It's a moving, fluid thing, a series of forces at play. It's not necessarily individuals. Military-industrial interests are at stake. That puts into play certain forces. We have had many incidents recently, with Oliver North, with Richard Secord, the whole Iran-contra business. We've seen the scale on which arms are moved around the world. We've seen secret deals. There's more going on than ever meets the eye, and there's more going on than is ever written about in the newspapers.

Q: Why did you pick Garrison as the focal point of *JFK*?

A: Because in Jim I found a worthy protagonist, a vehicle to include all the research that was done in the case. I respect Jim. He put himself out there and led with his chin. His was a flawed investigation, but he did his best. He was one of a very few who early on said that the government did it. Which was an astounding statement in 1967, a very scary one.

Q: It's still an astounding statement. Americans have the strong sense that their government is their government. They don't have the sense that, say, the Russians have had for generations, that the government belongs to the people who have seized power.

A: You really think that? Maybe you're right. I may be in the minority. I just think the American people smell a rat.

Q: Given our motley society, why couldn't a lone gunman have shot Kennedy? Why does it have to be a conspiracy?

A: Assassins through history have always proclaimed their act. They've been proud of it. They've killed for a political reason. But Oswald always said, "I didn't do it. I'm a patsy." And we have as enormous accumulation of physical evidence that makes it very difficult to buy that one gunman could have done that kind of shooting job.

Q: You stood in the window with that rifle and worked the bolt?

A: Not only that, but we created the motorcade. We had a massive motorcade moving through that ravine called Dealey Plaza. We fired. We heard the shots and echoes too. We did more of an enactment than the F.B.I. ever did, and by the way, their best marksmen were never able to match Oswald's feat.

Q: In *JFK* the media, including *Time* and *Life*, cover up the assassination conspiracy. Do you truly believe the press was C.I.A.-infiltrated?

A: I feel that the American reaction to the crime was to simplify it, to deal with good guys and bad guys and a lone gunman and John Wayne theatrics. The European press was much more skeptical, because they saw in this assassination political forces at play. The press in fact never did ask *why* Kennedy was killed. They immediately were, in a sense, trivialized by the questions of who and how. It all became a matter of scenery—Oswald, Ruby. Scenery distracts from the essential questions. Who benefited? Who had the power to cover it up? I don't point the finger of evil intention, but it is documented that the agency spent quite a bit of money to keep a leg up in journalism, that there were a lot of people working on their payroll.

Q: Specifically what evidence do you believe the press covered up?

A: Among other things, you have *Life* buying the Zapruder film and burying it and not showing it to the American public.* Eventually it was made available, but only 12 years later. Garrison was the first one, I think, to get it out in a public forum with the trial in 1969. He subpoenaed Time-Life and succeeded in getting the film shown to a limited audience.

Q: What is the importance of the Zapruder film?

A: I think the most conclusive thing it shows is the fatal head shot coming from the front, from the fence. In addition, it shows the time frame of the shots, which makes it very difficult to believe Oswald fired three shots in 5.6 seconds. And of course it raises the whole question of how Kennedy and Connally were shot by the same bullet.

Q: From what you're saying, you would have 400 of the most notable media people in America knowing about a conspiracy to kill Kennedy.

A: I don't know that 400 people have to know anything. I think there is such a form of informational equilibrium that preserves the status quo that you can virtually call it silent consent.

Q: Why did you put famous actors—Jack Lemmon, Walter Matthau, Donald

---

* In fact, *Life* printed the most relevant still frames in its next issue. But at the request of Zapruder, who feared "exploitation" of the tragedy, it did not allow the film to be shown as a moving image. In 1975 *Life* sold the film back to the Zapruder family for $1.

Sutherland, John Candy, Ed Asner—into small roles?

A: They help us along the road because the material might be in some sense dry and arcane to many people. Each actor has a little riddle or obstacle for Garrison, who has to work his way around it to move farther into the heart of the labyrinth, where the Cretan Minotaur lives.

Q: Isn't Garrison's wife, the character played by Sissy Spacek, simplified in the film?

A: I didn't misinterpret his wife at all. That's the way she was. Garrison's investigation threatened her family life. They had five kids, and he was not home. We didn't practice politically correct feminism to try to make her into something she was not. What we did—you could fault me for it—was put a woman D.A. into his staff. He did not have a woman D.A.

Q: Do you expect to see negative reaction to *JFK*?

A: I think older white males will have a major problem with it. I think the younger generation will be more open.

Q: The older generation has a memory of the event, the younger generation doesn't. What is your sense of responsibility to this younger, video generation, which will accept your movie as truth and history?

A: We did a lot of homework. I had a dozen technical advisers going over the script with a fine-tooth comb. Everything that we have in there we stand behind. What is speculation is clearly speculation. We did not throw in any facts that we felt were wrong. I did make some composites. I've admitted that. I made it very clear [in interviews], for example, that Garrison never really met with the character called "X," played by Donald Sutherland, who explains the dimensions of the CIA conspiracy.

Q: You have drawn together many threads of conspiratorial theory in the film. Are you endorsing everything or simply advancing them as possibilities?

A: I think I pulled back in the movie from some of my own beliefs and probably softened some of my own conclusions for fear of seeming too aggressive and bullying about information.

Q: With this film, aren't you joining the ranks of the conspiracy industry and commercializing a national tragedy?

A: It's a cottage industry but not necessarily a very lucrative one. The movie faces commercial risk. It has to appeal on a large level to justify itself.

Q: From many of your films it seems you see America as an ugly, disturbed country populated with sinister characters.

A: *Talk Radio* is the darkest film I've made, but I don't personally feel that way about America. I have a lot more hope for America. I see it as a totally homogeneous land and I love its vastness and its freedom. My mother is French. She was an immigrant who came over here in 1946. In a sense I'm half immigrant. I think that the best part of America is its lack of pretension and snobbism. If anything, in my work I've tried to veer away from the élites that I think I have corrupted and made cynical the American Dream. I hark back to an immigrant belief in the goodness of this country. I find it coming still from Asia, Mexico, Latin America, Europe. I think movies in a sense thrive on that democracy.

Q: Where were you on Nov. 22, 1963?

A: In my room during a lunch break at the Hill School in Pennsylvania. My reaction was very similar to Jim's in the movie. A fellow student ran into the room and said, "They just shot the President." It was shocking to me because Kennedy was a handsome young man. I loved his rhetoric. Politically, I was against him because I was for Nixon and Goldwater. But in my heart I could not help being moved by his charisma. I was very sad for the family. We watched TV the whole weekend, just like in the movie. Then we moved on with our lives. We didn't really think about it. That was the point.

Q: When did you begin to develop an intuition that maybe it wasn't Oswald alone, that maybe there was a conspiracy?

A: I began to distrust the government through my Vietnam experience, when I started to see the degree of lying and corruption that was going on. When I came back from the war, I began to redefine the way I had grown up. I started writing screenplays more aggressively protesting the authority of this government. I wrote *Platoon* and *Born on the Fourth of July*. I had heard the Oswald stories, but I had honestly been defeated by the size of the literature, and I didn't see its implications in my life, as to how it affected the beginnings of the Vietnam War. And then Garrison's book was given to me. I read it and saw its implications as a thriller—a whydunit.

Q: You have been called a chronicler of the '60s and the last of the '60s radicals. What does the '60s mean to you?

A: First of all, I was never a radical in the '60s. I was, if anything, very straight. I went to Vietnam. I was very slow in coming around. I do think the '60s is a determinant decade for the '90s, because people in my generation—I'm 45 now—are coming to power. We're the next power base of this country. We all grew up in the cold war. We were born in the dawn of the nuclear age. So the '60s is really determining what's going to happen in the '90s.

Q: You once said that Kennedy's assassination spawned the race riots, the hippie movement, organized protests and the drug culture. Do you think his death alone was responsible for this tide?

A: Yes, in a metaphorical sense. I think there was an erosion of trust in the government on the subconscious level. On the conscious level, we moved on. We buried Oswald and got rid of Ruby. The nightmare went away. But subconsciously the major fissure had occurred. Historians in the 21st century are going to point to this as a key moment in American history.

Q: Quite apart from whether there was a small, limited conspiracy, isn't the movie saying that it was in the general interest of Lyndon Johnson that Kennedy be assassinated and the war in Vietnam go forward?

A: Kings are killed. It is the nature of political powers. I have no problem believing this. I can see where certain people do, and I can see where you might think I'm crazy. The film is a bit subversive in its approach. But a film can often be subversive to the subconscious. It comes out and its often criticized and reviled, but it lasts. It's sort of like a tsunami wave. It starts out miles and miles from the beach. You hear a noise that just moves fast under the water. Then without warning it hits the beach, an explosion. Obviously this film is going to be denied; there will be some decrying and reviling. All the errors are going to be attacked. It will be discredited. Yet it will survive.

DECEMBER 23, 1991

THE NEW YORK TIMES

HOLLYWOOD WONDERS IF WARNER BROTHER'S LET *JFK* GO TOO FAR

Bernard Weinraub

What is the responsibility of a studio that produces a major film depicting a huge government conspiracy in the killing of President John F. Kennedy?

With the release of Oliver Stone's movie *JFK* the film community is asking about the ethical, artistic and even legal responsibility of the studio, Warner Brothers, which released the $40 million film that asserts Lee Harvey Oswald did not act alone and may not even have fired a shot in the Kennedy assassination. Instead, the movie, which opened Friday around the nation, implicates, directly and indirectly, the White House, the Central Intelligence Agency, the Federal Bureau of Investigation, the United States military, big business, anti-Castro Cubans, the Dallas police force and an assortment of fringe figures in New Orleans.

Hollywood is vexed by the film, and no movie in recent years has stirred the kind of discussion here that *JFK* has.

At issue is whether Warner Brothers, in helping finance and distribute the movie, adheres to Mr. Stone's provocative point of view, which has been attacked by critics in newspapers and magazines as a distortion of the facts. Or does Warner Brothers, like any studio, produce its films for one reason, to make money, brushing aside the artistic, political, moral and ethical implications of any film, including *JFK* which had the substantial involvement of the town's most powerful agency, Creative Artists Agency, representing Mr. Stone, the film's star, Kevin Costner, and numerous other actors.

One of the top producers in Hollywood, echoing a view commonly expressed here about the film business in general, said political and ethical questions about a film like *JFK* were simply dwarfed by money considerations: "All these guys sit in a room, look at what a picture will cost, look at Oliver's talent and track record, look at the fact that they'll get Costner and they say, 'This is a good roll of the dice for us.' All the rest really doesn't count."

The Role of the Studio

At the moment the issue confronting Hollywood is does a studio—or for that matter its parent company, Time Warner—view its role as merely giving total free rein to a prominent director, and in the process, hope to turn the movie into a financial success? Or at what point does a studio exercise its leverage and blunt the highly charged message of a film maker like Oliver Stone?

Warner Brothers is plainly delighted at Mr. Stone's promotion of the movie in the press, which he also attacks for accepting the reports of the Warren Commission, the official investigation that concluded that Oswald acted on his own in the assassination. On the other hand, the studio was caught off guard by the firestorm over the film.

Robert A. Daly, the chairman of Warner Brothers, and Terry Semel, the president, did not respond to phone calls about the studio's responsibilities. Neither did John Schulman, the senior vice-president and general counsel. But Mr. Semel told The Los Angeles Times before the film was released that when Mr. Stone made his proposal, "My immediate reaction was 'Wow! What a powerful and great idea for a movie.'"

Over the weekend, the film grossed $5.1 million, a bit disappointing, according to exhibitors. Preliminary figures, released by the Exhibitor Relations Company, which monitors films releases for theater chains, said *JFK* was tied for fifth with Disney's *Beauty and the Beast*. The top box-office films were Steven Spielberg's *Hook*, followed by *The Father of the Bride*, *The Last Boy Scout*, and *Star Trek VI*. Warner Brothers officials said that the three hour length of the film diminished the number of shows in movie houses and that audience exit polls had proved highly favorable.

Time Warner said the issue of a studio's responsibility was up to Warner Brothers. "Our operating divisions have total creative freedom," said Tod Hullin, the senior vice president for communications at Time Warner, in a statement. "This movie is a creative product and we do not interfere or comment on the results of the creative process."

A LOT OF DEBATE

And Robert G. Friedman, the president of Warner Brothers advertising and publicity, said in a statement that "controversial films raise a lot of questions and stimulate a lot of debate," and " we endorse and continue to endorse the right of responsible film makers to make their ideas heard and are proud to be a part of such an outstanding motion picture."

Film executives and movie makers have responded with uncertainty about the film. In the past numerous critically acclaimed films based on fact, like *Gandhi* or *Lawrence of Arabia* or *All the President's Men*, have altered fact in shaping a coherent drama. But the historical basis of the story remained intact. And few major films have, like *JFK* involved such a divergence of opinion from the official record.

Dawn Steel, a former president of Columbia Pictures, said: "An artist paints a picture the way he or she sees it. Film makers are artists. But when it comes to historical accuracy there may be a moral question here. I don't know what the answer to this is. We're making fiction here, we're not making a documentary. A movie can't be judged by the same standards that journalists judge a newspaper story. It's Oliver Stone's vision. It's called freedom of speech."

Frank Price, a motion picture executive who was also formerly a president of Columbia Pictures, said: "I don't think you as a studio have to be in agreement with the statement the artist is making. You're just backing the artist. But if a statement is one you find so unacceptable, that's where the dividing line comes. Here you're dealing with a respected film maker and you certainly give him every benefit of the doubt. Let's face it; everyone know's it's only a movie. He has actors and there's a premise. If you start to censor people's political point of view it's a real swamp."

TAKING A VIEW

In defense of Mr. Stone, Bert Fields, one of the most powerful entertainment lawyers in Los Angeles, whose law firm represents the director, said: "If you are doing what purports to be a book or film about history, it's hardly rare for an author or film maker to take a position. Look at *Richard III*. There was a violent controversy between those who believed Richard was a tyrant who murdered his two nephews. And those who think he was a wonderful king. Shakespeare represented one view, the view that was acceptable to his Queen. Nobody faulted Shakespeare. One has a right to take a view and present it as a fact."

But several studio chiefs, who would speak only on condition of anonymity, said they were disturbed by the way Warner Brothers was dealing with the film. "There is a difference between Oliver Stone presenting the truth, and the studio presenting this as truth; it's a fine line but, its there and the studio has made no differentiation," said the head of one major studio. "In this case they're not presenting it as Oliver Stone's version of the truth, as one man daring to tell his version, or something like that. They're saying, this movie is the truth. It's not irresponsible to make the movie, it's irresponsible to say, this is the truth."

Because the film deals with one of the most traumatic moments of United States History—the Kennedy assassination—some producers say the studio bears a special responsibility in releasing a movie that makes such sweeping allegations.

"The First Amendment, which is often cited in these circumstances, has nothing to do with the relationship of the studio and the film maker," said Thomas Baer, a movie producer and formerly a United States Attorney in Manhattan who was appointed by Robert F. Kennedy, then Attorney General. "It relates only to the relationship between the government and individuals. Accordingly, there is greater opportunity for studios to control film makers than there is for the government to control citizens. In this particular instance, since a living family's nightmare and a nation's torment are perceived by one person's skewed imagination, I would have hoped more control would have been exercised."

Warner Brothers strongly defended its decision to produce the film. In its statement, the studio said in part:

"Warner Brothers takes great pride in its history of presenting serious issue-oriented drama over the years, including *All the President's Men, The Killing Fields, Guilty by Suspicion* and the upcoming *Malcolm X.*"

"We accept that controversial films raise a lot of questions and stimulate a lot of debate. We believe debate is healthy. One of the most important foundations of our country is its defense of the right to free speech." Warner Brothers added that the movie "is a suspense drama that will cause audiences everywhere to ask fundamental questions about American institutions and the role that private and public citizens play in history.

"We endorse and will always continue to endorse the right of responsible film makers to make their ideas heard and we are proud to be a part of such an outstanding motion picture."

NEW YORK NEWSDAY

SWITCHING CHANNELS ON JFK MEMORIES

Jimmy Breslin

Television has burned the memory out of most of the populace, leaving them blank and embarrassed when asked to recall specifics of the times in which they lived. Those born after 1963 not only are without recall, but they also have so little to believe in that they look to horoscopes or to movies for truth. There is one movie out now, *JFK*, which is highly entertaining, and yet is a complete fake and a fraud. Of course it will be believed by many, and without the slightest whisper of warning, because they have no ideal of what has happened in the last 30 or 40 years.

Therefore, I today offer my recollections of the times in which President John F. Kennedy was shot in Dallas.

My memory, and it is a very good one, too, begins a couple of years before the assassination, with the great entertainment booking agent, the late Joe Glaser. He had at this time such acts as Barbra Streisand, Louis Armstrong and Ella Fitzgerald. Joe had a raspy voice, which was at its best with profanities. He had a sharp nose and gray hair slicked straight back. He wore expensive clothes and white socks that sagged. In his office on West 57th Street this day was a man in a dark suit who held a hat in his hand. He was balding, chubby and his face was pasty.

Joe said to me, "Here, say hello to my dear friend, Jack Ruby."

Ruby was from Dallas, Texas, where he owned a strip joint one flight up from a desolate street.

"Jack, I want you to see something," Joe said. He jumped up. Ruby and I followed Glaser through offices and to the mail room, which has a new Pitney Bowes stamp machine.

"This is the greatest stamp machine in the world," Joe said. "Nobody has one like it. They just built it. It does everything. It even seals the envelopes."

He went back to his desk, and began licking envelopes. He then licked loose stamps and punched them onto the envelopes. He took a stack of letters and sat on them like an old hen.

"Why are you doing it like that?" Jack Ruby asked.

"Because I don't use a stamp machine," Joe said.

"Joe, I'm rebuilding my whole joint," Jack Ruby said to Glaser.

"Great!"

"It's going to seat a thousand. I got to open big. I need Louis."

"You got him!" Joe Glaser flicked a switch. "Miss Church! Get me Louis right away."

Soon, onto the speaker comes the voice of Louis Armstrong. "Daddy, daddy, I love you," Louis says.

"Louis. I got Jack Ruby here. Jack Ruby from Dallas.:

Silence indicated that Louis Armstrong would not know Jack Ruby if he got hit with him. Joe Glaser fills the silence immediately. "Jack, as you know, is one of the dearest friends I have. The dearest! Jack is opening the biggest effin' place in the whole effin' world and we're goin' in and open it up for him."

"Oh, that's wonderful," Louis Armstrong said.

Jack Ruby, almost sobbing, yelled into the speaker, "Louis, how can I ever thank you?"

"By paying my daddy."

"I'll pay anything," Jack Ruby said.

Louis Armstrong's thrilling chuckle came over the speaker. "That's great." He called to Joe Glaser. "Daddy, since we're talkin', send me five thousand dollars."

Then Jack Ruby went back to Dallas and of course nobody heard from him.

Until the next year, when Jack Ruby again came into Joe Glaser's office. He said he was opening this huge new place in Dallas. "I want to open with Ella."

"You got her!" Joe Glaser shouted. "Miss Church. Get Ella on the phone."

Soon, on the loud speaker, came the voice of Ella Fitzgerald.

"Ella, I got Jack Ruby here."

"You got who?"

"Jack Ruby! What's our dearest friend from Dallas. Jack's opening the world's biggest nightclub in Dallas ... "

The next year, when Jack Ruby came up, he asked for Lionel Hampton.

So you now have a look at Jack Ruby as he actually was. Therefore, we go to Nov. 22, 1963 in Dallas. It is evening, and the hallway of the Dallas Police Headquarters is packed. Suddenly, a door opens and into the television lights, and they were still relatively new at this time and thus even more irresistible than they are now, comes a guy wearing a cowboy hat. He is handcuffed to this sallow-faced guy in a checked, short-sleeved shirt. Lee Harvey Oswald. Another Dallas detective, handcuffed to Oswald's other hand, follows. The crowd surges. I wind up with my chest against Oswald's. The detectives stand with Oswald in the hallway just long enough to have all those cameras on them. Then they push through the crowd and enter another office.

I believe it was Henry Machirella of *The New York Daily News* who said, "They are going to get this guy killed." I say I think it was Henry, because there were so many others saying the same thing. That was plain common sense and not some deep conspiracy.

On Sunday morning, I flew to Washington for Kennedy's funeral. In the middle of the flight it was announced that Oswald had been shot dead as he was coming out of the Dallas police station. When I got to Washington, I sat in my room in the Willard Hotel and watched rerun after rerun of Jack Ruby coming up the driveway and jamming the gun into Oswald's stomach and killing him.

A week or so later, when I got back to New York, there were messages from Joe

Glaser. And late one afternoon I went up to see him.

"How do you like what that crazy Jack did?" he said. When I asked Joe for the reason, he said. "Are you an effin' blind man? You saw the guy yourself. He had the whole sky in his head. He figured that if he shot this rat, Oswald, then he'd be the greatest patriot you ever seen. Nathan Hale! Patrick Henry! Jack Ruby!"

"And nobody put him up to it?" I asked.

"How effin' crazy are you? If somebody put him up to it, that means they got Jack Ruby, a complete effin' imbecile, sitting in a prison cell with their life in his hands. He says one word and everybody's gone. No, he got nobody to give up. He done it all by himself because he lives in illusion. Do you know what he thinks right now? That he's a bigger effin' hero in Texas than Davey Crockett."

And that is my story about Jack Ruby, who conspired with only himself to try to become a beloved American.

© Copyright 1991, Newsday. Reprinted by permission of the Los Angeles Times Syndicate International.

DECEMBER 24, 1991

LOS ANGELES TIMES

FACTS KNIT THE SINGLE-BULLET THEORY

Kenneth Klein

The new Oliver Stone movie, *JFK*, might lead moviegoers to suspect the conclusions of the Warren Commission, which investigated the assassination of President Kennedy. But the commission's findings have stood the tests of forensic analysis.

In September, 1976, the House of Representatives established the Select Committee on Assassinations to investigate the deaths of President John F. Kennedy and Martin Luther King Jr. In early 1977, I resigned as an assistant district attorney in New York County, assigned to investigate and try homicide cases, and accepted the position of assistant deputy chief counsel for the committee. I spent the next two years investigating the Kennedy assassination.

When I first heard of the "single-bullet theory," I was very skeptical. How could a single bullet found on a stretcher in Parkland Hospital enter the upper back of President Kennedy, emerge from the front of his neck, then enter the back of Texas Gov. John Connally, emerge from his chest and then shatter a bone in Connally's right wrist and cause a superficial wound to his left thigh?

Since the validity of the Warren Commission's finding that Lee Harvey Oswald was the lone assassin rested firmly on the validity of the single-bullet theory, the staff members of the select committee would have been thrilled to have disproved it. To have done so would surely have led to fame and fortune. Only one thing prevented us from doing so—the evidence.

First, the committee formed a panel of top forensic pathologists. These men had performed tens of thousands of autopsies and were experts at determining points of entry and the trajectories of bullets as they passed through human bodies. The panel concluded that two bullets struck the President from the rear. The panel also noted, and the committee found very significant, the ovoid shape of the wound in the governor's back. Such a wound indicates that the bullet had begun to tumble or yaw before entering. An ovoid wound is characteristic of one caused by a bullet that has passed through or glanced off an intervening object.

Second, the committee performed a trajectory analysis of the shots fired. We used the expertise of the forensic pathologists, acoustical and photographic analysts and an engineer from the National Aeronautics and Space Administration who plotted the trajectories. By coordinating the data from these experts, the analysis yielded three circles within which all shots originated. The southeast corner window of the Texas School Book Depository—the window from which the Warren Commission concluded that the single bullet was fired along with two other shots—was inside each of these circles.

Third, the committee considered the fact that the Zapruder "home movie" shows Kennedy's head moving backward after being hit. Of course, there are no other motion pictures of people being shot that could have been used for comparison purposes. Instead, the committee consulted an expert on gunshot wounds who determined that nerve damage from a bullet entering the President's head could have caused his back muscles to tighten, which, in turn, could have caused his head to move toward the rear. While such testimony was not considered decisive, it did lead the committee to conclude that the rearward movement of the President's head was not inconsistent with a bullet striking from the rear.

But the firearms evidence was the most important. The rifle found on the sixth floor of the Texas School Book Depository was analyzed by an independent panel of ballistics experts chosen by the committee. It was determined that the bullet found on a stretcher at the Parkland Hospital had been fired from the rifle recovered from the depository.

A remaining issue was determining whether the bullet found on the stretcher was the source of the bullet fragments taken from Connally's wrist. In making the determination, the committee had the benefit of neutron-activation analysis, a highly precise test that was not in existence at the time of the Warren Commission.

The essence of neutron-activation analysis is that every bullet has a unique composition. Using this analysis, it is possible to analyze precisely the composition of a bullet and a bullet fragment to determine whether the fragment came from the bullet. The analysis showed that it is highly likely that the bullet found on the stretcher was the one that passed through Connally's wrist, leaving tiny fragments behind.

That the single-bullet theory was not only a plausible explanation but, in fact, was the only reasonable explanation for the wounds suffered by President Kennedy and Gov. Connally is supported by the facts. The bullet that hit the President and the governor came from the rear; the trajectory of the bullet leads back to the Texas School Book Depository; the bullet was fired from a rifle found on the sixth floor of the depository; the bullet had been deflected before entering Connally's back, and the fragments in Connally's wrist came from the bullet found on the stretcher in Parkland Hospital.

Goodby fame. Goodby fortune.

Kenneth Klein is an attorney in Los Angeles.

Reprinted by permission of the author.

DECEMBER 25, 1991

THE NEW YORK TIMES

HISTORY BY DEFAULT: THE BLAME TRANSCENDS OLIVER STONE

Brent Staples

John F. Kennedy's assassination was the most traumatic spectacle of the television age, and because many still doubt that Lee Harvey Oswald acted alone, it remains an open-ended trauma. But even that doubt cannot account for all the criticism of the movie *JFK*, Oliver Stone's unpersuasive attempt to prove that Government conspirators arranged the assassination.

The criticism began while the movie was still being filmed. Political journalists have since tried to blow it off the screen. The critics even include former President Gerald R. Ford, a member of the Warren Commission.

This is more than a simple conflict between two versions of a historical event. The rancor over *JFK* arises from the realization that historical lies are nearly impossible to correct once movies and television have given them credibility.

The critics have two complaints: that the movie suppresses information well known to students of recent history, and that *JFK* is fiction so cunningly disguised that audiences will accept it as fact. The first speaks to simple misrepresentation. But the second describes a process—the fictionalization of fact—that took a quantum leap with television docudramas.

Mr. Stone does deserve a rhetorical thrashing for the film. His evidence for a Government conspiracy contains one factual misstatement after another. Perhaps the most notable misrepresentation is the movie's view of Jim Garrison, the New Orleans District Attorney in 1967 who dreamed up conspiracy charges against a retired businessman, Clay Shaw. Mr. Garrison was a malevolent force, not theFrank Capra good guy he's made out to be.

311

But Mr. Stone is just one of many who practice spurious history. Another is Alan Parker, whose film *Mississippi Burning*, based on the Ku Klux Klan's murder of three civil rights workers, was as falsified as *JFK*. In fact, the murders were solved thanks to a $30,000 bribe; in the film, a townswoman informs on her husband after an attack of conscience. In life, J. Edgar Hoover's FBI was hostile to the civil rights movement; the film makes FBI agents its heroes.

Mr. Stone is the most skilled player of this game. His films *Born on the Fourth of July* (about Vietnam), *The Doors* (the early rock era), and now *JFK* treat subjects that have strong emotions and much documentary film attached to them. His movies resemble wax museums in the way they strive to replicate their characters physically. Charged images lend power to his version of the story; bias is easily masked as history.

Not long ago, a film maker who took this kind of latitude would have changed names or added some kind of disclaimer. Today that kind of truthfulness seems quaint. Film makers no longer feel obliged even to acknowledge what they are doing.

The children of the video age get their information more from images than from words. They tend to believe uncritically what they see. They'll swallow *JFK* whole. Society cannot police art for inaccuracies; film makers are free to take whatever liberties they wish. But society can denounce bogus history—and study honest history. That means reading, critically. Otherwise Hollywood becomes the culture's historian by default.

THE LOS ANGELES TIMES

SUPPRESSION OF THE FACTS GRANTS STONE A BROAD BRUSH

Alan M. Dershowitz

Oliver Stone's new film, *JFK*, is the inevitable result of more than a quarter of a century of governmental cover-up of the facts surrounding the assassination of President John F. Kennedy. Stone takes full literary license not so much with the facts as we know them, but rather with the facts that have been kept from us by questionable claims of national security.

Stone's artistic rendition encourages the viewer to speculate wildly about a missive conspiracy—he calls it a *coup d'état*—involving the C.I.A., the FBI, the military and even Lyndon Johnson. In the mind of Stone's unlikely hero, then New Orleans Dist. Atty. Jim Garrison, there are connections among the assassinations of Robert Kennedy, Martin Luther King Jr. and John F. Kennedy. The invisible hand of the "military-industrial complex" is at work, violently preempting any change that might put an end to the profitable wars that fuel the defense industry. Six Presidents—two Democrats and four Republicans—have been part of the cover-up, since none has demanded disclosure of the classified files.

It's all a bit too politically correct and conspiratorial for my tastes, but it is precisely what is to be expected when the governments set out on a deliberate policy of keeping its citizens from making up their own minds on the basis of all the available facts.

It is now beyond dispute that the Warren Commission was denied crucial information by the C.I.A. and other intelligence agencies during its "investigation." Even Prof. John Hart Ely of Stanford University's law school—who was a lawyer with the commission and a law clerk to Chief Justice Earl Warren—now has some doubts about whether the commission was misled by intelligence agencies. Ely has acknowledged that the commission lacked independent investigative resources and thus was compelled to rely on the government's investigative agencies, namely the FBI, C.I.A. and military intelligence. He points of that in 1964 "one had to be a genuine radical" to believe that these agencies might be withholding significant information from the commission. Today—after Watergate, Iran-Contra and disclosures about J. Edgar Hoover's secret files—it would take a person of unusual naivete to ignore that possibility.

Ely still believes that the commission's conclusions were probably right. But he is not as confident as he was in 1964. If one discounts the information provided by government intelligence agencies and relies only on independently confirmable facts, the case for the commission's conclusions is hardly more compelling than some kind of conspiracy theory.

There are so many unexplained facts, such as acoustical and ballistics evidence, that are consistent with the presence of a second assassin. The deaths of so many witnesses (mostly by assassination and "accident") are also significant. Most important is the continued refusal of the intelligence agencies to declassify relevant information that can pose no plausible danger to our national security almost 30 years after the Kennedy assassination. Even the congressional committee that raised questions about some of the Warren Commission's conclusions has closed some of its files until well into the 21st century, when most of us who were alive when Kennedy was killed will be long gone. There is no excuse for such secrecy.

I can imagine how the suppressed material could be embarrassing to those who have suppressed it. I can even imagine how it could destroy reputations. But I cannot imagine how it could endanger the national security of the strongest nation in the world, especially since the Cold War is over.

The time has come to make full disclosure, to let the chips fall where they may and finally to learn as much of the truth as possible from the stale and incomplete evidence that today remains shrouded by a veil of secrecy.

The results of full disclosure may be disappointing. The suppressed evidence may not definitively resolve the "lone gunman" versus "small conspiracy" versus "massive conspiracy" dispute. It may simply provide more grist for the various conspiratorial mills. But we the people have the right to make up our own minds, on the basis of all the available evidence, about one of the most transforming events in American history.

No one who favors continued suppression of any available information about the murder of John Kennedy has the standing to criticize Oliver Stone's *JFK*. Until history comes forward with facts, art is entitled to paint with a broad brush. The best, indeed the only, answer to Stone's soft theories are hard facts. Those hard facts—at least those that have survived a quarter of a century of suppression—are in classified government files. If *JFK* contributes to the declassification of these suppressed facts, then Oliver Stone will deserve an Oscar for history as well as for cinematography.

Alan M. Dershowitz is a professor of law at Harvard University.

CHICAGO TRIBUNE

EDITORIAL

In the climactic scene of Oliver Stone's *JFK*, New Orleans District Atty. Jim Garrison, played by Kevin Costner, is depicted summing up his foredoomed conspiracy case for the jury.

The summation is more oration than argument, full of anguish and anger over the "conspiracy" that, in Garrison/Stone's view, resulted in the murder of President John F. Kennedy and turned the country away from peace and decency to war and greed.

In a revealing passage, Garrison/Stone compares America at that moment (late 1968, early 1969) to Hamlet, agonized by the murder of his father the king (Kennedy) and haunted by the presence on the father's throne of the usurper-murderers.

Stone, it seems safe to say, intended the Garrison peroration to clinch his case to America in 1991 that Kennedy was the victim of a right-wing *coup*, a conspiracy hatched by a military-industrial complex fearful that he was about to cut off their mother's milk—money—and end their adventure in Vietnam.

What the Garrison speech actually does, however, is make one wonder how firm was the man's purchase on reality. To listen to Costner/Garrison, virtually nobody since Nov. 22, 1963, had died of natural causes. Either they were poisoned or shot or otherwise done away with by "them," all to the end of keeping the conspiracy concealed and themselves in power.

What this entire, relentlessly didactic and polemical movie does is make one wonder about Oliver Stone. To some observers, there is nothing to wonder about. In their view, Stone's entire cinematic oeuvre—*Platoon*, *Wall Street*, *Born on the Fourth of July* and the rest—have been marked by dishonest renderings of history, simplistic moral constructs and a kind of puerile fatuousness about the 1960s.

Even without going that far, *JFK* gives cause to question this very gifted moviemaker's view of the world. Does he, at this late date, still buy the image of John Kennedy as incorruptible and the Kennedy administration as Camelot? Does he really believe that nation-as-Hamlet business?

JFK suggests he does, and that in a sense Stone has never aged, emotionally, beyond Nov. 22, 1963. Evil entered the world that day, imported by "them," and nothing has been right since.

The danger is that Stone's film and the pseudo-history it so effectively portrays will become the popularly accepted version. After all, what can scholarship avail against Kevin Costner, Sissy Spacek, Donald Sutherland, et al., on the big screen with Dolby stereo? What if, for example, there *was* a conspiracy, but not the one that Garrison/Stone identified?

That's why it is time that the documents and all the physical evidence from the Kennedy assassination—pictures, films, tissue samples and the rest—be made public and available for examination.

Two concerns have always been advanced for keeping these things secret until well into the next century: the sensibilities of the Kennedy family and fear that American national security, vis-à-vis the Soviet Union, might somehow be harmed.

Neither of those ought to be an obstacle now, if they ever should have been. If our history since Nov. 22, 1963, demonstrates anything, it is the cleansing effect of public exposure and the corrosive effect—as in *JFK*—of secrecy.

DECEMBER 26, 1991

NEW YORK NEWSDAY

STUDENTS SEEK THE TRUTH IN THE JFK CASE

John Hanc

Thursday, Oliver Stone dedicated *JFK* to "the young, in whose spirit the search for truth moves on."

But in a crowded pub in Greenvale on Monday night, the young sounded awfully restless. Not to mention disturbed, confused, angry, cynical, and yes, moved. About the movie, which they'd all seen by a prior arrangement with this newspaper. About the truth surrounding an event that took place nearly a decade before most of them had even been born. About the government, the military, the media ... all of which, they agree with Jim Garrison and Stone, were involved in a massive cover-up.

The real story, many of them believe, was never told to the American public. And the notion for having to wait until she's middle-aged to see the sealed government documents that may provide some answers doesn't sit well with 21-year-old Abby Archdeacon.

"Why should I have to wait until 2039 or whenever it is to find out the truth?" asked Archdeacon, a senior at the nearby New York Institute of Technology. "Why can't something be done?"

"Something was done," contended Frank Heller, 22, of Farmingdale. "They made a movie."

"But does it have to take this long to find out the truth?" asked Samantha Sedita, a college senior from Beechurst, Queens. "I could see two or three years. But thirty?"

"This is real life," chided 24-year-old Henry Chin-Hong from Brooklyn. "There were too many people, too many players involved [in the assassination]—and so they'll continue to teach it in a way that doesn't offend. It's like how they teach the history of the Third Reich to students in Germany ... they have to tread lightly."

How do they teach the assassination in schools?

"I don't get into it in any great detail," said Steve Waldman, a veteran high school studies teacher in West Islip. Like many others, Waldman said, he presents the official version and then touches briefly on a few of the alternative theories, choosing not to get mired in the maddening, often contradictory evidence of the conspiracy theories. "I do think kids will want to know the truth," he admits. "And I don't think anyone can give it to them."

Enter Oliver Stone.

"I was just so taken by this movie," said Sedita. "Because I'm sick of this government. It's such a joke. Like, we elect these people ... "

"Come on, we don't really elect anybody," said Jay Gershon, 22, of Dix Hills. "We're brought up to believe this is the land of the free and all that ... and they're kicking our teeth out."

"History was definitely altered," said Rob Lupo, 20, of Old Bethpage.

"I knew nothing about this," added Gershon. "I was dumfounded by the movie. It was mind-blowing."

Michael Delli Carpini, an assistant professor of political science at Barnard College, is pleased to hear students getting so riled up, so involved with the sins and omissions of their history books. He just wishes they'd chosen a different page to rip out and stomp on. "It's good for students to question these assumptions," He said. "But I'd have preferred to use a different event to teach them that lesson, whether it's what happened in Nicaragua, Chile, or event the FBI attempts to subvert the Black Panthers in the U.S."

As for the Kennedy assassination, he teaches in his American government classes that it was "basically an open and shut case" that Oswald acted alone. "When all the smoke clears, I guess I'm convinced that's what it was," said Delli Carpini, who had not yet seen the movie.

After sitting through Stone's version of the truth, many of the students had reached the opposite conclusion. "I believe what I saw," said Sedita. "I totally believe it."

"I always thought [Lee Harvey] Oswald was just a nut and another nut shot him," said Joe Zaso, 21, of Manhasset Hills. "That's basically what I was taught. But now I'm convinced it was a plot."

Of course, not all the students were ready to accept *JFK* as the last word. "I believe that here were definitely—no, I want to be a lawyer, so I'd better say 'most likely'—shots coming from the grassy knoll," said Julie Hyman, 20 a Barnard junior from Riverdale. "But [Garrison] went further ... a bit overboard. He didn't have the proof to incriminate everybody up to L.B.J. And the only proof Stone gives us is some guy coming out of the Lincoln Memorial and spilling the beans."

That character—the "Deep Throat" intelligence officer played by Donald Sutherland—talked about historical events. And so did the students, after watching the movie. Not just the Bay of Pigs, the Vietnam war and the killings of Martin Luther King and Robert F. Kennedy—all of which figured into the film—but the shootings of the Pope John Paul II and former President Ronald Reagan ("If Oswald was a patsy, why not Hinckley?" asked Lupo about John Hinckley Jr., the man who shot Reagan), the Iran-contra scandal and the untimely death of C.I.A. director William Casey, the invasion of Panama and President George Bush's past involvement with the C.I.A. and former Panamanian strongman Manuel Noriega, the S&L scandal, Desert Storm. Amidst the smoke and noise of the bar, all came under scrutiny; all could now be seen by this group of students as threads in a web of deceit, spun by sinister, omnipotent and anonymous individuals in the White House, the Pentagon, even the Time-Life Building.

Why, it was enough to make conspiracy theorists—those Zapruder film zealots who sounded so relevant in the '70s and so ridiculous in the '80s—glad to be alive and paranoid again in the '90s.

"I'm even worried about having my name used is this article," said Gershon. "Who knows who could be reading *Newsday*?"

Probably not William Kennedy Smith, who was also brought into the discussion: yes, even the acquittal of J.F.K's nephew in his rape case was further evidence of the same invisible network that took out his uncle. "Of course he was going to get off," said Heller, shaking his head.

Of course, what Heller and his friends were really talking about was the issue of power: how and by whom it's wielded in this country. And, perhaps more importantly, the need for average citizens to adopt the credo of a previous generation of college students: question authority.

"The lesson here," said Chin-Hong, "is not that you shouldn't trust your government at all ... but that you shouldn't follow it blindly."

John Hanc is a regular contributor to this newspaper.

Reprinted by permission of the author.

NEW YORK NEWSDAY

THE BLURRED VISION OF *JFK*

Oliver Stone's polemical version of the event of Nov. 22, 1963, has left some people wondering where truth ends and fiction begins. Other people don't wonder at all. A viewer's guide.

Steve Parks

"The key to the whole case is through the looking glass. Black is white. White is black."

In Oliver Stone's *JFK*, Kevin Costner as New Orleans District Attorney Jim Garrison uses those words to guide his staff through the conundrum of assassination evidence. They were searching for a peg on which to hang a conspiracy charge against Clay Shaw. They never found that peg, and Shaw, in a verdict that was delivered in less than an hour, was acquitted.

Unless you are a full-time student of assassination, you may find the torrent of evidence, witnesses and suspects crammed into *JFK* numbing and confusing. If you think you can't tell the players without a scorecard, here's a rundown of the key players and evidence in *JFK*:

THE EVIDENCE

◆ **The Zapruder Film:** The only reliable "witness" Garrison produced at the trial was a home movie. And Clay Shaw wasn't in it. Abraham Zapruder had purchased his 8-mm. Bell and Howell movie camera the day before President John F. Kennedy arrived in Dallas. He stood on top of a concrete pedestal overlooking Dealey Plaza, on what has become known as "the grassy knoll." His film establishes the time frame in which the shots were fired at the presidential limousine—5.6 seconds. It also suggests that the last shot was the fatal one. This color footage is shown repeatedly in *JFK*, at times in slow motion, and it is the authentic, undoctored Zapruder film.

◆ **The Magic Bullet Theory**: The so-called "magic bullet theory," as depicted accurately in the final courtroom scene in *JFK*, made it possible for the Warren Commission to conclude that there was only one gunman shooting at Kennedy. The problem for the Warren Commission was that it had too many bullets to account for and too short a time in which to fire them. Commission Counsel Arlen Specter, now a Republican senator from Pennsylvania, came up with a solution: His theory, which came to be accepted as fact by the Commission, claimed that the first shot that hit Kennedy also struck then-Texas Gov. John Connally, who was seated in front of Kennedy in the limousine. After striking Kennedy, the bullet is said to have entered Connally's body at the armpit, shattering a rib before exiting at the chest. It then hit Connally again, shattering his wristbone before exiting the arm and burrowing into his thigh. This virtually unscathed bullet was later recovered from a stretcher in Dallas' Parkland Hospital. No marksman has ever been able to duplicate the feat the Warren Commission ascribes to Oswald. Specter still defends his theory.

◆ **The Autopsy:** No one disputes that the autopsy of Kennedy was bungled, not even the doctors who performed it. The testimony of Dr. Pierre Finck as portrayed in the movie is accurate. The doctor admitted at the trial that he and the other two members of the autopsy team at the Naval Medical Center in Bethesda, Md., received "suggestions" from superior officers who looked over their shoulders. One of those suggestions was that the doctors should not probe the back wound to see if it went through the body and exited at the throat. Notes from the autopsy were destroyed by the team's leader, Cmdr. James Humes. Autopsy photographs shown in the movie appear to be authentic—black and white footage of the autopsy procedure is a re-enactment—but the most important piece of corroborating evidence—the president's brain—is missing. Oliver Stone did not make this up.

THE PLAYERS

◆ **Jim Garrison:** The district attorney who prosecuted the only trial ever conducted in the assassination of Kennedy, is known in New Orleans as the "Jolly Green Giant." As portrayed by Costner, Garrison is neither jolly nor a giant. But he does seem green. He's as naive as Jimmy Stewart in *Mr. Smith Goes to Washington*. Soft-spoken in his low-key intensity, Costner's Garrison is almost shy. The real Garrison is garrulous and audacious. He had the kind of gall that made it seem in character for him to claim he had "solved the assassination." Garrison may have been onto something, but he was bluffing. He knew he did not have a case against Clay Shaw. The trial was a fiasco and Garrison didn't even bother to show up in court for half the proceedings. Warren Report critics who flocked to Garrison when he was preparing for the trial abandoned him afterward, blaming him for discrediting all conspiracy theories with his overblown, unsupported claims that everybody from then-Vice President Lyndon Johnson to the NRA were in on the plot. Garrison plays Earl Warren in the movie.

◆ **Lee Harvey Oswald:** Stone is careful in his treatment of Oswald, played by Gary Oldman. Oswald rarely *says* anything in the movie that is not indisputably on the record, though he is shown in re-creations of various witnesses' stories. None of the film's information about Oswald's adult life is made up. Oswald did study Russian as a marine. He was assigned to Atsugi, a top-secret air base in Japan where American U2 pilots and ground personnel were trained. He left the Corps suddenly, claiming his mother was ill, and three days later boarded a ship in New Orleans bound for Europe. He showed up at the U.S. Embassy in Moscow and renounced his citizenship, and when the Soviets wouldn't accept him as a defector, he slashed his wrist. The Soviets let him stay, but shipped him off to Minsk where the KGB could more easily keep an eye on him. That's where he met and married Marina Prusakova. After about two years in the Soviet Union. Oswald asked to return to the United States with his Soviet-born wife. Despite his defection, despite the fact that Gary Powers' U2 flight was shot down shortly after Oswald showed up in Moscow, the defector was allowed to return home with no attempt to charge him with treason or any other crime. He settled in Dallas with his bride and their baby. Six months before the assassination, he left his family and moved to New Orleans, where he became involved with another set of characters.

◆ **Guy Banister**: Garrison's investigation of this former FBI agent led to a startling discovery about a couple of addresses. Banister, a fanatic racist and anticommunist played in *JFK* by Ed Asner, was working as a private investigator in New Orleans. He also ran guns for Cuban exiles who were training in Louisiana for another invasion of their homeland. Banister's office was located at 531 Lafayette Pl. When he arrived in New Orleans, Oswald opened the "headquarters" of the Fair Play for Cuba Committee at 544 Camp St. That sounds like a different address, but 544 Camp St. is the side entrance to 531 Lafayette. Oswald was the only member of the pro-Castro committee, and the Fair Play for Cuba leaflets he handed out were stored in Banister's office. If you look quickly at the news conference in *JFK*, just after the Dallas police have arrested Oswald, you'll see a man in the back of the room correcting a reporter who asks if Oswald is a member of the "Free Cuba" committee. "That's Fair Play for Cuba," the guy says. That guy—in real life and as represented in the film—was Jack Ruby.

◆ **David Ferrie**: If anything, Joe Pesci's manic portrayal of David Ferrie is understated. Ferrie had a rare disease that caused his hair to fall out, which accounts for the ridiculous wig and mismatched, painted-on eyebrows. He kept lab mice in his apartment, saying he was searching for a cure to cancer. He was also a priest in his self-proclaimed Catholic Church of North America. But he made a living as a pilot and his cause, like Banister's was arming the anti-Castro brigades training in the United States. And, like Shaw, Ferrie was homosexual. His death may have been untimely and suspicious, but natural causes were never ruled out. Ferrie was fingered by Garrison as the escape pilot for the team of shooters who killed Kennedy.

◆ **Clay Shaw**: Clay Shaw died shortly after being acquitted of conspiracy charges in 1969. Despite the assertions Garrison makes in the film, it was never established whether Shaw used the alias Clay or Clem Bertrand. In real life, Dean Andrews, the jive-talking witness played by John Candy in *JFK* described a Bertrand who was much younger and shorter than Clay Shaw. And it was never established whether Shaw was a C.I.A. employee, although Victor Marchetti, a former executive assistant to the director, says he was told that Shaw worked for the agency. Of course, this would not have made Shaw a conspirator anymore than his homosexuality or taste for fine food. Garrison's best evidence against Shaw was a series of witnesses from the small town of Clinton, La., who testified convincingly that they saw Oswald, Ferrie and Shaw together—these witnesses aren't in the film. Others have said the third man was Guy Banister, who resembled Shaw.

◆ **Willie O'Keefe:** This is one of the few fictionalized characters in *JFK*. Played by Kevin Bacon, he is a composite of three homosexual witnesses who placed Clay Shaw in the company of David Ferrie and Lee Harvey Oswald. O'Keefe's vivid film testimony recalling a conversation in which the three of them plot to kill the president is based on the story of Garrison's real-life star witness, Perry Raymond Russo. That Russo was his best witness to the conspiracy charge shows how weak Garrison's case was: Russo could not recall the conversation except under hypnosis.

◆ **Mr. X:** Played disarmingly by Donald Sutherland, Mr. X is another composite character. His meeting with Garrison on a park bench in Washington is fiction. The plot he propounds, however, is similar to one Garrison heard from former C.I.A. operative Richard Case Nagell. The film's Mr. X is more closely related to Fletcher Prouty, a former aide to the Joint Chiefs of Staff who Stone, not Garrison, talked to. Prouty has repeated the same scenario to many investigators and journalists. Prouty/Mr. X says he read a thorough account of Oswald's background in a New Zealand newspaper, just four hours after the assassination. News of Oswald's past went out on various wire services not long after his arrest, barely an hour after the shooting. Reporters at the time said the Dallas police made Oswald's profile available almost immediately. How did the cops get this information so quickly? Conspiracy investigators posit it came from a family connection. Gen. Charles Caball was deputy director of the C.I.A. at the time. His brother, Earl, then the mayor of Dallas, was in the fatal motorcade.

DECEMBER 26, 1991

NEW YORK NEWSDAY

THE MANY THEORIES OF A JOLLY GREEN GIANT

Michael Dorman

Inside the majestic old New Orleans courtroom, with its oak benches and solemn air, a prospective state witness showed up for the big trial wearing a toga. Asked by a court officer to identify himself, he replied: "Julius Caesar."

It was decided the interests of Justice would best be served by sparing the jury his testimony. But others of his ilk did testify, among them the prosecution witness who claimed he was being victimized by some sort of communist conspiracy. He testified that at least 50 or 60 people had hypnotized him against his will. And how, a defense lawyer asked, did he know he was being hypnotized? "When someone tries to get your attention—get your eye—that's a clue right off."

There was also the prosecution witness who testified he fingerprinted his daughter each time she came home from school so he could be sure a spy hadn't assumed her identity.

Such was the character of the case—to use the word charitably—assembled in 1969 by District Attorney Jim Garrison in his benighted attempt to convict businessman Clay Shaw of taking part in a conspiracy to assassinate President John F. Kennedy.

In those days, Garrison was known as the Jolly Green Giant. It was a curious appellation. He wasn't jolly. He wasn't Green. And, although he stood 6-foot-7, he was not a giant—least of all a legal giant.

To me, after watching Garrison in and out of the courtroom, he was simply a charlatan. At the very outset of his investigation, Garrison declared: "The key to the whole case is through the looking glass. Black is white. White is Black."

On that point, at least, he was consistent. If you pointed out a glaring failure of logic in a central element of his supposed case, he would puff slowly on his pipe, look you straight in the eye and tell you that you merely proved the truth of his theory. By the next day, he would have another theory.

Garrison could never seem to decide, for example, who was behind the conspiracy. First it was Shaw and a group of Cuban exiles. Then it was a band of former C.I.A. agents. Then it was the Dallas police. Then it was Texas oil barons. Then it was the right-wing Minutemen. Then it was White Russian emigres. Then it was munitions dealers. Then it was the Dallas establishment. Then it was "the invisible Nazi substructure." Then it was ...

He could never decide, either, how many gunmen there had been or where they had been positioned. At various times, he claimed assassins had fired from the Texas School Book Depository, from another building nearby, from the celebrated grassy knoll overlooking Kennedy's motorcade route, from some bushes, from behind a picket fence, and from a storm drain. In the end, Garrison, contended no fewer than 18 persons were involved in the assassination—at least three riflemen and perhaps more, a pair of coordinators with two-way radios, two spotters to distract a strategically placed police officer, a half-dozen members of the Dallas police homicide squad and a handful of others to handle training and logistics.

Yet, by his own account, he never made any attempt to identify or prosecute the actual assassins. "They all have nom de plumes," he said as if that explained it.

About the only one Garrison did *not* accuse of plotting the assassination was a man others think should have been his likeliest target: Carlos Marcello, the southern Mafia boss from Garrison's own hometown who has been described as the most powerful man in Louisiana. Others, including members of the House Assassinations Committee, have connected Marcello with purported mob plots to kill Kennedy. But Garrison said the mob was a "false sponsor"—set up in advance by the real plotters of the assassination to divert attention from themselves. he described Marcello as a "respectable businessman."

As for Clay Shaw, the former director of the New Orleans International Trade Mart—he first captured Garrison's attention when a witness named Dean Andrews reported that a homosexual calling himself Clay Bertrand had sought a lawyer immediately after the assassination to represent Lee Harvey Oswald. Andrews described Bertrand as a "boy," under 5-foot-8, with sandy hair. Shaw was past 50, stood 6-foot-4 and had white hair. Still, Garrison concluded that Shaw was Bertrand. After all, his first name *was* Clay and he *was* a homosexual.

From that, Garrison spun his entire web. When Andrews later said his whole Betrand story had been a hoax, Garrison insisted that must prove the story was true. Black was white and white was black.

Perhaps the most telling commentary on Garrison comes in an account once given men by the late Merriman Smith, the White House correspondent for United Press who covered every president from Roosevelt to Nixon. Smith won a Pulitzer Prize for his coverage of the Kennedy assassination and later was sent to New Orleans to write an assessment of Garrison and his allegations. Smith found himself at 3 o'clock one morning in the DA's home—drinking some weird concoction of Garrison's composed of distilled spirits and root beer.

At the time, Garrison was posing still another theory: that a rifleman had popped up from a manhole along the motorcade route, fired the fatal shot, then fled through the Dallas sewer system to another manhole. There, a truck was waiting to pick him up for the getaway. All of this ignored the routine Secret Service practice of sealing the manholes along presidential motorcade routes.

By Smith's account, Garrison was outlining the manhole theory when he dramatically reach into an attache case and whipped out a photograph. The image was fuzzy, but Smith could make out the shape of a truck.

"Are you telling me this is the truck?" he asked.

"Who's gonna say any different?" he said Garrison replied.

Then Garrison pulled out another picture—an equally fuzzy image of a rifle.

"Are you telling me this is the gun?" Smith asked.

"Who's gonna say any different?" Garrison repeated.

Michael Dorman, now a freelance writer, covered the Kennedy assassination for Newsday. In 1969, researching a magazine article, he went to New Orleans for the trial of Clay Shaw.

Reprinted by permission of the author.

OLIVER'S TWIST

Bill Marvel

The discussions and debates start even before the final credits roll. They spill over into the parking lot, and probably continue long into the night in kitchens and bedrooms all over the city.

Lone gunman or conspiracy? Mafia or C.I.A. or L.B.J.?

Oliver Stone's powerful and controversial film *JFK* has come to the town where it all began 28 years ago. And with predictable results.

At a packed screening at NorthPark 1 and 2 Cinema Sunday evening, several patrons stalked out, evidently offended as the circles of the alleged conspiracy widened to take in the FBI, C.I.A., Pentagon, Dallas police and even Lyndon Johnson.

The film centers upon the figure of New Orleans District Attorney Jim Garrison (Kevin Costner), the only prosecutor to ever bring anyone to trial in connection with the assasination, and upon the late Clay Shaw, the homosexual businessman who some believe was Mr. Garrison's victim and others believe was at the center of the alleged conspiracy.

Naturally, much debate about the film concerns its portrayal of Jim Garrison and the prosecution of Clay Shaw. We asked four students of the Kennedy assassination—call them assassinationologists—to watch *JFK* and then share some of their impressions and objections. Their remarks have been edited.

The four:

Dave Perry, an insurance company executive, became curious about the Kennedy assassination while in college. He was studying conspiracy rumors surrounding another assassination, that of Abraham Lincoln. In the late 1970s, he began investigating the Kennedy assassination in earnest. Five years ago, when his company transferred him to its Dallas office, he began making regular visits to the Dallas County Records Building and the Dallas Public Library.

Larry Sutherland is a free-lance journalist and former college teacher who has written articles about the assassination. He is the only panelist who leans—with some reservations—toward the lone-gunman theory.

Gary Shaw, a veteran student of the assassination, says he used to hang out at Jack Ruby's Carousel Club. He was convinced the day he watched on television as Ruby gunned down Lee Harvey Oswald that there was a sinister plot behind the Kennedy assassination. He is co-founder of the J.F.K. Assassination Information

Center here in Dallas.

Carl Henry, who teaches literature, creative writing and film at Dallas Baptist Academy, has been gathering assassination material ever since he picked up a copy of the *Atlanta Journal-Constitution* the afternoon of Nov. 22, 1963. By the time he was 14, he had managed to read his way through the entire twenty-six volume Warren Commission report, an experience that left him convinced that the report is filled with "inconsistencies and inaccuracies." He is a consultant to The Sixth Floor exhibit in the former Texas School Book Depository. He believes the Mafia played a prominent role in the assassination.

They were asked: Are there any serious errors in the film?

LARRY SUTHERLAND: One—his name is Jim Garrison. That is the most overt lie in the movie. He (Mr. Garrison) is portrayed essentially as a hero, and I don't think the historical record vindicates him in any way.

CARL HENRY: I think it's what was not shown in the film that was interesting. I counted the number of times the terms Mafia or mob were used in the film, and I came up with six. When we think about the assassination, there is a web of relationships, and one strand of that web was left out.

The original problem I had with the film is when you see Jim Garrison flying with Louisiana Sen. Russell Long, and they look out and see Washington, D.C. My understanding is that they were going between New Orleans and New York when that occurred, and there were three men on that trip. So that's when little alarm bells started going off in my head and I started watching it more carefully.

DAVID PERRY: You have to give him (Oliver Stone) a little poetic license here, though.

CARL HENRY: I was looking for poetic license, which I'm willing to grant. But I think that when you're dealing with this subject matter, people are going to be looking for things like that, and the fine details are what's really going to tell.

DAVID PERRY: Well, I went back and saw it a second time, because the first time I came away with some sort of mortification. I thought—like you did, Larry—that they made too much out of Garrison. But quite frankly (the second time) I came away with a far different impression. I think it requires a second look. I really do.

The first time I sat there and watched it, I was playing Trivial Pursuit with myself. You know—"Uh-oh. That's not correct, this is not right."

But I looked a second time, and I saw it differently. All he (Mr. Stone) did was tell Jim Garrison's story. And if you watch very closely toward the end of the film, he does not let Garrison off the hook. I remember vividly a scene in the courtroom where (Mr. Garrison) says, "Well, they'll all probably think I'm crazy," and the crowd in the courtroom bursts out, "Yeah, you probably are." And the judge kind of rolls his eyes.

LARRY SUTHERLAND: The (Clay Shaw) trial was a travesty. It rankles me that we can do a movie that disparaging about a guy named Clay Shaw when the only evidence we really have is that, yes, he may have had an association with the C.I.A. as being ipso facto a conspiracy, I don't believe most people would.

Clay Shaw was innocent, not guilty, had no involvement whatsoever in plotting to kill President Kennedy.

GARY SHAW: I'm going to defend Stone a little bit. Oliver Stone has stated publicly that Jim Garrison is basically a composite. The closing arguments (in the Shaw trial) were never even done by Jim Garrison. Stone has taken literary license. But that's his privilege. I think what he used as the words for Jim Garrison were the words that a lot of us have been saying for 28 years.

LARRY SUTHERLAND: The defense of Oswald in this movie overlooks incriminating evidence. It shows the witness who claims that it was not Lee Harvey Oswald who shot Officer Tippet, whereas I believe there are at least six witnesses who say it was.

GARY SHAW: I think that in a few minutes, you could tear up any of those six witnesses.

DAVE PERRY: The bottom line here is that everybody, including an awful lot of researchers, are nothing more than spin doctors. The Warren Commission was the first spin doctor. They were the ones that came out and hyped this thing up. What bothers me is that Jim Garrison and some of his staff, and Oliver Stone and some of his staff, all spin the facts.

When I went back and saw this film a second time, I didn't see the hero worship of Garrison you're getting, Larry.

LARRY SUTHERLAND: He's a martyr. At the end of the trial he's walking out almost like in the movie *Rocky*. Yes, he's beaten, but ...

CARL HENRY: I've seen *Platoon* and *Born on the Fourth of July*. And the common thread with these films and Oliver Stone's *JFK* is you have a David and a Goliath.

GARY SHAW: I see Garrison as leaving with his tail between his legs. I think he realized he got whipped, and I think that's more the impression than (that he's) the martyr.

LARRY SUTHERLAND: But, you know, if I had only seen that movie and believed what I saw, I'd come away thinking, 'Maybe old Garrison had a point.' And I think he probably did *not* have a point.

GARY SHAW: He did not have a case against Clay Shaw. But he had a very valid point, and that was that the government had not told us the truth about the assassination of the president, and that there was a conspiracy involved in that.

This is Oliver Stone's view. And I think the public needs to be aware of that, and he has stressed that.

CARL HENRY: But I think that he needs to expect that there are going to be those people who will go through it with a fine-toothed comb, and will be verbal.

GARY SHAW: The key thing about Oliver Stone's movie, and everybody's overlooking this, is that the government jumped in here and never asked the first question you should ask in a murder case, whether it be an assassination or the shooting of a cab driver. And that is: why? I'm saying they never asked "why?".

CARL HENRY: I think the film is the visual expression of what so far has been a written investigation. The generation now seems to be more of a visual generation. And I think its real important to see that we're not talking about just words on paper. We're talking about real events in time and space. To read ballistic reports and autopsy reports, to go through and read the words is one thing. But to see it on the screen ...

GARY SHAW: Here we have a three-hour movie that's going to speak to a whole generation of people that can get some insight and say, "I want to look further into this." That in itself is good.

CARL HENRY: What I would hope would happen is that people wouldn't shut their minds off after they see the film. That they would begin to question all the fine details of what he's out in there. I don't think he would say, "Quit thinking after you see the film."

DAVID PERRY: I cannot help but think that people are going to come out of the lobby of the theater after this movie is over, and they're going to say, "Boy, that was real interesting stuff. Now let's go home and put up the tree."

Reprinted by permission of the Dallas Morning News.

DECEMBER 29, 1991

THE WASHINGTON POST

THE PARANOID STYLE

Daniel Patrick Moynihan

It happens I was in the White House at the hour of John F. Kennedy's death. There were a dozen or so of us (I was an assistant labor secretary at the time) seated in a circle in presidential assistant Ralph Dungan's large southwest corner room on the first floor. We were a few doors down from the Oval Office, where the rug, or something, was being changed and the furniture emptied out. The president's famous rocking chair was resting on top of a pile of cabinets and such in the little anteroom just outside. (Come to think of it, this may be the only "proof" of a conspiracy that Oliver Stone's movie *JFK* somehow overlooks.) There was no formal announcement that the president had died—just a time when everyone knew. Nor did we do anything; there wasn't anything *to* do. Or not much, anyway. McGeorge Bundy got up and went over to a telephone, asking in a quiet voice that he be put through to the secretary of defense, Robert McNamara. The door opened, and in burst Hubert Humphrey, eyes streaming. He grasped Dungan, who had risen. "What have they done to us?" he gasped.

"They," of course, were those people down in Dallas. No one in particular, just the bunch that never did like Kennedy, one of them—or whatever—crazed enough to do some cowboy shootout thing. A little later I was interviewed on television, and from some unfathomed recess there rose the opening words of Prospero's soliloquy in "The Tempest": "Our revels now are ended." That is what had happened.

But there was another matter. What would the American people *think* had happened? Late in the afternoon I learned on the radio of the arrest of a man involved with Fair Play for Cuba, or something like that. Oh, my God! I thought, the Texans will kill him. Keep in mind that this was a nation only just coming out of a period of near hysteria on the part of some about the menace and influence of communism.

At midnight I went out to Andrews Air Force Base to meet the plane bringing back the Cabinet and subcabinet members, who had been halfway across the Pacific, heading for Japan, when the assassination occurred. I pleaded with any who knew me: "We must get hold of Oswald." No one had the foggiest idea what I was talking about. I went away with the sense that not enough of these people had ever been in a police station.

Oswald was killed presently, whereupon a complicated thing happened. I did not think there had been a conspiracy to kill the president, but I was convinced that the American people would sooner or later come to believe that there had been one *unless we investigated the event with exactly that presumption in mind.* John Macy, who was then Civil Service commissioner, is now dead, and so I must be careful in what I say he thought. But I believe he agreed, and I know he began to join me in meeting with people who might make a difference, and making the same argument I did. At one point I was carrying with me the 19th century "memoir" of Pastor Charles Chiniquy, *Fifty Years in the Church of Rome.* I used it as evidence of our utter credulity. Chiniquy tells of an "interview" warning Lincoln of a Catholic plot against his life. Lincoln agrees (according to Chinquy's fantastical account, responding as follows):

"I will be for ever grateful for the warning words you have addressed to me about the dangers ahead to my life, from Rome. I know that they are not imaginary dangers. If I were fighting against a Protestant South, as a nation, there would be no danger of assassination. The nations who read the Bible, fight bravely on the battle-fields, but they do not assassinate their enemies. The Pope and the Jesuits, with their infernal Inquisition, are the only organized powers in the world which have recourse to the dagger of the assassin to murder those whom they cannot convince with their arguments or conquer with the sword."

The president particularly regretted "the Roman Catholic traitors" that so infested the Union army. Let it be noted that Lincoln's secretary of war, Edwin M. Stanton, believed that the assassination had indeed been a Catholic plot. Note also that the copy of *Fifty Years* that I was carrying around had been specially reprinted for the 1960 presidential election, which is the only reason I knew about it.

We got nowhere, Macy and I. In truth, I probably got into trouble. I was heard as saying not that people were likely to think there had been a conspiracy unless we investigated properly, but that there *had* been a conspiracy. The Warren Commission did not see its work in anything like the perspective I had hoped for. It was Lyndon Johnson at his worst: manipulative, cynical. Setting a chief justice of no great intellect to do a job that a corrupt FBI was well content should not be done well. Edward Jay Epstein laid it out in a master's thesis written at Cornell a few years later.

More relevant to the present moment, however, is Richard Hofstadter's incomparable essay "The Paranoid Style in American Politics," which, as it happens, he delivered as the Herbert Spencer Lecture at Oxford within days of the Kennedy assassination. (It was published in Harper's Magazine a year later.) He begins: "Although American political life has rarely been touched by the most acute varieties of class conflict, it has served again and again as an arena for uncommonly angry minds."

Hofstadter begins with the panic in New England in the 1790's over the dangers to religion of the Bavarian Illuminati. On to the anti-Masonic era: them that is what drank wine from human skulls. Next "Catholics and Mormons—later Negroes and Jews lent themselves to a preoccupation with illicit sex." (Probably the most widely read contemporary book in the United States before "Uncle Tom's Cabin" was "Awful Disclosures" [1836], one Maria Monk's "account" of her escape from a convent/brothel in Montreal.) On to the John Birch Society.

Hofstadter (as also Daniel Bell) was at this time primarily concerned with the conspiratorial fantasies of the right—Ike as a tool of the Reds etc.—and certain of their characteristics, such as the redemptive role of ex-communists in exposing the conspiracies (similar to that of the ex-Catholic priests of yore.) But he knew well enough the paranoid style of the left also, as is illustrated in this passage:

" ... the clinical paranoid sees the hostile and conspiratorial world in which he feels himself to be living as directed specifically *against him*; whereas the spokesman of the paranoid style finds it directed against a nation, a culture, a way of life whose fate affects not himself alone but millions of others. Insofar as he does not usually see himself singled out as the individual victim of a person conspiracy, he is somewhat more rational and much more disinterested. His sense that his political passions are unselfish and patriotic, in fact, goes far to intensify his feeling of righteousness and his moral indignation."

It is in that sense a rationalizing mode. Facts are everything—and facts are *never* accidental. "For every error or act of incompetence one can substitute an act of treason." And always, of course, this is proof of "the existence of a vast, insidious, preternaturally effective international conspiratorial network designed to perpetrate acts of the most fiendish character."

And so to *JFK*. It *could* be viewed as a parody. The homosexual orgies in the New Orleans town house of the villain Clay Shaw are straight out of Maria Monk's nunnery in Montreal. The generals boozing it up as they plan the murder of their commander-in-chief are straight out of Ramparts in a slow week in the '60s. The black waiter who hears nothing is, well, MGM in the '30s. A John Birch look-alike is the fake erudition. Garrison is forever going on about those who practice to deceive, about riddles wrapped in mysteries inside enigmas. Of particular note: "Let justice be done, though the heavens fall." At one point I all but yelled out: "Jim! Use the code! *Fiat Justicia Ruat Coelum.*"

But it is not parody, and it is not funny. It could spoil a generation of American politics just when sanity is returning.

All of us in politics ought to see it: This is what citizens under 30 or 40 are going to be thinking soon. But don't despair. We have got through worse. As a matter of fact, an inadvertent illustration is there in the movie itself.

In one of the longer scenes, Jim Garrison meets with a renegade Pentagon officer who explains the whole plot. They sit on a park bench, with the Washington Monument at some distance in the background. Now if you just look closely at the monument, you will see that about a quarter of the way up, the color of the stone changes, gets lighter. That is because in the 1850's the pope donated a block of marble to the private association that was building the memorial. It was widely believed that there was a secret purpose in this act—that when the block was actually set in place, it would be the signal for the Masonic-Papist seizure of the White House. A band of alert citizens saw to it that the marble ended up on the Potomac instead. Work stopped, only to be resumed by the Corps of Engineers 30 years later, in time for the 1888 centennial, and that is the reason for the difference in color.

Don't despair, but maybe do read a little. The members of the Warren Commission could have done that for us. They could have known our past better.

Hofstadter closes with this pearl from the British historian L.B. Namier: "the crowning attainment of historical study" is to achieve "an intuitive sense of how things do not happen."

CHICAGO SUN-TIMES

STONE'S FILM TRASHES FACTS, DISHONORS J.F.K.

It is filmmaker Oliver Stone's own business whether he decides to produce a wildly inaccurate and distorted motion picture called *JFK* about the assassination of John F. Kennedy.

And it is Stone's own business if he wants to call it art. Just as it is his own business if he cares to think of it as a true depiction of reality.

Also, it is the movie studio's own business if it wants to plow a pile of money into a film without first considering its artistic value, or without first thinking about the studio's credibility.

It is the studio's own business, too if it believes that all the world's standards for good films are dwarfed by the studio's chance to parlay some big names into big money. Further, it is the studio's own business if it then tries to convince the world that it was merely pursuing its own concept of "creative freedom."

Finally, it is the studio's own business if it can't fathom the difference between a film that is "controversial" because it takes a serious look at a matter that has been in dispute for decades and a film that is controversial simply because it is patent nonsense.

Filmmakers, actors and studios are free to make all of this their own business, because that, after all, is what America is about.

Likewise, though, it is the public's own business if it decides that this goofy film is nothing more than a mush of fact, fiction and supposition, which taken together amounts to clumsy fantasy.

And it is the business of those who have a decent respect for history and truth if they choose to despise this film because it is propaganda. It is the business of those who lived through the awful events and who cherished Kennedy and his principles to feel that Stone, in trashing reality, has dishonored Kennedy and his legacy.

And it is the business of those who care about future generations , to worry, if they wish, about how Stone's legacy is a dose of heightened distrust and paranoia.

It, furthermore, is Oliver Stone's own business whether in the majesty of his mind he interprets the public's judgment of the movie as further evidence of a global conspiracy against Kennedy, New Orleans prosecutor Jim Garrison and now Stone himself.

Finally, it is the public's own business if it decides it can better spend the $13 or so for a couple of *JFK* tickets on something more worthwhile. Which seems to be the public's wont.

Despite one of the most massive publicity build-ups in memory, the movie in its first weekend took in only what the film industry describes as a disappointing $5.1

million.

Perhaps not insignificantly, that tied *JFK* for sixth place among the big holiday releases with another Hollywood fantasy—Disney's *Beauty and the Beast*. Way to go, public.

© Copyright 1991. Reprinted by permission of The Chicago Sun-Times.

DECEMBER 30, 1991

LOS ANGELES TIMES:

THE PLOT TO ASSASSINATE THE WARREN COMMISSION

Richard M. Mosk

As a member of the staff of the Warren Commission, I have concluded that there may have been a conspiracy. It was not to assassinate President Kennedy. Instead, it has been by publishers and the entertainment industry to distort history for profit. The Oliver Stone film *JFK* is the most recent example.

The *Times'* review of *JFK* (*Calendar*, Dec. 20) recognizes that the film is short on accuracy. But reviewer Kenneth Turan did not know by how much.

JFK constructed a conspiracy of the gay underground, the FBI, the C.I.A., the military, President Johnson, state officials and local police. Also included are the Warren Commission members and staff and even those in later Administrations, all of whom allegedly engaged in the ongoing cover-up.

That all of these individuals and organizations could effectively carry out such a monumental task and keep quiet for 28 years defies logic and common sense. For example, why would I, a young private-sector lawyer who had just completed active military service and whose father was close to President Kennedy, participate in a cover-up?

While the reviewers reject *JFK*'s preposterous thesis, they somehow are willing to accept many of the film's factual misstatements.

After decades of continuous misinformed, and, in many cases, fraudulent (and mostly profit-seeking) attacks on the Warren Commission, even well-regarded commentators, including film critics, now assume—incorrectly—that the commission was wrong or sloppy.

The Warren Commission concluded that Oswald, acting alone, shot President Kennedy from behind. *JFK* contends that there were multiple gunmen because Oswald could not have fired all three of the shots in 5.6 seconds; that one bullet could not have hit both Kennedy and Governor John Connally, and that Kennedy's head went back, suggesting he was hit from the front.

The probable time span of Oswald's three shots was around ten seconds, not 5.6, because one of the shots missed—most likely the first or the last.

Contrary to *JFK*'s speculation about shots from the front, over the years 19 doctors examined the Kennedy autopsy photographs and x-rays and concluded that all of the shots struck President Kennedy from the rear. Ballistics evidence demonstrated that the bullets came from Oswald's rifle found at the Texas School Book Depository, which was behind Kennedy.

Ballistics and medical experts explained that the backward movement of Kennedy's head when he was struck was not caused by the impact of a bullet in the front but by a predictable neuromuscular reaction and a "jet effect" from the explosion at the front of the head from which the bullet exited.

Scientific evidence (including neutron-activation analysis, which *JFK* dismisses as "mere physics") had repeatedly established the single bullet conclusion—that is, one shot struck Kennedy's neck, exited the front without hitting any bones and hit Gov. Connally causing all of his wounds. To inflict those wounds, the bullet did not have to be deformed or change course, as sarcastically suggested in *JFK*.

Over the years there have been a number of federal and state investigations of the assassination, none of which has unearthed anything new. After spending $5.8 million, a congressional committee in the 1970s supported the single bullet theory, but at the last moment found the acoustics evidence suggested the likelihood of a second gunman.

Subsequently, a ballistics acoustics group of the National Research Council determined that the committee's acoustics conclusion was wrong. The Justice Department thereafter also concluded there was no acoustical evidence of a second gunman shooting from the front.

Strangely, only a few well-informed commentators have noted how flawed *JFK*'s representations were about Kennedy Administration policies regarding Vietnam and other foreign policy matters.

No matter how incomprehensible it may seem, the overwhelming evidence establishes that the events occurred as found by the Warren Commission. And this is so, no matter how much we need to interpret the assassination as rational and orderly or to have it fit some particular dysfunctional world view.

Because of the power of film, many may well accept *JFK*'s false history about the assassination and other policies and events. For motion picture moguls after a fast buck to portray fiction as fact and to assassinate the characters of the living as well as the dead is irresponsible and inexcusable.

Richard M. Mosk is a Los Angeles attorney who served on the staff of the Warren Commission.

Reprinted by permission of the author.

LOS ANGELES TIMES

JFK IS NOT IRRESPONSIBLE—CHOOSING TO IGNORE THE EVIDENCE IS

Oliver Stone

Former Warren Commission staffer Richard M. Mosk makes several mistakes in his outcry against my film *JFK* (*Counterpunch*, *Calendar*, Dec. 30):

1—The idea that the shots occurred over 10 seconds is a relatively recent one. It dates from former President Gerald Ford and former commission counsel David Belin's Dec. 18, 1991, opinion piece in *The Washington Post*. It occurs nowhere in the assassination literature, not even in the Warren Commission volumes, which put the maximum time at 7.9 seconds.

JFK's time frame of 5.6 seconds is based on the visual evidence of the Zapruder film of the assassination—from frame 210 when J.F.K. is first visibly reacting to a shot in the throat to frame 313, the fatal head shot. Most researchers agree on this figure.

2—The neuromuscular reaction that Mosk claims accounts for the backward snap of Kennedy's head when struck by a bullet from behind could happen only if a major coordinating center of the brain is damaged. According to the x-rays and autopsy photos that Mosk champions as evidence of a shot from behind, those areas of the brain are intact.

Mosk's secondary explanation, the "jet effect"—a phenomenon wherein brain matter would exit back through the entry hole, driving the head backward—only works under certain pressure conditions, none of which exist in the human cranial vault.

3—While the "official" autopsy photos and x-rays do show all the shots coming from the rear, the 26 medical personnel who treated the President at Parkland Hospital testified to the Warren Commission that they saw an exit-type wound in the rear of the President's head, inconsistent with the photos and x-rays.

Neither the commission nor the 1976-79 House Select Committee on Assassinations showed the autopsy material to the Parkland doctors to clarify this point. We also know now that if the Bethesda Naval Hospital autopsy was not rigged, it was certainly a compromised affair. Dr. Pierre Finck, one of the three military doctors who signed the Bethesda autopsy report, testified at the Garrison trial that he was "ordered" by generals and admirals not to track the bullet through the neck.

Two FBI reports filed by agents in attendance showed that the same bullet only penetrated about two inches into the President's back and never exited from it, much less took the wacky course of the magic bullet through Gov. Connally.

4—Neutron activation analysis and other tests do not confirm the single-bullet theory. The NAA tests performed on the magic bullet and the fragments found in Connally's wrist for the Warren Commission were "inconclusive." The tests could only prove that the bullet passed through Connally's wrist—merely one of the seven wounds allegedly caused by the bullet.

No scientific evidence has ever proved that the bullet passed through Kennedy's body and there is convincing evidence that it did not. In addition to the aforementioned FBI reports, recently Gov. Connally once again reiterated he does not believe he was shot by the same bullet that hit Kennedy.

5—In overturning the "fourth shot" findings of the House Select Committee, the National Academy of Sciences unknowingly tested a second-generation dub of the Dallas Police Dictabelt, therefore invalidating their results.

The J.F.K. case is a simple homicide investigation but it has never been treated as such. It should be especially simple because we have the 8-millimeter home movie by Abraham Zapruder that shows exactly what happened to President Kennedy.

In response to the Zapruder film showing Kennedy's head snapping back in reaction to a shot from the front, the government produces a series of "experts" who tell you that what you see is not what really happened. Ask any homicide detective how many times they've had to take into account neuromuscular reactions, jet effects and seven wounds in two men with one undamaged bullet in all the gun-related murders they've investigated and you'll get an astounded stare in response.

Mosk, without offering any evidence, is quick to dismiss Kennedy's winding down of the Cold War as a possible motive for the murder. Not only do we have Kennedy's policy difference with the Joint Chiefs twice over Cuba and once over Laos, but we also have an early form of détente under way with Khrushchev (the October '62 deal: no U.S. invasion, no Soviet missiles), the groundbreaking signing of the Nuclear Test Ban Treaty and installation of the "hot line," the American University speech, the back-door negotiations with Castro—and the fact, not speculation, that repeatedly during his presidency, Kennedy turned down requests for combat troops in Vietnam despite heavy pressure from the Joint Chiefs.

Gen. James Gavin, a much-decorated general and ambassador, said in 1968: "I know he was totally opposed to the introduction of combat troops in Southeast Asia." We have Kennedy's statements to five men that he would withdraw the advisors from Vietnam: Rep. O'Neill, Sens. Morse and Mansfield, and aides Forrestal and O'Donnell.

Though his public statements were deliberately ambiguous in view of the forthcoming conservative attack in the 1964 election, he issued the first step in the withdrawal plan with the top-secret document National Security Action Memorandum 263 the month before his murder.

Is this not a place to begin a serious debate? By looking into the nexus of forces—political, business and military—that stood to profit from the $100-billion

Vietnam War? What Eisenhower warned us of as the "military-industrial complex"?

But Mosk is not interested in serious inquiry, he is looking only to whitewash the Warren Commission. It is a tragedy for this country that its "respectable" and "honorable" men, its jurists, government officials, media Establishment, continue to participate in the greatest lie ever put across on the American people. In accusing me of exploitation and irresponsibility, Mosk only disgraces himself.

Reprinted by permission of the author.

JANUARY 1992

GQ

THE CASE AGAINST JIM GARRISON

He was the only prosecutor ever to file charges in the J.F.K. murder. Unfortunately, says the author, his reel story doesn't quite match his real story

Nicholas Lemann

I know life is supposed to be full of surprises, but sometimes one comes along that exceeds the limits of what you should have to put up with. I never thought I'd see someone make an all-out effort to rehabilitate Jim Garrison, the six-foot-seven, booming-voiced district attorney of New Orleans during the years I was growing up there, and the only man to prosecute someone for conspiring to assassinate John F. Kennedy. Garrison lost his case after one hour of jury deliberation. The responsible wing of the assassination-conspiracy community—meaning writer-investigators, such as Harold Weisberg and Edward Jay Epstein—has regarded him as an embarrassment for nearly a quarter-century. Although until this past November he was still working in New Orleans, where he served many years as an elected state judge, most people there place him in the same category as the colorful, roguish political figures from Louisiana's past, along with Earl Long.

As with Uncle Earl, Big Jim's reputational deliverance has come from Hollywood: In Oliver Stone's movie *JFK*, the Garrison character, played by Kevin Costner, is the hero. Blaze at least avoided the mistake of taking Earl Long seriously; *JFK*, from all advance indications (I have not seen the movie as of this writing), will portray Garrison straightforwardly as a hero of the High Noon variety—as , in Stone's words, "one of the few men of that time who had the courage to stand up to the Establishment and seek the truth." There are enough good journalists around today who covered Garrison back in his heyday to guarantee that Stone will be called on this. Still, because of the momentum of

JFK's publicity, when it opens there will be an unavoidable feeling in the air that, well, by God, Garrison was onto something. It's easy to present the wide-spread opposition to him as a badge of honor. Courageous visionaries are always unpopular, aren't they?

In this case, though, everyone should face the unappealing truth: Establishment or no Establishment, Garrison was wrong. More than that: Garrison was a pernicious figure, an abuser of government power and the public trust, and if there's a deeper issue in American society that he exemplifies, it is that so many intelligent people prefer conspiracy-theorizing to facing this country's problems head-on.

Jim Garrison, actually Earling Carothers Garrison, was born in a small town in Iowa and grew up in New Orleans. In the sketchy biographical account he gives of himself in his books (*A Heritage of Stone* and *On the Trail of the Assassins*), he mentions, curiously, the influence of his grandfather but not of his father, and he doesn't say how his family wound up in the Deep South. If his father was a distant, cold or missing figure in his life, it wouldn't surprise me: People who have become fixated on the Kennedy assassination often are engaged in some sort of search for a lost father. Garrison had a generational link to Kennedy, too. He was born four years after Kennedy; served, like Kennedy, in World War II; and was elected district attorney of New Orleans a year after Kennedy was elected president.

In his early years in office, Garrison was a reformer. He got his job by upsetting a mossback incumbent and quickly made a name for himself by cleaning up the long-standing minor-vice rackets in the French Quarter that had existed under the unofficial sanction of the city and state political machines. In those days, New Orleans still thought of itself as the queen city of the South, not yet having succumbed to its present self-concept as a quaint tourist Mecca. Garrison, a young, articulate, handsome, well-read, crusading politician, was the object of a good deal of civic pride.

The official Garrison anecdote about how he decided to investigate the Kennedy assassination goes like this: In 1966, he got on a flight from New Orleans to New York and found himself sitting next to Louisiana Senator Russell Long, who told Garrison that he didn't find the Warren Commission's official report on the assassination credible. (Though Garrison doesn't mention this in any of his books, it seems relevant that Long is the son of an assassinated politician, the circumstances of whose death have always been in dispute.) Because Lee Harvey Oswald had spent the summer of 1963 in New Orleans, Garrison could, by stretching, claim that investigating the assassination was within his jurisdiction. He and his staff of assistant DA's, along with an eccentric crew of conspiracy theorists from around the country—the stand-up comedian Mort Sahl, for example, and Mark Lane, later famous as an adviser to mass-murderer-cult leader Jim Jones—went to work putting a case together (in secrecy, until the *New Orleans States-Item* blew their cover a year later).

The best thing the conspiracy theorists have going for them is the fact that if a lone assassin had shot President Kennedy from a sixth floor window, he would have had to have been a marksman of almost superhuman skill in order to kill Kennedy and wound Texas Governor John Connally Jr. in the few seconds when a clear shot to their car was possible. Without getting into the dense forest of four- and five-bullet (and two- and three-gunman) theories, clearly the most vulnerable point of the Warren Commission report is its contention that Oswald fired three shots and that one of them hit both Kennedy and Connally. The second-best thing conspiracy theorists have going for them is that Lee Harvey Oswald was not merely a loner and a misfit, but a loner and a misfit who had served in the U.S. Marine Corps, defected to the Soviet Union and then undefected and returned home. His extremely weird career involved spending time under the aegis of both superpower governments during the Cold War. The mechanics of Kennedy's murder and the details of Oswald's life are twin motherlodes for conspiracy theorists. But bear in mind that there is an enormous difference between, on the one hand, a few discrepancies, coincidences and lacunae, and, on the other, actual proof that there was a conspiracy.

When Oswald was living in New Orleans, he worked in a manual labor job at a coffee plant and, famously, formed a pro-Castro organization called the Fair Play for Cuba Committee, which got a good deal of publicity, considering it was a one-man, desk-drawer operation. To Garrison's mind, all this was a cover: The real situation was that Oswald was caught in the webbing of a powerful network of right-wing militarists, who had placed him at the coffee company and had manufactured a leftist identity for him, all in preparation for the time when he would be blamed for (but wouldn't actually commit) Kennedy's murder.

It's impossible to explain Garrison's theory adequately without first saying that the hallmark of the Kennedy-conspiracy theorists is that the burden of proof always lies with the Warren Commission, never with them. The full Warren Commission report takes up twenty-six thick volumes, filled with a mass of evidence and testimony. In additions to the shortcomings in the way the commission sequenced Oswald's shots, all of this information doesn't comprise a seamless web. There are loose ends and contradictions. On the other hand, the report does manfully shoulder the difficult task of presenting a comprehensive explanation of the assassination. While Garrison capitalizes on every flaw or imagined flaw, of the report, as if each discovery invalidates the entire twenty-six volumes, he holds himself to a significantly lower evidential standard, where the sketchiest connections are held to prove the existence of the conspiracy and he never has to explain precisely how he thinks Kennedy was murdered or by whom.

So: The Reily Coffee Company was at 640 Magazine Street, on the edge of downtown New Orleans. Two blocks away, at 544 Camp Street, was the office of W. Guy Banister, a former FBI agent and deputy superintendent of police in New Orleans. In 1963, Banister was a private detective and a right-winger involved in anti-Castro activities. And on Oswald's pro-Castro Fair Play for Cuba leaflets was a return address—544 Camp Street! Garrison is a man who thinks in terms of "links," and to him this is a rock-solid one; he had no trouble asserting, as a proven fact, that Oswald and Banister knew each other. (Banister died in 1964, before Garrison began his investigation.)

The next link, also unsubstantiated, is between Guy Banister and a weird character named David Ferrie. In 1963, Ferrie had been fired from his job as an Eastern Airlines pilot and was making a living as a civil-aviation pilot. He was also participating energetically in the underground homosexual life of New Orleans. According to Garrison, Ferrie performed, under Banister's direction, espionage-related piloting missions to Cuba and Central America during the early Sixties. On the fateful morning of November 22, 1963, Ferrie and two male "companions" had driven from New Orleans to Houston for a weekend trip. To Garrison, this was a transparent attempt to establish an alibi; Ferrie's real job had been to transport unnamed conspirators from Dallas to Mexico, in a private plane, a few days later. Ferrie died in 1967, a year into Garrison's investigation.

Next link: David Ferrie and Lee Oswald. Garrison asserts, again with no hard evidence, that the two men were in the same civil air patrol squadron in New Orleans and that Ferrie taught Oswald to fly and to shoot a high-powered rifle. Just before Ferrie died, the *New Orleans States-Item* broke the story that Garrison was investigating the Kennedy assassination, on the public's dime. (Afterward, a group of right-wing New Orleans businessmen funded the investigation privately.) The publicity increased the pressure on Garrison to produce a suspect, but the conspirators he had been focusing on—Oswald, Banister and Ferrie—were all dead. A final link was called for, and Garrison produced it: In March 1967, only a few days after the States-Item had blown his cover and Ferrie had died, Garrison arrested Clay L. Shaw, the retired director of the International Trade Mart in New Orleans.

Most of Garrison's suspects and witnesses were real fly-by-nighters, but Clay Shaw was a respectable figure. He was a tall, dignified, well-dressed white-haired man who, as head of the trade mart, had run a chamber of commerce-like organization. He wasn't rich or powerful, but he was settled, well-known, and upper middle class. He was also gay. It would have been inconceivable at the time for an openly gay man to hold the job Shaw had, so he necessarily had a secret life. At least part of the time, he traveled in the kind of social circles where people didn't use their last names and otherwise kept their participation quiet. This gave him just enough of a shadowy edge to make him useful to Garrison. In fact, a good part of Garrison's case had an aspect of persecution of homosexuals about it; he had relied on the closeted nature of gay life to lend plausibility to his vision of an underground world of conspirators.

Garrison asserted that Shaw had known Ferrie and Oswald; that Shaw had helped recruit Oswald to his role as the fall guy in the assassination; and that Shaw's ironclad alibi for November 22—he was in California making a speech—only strengthened the case for his involvement in the conspiracy. Remember, it has never been proven to the satisfaction of anyone, except Garrison and his admirers, that Lee Oswald, Clay Shaw, David Ferrie and Guy Banister even knew one another. It's a testament to Garrison's manipulative skills that he was able to turn this weakness into a strength by spending Shaw's entire trial endeavoring to prove that the four men had known one another, as if that was tantamount to nailing down their involvement in a conspiracy to kill the president. Virtually all of Garrison's oeuvre—meaning the Shaw trial, Big Jim's handful of lengthy interviews with sympathetic reporters, his two books about the Kennedy assassination and, presumably, *JFK*—is concerned with these "links," and nowhere does Garrison reveal how his four conspirators actually accomplished the murder or who fired the fatal bullets. (While we're on the subject of "links," I should mention, before Garrison or Stone does in a letter to the editor, that I have several of my own to the whole affair. My father and his brother are partners in a New Orleans law firm. One of the firm's long-standing clients is the very same Reily Coffee Company that had employed Lee Harvey Oswald. Another was the late Edith Stern, a liberal philanthropist, who was a friend and prominent supporter of Clay Shaw's. Also, my uncle worked on Garrison's campaign when he was first elected district attorney. And for twenty years, I've been a friend of Tom Bethell, a former investigator for Garrison who defected to the other side just before the Shaw trial began. To me, the lesson here is that, taking the "links" approach, just about everybody is a potential suspect.)

Garrison has always been similarly vague about the identity of the assassination plot's mastermind. In one typically Garrisonian locution of the subject, in a 1967 interview, he said "At midday on November 22, 1963, there were many men in many places glancing at their watches." Who were they? Who knows! Over the years, he has made dark, knowing references to the involvement of the FBI, the military-industrial complex and the oil business in the conspiracy, but his suspicions have centered on the C.I.A.. There is much, much less than meets the eye to Garrison's conclusion that the C.I.A. did it. All his evidence consists either of wild leaps of faith—David Ferrie is "linked" (to Garrison's satisfaction, though not to many others') to the C.I.A., therefore the C.I.A. killed Kennedy—or rank speculation. When exactly did the C.I.A. decide to assassinate the president? Who gave the order? How was the job carried out and then covered up? Garrison never comes anywhere near giving the answers to these questions.

In his more recent book *On the Trail of the Assassins*—on which *JFK* is based— Garrison says the assassination "was instigated and planned long in advance by fanatical anti-communists in the United States intelligence community." Well, who were they? A few pages later, Garrison says there is no evidence that the FBI's J. Edgar Hoover, Chief Justice Earl Warren, the C.I.A.'s Allen Dulles or President Lyndon Johnson "had any prior knowledge or involvement in the assassination, but I would not hesitate to classify all of these men as accessories after the fact." Why? What did they do? And how were the real planners of the assassination able to carry out their fantastically detailed conspiracy without the head of the agency's noticing?

Garrison consistently gets himself off the hook of questions like these by implying it's miraculous that he, a lone crusader has been able to chip away even some of the smooth façade presented by the immensely rich and powerful conspirators; he can hardly be expected to have gotten all the answers. And when he's going after his big fish, he's maddeningly elusive about exactly what accusation he is making. In his books, there is the implication, for example, that the big news media are somehow tied in to the conspiracy, but he's never actually said so directly. Back in the early days of the investigation, an editor from *Life* made friendly overtures to Garrison. A while later, as Garrison tells the story, the editor "suddenly flew in from New York. He seemed amiable enough, but he appeared to have lost a great deal of weight. He had deep circles under his eyes. His Ivy League clothes hung loosely on his thin frame. He informed me that *Life* would no longer be able to support me and work with me ... " We're supposed to think, aren't we, that the editor was tortured in some *Darkness at Noon*-style editorial dungeon. But Garrison doesn't say so. NBC's hostile coverage of the investigation is explained by its being "part of the warfare machine"; this thought hovers in the background of Garrison's unintentionally hilarious depiction of the depredations visited upon him when he appeared on the *Tonight Show*, which, in his retelling, is meant to make us wonder whether Johnny Carson was entirely uninvolved in the events of November 22.

Garrison presents the masterminds of the Kennedy assassination as being extremely far-reaching and clever—and yet, oddly enough, they were constantly making little mistakes that allowed Garrison to pick up their trail. Take the Clay Shaw trial. The obvious question was, Why didn't the conspirators entrust the hit to a more reliable crew? Garrison's key witness against Shaw, Perry Russo, was a young insurance salesman-cum-grifter who claimed to have overheard Shaw and Ferrie discussing the assassination at a party. Another witness, named Charles Spiesel—a paranoid accountant who regularly fingerprinted his own children and claimed to have been hypnotized by people on the street dozens of times—told a similar story about overhearing Shaw and Ferrie casually planning Kennedy's murder at a different party. It's not like the C.I.A., as Garrison describes it, to be so sloppy as to allow such conversations to take place. A third witness, prison inmate Vernon Bundy, testified that while preparing himself a heroin fix on the well-travelled banks of Lake Pontchartrain, he had seen Shaw handing money to Oswald. Wouldn't it have been wiser for them not to have made this transaction in a public place?

I remember feeling excited about Garrison's crusade, in the early days: Finally, something of national import was happening in New Orleans. In the late Sixties, the word "Sunbelt" had not yet been coined, but there was an unmistakable sense that, one century later, the South was finally going to stop obsessing about the Civil War and transform itself. It was also clear that while cities like Atlanta and Houston had jumped into this process with both feet, New Orleans was attracted in some deep way to eccentricity and torpor and endless sifting through the past. Thus, when the true nature of Garrison's inquest became apparent, there was a powerful reverberation: The trial's aftermath seemed like a metaphor for the state of the city—that the attention we were attracting because of the Shaw trial was going to be censorious, not admiring; that what we had on our hands, civically, was a tremendous embarrassment; that New Orleans was becoming known as the weirdo capital of the United States.

Almost immediately after the Shaw trial's humiliating end, Garrison began to downplay its importance. His first book, *A Heritage of Stone* (1970), barely mentions Shaw, and Russo, Spiesel and Bundy not at all, and presents the trial as having been an excuse to dispute the Warren Commission in a public forum. "We saw the verdict as pointing up the impossibility of presenting an espionage case in an American court of law," he says, explaining why he lost. Lately, Oliver Stone has begun to sound this note, too. "Yes, the jury returned a verdict of not guilty on Clay Shaw," he wrote in *The Washington Post*, but he went on to praise "the larger accomplishment of the trial." A second front in defense of Garrison's conduct opened up in 1975, when the renegade former C.I.A. agent Victor Marchetti revealed that Shaw (who had lived very quietly in New Orleans from the time of his acquittal until his death, in 1974) had been once affiliated with the agency's Domestic Contact Division, which debriefed civilian businessmen who regularly traveled overseas. Both Garrison and Stone discuss this as if its important new evidence.

Shaw's possible connection to the C.I.A. is another illustration of the problem with Garrison's whole way of thinking: Even if Shaw had been a career C.I.A. agent, that fact alone does not implicate him in the Kennedy assassination. Garrison still hasn't presented any convincing evidence of that. (Similarly, Garrison and Stone like to cite the conclusion of the House Select Committee on Assassinations, in 1979, that Kennedy "probably was assassinated as a result of a conspiracy," as proof that "the federal government" now agrees with them—but the House committee was an independent investigative operation; it didn't solve the case either, and it certainly didn't implicate Clay Shaw in the assassination.)

What's much more important, though, is the chilling line of argument Garrison and Stone are using to defend the trial. Garrison's writing is full of self-congratulatory references to George Orwell and Franz Kafka, but the essence of those writers' vision is that the most profound wrong a government can commit is to turn its powers against an innocent individual in order to advance a larger cause. Garrison was a public official who had prosecutorial power in his hands, and he used it to bring a man to trial when, by his own admission, he knew he didn't have a real case. With his use of innuendo, his carelessness in flinging the gravest charges at people, his belief that individual liberties (at least, Clay Shaw's individual liberties) are less important than his attack on what he imagines to be a vast conspiracy destroying America, Garrison does have a forbear, but it isn't Orwell or Kafka. It's Joe McCarthy.

Oliver Stone's parents split up when he was 16, in 1962. "The news of their divorce came as a total shock," he told *Time* five years ago. "... And when they were divorced, my father gave me the facts of life. He told me that he was heavily in debt. He said 'I'll give you a college education and then you're on your own. There's literally no money.'"

A few months ago Stone wrote in *The Washington Post*, "The murder of

President Kennedy was a seminal event for me and millions of Americans ... It was a crushing blow to our country and to millions of people around the world. It put an abrupt end to a period of innocence and great idealism."

It doesn't take a particularly adventurous foray into the realm of armchair psychology to see a parallel in the way that Stone describes these two almost simultaneous tragedies, one private and one public. That his own secure world suddenly came apart in the early Sixties might help explain why Stone would be drawn to the view that the Kennedy assassination had the same effect on national life—and why he was later drawn to Garrison. Like many demagogues before him, Big Jim has the ability to conjure up a simpler, better national past, which he equates with the innocence of childhood; the assassination ended those wonderful times, and tracking down the murderers holds out the larger promise of restoring (in his words) "the America I knew as a child."

The rational (or, more accurately, quasi-rational) accompaniment to this powerful emotional logic is the idea, fervently embraced by both Garrison and Stone, that John F. Kennedy was a man of peace who was planning to abort the Vietnam War. The C.I.A. or the military Establishment or the defense contractors or whoever became seriously alarmed about Kennedy when he signed the Nuclear Test Ban Treaty with the Soviet Union, in the summer of 1963, and when he signaled his intention to bring our troops home from Vietnam, they decided he had to be rubbed out.

Most of the evidence in support of the Kennedy-as-dove theory comes from books written after the assassination by the president's advisers, especially Arthur Schlesinger Jr. and Kenneth O'Donnell. Of course, what Kennedy would have done if he had lived is speculative, though Garrison doesn't treat it that way. But it's fair to say that the overall thrust of historical writing about Kennedy, in recent years, has been that he was a Cold Warrior at heart—certainly not someone with ambitious plans to dismantle the military-industrial complex and to effect, in Garrison's words, "a reconciliation with the U.S.S.R. and Castro's Cuba." Robert Kennedy, who was probably in a better position than anyone else to know what his brother's intentions in Vietnam were, had this to say on the subject in an in-depth, off-the-record interview conducted for the historical record in 1964, the year after his brother's death:

> INTERVIEWER: Did the president feel that we would have to go into Vietnam in a big way?
> KENNEDY: We certainly considered what would be the result if you abandon Vietnam, even Southeast Asia, and whether it was worthwhile trying to keep and hold on to.
> INTERVIEWER: What did he say? What did he think?
> KENNEDY: He reached the conclusion that probably it was worthwhile ... .

Not only is the Garrison-Stone case for the greater importance of the Kennedy assassination essentially a fantasy, it's strange that they feel it has to be made at all. Even if Kennedy wasn't planning to end the Vietnam War, his death was still a great tragedy. Garrison and Stone are trying to make it into something more: the main turning point in American history—which it wasn't. Garrison, for all these years, has been engaged in a witch-hunt, not a genuine attempt to solve a crime. Like all witch-hunts, his has been based on the idea that some vast, mysterious evil force has society in its grip. If the sense of pervasive corruption isn't there, then Garrison's mission (and, even more, his method) somehow completely loses its aura of virtue.

There is plenty that is wrong with American society, and Oliver Stone is one of the few directors with the clout and the interest in politics to be able to address it in mainstream films. Instead of going after a real problem, though, like economic decline or racial tension, he has chosen to pursue a made-up problem: a conspiracy that killed a president in order to heat up the Vietnam War and transform America from a sylvan, virtuous land into a military state. Stone won't get more than a handful of opportunities to make an important statement about this country. Too bad he wasted this one.

Nicholas Lemann is a national correspondent for The Atlantic. *He is the author of* The Promised Land: The Great Black Migration and How It Changed America *(Knopf).*

This article was originally published in *GQ* and is reprinted by permission of the author.

APRIL 1992

GQ

FOR THE DEFENSE

Zachary Sklar

Editor's note: Nicholas Lemann's essay "The Case Against Jim Garrison" [January] inspired more letters than any article we have published in recent years, almost all of them critical of Lemann's argument. The most comprehensive of these letters is the following, from journalist and screenwriter Zachary Sklar.

Evidently GQ has forgotten one of the fundamental rules of American journalism: Give the readers both sides of the story. The case for Jim Garrison is not to be found in your pages.

Lemann's glib charges are so sweeping that it's impossible to respond to all of them in a letter. I suggest anyone interested in Garrison's case read *On the Trail of the Assassins*, the former New Orleans district attorney's own account of his investigation. As the editor of this book, and co-screenwriter of Oliver Stone's JFK, I take issue with several of Lemann's unfounded assertions.

1. Lemann portrays Garrison as "a pernicious figure, an abuser of government power and the public trust," a D.A. who brought Clay Shaw to trial when "he knew he didn't have a real case," a D.A. who "engaged in a [McCarthy-like] witch-hunt."

The only evidence Lemann presents to support these accusations is that the jury found Clay Shaw not guilty of conspiring to kill the president. Yes, Garrison lost his case, but every D.A. in America loses cases. Garrison, three-term D.A. of New Orleans, and later a judge on the Louisiana state court of appeal, went through the proper legal channels when bringing charges against Shaw. A grand jury of twelve citizens voted to indict him. In a pretrial hearing, a panel of three judges ruled that Garrison had presented enough evidence to bring Shaw to trial.

What happened next is like what happened to Hemingway's old man, who caught a huge fish but found it eaten away by sharks before he could get it to shore. Garrison's investigation was sabotaged by the federal government. According to documents released years later per the Freedom of Information Act (FOIA), the D.A. was followed everywhere by the FBI. His phones were tapped, his offices bugged. Every request for extradition of witnesses from other states was denied—something that had never happened in his five previous years as D.A. His attempts to obtain important evidence, such as Lee Harvey Oswald's tax records and intelligence files, as well as photos and X rays from the Kennedy autopsy, were rebuffed. The U.S. attorney in Washington refused to serve subpoenas on CIA officials Allen Dulles and Richard Helms. Key witnesses died under mysterious circumstances (David Ferrie, Eladio del Valle, Rose Cheramie and Lee Bowers, to name a few), and others were threatened (Dallas Deputy Sheriff Roger Craig, Jim Hicks). Some of the D.A.'s files and a summary of his witness list were handed over to the defense before the trial, and the CIA was helping Shaw during it, according to Victor Marchetti, former executive assistant to CIA director Helms.

Some members of the national media jumped all over Garrison long before Shaw was found innocent, and we see their reckless charges recycled time and again—that Garrison bribed witnesses, that he was in cahoots with the Mafia, that he fondled little boys and so forth. Not one of these charges was ever proved, and to Lemann's credit, he didn't trot them out again.

These fabricated stories suggest Garrison was the victim of an old-fashioned smear campaign. A CIA memo dated April 1, 1967, and released under the FOIA, in 1977, lays out a strategy for discrediting critics of the Warren Commission. It urges agency operatives "to employ propaganda assets [writers and editors] to answer and refute the attacks of the critics. Book reviews and feature articles are particularly appropriate for this purpose." The memo goes on to suggest that the critics be labeled "politically interested," "financially interested," "infatuated with their own theories" and "hasty and inaccurate in their research." Sound familiar?

Garrison was attacked so vehemently in the press because he presented a message that most people were unwilling to accept in 1967: The CIA was involved in the assassination of the president. Today, after the revelations of Vietnam,

Watergate, the Church Committee, the Iran-Contra scandal, BCCI, etc., it is far easier to accept such a frightening possibility. But many in the mainstream press still cling to the Warren Commission's lone-gunman fairy tale, and they are the most vicious in attacking Jim Garrison.

2. Lemann says Garrison's case had "an aspect of persecution of homosexuals about it..." This is untrue. Shaw was a homosexual, but Garrison, who made a name for himself as a defender of gay rights when he refused to prosecute a bookseller for carrying James Baldwin's *Another Country*, went out of his way never to mention this in public or at the trial. Garrison considered Shaw's homosexuality irrelevant.

3. Lemann claims there is no evidence linking Oswald, Guy Banister, David Ferrie and Clay Shaw. Again, this is untrue. Four witnesses from Clinton, Louisiana, testified under oath at Shaw's trial that they had seen Oswald, Ferrie and Shaw together in Clinton the day of a voter-registration drive in September 1963. Delphine Roberts, Guy Banister's secretary, told the House Select Committee on Assassinations that Oswald and Ferrie worked out of Banister's office at 544 Camp Street. Jack Martin and David Lewis, both investigators who worked for Banister, confirmed this. Six witnesses told the House Committee that Oswald was in David Ferrie's Civil Air Patrol unit. Several homosexuals, whom Garrison chose not to call to the witness stand precisely to avoid the issue of Shaw's private life, signed sworn affidavits stating that they had seen Shaw and Ferrie together. Shaw denied under oath that he knew Oswald, Ferrie or Banister. The jury evidently believed him. But Judge Edward Haggerty, who presided at the trial, stated publicly that he believed Shaw lied and pulled a "con job" on the jury.

4. Lemann engages in some amusing armchair psychology. According to him, Stone believes in a conspiracy because Kennedy was killed a year after his parents' divorce; Garrison believes in a conspiracy because he's searching for a cold, distant father; and Senator Russell Long believes in a conspiracy because his own father was assassinated. Rather than try to dream up some psychological reason for each of the 73 percent of Americans who now believe there was a conspiracy, wouldn't it be easier for Lemann to admit that most people don't buy the Oswald-lone-gunman explanation because it just doesn't make sense?

5. Lemann worries about the "tremendous embarrassment" Garrison supposedly brought on New Orleans, "that New Orleans was becoming known as the weirdo capital of the United States." Evidently, most citizens of New Orleans do not agree with Lemann's view. After the Shaw trial, Garrison was reelected as D.A. by his biggest margin ever. Later, he was twice elected as a state court of appeal judge. If I were a resident of New Orleans, I'd be proud that my D. A. was the only elected prosecutor in America who had the guts to say the Warren Commission was wrong and conduct his own investigation.

6. Lemann is upset that Garrison hasn't provided all the answers to who killed the president. Well, who has? Certainly not the Warren Commission, which had millions of dollars and a huge staff. Not the House Select Committee on Assassinations, which concluded there was a "probable conspiracy" but did not

name names.

Isn't it a bit unfair of Lemann to ask Garrison to do what these governmental investigators could not do? He had a small staff, was forced to battle the government and the press at every turn and had no access to secret government files. None of us, including Garrison and Stone, would have to speculate if those files were opened.

7. Lemann complains that Stone should have made a film about "a real problem...like economic decline or racial tension," instead of a "made-up problem," such as a conspiracy to kill the president, which involved elements in our defense and intelligence Establishments. While Lemann obviously does not agree with Stone's hypothesis, surely he must see that a society dominated by wildly inflated military spending, covert operations and government lying and cover-ups is a real problem.

Martin Luther King Jr., as early as 1967, recognized that domestic problems such as economic decline and racial tension are directly linked to the vast amounts of money we spend on war and defense. It's too bad that so many otherwise intelligent people still don't get it.

APRIL 1992

GQ

Nicholas Lemann

In my dealings with the assassination-conspiracy community, I've persistently had the feeling that we see the world in such fundamentally different ways that it would actually be impossible to settle an argument. This feeling came back to me with the very first line of Zachary Sklar's letter: Printing both sides of the story has never been a fundamental rule of magazine journalism. Magazines are supposed to be feisty and opinionated. So it's with a sense of futility that I rebut Sklar's points.

1. Even if you accept Sklar's fantastic notion of a massive government effort, including several murders, to subvert Garrison's case (and of course I don't), it still doesn't prove that Shaw conspired to kill Kennedy.

2. Saying Garrison defended that bookseller doesn't disprove my contention about the Shaw case. Because they were gay, Shaw and Ferrie had a secret life, and Garrison used this to make them look like assassination conspirators. If they had been straight, he wouldn't have had even the flimsy case that he brought to trial. Does Sklar claim that the prancing, mincing Shaw in the movie *JFK*, so different from the real Shaw, isn't a gay stereotype?

3. I said "it has never been proved" that Oswald, Ferrie, Banister and Shaw knew

one another—and indeed, it hasn't been proved. There are no photographs, no letters—only an odd series of brief, onetime alleged sightings by people who didn't know them.

4. I engaged in armchair psychology because I think it's weird to make the leap—as Sklar once again does here—from the idea that the Oswald-lone-gunman theory may be implausible to the idea that therefore the CIA, the FBI, the Pentagon, LBJ and a cast of thousands must have conspired to kill Kennedy. That thought process reveals more about the thinkers than about assassination.

5. If someone has won the favor of the voters of New Orleans, believe me, it does not prove that the person is not embarrassing. To use just the closest at hand of many possible examples, the current governor of Louisiana has twice stood trial on corruption charges, and even though he just won an election, I'm still embarrassed, and I don't think his electoral success proves he has guts.

6. Sklar's script is much more courageous than Garrison's books, because Sklar does actually lay out a theory of the assassination—something Garrison has never done publicly. It's not that Garrison doesn't provide all the answers—it's that he provides none of them.

7. I still don't think *JFK* addresses a real political issue. Surely, with the end of the Cold War, Sklar doesn't believe that our society is dominated by the military today. In fact, the Sklar-Stone idea that it's healthy for Americans to regard the federal government with profound suspicion and mistrust is a perfect fit with Reagan Republicanism, which I doubt is the stated ideology of the makers of *JFK*.

JANUARY 1992

PREMIERE

OLIVER STONE TALKS BACK

JFK has created a storm of controversy. Here, the director answers his critics and explains the thinking behind his film

Oliver Stone

The dirty little secret of American journalism is that whenever you watch a TV news program or read a newspaper that includes coverage of something you saw or knew about or in which you actually participated, even a baseball game, *it's generally wrong*. Sometimes just a little, sometimes a lot, but wrong.

Now, if that's true, what about all the stories of which we don't have any firsthand knowledge? For that matter, what about history itself? According to Herodotus and Homer, history is gossip, stories heard around a campfire, passed down from bard to bard, father to son. Are we to believe our George Washington texts from primary school or Howard Zinn's multicultural *People's History of the United States*? In most textbooks, the assassination of President John F. Kennedy is reduced to a few short paragraphs following the party line and featuring the obvious names: J.F.K., L.B.J., Jackie, Earl Warren, Jack Ruby, and, of course, Lee Harvey Oswald, the "lone assassin." This is supposed to be "the truth."

There is a saying: "A lie is like a snowball—the longer it is rolled, the larger it is." The Warren Commission conclusion—that Oswald, acting alone, killed Kennedy—is that lie. America's Official Story. "History," in its original Greek sense (historia), means "inquiry," and in that light, my film, any film, any work of art, has the right to reexplore an event. Nevertheless, just by talking about a movie dealing with those events and preparing a first draft script, we had touched a raw nerve.

By late May 1991, barely six weeks into the shooting schedule, it was clear that *JFK* was no longer a film but a matter of "national security." I found an article entitled "ON THE SET: DALLAS IN WONDERLAND" splashed across the front page of the political Sunday Outlook section of *The Washington Post*, written by George Lardner, Jr., a reporter with considerable experience covering the C.I.A.. A grotesque cartoon topped the article, demonizing me like Saddam Hussein. It added 30 pounds to my girth, enlarged my fingers into sausages of greed; all that was missing was the foam dripping from my mouth.

Lardner's article accused me of both distorting and profiting from the J.F.K. murder, meanwhile quoting liberally from what I consider to be a stolen first draft of the script that he had acquired from a bitter researcher in the J.F.K. conspiracy community, who, I hear, continues, illegally, to sell copies of the script for $30 each. (Like all writers, I constantly revise my work—the shooting script was the sixth draft, different in crucial ways from the first.) Lardner seemed to be advocating precensorship of *JFK* or trying to discourage people from seeing the movie. He made it quite clear, given his reporting on the Jim Garrison investigation and the 1976-79 House Select Committee on Assassinations, that he did not want the event investigated any further by me, or by anyone else for that matter. Oddly enough, in the course of his attack on my film, he casually acknowledged that experts said there was a fourth shot (fired from the grassy knoll, not Oswald's Texas School Book Depository) and thus a conspiracy to kill J.F.K.!

Taking Lardner's cue, a *Chicago Tribune* columnist pronounced me a threat to history, and *Time* quickly followed with a full page-and-a-half review of the unseen film giving it far more space than it normally allocates to a finished film.

Of course, *Time* has its own dubious history in the J.F.K. affair: Time Inc. paid a huge sum for the 8mm film Abraham Zapruder shot at the scene and kept it locked in a vault for twelve years, refusing most requests to see it, on the grounds that the public would find it upsetting. *Time* has persistently misstated some of the facts of the case—some say for its own nonartistic purposes—to make sure that Jim Garrison is ensconced in the lunatic fringe of the paranoid conspiracy buffs.

Kennedy's death only becomes more troubling with time. Virtually every aspect of the case is fraught with questions that won't go away. Why did the crowd in Dealey Plaza, including the Dallas police and sheriffs, run up the infamous grassy knoll immediately after the shooting stopped? If Oswald was a lonely drifter, why did he have so many apparent ties to the U.S. intelligence community? How could Ruby walk into the Dallas Police Station and shoot Oswald with more than 70 policemen standing guard? If the assassination really was the work of a single disillusioned Communist, why is the government still withholding the records of the HSCA and some of the key Warren Commission files, on the grounds of "national security"?

It is completely beyond me, as a twice-wounded combat veteran, that grown men on government panels, some supposedly experts in wound ballistics and firearms, can sit through the 22-second Zapruder film and say that it looks like the fatal head shot came from behind. Or that the solitary, infamous "magic bullet " could cause seven wounds in Kennedy and Governor John Connally, breaking two dense bones, and emerge with virtually no metal missing, not to mention traveling along a path that defies the laws of physics. In the face of such implausibilities and new acoustics evidence, the 1979 *HSCA Report* acknowledged the 95 percent probability of a grassy-knoll shot, but immediately the government and the establishment media downplayed those official "fourth shot" findings in favor of the comfortable altogether unlikely Oswald-did-it-alone scenario.

You'd expect that the press would be as vigilant to the glaring problems with the Official Story and the lone-nut theory as they have been to our movie. But just as the government has failed twice at investigating the assassination, the national media has failed both at getting to the truth and at selling their "truth" to the public. According to a recent Gallup poll, 73 percent of Americans think there was a conspiracy to kill Kennedy. Only 16 percent believe the Warren Commission's conclusions.

The Washington Post, without even a hint of shame, ran a curious editorial just after the disclosure of the fourth-shot conclusion, warning the American public that simply because at least two "malcontents" were shooting at President Kennedy at the same time, it didn't necessarily mean that there was a conspiracy.

After reading widely in the assassination literature, I chose to make the story of former New Orleans district attorney Jim Garrison (played by Kevin Costner) the narrative framework of the movie. I was taken with the way in which a man starts to investigate one small corner of the conspiracy—in this case, the summer of 1963 in New Orleans, where Oswald passed the time—and comes to realize that a small-town whodunit has global repercussions. And moreover, he finds that his life and his family's life are darkened forever, all because he has opened up the floorboards and let in the light on a taboo subject that some powerful people wanted to remain hidden. Like a Capra everyman, he is darkened and sacrificed, yet wins his soul in the end. There are many flaws in the real Garrison (arrogance and paranoia, to name a couple), but we did not deal with them in the film, because you either had to make Garrison the issue or make Kennedy the issue. I chose Kennedy.

Personally, I've never found Garrison to be the "kook" pictured by a hostile press. Despite the caricatures of him as a modern Huey Long, he is an extremely well-read author of three articulate books, an eloquent and witty speaker, a street-popular, thrice-elected DA, a patriotic 27-year military man, an ex-FBI agent, and an appellate judge.

I took the dramatic liberty of having Garrison and his staff uncover much of the evidence that was really uncovered by other, uncredited researchers, such as Sylvia Meagher, Josiah Thompson, Mark Lane, Robert Groden, Peter Dale Scott, Paul Hoch, and Mary Ferrell. (It is typically Capraesque that private citizens have done the work while government bodies stagnated.) As a result, the film brings together several layers of research from the '60s, '70s, and '80s, we hope, in a seamless jigsaw puzzle that will allow the audience, for the first time, to understand what happened and why. As an outsider to conspiracy theories until the late '80s, I was always confused by competing theories—involving the Mafia, the C.I.A., Castro, anti-Castro Cubans, etc.—which, of course, allow the Lie to continue.

Today, even Garrison acknowledges the mistakes in his investigation and expresses doubt that the man he charged with conspiracy to kill the president, Clay Shaw (Tommy Lee Jones), was ever more than a fringe player. However, he did have evidence that appeared to connect Shaw and Oswald, and even more intriguing leads suggesting that Shaw was the mysterious "Clay Bertrand," who called a New Orleans attorney the day of the assassination and asked him to go to Dallas to represent Oswald.

Shaw appeared to have good intelligence-community connections—he served in the OSS in World War II and had a position on the board of a trade-show company expelled from Italy for espionage activities, among them raising funds for an assassination attempt on French president Charles de Gaulle, according to Italian and Canadian newspaper reports. There was also the puzzling business in rural Clinton, Louisiana, where, several people state, Shaw and right-wing activist David Ferrie were seen in a black Cadillac, chaperoning Oswald to a Congress for Racial Equality voter registration demonstration.

By getting the case into court, Garrison saw the chance to make the federal government talk truthfully about the assassination, or at least explain the fascinating relationships that Oswald cultivated. Garrison was trying against the odds—and perhaps wrongly—to reach a point of critical mass that would cause a chain reaction of people to come forward and talk, with the hope that the government would then crack and finally deliver the goods.

It was a calculated risk; the legal community condemned Garrison for his tactics. But even worse, it didn't work. The U.S. attorney in Washington declined to serve Garrison's subpoenas on members of the intelligence agencies. Governors from four states refused to extradite witnesses, and Shaw lied repeatedly on the stand, denying any association with Ferrie, Oswald, or members of the intelligence apparatus. Garrison had set out to prove conspiracy—first that there *was* one in

Dealey Plaza and then that Shaw was a part of it. By wresting the Zapruder film from the vaults of Time Inc. (he subpoenaed it), Garrison managed to undermine the claims of the Warren Commission. In post-trial interviews, the jurors indicated they were *convinced* that there was a conspiracy to kill Kennedy.

Despite some persuasive testimony, however, Garrison could not convince the jury that Shaw knew Ferrie or Oswald, and he was acquitted. Shortly after the trial ended, Garrison came across two photos of Shaw and Ferrie together at a party—proof positive that they knew each other. We include restagings of the photos as well as the situations in which they were taken, but we do not pretend Garrison had knowledge of them before the trial.

In the same frustrating vein, Shaw's C.I.A. ties were confirmed in later years by ex-C.I.A. director Richard Helms, who admitted Shaw had worked for the agency, and his executive assistant Victor Marchetti, who confirmed Ferrie's C.I.A. ties. Marchetti noted that during the Garrison investigation, Helms repeatedly voiced concern for Shaw's defense, urging the agency to do all it could to help him. These were the breaks Garrison never got.

I took the liberty of expanding on the thrashing Garrison administered to the *Warren Commission Report* , using the trial as a forum for presenting all the evidence of the J.F.K. case across the board—the Dealey Plaza witnesses, the medical evidence, Oswald's background, photographic evidence, the troubling murder of Dallas policeman J.D. Tippit, the government cover-up. While in no way claiming I now know everything, I allow my Garrison character to speculate to his staff and in the trial on what *might* have happened.

For many scenes, I took dialogue straight from the written record—the Warren Commission volumes and the Shaw trial transcripts—letting history speak for itself. I could not, of course, interview Oswald, Ruby, Ferrie, or Shaw—all of whom died years ago. We tracked down people who knew them. For Oswald (Gary Oldman) and Ruby (Brian Doyle Murray), there is a considerable historical record, audiovisual as well as written. Oswald remains an enigma, so I stuck tightly to the record for his dialogue, taking his lines verbatim from transcripts and news footage. I relied partly on my conversations with his wife, Marina, when we shot scenes of Oswald at home with his family. The picture that emerges is one of a devoted father and husband trying to make a new, difficult marriage work.

Eyewitnesses placed Ruby in Dealey Plaza at various times during the day, at Parkland Hospital after the shooting, and at the Dallas Police Station for a good part of the assassination weekend. Several people also reported seeing Oswald at Ruby's Carousel Club.

Ferrie (Joe Pesci) was a self-styled psychologist/hypnotist/priest, expert pilot, and vehement anti-Communist. He ran a New Orleans unit of the Civil Air Patrol, which had a cadet program that Oswald, as well as many other young boys, joined as teenagers, often to the dismay of their parents and the police. One scene called for Ferrie to make a partial confession to a Garrison investigator, Louis Ivon. The meeting did take place, very shortly before Ferrie's mysterious death, and Ivon remembers it well. The written record indicates that Ferrie was not one for subtlety or sugarcoating ("There is nothing that I would enjoy better than blowing the hell out of every damn Russian, Communist, Red, or what-have-you ... "), and it looked like he was about to break shortly before his death. In this scene, Ferrie is nervous, anguished, frightened, and vulnerable—and we're not quite sure if he's telling us the truth.

For one of Garrison's star witnesses, I created the character of Willie O'Keefe (Kevin Bacon), a young friend of Ferrie's and Shaw's doing time in Angola Penitentiary on prostitution charges. O'Keefe's trial testimony actually belonged to an insurance salesman named Perry Russo, who testified he attended a party at which Shaw, Ferrie, and Oswald discussed the upcoming assassination. I introduced elements of two other New Orleanians—Raymond Broshears and David Logan—to explore more fully the Ferrie-Shaw-C.I.A. connections in New Orleans in 1963.

Putting O'Keefe in prison was our choice, and, ironically, it made his character less credible, a problem Garrison knew well. Garrison's critics attacked his witnesses for being gays, junkies, political extremists. Garrison had little patience with this, telling reporters, "There are many attorneys who are brilliant liars, and there are dope addicts who have never learned to lie—and that's the case here."

Two composite anti-Castro Cubans appear in shadowy situations throughout the film, as in the puzzling incident in which they, with Oswald in tow, visit a Cuban woman, Silvia Odio, in Dallas shortly before the assassination. Silvia (like Oswald) is very real, but the two men are not based on anyone in particular and represent the active anti-Castro/Communist underworld of the Kennedy era, a movement not limited to Cubans. American mercenaries, organized-crime figures, right-wing fanatics, and the C.I.A. were all heavily involved in plots to subvert and destroy the Castro regime. To them, J.F.K. was soft on communism, and they made no secret of their hatred for him. Ferrie and Ruby ran with elements of this crowd, and so did Oswald, something highly unusual given his public pro-Marxist facade. The two Cubans, as well as ex-FBI agent Guy Bannister (Ed Asner) and his sometime associate Jack Martin (Jack Lemmon), help tie these murky associations together.

In reality, Garrison's legal staff consisted of a few assistant DAs and a fluctuating number of volunteer investigators, some of whom doubted his case and gave files and confidential information to the defense. Although I wanted to show the dissension within Garrison's office—and how it might have affected the trial—I needed to limit the number of people involved. I scaled down the investigative force to four assistant DAs and one chief investigator. One of the assistants is Garrison's Judas, and another is a woman, a deliberate nod to the corps of women researchers whose relentless efforts have helped keep the J.F.K. case alive.

So far as recreating the scene of the crime (Dealey Plaza) is concerned, we employed painstaking detail in turning the three-acre site back 27 years, moving streetlights and signs, cutting back trees, laying railroad tracks, printing exact replicas of the boxes in the Texas School Book Depository. But details are not facts, and the real issue was where the shots were coming from. Taking into account all the available photographic, eyewitness, and acoustic evidence, we hypothetically placed our shooters and fired our shots in an attempt to show mysterious figures, strange occurrences, and an all-out ambush on November 22.

But ultimately, I had to take the assassination out of Dallas and the conspiracy out of New Orleans and bring it all back to Washington, where it really began. To tell the bigger story—the reason why, as opposed to who or how—I drew from my own personal experience and from Garrison's post-trial writings. Three years ago, I met retired Air Force colonel L. Fletcher Prouty, whose 1973 book, *The Secret Team: The C.I.A. and Its Allies in Control of the United States and the World*, has become something of a classic on the inner workings of the government. Fletcher told me about his experiences as chief of special operations in the joint staff during the Kennedy Administration, the crucial early years of the Vietnam War. We loosely based a character known only as X on him. X meets with Garrison once before the trial and once after, to fill him in on the true meaning of Kennedy's murder.

Unfortunately, Prouty's long and loyal service to his country has been ignored by some today, who cite his association with the far-right Liberty Lobby. As offensive as this group is, Prouty's error in judgment in his later years in no way detracts from his insights into the highest levels of the American intelligence community during the '60s.

Just as the production was starting, I had the good fortune of being contacted by John Newman, an academic historian finishing up fifteen years of work on the Vietnam War during the Kennedy years. (His book, *JFK and Vietnam: Deception, Intrigue and the Struggle for Power*, will be out this month.) Newman's thorough policy analysis and dozens of interviews with military and government officials backed up a lot of what Prouty knew from first-hand experience and went way beyond it in scope and documentation. I added Newman's material to the X scenes.

The facts are that Kennedy was deeply ambivalent about the war in Vietnam. He said so privately to a number of his confidants—among them Kennedy aide Kenneth O'Donell, senators Mike Mansfield and Wayne Morse, and National Security Council staffer Michael Forrestal—and took tentative public steps toward withdrawing our combat advisers. There are three critical documents—National Security Action Memos (NSAMs) 111, 263, and 273—in Kennedy's Vietnam history.

In November 1961, the Joint Chiefs of Staff requested combat troops for Vietnam. Kennedy had turned down a similar request for Laos some months before, and with NSAM 111, he put more advisers into Vietnam but specifically *made no mention of combat troops*. The Joint Chiefs were not placated. How can we justify troops in Vietnam while ignoring Cuba, Kennedy asked. The pressure came to a head in the Cuban Missile Crisis of October 1962, when the Joint Chiefs again pushed Kennedy to invade Cuba. He refused, instead cutting a highly criticized deal with Khrushchev that included a promise not to invade Cuba if all offensive weapons were removed. Less than a year later, the Soviet Union, Great

Britain, and the United States signed the Nuclear Test Ban Treaty, a move that Kennedy called "a step toward reason." He also sought negotiations with Castro through back door channels; meanwhile, the C.I.A. continued—without his permission-its clandestine program with organized crime to assassinate Castro.

Sometime in 1962, Kennedy started to contemplate a withdrawal from Vietnam by 1965. While maintaining a strong public anti-Communist posture, by 1963 Kennedy knew that with a 1964 re-election victory, he could consolidate his grip on power and move more forcefully to end the Cold War. On October 11, 1963, he showed he meant business, issuing NSAM 263, a "top secret" directive that actually implemented an unannounced 1,000-man withdrawal by the end of that year.

Unfortunately, Kennedy had only six weeks to live. Barely *four days* after Kennedy was killed, there was a change in Vietnam policy when Lyndon Johnson, the new chief executive, signed NSAM 273, dated November 26, 1973. NSAM 273 paid lip service to the 1,000-man withdrawal but in fact contained escalatory language with respect to war policy. "Although 1,000 men were technically withdrawn, no actual reduction of U.S. strength occurred," said *The Pentagon Papers*.

Under the Johnson Administration, our government had no intention of withdrawing. In *Vietnam: A History*, Stanley Karnow quotes Johnson at a Christmas 1963 cocktail party, telling some of the Joint Chiefs, "Just get me elected, and then you can have your war," an anecdote that we take the liberty of transposing to the Oval Office. As we all know, a significant withdrawal from Vietnam did not happen for a full decade after the assassination, and not until after 58,000 Americans and about 1 million South Vietnamese had died. These are the facts, but hardly the history that we learn in school or in the newspapers.

By 1970, without the benefit of knowing Prouty or Newman, Garrison had reached the same conclusion. He believed that a primary reason J.F.K. was killed was because he wanted to end the military buildup in Southeast Asia.

In the end, the importance of a historical episode is not just its factual content but its emotional and ethical significance as well. Why did it happen? What does it mean? Was it a triumph or a tragedy? For whom? This process of evaluation, when undertaken by a whole society, eventually leads to the creation of a cultural myth. Unlike children's fairy tales, myths have always expressed the true inner meaning of human events. Myths are dynamic. They reinterpret history in order to create lasting, universal truths. For example, artists for centuries have tackled exactly the same historical and religious stories and produced a Christ with a thousand faces.

From Griffith to Kubrick, moviemakers have operated on the principle that the dramatic force of a story transcends the "facts." With *JFK*, we are attempting to film the true inner meaning of the Dallas labyrinth—the mythical and spiritual dimension of Kennedy's murder—to help us understand why the shots in Dealey Plaza still continue to reverberate in our nightmares.

In a sense, the *Warren Commission Report*, inadequate as a record of facts, was a stunning success as a mythical document. This is the real reason it was so widely accepted when it was first published in September 1964. Still grieving over the loss of the president, people wanted to accept its soothing conclusions, regardless of whether those conclusions were true, because they wanted to believe that the death of a president was a tragic accident, like a car wreck or a bolt of lightning. The gods had intervened—an act of a lone madman who, with poetic justice, was himself shot dead by another madman.

Our film's mythology is different, and, hopefully, it will replace the *Warren Commission Report*, as *Gone With the Wind* replaced *Uncle Tom's Cabin* and was in turn replaced by *Roots* and *The Civil War*. Our scenario views Kennedy as maturing by the end of his thousand days in office from a Cold Warrior into a visionary statesman (much like Gorbachev two decades later) who passionately sought détente abroad and an end to racial apartheid at home. Tragically, these progressive, humanitarian objectives sealed J.F.K.'s doom.

The assassination was America's first coup d'état, and it worked. It worked because we never knew that it even happened. And we, Kennedy's godchildren, the baby-boom generation that believed his stirring words and handsome image, are like Hamlet in the first act, children of a slain leader, unaware of why he was killed or even that a false father figure inhabits the throne.

Melancholy sons and daughters, we remain haunted by Kennedy's ghost and his unfulfilled dreams. Through the '60s, we watched in horror as the opponents of those dreams profited from the closing of the New Frontier. Since November 1963, we have endured Vietnam, Watergate, race riots, assassinations of progressive leaders, escalating war budgets, recession, poverty, crime, drugs, loss of trust in the government, and most of all, fear—the fear that makes law and order so falsely attractive.

Inevitably, J.F.K.'s death will come to be understood as the beginning of terrible times for the United States and that this tragic conjunction was not a coincidence. I think many Americans already suspect that, rightly or wrongly, November 22, 1963, marked the watershed when the enemy within wrested control of the nation's future from the hands of the people and their elected representatives.

We must start to change things. We must start by looking at the '60s not as history but as a seminal decade for the postwar generation coming into power in the '90s. Dan Quayle's thinking was shaped by the '60s as much as my own, and he may be our next president. We still have a choice. What is past is prologue. To forget that past is to be condemned to relive it.

Oliver Stone is the cowriter-director of JFK. This article was written while the film was still being edited. Various characters and events mentioned may not be in the final version.

Reprinted by permission of the author.

Z MAGAZINE

CONSPIRACY? ... NOT!

Michael Albert

Nowadays, wherever they go, leftists encounter many questions from newly political folks about this or that political episode—the October Surprise, the BCCI scandal, Irancontra, David Duke—with an emphasis on who did what, when, and with what foreknowledge and intent. They field far fewer questions about the *systemic* causes of trends and events. People study the membership of some rogue group. They ignore the structure of government and corporations. How did this "fashion" come about? Where is it taking us?

CONSPIRACY THEORY

A conspiracy theory is a hypothesis that some events were caused by the secret machinations of undemocratic individuals. A prime example is to explain Iran-contra as the rogue actions of Oliver North and co-conspirators. Likewise, another conspiracy theory explains the hostageholding in Carter's last presidential year as the machinations of a "secret team" to help Reagan win the presidency. A conspiracy theory of Karen Silkwood's murder would uncover the names of people who secretly planned and carried out the murder. Bending usage, we could even imagine a conspiracy theory of patriarchy as men uniting to deny women status, or a conspiracy theory of the U.S. government as competing groups seeking power for their own ends.

Conspiracies exist. Groups regularly do things without issuing press releases and this becomes a conspiracy whenever their actions transcend "normal" behavior. We don't talk of a conspiracy to win an election if the suspect activity includes only candidates and their handlers working privately to develop effective strategy. We do talk about a conspiracy if the resulting action involves stealing the other team's plans, spiking their Whiskey Sours, or other exceptional activity. When a conspiracy cause's some outcome, the outcome would not have happened had not the *particular* people with their particular inclinations come together and cheated.

Conspiracy theories may or may not identify real coteries with real influence. Conspiracy theories:

(a) Claim that a particular group acted outside usual norms in a rogue and generally secretive fashion.

(b) Disregard the structural features of institutions.

Personalities, personal timetables, secret meetings, and conspirators' joint actions, claim attention. Institutional relations drop from view. We ask, did North meet with Bush before or after the meeting between MacFarlane and Mr. X? Do we have a document that revealed the plan in advance? Do phone conversations implicate so and so? How credible is that witness?

INSTITUTIONAL THEORY

In an institutional theory, personalities and personal motives enter the discussion only as results of more basic factors. The personal actions culminating in some event do not serve as explanation. The theory explains phenomena via the roles, incentives, and dynamics of underlying institutions. An institutional theory doesn't ignore human actions, but the point of an institutional explanation is to move from personal factors to institutional ones. If the particular people hadn't been there to do it, most likely someone else would have.

An institutional theory of Iran-contra and the October surprise would explain how and why these activities arose in a society with our political, social, and economic forms. An institutional theory of Karen Silkwood's murder would reveal nuclear industry and larger societal pressures that provoked her murder. An institutional theory of patriarchy explains gender relations in terms of marriage, the church, the market, socialization, etc. An institutional theory of government emphasizes the control and dissemination of information, the dynamics of bureaucracy, and the role of subservience to class, race, and gender interests.

Institutions exist. Whenever they have sufficient impact on events, developing an institutional theory makes sense. However, when an event arises from a unique conjuncture of particular people and opportunities, while institutions undoubtedly play a role, it may not be generalizable and an institutional theory may be out of place or even impossible to construct.

Institutional theories may or may not identify real relationships with real influence on the events they explain. Institutional theories:

(a) Claim that the normal operations of some institutions generate the behaviors and motivations leading to the events in question.

(b) Address personalities, personal interests, personal timetables, and meetings only as facts about the events needing explanation, not as explanations themselves.

Organizational, motivational, and behavioral implications of institutions gain most attention. Particular people, while not becoming mere ciphers, are not accorded priority as causal agents.

THE DIFFERENCE

To see the difference between conspiracy theory and institutional theory we can compare a smattering of the views of two currently popular critics of U.S. foreign policy, Noam Chomsky and Craig Hulet, (a popular West coast and Midwest radio talkshow personality). Here is an indicative passage from each.

HULET: "This isn't about Kuwait. This isn't about oil. It has nothing to do with those things. And it certainly doesn't have anything to do with reinstalling a legitimate government [in Kuwait] when *for the first time* we're trying to install a legitimate government which is a non-military despotism listed by Amnesty International as committing the same heinous crimes against his people [as

Hussein] ... What I am suggesting is that *for the first time* we're going to expend American lives to put in a tyrant of only a smaller stature because of the size of his country ... there is a foreign policy that is being orchestrated in violation of U.S. Law, international law, and the U.S. constitution. Should that surprise anyone after Watergate, the Kennedy assassination? ...

"Why should Americans die to restore a dictator invaded by another dictator? First it was to protect Saudi Arabia. Everybody now knows he [Hussein] had no intention of going any further than Kuwait. So they dropped that as a reason. They came up with the next one, that this is about oil. Then all of a sudden oil prices, right in the midst of the war, drop to $21 a barrel, which was where it was before the war. So it obviously can't be about oil. So it can't be our vital interests at stake. Is it about a legitimate government? If it's about a legitimate government, then we're putting back in power a despot under the Breshnev doctrine, not the Truman doctrine. The Breshnev doctrine being that we treat all nations as sovereign equalities regardless of how despotic they are, and we keep them in power. *So for the first time* George Bush is now acting out the Breshnev doctrine rather than installing a free republic or keeping a free people free. [There follows a long discussion of the U.S. holdings and influence of the Al Sabah ruling Kuwaiti family, followed by listener questions primarily focused on the efficacy of impeaching George Bush to which Hulet's response is:] It's going to be up to the public whether or not George Bush—*and I agree, it's a ruling Junta*—is impeached. It won't be just up to Senators and Congressmen to make this decision. They won't make the decision unless public opinion supports this kind of action." [emphasis added.]

CHOMSKY: "If we hope to understand anything about the foreign policy of any state, it is a good idea to begin by investigating the domestic social structure: Who sets foreign policy? What interests do these people represent? What is the domestic source of their power? It is a reasonable surmise that the policy that evolves will reflect the special interests of those who design it. An honest study of history will reveal that this natural expectation is quite generally fulfilled. The evidence is overlwhelming, in my opinion, that the United States is no exception to the general rule—a thesis that is often characterized as a 'radical critique' ...

"Some attention to the historical record, as well as common sense, leads to a second reasonable expectation: In every society there will emerge a caste of propagandists who labor to disguise the obvious, to conceal the actual workings of power, and to spin a web of mythical goals and purposes, utterly benign, that allegedly guide national policy ... any horror, any atrocity will be explained away as an unfortunate—or sometimes tragic—deviation from the national purpose ...

"Since World War II there has been a continuing process of centralization of decision-making in the state executive, certainly with regard to foreign policy. Secondly, there has been a tendency through much of this period toward domestic economic concentration. Furthermore, these two processes are closely related, because of the enormous corporate influence over the state executive ... "

The common theme often evidenced by these two is distaste for U.S. foreign policy. The difference is that Hulet understands policy as the preferences of particular groups of people—in the Gulf War, "a junta" and the Al Sabah family—barely referring to institutions at all. Chomsky understands the policies as arising from particular institutions—for example, "the state executive" and corporations.

For Hulet, the implicit problem is to punish or "impeach" the immediate culprits, a general point applicable to all conspiracy theory. The *modus operandi* of the conspiracy theorist therefore *makes sense* whenever the aim is to attribute proximate personal blame for some occurrence. If we want to prosecute someone for a political assassination to extract retribution or to set a precedent that makes it harder to carry out such actions, the approach of the conspiracy theorist is critical. But the conspiracy approach is beside the point for understanding the *cause* of political assassinations to develop a program to prevent all policies that thwart popular resistance.

Conspiracy theorizing mimics the personality/ dates/times approach to history. It is a sports fans' or voyeur's view of complex circumstances. It can manipulate facts or present them accurately. When it's done well, it has its place, in uncovering culprits, but it is never a very enlightening approach.

For radicals trying to change society, the problem is to discern the underlying institutional causes of foreign policy. The *modus operandi* of the institutional theorist would not make much sense for discovering which individuals conceived and argued for a policy, or who in particular decided to bomb a civilian shelter. To understand why these things happen, however, and under what conditions they will continue to happen, institutional theory is indispensable and the motives, methods, and timetables of the actual perpetrators are largely beside the point.

Take the media. A conspiracy approach will highlight the actions of some coterie of editors, writers, newscasters, particular owners, or even a lobby. An institutional approach will mention the actions of these actors as evidence, but will highlight the corporate and ideological pressures giving rise to those influences.

A person inclined toward finding conspiracies will listen to evidence of media subservience to power and see a cabal of bad guys, perhaps corporate, perhaps religious, perhaps federal, censoring the media *from doing its proper job*. The conspiracist will then want to know about the cabal and how people succumb to its will, etc.

A person inclined toward institutional analysis will listen to evidence of media subservience to power and see that the media's internal bureaucracy, its socialization processes, and the interests of its owners engender these results as part of the media *succeeding at its job*. The institutionalist will then want to know about the media's structural features and how they work, and about the guiding interests and what they imply.

The conspiracy approach will lead people to believe that:

(a) They should educate the malefactors to change their motives, or

(b) They should get rid of the malefactors and back new editors, writers, newscasters, or owners.

The institutional approach will note the possible gains from changes in personnel, but also explain how limited these changes will be. It will incline people

(a) To wage a campaign of constant pressure to offset the constant institutional pressures for obfuscation, or

(b) To create new media free from the institutional pressures of the mainstream.

THE APPEAL OF CONSPIRACY THEORY

Conspiracy theory appeals to prosecutors and lawyers, since they must identify proximate causes and human actors. But why does it appeal to people concerned to change society?

There are a many possible answers that probably all operate, to varying degrees, on people who favor conspiracy theory. First, conspiracy theory is often compelling and the evidence conspiracy theories reveal is often useful. Moreover, description of the detailed entwinements can become addictive. Conspiracy theory has the appeal of a mystery—it is dramatic, compelling, vivid, and human. Finally, the desire for retribution helps fuel continuing forays into personal details.

Second, conspiracy theories have manageable implications. They imply that all was once well and that it can be okay again, if only the conspirators can be dealt with. Conspiracy theories therefore explain ills without forcing us to disavow society's underlying institutions. They allow us to admit horrors, and express our indignation and anger without rejecting the basic norms of society. We can even confine our anger to the most blatant perpetrators. That government official or corporate lawyer is bad, but many others are good and the government and law *per se* are okay. We need only get rid of the bad apples.

All this is convenient and seductive. We can reject specific candidates but not government, specific CEOs but not capitalism, specific writers, editors, and even owners, but not all mainstream media. We reject some manipulators, but not society's basic institutions. We can, therefore, continue to appeal to the institutions for recognition, status, or payment.

Third, conspiracy theory provides an easy and quick outlet for pent up passions withheld from targets that seem unassailable or that might strike back. This is conspiracy theory turned into scapegoat theory.

WHERE ARE CONSPIRACY THEORIES TAKING US?

It would be bad enough if endless personalistic attention to Iran-contra, the October Surprise, etc., were just attuning people to search after coteries, while ignoring institutions. This was the effect, for example, of the many Kennedy Assassination theories of past decades. At least the values at play would be progressive and we could hope people would gravitate toward real explanation of more structural phenomena.

But the fact is, the values inspiring conspiratorial ways of trying to explain events are currently drastically diverging from progressive values. Even some sectors of left activists have become so hungry for quick-fix conspiracy explanations they are beginning to gravitate toward any conspiracy claim, no matter how ridiculous.

Thus the field of conspiracy theorizing has become attractive and new entrants are no longer always progressive and sometimes even tilt toward reaction or downright fascism. The presentation of conspiracy theories has moved from little newsletters and journals to large audience radio talk shows and magazines and, at the same time, from identifying "secret teams" of C.I.A. operatives to imagining all-powerful networks of Arab financiers and worldwide Jewish bankers' fraternities.

There is an ironic analogy here to Republican Party politics. Many leftists now claim that the Republican Party's recent manipulations of race paved the way for David Duke by reacclimating the public to racial stereotyping and increasing its appetite for more. In somewhat the same way, isn't it plausible that the relatively huge resources thrown into progressive conspiracy writing, organizing, and proselytizing over the past decade is now coming home to roost? Of course, the changing times are partly responsible for growing public interest in conspiracies, but doesn't past behavior by progressives bear a share of responsibility as well?

WHAT TO DO ABOUT IT

Leftist institutionalist theorists generally ignore conspiracy theorists as irrelevant. To confront their arguments is to enter a miasma of potentially fabricated detail from which there is no escape. Nothing constructive emerges. But perhaps this view needs some rethinking. When Holly Sklar, Steve Shalom, Noam Chomsky, or any of many other left analysts talk about events, even about Iran-contra or the October Surprise, they pay attention to proximate facts but also the institutional context. That's as it should be, but apparently it's no longer enough. Those who have an institutional critique now have two additional responsibilities. First, they need to point out the inadequacy of left conspiracy theory, showing that at best it does not go far enough to be useful for organizers. Second, they need to debunk rightist conspiracy theory, removing its aura of opposition and revealing its underlying racist and elitist allegiances.

Likewise, when progressive radio shows and left magazines invite people to communicate with their public, it is good to be sure the guest is coherent, has effective speaking or writing style, talks about the issues, identifies actors accurately, and knows about the relevant history.

But it isn't enough. Fascists can fulfill these standards and still spout made-up statistics as if they were facts, disgusting allegations about social groups as if they were objective commentary, and nothing at all about real institutional relations, passing this whole mess off as a useful way to look at the world to understand and affect social events. Left media should take responsibility for its offerings. People expect that if commentators appear on our shows and in our publications they have a degree of integrity, honesty, and sensitivity. We should not lend credence to right-wing garbage, whether it is blatant or so well concealed as to be civil but malicious. Regarding progressive and left conspiracy theory: while it often uncovers important evidence, left media ought to indicate its limits and augment it with institutional and contextual analysis.

Michael Albert is a co-founder and editor of Z Magazine.

Reprinted by permission of the author.

FEBRUARY 1992

Z MAGAZINE

JFK AND US

Michael Albert

Before seeing *JFK* I wrote last month's column on conspiracy theory. Then I heard from friends what I, more or less, anticipated, that the film was a horrible misrepresentation that would put leftists in an impossible position. The main problems, I was given to understand, were: (1) the film made Kennedy a marvelous savior who would have taken the country down a peaceful, just road had he only lived long enough; and (2) the film snares viewers in an endless quagmire of details about conspirators, with no useful attention to institutions. In sum:

◆ *JFK* plot: John F. Kennedy's murder was a *coup d'état* and the country has since gone to hell in a handcart.

◆ *JFK* moral: Find a new Kennedy and keep him alive long enough to get the country back on track.

◆ *JFK* problem: *JFK* is liberal politics coupled to paranoid fantasy. Stone missed the point of what's now wrong with, and has always been wrong with, our country—the intrinsic oppressiveness of its basic institutions.

Obviously, with this advance billing, as I entered the theater I was ready for the worst. I expected clips of Kennedy speaking, Kennedy riding horseback, Kennedy looking good talking about humanity's needs, all juxtaposed to a typical thriller about evil C.I.A. renegades stealing our nation's fine institutions from good folks, like Kennedy, who were, until then, looking out for our well being and would do so again, if we just give them back the chance.

But that isn't the movie I saw. John F. Kennedy, except as target and corpse, was pretty much absent from *JFK*. *JFK* posits Pentagon, C.I.A., corporate profit-seeking militarism *from before Kennedy's election*, that Kennedy, for reasons left unstated, opposed. For Oliver Stone, this is why Kennedy was killed and why the murder should have been called a *coup d'état*. But Stone's "bad guy" is a *system* oriented to war and profitability—"the military-industrial complex"—and a lot of people obeying without questioning, not a few renegades stealing the government to set it on a new course.

Okay, *JFK* is wrong about Kennedy, and that's certainly a major flaw. Kennedy was not a good guy and would not have turned history on its head. Still, I remember being into Kennedy as a teenager, and it wasn't because he was a Cold Warrior, a concept which meant nothing whatsoever to me at the time. Some people may want to argue that the tendency for so many people to relate so positively to Kennedy was a proto-fascist phenomenon, but I don't think so. His policies were nothing new, but the mood swirling about John Kennedy aroused a new kind of social and moral concern and, whether intentionally or not, contributed significantly to awakening my generation to politics as morality. Of course that doesn't prove that Kennedy was an advocate of peace and justice, much less a paragon of virtue. Indeed, as Alex Cockburn in the *Nation* and others elsewhere have already indicated, there is no evidence that Kennedy would have quickly ended the war in Vietnam and decimated the C.I.A., if given the opportunity. As to the military industrial complex, before Reagan, John Kennedy was arguably its best friend.

So why did Stone employ the "he would have ended the war" hypothesis? It isn't hard to understand. Cockburn and other left analysts address the assassination *after* having looked at Kennedy's record and concluded that Kennedy was part of the establishment, not its enemy. Stone starts, instead, with the murder. He notes from its nature that the assassination had to be undertaken by a large, well organized group of actors. He further notes that the cover-up had to be undertaken by the government, right up to its highest levels. These are the facts—and the evidence in their favor is quite compelling—that Stone wants to explain. So Stone rejects the lone lunatic explanation, and seeks a motive for the establishment as a whole to kill Kennedy, and he comes up with one, however far fetched: Kennedy was doing things regarding foreign policy that the establishment was so opposed to that it killed him. What things? Well, how about policy reversal on the war and covert actions? So, Stone hypothesizes it was a *coup d'état* engineered by the U.S. government and corporate leadership.

The most compelling reason why we can deduce that Stone is wrong about this is important but has yet to be even mentioned in anything I've read about the film.

(1) It is not because this country isn't violent. Our's is arguably the most violent country in the world.

(2) It isn't because it's impossible for sons (or daughters) of capital (a) to be murderers and liars as Lyndon Johnson et. al. would have been in Stone's scenario, or (b) to oppose aims of capital, as J.F.K. would have done in Stone's scenario.

(3) Also, the argument against government-assassination doesn't depend on detailed analysis of films, testimony, bullets, and actuarial reports such as those that indicate the odds against so many potential witnesses having died so shortly after the assassination were billions to one. The facts show a conspiracy to kill Kennedy and then to cover up the killing, but unless there is a smoking gun

waiting to be entered in evidence, the facts don't show *who* was involved or *why*.

Therefore, to develop an argument able to rule out Lyndon Johnson, the Joint Chiefs of Staff, and the Boards of GM and Lockheed as the conspiring assassins, the only remaining option is to show that something about the history of the period indicates that they didn't do it. To understand this type argument, suppose Kennedy was what Stone says and much more. Suppose he had undergone some type of moral awakening and consciousness raising and had over night become the political/intellectual/moral equivalent of Martin Luther King, cum Rosa Parks, cum Robin Morgan,cum Noam Chomsky. This is borderline loony tunes, but not absolutely impossible. However, even then, and I don't think Oliver Stone believes anything like this level of transformation occurred, killing Kennedy would still *not top* the establishment agenda.

In short, why take the risk before trying other means to stay Kennedy's hand? Remember, even if Kennedy had become a paragon of peace and virtue, he did not have the country behind him. There were no mass movements seeking radical ends or any progressive change at all. So if you're the head of Lockheed or the C.I.A. or whatever else, why not just use threats of capital flight, media manipulation, and the other time-honored mechanisms available for restraining unwanted government initiative to so limit Kennedy's capacity to cause trouble that his time in office could be ridden out peaceably? If we want to claim that the Pentagon, C.I.A., and corporate America assassinated Kennedy, at a minimum we need to show that they had already tried coercing him via the safer, system-maintaining mechanisms they ordinarily use to get their way. Without trying that first step, they would never have gone on to the far more risky assassination. However, there is no such evidence.

If I wanted to tell a tale of the assassination with the government as killer, like Stone I'd try to find evidence that Kennedy represented a threat that needed to be extinguished. Knowing Kennedy wasn't a closet pacifist, however, I might try to argue that Kennedy was the point man for a growing movement of technocrats upset with the irrational, unplanned chaos of capitalism and intent on bringing it under the control of a corps of intellectual policy-makers and planners. In this persona, Kennedy with aides like MacNamara, Bundy, Schlesinger, et. al., would become a more believable adversary than he would as a closet pacifist. As the leader of technocracy, he would have had a growing constituency becoming increasingly excited at the prospect of government by the young and knowledgeable, for the young and knowledgeable. The problem irking corporate élites would not be the untenable claim that Kennedy was going to put power in the hands of working people, but the more plausible claim that he was going to put government in the hands of eager academics and professionals, not as servants to capital, but as rulers over capital. In this scenario, killing Kennedy would have been a preventive strike against a class uprising.

This hypothesis has the merit of being possible under the type of government and economy we have. Kennedy becomes a modern day Bolshevik, without the hammer and sickle, of course, but nonetheless seeking to institute rule by intellectual élites rather than property owners. Since Kennedy was rapidly arousing the class consciousness of his primary constituency, the coordinator class of managers and other intellectuals located "between labor and capital," he had to be stopped. Kennedy is not, in this rendering of history, a paragon of peace and justice, but a broker for intellectual order and managerial regulation. Regrettably for the theory, however, two problems arise. First, as for Stone's version, there was no real evidence of growing efforts to constrain Kennedy prior to the assassination, and this would surely have been present if the assassination occurred at the behest of capital and state. Second, after Kennedy was killed, the intellectuals stayed in Washington, if anything, enjoying greater power than before.

So what's a reasonable explanation for why Kennedy was killed and the assassination was whitewashed? I've always assumed that the Mafia—people who, after all, know how to kill other people and are highly skilled at it—plus some of their allies in government, did Kennedy in. Perhaps Kennedy was threatening their operations. Perhaps it was a family thing. Likely there were some crazy Cold Warrior/C.I.A. types involved, either out of anger over the Bay of Pigs, as a way to pay back Mafia debts, or, as Stone prefers, because they feared Kennedy would try "Vietnamization" rather than letting them do their thing in the war. In any event, presumably because there were some renegade government folks involved, or some crazy corporate folks, or because some FBI types were worried that maybe Cubans were involved, the cover-up was begun. Once underway it is easy to predict that it would grow so large that it incorporated government to the highest levels.

Would this explanatory theme plus all the rest of Stone's *JFK* have made a better movie? It would certainly have avoided false claims about Kennedy's aims. But *JFK* is a movie, after all, not a scholarly historical study. And it seems to me that as a movie, despite its historical flaws, *JFK* sends viewers out thinking not so much about renegade bad guys, as about the country *per se*, and not so much about Kennedy's virtues, as about the system's faults. The movie is brilliant drama, yet it conveys a ton of information, setting a valuable precedent about the possibility of entertaining and educating simultaneously.

Does *JFK* embody some of the problems of conspiracy theorizing I outlined last month? Of course, but fewer than I expected, and fewer, I think, than much of what the left has produced about Irancontra, October Surprise, etc. Moreover, this is a dramatic movie, not a history book or scholarly study. It is a product of Hollywood, not the community of leftists who have been studying the government and socio-economic system for decades.

JFK is directed at provoking the U.S. populace to think about the events, not at providing a careful analysis of the workings of society: it is a limited but fine aim, especially for a Hollywood movie.

The most revealing fact about the massive response to *JFK* is that, in all the hoopla about the movie, you rarely if ever hear anyone say, "but Kennedy couldn't have been killed by American leaders, by the government, by élites—*they don't do things like that.*" Critics claim that *JFK* is manipulative—as if *Bugsy* and every other Hollywood movie isn't. And what does that claim even mean? Saying the Director tugged at people's hearts or tried to get preferred results by having actors say what he wanted is merely saying he was making a movie. Critics claim *JFK* plays loose with history (though Stone repeatedly indicates that the film is hypothesis, not fact)—as if other films and TV, not to mention historical studies and legal accounts, don't play loose with history on a much grander scale. What differentiates *JFK* isn't that it bends circumstances, takes critical license, and incorporates history, it's that it does these things openly with a clear and politically charged purpose. In that sense, it is much less manipulative than most Hollywood films, and infinitely more serious. Critics don't claim, in their rush to judge *JFK* and Oliver Stone, that it is absurd to accuse our great leaders and institutions of so vile behavior as an assassination. And they don't do that because no one would buy it. Most people believe worse about the government, politicians, and big business than anything Oliver Stone has even intimated, much less sealed on celluloid.

The dynamics in *JFK* are compelling for audiences seeing the film not solely because of the obvious nonsense of the magic bullet and the effective way Stone uses the Zapruder film, the geography of the killing site, the revealing portrayal of the autopsy room, and Donald Sutherland's insider speech. it rings true because audiences take it for granted that rich and powerful people are amoral slugs who would do just about anything to further their own and their class's interests.

A point of advice that I hope Stone will take is that because so many people are critical, what we need from filmmakers as capable as Oliver Stone is a movie about winning a better world, about how a better world could work, and about what we could do to bring a better world into being. Those are the things people don't know and might have their consciousness raised by seeing addressed in public movie theaters. In the meantime, films like *JFK* and some of Stone's others are among the only rays of serious concern emerging from Hollywood. Constructively criticizing progressive film efforts makes sense. But some of the more aggressive attacks from the left on a project that has tens of millions of people talking about whether the U.S. government could, would, and did kill its own president over issues of war and peace seem misplaced. On the other hand, I can easily understand why mainstream commentators are having fits about Oliver Stone and his movies.

A WINNING ATTITUDE

On another, if tangentially related point: Is there anyone hunkering down as if to merely survive till death? That's the feeling I've been getting from many left folks. Progressive people seem to think our cause is dust. We are untidy corpses. History is their's. Morbidity is ours. Maybe they were even right and we were wrong all along. Sorry, but I don't get it, and I'm getting sick of it.

One manifestation of this accelerating losing attitude is widespread resignation among people who ought to know better about the possibility of something beyond capitalism. I've written about this before, but, once again, I defy anyone to contest the observation that in the past decade nothing whatsoever has happened to dim the worth of the idea of a society in which gender is not a power division; race, ethnicity,and religion are not grounds for denigration; politics is not disenfranchisement; the ecology is not a sewer; and the economy is not an arena of alienation and exploitation.

The demise of Soviet economies is the decline of a class-divided system of elite rule. The demise of Soviet politics is the decline of one party authoritarianism. These *are both better gone.*

The fact that the Soviet Union and other Eastern bloc countries are barreling toward economic calamity is a catastrophe, but says *nothing* about the potential of the human species to live better in *new* social circumstances.

The fact that the Soviet Union no longer exists as an international counterweight to U.S. international hegemony is a calamity for the Third World, but says nothing about the possibility of those countries following an egalitarian, democratic development path once imperialism is curbed.

Concern about the plight of millions of people in the East and Third World makes sense. But what the Soviet Union got for the past 75 years is what the Bolsheviks sought—political domination by a single party and economic rule by coordinators running planning boards and administering typically hierarchical workplaces. Only a nightmare has died, being replaced, regrettably, by another.

So why are so many good people acting as though we will have markets forever, we will have capitalists forever, and twiddle dee, tweedle dum politics is the epitome of democracy? This resignation is a *non sequitur.* Nothing has reduced the validity of left critique of markets, capitalism, racism, sexism, homophobia, etc. Nothing has diminished the logic or the morality of an appeal to find superior alternatives.

In fact, looking around, I feel considerable optimism. The state of our country is certainly depressing, but there are good prospects for change. People are upset and confused. Their trust in established institutions and authorities has plummeted. Their desire for a plan of action to make life better is growing. In short, the social arena has not been as open to radical (or fascist) critique in many years. It is therefore not hokum to say that this is a horrible time to wallow in depression. By doing so, we abdicate responsibility at a moment when the public is clamoring for answers and programs.

Ironically, while we're moaning and worrying about whether we were *ever* correct, Oliver Stone is telling the country that its government is a bunch of murderous amoral thugs and is getting away with it, and Jerry Brown (really, Jerry Brown) is running for President on the strength of a single claim—that our government is owned by capital and we need to take it back. The fact is, we have a lot of important things to say, and we ought to be doing so, loud and clear. I think a great many people are ready to listen and even take constructive action.
Michael Albert is a co-founder and editor of Z Magazine.

Reprinted by permission of the author.

THE WASHINGTON POST

CONSPIRACY THEORY WINS CONVERTS
Moviegoers Say 'JFK' Nourishes Doubts That Oswald Acted Alone

Robert O'Harrow Jr.

It has all the glitter of Hollywood, critics who deride it as conspiracy-theory fiction and a director intent on raising questions about one of the darkest moments in recent American history.

And in the Washington area over the holiday, it had fans who believed what it says is true about the assassination of President John Fitzgerald Kennedy.

"I came out of the movie feeling different about the government," said Russell Reed, 21, flushed after coming out of a theater in Herndon yesterday.

"It's deep."

Reed had spent the afternoon captivated by the movie *JFK*, which offers a dazzling, cosmic theory of who was behind the assassination of the president on Nov. 22, 1963, including the C.I.A., the Mafia, the Army and even Kennedy's vice president, Lyndon B. Johnson.

In some two dozen interviews at three area theaters yesterday and on New Year's Eve, people coming out of the movie made it clear they believe the film's elaborate theories, even though critics including former president Gerald R. Ford Jr. as well as historians and journalists of the 1960s sharply criticize the three-hour movie as a far-fetched, conspiracy-theory fantasy.

For many of those interviewed, *JFK* sparked remarkably dark opinions about what the U.S. government is capable of doing. Many said they would be surprised if the movie weren't true.

"I really see what the movie said could be possible," said Amanda Peel, 17, a senior at Walt Whitman High School in Montgomery County. "It really makes sense."

Isn't Amanda Peel's mother, a nursery school teacher, worried that her daughter's view of history now will be warped by the movie?

"I believe that could have happened, "said Ann Peel, standing outside the Uptown Theater in the District. "If there's a slight chance in a conspiracy and the government being involved it should come out ... I think fear is what has kept this under wraps."

The movie tries to demolish the official finding that one confused young man named Lee Harvey Oswald shot Kennedy from a sixth-floor perch in a Dallas warehouse. He worked alone, the standard theories and history books say, and died without having told his story when he was gunned down two days later.

Critics have had a romp with *JFK*. While Stone claims the military-industrial complex had Kennedy killed because he was about to pull out of Vietnam, a number of historians and journalists say Kennedy was a Cold Warrior who clearly favored continued U.S. support for the war.

Others say the movie relies almost completely on a bogus theory promoted through the years by a former New Orleans prosecutor, Jim Garrison. Garrison claims two New Orleans men conspired with Oswald to kill the president, even though the men were not in Dallas that day.

Despite such criticism, people such as David and Kathy Buell praise Stone for stirring up the mud. As far as they're concerned, Stone has done a good deed by raising questions, even if he doesn't have all the facts just right.

"I think it will get people talking and I think it should," said Kathy Buell, 34. "Too often we're blind sheep when it comes to what the government does ... and that's not good."

The Buells said they can't stand the idea the government was involved in a conspiracy. And they hate the thought that key documents from a congressional investigation in the late 1970s are sealed until 2029, as the movie points out.

In that investigation, the House Assassination Committee found in 1978 that a conspiracy involving more than one gunman was likely.

"The government should unlock the documents and let people find out what is in the documents," said David Buell, 30, who runs a computer business in the District.

Buell said he went into the movie believing that Oswald was the killer, but now he has serious doubts. As for the ethics of Stone stretching accepted history to push a theory, Buell said, if it works to break information free, then so be it.

"He knows what he is doing," Buell said.

"When you're playing against the system, everything is ethical."

Thomas Bailey, a safety consultant in Vienna, said he came out of the movie a whole-hearted believer there was a conspiracy in Kennedy's death, likely involving the government. But he said few in the 1960s—before events such as the Vietnam War and Watergate jaded people's views of government—would have ever believed such things.

"Thirty years ago, we were more naive. I think the public has been informed," said Bailey, 50, who watched the movie yesterday at Tysons Corner. "We need to be aware of our government."

"The government is not all clean," said his wife, Susan Bailey, 48, who recalled walking toward her college dorm in Richmond when shopkeepers placed radios out in the street as Kennedy's shooting and death were announced.

Jennifer Welti, 41, saw the movie in Herndon yesterday, and years after she "bought the whole official story," she now looks at Kennedy's death through the prism of the film, she said.

Asked whether the intense criticism of the movie bothered her, Welti said she is convinced the movie holds nuggets of truth about what really happened.

"If 50 percent is fiction, the other 50 percent should be looked at," she said. "It denies the whole fabric of what we believe our government to be about."

Some of those interviewed said they intend to look at the assassination more closely because of the movie.

"It makes a difference about what the government is about," said Rhonda Hill, 21, a theater student from Herndon. "It makes you doubt the government."

After emerging from a dark theater in Herndon, Teresa Blickenstaff, 34, a high school art teacher from Frederick, Md., said she felt ashamed after watching the movie.

"I find it almost embarrassing to be an American ... I'd be surprised if it wasn't true," Blickenstaff said. "I want to investigate it further because I want to know. I want to find out the facts."

© 1992 The Washington Post Co. Reprinted with permission.

JANUARY 5, 1992

THE PHILADELPHIA INQUIRER

NEW FILM FIRES A BULLET AT SPECTER'S RE-ELECTION

Katharine Seelye

U.S. Sen. Arlen Specter, already running for re-election during a recession, suddenly finds himself with another load of unwanted baggage—courtesy of Hollywood.

Back in 1964, Specter was an investigator for the Warren Commission and posited the single-bullet theory—that one bullet hit President John F. Kennedy and wounded Texas Gov. John B. Connally Jr., precluding the necessity of a second gunman in Dallas on Nov.22, 1963.

In a freak accident of bad timing for Specter, the controversial movie *JFK* now resurrects the single-bullet theory and portrays it as utterly preposterous—with the bullet zigging, zagging, halting in midair and even at one point making "a dramatic U-turn." With it comes Specter's name—and the derisive hoots of moviegoers across the country. More than three million people have seen the film so far.

For Arlen Specter, the three-hour *JFK* movie boils down to the ultimate three-second negative political spot—when he is still smarting from criticism for his performance in grilling Anita Hill during the hearings on Supreme Court nominee Clarence Thomas.

In the movie—widely discredited in the mainstream press—Kevin Costner, playing New Orleans District Attorney Jim Garrison, calls Specter "an ambitious junior counselor" and brands his theory "one of the grossest lies ever forced on the American people." At the mention of Specter's name, some members of some audiences in Philadelphia and elsewhere hoot, cheer, and applaud in apparent agreement with the disparaging reference.

Specter, who stands by the theory today and dismisses criticism of it as uninformed, mentioned in an interview last week of someday "owning" Time-Warner. Warner Bros. distributed the movie. Asked if he intended to sue for libel, Specter said: "No comment."

The movie comes at a time when Republican Specter faces re-election on a ticket headed by a Republican president whose popularity continues to crumble in the recession. It portrays the single-bullet theory as part and parcel of a massive, Washington-inspired cover-up at a time when the public is suspicious of Washington insiders.

And it comes on the heels of a nationally televised performance by Specter during the Thomas hearings that was widely criticized as insensitive to Anita Hill in particular and women in general—another "prosecution" by an ambitious counselor.

"I can't imagine this movie swaying large numbers of minds," said Todd Gitlin, a media analyst at the University of California at Berkeley. "But coming on top of a performance on the Judiciary Committee that many people viewed as brutal, I don't see how this could help."

Although many in the media have lambasted the movie as a travesty of history, Gitlin said, many moviegoers probably will not read the critiques, and the movie version is likely to become their reality. Numerous studies show that when people have no independent information on a subject, he said, "a mention in the media is more likely to be powerful, more likely to be remembered and more likely to be influential."

The movie-makers say they mentioned Specter's name not because of Anita Hill but because Specter played a a central role in laying the foundation for the falsehoods that they say permeated the official Warren report.

The film "was in the can before the hearings" were televised in mid-October, said Zachary Sklar, who co-wrote the screenplay with director Oliver Stone. Another scene, in which an actor playing Specter questioned a witness, was cut because the film originally ran more than four hours.

But Garrison's mention of Specter was not in the script until a late draft said the film's research coordinator, Jane Rusconi.

As Costner gradually learned more about Specter's role, Rusconi said, the actor asked that his name be inserted in the movie. Until then, the line blamed only "an ambitious junior counselor" for the single-bullet theory.

"Kevin asked who the ambitious junior counselor was," Rusconi said, "and I told him. And he asked, 'What does he do now?' And I said he was a senator from Pennsylvania, and Kevin said, 'I want to say his name.'

"When you're familiar with the material the way Kevin had become, and you know that the Warren Commission had no evidence and that someone dreams up this idea, you don't have the warmest of feelings for him."

But if Anita Hill was unknown to the movie-makers when they wrapped up filming, she and Specter had become household names by the time the movie was released last month.

"People got to know the man [during the hearings] and saw how he operates," said Dennis Barnebey, 44, a Philadelphia teacher, who was among those jeering at the mention of Specter's name at a recent showing of *JFK* at the Andorra shopping center.

Barnebey, who said he would sit out this election, said it did not matter if some details of the movie were inaccurate. "Clearly," he said, "something else happened than what the Warren Commission determined. That's obvious."

Asked why she clapped at the mention of Specter's name, Sheila Laney, 38, a hospital worker from Philadelphia, said: "Anita Hill."

She said the movie was especially powerful for her because, as a black woman, she thought the police would not always protect her in a white neighborhood.

"This film makes white people feel that way—that you can't trust the authorities," she said.

In addition, she said, her grandparents were strong Kennedy supporters. "We had come through the lynchings," she said, "and Kennedy was a beacon for them. Then he was killed. They didn't believe that it was only [Lee Harvey] Oswald. They didn't get technical like this [movie], but they just didn't believe it. My grandmother would say, 'They killed him. They killed him.'"

A *Nova* documentary broadcast in 1988 on PBS concluded that the single-bullet theory was valid "despite its implausible aspects." Nonetheless, only 19 percent of the American public believes Oswald acted alone according to a May survey by *The Washington Post.*

Specter said most people did not believe the theory because they had not read the 888-page Warren Commission report or examined the 17,000 pages in 25 volumes of supporting documentation. He noted, however, that the original commission members split 4-3 on whether to endorse the single-bullet theory.

Some, such as Robert Groden, an assassination analyst from Delaware County, contend that the evidence in the supporting volumes fails to support the commission's conclusions. He said eyewitness accounts and Kennedy's wounds confirm that a second gunman fired at the President from the front. Specter, who recreated the shooting in Dallas, said: "That is just plain untrue."

While highly critical of the movie, Specter added that it actually might help his re-election with some voters because "I had a key role in an important matter early in my career, and some people may find that impressive."

"But most voters are much more concerned with my proposals on things like getting the economy out of the recession or my pending legislation on extending health coverage," he said.

Specter's son, Shanin, an untitled campaign adviser, said voters were well-acquainted with his father. "They're not going to be fooled by a characterization of him in a movie," he said.

"If people believe Arlen Specter was behind a conspiracy to cover up the murderer of John Kennedy, then he wouldn't have been re-elected to the U.S. Senate or re-elected to the U.S. Senate. I don't believe Oliver Stone will change people's minds about Arlen Specter.

"Having said that, I recognize the movie is technically, from a cinematic standpoint a powerful film. I also regard it as a grotesque lie about many, many people in public life."

But will it become campaign fodder? Frank Mankiewicz, Robert F. Kennedy's campaign manager and now a public relations consultant hired to try to smooth the way for *JFK*, said it might.

"If there's anything about the movie that's convincing, it's that magic-bullet business," he said. "It's an absurd, silly, cockamamie theory. And if it becomes known as the Specter theory, I can see a candidate using it. Whatever vote or idea of Specter's on the economy comes along, all his opponent has to say is, 'It's another magic bullet. It won't work this time either.'"

Specter's opponent in the April GOP primary, State Rep. Stephen F. Freind, said he had not seen the movie and did not plan to use it in his campaign but trashed the single-bullet theory anyway.

"If you believe Lee Harvey Oswald acted alone," he said, "you believe in the tooth fairy. It adds up to a credibility issue ... There's this tremendous feeling of a cover-up, that we're not being leveled with."

Tony May, a Democrat and top political adviser to Gov. Casey, suggested that Specter's response to the movie would determine whether it hurt him.

"Was it the Watergate burglary itself, or the way Nixon responded to it, that brought down the presidency?" May asked. "Was it Willie Horton, or the way Dukakis refused to be engaged on the subject, that cost him the election? What is it that throws a candidate off his or her campaign plan and onto the defensive?"

The movie may put Specter on the defensive, said Marc Ross, a political scientist at Bryn Mawr College, "but it also puts him on the air. And Specter is articulate. He's good in those short sound bites." Ross dismissed the movie as "short-term noise."

Reprinted with permission from The Philadelphia Inquirer.

THE NEW YORK TIMES

REFLECTIONS ON THE GRASSY KNOLL

Stefan Kanfer

As Thoreau pointed out, sometimes the circumstantial evidence is overwhelming, as when you find a trout in the milk. In the case of the film *JFK*, the trout glistens and stinks by moonlight.

Under my supervision, a group of investigators went over the locations that Oliver Stone used in directing *JFK*, among them Dealey Plaza and the Book Depository in Dallas. On the first take, several pedestrians got in the way. On the second, the film was out of focus. On the third, I forgot to take off the lens cap. In *no case* did we get precisely the same results that Oliver Stone did. It seems fair to conclude that one person, unaided, could not possibly have made *JFK* I call this the Second Director Theory—that is, Oliver Stone shot the film with others. Perhaps one of them was on the Grassy Knoll. Once I looked closely, other incriminating pieces fell into place.

The film's co-producer is listed as A. Kitman Ho. This is obviously an invented name. It is an anagram for "Nam Hit O.K.," a reference to Mr. Stone's two previous films about Vietnam, *Platoon* and *Born on the Fourth of July*. The war had been over for a generation when the movies were made. No doubt the Federal Government, certain that the horse was safely dead, allowed Mr. Stone to beat it.

Then there is the Hollywood connections. The name Warner Brothers (the studio that released *JFK*) was derived from the late Jack, Harry and Sam Warner, whose autopsies have never been released to the general public. Warner Brothers made its reputation in the 30's with gangster films starring, among others, Edward G. Robinson.

Later it was responsible for cinema biographies, among them *A Dispatch From Reuters*, starring the same Robinson. This was a profile of the man who founded the syndicate that feeds information to newspapers around the world. Warner was also the studio that produced *Mission to Moscow*, about Joseph Davies, then U.S. Ambassador to the Soviet Union. The star of this film was Walter Huston, whose son John Huston appeared with Frank Sinatra in the film *The List of Adrian Messenger*.

Mr. Sinatra was the star of *The Manchurian Candidate*, a thriller whose plot centered around the assassination of a U.S. President. This film was released one year *before* the assassination of J.F.K. The self-same Warner Brothers is now a partner with Time Inc. (Time-Warner). *Time* magazine has recently put *JFK* on its cover. A 4-year-old child could spot the associations of organized crime, the

Soviet Union, the Government and the press. Unfortunately, there were no 4-year-olds on the Warren Commission, and the connections have gone unreported until now.

I am prepared to face the ridicule of historians. Let them scoff at my Second Director Theory. Let them call me self-important, dishonest, irresponsible, scurrilous, manipulative. After all, they said the same thing about Oliver Stone.

But I stand ready to offer a generous reward to anyone who can refute my theory. Furthermore, on the basis of research and innumerable interviews, I believe, and I think I can prove, that in the making of this lurid and shallow film Kevin Costner did not act alone.

JANUARY 7, 1992

DAILY VARIETY

STONE DOUBTS BUSH'S FAITH IN WARREN REPORT

David Robb

Oliver Stone says he doesn't believe President Bush's comments to reporters last week that Bush had no interest in reviewing the C.I.A.'s files on the John Kennedy assassination while he was head of the C.I.A. in 1976. "I don't believe him, especially in the light of the memos he wrote while at the C.I.A.." Stone said in a sharply worded statement released in response to Bush's comments about Stone's *JFK*.

Those memos, obtained by *Daily Variety*, suggest that Bush did have at least a passing interest in the Kennedy assassination while head of the C.I.A..

Stone also accused Bush of stonewalling the public on the facts surrounding the Kennedy assassination and urged the President to make public all government files on the assassination.

Stone's statement, released to Daily Variety, was in response to comments Bush made about Stone's *JFK* last Thursday while visiting Canberra, Australia.

At a press conference there, NBC news correspondent John Cochran asked Bush: "As a former C.I.A. Director, did you ever go back and read the C.I.A.'s findings during that period and satisfy any of your curiosity?"

'No curiosity'

Bush responded: "No, I didn't have any curiosity, because I believed ... the Warren Commission ... I saw no reason to question it. Still see no reason to question it."

Bush, who said he hadn't seen Stone's movie, went on to compare Kennedy assassination conspiracy theories to rumors that Elvis Presley is still alive.

"I don't know much about the movie," Bush said. "I haven't seen it, and there's all kinds of conspirational theories floating around on everything. Elvis Presley is rumored to be alive and well someplace and I can't say that somebody won't go and make a movie about that." Stone, whose office was contacted by Daily Variety Friday, fired back in a statement released over the weekend.

"For a man who one month ago denied there was a recession," Stone said. "I am not surprised he did not have more curiosity when he was head of the C.I.A. about Lee Harvey Oswald, Jack Ruby, and J.F.K—but, as with the recession, I do not believe him, especially in light of the memos he wrote while at the C.I.A..

"Mr. Bush is very much a part of the problem in this country, in that he has been a member of the executive branch establishment for 30 years. In which time he has had ample opportunity to stonewall the American people.

"I suggest first he see the film and second that he trust the American people with the truth of their history by allowing them to see the files of the government investigations of the J.F.K. case."

Despite Bush's claim last week that he "didn't have any curiosity" about the J.F.K assassination while head of the C.I.A. in 1976, C.I.A. documents obtained through the Freedom of Information Act by the Washington D.C.-based Assassination Archives & Research Center appear to paint a different picture of Bush's interest in the matter.

In one such memo, dated Sept. 15, 1976, C.I.A. director Bush asked his deputy director of central intelligence to look into news accounts linking Oswald assailant Jack Ruby to mobster Santos Trafficante.

Telltale memos

In that memo, Bush wrote: "A recent Jack Anderson story referred to a November 1963 C.I.A. cable, the subject matter of which had some U.K. journalist observing Jack Ruby visiting Trafficante in jail (in Cuba). Is there such a cable? If so, I would like to see it."

C.I.A. documents show that Bush was also curious about another 1976 Jack Anderson column which stated that newly released documents allegedly revealed that "the C.I.A. withheld data in J.F.K probe."

Evidence withheld

One of the assertions in that article was that shortly after the assassination of Kennedy, then—C.I.A. Director James McCone had briefed the new president Lyndon Johnson about a cable from the U.S. Embassy in Mexico City that suggested that "the Cubans may have been behind the assassination."

C.I.A. documents show that Bush wrote "is this true?" in the margin of Anderson's newspaper account of the Johnson briefing.

A few days later, Bush received a five-page C.I.A. memorandum that disputed the allegations contained in Anderson's column.

Still another C.I.A. document shows that Bush asked Seymour Bolten, a high-ranking C.I.A. official, whether another news article, allegedly connecting Lee Harvey Oswald to the C.I.A. would hurt former C.I.A. director Richard Helms, who had sworn before the Warren Commission that the C.I.A. had never "even contemplated" any contacts with Oswald.

"Will this cause problems for Helms?" Bush asked Bolten, in a memo dated Oct. 4, 1976.

What Bush was referring to was an article that appeared Oct.1, 1976, in the now-defunct Washington Star, which stated that contrary to Helms' sworn testimony, a newly released C.I.A. document indicated that a low-level C.I.A.

official had once considered using Oswald as a source of intelligence information about the Soviet Union. Oswald, who had defected to the Soviet Union in 1959, returned to the U.S. in 1962.

Bolten, responding to Bush's memo, wrote that "this article will further smear Dick Helms' reputation and probably cause him some anxious moments, but I do not see how it can result in any additional legal problems for him, as it is a gross distortion of the facts."

Several other C.I.A. memos, from then-C.I.A. Inspector General John Waller and other top C.I.A. officials to C.I.A. director Bush, addressed a wide range of other questions surrounding the Kennedy assassination—including such topics as whether or not Jack Ruby had met with Fidel Castro only a few weeks before the assassination and allegations that the C.I.A. was somehow involved in the plot to kill the president.

Altogether, the C.I.A. released two documents "in full" that dealt with then-C.I.A. director Bush and the Kennedy assassination investigation, while 16 other documents were released "in part." The C.I.A. noted that "a number of other documents are being withheld in their entirety."

Apparently, then, C.I.A. director Bush was "curious" about the assassination, which was back in the news in 1976 due to an investigation by Senators Gary Hart (D.Col.) and Richard Schweiker (R. Penn.), who had been appointed by the Senate Intelligence Committee to conduct a special study of the C.I.A. and FBI responses to the Kennedy assassination.

JANUARY 6-13, 1992

THE NATION

J.F.K. AND *JFK*

Alexander Cockburn

Whether J.F.K. was killed by a lone assassin or by a conspiracy has as much to do with the subsequent contours of American politics as if he had tripped over one of Caroline's dolls and broken his neck in the White House nursery.

Of course many people think otherwise, reckoning that once it can be demonstrated that the Warren Commission was wrong and Oswald was not the lone killer, then we face the reality of a rightist conspiracy engineered to change the course of history. (The idea of Oswald as a leftist conspiracy of one or more has perhaps fortunately never had the popularity one might have expected.) This is the view taken by Oliver Stone, who has stated in interviews, such as one in Spin, that "Kennedy was really moving to end the cold war and sign a nuclear treaty with the Soviets; he would not have gone to war in Southeast Asia. He was starting a backdoor negotiation with Castro." Instead of which good things, there was "the first coup d'état in America."

In *JFK*, Stone leaves no doubt about the coup's sponsors. A sequence in grainy black-and-white, presumably designed for extra vérité, shows L.B.J. planning the assassination with the Joint Chiefs of Staff. This is a $40 million equivalent of MacBird, though Stone's model is another Shakespeare play.

The core of this vision of history is put by Kevin Costner in his role as New Orleans District Attorney Jim Garrison:

> We have all become Hamlets in our country, children of a slain father-leader whose killers still possess the throne. The ghost of John Kennedy confronts us with the secret murder at the heart of the American dream. He forces on us the appalling question: Of what is our Constitution made? What is our citizenship—and more, our lives—worth? What is the future, where a President can be assassinated under conspicuously suspicious circumstances, while the machinery of legal action scarcely trembles? How many political murders disguised as heart attacks, cancer, suicides, airplane and car crashes, drug overdoses, will occur before they are exposed for what they are?

Stone wrote those words himself (and at one point even planned to have the ghost of J.F.K. appear to Garrison as he stood in his kitchen making a chicken sandwich while watching news of Bobby Kennedy's assassination). It's an important passage, for in its truly fascist yearning for the "father-leader" taken from the children-people by conspiracy, it accurately catches the crippling nuttiness of what passes amid some sectors of the left (admittedly a pretty nebulous concept these days) as mature analysis and propaganda: that virtue in government died in Dallas, and that a "secret agenda" has perverted the national destiny.

With this demented optic, left ultimately joins hands with right, as happened during the Gulf War when the para-Birchist Craig Hulet won an enthusiastic following amid radical circles for his conspiratorial account of the Bush regime's policy even though anyone with half a brain could see after about thirty seconds exactly where he was coming from. Out the window goes any sensible analysis of institutions, economic trends and pressures, continuities in corporate and class interest and all the other elements constituting the open secrets and agendas of American capitalism.

THE ANCESTRY OF *JFK*

The psychic bloodlines of *JFK* may be traced at least in part to Ellen Ray, who met Oliver Stone in an elevator in Havana and placed a copy of Garrison's *On The Trail of the Assassins* in his hand. Along with Bill Schaap, Ray had published Garrison's book and, as I vividly recall from several conversations, has long felt that history did a U-turn for the worse when conspiracy laid J.F.K. low. Why the publishers of *Covert Action Information Bulletin* and *Lies of Our Times* should take this position I'm not sure, unless we take a biographical approach and argue that maybe it all goes back to Ellen's Catholic girlhood in Massachusetts, with an icon of J.F.K. on the wall. But then lots of other people including Bill didn't grow up as R.C. Mass.-based Jack fans, so the reasons probably lie elsewhere.

Intellectual ancestry for the assertion that J.F.K. would have pulled the United States out of Vietnam can be traced back to an essay by Peter Dale Scott, "Vietnamization and the Drama of the Pentagon Papers," which appeared in Volume V of the Senator Gravel edition of the "Pentagon Papers," published by Beacon Press in 1972. This volume edited by Noam Chomsky and Howard Zinn, offered critical commentary designed to put the Papers in perspective.

Scott, now a professor of English as U.C. Berkeley, attempted to prove by philological analysis that whereas the official editors of the Papers working in the Pentagon—headed by Leslie Gelb and reporting to Robert McNamara—wanted to show there was continuity of policy between J.F.K. and L.B.J., the opposite was the case. Scott's focus was on National Security Action Memorandum 273 and on shifts in the verbal expressions of policies that occurred between the Honolulu conference of November 20, 1963, attended by J.F.K.'s top advisers, and L.B.J.'s November 24 policy meeting on Vietnam, the first in the wake of J.F.K.'s murder and including the same advisers, which led to the adoption of N.S.A.M. 273 immediately thereafter.

Scott lays enormous weight upon minute textual alterations, signaling these with urgent italic. Thus, on October 2 the Kennedy position was "The security of South Vietnam *is a major interest of the United States as other free nations [sic]*. We will adhere to *our policy of working with the people and Government of South Vietnam to deny* this country to communism and to suppress the *externally stimulated and supported insurgency* of the Viet Cong as promptly as possible. *Effective performance* in this undertaking is the *central objective* of our policy in South Vietnam."

Such, in Scott's yearning interpretation, was the language of benign intent, as contrasted with the N.S.A.M. 273 language of November 24: "It remains the *central objective* of the United States in South Vietnam to assist the people and Government of that country to win their contest against the externally directed and supported communist conspiracy. The test of all U.S. decisions and actions in this area should be the effectiveness of their contributions to this purpose."

To the sensible eye, those differences may be credited to the determination of an uncertain Johnson White House, following the assassination, to show the world its resolve, as opposed to the more anfractuous approach of a Kennedy White House trying to steer a path through the Buddhist crisis, the impending coup against Diem, the discontent of some liberals at growing involvement and the rage of conservatives that not enough was being done.

There was, however, no change in policy, and the measure of Peter Dale Scott's fantasizing may be gauged by his claim later in the same essay for the "overall Kennedy strategy for movement towards international relaxation of the cold war and conversion to a full-employment civilian economy at home." Military spending was slowing near the end of Kennedy's term for exactly the same reason it slowed near the end of Ronald Reagan's season in office. The largest and most rapid military buildup in the peacetime history of the United States had been accomplished. J.F.K. had doubled the number of Polaris nuclear submarines; increased Minuteman purchases by 75 percent, tactical nukes in Europe by 60 percent and the total number of weapons in the strategic alert force by 100 percent.

Kennedy, having fought the 1960 election partly on an imaginary missile gap, then acted as if this missile gap were genuine. In his vivid account in *High Priests of Waste*, Ernie Fitzgerald suggests that the military spending surge of the Kennedy years definitively undermined all rational standards of productivity and cost control achieved in the preceding seven decades (though an old auto worker from the Chrysler plant in Newcastle, Indiana, once remarked to me that such declines could be traced back to the cost-plus contracts of the Second World War). The idea that Kennedy was methodically tilting toward a full-employment civilian economy is preposterous.

Scott's essay has had a pertinacious half-life, and one of those paying tribute to it is a military historian named John Newman, one of Stone's advisers on the film. Newman's *JFK and Vietnam* first came into the offices of Sheridan Square Press, Ray and Schaap's publishing house, whence it was passed on to Stone, who assisted in its dispatch to Warner Books (part of the conglomerate backing *JFK*), which is publishing the book in February.

JFK and Vietnam is a serious book with two curious features. One is absence of any substantial evidence for the author's frequently repeated claim that by February or March of 1963 J.F.K. had decided to pull out of Vietnam once the 1964 election was won. Newman's only sources for this are people to whom J.F.K. would, as a matter of habitual political opportunism, have spoken in such terms, such as Senators Mike Mansfield and Wayne Morse, both of whom, particularly the latter, were critical of J.F.K.'s escalation in Vietnam. Against their recollections may be placed the accounts of those to whom J.F.K. spoke out of the other side of his mouth, such as Dean Rusk or even R.F.K.

The other curious feature is Newman's inference that the assassination should be re-examined in the light of his conclusion that L.B.J. reversed J.F.K.'s stance on Vietnam. Perhaps he wrote this late section of the book after association with Stone had commenced. The *ciné vérité* of L.B.J. hatching the coup with the Joint Chiefs was but a short step, and Newman was on hand for the press briefings on *JFK* in Los Angeles in mid-December, ready with scholarly backup.

THE JUNKYARD OF HISTORY

Oliver Stone looks upon the assassination as the coffin of all the bright hopes of the early sixties. To get a truer insight all you have to do is go to a junkyard or an auto museum and look at the colors. Bright hopes were really being born in the mid-fifties, with Detroit palettes of desert rose, aqua, even paisley. By the time of the New Frontier the colors had darkened into the dreary greens, tans and drab blues of combat. With their prophetic three-year lead times, the colors told the story. Kennedy had betrayed the hopes of people like Stone before he had stepped off the inauguration stand.

"Get a life," Captain Kirk once told some Trekkies. Get some history too. Critics of *JFK* like Tom Wicker have fretted that "in an era when mistrust of government and loss of confidence in institutions (the press not least) are widespread and virulent, such a suggestion [i.e., that representatives of the ruling élites murdered J.F.K.] seems a dubious public service." In fact the dubious public service is to suggest that J.F.K. himself was not a functional representative of those élites.

The real J.F.K. backed a military coup in Guatemala to keep out Arévalo, denied the Dominican Republic the possibility of land reform, helped promote a devastating cycle of Latin American history, including the anticipatory motions of the coup in Brazil, and backed a Baathist coup in Iraq that set a certain native of Tikrit on the path to power. He presided over Operation Mongoose, inflicting terror upon Cuba. At the very moment bullets brought J.F.K.'s life to its conclusion in Dallas, a C.I.A. officer operating firmly within the bounds of Kennedy's policy was handing poison to a Cuban agent in Paris, designed to kill Castro.

Lawrence J. Bassett and Stephen Pelz wrote in the 1989 collection Kennedy's Quest for Victory that "by putting American advisers in harm's way...he helped to engage American patriotism in a war against the Vietnamese people. By arguing that Vietnam was a test of the West's ability to defeat the people's war strategy and a test of American credibility in the Cold War, he raised the costs of withdrawal for his successor." J.F.K. sent in 16,000 advisers, sponsored the strategic hamlet program, launched napalm and defoliation upon the South and covert terror and sabotage upon the North. He never entertained the idea of a settlement as advocated by J.K. Galbraith when the latter was Ambassador to India.

Thomas Paterson, editor of this volume, put it well. Only out of respect for history "emerges unpleasant reality and the need to reckon with a past that has not always matched the selfless and self-satisfying image Americans have of their foreign policy and of Kennedy as their young, fallen hero who never had a chance. Actually, he had his chance, and he failed."

Reprinted by permission of the author.

THE NEW YORK TIMES

OVERKILL

By Garry Trudeau

Readers of The New York Times's sixth, seventh, eighth and ninth personal attacks on Oliver Stone this week could be forgiven for wondering if the beleaguered director of *JFK* has a point. Significant elements of the Establishment Media do seem hellbent on destroying his reputation.

Conspiracy or consensus? You don't have to be paranoid to re-create the key events of the last eight months—but it helps. From the top:

May 7, 1991: As Oliver Stone cruises down Hollywood Boulevard, he suddenly finds himself under fire. A troubled *Chicago Tribune* columnist named Jon Margolis is held responsible.

May 19: Stone, shaken by this vicious first strike, swerves to avoid a follow-up salvo from *The Washington Post*. The shooter, identified to readers only as "George Lardner Jr." has known ties to organized journalism.

June 3: While Stone returns fire at *The Post*, he is blindsided by *Time*'s Richard Zoglin, the first of the "Two Richards" at *Time* to draw a bead on him. Stone reloads and fires off a stinging rejoinder.

Oct. 15: Writing alone, a drifter by the name of Robert Sam Anson squeezes off several cheap shots at Stone. Numerous witnesses recall the attack originating from *Esquire*, whose offices are only seven blocks from *Time*'s.

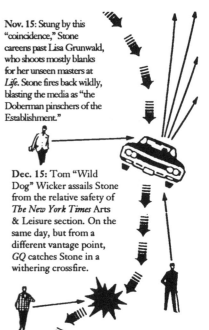

Nov. 15: Stung by this "coincidence," Stone careens past Lisa Grunwald, who shoots mostly blanks for her unseen masters at *Life*. Stone fires back wildly, blasting the media as "the Doberman pinschers of the Establishment."

Dec. 15: Tom "Wild Dog" Wicker assails Stone from the relative safety of *The New York Times* Arts & Leisure section. On the same day, but from a different vantage point, *GQ* catches Stone in a withering crossfire.

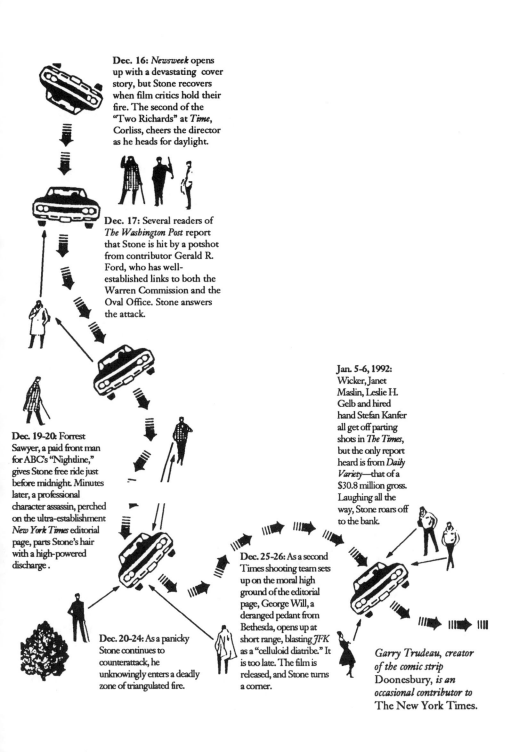

Dec. 16: *Newsweek* opens up with a devastating cover story, but Stone recovers when film critics hold their fire. The second of the "Two Richards" at *Time*, Corliss, cheers the director as he heads for daylight.

Dec. 17: Several readers of *The Washington Post* report that Stone is hit by a potshot from contributor Gerald R. Ford, who has well-established links to both the Warren Commission and the Oval Office. Stone answers the attack.

Dec. 19-20: Forrest Sawyer, a paid front man for ABC's "Nightline," gives Stone free ride just before midnight. Minutes later, a professional character assassin, perched on the ultra-establishment *New York Times* editorial page, parts Stone's hair with a high-powered discharge .

Dec. 20-24: As a panicky Stone continues to counterattack, he unknowingly enters a deadly zone of triangulated fire.

Dec. 25-26: As a second Times shooting team sets up on the moral high ground of the editorial page, George Will, a deranged pedant from Bethesda, opens up at short range, blasting *JFK* as a "celluloid diatribe." It is too late. The film is released, and Stone turns a corner.

Jan. 5-6, 1992: Wicker, Janet Maslin, Leslie H. Gelb and hired hand Stefan Kanfer all get off parting shots in *The Times*, but the only report heard is from *Daily Variety*—that of a $30.8 million gross. Laughing all the way, Stone roars off to the bank.

Garry Trudeau, creator of the comic strip Doonesbury, *is an occasional contributor to* The New York Times.

JANUARY 8, 1992

LOS ANGELES TIMES

SHADOWS ON THE AMERICAN STORYBOOK

The Establishment fears Oliver Stone because he could infect the young with the radical virus.

Tom Hayden

Why is there such an unparalleled media attack on Oliver Stone? His *JFK* is hardly the first controversial film of our time. The *Godfather* films alleged that the Mafia and the Vatican conspired in laundering drug money and killing a Pope, yet were reviewed calmly.

The media furor is about more than whether Stone takes license with certain facts, which he does, or whether he conclusively proves his conspiracy thesis, which he doesn't. The argument is really over the meaning of the 1960s.

The radicalism of that decade has been mostly dismissed in recent years as a cause that deservedly failed. There are no visionary heroes now, no civil-rights marches. Politics has become a cynical marketing game, funded by special interests. Media talk-show commentators are the official spokesmen for all opinion that they considered legitimate. Critics of our most recent war were mostly deleted from media coverage, which turned instead to commentary from retired military men.

Now comes Oliver Stone as an incarnation of the 1960s who cannot be dismissed. Like an Id from our past, he terrorizes the official subconscious with the fear that a new generation will be infected with a radical virus that was supposed to have been eradicated.

But the sensibility of Americans like Oliver Stone—and there are many of us—is rooted in experience. We came of age in a time of great idealism that was shattered by the killing of a President, which led to a very bad decade indeed. We became not has-beens but might-have-beens, doomed not to know what our lives would have been like if J.F.K. had not been murdered.

Our experience led us to believe that American democracy was not what it claimed to be, a process of peaceful interest groups competing for a voter majority within a framework of law. Instead, it was a system threatened by invisible élites, illegal conspiracies and faceless killers, some of them officially connected. Not monolithic conspiracies by any means, or even competent ones, but shadowy and pervasive nonetheless.

Our alienation deepened with Kennedy's murder, with the Warren Commission's unbelievable public-relations effort, with the subsequent escalation in Vietnam—and, above all, with the fact that the institution we trusted for the truth, the media, offered too little criticism too late.

Stone could have died fighting in Vietnam for a government that, by lying, broke his American heart. Thousands did die, along with millions of Indochinese, and countless others had their life hopes permanently changed for the worse.

Stone brilliantly expresses the unanswered cry of the 1960s. We do live in a culture that produces David Ferries, Howard Hunts, J. Edgar Hoovers, Oliver Norths, Watergate break-ins, Iran-Contra cover-ups and unsolved murders of our leaders.

The current attacks on Stone recall the C.I.A. memo in the late 1960s that suggested orchestrating an effort to defend the Warren Commission through existing "propaganda assets," that is, friendly journalists, "to answer and refute the attacks of critics."

The media has, in its current frenzy, indeed been acting as a "propaganda asset." But for whom? Not the C.I.A.—the media has criticized the agency often enough. Rather, the media is a "propaganda asset" for a storybook concept of democracy.

I would suggest that, unlike Stone, most successful journalists cannot bring themselves to believe that they live in a country where leaders could be murdered by interest groups. Instead, they cling to a fairy tale notion of democracy that lets them sleep at night.

But can they seriously claim that democracy is working as planned? It is easier to attack the in-your-face paranoia of Oliver Stone than to question the system that made him so. We need more haunted souls than comfortable sleepers in this country. We cannot repress and deny the past forever. Thank God Stone tries to wake us up.

Tom Hayden is a California Legislator. He was a leader in the student and anti-war movements of the 1960s.

Reprinted by permission of the author.

JANUARY 9, 1992

THE NEW YORK TIMES

JFK

Anthony Lewis

Oliver Stone's *JFK* may well move a generation to believe that a conspiracy lay behind the assassination of President Kennedy. That is its message, and a film that hits the emotions as skillfully as this one does can have a profound impact.

It is right, therefore, to take the movie seriously. Its charges could hardly be more serious. It suggests that Earl Warren, the revered Chief Justice, was party to covering up a murderous conspiracy. It tells us that our Government cannot be trusted even to give an honest account of a President's assassination.

The question is whether the film produces meaningful new evidence that should cause us to question the finding of the Warren commission that Lee Harvey Oswald alone killed John Kennedy. To those unfamiliar with the Warren report and its 26 volumes of evidence, much in the movie will appear new. But is it?

1. The audience was most moved, when I saw *JFK*, by Abraham Zapruder's film of the President's car moving in Dallas as he was killed. Kennedy's head snapped back. Surely, then, he must have been hit by a bullet fired from the front, not from the rear where Oswald was.

In fact, not just the President's head but his body moved backward. Medical experts told the commission that what happened was "a violent straightening and stiffening of the entire body," as one put it, "as a result of a seizure-like neuromuscular reaction to major damage inflicted to nerve centers in the brain."

Experiments with animals shot from the rear produced just such a reaction. The physical impact of a shot from the front would not move the body back.

The bullet that hit the President in the head broke apart. Two fragments were ballistically identifiable. Tests showed that they came from Oswald's rifle and could have come from no other.

Twenty medical experts examined the autopsy photographs and x-rays. Nineteen concluded that the shots that hit the President came from behind him.

2. The Zapruder film shows that about 5.5 seconds elapsed between a shot that wounded Kennedy and the one that killed him. Oswald fired three shots, one of which missed entirely. *JFK* argues that Oswald could not have fired three shots from an old-style rifle in 5.5 seconds.

But Oswald could have fired the shot that missed before the two that hit, or after them, rather than between the two as the movie assumes. Then he would have had 5.5 seconds for *two* shots: time enough. The Warren commission so found.

3. The movie makes much of alleged links between Oswald and Jack Ruby, who killed Oswald in the Dallas police station as he was being transferred to the county jail on Sunday, Nov. 24, 1963. It suggests that this killing was part of the cover-up.

The charge ignores unchallenged evidence. A postal inspector named Harry Holmes, a friend of the police captain in charge, was on his way to church that morning when he changed his mind and went down to the police station. He was taken in to Oswald's interrogation. When the police finished, they let Mr. Holmes ask questions—and he did, for 30 minutes. Without the accident of his presence, Oswald would have left the building long before Ruby arrived.

Every specific charge made in the movie similarly ignores extensive, for me dispositive, evidence. It gives weight to witnesses long since discredited. It does not mention the scientific findings that Oswald's gun fired the bullets that hit President Kennedy and Gov. John Connally.

Oliver Stone uses as his mouthpiece Jim Garrison, the former New Orleans District Attorney, who in real life bribed witnesses to prosecute an innocent man—and was laughed out of court. He alleges a conspiracy among the Army, the C.I.A., Lyndon Johnson and endless others: without a shred of evidence.

The best insight into Oliver Stone's character, for me, was his treatment of Chief Justice Warren. Earl Warren no doubt had his faults. But he loved this country with all his heart, and the assassination tore him apart. The notion that he would cover up that assassination is contemptible: a contempt well expressed by Stone's choice of the real Jim Garrison to play Earl Warren in the film.

I have no illusion that facts will dispel Oliver Stone's fantasy. Even to question the existence of a conspiracy is to risk being called a conspirator. Television is fascinated with the Stone phenomenon. It has no time for the man who knows more of the actual facts of the assassination than anyone else: David W. Belin, who was counsel to the Warren commission and has seen every document, every C.I.A. file.

No, the thirst for some deeper, darker truth is unquenchable in America. We want the answer. We want to open some file and find the conspiracy. But we never shall.

FEBRUARY 3, 1992

THE NEW YORK TIMES
LETTER

WARREN PANEL FINDINGS SHOULD STIR OUTRAGE

Oliver Stone

To the Editor:

Anthony Lewis's Jan 9 column is only one in a series of attacks in The Times on me and my movie *JFK*. and, in fact, on anything that questions the Warren Commission's findings on the assassination of President Kennedy. *New York Times* writers have done no investigation of their own; why do they continue to defend tooth and nail the commission's findings more than a decade after the House Select Committee on Assassinations sharply criticized and documented the deficiencies in the commission's investigations?

Mr. Lewis tells us, for instance, that medical experts told the commission the backwards snap of the President's head as seen in the Zapruder film was the result of a "seizure-like neuromuscular reaction" in response to damage to major nerve centers in the brain and not inconsistent with a shot from behind. This is entirely misleading and false.

Mr. Lewis is quoting from the House Select Committee on Assassinations report of 1973. Nowhere in the Warren Commission material is there an explanation of the backward movement of the President's head. Moreover, a Federal Bureau of Investigation "printing error" of crucial Zapruder film frames in the commission volumes gave the impression that the President fell *forward*—exactly the opposite of what the running film shows. The autopsy photos and x-rays show no damage to the major nerve centers of Kennedy's brain, making such a neuromuscular reaction impossible.

Mr. Lewis champions David W. Belin, former Warren Commission counsel, as "the man who knows more about the assassination than anyone else." According to Mr. Lewis, Mr. Belin has seen "every document, every Central Intelligence Agency file" relating to the assassination. But this is impossible. As Senate and House committees documented, the C.I.A. and other agencies deliberately withheld vital information from the Warren Commission.

There are many more inaccuracies in Mr. Lewis's column. The bullet fragments, allegedly from the head shot, lack any firm chain of possession or evidence; nevertheless, Mr. Lewis claims they are conclusively linked to Lee Harvey Oswald's rifle. Despite the opinions of 19 medical experts based on autopsy photos and X-rays that all shots came from the rear, there are still more than 20 doctors, nurses and technicians in Dallas who examined the President's body and saw a gaping exit wound in the right rear of the skull.

If there was a plan to kill Oswald during the jail transfer, the plotters would have waited to get Jack Ruby into place before bringing Oswald down, regardless of the surprise visit from Harry Holmes, a postal inspector. And so on. What we're looking at are discrepancies and contradictions in the Warren Commission's own evidence—problems the Government has never satisfactorily resolved.

Where was *The Times* when it should have been raising these questions? The day after the unindexed 26 volumes of the Warren Commission's hearings and exhibits were published, Mr. Lewis stated on the front page that the volumes "overwhelmingly supported" the commission report, implying he had read and analyzed all 20,000 pages overnight, a speed-reading feat that would make Evelyn Wood woozy.

Your editorial board, less intrepid, took two days to digest the volumes before announcing that the evidence within "brings to a close the inquiry." This is inexcusable on the part of Mr. Lewis and *The Times*, which claims to be a newspaper of record.

Inaccuracies aside, I find Mr. Lewis's charade of civil libertarian concern far more disturbing. Mr. Lewis asserts that Jim Garrison "bribed witnesses to prosecute an innocent man." The "bribed" witnesses all signed affidavits denying the allegations, and Clay Shaw—the "innocent man"—won an acquittal. I do not question that verdict. While Mr. Lewis and you excoriate Jim Garrison for taking a man to trial (after several hearings on the evidence), neither shows remorse in calling Oswald "Kennedy's assassin," though he was never tried, convicted or even allowed legal representation in Dallas.

In 1964, Mr. Lewis wrote of the Warren Report: "Few who loved John

Kennedy, or this country, will be able to read it without emotion." For some, like myself, the emotion is outrage. For Mr. Lewis and *The Times*, it's complacency.

Reprinted by permission of the author.

JANUARY 9, 1992

THE NEW YORK TIMES

KENNEDY AND VIETNAM

Leslie H. Gelb

On Oct. 11, 1963, President Kennedy issued top-secret National Security Action Memorandum 263. In it he called for stepped-up training for South Vietnamese forces so they could take over the duties of U.S. forces, thus permitting the bulk of Americans to withdraw by 1965.

Based mainly on that document, Oliver Stone's *JFK* movie asks us to believe one of the great historical "ifs" of the century: that if the young President has survived through a second term, the U.S. would have been spared the ordeal of full-scale war in Vietnam.

It is fair for Mr. Stone or anyone to take up that historical sword. But on a matter that remains so raw for so many Americans, it is gross of him to distort the record, and foolish to be so confident of decisions J.F.K. would have made in circumstances he never had to face.

Stone makes swaggering assertions about mighty unknowns. First, he maintains that J.F.K. was going to abandon South Vietnam to a Communist takeover. Second, he tells us that right-wingers (from the F.B.I. and C.I.A. to the Mafia) believed this, and killed the president to put Lyndon Johnson in the White House and insure that the U.S. would stay the course in Vietnam. I am competent only to address the first point.

To begin with, NSAM 263 was grounded in one of the few periods of genuine optimism about the war. So J.F.K. had some basis or believing the war might be won soon and that U.S. forces could be withdrawn—without a Communist victory. Put another way, J.F.K. might never have issued the directive if he had thought it would mean losing the war.

While some officials took the directive at face value, most saw it as a Kennedy bureaucratic scheme to regain control of the leaping American presence in South Vietnam—up from about 700 in 1961 to almost 17,000 in late 1963. The idea being to keep force levels from going up, order them to go down.

Most officials also viewed the withdrawal memo as part of a White House ploy to scare President Diem of South Vietnam into making political reforms. Without such reforms, many officials believed, the war they thought so vital would be lost. That is precisely how the State Department instructed the U.S. Embassy in Saigon to understand NSAM 263.

The clarifying event was, of course, the coup against Diem and his powerful brother-in-law, Ngo Dinh Nhu, on Nov. 1. The coup was fully supported if not inspired, by the U.S. in good part because of the fear that Nhu was conspiring with North Vietnam to "neutralize" South Vietnam. In other words, the Kennedy team felt that Diem and Nhu might be selling out to the Communists. Whatever J.F.K.'s precise intentions, the removal and killing of Diem profoundly increased America's political responsibility for the war.

As for Mr. Kennedy's underlying thinking about the war, that is a murky matter. In the last weeks of his life, he gave sharply diverse signals as befits a President trying to keep open his options, especially before an election. To CBS he said: "In the final analysis, it is [the South Vietnamese] who have to win or lose this struggle." Then he added, "But I don't agree with those who say we should withdraw. That would be a great mistake ... " To NBC he said he believed "the domino theory," whereby the fall of Saigon to Communism would lead to the collapse of America's position throughout Asia.

Brushing aside these complications, some have argued that Mr. Kennedy had gained self-confidence from successes like the Cuban missile crisis and would not have felt the need to prove himself in Vietnam—as did Lyndon Johnson. Soon after the assassination, Ted Sorensen painted a more tortured picture of J.F.K.'s thinking. "The struggle could well be, he thought, this nation's severest test of endurance and patience," the Kennedy intimate wrote. "He was simply going to weather it out, a nasty, untidy mess to which there was no other acceptable solution ... "

These words carry great weight. They echoed the private soul-searching of President Eisenhower and foreshadowed almost precisely the documented dilemmas of Presidents Johnson and Nixon. These torments are not to be trifled with by Oliver Stone, or anyone, however many men shot J.F.K. for whatever lunatic reasons on that tragic November day.

Wall Street Journal

JFK: TRUTH AND FICTION

Arthur Schlesinger, Jr.

What about Oliver Stone's *JFK*?

It comes at you with slam-bang intensity. It bombards you with flashes, images, sounds, like a music video. It is a virtuoso exercise in post-modernist film making.

But what does *JFK* have to do with truth? After all, the movie purports to tell the story of the murder of a president of the United States. What responsibility does a film maker have to the facts? Is even a virtuoso film maker justified in raiding history for his own purposes as if he were Shakespeare ransacking Holinshed's "Chronicles"? Is he justified in weaving fact, conjecture and fiction into an indecipherable mass posing as a bold, quasi-authoritative, historical narrative?

Let me say that Oliver Stone's premise in *JFK* is far from unreasonable. It is that in 1963 President Kennedy began to move toward the liquidation of the Cold War. Kennedy's American University speech that June called for an end to the "vicious and dangerous cycle in which suspicion on one side breeds suspicion on the other, and new weapons beget counter-weapons." He asked Americans to "re-examine our own attitude—as individuals and as a nation—for our attitude is as essential as theirs." He followed this speech by the negotiation of a test-ban treaty with the Soviet Union—an action he regarded as only a first step.

In addition (and Oliver Stone could have strengthened his case by mentioning it) President Kennedy authorized United Nations Ambassador William Attwood to explore the possible restoration of relations with Castro's Cuba. "The president gave him the go-ahead," Robert Kennedy said the next year, "and he was to go to Havana ... and see what could be done [to effect] a normalization of relationship."

STRONG EVIDENCE

Mr. Stone rests his case primarily on Vietnam. No one can say what President Kennedy might eventually have done about Vietnam. But there is strong documentary evidence as to his long-run purpose. From the beginning to end of his administration, he steadily opposed repeated military recommendations that he introduce an American expeditionary force. Having watched the French army fail in Vietnam in 1951, he had no desire to send the American Army into the same quagmire. "The last thing he wanted," said Gen. Maxwell Taylor, "was to put in our ground forces."

In the hope of enabling the South Vietnamese to save themselves, President

Kennedy did agree to modest increases in the number of U.S. military advisers assigned to the South Vietnamese army. But, as Roswell Gilpatric, the deputy secretary of defense, said later, "Resistance was encountered from the president at every stage as this total amount of U.S. personnel deployment increased."

In July 1962 President Kennedy instructed Robert McNamara, the secretary of defense, to start planning for the phased withdrawal of the American advisers. The target date for complete disengagement was the end of 1965. The military produced an acceptable plan in May 1963. Mr. Gilpatric later said, "McNamara indicated to me that this was part of a plan the president asked him to develop to unwind the whole thing."

President Kennedy's doubts about Vietnam were strengthened by Mike Mansfield, then Senate majority leader, once a professor of Far Eastern history, later ambassador to Japan. The president sent Sen. Mansfield to take a look at Vietnam in 1962 (as Franklin Roosevelt had sent Mr. Mansfield to take a look at Nationalist China in 1944). Sen. Mansfield recommended that the Americans pull out. President Kennedy subsequently told Sen. Mansfield that total withdrawal was the right course, but he could not do it until after the 1964 election. Otherwise, he feared, the Republicans might beat him in 1964 over the "loss" of Indochina as they had beaten the Democrats in 1952 over the "loss" of China.

But President Kennedy went quietly ahead with the first phase of withdrawal. In October 1963 he ordered the return of 1,000 advisers. Then came Dallas. President Johnson, listening to President Kennedy's more hawkish advisers and believing he was doing what President Kennedy would have done, issued National Security Action Memorandum 273 calling for the maintenance of American military programs in Vietnam "at levels as high" as before—reversing the Kennedy withdrawal policy. On March 27, 1964, President Johnson canceled President Kennedy's phased-withdrawal plan. In early 1965 he ordered in American ground forces.

So Oliver Stone's film has a defensible premise. But the conclusion he draws is indefensible. It is that, outraged by President Kennedy's policy of winding down the Cold War, a cabal of evil men in high government positions organized a great conspiracy based on the Joint Chiefs of Staff, the C.I.A., the FBI, the military-industrial complex, anti-Castro Cubans, the mob and Lyndon B. Johnson for the purpose of murdering the president and covering up the deed. Serious conspiracy arguments can be made; but the conspiracy theory in *JFK* is reckless, paranoid, really despicable fantasy, reminiscent of the wilder accusations of Joe McCarthy.

How much need we worry about the impact of *JFK*? Mr. Stone himself has equated history with *Rashomon*. *JFK*, he suggests, is merely an exploration of "possible scenarios of who killed Kennedy and why." Unfortunately his explosive style defeats the idea of the film as a judicious analysis of alternative theories.

Still, the paranoid thriller is a form that carries the seeds of its own disbelief. Nothing is more ludicrous in *JFK* than the scene in which Major X explains to Jim Garrison with the serene lucidity of a madman how the evil cabal is running and ruining the U.S.

Critics have expressed concern that young people for whom the Kennedy assassination is history as remote as the sinking of the Maine was to my generation will suppose *JFK* to be the literal truth. Maybe some will. But I would think that most have seen so much hyped-up speculation, surmise and invention in docudramas that they take these pseudo-historical exposures *cum grano salis*.

Still, for a people that prides itself on robust common sense, Americans have shown from the start an uncommon susceptibility to conspiracy theory. We've gone through panics over plots allegedly hatched by the Bavarian Illuminati, the Masonic Order, the Catholic Church, the slave power, the abolitionists, the international bankers, the anarchists, the Elders of Zion, the Comintern. Historian Richard Hofstadter wrote memorably about "The Paranoid Style in American Politics."

Of course, as the saying goes, even paranoids may have real enemies. The more enduring residue of *JFK* will be the questions the film raises about the adequacy of the Warren Commission inquiry. These questions are legitimate. There is no reason to regard the Warren Commission report as sacred. We now know that both the C.I.A. and the FBI withheld vital information from the commission. I think these agencies withheld the information for reasons of bureaucratic self-protection; but, whatever the motive, the result was an inadequate investigation.

Whether a more adequate investigation would have produced a different conclusion is a separate question, on which I remain agnostic. A powerful case can be made against the theory that the same bullet struck both President Kennedy and Gov. John Connally. This argues for a second gunman. *JFK* both makes that case and impairs it, since the viewer can never tell at any point in the movie where fact ends and fiction begins.

I find it difficult to exclude the conspiracy theory—or to accept it. Were the bumblers of the Dallas Police Department in the great conspiracy? the hospital's medical staff? the Secret Service? How far did the conspiracy extend? The wider the conspiracy, the more likely in this publicity-mad age that some survivor on the conspiracy's fringe would sell his memoirs to People magazine for $10 million. Nothing like this has yet happened.

RFK AND GARRISON

Robert Kennedy had his doubts about the Warren Commission. On Oct. 30, 1966, as we talked till 2:30 a.m. in P.J. Clarke's saloon in New York, he wondered how long he could continue to avoid comment on the report. He regarded it as a poor job but was unwilling to criticize it and thereby re-open the whole tragic business.

The next year Oliver Stone's hero Jim Garrison started making his sensational charges. RFK told me that he thought Garrison might be on to something. NBC, he said, was sending Walter Sheridan, a trusted investigator who had worked with him on the Jimmy Hoffa case, to New Orleans to find out what Mr. Garrison had. Robert Kennedy said to me some weeks later, "Sheridan is satisfied that Garrison is a fraud."

When I told this story to Oliver Stone, he replied rather sharply that Mr. Sheridan had come to New Orleans with his mind made up, almost implying that Mr. Sheridan too was part of the conspiracy. Conspiracy theory makes it dangerously easy to explain away all objections.

Mr. Stone is an earnest, appealing man. He fought bravely for his country in the horror of Vietnam. He has earned the right to brood and agonize over the reasons he and so many others were sent to kill and die in that war. He is an artist, and artists are often hopelessly loyal to their fantasies—and their fantasies often hopelessly abuse the truth. History will survive.

Mr. Schlesinger, a professor at the City University of New York, is the winner of two Pulitzer Prizes, including one for A Thousand Days, *on President Kennedy.*

JANUARY 13, 1992

TIME

TAKING A DARKER VIEW
The conspiracy theories reflected in JFK may not be persuasive, but they churn up a murky underside of America

Ron Rosenbaum

Some years ago, during a telephone interview, I finally succeeded in badgering Jim Garrison into naming the Name. For years Garrison had been telling people he had the whole case cold: he knew who gave the orders, who fired the shots and from where. Still, though he had talked a lot about the Big Guys behind the plot—intelligence agencies, the military-industrial complex and the like—he had never publicly named the name of the man he believed fired the fatal head shot from the grassy knoll.

I won't tell you that name, because Garrison didn't give me any evidence for singling out this person for historic infamy. On another day, I felt, he might have picked another name out of the hat.

Still, for one guilty moment I had the kind of thrill that assassination buffs live for. I had the Name everyone else was looking for and no one else had. Of course, it wasn't an entirely unknown name. Garrison told me the person had been questioned extensively by Warren Commission investigators, and when I looked him up in the Warren Commission testimony, I found he plays a kind of Rosencrantz-and-Guildenstern-level role in the Warren Report, that of a peripheral figure in a key place: he was a live-in manager and janitor at Jack

Ruby's sleazy strip joint, the Carousel Club. There's no doubt that the commission investigators were interested in his story—the transcript of his testimony runs more than 200 pages—but mostly because he was a source who might shed some light on the peculiarities of Jack Ruby's character (investigators repeatedly pressed the Name on whether Ruby had any sexual interest in his beloved dog Sheba).

Though reading the testimony didn't give me much intimation of an assassination revelation, it *was* a revelation of another kind. In telling his life story, of how he wound up in the Carousel Club in 1963, the Name was telling a story of an American life—of an America—far different from the one I'd known in my suburban hometown.

It was a story of guy who made his living in the carnival world; he worked as a barker with small-time freak-show acts like "the two-headed baby" and "the snake girl," he told the Warren Commission. He bummed around looking for roustabout jobs, met his first wife at a Salvation Army mission. When she left him in the summer of 1963, he hitchhiked all the way from the West Coast to Dallas looking for her. Picked up some work at the Texas state fair in a carny sideshow called "How Hollywood Makes Movies," which featured some of Jack Ruby's strippers. Made some connections and soon found himself living in the back room of the Carousel Club in the midst of Ruby's strange ménage, which included strippers, burlesque comics, stage hypnotists and, of course, the dog Sheba.

I remember reading this testimony, mesmerized by my sudden immersion in a carnival-sideshow underbelly of American life. (The 26 volumes of Warren Commission testimony are like a vast, inchoate Great American Novel in that respect.) I didn't feel I was any closer to solving the Kennedy assassination, but I did feel I had learned more about the America that produced both Kennedy and his assassin than was conveyed by the bland, complacent sitcom image of the nation and its institutions that prevailed in November 1963.

And that, I believe, is the real legacy of nearly three decades of revisionist Kennedy-assassination investigation. We may not ever know with certainty the Name or the Names. But we do have a much darker, more complex, less innocent vision of America, produced by the murk that has been churned up by the dissidents.

Consider the FBI. In 1963 few dissented from the view that its director, J. Edgar Hoover, was a peerless, incorruptible leader, a gangbuster nonpareil. He said so himself. Now, we may not want to agree with the conclusion of the latest FBI-centered conspiracy-theory book *Act of Treason: The Role of J. Edgar Hoover in the Assassination of President Kennedy*. The author, Texas attorney Mark North, accuses Hoover of deliberately withholding knowledge of a Mafia assassination plot against J.F.K. because he hated the Kennedy brothers and had enough dirt on L.B.J. to control him. But North's accumulation of documentary evidence of the ugly blackmail intrigues Hoover was weaving in the cellars of Camelot is perhaps even more damning that the allegations of treason.

Much of this has been reported earlier: the way Hoover pressured the Kennedys into letting him bug the bedrooms of Martin Luther King Jr.; how he subtly blackmailed the Camelot kids over *their* bedroom sports, including J.F.K.'s romps with the girlfriend of godfather Sam Giancana and (probably) with Marilyn Monroe. We know that while Hoover was passing around tapes of creaking bedsprings, he was letting the Mob grow unchecked and was going easy on deep sewers of Washington corruption like the Bobby Baker case to protect patrons like L.B.J.

Or consider the C.I.A.. To those who knew of it at all in 1963, it was still living off the glamour of its wartime OSS (Office of Strategic Services) legend—the dashing blue-blooded oh-so-special spies, American James Bonds. Even the black eye of the Bay of Pigs fiasco could be attributed to Kennedy's failure of nerve rather than to the Harvard and Yale ole boys who drew up the plans. From almost the very beginning, the C.I.A. has been a focus of Kennedy-assassination conspiracy theories (bitterness by some agents over Kennedy's Bay of Pigs "betrayal" was an obvious motive). This year the first and most relentless conspiracy theorist of them all, Mark Lane, has come out with a book, *Plausible Denial*, which targets high-level C.I.A. figures as the plotters behind the assassination. Lane presents what he calls new and conclusive evidence that the C.I.A. was setting up Oswald in the months before the assassination by having an Oswald impersonator meet with Soviet and Cuban agents in Mexico City, the better to frame him as a Commie assassin.

Again, even if we don't buy Lane's conclusion about C.I.A. complicity in the Kennedy assassination, 20 years of investigations have shown that the C.I.A. was no stranger to complicity in assassinations. We know how the best and brightest blue bloods bonded with the bloodiest and dirtiest Mafia hit men in plots to kill Castro. We know the freak-show side of the agency that used damaging mind-control drugs on unsuspecting citizens; we know that the agency's own top counterspy, James Angleton, paralyzed the place with his paranoid suspicions that KGB moles and false defectors had penetrated the C.I.A. in order to, among other things, conceal the Soviets' true role in the J.F.K. assassination. Even David Belin, the former Warren Commission's staff member who is fighting what he calls a "David and Goliath battle" to defend the Warren Commission's lone-gunman conclusion, declares in his book *Final Disclosure* that the C.I.A. blatantly deceived his beloved Warren Commission—specifically that it "deliberately withheld evidence" of the C.I.A.-Mafia plots against Castro.

Now consider the Kennedys themselves. Inevitably the darker, carnivalesque vision of America that has emerged in the wake of post-assassination investigations has not exempted them. Curiously, otherwise skeptical assassination buffs are among the last misty-eyed believers in Camelot. They still hold to the primal scenario sketched in Oliver Stone's *JFK*: a Galahad-like John Kennedy gallantly battling the sinister right-wing military-industrial complex to bring the troops home, ban the Bomb and ensure racial equality on the home front—a Kennedy killed because he was just too good to live.

You can hear other echoes of this naive vision in such conspiracy-theory compendiums as Jim Marrs' *Crossfire: The Plot That Killed Kennedy*, which was a key source for Stone. Marrs sums up his account of the Bad Guys in the plot, laboring to leave no one out: "Who done it? ... Powerful men in the leadership of the U.S. military, banking, government, intelligence and organized-crime circles ordered their faithful agents to manipulate Mafia-Cuban-agency pawns to kill the chief."

But what's more interesting is Marrs' arcadian vision of what America might be like today if J.F.K. had lived: "No divisive Vietnam War ... [no] Watergate, no other political assassinations, or the Iran-*contra*-Pentagon-C.I.A. attempt at a secret government. Détente with communist Russia and China ... [would have saved defense dollars] that could have been put to use caring for the needy and cleaning up the environment ... no organized-crime control over drugs, gambling ... even toxic waste ... " One feels Marrs believes that if Kennedy had lived the toxic waste just wouldn't have been as toxic *anyway*, because of all the fine, purifying Camelot vibes in the air.

By now, of course, an accumulation of sordid revelations has made J.F.K.'s Washington seem less like Arthur's Camelot than Capone's Chicago. J.F.K. himself, we know, was almost literally in bed with the Chicago Mob, sleeping with the godfather's mistress, for God's sake; his minions used Chicago mobsters as hit men against a rival head of state. He was enmeshed in sordid blackmail intrigues with Hoover; he was implicated in bugging King's bedrooms. Far from a noble peacemaker, he was a hawkish enthusiast for dirty tricks and covert ops, so Machiavellian that—according to Michael Beschloss's new book, *The Crisis Years*—he may even have given his blessing to Khrushchev's building of the Berlin Wall. In retrospect, J.F.K. resembles Marrs' Galahad less than a gang leader like *The Godfather's* Michael Corleone—the well-meaning son of a shadowy godfather (Joe Kennedy, with his bootlegging connections to the Mob), who can't escape his father's legacy or his family's cutthroat character.

In this respect the assassination theorists who seem most prescient, or at least realistic, are the odd couple of Malcolm X and L.B.J. It was Malcolm who provoked a storm of obloquy in the aftermath of the Dallas shooting when he said J.F.K.'s killing was "a case of the chickens coming home to roost." And it was L.B.J. who 10 years later gave a kind of gritty geopolitical substance to Malcolm's metaphor when he told an ex-aide that J.F.K. was "running a damned Murder Incorporated in the Caribbean"—all those C.I.A. assassination plots—and that he believed one of these plots must have backfired, or doubled back on Kennedy, in Dealey Plaza.

Perhaps this gets a bit too close to blame-the-victim. But could it be that the cumulative blackening of the sepulchers of Camelot is responsible for one of the most curious new trends in conspiracy-theory history—the increasing number of people coming forward not merely to claim they know who did it but to *confess* they did it?

One of the first to try this gambit was Charles V. Harrelson, the Texas hit man who happens to be the father of *Cheers* star Woody Harrelson. Cornered by cops seeking to arrest him for assassinating a federal judge in Texas, Harrelson, according to Marrs, told lawmen that he was the guy who killed Kennedy. By the time he backed off the story, assassination buffs had already convinced themselves that they had photographic evidence of Harrelson's presence in Dealey Plaza that day. They had "positively" identified him as one of the mysterious "tramps" arrested near the crime scene after the assassination—conveniently forgetting they had previously "proved" that two of the tramps were actually Watergate burglars E. Howard Hunt and Frank Sturgis.

Next to confess was Robert Easterling, a Mississippi ex-con who told journalist Henry Hurt in 1985 that he killed Kennedy on behalf of Fidel Castro. And then, in 1989, there was the son of a Dallas policeman who pushed his own (now dead) father forward as the grassy-knoll assassin, introducing some curious confessional documentation he claimed to have found in an attic. (The credibility problem of assassination buffs has not been enhanced by the double standard with which they seem to accept indiscriminately every self-proclaimed assassin or grassy-knoll eyewitness who comes forward, but tear to shreds any evidence or testimony that might support the lone-gunman theory.)

Recently, after seeing *JFK* I found myself curious about what had become of the man Jim Garrison once named as the hit man. I consulted some of the assassination buffs still speaking to me (though an agnostic on whether there was a conspiracy, I had written skeptically about the methodology of some of them), and one told me of a buff in Canada who made a specialty of tracking down lesser known figures in the case who might otherwise disappear into the mists of history.

Yes, the Canadian researcher told me, he had traced the still wandering whereabouts of the Name. And he wasn't the only one interested, he said. A former Warren Commission attorney had told him he still couldn't figure out why the Name made such a hasty exit from Dallas: 36 hours after the assassination, he left town and hitchhiked 2,000 miles north to Michigan. Another buff had theorized that the Warren Commission was interested in the Name because he bore as eerie physical resemblance to Oswald—which might have been an innocent explanation for some of the "Oswald" sightings in Ruby's Carousel Club. Other buffs wondered if he might not be one of the mysterious "Oswald impersonators" who was setting up the real, innocent Oswald to be the assassination patsy.

Declining to be led into this labyrinth of suspicion, I nonetheless asked the Canadian buff what had become of the Name's life after he fled Dallas. It seems he couldn't really escape—Nov. 22 continued to haunt him. The FBI followed him to Michigan and questioned him repeatedly; he had to go back to Dallas for Ruby's trial; he never found the wife he'd lost. And then in the early '80s, just when his life seemed to have settled down, renewed interest in the J.F.K. case made his name an object of speculation again: it appeared in a book on the organized-crime connections to Ruby and the assassination. His new wife read the book and began to get a little paranoid. She wondered about the serious car accident they had had; Was it really an accident? Eventually, things began to go awry; his marriage broke up, he lost his job. Last thing the Canadian buff heard, the Name was working as a night security guard in a mill, "boarding with some people," without a traceable phone number of his own.

Looking back, it doesn't seem that much of a mystery why the poor guy fled Dallas so abruptly. His life took a wrong turn down there and never recovered. So did ours. We're all still fleeing Dallas, but it's too late to escape.

JANUARY 14, 1992

THE BOSTON GLOBE

THE 'GIMMICK' IN J.F.K'S VIETNAM WITHDRAWAL PLAN

John Newman

Bruce Palmer, a highly respected general, wrote in 1984 that, in his view, President John F. Kennedy would not have committed major US combat forces to Vietnam "and that quite a different story would have unfolded" had he lived. Palmer served as the No. 2 man for the Army's deputy chief of staff of operations (and later as Gen. Westmoreland's deputy in Vietnam) during the time when Kennedy implemented his withdrawal plans—October 1963.

Today, in the whirlwind of controversy provoked by the movie *JFK*, a concerted attempt has been launched to discount Kennedy's withdrawal plan and discredit the notion that he never would have sent combat troops as Johnson did. Leading this attack is George Lardner of *The Washington Post*, who has marshaled author Stanley Karnow into the fray. Karnow now claims Kennedy's order to withdraw 1,000 advisers in 1963 was a "gimmick."

Even scholar William Gibbons has signed up to Lardner's cause, arguing that a directive prepared for Kennedy the day before his death "demolishes the whole argument" that Kennedy had decided to pull out and that he would not have continued the war.

Karnow's loosely sourced work, *Vietnam: A History*, argued that the prediction that the US could be out of the war by 1965 was "evidently made for domestic political consumption at Kennedy's insistence," but the "gimmick" charge with respect to the 1,000-man withdrawal is new. Neither in his book nor now does Karnow produce a source or cite a document to back up his claims.

Gibbons, who recently told Lardner the 1,000-man withdrawal was a device to pressure Diem into assuming more of the war burden, made no such claim in his work *The US Government and the Vietnam War*. That work only shows that the idea of using the 1,000-man withdrawal as a pressure device was Gen. Taylor's (then chairman of the Joint Chiefs of Staff), not Kennedy's.

Now Gibbons points to the directive NSAM-273 as evidence that Kennedy would have continued the war—"covert action and all." Gibbons argues that because NSAM-273 was prepared for Kennedy, he would have approved it. Kennedy never saw NSAM-273—it was authored the day before his assassination. Moreover, the draft prepared for Kennedy constrained those covert operations to using South Vietnamese forces, while Johnson signed a different version only days after the assassination that dropped this constraint and opened the door to direct US actions against North Vietnam.

In a bit of journalistic license, Lardner fabricates a new clause in NSAM-273 to make it appear as if it specifically mentions an approval of the 1,000-man withdrawal. Pure fiction, NSAM-273 contained one sentence that mentioned withdrawal in a generic sense and only then in the context of a slippery White House statement of Oct. 3, 1963. That statement said withdrawal could take place if the war effort continued to bear fruit. NSAM-273 failed to address the 1,000-man withdrawal specifically or Kennedy's top secret order—NSAM-263—of Oct. 11, 1963, which implemented it.

There is a political subtext behind all this irresponsible journalistic fiction: an attempt to tar Kennedy with the brush of intervention in Vietnam and convince the American public that Johnson simply did what Kennedy would have. This notion does not sit well with many who discussed Vietnam with Kennedy. "Let us not lay on the dead the blame for our own failures," wrote James Gavin—a much-decorated general and ambassador—in 1968. Having discussed military affairs with Kennedy for 15 years, Gavin contended: "I know he was totally opposed to the introduction of combat troops in Southeast Asia."

Whom are we to believe? What are the facts? Kennedy repeatedly turned down the idea of sending combat troops to Vietnam. He did so when all the arguments that could be mustered for sending them had been made—the same arguments, incidentally, which led Johnson to approve sending combat troops in 1965. With respect to withdrawal from Vietnam, Kennedy's public statements were sometimes ambiguous and more often misleading.

Privately, Kennedy made no secret of his anguish over the war or his intention to withdraw the American advisers. In the months before his death he made this abundantly clear to Sens. Mike Mansfield and Wayne Morse, US Rep. Thomas P. O'Neill Jr., and his aides Mike Forrestal and Kenneth O'Donnell.

Kennedy's public statements contradicted his private ones. Why? Kennedy publicly conveyed the impression that the US would stay the course in Vietnam because he feared the advocates of intervention might undermine his reelection in 1964.

The declassified documentary record is more explicit. Kennedy's NSAM-263 implemented the withdrawal plan. If, as Karnow theorizes, the pullout was staged for "domestic political consumption," it was certainly a strange way to influence the voting public, as Kennedy specifically ordered the withdrawal to be kept secret. The secret presidential order to begin the withdrawal seems to buttress the case that Kennedy was feigning right while moving left—not the reverse.

The facts are that Kennedy was withdrawing from Vietnam when he died and that Johnson crossed the line that Kennedy repeatedly refused to cross—the dispatch of American combat troops to Vietnam.

History has taught us John Kennedy was a flawed man. He may also have been, if only for political considerations, purposely deceptive. Vietnam, the record shows, was one such instance. It is crucial that we understand that record and not employ it as a shuttlecock in a debate over a movie. To do otherwise trivializes not only Kennedy's life but also the price that our nation paid for his death.

Reprinted by permission of the author.

JANUARY 15, 1992

SPEECH TO THE NATIONAL PRESS CLUB

Oliver Stone

Thank you Kathryn, thank you ladies and gentlemen, I think I have George Lardner to thank for the turnout here today. Thank you, George, for coming.

I have been accused by a number of people, some of them journalists, of a distortion of history. And, if there is any common thread of attack running through the claims of those critics of *JFK* it is a notion that somehow there is an accepted, settled, respected, carefully thought-out and researched body of history about the assassination of John F. Kennedy, all of which I have set out deliberately to subvert, using as my weapon the motion picture medium and taking as my target the impressionable young who will believe anything as long as it is visual.

This "distortion of history" charge has come at me from all quarters, although almost entirely—it must be said—from people old enough to know better. And it ignores, deliberately and carefully, the fact that there is *no* accepted history of these events and this terrible time remains the most undocumented, unresearched, unagreed-upon, non-historical period of our history.

One can read in history books the standard two paragraphs that John F. Kennedy was shot by a lone gunman who, in turn, was killed by another earnest vigilante and lone gunman. End of story. But that theory, put forward in 26 unindexed volumes by the Warren Commission, was never even believed from the day it was issued by a majority of Americans—and the number of people who disbelieve it increases each year.

Are we really to believe that settled, agreed, sanctified *history* includes that Lee Harvey Oswald wrote away—under an easy-to-trace alias—for an inaccurate mail-order Italian rifle called, by the Italian army, the "humanitarian rifle" because it never killed anyone when deliberately aimed, when he could have anonymously bought an accurate weapon at any street corner in Dallas? Is it sacred *history* that this semi-literate high school dropout from Fort Worth, Texas, professing Marxism, was taken into a secret, highly-trained Marine unit at an air base where the U-2 flights originated in Japan?...given courses in the Russian language and then permitted to leave the Marine Corps on three days' notice on a trumped-up claim of illness of his mother—who, days after his death, was the first to make the claim her son was working for American intelligence? Is it settled *history* that he then defected to the Soviet Union with a request for travel that included a reference to an obscure Ph.D.'s-only graduate institute in Switzerland? Are we to believe that it is now *history*, not to be disturbed except by people like me, that he then went to the United States Embassy in Moscow, announced his intention to defect and to turn over U.S. secrets to the Russians—and was permitted to go on his way? Is it part of our *history*, which cannot be touched, that he then returned 18 months later to the same U.S. Embassy, announced his intention to resume American citizenship and was handed his passport and some funds to enable him to return home?

Must one be a Disturber of the Peace to question the history that says Oswald was met by a CIA front representative when he returned to the United States, that he was never debriefed by an intelligence organization, although 25,000 tourists that year were so debriefed? Must one be a Distorter of History to question why he then merged into the fierce anti-Communist White Russian community of Dallas although he kept up the absurd front of Marxism? Or into the equally rabid anti-Communist circle of Guy Bannister in New Orleans? Or how did Oswald just come to have a job a few weeks before at the Book Depository overlooking the precise point in the motorcade where Kennedy's car took that unusual 11-mile-an-hour-curve? Or how Oswald came to be spotted by Patrolman Marion Baker only 90 seconds after the sixth floor shooting, on the *second* floor, having a Coca-Cola and showing no signs of being out of breath? Or the too neat stashing of the rifle without prints and the three cartridges neatly laid out side-by-side at the window? Or Oswald's cool and calm behavior that weekend, or his claim, his statement, that he was a patsy?

Am I a Disturber of History to question why Allen Dulles, who was fired by JFK from the CIA, which JFK said he would splinter into a thousand pieces, why, why was Mr. Dulles appointed to the Warren Commission to investigate Mr. Kennedy's murder? And so on, and so on, and so on.

To accept this settled version of history which must not be disturbed lest one call down the venom of leading journalists from around the country, one must also believe the truly absurd single-bullet theory of the Warren Commission. This holds that one bullet caused seven wounds in Kennedy and Connally, breaking two dense bones and coming out clean. No metal missing, no blood tissue or anything on it; its path, as you know, utterly ludicrous, entering Kennedy's back on a downward trajectory, changing direction, exiting up through his throat, pausing for 1.6 seconds before deciding to attack Connally, then turning right, then left, then right again, hitting Connally at the back of his right armpit, heading downward through his chest, taking a right-turn into Connally's wrist, shattering the radius bone and exiting his wrist. The bullet launches one last assault, takes a dramatic U-turn and buries itself in Connally's left thigh. Later the bullet turns up 5 miles from the scene of the crime, on a stretcher in a corridor at Parkman Hospital in pristine condition.

No, ladies and gentlemen, this is not history, this is myth. It is a myth that a scant number of Americans has ever believed. It is a myth that has sustained a generation of journalists and historians who have refused to examine it, who have refused to question it, and above all who close ranks to vilify those who do. So long as the attackers of that comforting lone gunman theory could be dismissed as kooks and cranks and the writers of obscure books that would not be published by "reputable" publishing houses, not much defense was needed. But now that myth is under attack by a well-financed and—I hope—well-made motion picture with all the vivid imagery and new energy the screen can convey. Now, either enormous amounts of evidence have to be marshaled in support of that myth or else those who question it must be attacked. There is no evidence; therefore the attack is on.

Some journalists of the 60s are self-appointed Keepers of the Flame. They talk about this history and fight savagely those who would question it. But confronted with the Crime of the Century, with no motive and hardly any alleged perpetrators, they stand mute. Where in the last 20 years have we seen serious research from Tom Wicker, Dan Rather, Anthony Lewis, George Lardner, Ken Auchincloss into Lee Harvey Oswald's movements in the months and years before November 22, 1963? Where have we seen any analysis of why Oswald—who many say adored Kennedy—alone among assassins in history would not only deny his guilt, but claim he was a patsy? Can one imagine John Wilkes Booth leaping to the stage at Ford's Theater, turning to the audience and shouting, "I didn't kill anyone, I'm just a patsy"?

One might ask of the journalists who have suddenly emerged as the Defenders of History what is *their* sense of history? How much work has the sage of Bethesda, George Will, done in the 20 years he has been a columnist to try to uncover the answers to some of the dark secrets in Dallas, '63? Will Tom Wicker and Dan Rather spend their retirement years examining closely the possibility of a second or a third gunman, or will they content themselves with savaging those who do? Why has no one questioned Richard Helms, who lied to the Warren Commission when he said the CIA had no knowledge of Lee Harvey Oswald, when we know now that there was, as of 1960, an increasingly thick 201 file on Oswald? Or why is no one asking for the files of Operation Mongoose, which may be at the very heart of this conspiracy? Or why is no one questioning Mr. Hoover's memo of 1961 outlining the fact that someone was using Oswald's name while he was in Russia to buy trucks for the Guy Bannister apparatus in New Orleans? Why are none of the reporters questioning Col. Fletcher Prouty in depth? Or historian John Newman? Or Marina Oswald Porter, who says her husband was working for something bigger? Or questioned the hit man, Charles Harrelson, who is in maximum security? Let them deny what they will, but at least *ask* them. There is more truth-seeking going on now in Russia than there is in our own country. What *JFK* has brought out is that those who talk the most of history have no commitment to it either.

The central historical question raised by *JFK*, of course, has to do not with the tramps in Dealey Plaza, not with who might have been firing from the grassy knoll, not with by what coalition of Cubans, exiles, mobsters, rogue intelligence officers the conspiracy might have been concocted, but the darker stain on the American ground in the '60s and '70s—Vietnam. It is Vietnam which has become the "Bloody Shirt" of American politics, replacing the slavery issue of a hundred years before. Just as we did not resolve, if we ever did, the great battle over slavery until 100 years after the Civil War, when we passed the Voting Rights Act of 1965, so it becomes clear that the Vietnam War remains the watershed of our time and the divisions of our country among our people opened up by it seems to gape wider and wider with each passing year.

JFK suggests it was Vietnam that led to the assassination of John Kennedy. That he became too dangerous, too strong an advocate of changing the course of the Cold War, too clear a proponent of troop withdrawal for those who supported the idea of a war in Vietnam and later came to support the war itself. Was President Kennedy withdrawing from Vietnam? Had he indicated strongly his intention to do so? Had he committed himself firmly, and against all hawkish advice to the contrary, to oppose the entry of U.S. combat troops? The answer to these questions is unequivocally yes. As Arthur Schlesinger, Jr. has attested and Maj. John Newman, a young historian here on this dais who has devoted himself to a ten-year study of this, can attest. His book, *JFK and Vietnam*, a major work coming next month, will surely contribute more heavily than any other volume of immediate military history to the solution of these questions.

Major Newman makes it very clear President Kennedy signaled his intention to withdraw from Vietnam in a variety of ways and put that intention firmly on the record with national Security Action Memorandum 263 in October of 1963. Those who try to say it was no more than a call for a rotation of troops or a gimmick and that the Johnson NSAM 273 within a week of the assassination merely confirmed the policy, ignore the obvious question. If LBJ was merely continuing Kennedy's policies, why was it necessary to reverse the NSAM?

So the protectors of Vietnam, the new wavers of the bloody shirt, leap to attack the central premise of *JFK*. Oliver Stone is distorting history again, they say. Even *suggesting* that John Kennedy was positioning us for a withdrawal from Vietnam—by even suggesting that—I am distorting history. But these Defenders of History had very little to say five years ago when it was suggested, in a motion picture, that Mozart had not died peacefully but had been murdered by a rival and second-rate composer. Where were all our cultural watchdogs when Peter Shaffer was "distorting history" with *Amadeus?* The answer, of course, is that it wasn't worth the effort. Eighteenth Century Vienna, after all, is not 20th Century Vietnam. If Mozart was murdered by Salieri, it would not change one note of that most precious music. But, if John F. Kennedy were killed because he was determined to withdraw from and never send combat troops to Vietnam, then we must fix the blame for the only lost war in our history, for 56,000 American dead, and for an as yet unhealed split in our country and among our people.

I have been ridiculed, and worse, for suggesting the existence of a conspiracy—as though only kooks and cranks and extremists suggest their existence. But this is the wrong city in which to ridicule people who believe in conspiracies.

Is it inconceivable that a President of the United States could sit at the heart of a criminal conspiracy designed to cover up a crime? We know *that* happened—we would have impeached him for it had he not resigned just one jump ahead.

Is it so far-fetched to believe in a high-level conspiracy involving the White House, the Joint Chiefs, the Air Force and the CIA to bomb a neutral country and lie about it in military reports to the rest of the country? But it happened. Perhaps more than once.

Is it inconceivable the National Security Council leadership, with or without the knowledge of the President of the United States and with the collaboration of the director of the CIA (not just a few rogues), could have engaged in a massive conspiracy to ship arms to our sworn enemy with a casual hope that a few hostages might be released as a result? But it happened.

Does it offend our sense of propriety to suggest an Assistant Secretary of State for Latin America might have regularly lied to Congress about raising money abroad to perform things the Congress had forbidden us to do? But *that* happened.

Is it inconceivable that a campaign manager, later to become the CIA director, negotiated with a foreign country to keep American hostages imprisoned until after a Presidential election in order to ensure the election of his candidate? We shall see. But I think no one thinks any more it is out of the question.

So when "JFK" suggests that a conspiracy involving elements of the government, people in the CIA, people in the FBI, perhaps people associated with the Joint Chiefs, all in the service of the military-industrial complex that President Eisenhower warned us about, might have conspired to kill John Fitzgerald Kennedy because he was going to change sharply the direction of American Foreign policy, is it not appropriate at least to look there for evidence? What was Allen Dulles really up to in those months, or Charles Cabell, also fired by JFK, or his brother Earl Cabell, the Mayor of Dallas?

Thomas Jefferson urged on us the notion that when truth can complete in a free marketplace of ideas, it will prevail. There is as yet no marketplace of history for the years of the Kennedy assassination and immediately afterward. Let us begin to create one. What I have tried to do with this movie is to open a stall in that marketplace of ideas and offer a version of what might have happened, as against the competing versions of what we know did not happen, and some other possible versions as well. I am happy to say, based not only on the nine million people who have already seen the movie, but on the attitude towards the facts they take with them away from the movie, that our new stall in that marketplace of ideas is doing a very brisk business and we expect by the time this film is played out in video cassettes, etc., that another 50 or so million Americans will have a little more information on their history.

I am very proud that "JFK" has been a part of the momentum to open previously closed files in the matter of the assassination. Cong. Louis Stokes of Ohio, who chaired the House Select Committee on Assassinations, has announced his willingness to consider the opening of the files closed until, as you know, the year 2029. I am hopeful his consideration will ripen into approval. In addition, Judge William Webster, formerly the director of the Federal Bureau of Investigation and of the CIA, has indicated his strong opinion that all of the files, *all* of the files—House, Committee, CIA and FBI among them—be made public, a proposal I was extremely pleased last weekend to see endorsed by Sen. Edward Kennedy. In the meantime, we are grateful to Congressman Stokes, Cong. Lee Hamilton, Judge Webster, Senator Kennedy and others who have indicated a willingness to consider opening these files. Now if the Army and Navy intelligence services will join suit, it is my hope the American people will have the full truth of the assassination.

Thank you.

Reprinted by permission.

JANUARY 16,1992

THE NEW YORK TIMES
EDITORIAL

GET THE REST OF THE J.F.K. STORY

Oliver Stone, the film maker, was wrong to use trick photography and spurious evidence to charge that the murder of John F. Kennedy was a coup by the nation's highest officials. But he is right to call for release of assassination documents that have been sealed for decades and are scheduled to remain so for decades more.

Without endorsing Mr. Stone's conspiracy theories, the Kennedy family and a growing number of public officials are giving welcome encouragement to a fuller historical account of a national tragedy. They need to press the case for wider disclosure—without illusions that new data will appease the insatiable conspiracy theorists.

America, where free speech prevails, has no official history and does not sponsor orthodox stories, impervious to new evidence, about its past. The Warren commission report, which concluded that Lee Harvey Oswald was the lone killer, never was more than a conscientious attempt to explain the crime and account for as many of its mysteries as possible. It now makes sense to release as much of the underlying evidence as possible.

The easiest disclosure would be the release of overclassified documents in files generated by the House committee that published two dozen volumes of material before running out of time and money in 1979. Its chairman, Louis Stokes, favors careful declassification. For documents generated by the C.I.A., F.B.I., Secret Service and other agencies, the executive branch needs to designate an official to collect and screen scattered archives.

Some secrecy is defensible. Some personnel files merit continued confidentiality. Consent must be sought from some informants who spoke to investigators under promises of confidentiality. Some intelligence-gathering sources and methods still deserve respect and protection.

True, every refusal to disclose, reasonable or not, will continue to be grist for conspiracy theorists, and the newly released documents will beget new questions. But that's the American approach to information and history.

Oliver Stone, who directed the $40 million movie *JFK* is not engaged in a fair-minded inquiry. He continues to libel Clay Shaw, a New Orleans businessman who was acquitted of conspiring to kill the President. And he continues to ridicule the Warren commission's theory that one of the bullets fired in Dallas in November 1963 hit both the President and Gov. John Connally of Texas. Yet the House committee, while concluding there probably was a conspiracy, confirmed that fragments from a supposedly pristine bullet wounded the Governor.

Nevertheless, the public's right to information does not depend on the integrity or good faith of those who seek it. Congress and the executive branch would serve the public by maximizing disclosure of the facts surrounding that fateful day in Dallas.

ENTERTAINMENT WEEKLY

THE ZAPRUDER FILM: SHOTS SEEN ROUND THE WORLD

Richard B. Stolley

Richard B. Stolley was the Los Angeles Bureau Chief of Life *magazine when his assignment to cover the events in Dallas led to one of the great scoops in journalism: obtaining exclusive rights to Abraham Zapruder's film of the President's assassination. Here, Stolley, now editorial director of Time Inc. Magazines (including this one), recounts that experience in detail.*

"Dick, Kennedy's been shot in Dallas!"

Within an hour of the shout that brought me running out of my office, I was on a plane to Texas with another correspondent and two photographers. In the air we learned that the President was dead and that someone named Lee Harvey Oswald had been arrested. By dusk, I was setting up office in a downtown hotel.

At about 6 p.m., I got a phone call from one of the magazine's part-time reporters, Patsy Swank. She was at Dallas police headquarters, she said in a confidential whisper, Oswald was being interrogated in an office not far away, and the corridors were in a chaotic mob of cops and reporters. What Patsy said next was electrifying: She had been tipped by a Dallas police officer that the assassination had been filmed in its entirety by a local garment manufacturer, whose name started with a "Z." She sounded out the syllables. I picked up the Dallas phone book, ran my finger down the Z's, and there it was: Zapruder, Abraham. I called the number. No answer. I called again every 15 minutes or so until 11 pm. Then a weary voice answered.

It was Zapruder himself. He had been driving around trying to calm his nerves. After photographing the shooting, he had literally stumbled back to his office nearby muttering, "They killed him, they killed him." Zapruder's secretary described him as "incoherent, in a state of shock," but clutching the camera containing what would become the most famous home movie of all time.

Incredibly, nobody in authority was much interested in it. Zapruder had contacted the Dallas police, but by mid-afternoon they had Oswald in custody and the film seemed of marginal importance. Both the Secret Service and the FBI said it was his property to dispose of as he saw fit but that they would like copies. Zapruder took his 8 mm film to a Kodak lab, and by evening had the original and three copies in hand.

I questioned him as gently as I could. Yes, it showed everything. Yes, I was the first journalist to contact him. No, I could not come out to his house at that late hour. He was too exhausted, too distraught. He seemed genuinely grateful that I did not persist, and asked me to be at his office at nine the next morning.

I got there at eight: By now other reporters would surely have learned about the film and be in hot pursuit. Standing in the hall at Zapruder's dress factory were several grim-faced men in dark suits—Secret Service agents about to see evidence of their catastrophic failure to protect the President. Zapruder invited us in, darkened the room, and started the film.

It begins with a few frames of employees from his office, then of Dealey Plaza and, suddenly, the motorcade is turning the corner. We held our breath. The President is smiling and waving. The limousine is briefly obscured behind a highway sign. It emerges and now Kennedy's waving arms are clutching his throat, a puzzled look on his face. Governor Connally's mouth is open wide, as if howling in pain.

Remember, this is pre-camcorder; there is no sound, except the creaking of the projector. The camera jerks almost imperceptibly with every shot. The third and last is to the right side of Kennedy's head, caught in sickening frame 313. Brain matter and blood spray up and forward, a trajectory that would have been impossible if the shot had come from anywhere but behind (*JFK* and many conspiracy theorists argue that it came from the grassy knoll in the front).

The furiously bleeding President collapses into his wife's lap. After a split second of terrified contemplation, Jackie clambers out onto the truck of the limousine, until a Secret Service agent pushes her back into the car. It speeds off for Parkland Hospital.

As those of us in the room tried to recover our composure, I knew that *Life* magazine had to have this film. It was a complete photographic record of the death of the President, a unique historical document. I doubted any other existed, and I was right.

By this time I could hear enough commotion outside to realize that other journalists had arrived. I went out to determine who my competition was: the Associated Press, *The Saturday Evening Post*, a newsreel, so far. Zapruder showed the film again to the other journalists, but agreed to talk to me first. We went into his little office and I knew I had to make a deal, right then, or I would likely lose the film. He understood its value to his family's financial future, but was worried about "exploitation," a word he used time and again.

During the night, he told me, he had had a nightmare in which he walked by a sleazy Times Square movie theater and a man on the sidewalk was luring people inside with the promise: "See the President get killed!" I vowed that *Life* would treat his pictures with taste and respect. In less than half an hour, we had agreed on a price—$50,000 for all print rights—and I snuck out the back door of the factory with the original film and one copy, leaving poor Zapruder to face the angry journalists in the hall.

The next day, after the *Life* editors in New York had seen the film, I was instructed to try to tie up all rights, print and motion picture. On this mission, I was competing with Dan Rather and CBS, but Zapruder seemed so relieved to be dealing with a familiar face that we quickly reached an agreement: a total of $150,000, in annual installments of $25,000.

This grainy snippet of film henceforth became the most crucial bit of evidence in the Warren Commission's investigation of Kennedy's death. It was critical in establishing the timing of the shots, the position of those in the limousine, the reaction of onlookers and much more. It also dragged *Life* into the thicket of conspiracy theories that began springing up as soon as the Warren report offered its lone-gunman explanation. Indeed, there have been hints over the years that I personally was part of the plot. These are the facts:

◆ I wasn't. One reason my name crops up is probably that I still think the Warren report has a better grip on the reality of Nov. 22 than any of the conspiracy buffs and have said so. My role in the assassination investigation was strictly that of a reporter. I was never interrogated by any government agency or by the Warren Commission; I never met any of the alleged conspirators.

A name mentioned far more often is that of the late C.D. Jackson, who was publisher of *Life*. Because he had served in military intelligence, the theories go, he had both a motive and an opportunity to influence how the magazine handled the Zapruder film. The truth is that all decisions involving its use (or nonuse) were made only by editors, not by anyone on the publishing side.

◆ *Life* did not bury the Zapruder film for 12 years, as Stone charges. All the relevant images were printed immediately except for frame 313. We felt publishing that grisly picture would constitute an unnecessary affront to the Kennedy family and to the President's memory. Today, that may seem a strange, even foolish, decision. But this was 1963, a few years before Vietnam brought carnage into American living rooms. The head wound was described only in words in that issue. *Life* published frame 313 in 1964 and several times later, and for years urged that the Kennedy investigation be reopened.

◆ *Life* decided not to sell the Zapruder film for TV or movie showing for reasons of both taste and competition. Copies were given to the Secret Service and to the Warren Commission. When New Orleans district attorney Jim Garrison subpoenaed the film for his trial of alleged conspirator Clay Shaw, *Life* complies. There was no reluctance on the magazine's part, as *JFK* suggests, although it now seems clear that security at the trial was so lax that the film was illegally duplicated, and bootleg copies were soon sold all over the country. They were shown at conspiracy lectures for years, maybe even a time or two on local TV. My files are full of letters from conspiracy buffs commenting on the film.

◆ There have been charges that *Life* tampered with the film, removed or reversed frames, diddled with it to confound the truth. Nothing like that ever happened. I have inspected the film many times, as have others; the frames are all there, in the proper order.

In 1975, *Life* sold the Zapruder film back to his family (Abe died in 1970) for one dollar. His son, a Washington tax lawyer, does a brisk business in renting it for one time use. (Oliver Stone, for instance, says he paid $40,000 to use the film in *JFK*.) The original is kept in the National Archives, part of the official history of the event that for many of us defined the last half of the twentieth century.

Since seeing *JFK*, I have been wondering what that history would be if a middle-aged businessman had not brought his camera to Dealey Plaza. Without knowing that the film went through Zapruder's camera at 18.3 frames per second, we would have no precise way of timing the shots. There would presumably be no controversy about Oswald's ability to fire that often and that accurately. We would probably assume the first shot passed through Kennedy's neck virtually unmarked; thus, the so-called pristine, or "magic" bullet. We would think the second shot hit Governor Connally alone (as he has always believed).

We would ...well, you get the idea. There would still be conspiracy theories, since serious questions do remain unanswered. but it is hard to believe that an entire industry of financially rewarding intrigue would have sprung up and still flourish three decades later. No Zapruder film; possibly no wild allegations, totally unproved, of dark crimes committed at the highest levels of American government and society.

As a country, ironically, we might be better off.

© 1992 Entertainment Weekly Inc., reprinted by permission.

JANUARY 19, 1992

THE MIAMI HERALD

J.F.K.'S MURDER: WHERE ARE THE MEDIA?

Robert Hennelly

Unfortunately the firestorm over Oliver Stone, flamboyant filmmaker, and his making of the movie *JFK* have upstaged one very relevant question that emerges out of the controversial film. Who decided that thousands of pages of files on the Kennedy assassination should be kept from the American public well into the next century, and what possible national security interests could be served by the continued suppression of the documents?

In true fluff over substance, American media style, Stone is reduced to a caricature of wild genius, a once drug-crazed, womanizing gun-toting, paranoid who is lamenting the loss of a father. The focus on the trivialities of personality conveniently prevents us from having to confront the tough question his film raises.

Where have the American media been on this major story of our time? They have relegated continued digging on the topic to the supermarket tabloids, which in turn split their resources between finding Josef Mengele and Elvis Presley. The mainstream media reserved for themselves the formidable tasks of going to court to get the actual tape of the Challenger astronauts in their final moments of mortal terror or the chasing of every succulent detail of the William Kennedy Smith rape trial, including the accuser's driving record.

Years ago, a congressional committee investigation raised the serious possibility that indeed a fourth shot was fired in the Kennedy assassination, contradicting the Warren Commission report, and got about as much media play as the recent exhumation of President Zachary Taylor's body did: It was reduced to a historical curiosity. According to polls, most Americans don't believe that august body's version of the events of Nov. 22, 1963.

Stone's grisly film withstanding, serious questions remain about the assassination, the handling of the police and federal investigation, and the continued secrecy surrounding much of the primary evidence. Sen. Edward Kennedy, the president's brother, has now called for the release of documents that have remained out of reach of the American public for nearly 30 years.

The America of 1963 was a much different place. We believed our leaders. When the air-raid sirens sounded, we got under our desks. When we were told to hate communists, we did. Whatever Walter Cronkite said had to be true. He was like Moses. "Hey, it has to be true—I saw it on TV."

It was before Watergate, Iran-contra and dozens of Pentagon procurement scandals, and before the public's discovery of the FBI's covert surveillance of legitimate political movements. It was before the murder of Chilean President Salvador Allende and before we had a lowly lieutenant colonel running a covert free-lance foreign policy from his office in the White House.

In 1963, the nation was paralyzed for days with grief. The powers that be offered the nation a hypothesis that became, with polished media projection, a mythopoetic that helped ease the pain. I say hypothesis because Harvey Oswald's freelance execution by Jack Ruby ensured he would have no trial. The Warren Commission has been permitted to suffice as one in history.

The historic record is rife with questions. Considerable questions remain about the way the autopsy of President Kennedy was handled. The one piece of extant evidence the public has seen, the Zapruder 8mm film, seems to contradict the Warren Commission findings. And then there is the magic bullet ...

Since those tragic days the size of the intelligence community's black budgets has ballooned. What we can't know fills libraries. Meanwhile, our intelligence community has proven itself anything but intelligent.

The keepers of the secrets missed the biggest global reorganization in modern history, permitted our own Commerce Department to license components for Saddam Hussein's war machine and over-stated by orders of magnitude the level of Soviet military buildup, leaving us deep in debt as we armed to meet the evil empire. Those are the screw-ups we know about. Imagine what we missed.

The C.I.A. and FBI have files on Oswald and the assassination of John F. Kennedy. The Cold War is over and we are still treated like children by some faceless, nameless big daddy with the big picture. There is no greater crime against the people than their co-option and suppression of their history.

Oliver Stone's movie disturbed me. The re-creation of the autopsy of my boyhood hero sickened me, as did the weighing of the dead man's brains.

Finally, the Zapruder film was played with as much frequency in the film as the major networks aired the explosion of the Challenger. In both cases the media became a bludgeon, working a terrorist massage designed to illicit psychic pain but most importantly to get your attention and hold it.

In an age when most young Americans have no sense of history or geography and don't like to read much, there is the real potential that Oliver Stone's spine-tingling mythopoetic of John Kennedy's tragic death will replace the Warren Commission as the next popular perception. By the government's continued suppression of the documents relating to the Kennedy assassination, it will guarantee it.

Reprinted by permission of the author.

JANUARY 21, 1992

THE WASHINGTON POST

SEEKING J.F.K.'S MISSING BRAIN, 'SECRET' FILES
National Archives Has Surge of Public Requests to See Evidence Related to Assassination

Michael Isikoff

Is President John F. Kennedy's brain really missing from the National Archives? And what about those "secret" assassination files that can't be opened for another 37 years?

If you've seen *JFK*, Oliver Stone's three-hour docudrama about a sinister conspiracy to kill the president, you might be wondering the same thing. Such questions have caused more than a few headaches at the National Archives, staff members said last week. The movie has generated a surge in public requests to inspect evidence relating to Kennedy's slaying.

"There's always been interest in this from Day One, but in the last few months we've been very busy," said Michael R. McReynolds, who, as director of the "Textual Reference Division, oversees the records of the Warren Commission that in 1964 completed its investigation of the Nov. 22, 1963, Kennedy assassination. "We're getting a lot of letters from people asking for information and to see documents. Almost all of them want to see autopsy photographs."

As official custodian of the nation's records, the Archives retains hundreds of thousands of pages of Warren Commission records-more than 360 cubic feet of material: from the Italian-made Mannlicher-Carcano rifle used by Lee Harvey Oswald to pictures of the strippers who worked at Jack Ruby's Dallas nightclub, the Carousel.

But while 98 percent of this material is theoretically open to the public, the businesslike McReynolds explained that you can't just wander in the off the street and take a peek. Under an agreement with the Kennedy family, for example, the autopsy material has been restricted to "serious" researchers, and the Archives applies the same standard to material evidence.

"We have a lot of people who walk in and say, 'Can I see the rifle?'" said McReynolds, leading a reporter on a tour through the dimly lit rooms where the records are kept. "We say, 'No ... It's not a serious request.'"

Meanwhile, the Archives has accelerated its review of the remaining 2 percent of classified Warren Commission evidence, which is segregated in 20 boxes in a secure vault. McReynolds and other Archives officials indicated last week that at least some of that material will never be made public.

There are, for example, Oswald's tax returns. "That's protected by statute," said Jill D. Brett, an Archives spokeswoman.

But much of the interest generated by Stone's movie centers on another set of assassination documents also stored at the Archives: the unpublished records of the House Select Committee on Assassinations, turned over to the Clerk of the House in 1979 and sealed until the year 2029. Conspiracy theorists have long contended that these "secret" records - not subject to the Freedom of Information Act - hold critical clues to the assassination.

Among the 400 cubic feet of documents in the committee files, for example, are records of staff interviews, files on informants and, perhaps most intriguing, a 200-plus-page report written by a committee staff member about Oswald's trip to the Cuban and Soviet embassies in Mexico City a few months before the assassination.

James Lesar, a Washington lawyer who heads the privately funded Assassinations Archives and Research Center and who has been suing the government for more than a decade for release of the files, said he believes the report questions whether "it was Oswald that visited those embassies. And if it was not Oswald, then who the hell was it?"

Stone makes much of the "secret" files in *JFK*. and when the director spoke before the National Press Club last week, his publicists passed out red, white and black "J.F.K Free the Files" buttons. Archives officials insist the sealing of those assassination committee records is not as suspicious as Stone makes it sound.

Under a House rule, *all* unpublished records of House committees are sealed from the public for 30 years, and certain categories - such as minutes of executive session meetings - are sealed for 50 years, said Bob Corren, who oversees committee records at the Archives. "Records of the Merchant Marine Committee … the Agriculture Committee, they're all closed," said Corren, who added that he has never taken a look at the J.F.K files.

Lesar and other committee critics say Rep. Louis Stokes (D-Ohio), who was chairman of the former House Select Committee on Assassinations, G. Robert Blakey, Have consistently opposed calls to release the files. But now, momentum to do so is mounting. Stokes last week said he was "exploring the possibility" of supporting a House resolution that would unlock the files.

Over at the Archives, staff members are more concerned about another assertion in Stone's movie—in the epilogue—suggestion that the Archives somehow lost the president's brain.

"It's important to us that we clear this up," said spokeswoman Brett.

The claim was first made by Cyril Wecht, a prominent Pittsburgh pathologist and longstanding Warren Commission critic, after he was permitted to examine Kennedy autopsy records at the Archives in 1972. An inventory of materials that had been turned over to Kennedy's former secretary, Evelyn Lincoln, at the National Archives by Kennedy's personal physician, George G. Burkley, in April 1965 had listed nine categories of autopsy-related items, including a "stainless steel container—seven inches in diameter—containing gross material" and microscopic tissue slides.

Wecht said that seven years later when he opened the material that had been locked in a footlocker, the stainless steel container and slides were gone. "There's something very sinister about this," Wecht said yesterday. "It's the most important piece of physical evidence in the case. At the very least, they [the Archives] were inept and negligent."

But Brett contends the charge is unfair. In fact, she said, the material turned over by Burkley belonged to the Kennedy family. She said that a few days after Burkley gave the material to Lincoln in 1965, a secretary to Sen. Robert F. Kennedy retrieved it. Not until Oct.29, 1966, did Burke Marshall, a lawyer for the Kennedy family, return the material in a footlocker to the Archives and officially deed its contents to the government.

"We have no idea what happened to the gross material and tissue slides," said Brett. "But the point is they were never in the custody of the National Archives ... The movie implies they were part of the [Archives] records and that's not accurate."

© 1992 The Washington Post. Reprinted by permission.

JANUARY 22, 1992

REUTERS

BOREN SEEKS OPENING OF ASSASSINATION PAPERS

Senate intelligence committee Chairman David L. Boren (D-Okla.) said yesterday that all government papers on President John F. Kennedy's assassination should be opened to clear the air on whether federal agencies were involved in the incident.

Boren is the latest legislator to say the documents should be opened in the controversy over the movie *JFK*, which portrays federal agencies as conspiring to kill Kennedy in 1963 so he could not end the Vietnam War.

Boren said all government documents, including those now classified, should be open to legitimate historians. He said the committee will conduct a study on how this could be done.

"I have no information or knowledge which would lead me to believe that our government agencies were involved in any kind of plot in relation to the death of President Kennedy," Boren said in a statement.

"But it is time to find an appropriate way to clear the air," he said.

Rep. Louis Stokes (D-Ohio), who was the chairman of a 1979 House investigation of the assassination, said last week that he was exploring the possibility of having the House open files sealed after that investigation.

The House investigation concluded Lee Harvey Oswald fired the shots that killed Kennedy in Dallas. It concluded there was no government or Cuban conspiracy to kill Kennedy but said it could not rule out a conspiracy by gangsters.

The National Archives has said about 2 percent of the documents collected by the official Warren Commission investigation in 1964 remain classified.

It said papers not already published in a voluminous House investigation report are sealed only because of a House rule that seals all such unpublished papers for 30 years.

Stokes said he was confident the sealed papers would reveal no significant new information on Kennedy's assassination.

JANUARY 15, 1992

UNIVERSAL PRESS SYNDICATE

PUNDITS GO ASTRAY TAKING AIM AT *JFK*

Roger Ebert

Thank god for President Bush's stomach flu. It gave the op-ed pundits something to write about other than Oliver Stone's *JFK*. Never in my years as a newspaperman have I seen one subject pummeled so mercilessly and joylessly as this movie that questions the official wisdom on the assassination of Kennedy. Saddam Hussein did not receive half the vituperation the op-ed crowd has aimed at *JFK*. Nothing Oliver North did was remotely as shocking to them as this film by the other famous Oliver.

It is always a little daunting when the deep thinkers of the editorial department venture out to the movies. There is condescension in their voices when they return. They're going to set us straight. What is strange about *JFK* is that few of the pundits seem actually to have SEEN the movie. You will search the clippings in vain for their visceral response, for their answer to the question: Politics aside, how was it as a movie?

I think it is a terrific movie experience. Audiences seem to agree. But it's important to draw a distinction between the movie's politics, and its entertainment value. The op-ed team seems to begin with the premise that if they disagree with a movie, if it offends their ideological and historical beliefs, then that makes it a bad movie. It does not. It makes it a movie they disagree with. Quality is a separate question. Even if I disagreed with the arguments in each and every frame of *JFK*, even if I thought the whole film was an irresponsible paranoid fantasy, I would have to admit that it engaged my attention, it entertained me, it challenged me, and it made me think.

That cannot be said about many movies in the course of a year. Here on the movie beat, I see a lot of movies that are shameful, lazy, corrupt, boring and exploitative. *JFK* isn't one of them. It's a labor of love and risk by Oliver Stone, who has dramatized the doubts many people have about the official version of Kennedy's death. He is entitled to his beliefs.

If it has done nothing else, *JFK* has achieved the remarkable feat of making the op-ed people livid with anger—greater anger, apparently, than was generated by Watergate, or Irangate, or the vast looming specter of Vietnam, or such issues as gun control. Most of the pundits pride themselves on a certain measured tone; why does this movie make them so mad they lose their cool?

Consider political columnist Tom Wicker. He attacked the film in the entertainment section of the Sunday *New York Times*, a week before it opened. Oliver Stone responded in a letter to the editor, where he made the mistake of referring to himself as an artist. Wicker chose not to reply to anything of substance in Stone's letter, limiting his response to a smartass comeback: "The director of '*JFK*' is not, as he claims, an artist. He is a polemicist."

Here you see the anger. Wicker doesn't answer the letter; he dismisses it in a show-off moment I imagine he is ashamed of by now. Tom Wicker should know that it is possible for the same man to be an artist and a polemicist, that it is not forbidden for an artist to express political opinions.

Dan Rather is as angry as Tom Wicker. He has attacked the movie twice on the CBS news. Why are these guys so worked up? There is one obvious reason, one not so obvious:

1. If Stone is right, then their own reporting on the Kennedy assassination is discredited. They got the story wrong. They have spent the last 30 years tacitly acting as if there were no substantial stories still to be generated by the Kennedy assassination. What are they going to do now? Thank Stone for directing their attention back to some of the bothersome questions in the case?

2. It is human nature to reserve a special dislike for those whose lives are a rebuke to our own. In the 1960s, this same generation of op-ed guys saw themselves as anti-establishment, hard-nosed reporters who brushed aside official versions. Today, the former anti-establishment rebels are themselves the establishment. Then here comes that nuisance Ollie Stone, like the Ghost of Christmas Past, rattling the skeletons in all those old cupboards and upsetting everyone.

Even if Stone is completely wrong, isn't there a story in the fact that two-thirds of Americans believe we don't know the full story of the Kennedy assassination? Even if Stone is a paranoid polemicist, why can't those government files on the assassination be opened until after most of us are dead? What's in them? Why aren't the op-ed guys demanding to see them? Why is Stone a nut for wanting them to be unsealed?

A man named Robert Warshow once wrote a few words that I have pinned to the wall in front of me. He wrote: "A man watches a movie, and the critic must acknowledge that he is that man."

In other words, a critic must acknowledge the feelings he really had, the thoughts he really formed,the opinion he really believes. Even if you hate everything a movie stands for, you have to acknowledge how it made you FEEL.

Sometimes Warshow's credo gets me into tricky situations, as it did not long ago when I was reviewing a skillful but reprehensible movie named *The Last Boy Scout*. I had to acknowledge the craft of the movie even while deploring its debasement of women and its basic indecency. As a polemicist, if you will, I disagreed with the film. But as the man who was watching the movie, I had to admit that it delivered. I wrote: " ... this film panders with such determination to the base instincts of the action crowd that it will, I am sure, be an enormous hit."

The ads for *The Last Boy Scout* have dishonestly distorted that sentence. They quote me in big letters: "An enormous hit!" Well, at least I can live with what I did write.

What about the op-ed guys? Did they watch *JFK*? How did it make them feel? What did they think about the performances, the energy, the skillful mixture of documentary and reconstructed footage? Did they admire Stone's sheer technical ability to keep us interested through 188 minutes of densely woven fact, fiction and speculation? Did they consider what an indigestible mass of disorganized material the movie COULD have been? Did they see it as a movie at all? Or did they have their op-ed blinkers on, and only judge it in terms of their politics?

"A man watches a movie, and the critic must acknowledge that he is that man."

Clip it out. Stick it where you can see it. It's not only about the movies.

© Copyright 1992 The Ebert Company, Ltd. Distributed by Universal Press Syndicate.

JANUARY 27, 1992

AP

CRITIC SEES STARS AFTER EDITOR KILLS REVIEW OF *JFK*

Film critic Pat Dowell never wrote a review her editors wouldn't run. But that was before she gave 3 1/2 stars to *JFK*.

She's now the ex-critic of *Washingtonian* magazine, after resigning when editor Jack Limpert spiked her words of praise for the controversial movie.

"The idea that the president, the Pentagon and the C.I.A. are all acting in concert" to assassinate John Kennedy and cover it up "is bizarre, just crackpot, preposterous," Limpert said Friday.

His view after seeing the film: "the dumbest movie about Washington ever made."

Dowell's unpublished critique called it "a brilliantly crafted indictment of history as an official story."

When Limpert sent her a note saying he'd pulled the review from the February issue of the *Washingtonian*, Dowell made him an offer.

She wouldn't resign in protest, she said, if he ran her review in the March issue. "I didn't really expect him to take me up on it." she said Friday.
He didn't.

WALL STREET JOURNAL

A CONCOCTION OF LIES AND DISTORTIONS

The following is a copy of a letter sent by Joseph A. Califano Jr. to Rep. Louis Stokes (D. Ohio)

Joseph A. Califano Jr.

As an aide to President Lyndon Johnson from 1965 until he left office in January 1969, let me add my voice to those who are urging you and the House to release all files related to your investigation of the assassination of John Kennedy and the Warren Commission report, as well as the executive branch files relating to the investigation of Teamster president James Hoffa and the activities of the Kennedy administration in connection with the assassination attempt against Fidel Castro.

The Oliver Stone movie *JFK* is a disgraceful concoction of lies and distortions designed, among other things, to leave the impression that there was a massive conspiracy among all elements of American society—government, business, the media, to kill President Kennedy, and that one of the conspirators was President Johnson. The movie may make Mr. Stone and Time-Warner lots of money, but it is still a big lie.

The film is particularly offensive with respect to Johnson, who called the Kennedy assassination "the foulest deed of our time" and said when he faced a joint session of Congress shortly thereafter, "All I have I would have given gladly not to be standing here today." In addition to working as Lyndon Johnson's closest domestic aide for three and a half years, I have spent the last four years researching and writing "The Triumph and Tragedy of Lyndon Johnson."

Johnson believed, as he said to me, that Fidel Castro was responsible for Kennedy's assassination. In a reference to attempts by the Kennedy brothers to assassinate Castro, Johnson told me, "Kennedy tried to get Castro, but Castro got Kennedy first." After assuming the presidency, Johnson ordered a stop to all covert activity to eliminate Castro. Moreover, L.B.J. was so convinced that Castro assassinated Kennedy that he asked the FBI to take special precautions to protect him and his family from an attempt by Castro on his own life. Johnson did not agree with the Warren Commission's report that Lee Harvey Oswald acted alone. In late 1966 and early 1967, he discussed with me reopening the investigation, but decided against it because he did not believe it was in the interest of the country and he did not want to inflict any additional pain on the Kennedy family.

Mr. Stokes, you did take the time in a thorough House inquiry to re-examine the Warren Commission findings and conduct your own investigation. In these circumstances—and particularly with this scurrilous film giving millions of young Americans a false revisionist history lesson—I believe that it is imperative that the House open to the public all the files accumulated in the course of your investigation.

JANUARY 30, 1992

THE WASHINGTON POST

FORD URGES HOUSE LEADERS TO SEEK RELEASE OF ALL RECORDS ON KENNEDY ASSASSINATION

George Lardner Jr.

Former President Gerald R. Ford, the only surviving member of the Warren Commission that investigated the 1963 assassination of President John F. Kennedy, has asked House leaders to press for release of all files concerning the assassination.

Ford urged public disclosure of all materials at the C.I.A. as well as the records of the House Select Committee on Assassinations and the relatively few of the Warren Commission papers still under seal.

He made the request in letters sent last week to House Speaker Thomas S. Foley (D-Wash.) and to Rep. Louis Stokes (D-Ohio), who was chairman of the assassinations committee. Stokes has said recently that he favors disclosure of most records still under seal to counter the charges of government involvement in Kennedy's death and a subsequent coverup made in the movie *JFK*.

The only restrictions Ford said he would retain are those laid down by the Kennedy family, limiting access to the autopsy photographs and x-ray materials to qualified medical experts. These limitations, he noted, "could, of course, be removed at the request of the Kennedy family."

Ford emphasized that he still holds firm to the Warren Commission's finding that Lee Harvey Oswald, acting alone, was the one who killed Kennedy. According to public opinion polls, most Americans disagree. Ford said he hoped disclosure of the records would "resolve any legitimate doubts of others."

Ford also urged that the National Research Council appoint "a new panel of outstanding scientists" to review the acoustical evidence that led the House committee in 1979 to conclude that a fourth shot had been fired at Kennedy from the grassy knoll in Dealey Plaza and that he was probably killed as the result of a conspiracy.

In his letter, Ford asserted that "all" of the Warren Commission records having "any primary relevance" to the question of who killed Kennedy and whether there was a conspiracy were made available to the public in 1964.

Less than 5 percent of the commission documents remain under seal. But hundreds of thousands of pages of C.I.A. and FBI records are still being withheld.

JANUARY 31, 1992

THE WASHINGTON POST

EX-WARREN STAFFERS URGE JFK DATA RELEASE

George Lardner Jr.

Thirteen former counsel and staff members of the Warren Commission yesterday urged all government agencies, including the FBI and the C.I.A., to make public all records compiled in investigating the 1963 assassination of President John F. Kennedy.

In a joint statement they said the reasons for secrecy had dissipated after 28 years and officials should be guided by a bias in favor of public disclosure.

Adding to growing pressure for disclosure generated by the movie *JFK*, the 13 also delivered a letter to the Archivist of the United States, Don W. Wilson, asking his help in releasing the remaining 2 percent of Warren Commission evidence that is still under seal.

Wilson could not be reached for comment, but a spokeswoman, Jill D. Brett, said "the 2 percent still closed are covered by restrictions over which the archives has no control." These restrictions include privacy law regulations, national security classifications, protections for confidential informants and other statutory limitations such as those applicable to Lee Harvey Oswald's tax returns.

The 13 former staffers who investigated Kennedy's assassination said they "remain convinced beyond a reasonable doubt" that Oswald alone fired all the shots that killed Kennedy and that "based on the record as a whole," there was no credible evidence of a conspiracy on the part of the C.I.A. or any other government agency or anyone else.

The signers included the former general counsel of the commission, J. Lee Rankin, 11 of the 14 assistant counsels for the panel and a former staff member.

Among them were Sen. Arlen Specter (R-Pa.), Ohio state court judge Burt W. Griffin of Cleveland and David W. Belin, A Des Moines lawyer who unsuccessfully sought release of all the files in 1975 in a Freedom of Information Act request.

Washington lawyer Howard P. Willens, a spokesman for the group, said they want to dispel charges of a governmental coverup following the assassination and are confident that public disclosure would bear them out on that point, even though the debate over what happened in Dallas Nov. 22, 1963, probably will never end.

The recent movie by director Oliver Stone about the assassination contends there was a far-reaching conspiracy and coverup on the part of senior government officials, the military-industrial complex and others. Willens said the controversy over the movie brought the former staffers back together.

He added that bringing about full disclosure will likely take a long time but said he hoped the joint statement would help start the process.

© 1992 The Washington Post. Reprinted by permission.

FEBRUARY 1992

PLAYBOY

THE CONSPIRACY THAT WON'T GO AWAY.

Carl Oglesby

We are in a screening room atop the Westin Hotel in New Orleans. It is July 1991 and Oliver Stone is in town filming *JFK*, his latest assault on establishment sensibilities, a movie with the premise that we do not yet know the truth about the assassination of President John F. Kennedy in Dallas on November 22, 1963.

Stone has already filmed the Dallas scenes. He has brought his company to New Orleans because *JFK* is based on the work of Jim Garrison, a young and aggressive district attorney at the time of the J.F.K. murder. The lights dim and an image flickers to life on the screen. The clapper board reads *JFK*, SCENE 30. We are in a cell in the Dallas County Jail. It is June 1964, seven months after Dealey Plaza.

The prisoner is Jack Ruby, a stocky, nervous middle-aged man whom the whole world watched murder accused J.F.K. assassin Lee Harvey Oswald on live TV two days after Oswald's arrest. Facing Ruby across a table, erect and somber in a black suit, sits Earl Warren, Chief Justice of the Supreme Court and the reluctant chairman of the Report of the President's Commisssion on the Assassination of President John F. Kennedy.

It is a tense moment. Ruby has insisted on testifying even though no one wants him to, least of all Warren himself. "Do you understand that I cannot tell the truth here in Dallas?" Ruby says. "That there are people here who do not want me to tell the truth?"

But Warren says only, "Mr Ruby, I really can't see why you can't tell us now."

Ruby's desperation is palpable. "If I am eliminated," he says, "there won't be any way of knowing." He waits for a reaction, but Warren seems a genius at not getting on Ruby's wave length. He does not ask, "Knowing what?"

Finally, exasperated, Ruby blurts it out: "A whole new form of government is going to take over our country," he says, "and I know I won't live to see you another time. My life is in danger here. Do I sound screwy?"

And Warren's voice resonates in its most mournful basso, the words lingered over, tasted, given all their weight: "Well, I don't know what can be done, Mr. Ruby. Because I don't know what you anticipate we will encounter." Now the camera turns more closely on the heavy, solemn figure of Warren and, for a moment, it almost is Warren, the right age, the right look of stolid pride.

But the figure isn't Warren at all, of course. It's Jim Garrison. Not Kevin Costner, who plays the part of Garrison in the film, but Garrison himself, the real Garrison, all six and a half feet of him. No soul in all creation stands more opposed to Warren on the question of what happened in Dallas than does Garrison, the embattled naysayer of New Orleans, who was one of the first to hold that J.F.K. was felled by conspiracy, that the same conspiracy acted through Ruby to kill Oswald and thus prevent a trial, and that the commission to which Warren gave his name was the front line of the most serious cover-up in American history.

"Warren must have spun madly in his grave," mused Garrison the next afternoon as we talked about this scene. "I can only hope the afterlife has sharpened his taste for irony."

Yet Stone was not just indulging his own taste for irony in casting Garrison in this role. "Between adversaries," Stone told me, "there can sometimes be great respect." Had Stone not seen in Garrison that respect for the adversary, his casting move could easily have backfired. Let Garrison's portrayal of Warren seem the least bit vindictive and the entire movie could come out looking like a cheap shot.

Garrison leaned forward with delight. "I'll swear I never said it," he remarked in his soft New Orleans drawl, "but I think it was a minor stroke of genius for Oliver to offer me this role. The great thing about it is that the screenplay uses Warren's words. And the more I studied them, the more I could see that Warren had developed such empathy with Ruby that he couldn't control himself completely. Although I've never forgiven Warren for what he did, he was a basically warm human being. You could tell he felt sorry for Ruby even as he evaded him. And in that final line, he told him more than he intended to. He confessed his own weakness."

His smile brightened. "And I think I was just the actor to bring this out. If Warren could see it, I think he'd smile."

Garrison's enactment of Warren seems a perfect summation of a career that has been to an uncommon degree shaped by irony, by a relationship with the mass media predicated on equal parts of mutual need and rejection. *JFK* is based on Garrison's 1988 memoir, *On the Trail of the Assassins.* This in itself is satisfying to Garrison, now a retired Louisiana appeals-court judge. He finds it satisfying to see himself portrayed by. an actor as convincing and warm as Kevin Costner in a movie directed with the artistry and drive of Oliver Stone.

But the mere news that Stone was making this movie was enough to reawaken the media furies that have bedeviled Garrison since he first joined the great hunt for the J.F.K. conspiracy in 1966.

As early as last May, when Stone had barely begun production, *Chicago Tribune* columnist Jon Margolis angrily assured his readers that *JFK* was going to be not just a bad movie but an evil one, "morally repugnant" because it sympathetically treated Garrison's "fantasies" that a conspiracy was responsible for the J.F.K. assassination and that federal agents were probably involved. George Lardner of *The Washington Post* entered the fray with two long diatribes in which he grudgingly admitted that "a probable conspiracy took place," while insisting that this was "not an acknowledgement that Garrison's investigation was anything but a fraud." Then came *Time* magazine to dismiss Garrison as somewhere "near the far-out fringe of conspiracy theorists."

A man less confident of his vision may have been shaken, but Garrison long since has become inured. "Being attacked with such vehemence from so many sides and for such a variety of reasons, I admit, is not conclusive proof that one is right," he says with a smile and a shrug. "But surely it goes a long way."

The controversy that rages around Garrison is set against the fact that he started out so all-American. He was born in 1921 in Denison, Iowa, to a family of tall lawyers that soon moved to New Orleans. At the age of 19, in 1940, he joined the U.S. Army and, in 1942, was commissioned as a lieutenant in the field artillery. He volunteered for flight training and spent the war on the European front flying light airplanes on low-level and often-dangerous spotter missions. He saw combat in France and Germany and was present at the liberation of Dachau.

He came back to New Orleans, earned his law degree at Tulane and joined the FBI, which sent him to Seattle to check out the loyalty of defense employees, a job he soon found "greatly boring." He left the FBI and returned to New Orleans to go into pivate practice as a trial lawyer. Then he went to work in the district attorney's office. He ran for a judgeship in 1960 and lost, but then, in 1961, quarreled publicly with Mayor Victor Schiro—whom he accused of "laxity in law enforcement"—and District Attorney Richard Dowling, whom he called "the great emancipator" because he "lets everyone go free."

This was the first burst of controversy in his carrer and it immediately propelled him to a higher orbit. He campaigned for D.A. in 1961, without the backing of the Democratic Party and without a big war chest. But he had the strong support of both blacks and blue-collar whites, a unique coalition in the South of the early Sixties. "To my surprise and to the astonishment of many others," he says, "I was elected."

He moved immediately to make good on his election promises. "If this entailed raising the level of confrontation," he recalls, "my attitude was, well, let the good times roll." He clamped down on organized gambling and prostitution, made Bourbon Street safe for tourists, challenged police corruption and criticized eight criminal-court judges for refusing to approve funds for his fight against racketeering. The judges sued him for defamation of character and won a judgment of $1000; but he appealed, arguing that elected judges were not exempt form public criticism. He won a reversal.

Jim Garrison was on the map.

So was Fidel Castro.

Castro overthrew Cuban dictator General Fulgencio Batista and took power in 1959. He announced a communist program. Cubans opposed to his government began flocking to Miami and New Orleans. Many of them formed counterrevolutionary organizations with such names as Alpha-66, the Cuban Revolutionary Council, Free Cuba, the Cuban Expeditionary Force and the Cuban Brigade. All were sponsored by the C.I.A..

Their aim was to reverse Castro's revolution. This was the objective of their major military assault, Operation Zapata, organized by the C.I.A. and the U.S. military. The world came to know Operation Zapata better as the Bay of Pigs fiasco of April 1961. This attempted invasion failed to inspire the mass uprising that was its major strategic premise. The Zapata guerillas were pinned down on their beachheads without a chance to declare a provisional government. Instead of sending in U.S. military support, J.F.K. opted to cut his losses, standing by as the invasion force was captured and paying a humiliating ransom to rescue the prisoners. An angry self-pity soon gripped the anti-Castro militants and their U.S. supporters. They blamed Operation Zapata's failure on Kennedy. He had put them on the beach, then fled.

Then J.F.K. betrayed them again, as they saw it, in October of 1962, when a spy plane revealed Soviet missile bases under construction in Cuba. In the year and a half since the Bay of Pigs, the C.I.A. had helped the exiles stage a series of commando raids against a variety of Cuban targets. But in the secret deal that ended the Cuban Missile Crisis with the dismantling of the Soviet bases, J.F.K. promised that this activity would end.

This arrangement deeply affected an ultra-right-wing acquaintance of Garrison's named W. Guy Banister, a key player in the anti-Castro games of New Orleans. Banister served in the office of Naval Intelligence during World War Two and after the war joined the FBI, rising to head its Chicago bureau. He left the FBI to become deputy chief of police in New Orleans, then resigned in 1957 to set up a private detective agency.

In 1962, at the time of the Cuban Missile Crisis, Banister was involved in running a C.I.A. training camp for anti-Castro Cuban guerrillas on Lake Pontchartrain, north of New Orleans. Garrison had no idea at the time that Banister was involved in this activity. But he did know that Banister was not just another gumshoe for hire.

Guy Banister Associates, Inc., hung out its shingle, according to Garrison, "across the street from the building that housed the local offices of the C.I.A. and the FBI. And across from that building was the New Orleans quarters of Operation Mongoose." Operation Mongoose was an array of anti-Castro projects being run by the C.I.A., the Defense Department and the State Department under the coordination of Air Force Major General Edward G. Lansdale. Its C.I.A. component called Task Force W was dedicated to the assassination of Castro. Its deepest secret was the fact that the C.I.A. had contracted out his murder to the Mafia. Its headquarters was the meeting place for Cuban exiles coming in from Florida. "They were sleeping in the hallways," says Garrison.

Banister's key associate in these anti-Castro operations was a peculiar man named David Ferrie. Ferrie was an ace pilot, a kitchen-sink scientist, an omnivorous reader in the occult, a well-known denizen of the New Orleans gay scene, a militant activist against Castro and a great hater of J.F.K. His on-the-job homosexual activities had cost him his pilot's job at Eastern Airlines, but he had flown several clandestine flights to Castro's Cuba and was part of the training staff at the Lake Pontchartrain guerrilla camp. A rare chronic disease (*alopecia praecox*) having taken all his hair, he wore a wig made out of mohair and drew on his eyebrows with a grease pencil. He worked out of Banister's office, but he also served as a free-lance investigator for G. Wray Gill, a lawyer who represented Carlos Marcello, the Mafia godfather of New Orleans. Ferrie reputedly flew Marcello back into the United States after his deportation by Robert Kennedy in 1961. On the day of J.F.K's murder, Ferrie was with Marcello in a New Orleans court as Marcello won a verdict against R.F.K's effort to deport him again.

But far stranger still among Banister's associates in the summer of 1963 was a young ex-Marine named Lee Harvey Oswald.

At first look, Oswald seems to be a creature of contradictions. On closer examination, the contradictions become complexities.

There was, on the one hand, the patriotic Oswald, a true-blue if emotionally mixed-up American kid raised in and around New Orleans, New York City and Fort Worth by his widowed (and twice-divorced) mother with help of aunt Lillian and uncle "Dutz" Murret, a bookie in the Marcello gambling net. As a teenager in New Orleans, Oswald joined the local Civil Air Patrol and there met David Ferrie, its commander, in 1955. He tried to join the Marines but was rejected for being underage. He went home and memorized the Marine Corps manual, and came back to try again as soon as he reached 17 in October 1956, this time succeeding.

Oswald served his three years ably, rated "very competent" and "brighter than most" by his officers. The Marines cleared him for access to the performance characteristics of the top-secret U-2. They put him in a program of Russian-language training and instruction in the basics of Marxism-Leninism, as though he were being prepared for intelligence work. Indeed, a Navy intelligence operative named Gerry Hemming had thought as far back as 1959 that Oswald was "some type of agent." The House Select Committee on Assassinations noted that "the question of Oswald's possible affiliation with military intelligence could not be fully resolved."

On the other hand, there was Oswald the traitor. With only three months to go in the Marines, rather than await the normal discharge process, he applied for a hardship discharge for no good reason (citing a minor and already-healed injury to his mother's foot), then hurried to the Soviet Union. After two and a half years of Soviet communism, Oswald recanted. Now with a Russian wife and a daughter in tow, he returned to the United States, explaining in a written statement that "the Soviets committed crimes unsurpassed even by their early-day capitalist counterparts."

So was he a good patriot again? No, now he announced himself to be a member of the Communist Party and became the founding and sole member of the New Orleans chapter of the Fair Play for Cuba Committee, three times passing out pro-Castro leaflets in New Orleans.

Yet, paradoxically, Oswald's frequent companion that summer in New Orleans was the militant anticommunist David Ferrie, with whom he had joined in loud public condemnation of Castro and J.F.K. During this same period, Oswald also spent time with Banister. He stamped Banister's office address on his pro-Castro leaflets and stored his extra copies there. He and Banister twice visited the campus of Louisiana State University and made themselves conspicuous in discussions with students in which their main theme was that J.F.K. was a traitor. Not once during this time Oswald associate with anyone actually sympathetic to Castro.

Oswald left New Orleans on September 25, 1963, and on the next day in Mexico City, according to the Warren reconstruction, registered as O.H. Lee at the Hotel del Comercio, a meeting place for anti-Castro Cuban exiles. He spent the next several days trying to get visas for travel to Cuba and the Soviet Union. In the process, he got into a prolonged row with Cuban consular official.

The C.I.A. had the Soviet and Cuban embassies staked out. It was later able to produce several photos of Oswald taken at these sites—as well as to supply tapes of several phone conversations between a Soviet embassy official and a man calling himself Oswald. There was a problem with the photos: They showed a large, powerfully built man in his mid-30s not in the least resembling Oswald. And there was a problem with the tapes: The C.I.A. destroyed them, and the transcriptions contained garbled Russian, whereas Oswald was considered to be fluent in Russian. Even the row with the Cuban official presented a problem: Interviewed by the Select Committee on Assassinations in 1978, the official said his Oswald was not the same one as the man arrested in Dallas. Moreover, two C.I.A. spies working inside the Cuban consulate in 1963 agreed that "the real Oswald never came inside." They told the House Committee that they sensed "something weird was going on" in the Oswald incident.

There is also abundant evidence that Oswald was often impersonated quite apart from the alleged Mexico City trip.

ITEM: An FBI memo dated January 3, 1960 noted that "there is a possibility that an impostor is using Oswald's birth certificate." The real Oswald was in the Soviet Union at this time.

ITEM: Two salesmen at the Bolton Ford dealership in New Orleans were visited on January 20, 1961, by a Lee Oswald in the company of a powerfully built Latino. Oswald was looking for a deal on ten pickup trucks needed by the Friends of Democratic Cuba. On this date, Oswald was in the Soviet Union.

ITEM: On September 25, 1963, a man calling himself Harvey Oswald showed up at the Selective Service office in Austin to request help in getting his discharge upgraded from undesirable. On this date, Oswald was supposedly in transit to Mexico City.

ITEM: A highly credible Cuban *émigrée*, Sylvia Odio, told the Warren Commission that she was visited in Dallas by Oswald and two other men recruiting support for the anti-Castro cause. On the date of this encounter, the Warren Commission placed Oswald either in New Orleans or en route to Mexico.

ITEM: On November 1, 1963, a man later identified by three witnesses as Oswald entered a gun shop in Fort Worth and made a nuisance of himself while buying ammunition. The Warren Commission had evidence that Oswald was at work in Dallas that day.

ITEM: On November 9, 1963, when Warren Commission evidence placed Oswald at home in Irving, Texas, a man calling himself Lee Oswald walked into a Lincoln-Mercury showroom in Dallas and asked to take a car for a test drive. The salesman found the ride unforgettable in that Oswald reached speeds of 70 miles an hour while delivering a harangue about capitalist credit and the superiority of the Soviet system. Oswald, in fact, did not know how to drive a car.

Curiouser and curiouser, this Oswald who was all over the map and all over the political spectrum, in New Orleans and Fort Worth and Austin and Mexico City all at once, here a radical and there a reactionary. What to make of this man?

"This question became a very practical one for me," says Garrison, "on the day the President was killed and Oswald's picture was flashed around the world. As his résumé filled in over the next day and we found that he'd spent that summer in New Orleans, it became my duty as D.A. to see what we could find out about him."

Garrison soon discovered Oswald's ties to Ferrie. He brought Ferrie in for questioning on Monday the 25th, the day after Ruby murdered Oswald, then turned Ferrie over to the FBI for further questioning. "In those days," Garrison recalls, "I still believed in the FBI. They questioned Ferrie, found him clean and released him with a strange statement to the effect that they wouldn't have arrested him in the first place, that it was all my idea. Then they put a SECRET stamp on their forty-page interrogation report. But what did I know? I had burglaries and armed robberies to worry about. I went back to the real world. I was happy to do so."

Garrison's happy life in the real world came to an end for good about three years later. He at first saw no problem when the Warren Report was published in September 1964, holding that Oswald was a lone nut and Ruby another one. "Warren was a great judge and, one thought, wholly honest." Here and there a few spoilsports—Mark Lane, Edward J. Epstein, Harold Weisberg, Penn Jones, Sylvia Meagher, Josiah Thompson—were discovering problems with Warren's double lone-nut thesis, but Garrison was inclined as most Americans were to go along with it. "It seemed the easiest position to take," he says "especially since the war in Vietnam was getting nasty and Americans of critical spirit were now caught up more in the mysteries of Saigon than in those of Dealey Plaza."

Then in 1966 came a fateful chance meeting with Louisiana's Senator Russell Long. The conversation turned to the Kennedy case. Long astounded Garrison by saying, "Those fellows on the Warren Commission were dead wrong. There's no way in the world that one man could have shot up Jack Kennedy that way."

Garrison immediately ordered the Warren Report plus the 26 volumes of its hearings and exhibits. He plunged in, dedicating his evenings and weekends to the case.

He expected to find "a professional investigation," he says, but "found nothing of the sort ... There were promising leads everywhere that were never followed up, contradictions in the lone-assassin theory that were never resolved."

In particular, he was troubled by evidence that:

◆ Shots were fired from the so-called grassy knoll to the front and right of J.F.K. as well as from behind.

◆ The maximum number of shots the alleged murder weapon could have fired was inadequate to account for the total number of bullet holes found in Kennedy and Texas Governor John Connally (who barely survived) unless one of the bullets had magically changed its direction in mid-flight.

◆ Nitrate tests performed on Oswald when he was arrested supported his claim that he had not fired a rifle in the previous 24 hours.

◆ Oswald appeared to have been trained as an intelligence agent in the Marines, which implied that his awkward display of sympathy for communism was phony.

Any one of these possibilities, Garrison realized, was enough to reduce the Oswald-acting-alone theory to ruins. "I was stunned," he says. "There were nights I couldn't sleep."

Finally, in November 1966, as he puts it, "I bit the magic bullet." Basing his jurisdiction on Oswald's 1963 summer in New Orleans, he secretly opened an investigation into the President's murder.

Of the four New Orleanians of primary interest to Garrison, the most interesting of all was Oswald himself, since Oswald had in a sense become Garrison's client. But he was dead. Next most interesting was Guy Banister, clearly at the center of New Orlean's anti-Castro scene. But Banister had died, too, of a heart attack in 1964.

Third came David Ferrie, quite alive in 1966. Garrison's investigators started compiling a portrait of Ferrie as a talented and impassioned anticommunist, a far-right soldier of fortune whose relationship with the reputedly procommunist Oswald during the summer of 1963 posed a question crucial to the clarification of Oswald's purposes—namely, as Garrison puts it, "What the hell were these guys doing together?"

By reconstructing the 1963 relationships of Oswald with Ferrie and Banister, Garrison hoped finally to make sense of the bundle of contradictions that was Oswald. But he never got a chance to do a proper job of it.

A bright young reporter for the *New Orleans States-Item*, Rosemary James, was routinely nosing through the D.A.'s budget in February 1967 when she noticed some unusual expenses. Garrison's men had spent some $8000 during the pervious three months on such things as trips to Texas and Florida. What could they be up to? A few questions later and she had the story.

D.A. HERE LAUNCHES FULL J.F.K. DEATH PLOT PROBE read the headline on the February 17 *States-Item*. MYSTERIOUS TRIPS COST LARGE SUMS. James's lead ran, "The Orleans parish district attorney's office has launched an intensive investigation into the circumstances surrounding the assassination of President John F. Kennedy."

In the ensuing pandemonium, Garrison found himself under enormous pressure from city hall and the media. He felt he had begun to build a strong conspiracy case against Ferrie in that Ferrie clearly hated J.F.K. and clearly had a tie to Oswald, but that it was still not time to arrest him. His staff was meeting to debate the timing of Ferrie's arrest when word came that Ferrie had been found dead in his apartment, killed by a brain aneurysm. The coroner ruled the cause of death as natural, but Garrison saw indications of suicide: an empty bottle of Proloid—a medicine that could have pushed the hypertense Ferrie's metabolism over the red line—plus two typewritten and unsigned suicide notes.

Within hours came a report that Ferrie's militant anticommunist comrade, Eladio del Valle, had been found in a car in Miami, shot point-blank through the heart and with his head hatcheted open.

Now what? The stage was filled with enough dead bodies for an Elizabethan tragedy, and two of Garrison's key suspects were among them. Just one other was left.

Clay Shaw, born in 1913, was one of New Orlean's best known and most impressive citizens, a charming, richly cultivated and cosmopolitan businessman, a much-decorated Army officer during World War Two detailed to the Office of Special Services and a founder and director of the International Trade Mart, a company specializing in commercial expositions. Shaw retired in 1965 to pursue interests in the arts, playwrighting and the restoration of the French Quarter, where he lived. He was a silver-haired, handsome *bon vivant* with high cheekbones, a ruddy complexion and an imposing six-foot-four frame.

Garrison had come to believe that he was part of the J.F.K. conspiracy. Research had turned up indications that Shaw was the mysterious Clay Bertrand who had phoned New Orleans attorney Dean Andrews on the day after the J.F.K. hit to see if Andrews could arrange legal representation for Oswald. Garrison had found that Shaw led a double life in the New Orleans gay community and that Shaw was a friend of Ferrie's, who had been his pilot on at least one round trip to Montreal. Garrison had a witness, Perry Russo, who claimed to have been present when Ferrie, Shaw, and a man Russo thought was Oswald discussed assassinating J.F.K.

More important, one of the D.A.'s assistants, Andrew Sciambra, had discovered an Oswald-Shaw link in Clinton, a rural Louisiana town. Dozens of people had seen Oswald in Clinton on two occasions in early September 1963, once as a passenger in a battered old car driven by a young woman and later in a shiny black Cadillac with two other men who waited for hours while Oswald, the only white in a long line of blacks, tried unsuccessfully to register to vote. Five Clinton witnesses testified that the men with Oswald were David Ferrie and Clay Shaw. The local marshal, curious about strange Cadillacs in town, traced the license plate to the International Trade Mart. He talked to the driver and later, at the trial, identified him as Shaw.

Garrison knew that such fragments didn't add up to an airtight conspiracy case. When I asked him if he was surprised to lose, he said, "Not really. I'm too good a trial lawyer. So why did I go to trial against Clay Shaw? Because I knew that somehow I had stumbled across the big toe of someone who was involved in one of the biggest crimes in history. And I was not about to become the person who did that and then let go and said, 'Oh, I might be violating a regulation.'"

Looking back, does he think this was an error?

"If it was an error, then it was an error that I was obliged to make."

But Garrison did not leap blindly into the prosecution of one of New Orlean's leading citizens. He first presented his evidence to a panel of three judges. They told him he had a case. Then he presented the evidence to a 12-member grand jury. The grand jury also ruled that there was sufficient evidence to try Shaw. And at that point, the decision was out of Garrison's hands: The law required him to proceed. Shaw's lawyers went all the way to the Supreme court with an argument that the case should be thrown out, and they lost. After Shaw was acquitted, he filed a $5,000,000 damages suit against Garrison for wrongful prosecution; the Supreme Court dismissed it.

But Garrison's case ran into many strange problems. One of his assistants provided the list of state's witnesses to Shaw's attorney's. An FBI agent with detailed knowledge of anti-Castro projects in New Orleans refused to testify for the prosecution, pleading executive privilege. The U.S. Attorney in Washingon, D.C., "declined" to serve Garrison's subpoena on Allen Dulles, C.I.A. chief at the time of the Bay of Pigs, who was in a position to clarify the relationship between Ferrie, Banister, Shaw and the C.I.A.. The governors of Ohio, Nebraska, and other states refused on technical grounds to honor Garrison's requests for the extradition of important witnesses. A federal agent told Garrison privately—but refused to testify—that Ferrie, Shaw, and Banister were involved in handling

Oswald. A witness critical to establishing that Shaw used the alias Clay Bertrand, a key issue, was not allowed to present his evidence.

Some of these difficulties may have arisen because, as later became known, both Shaw and Ferrie were contract agents of the C.I.A.. This was revealed in 1974 when a former aide to C.I.A. director Richard Helms, Victor Marchetti, noted he had heard Helms wonder aloud if the C.I.A. were giving Shaw and Ferrie "all the help they need."

Without this knowledge, the jury got the case on March 1, 1969, two years to the day after Shaw's arrest. It took a little less than an hour to conclude unanimously that Shaw was not guilty of conspiring to kill Kennedy. In posttrial interviews, some jurors said Garrison convinced them that a conspiracy existed but not that Shaw had been a part of it. The Garrison who two years previously had promised, "We are going to win this case, and everyone who bets against us is going to lose his money," could now sit down for a long, slow chew.

The loss didn't hurt him at the polls. He recorded his most lopsided victory ever in the election of 1969.

But the story wasn't over.

Garrison had just risen from his breakfast and was still in his pajamas and robe when the doorbell rang. It was a posse of IRS men, there to arrest him on a charge of allowing pinball gambling in exchange for a bribe.

This was June 30, 1971. About two years later, in August 1973, the trial was held, Garrison arguing his own case (with the donated help of F. Lee Bailey). His defense revolved around one powerful basic point, namely, that the government's star witness against him, his former wartime buddy and colleague, Pershing Gervais, had been bribed by the government to make the accusation.

Garrison was acquitted of the bribery charge as well as of a follow-up charge of tax evasion the government pressed against him in 1974. "A thing like that," he says, "can be enjoyable if you have a cause and you're wrapped up in it. I'd say it was one of the high spots of my life. It was nothing to feel sorry about. I never went to bed with tears on my pillow."

But another kind of attack on Garrison began about this time, most often in the work of other conspiracy theorists who began to wonder why Garrison said nothing about Mafia involvement in the J.F.K. hit. There were Mobsters all around Jack Ruby. The New Orleans godfather, Carlos Marcello, was right in Garrison's back yard. A Marcello lawyer worked with Ferrie. Ferrie was with Marcello the day J.F.K. was shot. Yet Garrison seemed to ignore all this.

The charge is raised by writers (notably G. Robert Blakey and John H. Davis) who champion a Mafia-did-it theory of the crime and who themselves spend little ink on the evidence pointing to renegade federal agents. But Garrison's position on Mafia involvement was reflected in the 1979 report of the Select Committee on Assassinations (Blakey was its chief counsel), which stated that "the national syndicate of organized crime, as a group, was not involved in the assassinations." As for the presence of individual Mobsters, Garrison was among the first to see it.

An FBI memo of March 28, 1967 reported that "Garrison plans to indict Carlos Marcello in the Kennedy assassination conspiracy because Garrison believes Marcello is tied up in some way with Jack Ruby." According to another FBI memo, June 10, 1967, "District Attorney Garrison believes that organized crime was responsible for the assassination," the memo going on to explain Garrison's fear that the Mafia wanted to blame the crime on Castro and thus spark a U.S. retaliation that would lead to restoration of the Mafia's control of Cuban casinos.

More recently, Garrison has written that "Mob-related individuals do figure in the scenario." After all, the C.I.A. and the Mafia shared an interest in Castro's overthrow, as is evident in their murderous alliance of Task Force W.

But Garrison does not believe that the Mafia could have set up Oswald, controlled the investigation of the crime and influenced the conclusions reached by the Warren Commission. "The C.I.A. hired the Mafia," he points out, "not the other way around. If Carlos Marcello had killed J.F.K. on his own, he would never have gotten away with it."

The merits of the C.I.A.-*vs.*-Mafia debate aside, however, this was not a great time for Garrison. He lost a close race in the next election, and in 1974 left the D.A.'s office after 12 years of service. He spent the next few years in what he call his interregnum, a period of relative quiet in which he wrote his one novel, *The Star-Spangled Contract*, a fictional treatment of the J.F.K. hit. That period ended in his successful campaign for a seat on the Louisiana court of appeals in 1977. He was inaugurated to a ten-year term in 1978 and reelected in 1987. He reached mandatory retirement age of 70 in November 1991.

During the Seventies, the J.F.K. case suddenly shot forward. Watergate and the resignation of President Nixon had already put the country in a mood to listen to conspiracy theories when Mafia boss Sam Giancana was shot down in his home on June 19, 1975, five days before he was to testify to Senate committee. On July 28, 1976, mafioso John Roselli was asphyxiated, dismembered and dumped into Miami's Dumfoundling Bay. Giancana and Roselli had both been deeply involved in the C.I.A.-Mafia plots. The atmosphere created by these events persuaded the House of Representatives by a vote of 280-65 to enact H.Res.1540, which established the Select Committee on Assassinations.

That was September 17, 1976. Two and a half years and $6,500,000 later, this committee reported its findings: that conspiracy was "probable" in the death of J.F.K. and a "likelihood" in the 1968 death of Martin Luther King, Jr. In the neither case could the House committee offer a solution.

But then came the Reagan years. The new Justice Department found the conspiracy evidence unconvincing and decided not to bother about it. And there the case has stood for the past decade—"stuck" as Garrison says, "not for want of something to do but for want of a government with the will to do it."

But Garrison is not resigned.

"Who killed President Kennedy?" he demands, just as though he still expected an answer. "That question is not going to disappear, no matter what the government does or does not do. It may fade into the background sometimes, but something will always evoke it again, as Oliver's movie is about to do now. It's basic to who we are as a people. We can no more escape it than Hamlet can escape his father's ghost."

But what can Hamlet do three decades later?

"There's a lot to do," says Garrison, "and since well over half the American people still gag on the lone-nut theory, there would appear to be a supportive constituency."

Garrison's program:

"First, open the files that the Warren Commission and the House committee classified as secret until the year 2039.

"Second, declassify the House committee's so-called Lopez Report, a 265-page document on Oswald's supposed trip to Mexico. Lopez himself has said he believes Oswald was set up. Why is this report still secret?

"Third, declassify all the files on Operation Mongoose and the C.I.A.-Mafia murder plots. The Mongoose group seems to be at the center of the J.F.K. conspiracy. We need to know every detail about it.

"And, no, these steps will not crack the case, but they will help us understand it better, and we can move on from there."

Someone else who had put so much into such a cause and who had so often been abused for his pains might feel defeated to have to settle for such small demands as these, and to realize that, small as they are, they are almost certainly not going to be met.

But Garrison doesn't see it that way. "The fight itself has been a most worthy one," he says quietly. "Most people go through their lives without the opportunity to serve an important cause. It's true that I've made some mistakes and had some setbacks. But who knows? To manhandle a line from *The Rubáiyát*: The moving finger has not stopped moving on yet. The full story's not in."

His smile becomes a beam. A light dances in his eyes.

"Clarence Darrow lost the Scopes trial," he says. "But who remembers that today?"

VANITY FAIR

FOOTFALLS IN THE CRYPT

Oliver Stone's new movie, J.F.K, has something to alienate everyone, from Establishment theorists to the gamut of conspiracy buffs. But as Norman Mailer writes, by daring to plumb the depths of America's nightmare obsession on the big screen, the controversial director has posed some very unsettling questions.

Norman Mailer

What is one to make of *JFK*? It is not routine to take it on, for Oliver Stone presents a nice problem in critical assessment. These years, when the best film directors have preferred to ignore the largest themes, Stone has gone bucking ahead with all the full-backed intensity of a heavyweight willing to endanger his body against any opponent.

Platoon, his first major success, is an example. It's story barely holds together, yet there is no need for the film to do more. Stone, better than anyone before, is showing us what it is like to endure the physical misery of a patrol on a jungle trail. The minute-by-minute experience of slime, bugs, exhaustion, and occasional combat is conveyed; by the unspoken logic of film, that is enough. Good films need be no better than good or interesting one-night stands. They do not have to change lives, provided they show us something we had not known before. *Platoon* did that. It offered a sense-filled correlative for what veterans of the South Pacific and Vietnam had been trying to explain for a long time. Since it also had the advantage of a fine job by Tom Berenger and a performance by Charlie Sheen that grew as it went along, *Platoon* worked.

So did *Wall Street*, if at a lower level. Michael Douglas, Daryl Hannah, Charlie Sheen, and Martin Sheen did responsible work, but the story drawn from the history of a couple of financial worthies who made newspaper headlines for their white-collar crimes, was a contrivance, the cinematography was conventional, and the moral was homiletic. It seemed apparent that Stone, whatever his willingness, was not a man with a vocation for irony.

Born on the Fourth of July, however, came near to being a great movie. It gave us a view of the torture rack that bound those Americans who went over to Vietnam with a set of conventional beliefs, only to return with no conviction more fiercely held than that morality was equal to surrealism. In one of the best scenes ever filmed in any American movie, Willem Dafoe and Tom Cruise, marooned in their wheelchairs on a clay-dirt road in clay-red Mexican mountains, commence to argue over who has actually shot a baby in Vietnam and who is merely pretending to have it on his conscience. Before the verbal duel is over, each is spitting in the other's face. The wheelchairs tangle, fall over, and the two paraplegics wrestle on the ground, enraged that the other will not believe that, yes, I am guilty of a greater horror than you. Tumbling down together into a gully, they lie half-conscious in the dust, helpless to move, and never are we more aware of their broken spines. That scene captures as much of the war in Vietnam as did Coppola's Valkyrie ride of helicopters in *Apocalypse Now*. Yes, *Born on the Fourth of July* was close to being a great movie, but the logic of its inner development was tenuous, and so, despite Cruise's exceptional performance as Ron Kovic, we were only partially convinced that he ends as a radical. Yet what a large and ambitious attempt had Stone undertaken. The size of the gamble underwrote the cruder means. Lack of fear can take an artist into places his skill does not permit.

By the time Stone made *The Doors*, he must, given his box-office successes, have been choked with hubris. *The Doors* has to be one of the truly bad movies of all time, albeit with a prodigious distinction, for it is also virtuoso. It has not one mass scene, but three dozen. Since the demands on a film crew shooting a single mass scene are uncountable, the toll on assistant directors must have been catastrophic. *The Doors*, almost two and a half hours long, probably has two hours of scenes with fifty to five hundred extras. It provides us with the experience of a rock world, but at the harsh cost of living in it. Half-glimpsed wonders of a half-muttered and half-uttered Dionysian life just about convert us to the Apollonian.

It is possible, given Stone's enormous ambition to take on none but the largest American themes, that he had decided this once (since rock's apocalyptic promise to break through into a brave new consciousness was now two decades dead) that he would shift his interest from wild frontiers onto unparalleled technical difficulties; he certainly brought that much off. At a time when other directors, for lack of heart or certainty of theme, have all been heading toward technical splendor, *The Doors* goes even further into kaleidoscopic cinematography. All of Stone's faults, however, were compounded—his lack of grasp for what a good script can be, his heavy-handed hold on mystical states, and his disjunctive narrative sense of how protagonists can grow, or be destroyed. It may be that the virtue of *The Doors* is that it cleared the decks for something larger.

We come, then, to *JFK*. It is the boldest work yet of a bold and clumsy man, but the first thing to be said about it is that it is a great movie, and the next is that it is one of the worst great movies ever made. It is great in spite of itself, and such greatness owes more to the moxie of the director than to his special talents. Nonetheless, it is an incomparable experience which moves into parts of our heart that we have anesthetized for years.

So one's first judgment is that it cannot be discussed as just a film; it is not of the first interest to talk about where *JFK* works cinematically and where it does not. One does better to treat it as a psychic phenomenon, a creature in the dream life of the nation, and this is legitimate; film, at its most compelling, lives in our mind somewhere between our memories and our dreams. One of the most advanced art forms of the twentieth century is, therefore, one of the most primitive as well, or, at least, such a claim can be invoked when we are dealing with the sinister edge of serious film on a large screen in a dark theater. In that sense, Stone's instinct proved superb.

Subjects as heroic in scope as J.F.K. can be uniquely suited to film as is a good kill to a tribe of hunters, and if the prize was obtained at considerable peril to the chief hunter, then it barely matters how the meat is cooked. Need, and the nature of the exploit, flavors the repast.

JFK is bound to receive some atrocious reviews, perhaps even a preponderance of unfavorable ones, and, as has been the case already, more than a small outrage is likely to be aroused in the Washington Club (that is, *The Washington Post*, *Newsweek*, *Time*, the F.B.I., the C.I.A., the Pentagon, the White House, and the TV networks on those occasions when they wish to exercise their guest privileges).The Establishment has found that Oswald-as-the-lone-assassin serves a multitude of useful purposes, in much the way that a public figure who wraps himself in propriety, no matter how greasy his private life may be, has a dependable political seat. Studying such prizes on television, we know they lie—the gross and subtle folds of corruption on the average senatorial face are hardly the lineaments of virtue—but we can also recall that nobody who played at being a puritan during the Thomas-Hill hearings had to move off his dime. Rectitude planted all the flags.

Ditto for the lone assassin. The F.B.I. was the first to endorse the idea, and this but two weeks after the death of J.F.K. In 1964 the Warren Commission came down four-square behind that finding. Over the years, however, the Warren Commission lost its credibility. The polls give the figure: a majority of Americans now believe there was more than one killer. That, however, is naught but belief. It is the actions of men that make history, and the majority of action in this case has been taken over by The Washington Club—they have circled their wagons around the lone assassin.

It does not matter that in 1978 the House Select Committee on Assassinations decided, on the basis of the acoustic evidence, that there had been a fourth shot. Since it was agreed that no rifleman, no matter how skilled, could get off four aimed rounds from a Mannlicher-Carcano bolt-action rifle in 5.6 seconds, that meant there had to be a second assassin. While this opened a fell crack in the granite wall of lone-assassin solidarity, the committee's thirty month mandate expired even as it was making the discovery, and its work was not extended. Instead, the Department of Justice was handed its files, with a full invitation to look into the new findings. The Department of Justice and the F.B.I. are still looking—that is about equal to saying that the files pertaining to the case have presumably not been destroyed. Of course, about as much may now be left of such documents as still adheres to an automobile after it has been abandoned on a slum street in the South Bronx. And the House committee's own back up records and unpublished transcripts have been sealed as "congressional material." They won't be made public until the year 2029. We may be witting to the all-but-absolute certainty of a fourth shot by a second assassin, but we are still living in the land of upper maintenance men; they look to keep their establishment intact. So in 1988 the Department of Justice announced that the House committee had misinterpreted the acoustic evidence. How not? The price is too prodigious if there was more than one demented gunman. Two assassins not only have to be able to function in concert, but, by their effectiveness itself, suggest a support system, which is to say a larger conspiracy.

At this point, many an old horror arises. Did Castro have a hand in it? the American left must try not to ask itself again. No, of course not, he had too sure a sense of the consequences is the reflexive reply, but then, who can be certain that individual members of the D.G.I., Castro's intelligence service, had not been engaged in some mutually deceptive game with Cuban exiles in Florida and Texas? Even worse for the national polity is that our political center must ask itself, Could Lyndon Johnson, who, we now seem to be learning, was capable of just about any deed, have ordered it? Certainly not, replies the center, and just as reflexively. Yet how could Lyndon Johnson, even if wholly innocent, have ever been certain that some of that bold Texas money, nudging him through the years, had not decided to take a flier on its native son? Nor could Richard Nixon be certain of immaculate innocence. He had been in contact with Cuban exiles for many years, and some of them had not been without murderous ideas. Could the C.I.A. know its own stables were clean after their hit-man dealings with the Mafia? Rogue elephants were capable of fancy steps that put ballet dancers to shame. And then, for that matter, who was Oswald? By now, there is more evidence to suggest that he was sent to Russia as a ploy of U.S. intelligence than that he went over on his own. Could the Pentagon afford to look closely into its most special contingents? Could the F.B.I. live with a second rifle after all these years of being signally unable to improve on the absurd tale of one gun? Could those headmasters of the Washington Club's conscience, *The Washington Post* and its often concordant satellites, *Time* and *Newsweek*, live with an unresolved conspiracy after being for decades loyal apostles of the lone assassin? No, it was to the interest of left, center, and right to remain unaffected by the House select committee's findings. Even if, in light of the new evidence, a second assassin could not be denied, it had to be realized when you got down to it, that a lone assassin was what we had been living with all along. Headmasters do not traffic with the novel and the unforeseen.

When Oliver Stone charged, therefore, in full panoply with all his filmmaking teams and equipment into the valley of assassination enlightenment, there were heavy guns emplaced on the right, and on his left were all the inflamed ragtag assassination buffs. They had been working in relative solitude for decades, laboring on in the private, inspired, and isolated hope that one day they would uncover the mystery and be renowned forever.

It was a fantasy. The best and most skilled of the assassination buffs knew as much by now. To the degree that the murder of J.F.K. was a conspiracy, so could one assume that the most salient evidence and the most inconvenient witnesses had been removed long ago. Yet a buff could only persevere. It had become one's life. It had become, so far as the universal need for personal power is concerned, a way of life. If one could not solve the assassination, one could at least mow down the theories of other researchers who tried to squat in proximity to the barren acres of one's own land grab.

So, the parvenu, Oliver Stone, endowed with all the wealth, muscle, and arrogance of a $35-to-$40-million budget, and no great willingness to become enmeshed with the majority of assassination buffs, naturally encountered trouble on both flanks. The buffs might not have been a well-organized army like the Washington Club—no, by comparison, they were Bushmen with blowguns—but some of them were ready to collaborate with the big guns on the right.

The attacks began before movie shooting even commenced. George Lardner Jr., the resident writer on intelligence matters for *The Washington Post* (which is to say the friend and confidant of many an F.B.I. and C.I.A. man), obtained a stolen copy of the *JFK* script, and did a long piece about Stone for the Club on May 19, 1991:

> His hero: former New Orleans district attorney Jim Garrison, whose zany investigation of the assassination in the late 1960s has almost faded from memory ... Oliver Stone is chasing fiction. Garrison's investigation was a fraud.
>
> Stone has said that he considers himself a "cinematic historian" and has called the assassination "the seminal event of my generation." But Harold Weisberg, a longtime critic of the F.B.I. and Warren Commission investigations of the assassination ... protests: "To do a mishmash like this out of love for the victim and respect for history? I think people who sell sex have more principle."
>
> ... DA Costner assails the murder as a"coup d'état"—hold your breath— ordered up by "a shadow government consisting of corrupt men at the highest levels of the Pentagon, the intelligence establishment and the great multinational corporations," carried out by elements of the intelligence community and covered up "by like-minded individuals in the Dallas Police Department, the Secret Service, the F.B.I., and the White House–all the way up to and including J. Edgar Hoover and Lyndon Johnson, whom I consider accomplices after the fact."
>
> The screenplay ends the Sunday Oswald was killed with a White House scene of Johnson meeting with his Vietnam advisers. "He signs something unseen" and tells them, "Gentlemen, I want you to know I'm personally committed to Vietnam. I'm not going to take one soldier out of there till they know we mean business in Asia."
>
> That is nonsense ... All the hoopla, of course, will obscure the absurdities, and palpable untruths in Garrison's book and Stone's rendition of it.

The manuscript smuggled over to Lardner had been a first draft, and Stone and his co-writer, Zachary Sklar, were to rewrite the script five times. Stone would later reply, "I've taken the license of using Garrison as a metaphor for all the credible researchers. Lardner ... narrows the focus of the picture to his enmity for Garrison, whereas this is not the specific Jim Garrison but an all-encompassing figure."

Played by Kevin Costner in restrained and dignified fashion, the Jim Garrison of the film is, by any rough and living measure, too good to be true—an honorable

D.A. consumed by an inner passion to find the light and save the land. If the real Jim Garrison had to be outrageously brave, staggeringly ambitious, willing like many a district attorney before him to cut a few corners, and vain enough to take on the moon, Costner is directed to play him as heir to Mr. Deeds and that particular Mr. Smith who once went to Washington. Wide-eyed, open, fearless, and consumed by his work, he is indefatigably fueled by his ideals. His only vulnerability (other than to the classic nagging of his wife, Sissy Spacek, who finds the children and herself ignored as a result of the exigencies of inquiry) is that he is innocent of guile and so has no built-in bulwark against the tide of horror he feels as he encounters the all-pervasive manipulations that are stifling his attempts to uncover the true conspirators responsible for the death of J.F.K.

In this mythic Wagnerian vein, the movie goes back to the primitive roots of silent film when each character was an attitude or a force or a spirit or a project—I will clear the forest, I will find the magic sword. Garrison/Costner takes off after evil, and is unhorsed over and over again by a variety of foul obstacles (the C.I.A.) and treacheries (a trusted associate). Always he gets up, always he goes on. At the end, defeated in his attempt to convict the immediate target, Clay Shaw, of conspiracy to murder the president, Garrison/Costner is nonetheless redeemed because he is in the right. He will prevail, or if he does not, the good fight will prevail, and if not in this venture, than in another. Many a silent film was built on the vision that virtue is equal to light and will take us through the dark—it was what the pianist was always telling us from the pit.

There should be no surprise, therefore, if the narrative jerks and manhandles us around many an unnegotiable turn. The film has a large conspiracy thesis that cannot be encompassed by the likes of Clay Shaw and David Ferrie and the supposed link between them as homosexuals. That does not provide us enough drama to assure us, as Lardner warned, that the Pentagon masterminded the assassination in response to J.F.K.'s desire to take us out of Vietnam. Nor does it prepare us for Garrison/Costner's final measure of the conspiracy, which includes elements from the C.I.A. and the Mafia, the F.B.I. the Secret Service, the Dallas police, and yes, J. Edgar Hoover and Lyndon Johnson, accomplices after the fact who directed the cover-up. It is a paranoid installation the size of a space city on the moon, yet we come face-to-face with it in just two scenes, each didactic, each expository, and neither emerges from the action.

In the first, Garrison/Costner, all but defeated by the three-quarter point of the film, weary, spiritually burdened, and in need of charging his missionary batteries, decides to visit Washington, D.C., and look around, ask around. He pays a visit to the Lincoln Memorial, and as he emerges onto the portico, a mysterious figure in a dark raincoat and a small gray checked fedora of precisely the sort that we expect an intelligence officer to wear comes into the frame and introduces himself. It is Donald Sutherland. In the next few minutes Sutherland explains it all—who killed Kennedy and how, and what steps Garrison/Costner can take. It was the military—Sutherland now offers—who did it, and with a wise smile he informs us of how he knows of what he speaks: as a member of an ultra-covert military outfit, he has long been geared for elite, high-tech snuff jobs. As they stand side by side in a drizzle, Sutherland fills Garrison/Costner in on how the Pentagon set up the assassination. "Testify," says our hero. "No chance," says the informant, and in another moment he is gone. It is all but the return of Deep Throat.

It could have been one of the more embarrassing moments in recent film history. Given our contemporary film canons, the use of such a scene is analogous to approaching the bed of one's beloved with a dildo larger than oneself. Yet Sutherland shows us what a talented actor using quiet means can accomplish in a scene that might be intolerable if anyone else tried to bring off this expository implant.

A little later, in the penultimate scene, at the conclusion of the Clay Shaw trial, Garrison/Costner comes up with a speech to the jury that is beyond the reasonable limits of any court; in that speech the cause of Kennedy's death is restated. He desired to get out of Vietnam, says Garrison/Costner, and Lyndon Johnson wanted to keep us there. So we have had a changing of the guard. Before it was over, every dark force in America had made its contribution. A case that has not been proved at all in the scene-to-scene details of the film now again delivers a final and arbitrary conclusion. We have been treated to not one *deus ex machina* of exposition but two, and at the very end, case lost (and indeed we, the audience, have been given no more real connection between Clay Shaw and the assassination conspiracy than was the actual jury), Garrison/Costner, reunited with his wife by the force of his pleading in court, walks out hand in hand with her and with their children, and we see the family in a corny long shot at the other end of the courthouse lobby.

How, then, is *JFK* a great movie?

Let us commence with what is needed for a great history (as opposed to a great movie). Such a work not only would require a comprehension of the forces and tides that shape and convey an era, but would also be obligated to possess a special species of pointillism; its thousand diverse points of light ought to be details chosen well enough to buoy the history with resonance. That, however, cannot be asked of any movie. Films, we are bound to repeat, live between memory and the dream. A great film may be epic, operatic, panoramic, stoic, and certainly it can be mythic and embody the more powerful legends of our lives, but any attempt at cinematic history has to be an oxymoron. Oliver Stone, like many a movie man before him, has mislabeled the product. He has not made a cinematic history, and, indeed, to hell with that! He has dared something more dangerous: he has entered the echoing halls of the largest paranoid myth of our time—the undeclared national belief that John Fitzgerald Kennedy was killed by the concentrated forces of malign power in the land. It is not only our unspoken myth, but our national obsession: we have no answers to his death. Indeed, we are marooned in one of two equally intolerable spiritual states, apathy or paranoia.

That is a large remark, but it may fit the condition of our time. Since the death of J.F.K., we have suffered the moral disruption of Vietnam, the assassinations of Martin Luther King, Jr. and Robert F. Kennedy, the flatulent host of petty mysteries concerning Watergate—why ever did it happen, and what, in fact, took place? Like a battered wife, we have borne our national obsession through Carter and stagflation to be revived for a time by the Pied Piper; he, in turn, wrecked our economy in the course of cheering us up and defeating the Evil Empire. Of course, that Evil Empire was already on the way to expiring in its own dust, but we were ready to accept much hypocrisy (and future bankruptcy) to avoid living with dread.

For what is an obsession but a black hole in our psychic space, a zone of ambiguity into which our energies flow and do not return? A nearer example to many of us: when a marriage ends in uncertainty and neither mate knows within who is more at fault for the divorce, then an obsession has commenced. One goes back again and again to the question: Was one more right than wrong, or more wrong than right? Fear stirs, precisely the fear of spiritual consequence. It is then that the ego—its hand on the throttle that will keep us moving forward— discharges funds of assurance. One must keep up the certainty that one is right even when one does not know, and somewhere, off to one side, one wonders if one's will is being corroded.

If that is the cost of personal obsession, what is one to make of the million-headed, or is it, rather, the hundred-million-headed, deficit of the national obsession? There have been moments in our history when all Americans have found themselves together for an hour in the same stricken space. Pearl Harbor was such a day, and the death of Franklin Roosevelt may have been another. The hour in which we learned of the bomb on Hiroshima had to be another. On that day, the new concept of atomic energy spoke with equal force to the idea of a new civilization and to the terror that all civilization would be destroyed. If that is, by now, an international obsession so large that the fears are cosmic, the assassination of J.F.K. remains as the largest single event in the history of nearly all Americans who were alive that day. No afternoon in the recollection of our lives is equal to November 22, 1963, and in its aftermath we lost our innocence and had to decide whether life was absurd (for one demented assassin could swing the ship of state wholly off its course) or, worse, whether the route of the ship of state had been so determined that even a president, wishing to change the given, was hurled off the bridge. We have lived with that question ever since. Do we descend into paranoia, or suffer the tedium of an apathy that tells us we will never know and so may as well accept the theory of Oswald as the sole killer? There is a profound reason why the Washington Club clings to the lone assassin and the incredible bullet that passed at many an angle through both Jack Kennedy's body and John Connally's body—apathy is easier to endure than livid inquiry; a dubious set of unsatisfactory facts disrupts much less than does an all-out full-scale investigation. Just as a good lawyer never asks a question to which he does not have the answer, at least not if he can help it, so the Washington Club does not pursue the assassination. For no one knows, unless there is someone who does know, where it may all end.

JFK is false probably to the likelihoods of whatever conspiracy did take place, since it is all but inconceivable that a major plot involving the C.I.A., the F.B.I., and the White House could ever hold together through the decades. Yet, the horror persists: if the assassination were not an absurdity committed by one man in a surrealistic universe, nor even a foul deed brought off by a few determined operators who managed to remain undiscovered because the real powers of the nation were all terrified of their own possible implication, so terrified that evidence was buried and all real inquiry paralyzed—no, what if it were even worse than that, what if the assassination was designed by powerful people for large purposes? Once, as a guide for approaching political questions that do not have a quick answer, Lenin laid down the axiom "Whom? Whom does this benefit?" and by that measure, yes, to the degree that history conforms more or less directly to the needs of power and policy, then, yes, if Kennedy was going to end the war in Vietnam, he had to be replaced; Lyndon Johnson was the man to do it.

History, rarely tidy, is not always so functional. Stone's movie offers us the overarching paradigm, not the solution, and that becomes a large part of its power. It is a crude movie driven home with strong colors and heavy strokes, as indeed all of his films have been. He is one of our few major directors, but he also can be characterized as a brute who rarely eschews the heavy stroke. All the same, he has the integrity of a brute, he forages where others will not go, and the result is that we live for three hours in the ongoing obsession of our national lives. (Be it recognized that, while our psyches are obviously devoted in the main to our private concerns, larger and larger grows the national sector of our souls.) So we descend again into that obsession to which we know it is better not to return, that dark land where no answers are provided. It is amazing how powerful the film becomes. Even when one knows the history of the Garrison investigation and the considerable liberties that Stone has taken with the material, it truly does not matter, one soon decides, for no film could ever be made of the Kennedy assassination that would be accurate. There are too many theories and too much contradictory evidence. Tragedies of this dimension can be approached only as myths. Here, the one that we are witnessing exerts upon us the whole force of Greek drama, and we return again and again to that national chorus of which we were a part on November 22, 1963—we live again in the mystery, the awe, the horror, and the knowledge that a huge and hideous event did, yes, take place on that day, and the gods had warred, a god fell, and the nation could never be the same.

It did not have to be Oliver Stone who made this film. Another director and another script bearing on the same events would have been as powerful if it had dared as much, but Stone is entitled to the kudos he will probably not receive, for he was the first to enter into the caves of the obsession and live in them through the year and more of writing, shooting, editing, and being assailed by the media; he was the first moviemaker to be fevered by the heat and chilled with the terror that what he was daring to say about this assassination could keep him sleepless, and will, I expect, until he learns whether this huge gamble, this spelunker's reconnaissance into the caverns of the American horror, will be well received at the box office or rejected by a new generation of television Americans who will choose no aesthetic experience powerful enough to stay with them until the morning after. If so, then the question to ask is whether the attempt to capture greatness has become the most unacceptable aesthetic endeavor of them all. In that case, *JFK*, the crudest of the great movies, but a great movie, will have to rest in peace.

That is one scenario. If, on the other hand, *JFK* proves successful, then there is no way in which the point will not be raised by Lardner & Co. that Stone's mythic presentation of the murder of President Kennedy is a monstrous act, for it is going to be accepted as fact by a new generation of moviegoers. One can only shrug. Several generations have already grown up with the mind-stultifying myth of the lone assassin. Let cinematic hyperbole war then with the Establishment's skewed reality. At times, bullshit can only be countered with superior bullshit. Stone's version has, at least, the virtue of its thoroughgoing metaphor.

A coda. Reviewing Thomas Reeve's book on John Fitzgerald Kennedy's private life, *A Question of Character*, Jonathan Yardley, the book-review whip for *The Washington Post*, offered these neo-puritanical comments the Sunday after Lardner's attack on Oliver Stone appeared:

> [Reeves] undertakes to assess Kennedy not merely in political or mythological terms but in moral ones ... Though Reeves does not come right out and say so, his analysis suggests that the assassination of John F. Kennedy, however cruel and ghastly, may have spared the nation something even worse than the prolonged orgy of grief and hagiography that followed it. He suggests that the gentlemen's agreement by which details of Kennedy's private life were kept secret might well have been violated, for whatever reason, during his second term, and that a vote of impeachment might well have followed.

> This, had it come to pass, could have been more damaging even than Watergate. This spectacle of a president in the United States on trial for illicit liaisons within and without the White House, for questionable relationships with ranking figures of the underworld—this would have been more than the United States of the mid-1960s could have stomached. The proceedings would have torn us apart in ways we can scarcely imagine, and left us with a cynicism about politics by contrast with which the residue of Watergate would seem a mild case of disenchantment. Better that the handsome young president died a mythical if not actual hero, and that the true story of his character emerged so tentatively and gradually that we were given time to come to terms with it. Had we been forced to bear in a single blow the full import of the story Thomas Reeves tells, it would have shattered us.

What this singular assessment provides is the new notion that the determination to get rid of Kennedy, if it had failed in the overt attempt, might well have moved on to impeachment, a more protracted affair. So we are free to wonder, having been given not only the presidential models over the last three decades of Johnson, Nixon, Ford, Carter, Reagan, and Bush, but also the secondary examples of Humphrey, McGovern, Mondale, and Dukakis, whether any protagonist as innovative, flexible, daring, ironic, witty, and as ready to grow as Jack Kennedy ever did have a chance to change the shape of our place.

Or is it that we will do anything to get rid of an obsession, even buy the proposition that the guy who gives us the problem in the first place is better off dead? The Washington Club has many mansions, and Yardley Court is the newest.

Reprinted by permission of the author and the author's agents, Scott Meredith Literary Agency, Inc., 845 Third Avenue, New York, New York 10022.

FEBRUARY 1992

Z MAGAZINE

JFK

Edward S. Herman

Oliver Stone's movie *JFK* had caused a remarkable mainstream media reaction that can be likened to a rush to the barricades by defenders of the faith. The attacks started even before the film was completed, and escalated as it began to be shown around the country in December. As *New York Times* editorial board member Brent Staples acknowledged on December 25, the mainstream media have been trying "to blow it off the screen" ("Hollywood: History by Default").

The media's explanation for their response is that the movie is purveying errors and falsifying history. Stone's defenders, however, point out that the movie is not a documentary, and that the mainstream media have not treated with similar intense scrutiny for error and open hostility the hundreds of anticommunist and other films shown on U.S. screens over the past half century that rewrote history. This suggests that *JFK* is being attacked because of its politics, not its untruthfulness.

Brent Staples argues that the movie's menace lies in "the realization [by media pundits] that historical lies are nearly impossible to correct once movies and television have given them credibility." Staples implies that it is Oliver Stone who threatens to inject lies into the historical record of explanations of the Kennedy assassination, and that Stone's critics are defenders of the truth. In reality, the exact reverse is correct. That is, the Warren Commission Report and the theory of Oswald as lone assassin shooting a magic bullet are the "historical lies"—

accepted by the establishment, and supported by movies, TV and the press. The establishment institutions never seriously questioned the Warren Commission report, nor applied to it the critical scrutiny and investigative zeal they apply to *JFK*; they never followed up on the 1979 congressional assassination committee report which suggested the likelihood of a multi-person operation and conspiracy, nor did they complain when its files were made unavailable to the public until 2029; and they have constituted a solid phalanx fending off successive attacks and questions about the preferred model.

An excellent case can therefore be made that it is the elements of *truth* in *JFK* that have aroused hostility, not its debatable claims. Arguably, the most compelling and important feature of the movie is its unrelenting review, one after another, of the points that make the single assassin—magic bullet—Warren commission theory of the assassination completely untenable. Most notable is the showing, several times, and in slow motion, of the Zapruder film of the actual shooting—hard evidence incompatible with the standard version. The critics of *JFK* never mention this powerful attack on the version of the assassination they implicitly defend; they only focus on the film's alleged errors.

JFK is also offensive to defenders of the faith for its stress on the militarization of the United States and the power of the military-industrial complex (MIC) to override civilian authority and render democratic government inoperative. The movie begins with President Eisenhower's farewell address warning about the MIC, and it refers sardonically and more than once to the history of open and covert Pentagon and C.I.A. interventions, from Iran in 1953 to Nicaragua/Iran-contra in the 1980s. The film suggests that these activities are the norm, and it portrays the military-intelligence leadership in a very unsavory light. The slant and critical argument in the move are completely antithetical to the media's and Hollywood's longstanding adherence to, and promotion of, cold war ideology.

JFK does expound the view that Kennedy was killed by a conspiracy of officials at many levels, who wanted him out of the way because he was threatening to curb the C.I.A. and close out the Vietnam war. In this view, the Kennedy assassination was a coup d'état. This explanation is debatable, but Stone does allow opposition viewpoints to be expressed in the film—there is, in fact, more openness on this question in *JFK* than one can find in the reviews by its critics. The defenders of the faith use the contestability of Stone's model to discredit the film as a whole, ignoring the strengths and legitimate facts and questions raised. This is testimony to the ideological-political coloring of the criticisms.

JFK also stresses the cover-up of the Kennedy assassination by government and media in tandem. He provides numerous pieces of evidence of the destruction and misrepresentation of data, failures and perversion of police-intelligence procedure, and media connivance in closing down the inquiry prematurely, from the moment Kennedy was shot to *JFK*. The Zapruder film, for example, was bought by Time and Life, and then kept out of the public domain for many years. The media's response to Stone's film follows a long tradition of protecting a "historical lie" that they have failed to investigate critically since November 22, 1963.

Stone's menace runs deeper. If not discredited now, he might some day look with a similarly jaundiced eye at the Iran-contra Report, hearings, and media treatment; or, even more frightening, he might examine the great Persian Gulf war as possibly related to the political interests of George Bush and the threatened budget of the MIC (which had been looking frantically for a "mission"), instead of as a triumph of virtue against naked aggression. This would never do.

DOUBLESPEAK APPENDIX

BUYER'S RESISTANCE. A condition in which the citizenry, overburdened with debt and unemployed or fearing job loss, refuses to buy overpriced goods.

BUSH LONG-RUN JOBS PROGRAM. Lowering the capital gains tax.

BUSH SHORT-RUN JOBS PROGRAM. A little money for road-building, a bit of Japan bashing, and a lot of hokum.

CONSPIRACY THEORY. A critique or explanation I find offensive.

HISTORICAL LIES. Lies, partial lies, or truths that conflict with well-established official lies; as in: "The rancor over *JFK* arises from around the realization that historical lies are nearly impossible to correct once movies and television have given them credibility" (Brent Staples).

MAGIC BULLET. One that wends its way through several bodies, smashing bones on the way, but ends up in pristine condition conveniently located for police attribution to the gun of choice.

Edward S. Herman is an Adjunct Professor of Communication, Annenberg School, University of Pennsylvania.

Reprinted by permission of the author.

THE NEW YORK TIMES
LETTERS

NO EVIDENCE FOR A CONSPIRACY TO KILL KENNEDY

William Manchester

To the Editor:

After the assassination of President Kennedy, his widow and his brother Robert asked me to inquire into the Dallas tragedy and write an account of my findings.

This task became my sole concern for the next three years. I was answerable to no one. I accepted no money from the Government or the Kennedys, and I stipulated that the author's royalties would be donated to the John F. Kennedy Library in Boston. My only assistants were volunteers. I was especially grateful for the help of Jim Lehrer, who was then a young reporter for *The Dallas Times-Herald*.

In Texas, in Washington and elsewhere, I questioned everyone who might shed light on the event. That included members of the Secret Service, who had never been available to interrogation by an outsider; the physicians who performed the autopsy on the President's body at Bethesda Naval Hospital; the Kennedy family; Kennedy and Johnson aides; members of the Cabinet and the Supreme Court; the Joint Chiefs of Staff; the Congressional leadership, the Central Intelligence Agency and the Federal Bureau of Investigation, including J. Edgar Hoover.

In Texas, I went over the motorcade route, searching for and finding men and women who had been spectators that Friday, Nov. 22, 1963. Abraham Zapruder went over his remarkable film with me and showed me where he had been and what he had seen. In Irving, Tex., the Paines, with whom Lee Harvey Oswald spent the night of Nov. 21, were interrogated at length. So were Dallas policemen, Gov. John Connally, E.M. (Ted) Dealey, Maj. Gen. Edwin A. Walker, employees of the Texas School Book Depository, Bill Whaley, the taxi driver who unwittingly carried Oswald in his flight from the depository; and doctors, nurses and orderlies at Parkland Memorial Hospital. In Washington, I had the President's first coffin—inadvertently damaged at Love Field—uncrated for inspection.

I needed no authority to assess Oswald's marksmanship. As a World War II Marine, I had qualified as an expert rifleman on the Parris Island, S.C., range. Oswald, a former Marine, had also qualified. In Dallas he was equipped with a bolt-action, clip-fed, 6.5 millimeter Mannlicher-Carcano rifle and a four-power telescopic sight. His target—the Presidential limousine—was only 88 yards away from his sniper's nest. At that distance, with that scope, a trained marksman could scarcely miss.

In any gathering of evidence, time is crucial. During the first eight months of my inquiry, Warren Commission investigators were also in the field, but after that I was alone. Had anyone else been active there, I would have known of it. The witnesses I was interrogating would also have been questioned then.

When Chief Justice Earl Warren's report was complete, he asked me to sign it as a representative of the Kennedy family. I felt that would be presumptuous and inappropriate; my own work was far from finished, and I was far from ready to endorse the commission's findings. Nevertheless, in the end I concluded that its report was correct on the two main issues. Oswald was the killer, and he had acted alone.

The Death of a President was published by Harper & Row on April 7, 1967. More than 550,000 copies were sold in bookstores and 800,000 more through the Book-of-the-Month Club. It astonishes me that anyone undertaking a portrayal of the assassination should be unaware of it. When a Congressional committee was looking into rumors of a plot to kill Kennedy, its chief counsel and chief investigator approached me, and I opened my files to them. I have never heard from a motion picture producer or director on such a mission.

Those who desperately want to believe that President Kennedy was the victim of a Conspiracy have my sympathy. I share their yearning. To employ what may seem an odd metaphor, there is an esthetic principle here. If you put six million dead Jews on one side of a scale and on the other side put the Nazi regime—the greatest gang of criminals ever to seize control of a modern state—you have a rough balance: greatest crime, greatest criminals.

But if you put the murdered President of the United States on one side of a scale and that wretched waif Oswald on the other side, it doesn't balance. You want to add something weightier to Oswald. It would invest the President's death with meaning, endowing him with martyrdom. He would have died for *something.*

A conspiracy would, of course, do the job nicely. Unfortunately, there is no evidence whatever that there was one.

Reprinted by permission of the author.

THE NEW YORK TIMES
LETTERS

IN 60'S, THEY MISSED ASSASSINATION EVIDENCE

Alfred Lee

In "No Evidence for a Conspiracy to Kill Kennedy" (letter, Feb. 5), William Manchester calls Lee Harvey Oswald a "wretched waif"; in *The Death of the President,* and "incoherent hater, nothing more."

A pending file on Oswald sat on a supervisor's desk at Federal Bureau of Investigation headquarters the morning before the assassination of President Kennedy. The Central Intelligence Agency file on Oswald awaited action the same morning. The Soviet Embassy had just opened a mysteriously worded letter from Oswald delayed by the F.B.I.'s having plucked it from the mail and photographed it.

Oswald and I were contemporaries. Just about no one else in our generation had a distinctive, eyebrow-raising personal history by the time he turned 24. Mr. Manchester stood in the front row of the chorus that kept saying Oswald was a lonely, pathetic twerp who turned assassin for reasons of ego. One can't help wondering whether all that oratory proselytized Sirhan B. Sirhan and the other copycat lone nuts of later Presidencies and campaigns.

The Death of a President is a superbly readable, richly detailed account which probably explains a number of riddles turned up by later authors. Weren't the two coffins in the emergency room in Dallas—one ceremonial bronze and one a simple gray—the same two that arrived in Washington, according to the detective work of David Lifton in *Best Evidence* (1980)? Mr. Lifton needlessly inferred a sinister intrigue from reports of two coffins.

Neither the Warren Commission nor Mr. Manchester wrote anything pertinent to the debate of one versus two gunmen. They lacked the technical imagination to perceive the evidence. The House Assassinations committee in 1978 asked a team of scientists nominated by the Acoustics Society of America to analyze a recording made on the Dallas Police radio system during the shooting.

Drawn as a spectrograph, the sound depicted two shots in very rapid succession from the warehouse window, closer together than the F.B.I. originally said was possible, then a third shot from the grassy knoll, where several witnesses heard a shot and saw a puff of smoke. (The Warren Commission was so naïve about guns that one lawyer later wrote that the "smokeless powder" of modern ammunition doesn't give of smoke, but it does.) The fourth shot, the head shot in the Zapruder home movie, was fired from the same window as the first and second shots.

The acoustic experts reported that the probability of a grassy knoll shot was better than the threshold figure of .95 often used in statistics. The data conservatively computed to a probability of .9999999988, a billion to one, nullifying the lone-nut theory.

The inquiries of the 1960's missed the evidence the first time around and ring hollow now.

The writer, who is working on a book about the Kennedy assassination, teaches a course on spy fiction at New Jersey Institute of Technology.

Reprinted by permission of the author.

FEBRUARY 16, 1992

IMAGE MAGAZINE
SAN FRANCISCO EXAMINER

THE STONING OF OLIVER

Todd Gitlin

Why the journalistic barrage at Oliver Stone? Whom did he shoot? The first thing to understand is that the *JFK* controversy is the latest in a series of credibility scandals. In recent years, reputable journalists have been sounding alarms about infotainment—the blurring of lines between news and amusement. TV news uses re-enactments, coming attractions and theme music, while entertainment resorts to the shaky hand-held camera, grainy film and other conventions of documentary and behind-the-scenes reporting. Consider that Oliver Stone and the *NBC Nightly News* both avail themselves of theme music composed by the very same bombastic John Williams. As proper postmodernists, we all know that images are arranged and contrived; that the polyform villain in *Terminator 2* was produced by Industrial Light & Magic in Marin County; that Demi Moore's belly and Arnold Schwarzenegger's face and every centerfold's body have been airbrushed for effect. In fact, as a culture, we delight in being led backstage to inspect the mechanics of fakery. People like mini-documentaries on *The Making of…* this, that and the other.

Still, whenever we are signaled that we are getting the news, nonfiction, the inside story—and when Warner's advertising campaign calls Stone's movie *The Story That Won't Go Away*—people expect the straight stuff. The more corrupt the public language, the more people want the luxury of suspending disbelief. For all our postmodern savviness. our everyday cynicism, we want to believe there remains a truth that hasn't been retouched. Curiously, no one believes in truth like a person surrounded by liars.

So, not surprisingly, our culture keeps stumbling into credibility scandals. A decade ago Janet Cooke was fired by *The Washington Post* and stripped of her Pulitzer Prize when the child heroin addict she had profiled turned out to be fictitious. Janet Malcolm of the *New Yorker* suffered a loss of prestige as many readers came to suspect that she had cooked up some quotations attributed to Jeffrey Masson. A *National Geographic* cover became scandalous when it was revealed that, with the use of electronic equipment, the editors had moved the Egyptian pyramids closer together to fit them onto their cover. ABC News came under fire for using an actor to "recreate" the passing of secrets by the accused spy Felix Bloch; Connie Chung, under the imprimatur of CBS News, made re-creations part of her weekly ritual, and took heat for it, even in-house. A *TV Guide* cover purporting to show Oprah Winfrey's reduced body became scandalous when an editor admitted that the body actually belonged to Ann Margret.

Journalism has an occupational credo: The truth is supposed to be tamper-proof. But there they are, newspapers and networks, losing circulation in the era of *Not-so-Hard Copy* and *Not-So-Inside Story* and *A Current-Wink-Wink-Affair*. Straight-arrow journalism finds itself far down a slippery slope moving toward more photo ops, celebrity profiles and various other forms of entertainment, because of their proprietors' belief that their only responsibility is not to be boring.

So it is precisely the serious journalists, the ones who still believe in the sacred mission of truth-telling—the Anthony Lewises and Tom Wickers—who are most alarmed about what their own business is coming to. Never mind that so-called *Eyewitness News* is full of contrivance: The "character" walks into her office building, the professor processes words on cue, the president and the ambassador chat, the victim's mother poses next to his photo—*because the correspondent has asked them to*. In principle, factuality remains sacrosanct. Facts are not supposed to be factoids.

So journalists these days are prone to blowing the whistle on credibility scandals. And *JFK* certainly has its fictions and its deep flaws—not least, the jailhouse witness played by Kevin Bacon, who was actually a composite, and the utterly incredible character "X." But still, why the intensity of the media's panic? Why a preemptive strike by George Lardner Jr. in *The Washington Post* on the basis of a first draft of the script, months before its release? Why an outraged *Newsweek* cover story?

Now, Hollywood history is saturated with historically dubious movies. Among them are the hero-worshipping Westerns that romanticized cowboys and drastically underestimated the settlers' violence against the indigenous peoples. But the only time I can recall even a trace of media animosity toward a movie before *JFK*, on the basis of its factuality or lack thereof, is the case of Costa-Gavras' *Missing*, which, for example, Flora Lewis of *The New York Times* attacked as unfair to the American ambassador to Chile.

So why cast so many stones at Oliver?

I offer two speculations. One is that the movie damages a deep and unexamined, even unarticulated, idea that Americans—including journalists, for all their famous cynicism—harbor about the national essence. America is the land of innocence, the shiny new world. In America, presidents do not get killed by conspiracies. Leave aside Lincoln, the victim of a political conspiracy if there ever was one; the myth springs back, perennially born again. Now, if the president of the United States can be assassinated, and the chief justice of the Supreme Court, leading members of the House and the Senate, the former director of the Central intelligence Agency and other pillars of authority can be wrong about who did it— can be at best sloppy and blind, at worst deceptive—then what remains of the idea that in America we are free to know the truth and the truth shall make us free? The creed insists that the government is, ultimately, our own. If secret forces can overturn the popular will, what becomes of our innocence? Along comes *JFK*, which, for all its bombast, questions the mythic sense of the country's reality. As the historian Ruth Rosen points out, Oliver Stone dizzies us by starting his movie with the Camelot myth, invoking that Christ-like John F. Kennedy who had the grace to walk among us during his, and our, glory days. Kennedy, we are given to believe, would have salvaged the endangered American innocence. Instead, he was crucified. Having set up American glories, Stone punctures them. In the process, he wrenches American ideals to the breaking point.

And there is something else that must nettle the press. Striking directly at the viscera, the movie shames the press, tears at its occupational pride—its belief in its capacity to tell the big, empire-shaking, life-warping stories of the time, the stories about the legal and illegal crimes that mow down the forests and throw out the workers and undermine the social contract.

Well, the movie damn well *ought* to shake, rattle and roll the press. For all the retrospective self-congratulation to the effect that the press punctured the pretensions of the war in Vietnam, there was plenty of puffery, even from St. Walter Cronkite, while the press missed many of the big stories of the war— including the fakery of the 1964 Tonkin Gulf incident that led Congress to write a blank check for Johnson's subsequent escalation of the war. The My Lai massacre was uncovered by Seymour Hersh, who was, at the time, working for a minuscule news agency; he and others spent months getting the establishment press to show interest. As for Watergate, credit where credit is due to the remarkable tenacity of Bob Woodward and Carl Bernstein and their editors; but most of the press missed the Watergate story altogether until late in the game—and then most of the investigative work was done by official government bodies, by the General Accounting Office and the congressional committees, not the fearless press. The Iran-contra link was uncovered by a newspaper—in Beirut. The discovery that 93 percent of the bombs dropped on Iraq last year were "dumb" bombs, and that 70 percent missed their targets—claiming many civilian lives—was left to the Pentagon.

And talk about momentous events of our times: For all the talking MacNeil-

Lehrer heads and all the think-tankers, who in the press intimated that Communism was rotting from within, that dissident groups considered marginal were about to become governments? Who in the press dared suggest that George Bush intended to go to war from early August 1990 on? Who told the American people what the savings and loan thieves were up to? Who, today, is interested in the Justice Department's disinterest in BCCI? And for that matter, considering the endless anniversary stories on John F. Kennedy—you can guarantee one a year—where is that famous journalistic curiosity about the unsolved murder?

Oliver Stone's movie, for all its profound flaws, produces a scandal partly because it disputes the myth that the world is as the press reports it, day after day. In its lurid and overblown way, the movie says: While reporters are dutifully at their beats, history is being moved and shaken by covert actors. It says you can work the White House beat day in and day out for years, your talking anchorheads can fly around the globe as much as they like, and they won't get any closer to the deals, the deep stuff. It says you may be able to see the homeless people in the streets, but you haven't been paying attention to the real estate transactions and tax abatements that help put them there. Most pointedly it says, as the Vietnam veteran Oliver Stone wants to say, and say, and keep on saying: The awful war in Vietnam didn't just happen: *Someone* was responsible.

Journalism, in other words, is staggered by the world. It has little grasp. It doesn't know who is responsible, and often enough it doesn't seem to care. So to many a horrified reporter and columnist, Stone is an interloper. He is not only sloppy and gullible, he is a transgressor. The gall of the man! He is obsessed with Vietnam; doesn't he know—to use the popular dismissal of the day—that Kennedy is *history*? Stone crosses the border in a lightning raid and kidnaps the Kennedy saga. He is a terrorist of the cinema. He is that most irritating of interlopers, the one who jabs at a bad conscience. The guardians of the truth blast him with loathing, but in the crevices of their souls they look upon him with fear: the secret fear that their own profession has become deeply irrelevant to its ideals; the fear that routinely they've missed the goods; the realistic fear that they're not being read. And perhaps even the fear that they have become collaborators, in ways too many to name here, in the vast corruption and hollowness that America has become. Something is severely wrong, and like Dylan's Mr. Jones, the media don't know what it is.

Brecht has Galileo say: Unhappy is the country that has need of heroes. Unhappy is the journalism that has to wait for Oliver Stone to do its proper work—to do it for better and/or worse—to do the indispensable work of tracking the big game; to hazard an answer, however glib, to the question, What the hell is going on in this country? The movie doesn't tell us, but it has clues and a hypothesis. Eyewitness News doesn't have even that.

Todd Gitlin, professor of sociology at U.C. Berkeley, is the author of Inside Prime Time *and* The Sixties: Years of Hope, Days of Rage. *His first novel will be published this fall by Farrar, Straus & Giroux. This essay was excerpted from a speech delivered at a forum on* JFK *sponsored by* Tikkun *magazine.*

Reprinted by permission of the author.

FEBRUARY 17, 1992

<hr/>

NEW YORK

THE BIG 'LIES' OF 'JFK'

David W. Belin

In the furor over the film JFK, *it is easy to lose sight of just how exhaustive the investigation of the assassination of John F. Kennedy by the Warren Commission was. The commission over nine months accumulated eyewitnesses and expert testimony, and ballistic and other physical evidence that eventually filled 26 volumes and a summary report. The overwhelming weight of that evidence points to Lee Harvey Oswald as the lone gunman. David W. Belin was a counsel and a key investigator for the Warren Commission and is author of* Final Disclosure: The Full Truth About the Assassination of President Kennedy *and* November 22, 1963: You Are The Jury. *(Royalties from both books went to charity.) Belin, who now practices law in Des Moines and New York, is deeply troubled by the revisionist history presented in* JFK, *as well as in the book on which the movie is based—On the Trail of the Assassins, by former New Orleans district attorney Jim Garrison—and* The Men Who Killed Kennedy, *a recent five-hour series on the Arts and Entertainment Network. He claims that in* JFK *alone, there are "more than 100 major lies and omissions." In a memo written to his files and made available to* New York, *Belin attempts to refute several of what he considers the worst transgressions of the film, the book, and the A&E series:*

The basic format underlying the spread of lies about the murders of President Kennedy and Dallas police officer J. D. Tippit on November 22, 1963, is to cover up the overwhelming weight of the evidence and to paste together scraps of testimony to form a case for conspiracy while covering up the guilt of Lee Harvey Oswald, who was the lone gunman. The Oliver Stone-Kevin Costner film *JFK*, as well as the book by Garrison and the recent five-hour A&E television series, has adopted this format. Four vivid examples involve the critical testimony of postal inspector Harry Holmes, cabdriver William Scoggins, shoe-store manager Johnny Calvin Brewer, and steamfitter Howard Brennan—some of the key witnesses whose testimony I took while I served as counsel to the Warren Commission. Together with California attorney Joseph Ball, I was assigned to what was called Area II: the determination of who killed President Kennedy and who killed officer Tippit.

Postal inspector Holmes's testimony independently disproves the central thesis of the film *JFK*, that the killing of Oswald by Jack Ruby was the ultimate act proving the existence of conspiracy. William Scoggins was the most important witness to the murder of Tippit and actually saw Oswald from a distance of as close as twelve feet. Johnny Calvin Brewer is the Dallas citizen who was responsible for the apprehension of Oswald in the Texas Theater. Howard Brennan was the witness who actually saw the gunman fire from the southeast-corner, sixth-floor window of the Texas School book depository building, went to the police, told them what he had seen, and described the gunman as young, white, slender, about five feet ten, weighing about 160 pounds—a description remarkably close to Oswald's. None of the crucial testimony of these witnesses appears in *JFK* or in Garrison's book, which forms a large part of the foundation of the Stone movie. Here are a few highlights from their testimony.

1. POSTAL INSPECTOR HARRY HOLMES

On Sunday morning, November 24, 1963, Holmes was on his way to church with his wife. At the last minute, he decided instead to go to the Dallas police station to see if he could help his friend Captain Will Fritz. Holmes had been assisting Fritz in the investigation of the murder of President Kennedy and the murder of Officer Tippit, the Dallas policeman who was killed by Oswald about 45 minutes after the Kennedy assassination and whose murder is really the Rosetta stone to understanding the truth about the assassination. Holmes entered Captain Fritz's office, where Oswald was being interrogated by Fritz and representatives of the Secret Service and the FBI. During their interrogation, Fritz turned to Holmes and gave him the opportunity to ask questions. Holmes jumped at the chance, and the session was extended approximately another half-hour.

Jack Ruby, meanwhile, had come downtown to the Western Union office to send a money order to one of his employees. The time stamp on the money order showed that he was at the Western Union office at 11:17 A.M.. Jack Ruby went from the Western Union office to the basement of the nearby police station, where he joined a group of reporters awaiting the transfer of Oswald to the county jail. Oswald was killed at 11:21 A.M. If Harry Holmes had just continued on to church that morning, the interrogation session would have ended and Oswald would have been transferred long before Jack Ruby ever got to the Western Union office. Obviously, if Jack Ruby were part of a conspiracy, he would have been downtown at least a half-hour earlier. And common sense dictates that a conspiratorial "hit man" would not kill his target in the middle of a police station.

But nowhere will the movie audiences seeing *JFK* ever learn about postal inspector Holmes, whose testimony is one of many elements showing that Jack Ruby was not conspiratorially involved. Nor will they ever learn about the testimony of Jack Ruby's rabbi, Hillel Silverman, who, on the basis of his many visits with Ruby in prison, is convinced that Ruby was not involved in any conspiracy. Nor will they ever learn about Jack Ruby's lie detector test and the results, which, although not 100 percent accurate, confirmed that Ruby was not part of a conspiracy.

2. WILLIAM SCOGGINS AND THE TIPPIT MURDER

Nowhere in *JFK* (or in the A&E series) does the viewer ever learn that six eyewitnesses, including cabdriver William Scoggins, who was twelve feet from Oswald, witnessed Oswald at the Tippit-murder scene or running away from the Tippit-murder scene with gun in hand, and positively identified him as the gunman. As Oswald reloaded his gun, he tossed cartridge cases into the bushes as he headed towards Scoggins cab, and four of these cartridge cases were turned over to the police. Ballistically, it was determined that they were fired from the revolver Oswald pulled out in the Texas Theater as police approached. Cartridge cases are an absolute means of ballistic identification. Because Oswald's revolver had been rechambered and because of the mutilated condition of the bullets in Tippit's body, FBI experts could not absolutely identify the bullets as having been fired from Oswald's revolver. But an independent expert retained by the Warren Commission was able to confirm that one of the bullets did indeed come from Oswald's revolver. Of course, the movie, as well as the A&E series, covers up the ballistic testimony, which is overwhelming when combined with the eyewitnesses and Oswald's pulling his gun.

3. JOHNNY CALVIN BREWER AND THE ARREST OF OSWALD

Oswald was apprehended in the Texas Theater because an independent citizen, Johnny Calvin Brewer, who worked in the neighborhood where the Tippit murder took place, became suspicious of Oswald as Oswald ducked into Brewer's shoe store as police sirens were heard and then immediately left as sirens faded. Brewer trailed Oswald to the Texas Theater, had the cashier call the police, and pointed Oswald out to the police as they entered the theater and the house lights were turned on. All of this is covered up in the movie, as well as in the Garrison book (and in the A&E series).

4. HOWARD BRENNAN, WHO SAW THE ASSASSIN FIRE

Howard Brennan was seated on a retaining wall facing the Texas School Book Depository building and, after hearing what he first thought was a firecracker, looked up and actually saw the gunman take aim and fire the last shot. Brennan went to the police and told them what he had seen, and it was his description of the gunman that was broadcast on the Dallas police radio approximately fifteen minutes after the assassination. When police entered the book depository and went to the sixth floor assassination window, they found three cartridge cases, which were determined to have been fired from Oswald's rifle, which was found from the back stairway in the northwest corner of the sixth floor. They also found a large homemade paper bag undoubtedly used to carry the rifle into the building, and it contained the left-index-finger print and the right-palm print of Oswald. Oswald's palm print was also on the rifle. It was also determined scientifically that Oswald's rifle had fired the bullet that struck President Kennedy's head—two portions of that bullet were large enough to be ballistically identifiable. (This is independent proof that Kennedy was not struck in the head by a shot fired from the grassy-knoll area, despite the movement that one sees from the Zapruder film.)

Neutron-activation-analysis tests on the bullet fragments from Governor Connally's wrist subsequently proved that they came from the nearly whole bullet that fell off his stretcher. Ballistic tests proved that bullet was fired from Oswald's rifle. Connally's doctors all agree he was hit by one bullet, which was the bullet that first passed through President Kennedy's neck. Governor Connally was right in line to receive the shot. Nineteen out of twenty medical experts who served on the four independent panels that over the years have examined the autopsy photographs and x-rays of President Kennedy have confirmed that all of the shots came from the rear. Of course, this is omitted in *JFK*, as it was in the A&E five-hour series.

In the 1975 report of the Commission on C.I.A. Activities Within the United States (the Rockefeller Commission), there are summaries of the findings of three of the investigative panels (separate from them, there is the 1979 report of the House Select Committee on Assassinations). In all four, the medical experts determined that all of the shots came from the rear and there is specific discussion of the head movement of the president when the fatal bullet struck. *JFK* uses the head movement as proof of a bullet from the front, despite the unanimous findings to the contrary by the physicians on these panels, and despite the irrefutable ballistic evidence that the bullet came from Oswald's rifle. According to the report of Dr. Alfred Olivier, "the violent motions of the President's body following the head shot could not possibly have been caused by the impact of the bullet." He attributed the popular misconception on this subject to the dramatic effects employed in television and motion-picture productions. The *impact* of such a bullet, he explained, can cause some immediate movement of the *head* in the direction of the bullet, but it would not produce any significant movement of the *body*. He also explained that a head wound such as that sustained by President Kennedy produces an "explosion" of tissue at the area where the bullet exits from the head, causing a "'jet effect' which almost instantly moves the head back in the direction from which the bullet came." The 1979 House Select Committee report also concluded that the head shot, as well as the shot that passed through President Kennedy's neck and then struck Governor Connally, came from Oswald's rifle and was fired by Oswald. Of course, none of these facts is included in *JFK*, in A&E's *The Men Who Killed Kennedy*, or in Garrison's book.

IN DEFENSE OF WARREN

When will Hollywood produce a movie that includes the heart of the testimony of Holmes, Scoggins, Brewer, and Brennan—a movie that tells the truth? When will the A&E network produce five hours of commercial television that presents the truth? When will the responsible leaders of our free press, who owe so much to Earl Warren, stand up for the truth, expose the techniques that have been used to disseminate the big lie that there was a high-level coup d'état involving the C.I.A. or organized crime or both, and the big lie that Lyndon Johnson was part of the cover-up (Garrison calls him an accessory after the fact), and fully defend Earl Warren's name from the slanderous charges that have been made against him and the Warren Commission?

There are some who assert in the face of this conspiracy barrage by the mass media that we will never know the truth. That simply is not accurate. The truth is known: Lee Harvey Oswald was the lone gunman who killed President Kennedy and Dallas police officer J.D. Tippit. (To reinforce that truth, in 1975 I filed a Freedom of Information Act request, seeking the release of all remaining Warren Commission files. Unfortunately, the fruits of that filing produced less than 5 percent of the remaining material.) However, all the salient evidence is already available. If the press were ever to approach that evidence with the kind of diligence and fairness that the American people have the right to expect, then the overwhelming majority of Americans would not only understand the truth but would also understand the techniques of the big lie, so that the kind of deception used by the producers of *JFK* would be exposed for all to see. The press owes that obligation to the memory of President Kennedy, to the memory of Earl Warren, and, indeed, to the American people. To paraphrase Walter Lippmann, the time had come for the press to devote sufficient effort to help the truth emerge for all America and, indeed, for all the world to know. The time has also come for the press to rise to the defense of Earl Warren from the reckless charges that are being made by those who not only seek to cover up the truth but who, in the course of making money out of the Dallas tragedy, slander the name and reputation of an individual who stood for truth and justice.

MARCH 9, 1991

NEW YORK MAGAZINE
LETTER

TURN TO STONE

Oliver Stone

In his attack on my film *JFK*, Warren Commission apologist David W. Belin defends a position that is entirely indefensible ["The Big 'Lies' of *JFK*" February 17]. Since the commission's report was released in 1964, its findings have been debunked by both the private and public sectors—Edward Jay Epstein's *Inquest* (1966) and Sylvia Meagher's *Accessories After the Fact* (1967) as well as the findings of the Schweiker-Hart Subcommittee of the Senate Intelligence Committee (1976) and the House Select Committee on Assassinations (1976-1979). The consensus of those who have studied the workings and evidence of the commission is summed up by the HSCA report's remarks that "the style of the commission's staff was not one of criminal investigation" and that its report "was not, in some respects, an accurate presentation of all the evidence available to the commission."

Likewise, Belin's "evidence" is hardly that of a skilled trial attorney. He championed the testimony of Howard Brennan, who saw a man fire a rifle out of the sixth-floor window of the Texas School Book Depository. Brennan's testimony had several inaccuracies in its description of the gunman. Brennan did identify Oswald in the third lineup and then claimed he made no identification the first two times because he feared for his family's safety. There is no doubt that Brennan saw a gunman in the window; that the gunman he saw was Oswald, alone on the sixth floor, is questionable. The commission's own evidence reveals several witnesses who said they saw *two* men, one—who was probably not Oswald— holding a rifle, in the same window at the time of the shooting. Belin disregards their testimony entirely. Similarly, he disregards parts of the testimony of his other "crucial" witnesses—including postal inspector Harry Holmes—that don't fit the Commission's conclusions.

Belin's claim that Holmes's last-minute questioning of Oswald proves that Ruby acted alone in killing the accused assassin is nonsense. Holmes's own testimony does not support Belin's assertion that his surprise visit to the police station delayed the transfer of Oswald to the Dallas County Jail. When Holmes showed up at the station on Sunday morning, Captain Will Fritz said, "We are getting ready to have a last interrogation of Oswald before we transfer him. Would you like to join us?" Clearly, Holmes did not disrupt the schedule of events—he merely joined a meeting already in the works.

Belin's extreme selectivity may be due to the fact that he was privy to only a fraction of the commission's work. As an assissistant counsel on a consulting basis, Belin interviewed fewer than 100 of the 25,000 commission witnesses; the chapter of the report he co-wrote (with Joseph Ball) was rewritten by another counsel because it was deemed "inadequate"; according to Ball, this was for stylistic reasons. He was not present at any other hearings, nor could he sit in on the executive sessions of the commission.

Clearly, defending his own credibility by his defense of the Warren Commission is more important to David Belin than any concept of justice in the murder of President Kennedy. What gave rise to the public's doubt of the Warren Report was not a mass desire to seek solace in conspiracy theories (a dubious comfort if ever there was one) or the workings of some profit-oriented network of, as Belin calls them, "assassination sensationalists." In fact, the Commission's own evidence did not support many of its conclusions (including the absurd "single magic bullet" theory). That failure, added to the insightful, comprehensive analysis of researchers and academics like Epstein and Meagher, made the overwhelming majority of the American public believe President Kennedy was killed as a result of a conspiracy. Commission defenders like Belin have not been able to resolve the contradictions in their own material, thus they cannot resolve the public's doubts.

Most important, one has to question the ethics of any American attorney who calls Lee Harvey Oswald—who was never tried, convicted, or even allowed legal representation—Kennedy's assassin, and not the "alleged" or "accused" assassin, thereby violating the most fundamental principles of our legal system.

The article's most preposterous claim, however, is not Belin's but *New York*'s. The introduction says the piece is a "memo written to [Belin's] files and made available to *New York*." Similar Belin articles recently appeared in *The Wall Street Journal*, in *The Washington Post*, and across the nation through the *Post*'s syndication service. So much for exclusivity.

Reprinted by permission of the author.

MARCH 7, 1992

THE NEW YORK TIMES

EARL WARREN'S ASSASSINS

David W. Belin

Former Chief Justice Earl Warren, one of the great Americans of this century, is being honored on Monday by the issuance of a postage stamp. At one time he was best known for his leadership in breaking down the barriers of discrimination through the landmark decision of Brown v. Board of Education.

But today, America's young people know him best as he is portrayed in the Warner Brothers film *JFK* as a liar, an incompetent and as someone who participated in a cover-up of the truth about the assassination of President John F. Kennedy.

What far right-wing extremists tried to persuade a majority of Americans to believe in the 1960's with their "Impeach Earl Warren" billboards, Hollywood has been able to achieve in the 1990's in its impeachment of the integrity of a great Chief Justice.

Earl Warren is not the only victim. The Kennedy assassination is called a "coup d'état," a "public execution" by elements of the C.I.A. and the Department of Defense, while President Lyndon B. Johnson is called an accessory after the fact—in other words, a murderer.

When the film not only alleges conspiracy but names the guilty parties, it goes beyond just artistic license and entertainment. It crosses the threshold of slander and character assassination—a 1990's version of McCarthyism.

As if telling these lies were not enough, Warner Brothers has now gone one step further, and has helped finance the mailing of 13,000 copies of a "*JFK* Study Guide" to high school social studies and college history departments. The text supposedly has been "approved" by Warner Brothers and is accompanied by a film poster and a two-page exercise sheet.

All of this is in the context of a film that professes to speak the truth. "Dedicated to the young, in whose spirit the search for the truth marches on," declares the film at the end. "The truth is the most important value we have," proclaims Kevin Costner as he portrays New Orleans District attorney Jim Garrison.

In fact, to incorporate *JFK* in any school curriculum misrepresents the truth the same way that Oliver Stone, the film's producer, director and screenplay co-author, misrepresents the most important facts in speaking and writing about the assassination. In a recent letter to New York magazine, Mr. Stone used the 1979 report of the House Select Committee on Assassinations as a primary authority for his attacks on the Warren Commission. But he covered up the fact that the panel's ultimate conclusion was that "Lee Harvey Oswald fired three shots at President John F. Kennedy." Two shots hit and one shot missed. That's what the Warren Commission found.

JFK claims that the shot that killed President Kennedy was fired from the front. The House committee's report directly contradicts this, concluding "that President Kennedy was struck by two, and only two, bullets, each of which entered from the rear." Like the Warren Commission, the House panel also "concluded that a single bullet" passed "through both President Kennedy and Governor Connally." Will these findings be in the *JFK* study guide?

What about the murder of Police Officer J. D. Tippit—the Rosetta Stone to understanding the assassination of President Kennedy? "*JFK* asserts that Oswald was a "patsy" and did not do it. But like the Warren Commission, the House report concluded "that Oswald shot and killed Officer Tippit."

The committee further concluded that "this crime, committed while fleeing the scene of the assassination, was consistent with the finding that Oswald assassinated the President."

The fundamental differences between the committee's report and the Warren Commission's findings stem primarily from acoustical evidence. The majority of the House committee claimed that this evidence indicated the presence of a second gunman who missed everything. But this evidence was subsequently disproved by the May 14, 1982, report of the Committee on Ballistic Acoustics of the National Research Council, which found no scientific validity for it.

Perhaps the ultimate irony in *JFK* is the proclamation of Mr. Costner: "Hitler said, the bigger the lie, the more people will believe it." Warner Brothers, Mr. Stone and Mr. Costner are proving that to be true, making millions of dollars along the way. Furthermore, they want to spread the disinformation of *JFK* into our public schools, in effect brainwashing students through the power of a commercial film and rewriting history the Hollywood way. And for this, the film has received eight Academy Award nominations.

For Hollywood to give any Academy Award to this massive misrepresentation of truth and character assassination of Earl Warren would be vivid evidence of the depths to which Hollywood's standards of integrity, truth and justice have fallen.

David Belin is former counsel to the Warren Commission.

THE NATION

IN DEFENSE OF THE WARREN COMMISSION

Alexander Cockburn

In mid-February, for the benefit of television viewers in Australia, I found myself squaring off on the subject of *JFK* against Fletcher Prouty and Carl Oglesby. Perched on a stool beside me in a Los Angeles studio was Wesley J. Liebeler, a 60-year-old professor of law at U.C.L.A Originally from North Dakota and conservative/libertarian in political out-look, Liebeler was one of the staff counsels on the Warren Commission. Later, in a week when *JFK* got eight Academy Award nominations, and when Richard Heffner, a Rutgers professor who is also chairman of the motion picture industry's film rating system, announced in the *Los Angeles Times* that *JFK* marked the end of the Gutenberg era and the dawn of a new way of telling history, I drove up to Zuma Beach and interviewed Liebeler.

AC: What about the speed at which Oswald would have had to fire his Mannlicher-Carcano? Critics of the Warren Commission say Oswald could never have loosed off the shots in so short a time.

WJL: The clock for the whole thing is the Zapruder film, which runs at 18.3 frames a second. The film shows only two shots striking the people in the car. A time fix on the first shot can't be precise, for reasons I'll come back to. But the time of impact of the second shot that struck is precise. That was at frames 312-313, of the Zapruder film. At frame 313 the head just explodes. So either at 312 or 313, which is practically the same instant. And that's the last shot for which there is any evidence of anything in the car being struck.

The first shot hits, in the view of the Warren Commission, between frames 210 and 225. The commission came to that conclusion based on the Zapruder film, which shows that at a certain point Kennedy was reacting to a shot. He raises his hands up. During part of that time the limousine is behind a road sign, so it can't be seen for about .9 of a second. So you can't tell how long before the reaction the shot actually struck.

The House Assassination Committee (1978) said the first shot struck around frame 190, which is a little sooner, about a second. So to establish the time frame the Warren Commission subtracted either 210 or 225 from 312, and divided that by 18.3. Let's say 210. This gives us 5.6 seconds. Take 313 and subtract 225, and divide that by 18.3 and that gives 4.8 seconds. So the commission said that the time lapse between the first shot that hit and the second shot that hit was between 4.8 and 5.6 seconds.

If we assume that three shots were fired, you have the question of which shot missed. The House committee concluded that the first shot missed. The Warren Commission never decided on the matter. The evidence is consistent with the proposition that the first shot missed. If so, all Oswald had to do was fire one more shot. So in fact he would have had from 4.8 to 5.6 seconds to fire one shot, not three shots.

AC: So, on that explication, he's waiting with his gun aimed. The car comes along, he shoots and misses. But there's no time fix as to when he might have fired that shot. It wasn't in the famous 4.8 to 5.6 second interval. He reloads and then fires the shot that hits the President in the neck between frames 210 or 225 according to the Warren Commission, or 190 according to the House committee.

WJL: Right. Now he has to reload (which takes a minimum of 2.3 seconds), work the bolt once and fire the third shot that's fired (the second shot that strikes). And he has, according to the Warren Commission, 4.8 to 5.6 seconds. That is even time enough to fire twice, which he would have had to do if the second shot missed. If, as the House committee said, the first shot that hit was fired at frame 190, then Oswald had 6.72 seconds to fire either one or two shots. That is 313 minus 190, divided by 18.3. There was enough time.

You know, people harp on about the Warren Commission, which is fine. But the House Assassination Committee confirmed every single finding that the Warren Commission made—every one, except on the conspiracy question.

AC: Well, what about that?

WJL: The only evidence for conspiracy that the House committee had was a Dictabelt tape that recorded police radio transmissions. That was discovered long after the event in a file cabinet in the Dallas Police Department. There were two different radio frequencies that the Dallas Police Department used to transmit messages back and forth among the police. Both those frequencies were separately recorded. The Warren Commission didn't know anything about this evidence. When you listen to the Dictabelt there's no sound of shots at all. But the House committee took this Dictabelt and gave it to an audio consulting firm in Boston that did an analysis and found some pulses. The Dictabelt had been recording from a motorcycle somewhere that had its microphone stuck open. The consultants claimed they could distinguish four different pulse phenomena, three of which could be made to correspond to the shots we've just talked about, if you pushed the first shot back to frame 190. And there was a fourth pulse. So the consultants went down to Dealey Plaza, set up microphones, fired off rifles and established what they called an audio footprint, and said initially that there was a 50-50 probability of a shot fired from the grassy knoll. This was in September of 1978. Then in December, right before the House committee closed up shop on the hearings, the audio consulting firm came up with a 95 percent probability on this same shot. So on the basis of that evidence the 1978 House committee concluded there was probably a conspiracy, that there was a guy on the grassy knoll shooting, though he didn't hit anybody. Robert Blakey, the committee's chief counsel, then gave the Dictabelt to the Justice Department to be analyzed further. Later he wrote a letter to *National Review* saying that if the Justice Department's investigation of the tape didn't bear out the 95 percent probability of another shot, he'd retract the whole conspiracy theory.

Well, the Justice Department turned all this over to a panel of acoustic experts set up by the National Research Council. They figured out that sounds on both Dictabelts could be matched, and since the one had a time reference, they could fix the time frame on the other Dictabelt as well. The N.R.C. acoustic committee then concluded that the sounds on the second Dictabelt were recorded more than a minute after the assassination occurred. So they didn't have anything to do with the shots in Dealey Plaza.

AC: The other thing that seems to cause people a lot of problems is the "single-bullet theory"—the first shot that hit Kennedy and also John Connally.

WJL: The first shot that hit went through the top of Kennedy's back, came through the throat to the right of his trachea, didn't hit any bones. Governor Connally was struck right below the right armpit in the back. The bullet went down through his chest cavity, came out just below his right nipple, struck him on the back side of his right wrist at the joint, broke the wrist and came out the front of his wrist and entered his thigh, making a very shallow hole.

The pathology panel of the House committee and also the Warren Commission concluded that the damage to Connally was done by one bullet. Work it backwards. If his hand was on his thigh, which is consistent with the Zapruder film, you know that the bullet wasn't going very fast when it came out the underside of the wrist, which has implications about how fast it was going when it entered the wrist. If it had already gone through Connally's chest cavity and the President's neck it had been slowed down. A wounds ballistic expert testifying to the House committee established that there's a range of velocity within which a bullet will break a bone without hurting the bullet, provided it's not going to fast.

Warren Commission Exhibit 399 is the so-called "magic" or "pristine" bullet. It is neither one. It is in good shape, but eight of the nine forensic pathologists on the House committee medical panel agreed that it had gone through the president's neck or upper back and then inflicted all of Connally's wounds. Ask yourself where the bullet went after it came out of the President's neck if it didn't hit Connally. After coursing downward through the President's body, where it hit no bone to deflect it, either it's got to hit Connally, who is sitting right in front of him, or it's got to hit the car. It didn't hit the car.

The Warren Commission did a re-enactment of the assassination which showed that the President and Governor were located in a way that the bullet would have gone directly from the exit wound in the President's neck into Connally's back. The House committee used a different method of calculating the trajectory and unequivocally confirmed the Warren Commission findings that one bullet—CE 399—did go through the President and inflict the Governor's wounds. The House committee said flatly that the trajectory it established supported the single-bullet theory.

Oliver Stone's treatment of this question is simply a lie, and he knows it. The House committee confirmed the Warren Commission's findings on this point without qualification. But with the conspiracy Stone has fabricated, the addition of the House of Representatives won't cause any further problems. He's got half the country in on it now.

I have challenged him to debate the validity of the Warren Report. Naturally he issued a press release saying he'd be happy to do it, but he never responded to me. He's engaged in scholarship by press release. I repeat my challenge.

AC: In the Zapruder film, at frame 313, when the second bullet strikes, Kennedy's head jerks back convulsively, and people have reckoned this implies a shot from the front.

WJL: If you look at Kennedy's head, right at frame 313, just as the bullet strikes it, it doesn't move backward. It moves slightly to the left and downward, just for two or three frames, which is consistent with a bullet striking it from behind and nowhere else, because the momentum of the bullet is imparted instantly.

Then shortly after frames 312-313 the President's body goes backward. The House committee said there are two explanations. One is the jet effect, caused by the skull and brain exiting and forcing the head back and to the left. Combined with that effect, the committee said, was a neuromuscular reaction. The medical evidence is the best way to determine the direction of the shots that hit the President. Take the skull. The entry wound in the back of his head is "coned" on the inside of the skull. What can be constructed of the exit wound from the skull is coned on the outside. The House medical panel all agreed to these conclusions, and also that the wound on the President's upper right back could only be an entrance wound. Eight of the nine pathologists on that panel concluded that the President was struck by two *and only two* shots. The medical evidence excludes the possibility that the President was struck by a shot fired from any direction other than behind him.

AC: Why didn't the Warren Commission have access to the autopsy photographs and x-rays?

WJL: Warren didn't want to press Bobby Kennedy, who controlled them, for their release. The worst consequence was the idea that someone was trying to hide something. Without these materials the autopsy surgeons described to the commission their recollection of the wounds, and their medical artist drew the diagrams showing the entrance wounds in the wrong place.

AC: What happened to Kennedy's brain?

WJL: The brain was under Robert Kennedy's control when it disappeared. It is widely believed that he destroyed it. He was afraid that these materials might end up on public display.

committee said flatly that the trajectory it established supported the single-bullet theory.

Oliver Stone's treatment of this question is simply a lie, and he knows it. The House committee confirmed the Warren Commission's findings on this point without qualification. But with the conspiracy Stone has fabricated, the addition of the House of Representatives won't cause any further problems. He's got half the country in on it now.

I have challenged him to debate the validity of the Warren Report. Naturally he issued a press release saying he'd be happy to do it, but he never responded to me. He's engaged in scholarship by press release. I repeat my challenge.

AC: In the Zapruder film, at frame 313, when the second bullet strikes, Kennedy's head jerks back convulsively, and people have reckoned this implies a shot from the front.

WJL: If you look at Kennedy's head, right at frame 313, just as the bullet strikes it, it doesn't move backward. It moves slightly to the left and downward, just for two or three frames, which is consistent with a bullet striking it from behind and nowhere else, because the momentum of the bullet is imparted instantly.

Then shortly after frames 312-313 the President's body goes backward. The House committee said there are two explanations. One is the jet effect, caused by the skull and brain exiting and forcing the head back and to the left. Combined with that effect, the committee said, was a neuromuscular reaction. The medical evidence is the best way to determine the direction of the shots that hit the President. Take the skull. The entry wound in the back of his head is "coned" on the inside of the skull. What can be constructed of the exit wound from the skull is coned on the outside. The House medical panel all agreed to these conclusions, and also that the wound on the President's upper right back could only be an entrance wound. Eight of the nine pathologists on that panel concluded that the President was struck by two *and only two* shots. The medical evidence excludes the possibility that the President was struck by a shot fired from any direction other than behind him.

AC: Why didn't the Warren Commission have access to the autopsy photographs and x-rays?

WJL: Warren didn't want to press Bobby Kennedy, who controlled them, for their release. The worst consequence was the idea that someone was trying to hide something. Without these materials the autopsy surgeons described to the commission their recollection of the wounds, and their medical artist drew the diagrams showing the entrance wounds in the wrong place.

AC: What happened to Kennedy's brain?

WJL: The brain was under Robert Kennedy's control when it disappeared. It is widely believed that he destroyed it. He was afraid that these materials might end up on public display.

AC: Do you think the Warren Report was flawed?

WJL: It was too oracular, overwritten. Also I think it relied too heavily on eyewitness testimony. The problem is that people will testify to damn near anything. So the commission had one eyewitness testifying that he saw Oswald sticking a rifle through the sixth-floor window——

AC: But there was another witness next to him who saw Oswald and another man beside him.

WJL: Right. That's the problem. The only way you can avoid that is to look at evidence that can be replicated. Evidence that is here today, will be here tomorrow and 100 years from now: the autopsy photographs; the autopsy X-rays; the ballistics tests. The bullet that was found on the stretcher was fired from Oswald's rifle to the exclusion of all other rifles; the two big fragments in the car were fired from that rifle to the exclusion of all other rifles; that rifle was on the sixth floor of the School Book Depository; it had Oswald's print on it; there was a brown paper bag there that had Oswald's palm print on it; it was a long bag that would have held a rifle. At this point it would be nice to have an eyewitness who said that when he gave Oswald a ride to work that morning he had the bag with him, and there was one. But fine, never mind how the bag got there. We know it was Oswald's rifle because he rented a post office box and his handwriting is on the application; he ordered the rifle and his handwriting is on the paper he ordered the rifle with; he wrote out a money order and his handwriting is on that; and the rifle was sent to his post office box. There are a number of pictures of Oswald with a rifle. The House Assassination Committee, with improved enhancement techniques that the Warren Commission didn't have, was able to prove it was the same rifle. The negative was found and it had been taken from Oswald's camera to the exclusion of all other cameras. George do Mohrenschildt had a copy of that picture with Oswald's handwriting on the back. There's no evidence of tampering on the negative; the scratch marks are the same. The picture was taken six months before the assassination. We have photographic evidence, like the Zapruder film. On the Tippit shooting, we've got forensic evidence that shows clearly Tippit was killed by bullets from the gun Oswald was carrying when he was arrested. So you can make out a pretty good case just on the basis of the physical evidence.

Why did Oswald kill the President? The man was a malcontent, not happy, not stupid by any stretch of the imagination, but unhappy and discontented. I guess your typical liberal [laughs]. Not that. I guess he would have as much contempt for liberals as you or I. He was a revolutionary of one form or another. I drafted a psychological profile of Oswald for chapter seven of the report. It was reviewed by a panel including the chief of psychiatry at the Mayo Clinic, who threw my draft down and said, "This is very interesting stuff, but it tells me a lot more about you, Liebeler, than it does about Oswald." So how the hell do I know why Oswald killed the President?

Reprinted by permission of the author.

THE NATION

EXCHANGE: JOUSTING AFTER CAMELOT

The Sword and the Stone

Zachary Sklar

I'm afraid my friend Alexander Cockburn has missed the main point of Oliver Stone's *JFK* ["Beat the Devil," Jan. 6/13]. As co-screenwriter of the film, I can assure Alexander that its intent was not to transform John Kennedy into a white knight who single-handedly would have ended the cold war had he lived. Rather, it was to show that the economic, military and intelligence institutions committed to fanatical anticommunism were far more powerful than any elected official and would stop at nothing to continue their enormously profitable cold war crusade.

Historians differ on whether Kennedy would have pulled out of Vietnam, continued limited assistance or escalated the war by committing massive numbers of U.S. combat troops. Cockburn and others argue that Kennedy was elected as a cold warrior, built up the military, made a number of hawkish public statements defending U.S. involvement in Vietnam and thus could have been expected to do just what Lyndon Johnson did later.

That position, while largely accurate about Kennedy's early years in office, ignores crucial evidence. As John Newman shows in his book *JFK and Vietnam*, Kennedy turned down numerous requests from his advisers and the Joint Chiefs of Staff to send troops to either Laos or Vietnam. While Cockburn may dismiss as "political opportunism" Kennedy's private statements to Senators Mike Mansfield and Wayne Morse, as well as to aide Kenneth O'Donnell, that he intended to withdraw all U.S. advisers from Vietnam after the 1964 elections, it is more difficult to dismiss National Security Action Memorandum 263. Signed by Kennedy on October 11, 1963, it unequivocally ordered the withdrawal of 1,000 U.S. advisers by the end of 1963. The existence of that memorandum is *fact*. The *speculation* is that Kennedy might not have carried out the order had he lived.

Cockburn quotes part of NSAM 273, signed by Lyndon Johnson four days after Kennedy's assassination, and says it contained no change in policy from a draft written before the assassination. This interpretation neglects entirely paragraph 7 of that document, which gave the go-ahead for *U.S. forces* to develop covert military operations against North Vietnam. In the early draft, such operations were to be carried out by *"Government of Vietnam resources."* The distinction is important because it was such covert operations by U.S. Navy ships that led to the Tonkin Gulf incident, which in turn opened the door for U.S. troops to be sent en masse to Vietnam.

JFK presents the hypothesis that Kennedy was assassinated because those institutional forces with a vested interest in the cold war perceived him as a threat. Allen Dulles, Gen. Charles Cabell and Richard Bissell, all fired from the highest echelons of the C.I.A., felt Kennedy had betrayed them at the Bay of Pigs by refusing to provide air cover. Cuban exiles and right-wing mercenaries trained by the C.I.A. under Operation Mongoose for a second invasion of Cuba were enraged at Kennedy for ordering their training camps raided and all their weapons and ammunition confiscated in the summer of 1963. (The head of Operation Mongoose, Gen. Edward Lansdale, had spent much of his career conducting black operations in Southeast Asia and had lobbied for the ambassadorship to Vietnam, but Kennedy rejected him.)

The Joint Chiefs and others in the Pentagon felt Kennedy had caved in to the Communists in October 1962 by reaching, over their objections, a secret agreement with Khrushchev not to invade Cuba in exchange for withdrawal of Soviet missiles from the island. Kennedy had also signed a nuclear test ban treaty with the Russians in the summer of 1963, again over the objections of the Joint Chiefs. And he had initiated back-channel overtures to Fidel Castro to try to normalize relations with Cuba—a process that was under way, according to Castro, when Kennedy was killed.

All this had the Pentagon and the intelligence community in an uproar. Cockburn and others on the left may view Kennedy as just another cold warrior, but *JFK* makes the case that the right saw him as an appeaser of communism and had him executed for that reason. It is possible to acknowledge Kennedy's cold war history and at the same time believe he had changed enough—or talked about change enough—to be perceived as a genuine threat to war profiteers on the right.

Finally, Alexander's idea that "the psychic bloodlines of *JFK*" may be traced to Ellen Ray's "Catholic girlhood in Massachusetts, with an icon of J.F.K. on the wall" is amusing but makes about as much sense as the notion that Cockburn's view of *JFK* may be traced to his own childhood surrounded by icons of Stalin. Has Alexander forgotten that Ellen was raised in Nebraska and that her father was an unapologetic atheist?

Reprinted by permission of the author.

THE QUEST FOR THE GRAIL

Peter Dale Scott

Orwell once made a remark to the effect that only an intellectual could say something so stupid. I was reminded of it reading Alexander Cockburn's efforts to use the undoubted fictions in Oliver Stone's *JFK* as a pretext for denying two of its incontrovertible facts: that in late 1963 Kennedy had authorized an initial withdrawal of 1,000 U.S. troops from Vietnam, and that, in a high-level meeting right after Kennedy's murder, Johnson redirected U.S. Vietnam policy from this

Cockburn suggests that my "fantasizing" about Vietnam is in Oliver Stone's movie because of John Newman's *JFK and Vietnam*, which "first came into the offices of Sheridan Square Press ... whence it was passed on to Stone, who assisted in its dispatch to Warner Books (part of the conglomerate backing *JFK*), which is publishing the book in February." But the fantasizing here is Cockburn's. Newman, a professional historian, sent his book first to Warner, which signed a contract for it in April 1991. Stone never saw the manuscript until August. The book will gain a large and respectful readership—not because of corporate linkages, or someone's Catholic girlhood, but because it meticulously documents allegations I could make only tentatively twenty years ago in an article. That article absolutely did not assert, as Cockburn implies, "that J.F.K. would have pulled the United States out of Vietnam."

What Kennedy would or would not have done, had he lived, is of course speculation. But his policies at the time of his death are a matter of record, a strenuously suppressed record, to be sure, but a record I was able to reconstruct deductively form the "Pentagon Papers." The most cowardly feature of Cockburn's essay is his decision to attack my tentative reconstruction from limited evidence in 1971 rather than from Newman's massive documentation of the same basic case today. That argument included the following propositions:

1) Kennedy planned, over the most vigorous dissent of his Joint Chiefs, "to withdraw 1,000 US. military personnel [from Vietnam] by the end of 1963." This withdrawal was in accordance with a more long-range program to train Vietnamese, making it "possible to withdraw the bulk of U.S. personnel ... by the end of 1965."

This language did not come from antiwar Senators Mike Mansfield and Wayne Morse, as Cockburn asserts. This language is taken from the Top Secret Military Recommendations to the President by Defense Secretary Robert McNamara and Gen. Maxwell Taylor on October 2, 1963. The "presently prepared plans" to withdraw 1,000 troops, which they then recommended announcing, had in fact been approved at a conference the preceding May.

2) In NSAM 263 of October 11, Kennedy secretly approved the McNamara-Taylor recommendation "to announce in the very near future" withdrawing 1,000 troops, "as an initial step in a long-term program to replace U.S. personnel." He directed then "that not formal announcement be made of the implementation" of these plans, but in November the secrecy was lifted, with the President suggesting that the details would come from a top-level Honolulu conference on November 20. *The New York Times* published the announcement on November 21, one day before the assassination in Dallas.

3) Two days after the assassination, Johnson and his top advisers (all Kennedy holdovers) approved a new policy statement, finalized as NSAM 273 of November 26. With respect to the 1,000 men, the text was highly ambiguous, if not deliberately misleading. It implied continuity with previous *objectives* of withdrawing troops (as had been announced publicly on October 2) but failed to reaffirm NSAM 263, which had implemented the plan to withdraw them.

Here is the language: "The objectives of the United States with respect to the withdrawal of U.S. military personnel remain as stated in the White House statement of October 2, 1963." Of course the *objectives* remained the same: No one wanted the U.S. troops to fight there forever. But the *implementation* of troop withdrawal, an implementation so controversial that to this day many people deny and lie about it, had been replaced by the earlier objectives and nothing more.

4) Let us now turn to the key policy innovation of Johnson's NSAM 273, that the United States would begin carrying the war north. For the first time in any presidential directive, NSAM 273 authorized prompt planning for "different" (i.e., escalating) levels of U.S. activity against North Vietnam, up to and including bombing. These operations, which led to the August 1964 Tonkin Gulf incident, had in fact been discussed for some time inside the Pentagon but had never before been presented for presidential authorization.

5) There has been a flood of cover-up and lying about this policy innovation by L.B.J. In the secret "Pentagon Papers" an account of NSAM 273 claimed that it "revalidated the planned phased withdrawal of U.S. forces announced publicly ... limited cross-border operations to an area 50 kilometers inside Laos ... No new programs were proposed or endorsed." This Pentagon lie is virtually repeated by Cockburn when he assures *Nation* readers that "there was ... no change in policy." The secret summary of another of the "Pentagon Papers" stated categorically that the "U.S. did effect a 1,000 man withdrawal in December 1963," but the paper being summarized had also just as categorically denied this.

Recent controversy has revived the lying. Although both NSAMs were declassified in the 1970s, the obfuscation of the record in *The Washington Post, The New York Times*—and now *The Nation*—continues. George Lardner wrote in the *Post* last July that NSAM 273 "ordered the withdrawal [of 1,000] troops to be carried out." (It didn't.) Michael Specter in the *Times* is longer, and worse: NSAM 273 "continued Kennedy's policies, and historians have shown that it was drafted the day before Kennedy journeyed to Dallas." But on November 21, the day in question, Kennedy was in Texas and never saw the draft prepared for his signature. He may of course have heard it over the telephone. But the draft spoke only of additional resources for activities against North Vietnam by the Saigon government. NSAM 273 deleted this restriction and sanctioned the plans for U.S. operations that began shortly thereafter. This alone is proof of the change in policy that occurred under L.B.J. on November 24.

Of the three obfuscations, Cockburn's is the longest, and the worst. Dipping deep into my article, he quotes extensively not from my argument but from NSAM 273 and an earlier Kennedy-era statement of October 2, 1963. He suggests, quite falsely, that I merely compared the two, laying "enormous weight upon minute textual alterations" and "signaling these with urgent italic." But it was three texts, not two, I was comparing, in three parallel columns. And the point of the italic was to show that in 1963, as earlier in 1961, Kennedy had refused to make the final commitment to an overriding objective—"to win"—that Johnson made so swiftly in NSAM 273. In other words, Cockburn makes my three-part sandwich look beefless by himself removing the beef. Despite the space he devotes to trashing me, only one of my sentences is quoted, and that one to misrepresent it.

No one can deny that Kennedy was a hawk, at least until the shock of the 1962 Cuban missile crisis. But after that crisis he explored new and more conciliatory policies in the Caribbean as well as Vietnam. Here Cockburn is totally unreliable. How can he claim that Kennedy "never entertained the idea of a settlement as advocated by [Ambassador] J.K. Galbraith"? Galbraith's idea was for a quid pro quo based on a *phased American withdrawal* (my urgent italic), precisely what Kennedy set in motion in 1962 and them implemented with NSAM 263. And how can he blame Kennedy for the 1963 coups in Guatemala and the Dominican Republic? Kennedy refused to recognize the military juntas that took over there and in Honduras—another policy that was swiftly reversed by Johnson. Thomas Mann, the U.S. Ambassador to Mexico who had been deeply involved in the Guatemala coup, had announced in mid-1963 that he would retire; instead, Johnson promoted him to preside over the new policy of encouraging coups in Latin America, like the one in Brazil in 1964.

I cannot prove that Kennedy, had he lived, could have pursued these policy divergences to any different outcome. But in 1963 there were both bureaucratic and corporate pressures for him to do so. To say this may be an affront to those single-minded foundationalist Marxists who talk, like Cockburn, of "the open secrets and agendas of American capitalism." The fact remains that in late 1963 a worsening balance of payments forced Presidents to choose between defending the dollar and security for overseas investment. Kennedy was inclined to the former before Johnson chose the latter.

Those familiar with my research into deep politics (unacknowledged political processes) and parapolitics (the exploitation of these, as in the C.I.A.-Mafia connection) will appreciate how consistently such research is resisted by the establishment left (*The Nation*) in almost the same terms as the establishment center (*The Times*). Both consistently deny that covert forces can influence politics as well as implement them. Both thus illustrate the hyperstructuralism of "power systems" analysis, which anti-foundationalists see linking Talcott Parsons to Michel Foucault. The center writes out of false optimism, the left out of false despair. But both write out of false consciousness, to rationalize their disempowerment.

The result is a shared resistance to new facts, like those about the assassination, to which their hyperstructuralism cannot give meaning. (One thinks of the Nicaraguan Communists who, like their opponents from the center and right, joined the UNO coalition to resist the Sandinistas.) And increasingly, as we have just seen, a shared distortion and repression of other facts, such as the documented Vietnam policy change.

Reprinted by permission of the author.

MORTE D'ARTHUR

Michael Parenti

My friend Alexander Cockburn has no tolerance for those who wish to uncover homicidal conspiracies like the Kennedy assassination. He says there are more important things to worry about. He never actually denies there was a conspiracy to kill the President; he just thinks U.S. foreign policy would have remained pretty much the same had John Kennedy lived or died, for J.F.K. was an anticommunist cold warrior, committed to counterinsurgency and military interventionism. Therefore, how he died is a matter of no great moment.

Alexander argues from a structuralist position, to wit: When we try to reduce great developments of history to the hidden machinations of conspiracy, "out the window goes any sensible analysis of institutions, economic trends and pressures, continuities in corporate and class interest and all the other elements ... of American capitalism." How true. Yet this does not mean we can discount the role of human agency in history. The great "continuities in corporate and class interest" do not happen of themselves like reified, disembodied social forces. The function of state leaders is to act as willful and conscious agents in re-creating the conditions of politico-economic dominance. They may not always get the results they want, but they do so often enough.

To achieve their goals they will resort to every form of mass manipulation and every means of force and violence—even against one of their own whom they have come to see as a liability. Thus, specific acts of assassination—be they by death squads in El Salvador or hit squads in Dealey Plaza—cannot be treated as exclusive of, or in competition with, the existence of broader systemic forces. They are part of what keeps those forces in control.

While the larger structural trends may set the outer limits of policy or exert strong pressures on leaders, this does not mean that all important policy is predetermined. Short of betraying fundamental class interests, different leaders can pursue different courses, the effects of which are not inconsequential to the lives of millions of people. Thus, it was not foreordained that the B-52 carpet bombing of Cambodia and Laos conducted by Nixon would have happened if Kennedy, or even Johnson or Humphrey, had been President. It was not foreordained by the imperatives of global capitalism that the United States invade Panama or heartlessly slaughter Iraqis. If Alexander thinks these things make no difference in the long run, he had better not tell that to the millions of Cambodians, Laotians, Salvadorans, Iraqis and others who still grieve for their shattered lives and lands.

John Kennedy was himself something of an assassin. He probably ordered the murder of Diem, a class cohort who had become a serious liability. He plotted attempts on Fidel Castro, a class enemy. But Kennedy also did withdraw 1,000 troops from Vietnam. He did have serious conflicts with the C.I.A. He did close the armed C.I.A. camps that were readying for a second Bay of Pigs. He did give Khrushchev a guarantee he would not invade Cuba. He did, in his American University speech, call for a re-examination of U.S. attitudes toward the Soviet Union. He was unwilling to intervene in Laos and instead negotiated a cease-fire and coalition government—which the C.I.A. refused to honor, preferring to back a right-wing militarist faction that continued the war.

Kennedy was seen by the national security establishment as a danger. Right-wingers referred to him as "that delinquent in the White House." That Alexander doesn't see him that way does not mean the C.I.A. shared his view. In any case, even if Kennedy was a total C.I.A. tool, the fact that the President can be assassinated with impunity by elements in the national security state raises grave questions about the security of us all. It is a momentous crime that should be uncovered. Exposing such crimes is an important part of democratic fightback, an important part of our struggle to delegitimate the national security state. This is why Oliver Stone's *JFK* does a great service.

Reprinted by permission of the author.

COCKBURN REPLIES

Alexander Cockburn

The main point of *JFK*, writes one of the co-authors of its script, Zachary Sklar, was to demonstrate the existence of institutions more powerful than any elected official. The main point of my column was that J.F.K. always acted within the terms of those institutions and that, against the script's assertions, there is no evidence to the contrary. The film is premised on a lie. By its standards of analysis the "national security state" should have murdered L.B.J. during the 1964 presidential campaign on the ground that Barry Goldwater was more in tune with its interests, and should similarly have assassinated Ronald Reagan after the Reykjavik summit, where he nearly gave Gorbachev the store while lauding Lenin (for which enthusiasm he was sharply reproved by *The Washington Post*).

Both Sklar and Peter Dale Scott invoke John Newman's recent book *JFK and Vietnam* to buttress the thesis that whereas J.F.K. was committed to withdrawal from Vietnam, L.B.J. reversed this posture within days of the assassination in Dallas. Newman's work is a stew of muddled chronologies and unproven assertions that Kennedy was a closet dove seeking to maneuver around the superhawks, like Gen. Maxwell Taylor. Aside from some conversations recollected by men such as Kennedy's political operative Kenny O'Donnell or Senators Wayne Morse and Mike Mansfield, Newman offers nothing to back up his claim that J.F.K. nourished, little more than a year after the start of his presidency, a plan for disengagement. Meanwhile, Newman has to deal with J.F.K.'s numerous

There were plenty of those. Mid-July 1963, as quoted in J.F.K.'s *Presidential Papers*: "In my opinion, for us to withdraw from that effort would mean a collapse not only of South Vietnam, but Southeast Asia, so we are going to stay there." September 9, 1963, to David Brinkley: "What I am concerned about is that Americans will get impatient and say because they don't like events in Southeast Asia, or they don't like the government in Saigon, that we should withdraw. That only makes it easy for the Communists. I think we should stay." The public record shows J.F.K. was always hawkish. With a willful credulity akin to religious mania, Newman insists that J.F.K. was dissembling, concealing his private thoughts, throwing the hawks off track. Out of such data-free surmises he constructs his fairy tale. The evidence he assembles to underpin these false surmises proves exactly the opposite of his thesis.

What in fact was going on during his phase of the Vietnam War is not complicated. As Scott concedes in his letter, the famous 1,000-man withdrawal was proposed by Secretary of Defense Robert McNamara and General Taylor (though Scott seems to find nothing odd about the fact that the "strenuously suppressed record" of J.F.K.'s pacific strategy originated in part with superhawk Taylor) because, buoyed by euphoric reports from the field, at that time they thought the war was going according to plan and victory was in sight. There were also domestic political reasons for the adoption of such a course. But a qualifier was always there. Withdrawal of advisers could begin, "providing things go well," to quote one Pentagon official. Take J.F.K.'s answer in a May 22, 1963, press conference: "We are hopeful that the situation in Vietnam would permit some withdrawal in any case by the end of the year, but we can't possibly make that judgment at the present time. There is a long hard struggle to go." The minutes to the discussion of NSAM 263 have J.F.K. saying the same thing: "The action [withdrawal of 1,000 men] should be carried out routinely as part of our general posture of withdrawing people when they are no longer needed." And in implementing the withdrawal order, J.F.K. directed that "no further reductions in U.S. strength would be made until the requirements of the 1964 [military] campaign were clear." Remember that already by the end of 1961 J.F.K. had made the decisive initial commitment to military intervention, and that a covert campaign of terror and sabotage against the North was similarly launched under his aegis.

In his letter and also in his 1972 essay Scott makes a big point of contrasting J.F.K.'s supposed reluctance to articulate an overriding military "objective" in Vietnam against L.B.J.'s endorsement (in the opening paragraph of NSAM 273, signed on November 26, 1963) of the "win" posture as soon as he assumed the presidency. This distinction is pure philological fakery. On November 13, 1963, *The New York Times* published an interview with Michael Forrestal, a senior member of J.F.K.'s National Security Council, in which he said, "It would be folly ... .at the present time" to pursue "a negotiated settlement ... between North and South Vietnam." J.F.K. himself, in a November 14 press conference addressing the situation in the wake of the Diem coup and discussing the upcoming Honolulu summit on Vietnam policy, said: "We do have a new situation there, and a new government, we hope, an increased effort in the war." He added, "Now, that is our object, to bring Americans home, permit the South Vietnamese to maintain themselves as a free and independent country and permit democratic forces within the country to operate—which they can of course, much more freely when the assault from the inside, and which is manipulated from the North, is ended. So the purpose of the meeting in Honolulu is how to pursue these objectives."

Thus, J.F.K. was defining victory—to be followed by withdrawal of U.S. "advisers"—as ending the internal Communist assault in the South, itself manipulated from the North. Scott charges me with misrepresenting his argument that this posture can be sharply distinguished from the aggressive formulations in the opening statements of NSAM 273. I'm afraid that it is Scott who is being less than forthright with the historical data. In January 1991 the November 21 draft of NSAM 273, as drawn up by J.F.K.'s special assistant for national security affairs, McGeorge Bundy, was declassified. It is cited by Scott's hero, Newman, in a book Scott has endorsed for its "massive documentation" and therefore has presumably read.

As Newman acknowledges, the upshot of the Honolulu meeting was that for "the first time" the "shocking deterioration of the war was presented in detail to those assembled, along with a plan to widen the war, while the 1,000-man withdrawal was turned into a meaningless paper drill." The next day, back in the White House, Bundy put the grim conclusions of the meeting into the draft language of NSAM 237, which, as he told Newman in 1991, he "tried to bring ... in line with the words that Kennedy might want to say." Here is the first paragraph, which Newman says "reiterated the essence of Kennedy's policy":

> It remains the central object of the United States in South Vietnam to *assist* the people and Government of that country to win *their* contest against the externally directed and supported Communist conspiracy. The test of all decisions and U.S. actions in this area should be the effectiveness of their contributions to this purpose. (11/21/63)

Compare that with what Scott argues is the radical shift of NSAM 273 as finalized five days later under L.B.J.:

> It remains the *central objective* of the United States in South Vietnam to assist the people and government of that country *to win* their contest against the externally *directed* and supported Communist *conspiracy. The test of all U.S. decisions and actions in this area should be the effectiveness of their contributions to this purpose.* (11/26/63)

The italics in the first version are added by Newman, and in the second by Scott. They furnish an amusing example of two men trying to tilt, in different directions, virtually identical words. So Scott's whole edifice collapses, helped on its way by the words of the speech J.F.K. was to have delivered at the Dallas Trade

Mart on November 22: "Our assistance to these nations can be painful, risky and costly, as is true in Southeast Asia today. But we dare not weary of the task."

There is no beef either in the famous paragraph 7 of NSAM 273, which in the fantasies of Scott and Newman and Sklar is crucial, and which runs in toto as follows: "Planning should include different levels of possible increased activity, and in each instance there should be estimates of such factors as: A. Resulting damage to North Vietnam; B. The plausibility of denial; C. Possible North Vietnamese retaliation; D. Other international reaction. Plans should be submitted promptly for approval by higher authority." If this paragraph had been drafted on November 20 instead of November 24, Scott, Newman and the others would be excitedly italicizing "*possible* increased activity" as evidence that J.F.K. was avoiding concrete military commitment.

J.F.K. in the last days of his Administration, and L.B.J. in the first days of his, defined victory in the same terms, and both were under similar illusions. As L.B.J. recalled, looking back on his first presidential session on Vietnam on November 24, 1963, "Most of the advisers agreed that we could begin withdrawing some of our advisers by the end of the year and a majority of them by the end of 1965." To conflate such a position with what Galbraith was urging is ridiculous.

What with all his heavy breathing about "deep politics" and "parapolitics," Scott either doesn't know or care very much about the actual, accessible historical record. To start with, he should read more Latin American history. J.F.K. most certainly can be blamed for the coups in Guatemala and the Dominican Republic. To take the latter: J.F.K.'s officials prevented Juan Bosch from mobilizing popular support, the only way a military coup could have ben averted. They blocked land reform and obstructed his attempts to build a strong labor movement. They also refused to let him bring the armed forces under loyal leadership. In November of 1962, U.S. Ambassador John Bartlow Martin pressed the Dominican ruling council to harass and beat opposition figures. Robert Kennedy sent detectives to teach the art of riot control. In 1963, in Ambassador Martin's words about Bosch, the U.S. Embassy decided to "let him go." J.F.K.'s State Department recognized and supported the coup makers after a brief interval. In 1965, L.B.J. repeated J.F.K.'s achievement in nullifying the pro-constitutionalist threat. There was no "new policy" of L.B.J., encouraging coups in countries like Brazil. In 1962 R.F.K. went to Brasilia expressly to lecture President João Goulart on Brazil's "disturbing drift to the left," meaning proposed land reform. Military assistance and supplies of riot control equipment were remitted to the security forces in increasing amounts. C.I.A. slush funds were distributed to right-wingers, and in that same year the prime U.S. adviser to the eventual coup makers, Gen. Vernon Walters, transferred from Rome to Rio as military attaché. Walters later recollected that at the time of his transfer he was told that President Kennedy would not be averse to Goulart's overthrow. Perhaps this is all too "foundationalist" for Scott.

So far as corporate and bureaucratic pressures are concerned, Wall Street didn't turn against Vietnam until 1968, following the min-recession of 1966-67 and the Tet offensive. All in all, Scott reminds me of an amateur paleontologist scrambling off the fossil heap with the jaw of a dog, which he clamorously misidentifies as irrefutable proof of the missing link. His self-serving characterizations of the "establishment left" strike me as silly, also as evidence of a rather pathetic persecution mania. First he shouts for attention, then he says I was unfair for citing him rather than Newman. Scott has done some interesting work (e.g., on the Indonesian coup of 1965), but his foolish performance here is indicative of how J.F.K. addles intellectuals. Incidentally, in the "what if" department, one can easily argue that J.F.K., confident of having the liberals on his side, would have escalated harder and quicker than L.B.J., who had no such confidence in liberal support.

Michael Parenti is fighting a straw man. I never discounted the role of human agency, any more than did those who in 1968 thought Richard Nixon more likely to get the United States out of Vietnam than Hubert Humphrey, a highly tenable position. Would Bill Clinton or Paul Tsongas be "better" for Cuba in 1993 than George Bush? Maybe. Would Bush be "better" for the Palestinians? Possibly. There are, nonetheless, tendencies in U.S. capitalism, reflected in the policies of the élites, that have been demonstrably bad for Cuba and for Palestinians, whatever individual has been inhabiting the White House. Kennedy never challenged those tendencies or ran athwart them. (It was L.B.J. who ended Operation Mongoose.)

"Even if Kennedy was a total C.I.A. tool," Parenti concludes, "the fact that the President can be assassinated with impunity by elements in the national security state raises grave questions about the security of us all." Many of those writing to *The Nation* to abuse me apropos *JFK* made the same claim. But it isn't "a fact." It's a supposition, and even assuming the supposition were true, how was Parenti's safety placed in grave question? In politico/military/national security terms, probably the greatest threat to Parenti's safety came when J.F.K. brought the world to the brink of destruction during the Cuban missile crisis.

JFK teeters between fascism and liberalism. In the idiom of the former, Stone has Garrison speak of the betrayed and slain "father-leader" whose children we are and whose revenge must be consummated before America can be free. On the liberal side of the ledger, Stone constantly promotes the idea, both in *JFK* and in other pronouncements, that J.F.K. was a good President, would have pulled out of Vietnam, made peace with Castro, caused the lion to lie down with the lamb.

Stone tries to have things both ways. He maintains that *JFK* is all true until someone demonstrates forcibly that it isn't. Then he tilts the other way and claims he is trying to construct an alternative myth. We should leave this "alternative myth" talk to the deconstruction industry. Myth making is two-edged sword. Disraeli promoted a Jews-run-the-world theory; not so many years later the authors of the *Protocols of the Elders of Zion* happily expanded on the theme. The wizardry of the film lab, which can produce a grainy news film of L.B.J. making deals with the masterminds of J.F.K.'s assassination—part of Stone's mythic truth—can also produce Arafat urging Sirhan to kill R.F.K. Every artist deals in myth, but anyone arguing for Stone's manipulation of history should be aware of the morally tricky terrain and of the downside of myth making.

There's no "golden key" (e.g., the "truth" about the Kennedy assassination; "proof" that George Bush flew to Paris on October 20, 1980) that will suddenly render the overall system transparent and vulnerable. People who look for golden keys are akin to those poor souls who thought the future could be decoded by measurements in the Great Pyramid.

A couple of house-cleaning points. The passing of Newman's book to Warner via Ellen Ray, Bill Schaap and Oliver Stone was something mentioned to me by Zack Sklar in the same phone conversation I had with him in Los Angeles, when I called him to get the exact words of Kevin Costner's Hamlet speech. Zack very decently looked up the script and dictated the passage to me, adding amid my reproaches for his role in formulating such revolting sentiments that it had been Stone's work alone. It turns out that Stone lifted the passage almost intact from Carl Oglesby's afterword to Jim Garrison's *On the Trail of the Assassins*. And I'm sorry to have said Ellen Ray started the whole cycle on account of Catholic girlhood in Massachusetts. I thought it was true when I wrote it, and didn't think it a particularly low blow. Frankly I was and remain baffled by the spectacle of the editors of *Covert Action Information Bulletin* and *Lies of Our Times* promoting false history and bad politics.

Parenti says the left should support Oliver Stone and his *JFK* because the film does a "great service" in the delegitimation of a national security state that exterminated a leader who dared entertain critical views about such a state. This is core bunkum. What "great service" is being done here? The answer offered by one letter writer was that "*JFK* is one of the most important films of our time because Stone is literally *causing millions of people to think* [his italics], to wonder and ask questions. As a bonus, perhaps they will go to the polling booths in November to demand answers." But people are being asked to think about something that isn't true, so they'll be asking the wrong questions and thus getting useless answers. The effect of *JFK* is to make people think that America is a good country that produced a good President killed by bad élites who also nearly destroyed the good investigator of the crime. This is an infantile, inactivist prescription for politics, essentially inviting people to put their faith in another good President, whose inevitable foul-up can then be blamed on the same bad élites. In New Hampshire in mid-February, Daniel Patrick Moynihan stood in Nashua, citing it as J.F.K.'s first campaign stop in 1960, quoting J.F.K.'s call for "a new generation to lead this nation" and adding in praise of the candidate standing next to him, "John Kennedy was right then and Bob Kerrey is right today." This is the answer people leaving *JFK* and searching for answers in the polling booths will get. For the left in 1992, trying to figure out how to foster the mass movements of tomorrow, *JFK* offers nothing but another dose of lies about the past.

THE VILLAGE VOICE

JFK: HOW THE MEDIA ASSASSINATED THE REAL STORY

Robert Hennelly and Jerry Policoff

If the assassination of John Fitzgerald Kennedy was one of the darkest tragedies in the republic's history, the reporting of it has remained one of the worst travesties of the American media. From the first reports out of Dallas in November of 1963 to the merciless flagellation of Oliver Stone's *JFK* over the last several months, the mainstream media have disgraced themselves by hewing blindly to the single assassin theory advanced by the F.B.I. within hours of the murder. Original, enterprise reporting has been left almost entirely to alternative weeklies, monthly magazines, book publishers, and documentary makers. All such efforts over the last 29 years have met the same fate as Oliver Stone's movie: derision from the mainstream media.

At first, the public bought the party line. But gradually, as more and more information slipped through the margins of the media business, and finally through the efforts of Congress itself, the public began to change its mind. Today, according to a recent New York Times/CBS poll, an astounding 77 per cent of Americans reject the Warren Report's conclusions. How did such a tremendous credibility gap come about? And, assuming that the majority of Americans are right, how did a free press so totally blow one of the biggest stories of the century? To find out, *The Village Voice* has reviewed hundreds of documents bearing on the media's coverage of the assassination and has discovered a pattern of collusion and co-optation that is hardly less chilling than the prospect of a conspiracy to kill the president.

In particular, *The New York Times*, *Time-Life*, CBS and NBC have striven mightily to protect the single-assassin hypothesis, even when that has involved the suppression of information, the coercion of testimony, and the misrepresentation of key evidence. *The Voice* has discovered that: Within days of the assassination, the Justice Department quashed an editorial in *The Washington Post* that called for an independent investigation; within weeks the F.B.I. was able to crow that NBC had pledged not to report anything beyond what the F.B.I. itself was putting before the American people; only four hours after the murder, *Life* magazine grabbed up one of the main pieces of evidence-the Zapruder film—misrepresenting the content to millions of readers in its very first post-assassination issue and then continuing the lie with ever-changing captions and Zapruder frames in its special issue supporting the Warren Commission report; in

1967, a supposedly independent CBS documentary series on the assassination was in face secretly reviewed and seemingly altered by former Warren Commission member John Jay McCloy, through a "Dad says" memo written by his daughter Ellen McCloy, then administrative assistant of CBS News president Richard Salant; within that same CBS series , the testimony of Orville Nix- an amateur filmmaker who captured "the grassy knoll" angle on tape—was tailored to fit the requirements of CBS's Warren Commission slant

Much of this unethical and immoral practice was accomplished under the pretext of "sparing the Kennedy family." Indeed, the coverage of the assassination was complicated by the cross-identification between reporters and the president. The Kennedys were the first, and possibly the last, American political family to so thoroughly cultivate the fourth estate; in the aftermath of the assassination, the media completely relinquished its usual skepticism and opened the door for the government to do whatever it found most expedient.

What possible motive could the national media have for failing to properly investigate the Kennedy murder? Perhaps they were genuinely seduced by this "Camelot" they themselves created. And if anyone was going to end Camelot, far better for the memories, far better for the family, that it be a lone psycho than a conspiracy. And if the media were solicitous to the Kennedys in this way, they were positively patronizing to the citizenry. It was Vietnam all over again: the war was good for the country, so don't report how badly it was going; a conspiracy to kill the president would be demoralizing at home and humiliating abroad, so sweep under the rug any evidence pointing in that direction. And then of course there was the national security issue. Many of the editors who were calling the shots on assassination coverage had come out of World War II. Their country took precedence over the truth- the C.I.A. and F.B.I. were entitled to the benefit of the doubt; the "free press" was sometimes confused with the Voice of America. J. Edgar Hoover, supreme patriarch of the F.B.I. and all-powerful with a distraught Robert Kennedy out of the way, knew just how to exploit the opportunity. Deputy Attorney General Nicholas Katzenbach recalls that Robert Kennedy, attorney general at the time, was so despondent he didn't even see the point of an investigation. "What the hell's the difference? He's gone," Katzenbach remembers R.F.K. saying before handing over the reins.

Just three days after the assassination, an internal Justice Department memo from Katzenbach to Bill Moyers, then a top aide to Lyndon Johnson, spelled out the Justice Department strategy, a strategy that would prevail to a shocking degree right through the end of the decade:

"1. The public must be satisfied that Oswald was the assassin; that he did not have confederates who are still at large; and that the evidence was such that he would have been convicted at trial.

2. Speculation about Oswald's motivation ought to be cut off, and we should have some basis for rebutting thought that this was a Communist conspiracy or (as the Iron Curtain press is saying) a right-wing conspiracy to

blame it on the Communists. Unfortunately the facts on Oswald seem about too pat—too obvious (Marxist, Cuba, Russian wife, etc.). The Dallas police have put out statements on the Communist conspiracy theory, and it was they who were in charge when he was shot and thus silenced."

Katzenbach, whose memo sets out the Warren report results a year before the commission reached them, suggests that a "Presidential Commission of unimpeachable personnel" be appointed to examine evidence and reach conclusions. In closing he writes, "I think, however, that a statement that all the facts will be made public property in an orderly and responsible way should be made now. We need something to head off public speculation or Congressional hearings of the wrong sort."

Such a statement was indeed made, and of course the facts, the files, the evidence never were made public in their entirety. As it turned out, the speculation took years; new Congressional hearings, decades. Today, Katzenbach realizes that allowing Hoover's agents to control the flow of information was a little like letting the fox guard the henhouse. The Senate Church committee report that came out in 1976 confirmed that while investigating the murder "top F.B.I. officials were continually concerned with protecting the Bureau's reputation." Even Katzenbach concedes that Hoover would never "let the agency be embarrassed by any information on the bureau itself. He just would never show it. But how would you know it? What could you do?"

According to an F.B.I. memo obtained by *The Voice*, it didn't take the F.B.I. or the Justice Department long to get the the press under control. On November 25, 1963, the White House learned that *The Washington Post* planned an editorial calling for the convening of a presidential commission to investigate the assassination. Though Lyndon Johnson planned to do just that, the strategy was to get the F.B.I. report out first. The memo states that Katzenbach called *Washington Post* editor Russell Wiggins and told him that "the Department of Justice seriously hoped that the '*Washington Post*' would not encourage any specific means" by which the facts should be made available to the public.

The memo also describes a conversation an F.B.I. agent had with Al Friendly, *The Washington Post*'s managing editor, discouraging publication of the editorial and suggesting that it would "merely 'muddy the waters' and would create further confusion and hysteria." The editorial never appeared. Later that day Hoover triumphantly boasted in another F.B.I. memo that "I called Mr. Walter Jenkins at the White House and advised him that we had killed the editorial in *The [Washington] Post*."

The F.B.I. had the electronic media wired as well. A December 11, 1963, teletype from the F.B.I. office in New York to J. Edgar Hoover indicates that NBC had given the bureau assurances that it would "televise only those items which are in consonance with bureau report [on the assassination]." The eight-page F.B.I. message details the substance of NBC's research, including the development of leads. "NBC has movie film taken at some one hundred and fifty feet showing a Dallas Police Dept. officer rushing into book depository building while most of police and Secret Service were rushing up an incline towards railroad trestle [in front of the motorcade]."

THE NEW YORK TIMES

The paper of record, *The New York Times*, led the newsprint pack with the official story. Months before the Warren Commission report was released *Times* writer Anthony Lewis got a special exclusive preview and his June 1, 1964, page-one article presented its findings in positively glowing terms; over the years he has continued to attack Warren Commission critics as well as Oliver Stone's film.

Lewis has told *The Voice* that his close ties with the Kennedys, specifically Robert, made "it very painful to me personally. Over the years I felt I did not want to get involved as a counterexpert or expert. Maybe with all that has happened, Vietnam and Watergate, today's reporters would have come to it with more resistance. There was at the time a predisposition for the society as a whole to believe."

But can "lost innocence" account wholly for the mangling of history and management of information that the major media engaged in during that period? For *The Times*, creating a supportive climate for the Warren report seemed an institutional imperative. *The Times* was going to run the report in the paper and then go commercial with it: collaborating with the Book of the Month Club and Bantam Books to publish it in September of 1964.

On May 24, 1964, Clifton Daniel of *The Times* wrote Warren Commission Chief Counsel J. Lee Rankin expressing gratitude to Chief Justice Earl Warren for facilitating publication of the Warren report. Certainly any vigorous critical evaluation of the Commission's findings at this juncture would have jeopardized this great relationship.

The Times did not quit with the Warren report. Two months after the Warren report was released, *The Times* collaborated with McGraw-Hill and Bantam on *The Witnesses*, a book of testimony from the Warren Commission hearings edited by *The Times*. The accounts of those witnesses whose testimony deviated the slightest from the official story were simply edited out. Not included, for instance, was one man's testimony to the Warren Commission that on the day of J.F.K.'s murder he had see two men on the sixth floor of the Texas Book Depository, where the official lin, says there was just Oswald. The F.B.I. told this witness to "forget it." His references to shots coming from the railroad yards in front of the president were also deleted. In addition, the section of the transcript where three Secret Service agents' autopsy observations contradict the official autopsy report was deleted. No wonder readers of this expurgated version of the commission's report became true believers.

With the issuance of the Warren report, Oswald became the assassin. (Although from the very beginning—with a November 1963 *Life* article on Oswald headlined "The Assassin: A Cold Lonely Man Who Resented All Authority"—there was no presumption of innocence and little inclination to consider other explanations.) As time went on and inconsistencies began to surface, it became harder to accept the Warren report findings. *The Times* did its best to downplay this revisionist thinking, with one of the most blatant examples being John Leonard's December 1970 *New York Times* review of two Kennedy assassination books—Jim Garrison's *A Heritage of Stone* and James Kirkwood's *American Grotesque.* In the early edition of the paper the headline read, "Who Killed John F. Kennedy?" and the review itself contained two long paragraphs challenging the Warren Commission, subtitled "Mysteries Persist." "But until somebody explains …," wrote Leonard, "why a 'loner' like Oswald always had friends and could always get a passport— who can blame the Garrison guerillas for fantasizing? Something stinks about the whole affair." Within hours, these hard-hitting paragraphs disappeared from the review and the headline was altered to read, "The Shaw-Garrison Affair."

Leonard told *The Voice* he was never able to trace down the person responsible for the changes. "Not the bullpen, not the culture desk, not even Abe Rosenthal knew how it happened. We've every right to be paranoid," Leonard says.

TIME-LIFE

While *The Times* was busy selling the Warren Commission story, *Life* magazine went one step beyond that, actively intervening to spirit away crucial physical evidence in the case. Aside from swooping down on Oswald's wife and mother and sequestering them in a hotel room to protect *Life*'s exclusive interviews, *Life* was in Dallas making arrangements to buy the original Zapruder film only four hours after the assassination. Of the four existing home movies taken that day in Dealey Plaza, the 8mm film, shot by a middle-aged dress manufacturer, was considered to be the best record of J.F.K.'s murder. According to Richard Stolley, who is currently the editorial director of Time Inc. and who handled the Zapruder transaction for *Life*, the order to acquire the film and "withhold it from public viewing" came from *Life*'s publisher, C. D. Jackson. And who was C. D. Jackson? A staunch anticommunist who played a crucial role in the direction of U.S. policy throughout the 1950s, both as "psychological war advisor to Eisenhower and as a member of anticommunist front groups, Jackson's publication had long been known for "always pulling chestnuts out of the fire for the C.I.A.," as the late Drew Pearson once put it.

Having shelled out $150,000 for the film (the Zapruder family attorney claims the number was even higher), Stolley headed back to New York with the original print under his arm, leaving investigators with a copy that was next to worthless in terms of forensic analysis. By permitting the chain of custody to include Life magazine, and by accepting a mere copy of a crucial piece of evidence, the law-enforcement authorities were well on their way to compromising their investigation.

The critical Zapruder film was kept exclusively in the hands of Time Inc. and out of the public's reach for the next 12 years, allowing *Life* to take the American people on one of the longest rides ever in American journalism. In its very first issue after the assassination, *Life* seriously misrepresented the content of the Zapruder film, a practice that would continue until the film finally gained general release in 1975.

The doctors at Parkland Hospital, who had worked on the president, had reported that he had suffered an "apparent" entrance wound to the throat. Since the book depository, from which Oswald had allegedly fired, was to the presidential limousine's rear, how, some were beginning to wonder, did the president suffer a frontal throat wound? Life's December 6, 1963, edition gave a simple and conclusive explanation, based on the Zapruder film, an answer only *Life* could provide.

Wrote *Life* "The 8mm [Zapruder] film shows the President turning his body far around to the right as he waves to someone in the crowd. His throat is exposed to the sniper's nest just before he clutches it."

This description of the Zapruder film went a long way toward allaying fears of conspiracy in those early days, for it explained away a troublesome inconsistency in the lone assassin scenario. There was only one problem: The description of the Zapruder film was a total fabrication. Although the film shows Kennedy turning to the right—toward the grassy knoll, that is—at no time does he turn 180 degrees toward the book depository. Indeed, by the time he is hit, he is once again turning toward the front.

Even this yeoman's effort pales, though, beside *Life*'s October 2, 1964, edition, which was largely committed to the newly released Warren report. Rather than assign a staff writer the job of assessing the committee's work, *Life* gave the assignment to Warren Commission member Gerald Ford.

But it is not the articles in that edition of *Life* that are so extraordinary, but the pictures, and the pains that were taken to rework them so they fit the Warren report perfectly. The October 2, 1964, issue underwent two major revisions after it hit the stands, expensive changes that required breaking and resetting plates twice, a highly unusual occurrence. That issue of *Life* was illustrated with eight frames of the Zapruder film along with descriptive captions.

One version of caption 6 read: "The assassin's shot struck the right rear portion of the President's skull, causing a massive wound and snapping his head to one side." The photo accompanying this caption—frame 323—shows the president slumped back against the seat, and leaning to the left, an instant after the fatal bullet struck him. The photo makes it look as though shots came from the front—the railroad trestle—or the right—the grassy knoll.

A second version of the issue replaces this frame with another, the graphic shot of the president's head exploding (frame 313). Blood fills the air and all details are obscured. The caption, oddly enough, remained the same—describing his head snapping to one side.

A third version carries this same 313 slide—frame 323 has been thrown on the dumpheap of history—but now with a new caption, one that jibes perfectly with the Warren Commission's findings. "The direction from which shots came was established by this picture taken at instant bullet struck the rear of the President's head and, passing through, caused the front part of his skull to explode forward."

Nice try. Of course, as all the world would learn years later, it was the back of the president's skull that would explode, suggesting an exit wound, and sending Jackie Kennedy crawling reflexively across the trunk of the limousine to try to salvage the pieces. But this would not be fully understood until the Zapruder film itself had been seen in its entirety. For the moment, the only people in a position to spot *Life*'s error were the Secret Service, the F.B.I., and possibly the busy pressmen at R. R. Donnelly who must have piled up a lot of overtime trying to keep up with the ever-changing facts. (*Life* wasn't the only publication on the assassination to have bizarre layout problems. The Warren Commission Report itself never addressed the backward motion of the president's head, thus sparing itself the burden of having to explain it. This omission was facilitated by the reversal of the two frames following the explosive frame 313 in the Warren Commission's published volumes, which considerably confused the issue by making it seem as if the head jerked forward. J. Edgar Hoover later blamed the switch on a "printing error.")

Life's exclusive monopoly on the Zapruder film came in just as handy for Dan Rather, CBS's New Orleans bureau chief, who was permitted by Zapruder to see the film before it was whisked off to the vault. Rather told the world he had seen the film and that the president "fell forward with considerable force." (CBS spokesman Tom Goodman told *The Voice* that Rather only got to see the film briefly and viewed it on a "crude hand-cranked 8mm machine.")

What was the effect of these misrepresentations of the Zapruder evidence? One can only guess, but they could well have been crucial to the public's faith in the single assassin theory. British journalist Anthony Summers, author of the book *Conspiracy*, speculates that "if they had shown the film on CBS the weekend of the assassination or at any time the following year there would not have been anyone in America who would not have believed that the shots came from the front of the President and that there was therefore a conspiracy."

Meanwhile, *Life*'s sister publication, *Time*, did its best to swat away any and all conspiracy talk. *Time* countered the ground swell of conspiracy rumors in Europe with an article in its June 12, 1964, issue. Entitled "J.F.K.: The Murder and the Myths," the article blamed the speculation on "leftist" writers and publications seeking a "rightist conspiracy." Proponents of further investigation suffered fates similar to that of Thomas Buchanin, who in 1964 wrote the first book critical of the Warren Report, *Who Killed Kennedy*. Buchanin's thesis was groundless, *Time* argued, because he had allegedly been "fired by the Washington Star in 1948 after he admitted membership in the Communist party."

By late 1966, however, it was getting harder for the media to hold the line. Calls for a reexamination of the Warren report now came from former Kennedy aides Arthur Schlesinger and Richard Goodwin, *The Saturday Evening Post*, the Vatican newspaper L'Osservatore, Walter Lippmann, Cardinal Cushing, William F. Buckley and the American Academy of Forensic Sciences. It was in this climate that The New York

Times initiated its first independent investigation of the assassination.

By 1966 *The Times* seemed to be moving away from its stance of unquestioning support for the Warren report. In a November 1966 editorial the paper acknowledged that there were "Unanswered Questions." Harrison Salisbury, then editor of the op-ed page, called for a new investigation in the pages of *The Progressive*. Salisbury, who had been a solid supporter of the Warren Commission initially, also told *Newsweek* that *The Times* would "go over all the areas of doubt and hope to eliminate them." That investigation lasted for less than a month. The best look inside the brief investigation came in a *Rolling Stone* interview with *New York Times* reporter and assassination investigation team member Martin Waldron. Waldron told *Rolling Stone* that the team found "a lot of unanswered questions" that *The Times* did not choose to pursue.

Even *Life* was beginning to feel the pressure to address the critics and their substantive observations. In 1966 Ed Kerns, Dick Billings, and Josiah Thompson were given the green light to review the Kennedy murder, which would culminate in a magazine series taking a critical look at the Warren Report. Their efforts produced the November 25, 1966, *Life* cover story. "Did Oswald Act Alone? A Matter of Reasonable Doubt." Accompanying the article was an editorial that called for a new investigation. Paradoxically, *Time* in the same week editorially attacked the "phantasmagoria," dismissing both the Warren Commission's doubters and the calls for a new investigation.

Questioned by *The New York Times* about the editorial schism at *Time-Life*, Hedley Donovan, editor in chief of both magazines, said, "We would like to see our magazines arrive at consistent positions on major issues, and I am sure in due course we will on this one."

Indeed. Within months, Billings was told by a superior he won't name, "It is not *Life*'s function to investigate the Kennedy assassination." The investigative team was disbanded. The first article in the series was also the last. But team member Thompson, a former philosophy professor turned private detective, had laboriously made 300 four-by-five transparencies of the suppressed film. After his work with *Life* he kept this cache and resumed work on his book *Six Seconds in Dallas*. Thompson and his publisher, Bernard Geis, sought unsuccessfully to get permission from *Life* to use the Zapruder shots. They offered to turn over all the proceed from the book to the print giant. The answer was still no.

Without the use of the images of the Zapruder film, or at least some facsimile of them, Thompson would have a hard time clinching his argument that Kennedy was hit from the front in the notorious head shot, Zapruder frame 313. After consultation with an attorney, Thompson and Geis decided to have an artist render drawings based on Thompson's slide-by-slide copy of the contraband film.

When the book was ready to be distributed by Random House, the *Time-Life* steamroller puffed into action and threatened Random House with legal action in the event they went ahead and distributed the book. According to Geis, Random House was ready to cave in to Time-Life, and Geis geared up to send trucks over to the Random House warehouse to pick up the books. In the eleventh hour Random House reconsidered and decided to publish *Six Seconds in Dallas*, thus giving the American public its first view, albeit as an artist's rendering, of the most compelling piece of evidence from the assassination of Kennedy. *Life* was so furious that it took Thompson and his publisher to court on a copyright infringement; the magazine lost because it could not claim financial damage—after all, Thompson had offered all the proceeds to Life.

Despite Thompson's expensive victory (all the legal fees fighting Time Inc. consumed the income from his book), the company's grip on the film remained every bit as strong as it had been.

Such efforts, large and small, mostly succeeded in keeping the Warren critics marginalized. But finally, the lid blew off in 1975 when activist Dick Gregory and optics expert Robert Groden approached Geraldo Rivera with a newly unearthed clear copy of the Zapruder film. Finally, the American public was to see the Zapruder film in its entirety, unmediated by any editors or censors.

ABC's *Good Night America* show was the first national television airing of the film to include the deadly frame 313. (Pirated copies had started to crop up in the mid '60s but were of such poor quality they had no dramatic impact.) "It was one of those things where I said [to ABC], 'It gets on or I walk,'" Rivera told *The Voice*. ABC relented, but only after Rivera agreed to sign a waiver accepting sole financial responsibility if *Time* or the Zapruder family sued.

Rivera maintains that Time-Life did not sue because "they were blown away by the reaction to the program." The airing of the Zapruder film on Rivera's show was a catalyst for renewed interest in the murder and ultimately culminated in four congressional investigations into various aspects of the controversy. It is probably no accident that Time-Life sold the original film back to Zapruder's estate for one dollar the following month. (Today, for $75—with costs waived for poor scholars—you can view a VHS copy of the film. The Zapruder estate recently turned down an offer to turn the frames into baseball cards.)

Oliver Stone's movie *JFK* relies on the Zapruder film to support the film's central contention that Kennedy's fatal wound came from the front, and that therefore a conspiracy existed. Referring to the 8mm film, Stone told *The Voice*: "It was key. It is the best smoking gun we have to date."

Despite the compelling use of the Zapruder film in Stone's movie, the man who helped acquire it for Time-Life remains convinced that the Warren Commission got it right and that Oswald did in fact shoot Kennedy from the book depository. "There is nothing in the Zapruder film which contradicts the Warren Report," says Dick Stolley. Oddly enough, the man who shot the film, Abraham Zapruder, according to an article authored by Stolley in the November 1973 *Esquire*, told the *Life* reporter, "My first impression was that the shots were coming from behind me"—that is, from the infamous grassy knoll.

Stolley now maintains that the urge to control the Zapruder film had to do with beating out the competition. If the competition was a contest to suppress the most evidence possible, then *Life* certainly won hands down. But if the competition Stolley refers to is journalistic competition, One wonders why *Life* bothered. Take, for instance, the case of CBS's documentary series on the assassination, which aired in June of 1967.

CBS

CBS decided to go ahead with a documentary series in the fall of 1966, as the cynicism about the assassination continued to mount. Books on the subject were starting to stimulate a national debate. Reports on the suppression of crucial evidence—including the fact the Warren Commission never even saw the actual autopsy photos and x-rays of J.F.K.—had became parlor talk around the country. Buzz phrases like "magic bullet" were being used for the first time to express a growing cynicism. Public opinion polls indicated that a majority of the respondents had begun to doubt that Oswald was the whole story.

The CBS effort was nothing if not monumental. Whereas those who had come before had used fixed targets to test the magic bullet hypothesis, CBS went a giant step further, rigging up a moving target. But the money and manpower thrown at the project was undercut all along the way by errors in procedure and logic; if not motive. For instance, in trying to determine whether Oswald could possibly have fired all the rounds believed to have been squeezed off in Dealey Plaza, CBS used a rifle that was faster than Oswald's: capable of three shots in 4.1 seconds as opposed to 4.6 seconds for Oswald's. The 11 CBS marksmen fired 37 firing runs of three shots each; of those, an amazing 17 of the 37 runs were disqualified as Cronkite said "because of trouble with the rifle." And, even with their faster guns and time to practice, the 11 marksmen averaged 5.6 seconds to get off their three shots, with an average of 1.2 hits. Oswald, a notoriously bad shot firing with a slower gun, is alleged to have done much better-three shots and two direct hits in 5.6 seconds, with no warm-up. CBS neglected to inform its viewers of the poor total average hit ratio.

How did CBS interpret these rifle tests? "It seems reasonable to say that an expert could fire that rifle in five seconds," intoned Walter Cronkite. "It seems equally reasonable to say that Oswald, under normal circumstances, would take longer. But these were not normal circumstances. Oswald was shooting at a president. So our answer is: probably fast enough."

Such lapses may well be explained by a perusal of internal CBS documents, generated in preparation for the 1967 documentary, that have been obtained by *The Voice*. The documents show the highly unusual role played by one Ellen McCloy, who for years had served as the administrative assistant to Richard Salant, head of CBS News. During the production of the CBS series, McCloy was one of only a handful of people who was cc'd on all 10 memos obtained by *The Voice* concerning the work in progress. (McCloy and Salant contend there was nothing unusual in this arrangement as she routinely received copies of Salant's correspondence.) But in this instance, she was more than a passive recipient, filing duplicates for her boss. She was passing along not her own opinions but those of "Dad." Ellen McCloy's father, John J. McCloy, had not only served on the Warren Commission but had been Assistant Secretary of War, High Commissioner for West Germany, chair of the World Bank, chair of Chase Manhattan Bank, and head of the Ford Foundation. According to Kai Bird, author of the soon to be released biography *The Chairman: John 'Jay McCloy—the Making of the American Establishment* McCloy was "the guy who greased the wheels between the world of Wall Street big foundations, and Washington." McCloy himself acknowledged his agenda: showing that America was not "a banana republic where a government can be changed by conspiracy."

Not only did McCloy appear in CBS's documentary, he also lurked about in the shadows, helping to steer and shape. A handwritten note on CBS stationery from Ellen McCloy to Les Midgley, producer of the series, gives the reader a feel for the close relationships between the McCloys and the CBS bunch. The memo reads:

> One comment that *Dad* [emphasis added] made after reading the 'rough script' Mr. Salant wanted me to pass on to you. It concerned a sentence (—or two—) that appears on the top of page 5C .... *Dad* said: 1) he had no recollection of the President (L.B.J.) asking or urging the members of the Warren Commission to act 'with speed.' 2) The phrase 'In less than a year' again implies that the commission might have acted in haste. *Dad* suggests that you might say 'after 8 1/2 months.... '   —Ellen

Or again:

> *Dad* asked me to give you the enclosed. He said it shouldn't be considered a bribe ... maybe it's just a gift as the result of the birth of Luci's baby. 'The old man' thanks you very much for the booklet!!! —Ellen

On July 20, 1967, Midgley sent a letter to John McCloy thanking him for his "extremely kind and generous comments," adding, "Another member of your family also sweated this all out with us and did a fine job."

Salant now contends that Ellen McCloy's presence on the CBS payroll did not prejudice the documentaries. "Should who her father was have disqualified her from the job?" he asks. "She was a very able lady. She worked for me for six years."

Ellen McCloy concurs that she herself did nothing to influence the editorial content of the documentaries. "I would act as a conduit," McCloy explained. "I would take things home and they would ask me to ask my dad this or that."

He and producer Midgley remain proud of the series, and believe it holds up. "It still is the major journalistic inquiry into this 25 years later ... it was an independent inquiry." But the McCloy memos, and a few others, certainly raise a question about how open-minded and thoroughgoing CBS was. Take, for instance, this April 26, 1967, memo from Salant to Midgley: "Is the question of whether Oswald was a C.I.A. or F.B.I. informant really so substantial that we have to deal with it?"

The answer was, maybe. In CBS's June 28, 1967, program, Cronkite does indeed refer to Oswald's F.B.I. connection in the following fashion:

The question of whether Oswald had any relationship with the F.B.I. or the C.I.A. is not frivolous. The agencies, of course, are silent. Although the Warren Commission had full power to conduct its own independent investigation, it permitted the F.B.I. and the C.I.A. to investigate themselves—and so cast a permanent shadow on the answers.

Although Salant asserts to this day that CBS was only after the truth, a recently released documentary indicates otherwise. Danny Schechter's *Beyond 'JFK': The Question of Conspiracy*, features Walter Cronkite conceding that CBS News in 1970 censored Lyndon Johnson's own doubts about the lone-assassin theory. Cronkite tells Schecter that Johnson invoked "national security" to get CBS to edit out his remarks long after they had been captured on film Cronkite and CBS of course, reflexively complied.

But perhaps nothing revealed CBS's prejudice in the series more tellingly than the network's treatment of Orville Nix, a man who was wielding a movie camera across from the grassy knoll on that fateful day.

Nix, who had worked for the General Service Administration as an air conditioning repairman in the Dallas Secret Service building, sold his footage to UPI for $5000 in 1963. But, according to his granddaughter Gayle Nix Jackson, the film only brought him heartache. "The F.B.I. had issued a dictum to all of Dallas's film labs that any assassination photos had to be turned over to the F.B.I. immediately," recalls Gayle Jackson. "The lab called my granddad first and, like the good American he was, he rushed it to the F.B.I.." Nix had to turn his camera over to the F.B.I. as well. "They took the camera for five months. They said they needed to analyze it. They returned it in pieces," recalls Jackson.

In 1967 Nix dutifully turned out for the CBS re-creation. Recalls his granddaughter: "His turn came to reenact what he saw. They said, 'Mr. Nix, where did the shots come from?' He said, 'From over there on that grassy knoll behind the picket fence.' Then it would be, 'Cut!' We went through this six or seven times and each time it was 'Cut!' And then a producer stepped forward and said, 'Orville, where did the Warren Commission say the shots came from?' My granddad said, 'Well, the Texas Book Depository.' The producer said, 'That's what you need to say.'"

CBS producer Bernard Birnbaum, who worked on the documentary, denies the exchange. "We never tried to put any words in anybody's mouth, absolutely not," he told *The Voice*. Birnbaum says CBS did give Warren Commission critics air time and cites a segment of the documentary where another eyewitness contends shots came from the grassy knoll. "We were looking to disprove everything," he insists.

According to Jackson, her grandfather also told CBS that there were four shots fired during the assassination, an observation subsequently endorsed by the House Select Committee on Assassinations in 1975, based on controversial acoustical evidence. But what did the CBS viewing audience hear from Nix? "Bang, bang, bang," as if to suggest that Nix also subscribed to the three-bang theory.

After being browbeaten by CBS, Orville Nix, a normally mild-mannered man, became furious. "He was hitting the steering wheel on the ride back home saying, 'Why are they trying to make me feel like I am insane?'" Jackson recalls. She remembers that a year or so later, when District Attorney Jim Garrison called for Nix to testify, her grandfather wouldn't talk. He was afraid for his life.

How many other witnesses experienced the Orville Nix you-never-heard/saw-that phenomenon we will never know. But one other was Kenny O'Donnell, a confidant and adviser to J.F.K. who was in the motorcade. In Tip O'Neill's book *Man of the House*, O'Neill describes a conversation with O'Donnell, who told him he was sure that two shots had come from the fence behind the grassy knoll. O'Neill said to O'Donnell, "That's not what you told the Warren Commission." O'Donnell responded, "You're right, I told the F.B.I. what I had heard, but they said it couldn't have happened that way and that I must have been imagining things. So I testified the way they wanted me to. I just didn't want to stir up any more pain and trouble for the family."

Since Orville Nix's death in 1988, his granddaughter, a former loss-prevention executive, has been waging a one-woman war to get the original film back from UPI. She wants it analyzed to reveal the details that a copy does not provide. "You know my granddad believed in the Texas handshake, and that is how he made his deal with UPI." According to Jackson, the rights to the film were to revert to Nix's estate in 1988. After initially getting a green light from UPI for the return of the film, the then-media giant informed her that the attorney that granted her request was "no longer with the company." She was told to wait until 1991. Then on June 4, 1991. came a note from UPI's general counsel. Frank Kane. "UPI agrees that, in accordance with the oral agreement ... UPI hereby releases all rights over the Nix Film to Mr. Nix's heirs and assigns."

There was only one problem. UPI no longer had the film. Jackson received a letter saying the film had gone to the Warren Commission and was supposedly housed in the National Archives. With the Warren Commission out of business, she contacted the National Archives only to learn that the original was not there either.

The last official place the film was said to have been was in the House Select Committee on Assassinations files. That Committee was convened in 1975 to investigate the assassinations of John Kennedy and Martin Luther King. The chief counsel for the HSCA, G. Robert Blakey, who has a penchant for gagging his staff via mandatory secrecy oaths, came clean with Nix's granddaughter about the fate of the family heirloom, says Jackson. "Blakey's the only one who takes full responsibility for the loss of the film because it was his committee that was supposed to assure that all evidence was returned to the rightful owner," Jackson says. So much for posterity's view of the grassy knoll on November 22, 1963.

A former HSCA staff member, Gaeton Fonzi, recalls that back at the time of the hearings the staff "heard rumors that Blakey planned to classify all of the committee files, but we didn't believe them because that would be too reminiscent of what the Warren Commission had done." In fact, many of the files were classified and this same man, Blakey, is the one who has been recently assigned to help draft legislation about what will be released from the original Kennedy assassination files.

FACT COLLIDES WITH FICTION

Today, there are hundreds of thousands of documents relating to the Kennedy assassination kept from public scrutiny in classified files. But it is growing harder for the American public to accept the government's suppression of these files. The Cold War's over, right? *The New York Times* runs photos of East Germans knee-deep in covert Stasi files. *60 Minutes* takes us into the depths of the KGB labyrinth to find Lenin's brain, yet the nation has to be content with Bob Gates offering up state secrets from World War I.

What is the C.I.A. hiding and what were they afraid to let Americans know about 1963? (With Allen Dulles, former director of the C.I.A., on the Warren Commission the intelligence community had a staunch protector.) Had the government opened its files to assassination investigators tracking the complex globe-trotting of Lee Harvey Oswald between 1959 and 1963, the 1960-1962 attempts on Fidel Castro's life—exploding cigars and poisoned milkshakes—might have been exposed. Years before that information finally leaked out, the public might have learned that the U.S. itself was in the business of assassinating heads of state. Hadn't the White House looked the other way while South Vietnam's President Ngo Dinh Diem was being struck down, just two weeks before J.F.K.'s murder?

It could be argued that, had the media done their job in pursuing the Kennedy assassination story, they would have exposed the situational ethics of America's security apparatus years before Vietnam became a domestic civil war, or Watergate and Iran-contra national disgraces.

Motive in this crime of omission was no doubt a confluence of many elements: a blind patriotism, an institutional paternalism, and a determination to admit no mistakes. Once wedded to the Warren Commission, the editors and reporters who covered the assassination considered even a whisper of conspiracy a form of infidelity. All others, from Mark Lane to Oliver Stone and the hundreds of enterprising reporters in between, were traitors, hysterics.

Throughout the early 1960s, when Walter Cronkite said, "That's the way it is ..." we had no reason to doubt him. The bashing of Oliver Stone's movie *JFK* by the bastions of the American media—CBS, *The New York Times*, *Time*, *Newsweek*, and *The Washington Post*—is said to spring from the sincere desire on the part of the keepers of America's memory to see that our sacred history does not fall prey to revisionist charlatans. While Stone's film does take serious liberty with history, the virulence with which the film has been attacked seems to say more about a defensive press that missed and continues to miss a major story than it does about any flaws in *JFK*.

"When it came to this [reporting on the assassination], the working press was a lobster in a trap," Bill Moyers told *The Voice* "Back then, what government said was the news.... In the 1950s and early '60s, the official view of reality was the agenda for the Washington press corps ... I think it is quite revealing that it's Oliver Stone that's forcing Congress to open up the files and not *The Washington Post*, *The New York Times*, or CBS."

THE MEDIA ON THE MEDIA

Anthony Summers, BBC reporter and author of the book *Conspiracy*. "As I did more and more work on this I became increasingly more ashamed for my mainstream American colleagues ... In 1978 I went to Dallas, 15 years after the assassination, knocking on doors of witnesses. My preamble would be "I'm sure you spoke to everyone back in 1963," and the response would be, much to my surprise, 'No. Where have you been all these years?' The media and in some cases law enforcement, had never spoken to them."

Helen Thomas, UPI correspondent and the unofficial dean of the White House Press Corps, was on the spot reporting the day of the assassination: "We all phoned in stories with tears in our ears, [yet] we never defaulted." Thomas goes on to acknowledge shortcomings in the follow-up reporting: "After Watergate, today we are more skeptical and ther will always be questions. The killing by Ruby of Oswald did raise a question mark ... We were all remiss, period."

Arthur Schlesinger, historian and former special assistant to J.F.K., on Kennedy's murder: "It does seem apparent that a lot of loose trails would have been picked up on by a more alert press."

James Reston, of *The New York Times*, on J.F.K.: "I was always suspect of the charmers. Roosevelt was the first ... You can't avoid the really critical point about the investigation itself into one of the greatest tragedies since Lincoln. It was very natural reaction to the tragedy when the country stopped, but it should have never stopped with so many unanswered questions."

Tom Wicker, covering the assassination as a breaking news story for *The New York Times*, on the presumption of Oswald's guilt: "Nobody ever tried John Wilkes Booth either ... an official report labeled him [the assassin]."

Earl Golz, a reporter for *The Dallas Morning News* and one of the few journalists to follow up on important leads in the Kennedy and Oswald murder stories in the 1970s (including a scoop about the F.B.I.'s dealings with Oswald before the assassination): "I had continuous fights with my editors. Many of them were reporters back in 1963 who were spoon-fed by the F.B.I.." In 1973 Golz used the publication of one of his stories in *The Village Voice* as leverage against his local editors: "I kind of blackmailed them to run it. I said, 'How is it going to look if *The Village Voice* runs this and the *Dallas News* refuses to run it?' They ran it."

Bill O'Reilly, anchor for *Inside Edition* and reporter who announced on February 5 of this year that sealed documents from the House Standing Committee on Assassinations revealed the C.I.A. had lied when they denied a link between Oswald and the agency, and that the C.I.A. had 11 agents infiltrating Jim Garrison's investigation in New Orleans:

"*The New York Times, The Washington Post,* and *The Boston Globe* wouldn't even assign a reporter [to look into this discovery]. They said, 'sorry, we'll pass.' I don't understand it. I thought the press in the U.S. was supposed to seek the news. I am absolutely shocked."

Reprinted by permission of the authors.

APRIL 1992

GOLD COAST

THE KENNEDY ASSASSINATION
STEPPING ON STONE: WHO CAN YOU TRUST?

Gaeton Fonzi

Back in June, I received a letter from Mary Ferrell in Dallas. Mary was among the first critics of the Warren Commission Report and now, almost three decades later, remains one of the most respected researchers dealing with the assassination of President John F. Kennedy. She has never attempted to commercialize her efforts, nor has she shown a narrow-minded devotion to any particular conspiracy theory. So it was particularly significant that Mary Ferrell decided to send a letter to me and other researchers concerning the film that Oliver Stone was making about the Kennedy assassination.

Mary was upset. She was disturbed that Stone was drawing a lot of fire before his film was even finished. She cited sharp attacks from both *Time* magazine and *The Washington Post.* Then *The New York Times* legitimized the criticism with a major piece headlined, "Oliver Stone Under Fire Over the Killing of J.F.K."

What concerned Mary was that the media campaign would likely pick up as Stone moved toward completion of his film and that reporters would probably go hunting among assassination researchers and so-called experts for critical comment to bolster their negative perspectives.

In her letter, Mary pointed out that Stone's movie was a work of fiction, not a documentary. She suggested that "it ill behooves the critical community to detract from Mr. Stone's efforts, particularly before we know the true contents of his production." And, reflecting the decades of frustration in her efforts to get the American public to take a keener interest in one of the most important events in history, Mary noted: "If Oliver Stone's efforts cause massive attention to be focused on the John F. Kennedy assassination, our interests will be well served."

Mary Ferrell's letter seemed justified. Rarely, if ever, has a movie been attacked so vehemently before anybody even saw it and while, in fact, it was still in production.

But the core of the premature condemnation of Stone was not because he was doing a film about the Kennedy assassination but because he had selected Jim Garrison's novel, *On the Trail of the Assassins*, as the base for the movie story and Garrison's assassination theory as its perspective.

Garrison, as you likely know, was the district attorney of New Orleans in 1966 when, in a casual airplane conversation with Senator Russell Long, he was shocked to learn that the veteran Congressional insider had doubts about the validity of the Warren Commission Report. Long suggested that Garrison read not only the Report, but compared its conclusions to the 26 volumes of evidence the Commission quietly released four months after it trumpeted its Report. Garrison did and was shocked when he realized that the Commission's own published evidence did not justify its conclusions. Probing deeper, Garrison stumbled upon information linking Lee Harvey Oswald to certain New Orleans characters and, with that, opened a full-blown criminal investigation into the murder of President Kennedy.

As a result of his erratic conduct during that investigation, the hasty charges he filed against New Orleans businessman Clay Shaw and Shaw's quick acquittal by a jury, Garrison was thoroughly discredited in the news media and by many assassination researchers. He was accused of tampering with evidence, manipulating witnesses and conducting a fraudulent investigation.

Garrison never bowed, even after the Clay Shaw trial debacle. With stentorian vigor, he continued to proclaim his sweeping, broad-brush conclusions about the means, methods and motivations behind the Kennedy assassination. The fact that he had slugged through or around some awful swampy strands of evidence to reach his hammock of solid declarations bothered Garrison not a bit. His point was always the same: Hell, who cares if not all the evidence holds up, look where it leads!

I can see how Oliver Stone would be enthralled by Jim Garrison and his unclouded conclusions about the Kennedy assassination. I recently heard Gary Oldman, who plays the role of Oswald in the film, say of Stone: "The thing about Oliver is that he never stays on the fence. He's not afraid to come down on one side or the other."

Men of lesser pluck have been swallowed by Jim Garrison. A huge, six-foot-six hulk with a melodious voice and a thespian's talent for dramatic intonation, Garrison has the ability to wrap the wildest conclusions in a honeycrust of charm and sincerity. And, on a one-to-one encounter, it's difficult to resist the force of his personality and impossible not to like the guy. I did and still do.

I first met Garrison in 1975 when I was a staff investigator for U.S. Senator Richard Schweiker, then heading a subcommittee of the Senate Intelligence Committee looking into the J.F.K assassination. Schweiker, like most Americans, had accepted the conclusions of the Warren Commission Report without delving into its evidence. But when, as a member of the Intelligence Committee, he learned that the C.I.A. had a long and secret working relationship with Organized

Crime, it shattered a lot of his assumptions about the workings of some government agencies. He decided to review those assumptions. One of the areas of review was the Warren Commission Report. Schweiker set up a subcommittee to investigate the Kennedy assassination only after he had personally evaluated the Commission Report and its volumes of evidence. He especially doubted the Commission's conclusions that Lee Harvey Oswald was a lone nut who had acted precipitously. After delving into the evidence, Schweiker concluded that Oswald was, in fact, a very bright guy whose activities "bore the fingerprints of intelligence." Because that conclusion was partially based on evidence stemming from Oswald's activities in New Orleans, I eventually came to contact Jim Garrison

At our first meeting, I spent a long evening listening to Garrison not only expounding his macrocosmic conspiracy theory, but also detailing some of the many leads his investigation had uncovered. Those critical of Stone's adherence to Garrison's perspective should keep in mind that Garrison's investigation was founded on specific facts about Oswald's adventures in New Orleans.

If Oswald had a political motivation to kill President Kennedy, the Warren Commission concluded, it stemmed from his leftist viewpoint, as demonstrated the summer before the assassination when he handed out pro-Castro leaflets on a New Orleans street corner. He was arrested after a scuffle with an anti-Castro activist and subsequently appeared on a local radio station debate proclaiming his pro-Castro philosophy. He said he headed the local branch of the Fair Play For Cuba Committee. Actually, it was a one-man branch that lasted only long enough for Oswald to publicize himself as a pro-Castro activist. Later investigations into the background of the anti-Castro Cuban he had fought with and into the radio personality who had invited him on his show revealed that both had ties to C.I.A. fronts and the whole incident appeared to be staged.

That's more than an assumption. On some of the leaflets Oswald had handed out the New Orleans address of the Fair Play for Cuba Committee was listed as 544 Camp Street. That was a seedy corner building with a side door that had another address: 531 Lafayette. The Warren Commission's FBI reports tracking Oswald's activities in New Orleans would fail to mention that second address. It happened to be the address of a former highranking FBI agent named Guy Banister. Retired from the Bureau, Banister had opened a private detective agency and was an active John Birch Society right-winger. He was also heavily involved in supplying arms to anti-Castro groups. Records would later reveal that some of his activities were funded by the C.I.A..

A decade after Garrison's investigation, the House Select Committee on Assassinations learned that Oswald had a working association with Banister and a much closer relationship with one of Banister's investigators, David Ferrie. With garish red wig and false eyebrows, Ferrie was a geeky-looking misfit with a brilliant mind and a disordered life. He was a skilled pilot who flew missions for the C.I.A. during the Bay of Pigs invasion and later was involved in running an anti-Castro training camp for Cuban exiles around New Orleans, including members of the Cuban Revolutionary Council, which was also headquartered in 544 Camp Street.

It was Oswald's links to Banister and Ferrie which, in turn, led Garrison to Clay Shaw. Both Shaw and Ferrie were prominent players in New Orleans' homosexual community. And Shaw, too, it would later be learned, had also been a contract agent for the C.I.A..

At Clay Shaw's trial, Jim Garrison attempted to use a variety of sleazy characters to link Shaw and Oswald in the planning of the Kennedy assassination. His best witness, however, would have been David Ferrie. But by the time the trial came around, David Ferrie was dead. Although the coroner concluded that he had died of a cerebral hemorrhage, Ferrie left two suicide notes, both typewritten and unsigned. Another potential Garrison witness, Eladio Del Valle, a close friend and an associate in Ferrie's anti-Castro activities, was killed in Miami a few hours after Ferrie died. Nothing mysterious about his demise, a closeup bullet in the heart. Case yet unsolved.

Garrison's interest in Ferrie went beyond the Oswald connection. Immediately after the Kennedy assassination, Ferrie had driven over a thousand miles to go on what he said was a "goose hunting" trip to Texas. Later investigation revealed that he had simply gone to a skating rink in Houston, waited at its phone booth for two hours until he received a call, and then returned to New Orleans. Garrison believed that Ferrie was kept on line in case his piloting skills were needed immediately after the assassination. Bracing that belief was Ferrie's association with New Orleans Mafia boss Carlos Marcello. Ferrie had secretly flown Marcello back into the United States following Marcello's famous deportation by Attorney General Robert Kennedy in 1961.

There was another key Ferrie link which intrigued Garrison. On the evening before President Kennedy's assassination, Jack Ruby had met with a man named Lawrence Meyers at the Cabana Motel in Dallas. Meyers was an old Chicago chum of Ruby's. With Meyers was a woman named Jean West, whom Meyers would later describe as "a rather dumb but accommodating broad." Garrison discovered in the record of David Ferrie's telephone calls one that he had made on the day that Oswald left New Orleans for his mysterious trip to Mexico City. The call was to a Chicago number registered to Jean West.

Do all those details raise some interesting questions? Sure as hell do. Were any of those questions pursued by the Warren Commission. Sure as hell weren't.

The point is that Garrison's investigation wasn't a wild foraging through an irrelevant thicket of evidence. And if he eventually came to design broad, extravagant conclusions about the C.I.A., the Mafia and anti-Castro Cubans being involved in the assassination of President Kennedy, he wasn't weaving them out of fanciful strands. And although Garrison's investigation was ridiculed and derided by the media, termed a farce and a fraud, it was later discovered that the C.I.A. maintained an intense interest in its progress and direction. A disillusioned Victor Marchetti, executive assistant to the Agency's deputy director, resigned from the C.I.A. in 1969 and reported that then Director Richard Helms ordered that the

Agency provide all the help Clay Shaw needed to fight Garrison's case against him. And, as a staff investigator for the House Select Committee on Assassinations, I was shocked to learn that the C.I.A. had infiltrated almost a dozen covert operatives into Garrison's staff of investigators. So Garrison was not only attacked from the outside, but also subverted from within.

Whatever excesses or improprieties Garrison pulled during the conduct of his investigation were irrelevant to the fact that he raised valid questions about valid areas of evidence that were never pursued by the Warren Commission.

Nor was the subsequent House Select Committee investigation a complete or even competent effort.* And that's undoubtedly part of the basis of Oliver Stone's acceptance of Garrison's conspiracy theory. For sure, he doesn't sit on the fence: "I think the artist's obligations are to interpret history as he sees fit," Stone says.

For that, as Mary Ferrell forewarned, Stone took a barrage of hard knocks before *JFK* ever got in the can. But those raps now appear mild compared with the major media's negative frenzy when the movie was released last month. *The New York Times* put its big gun, Tom Wicker, up front. "Oliver Stone," said Wicker, "transforms a discredited theory into the sole explanation for the assassination." (Institutionally, *The Times* has been oddly critical of criticism of the Warren Commission Report since its release. That newspaper, coincidentally, was the first to give the Report its editorial imprimatur, and then immediately published a hardback commercial edition of it.)

Perhaps the most pernicious attack on Stone came from *Newsweek* with its cover-plus-eight-page treatment. Blared its cover lines: "The Twisted Truth of *JFK*: Why Oliver Stone's New Movie Can't Be Trusted."

Oddly subverting the validity of an assessment by its own movie critic, David Ansen ("... above and beyond whether Stone's take on the assassination is right, his film is a powerful, radical vision of America's drift toward covert government ... Two cheers for Mr. Stone, a troublemaker of our times."), *Newsweek*'s cover story declared: "*JFK* is not just an entertainment, it's a work of propaganda." It subtly attempted to twist its analysis to fit its point: "In effect, Stone is inviting America to adopt an alternative version of history. His film categorically rejects the report of the Warren Commission, the imperfect but painstaking government investigation ..."

Painstaking? Hardly. The Warren Commission investigation relied on five volumes of reports gathered in less than three weeks by the FBI. Those reports were consistently loose-ended, incomplete and devoid of follow-up—often, it appeared, deliberately so.

As for Stone's "alternate version of history," let's get specific for a moment. *Newsweek* decries Stone depicting a mysterious figure surreptitiously depositing the "pristine bullet" on a gurney in the corridor at Dallas' Parkland Hospital. That, it claims, is Stone's fiction. Well, what are the facts? Since *Newsweek* neglects to provide them, here they are: The "pristine bullet" *was* found on a gurney in the corridor at Parkland Hospital. That may be one of the most significant facts in all the evidence pointing to a conspiracy in the Kennedy assassination. Without that "pristine bullet," the Warren Commission's lone assassin theory collapses.

Here's why: Even the Warren Commission concluded that Oswald could not have fired the 25-year-old, bolt-action Italian rifle with a misaligned sight faster than once every 2.3 seconds. (After a lot of practice and numerous attempts, that's the minimum time it took the Commission's hired expert marksman to fire it *without* aiming.) The problem was that the famous Zapruder film revealed that Governor Connally had been hit no later than 1.6 seconds after the first shot hit Kennedy. To solve the problem the Commission—specifically staffer (now U.S. Senator) Arlen Specter—devised what came to be known as the Magic Bullet theory. This bullet first struck Kennedy's back, went through his upper chest, emerged from his throat, went on to strike Connally's back, pierced a lung, severed a vein, artery and nerve, broke the right fifth rib, destroying five inches of the bone, emerged through his chest and then plunged into the back of Connally's right forearm, broke a thick bone and distal end of the radius, came out the other side of his wrist, and finally embedded in his left thigh. The bullet did all this damage to two human beings and yet emerged virtually pristine, losing only about .65 percent of its original weight, less than it would have if it had been fired through water. Never mind that there were more bullet fragments in Connally and in the limousine than was lost from the almost pristine bullet. And never mind that the FBI could not duplicate the results by firing identical rounds through all kinds of material, including human cadavers, without producing a grossly deformed bullet. Without the Magic Bullet theory, there had to be at least two assassins.

So after it did its tragic routine (including some nifty spins and sharp turns to accommodate its dedicated trajectory as defined by the wounds), where did the bullet end up? One would assume, given the theory, deeply embedded in Connally's left thigh. But that's not where it was found. It was found on one of two gurney's in the corridor at Parkland Hospital—and, from doctors at Parkland Hospital reported that the right side of the President's head was missing—contrary to what the later "authentic" x-rays and photographs taken by the military doctors at Bethesda claim to reveal.

Where was the media when the Warren Commission claimed Jack Ruby killed Oswald as the result of an emotionally-driven, spontaneous impulse while the evidence revealed that Ruby had stalked Oswald since his capture, was a crony of Oswald's police protectors, had close connections to Organized Crime and later, in prison, unsuccessfully begged Commission Chairman Earl Warren to be taken back to Washington where, in protection, he would reveal the truth about why he killed Oswald?

And where was the media to demand answers from the Government—*still* not forthcoming—when hard, undisputed evidence emerged that President Kennedy's body was wrapped in a white sheet and placed in a bronze casket in a Dallas funeral home and yet arrived at Bethesda Naval Hospital for autopsy, supposedly right off Air Force One, in a black plastic body bag and a plain military-style coffin?

And where was the media even years later when the House Select Committee on Assassinations, mandated by Congress to conduct "a full and complete investigation" of Kennedy's assassination, relegated its priorities to political expediencies, forced at the last moment by acoustics evidence to admit that the President's murder was a conspiracy, yet packed its bags and went home without attempting to pursue the truth about *who* the conspirators were?

Where was the media outrage to equal the outrage it now manages to muster about Oliver Stone's movie?

Forget the media's outrage about *JFK*. You don't have to believe Stone's "propaganda." But this is the reality: President John F. Kennedy is dead. And you don't know the truth about how or why he was assassinated. You don't know who decided to invalidate your right to democratically choose your President. The reason you don't know is because your Government and your Constitutionally-protected mechanism for tracking how your Government serves you—the country's mass media—failed you. And they are continuing to fail you. Your Government, ever since the issuance of the Warren Report, has undermined your belief in the strength of the democratic process, that the individual voter matters. And the major media has been negligent in reporting a truthful perspective about your Government's operations. Too often, from Vietnam to Iran-Contra to the strength of the Soviet monolith, it has reported the Government fed facts while ignoring the truth. As a result, you've lost your faith in the worth of your vote, you feel more powerless than ever.

And now they're telling you Oliver Stone's movie can't be trusted.

Gaeton Fonzi is a veteran journalist who spent three years as a U.S. Government investigator working for both The Church Committee on Intelligence and the House Select Committee on Assassinations

Reprinted by permission of the author.

NEW YORK TIMES

VALENTI CALLS 'J.F.K.' 'HOAX' AND 'SMEAR'

Bernard Weinraub

In a highly unusual and angry statement, Jack Valenti, the president and chief executive of the Motion Picture Association of America and a former top aide to President Lyndon B. Johnson, denounced the film "J.F.K." today as a "hoax," a "smear" and "pure fiction" that rivaled the Nazi propaganda films of Leni Reifenstahl.

Mr. Valenti, a film industry spokesman and lobbyist in Washington, has kept silent until now about the Oliver Stone film, which opened in December. He emphasized that he was making a personal statement that "has not connection to my responsibilities in the movie industry."

"Indeed, I waited to speak out because I didn't want to do anything which might affect this picture's theatrical release or the Oscar balloting," he said.

In the seven-page statement, Mr. Valenti said Mr. Stone's film was "a monstrous charade" based on "the hallucinatory bleatings of an author named Jim Garrison, a discredited former district attorney in New Orleans." The movie implies that President Johnson was part of a Government conspiracy in the assassination of President Kennedy.

"Does any sane human being truly believe that President Johnson, the Warren Commission members, law-enforcement officers, C.I.A., F.B.I., assorted thugs, weirdos, Frisbee throwers, all conspired together as plotters in Garrison's wacky sightings?" he asked. "And then for almost 29 years nothing leaked? But you have to believe it if you think well of any part of this accusatory lunacy."

"In scene after scene Mr. Stone plasters together the half true and the totally false and from that he manufactures the plausible," Mr. Valenti said in his statement. "No wonder that many young people, gripped by the movie, leave the theater convinced they have been witness to the truth."

"In much the same way, young German boys and girls in 1941 were mesmerized by Leni Reifenstahl's 'Triumph of the Will,' in which Adolf Hitler was depicted as a newborn God," he said. "Both 'J.F.K.' and 'Triumph of the Will' are equally a hoax. Mr. Stone and Leni Reifenstahl have another genetic linkage: neither of them carried a disclaimer on their film that its contents were mostly pure fiction."

What makes the statement especially unusual is that as head of the Motion Picture Association since 1966, the Texas-born, Harvard-educated Mr. Valenti has sought to keep his employers, the movie studios, as happy as possible without stirring controversy despite his high profile in Hollywood and Washington. One of those employers, Warner Brothers, produced "J.F.K.," which has raised considerable debate over its blend of speculation, fiction and fact.

In a telephone interview, Mr. Valenti said he delayed attacking the movie because of his job. "Warner Brothers is a member of my association, and I owe them a fidelity to my responsibility," he said. "While this is a personal statement, I did not want to do anything that, in the slightest way, would affect this picture's journey and its chances of winning as Academy Award." The movie, which won Academy Awards on Monday night for cinematography and editing, has grossed more than $68 million in the United States and is expected to prove a strong box-office success in Europe.

Mr. Valenti said he had told Warner Brothers that he planned to issue a statement but had not provided the text to the studio. "They recognize that I am in a difficult position, but I told them that this was such a personal thing, it goes deep into my vitals," he said. "I owe where I am today to Lyndon Johnson. I could not live with myself if I stood by mutely and let some film maker soil his memory."

Mr. Stone, who received a copy of the statement from Mr. Valenti late this afternoon, said by telephone: "While I respect Jack Valenti's enduring loyalty to President Johnson, I find his emotional diatribe off the mark. The overwhelming majority of Americans—and not just the young, whom Mr. Valenti puts down as too impressionable—agree with the central thesis of my film: that President Kennedy was killed by a conspiracy, which included people in the Government."

He added: "I am enormously proud of the artistic and political impact which 'J.F.K.' had had. I hope Mr. Valenti, now that he has vented his spleen, will join in supporting the joint House-Senate resolution that all Government files in the assassination of President Kennedy be opened so that the American people can have a fuller understanding of that tragedy and its continuing implications for our democracy."

Robert A. Daly, the chairman of Warner Brothers, said the company supported Mr. Stone but understood Mr. Valenti's fury. "Our feeling is very simple," he said. "we support the movie. We think it's a wonderful movie. We have the utmost regard for what Oliver Stone did. As far as Jack Valenti is concerned, the fact that he's loyal to L.B.J. is admirable, and I would hope anybody who worked for me for all those years would be that loyal. I have nothing but the highest regard for Jack."

Mr. Daly said that if the Warren Commission files are opened because of pressure generated by the film, he was convinced that some of the movie's speculation about more than one assassin would be borne out.

'I Was There'

Mr. Valenti began working for Mr. Johnson in 1955 when he was the Senate majority leader and later served at the White House as Mr. Johnson's assistant form 1963 to 1966. Mr. Valenti handled the press during the visit of President Kennedy and Vice President Johnson to Dallas on Nov. 22, 1963, when Mr. Kennedy was assassinated.

In his statement, Mr. Valenti said: "My own rebuttal to Mr. Stone comes down to this: I was there, and he wasn't."

Mr. Valenti said in his statement that he stood beside Mr. Johnson when he was sworn in on the plane carrying Kennedy's coffin, that he lived at the White House for two months afterwards, that he lived at the White House for two months afterwards, that he "read every paper that crossed the President's desk, including the most top-secret documents, and was an ear-witness to many of his most confidential phone conversations." He continued: "I was there when President Johnson ruminated about the assassination, and the urgency to enlist the most prestigious citizens within the Republic to inspect this murder carefully, objectively, swiftly."

After naming some of the members of the Warren Commission, which Mr. Stone has denounced because of its conclusion that Lee Harvey Oswald acted alone in killing Mr. Kennedy, Mr. Valenti said: "To indict these men of honor, along with Lyndon Johnson, is vicious, cruel and false."

He added, "No matter is brilliant creative skills, and they are considerable, Mr. Stone has with deliberate forethought put on the screen a monstrous charade about President Johnson that ranks right up there with the best work of old-guard Soviet revisionist historians."

APRIL 7, 1992

THE ADVOCATE

HEART OF STONE
Writer-Director Oliver Stone Opens Up on Sex, JFK, *and Harvey Milk*

Jeff Yarbrough

Actor-producer George M. Cohan once told a member of the press,"I don't care what you say about me as long as you say something about me and as long as you spell my name right." Mr. Cohan, meet Mr. Stone.

Writer-director Oliver Stone has, over the last decade, been catapulted to a level of stardom rivaled only by the lead players in his films. Even with actors like Kevin Costner (*JFK*), Val Kilmer (*The Doors*), Tom Cruise (*Born on the Fourth of July*), Michael Douglas (*Wall Street*), and Charlie Sheen (*Wall Street* and *Platoon*), his involvement in a film sometimes renders the actors and their performances unmemorable. Frankly, the star of an Oliver Stone film is Stone himself.

Much of Stone's star status is owed to the press coverage generated by him and his films (some of this status is, of course, owed to his talent)."There's something inside Oliver that forces him to oversell everything," says *Rolling Stone*'s senior editor, Peter Travers. "He's like [showman] Mike Todd. He'd go up in a hot-air balloon with signs all over it if he could." Film critic Travers summed up his views on Stone in his review of the 1991 film *The Doors*, writing that Stone is "part poet, part provocateur, part snake oil salesman "

"He's a master of self-promotion," says Michael Sragow, a film critic for the *San Francisco Examiner* and a frequent film reviewer for *The New Yorker*. "But he's not alone. He and Spike Lee both tackle incendiary subjects [in their films], then go out and fan the flames on all of the media's available levels—and all the while offer no solutions to the problems that their films raise"

The key to the media's fatal attraction to Stone is his ability to weave a complex, polemical web in and around almost every film he makes. Forget lame comparisons of Brian De Palma (*Dressed to Kill*) and Kenneth Branagh (*Dead Again*) to master audience and media manipulator Alfred Hitchcock. Stone is the director whose name—much like the Master's—instantly identifies the contents of his films. Hitchcock's name signaled suspense. Stone's signals controversy.

"L.A. is stressville for me," says Stone from behind a mahogany desk at his company's offices in Santa Monica, Calif. "Too much going on ..." Indeed, Stone's company, Ixtlan Productions, is at present involved—in some capacity—in over a dozen films. Stone's current film in release, *JFK*, nominated for eight Academy Awards, including Best Picture and Best Director, has just opened internationally and is doing "spectacular business," according to *The Hollywood Reporter's* international editor, James Ulmer. "*JFK* is a huge hit overseas," he says. "It had one the strongest openings in Paris ever." Stone, who recently returned from a promotional trip to Europe and South America to boost *JFK*'s international profile, says, "We hit ten countries in 21 days It's doing well everywhere. It's a universal film."

It is also a wildly controversial film. In fact, it is difficult to imagine a film more controversial than *JFK*. Stone has singlehandedly brought interest in the assassination of President John F. Kennedy, a murder that took place almost 30 years ago, to a state of national—and now international—frenzy. Even Congress, a body of politicians who move on most issues with the grace and pace of a brontosaurus, have been tweaked by Stone's film. In January, an article in *The Washington Post* quoted House speaker Thomas Foley as saying that *JFK* "has renewed demands to unseal [government] files that could add relevant information" about the assassination. Without Stone's *JFK*, those files may continue to gather dust until 2019.

Like the halls of government, the halls of virtually every media outlet in the United States have also buzzed regarding Stone's film version of the assassination. *The New York Times* said Stone "is not engaged in a fair-minded inquiry." *The Chicago Tribune* wrote, "This is not artistry, it is flim flam. This is not mythmaking, it is exploitation. This is not high drama, it is low propaganda." *New York* magazine printed that "there are more than 100 major lies and omissions" in the film. Most of the film's criticisms concern the fact that Stone has produced a document in *JFK* that will stand as a historical representation for all of those who know little or nothing about the assassination. "Kids are swallowing it whole," says critic Sragow.

At those kids' fingertips are volumes of information on the conspiracy to kill the president. Earlier this month, *The New York Times Book Review* contained two titles in its top-selling 15 that were related to the assassination. On the paperback list, three out of ten best-sellers—including *On the Trail of the Assassins*, written by former New Orleans district attorney Jim Garrison (played in *JFK* by Kevin Costner), which was listed at number one—were assassination-related.

Despite all this interest in the film and renewed interest in the assassination, one issue that has gotten little play since the movie's opening is the subject of homophobia and *JFK*. Despite criticisms—mostly in the gay press—of the film's alleged homophobia (*Rolling Stone*'s Travers has also referred to certain scenes in *JFK* as "scarily homophobic"), little has been said on the matter by Stone.

Until now.

Last January, Stone was "outraged" by an article written by *The Advocate*'s film critic, David Ehrenstein. In "*JFK*—A New Low for Hollywood," Ehrenstein attempted to refute *JFK*'s theory that there was "a gay cabal out to kill Kennedy." The article spouts evidence that Ehrenstein feels discredits Stone's version of the events. He quotes from James Kirkwood's *American Grotesque*, a book that attempts to prove that Garrison was on a personal vendetta to get international businessman Clay Shaw (Tommy Lee Jones in *JFK*). *American Grotesque* paints Garrison as unstable and a wife beater—the antithesis of the Garrison in Stone's film. Following the article was Ehrenstein's review of the movie, in which he pronounced *JFK* "the most homophobic film ever to come out of Hollywood." The critic bristled at what he called the movie's "constant contrast between purer-than-driven-snow straights and slimy, sweaty, whimpering gays".

Following the appearance of Ehrenstein's views in *The Advocate*, Stone started receiving hate mail. Most of this mail expressed outrage at Stone's involvement in the production of *The Mayor of Castro Street*.

Stone is executive producing *The Mayor of Castro Street* for Warner Bros. The film, based on Randy Shilts's biography of openly gay San Francisco supervisor Harvey Milk, will chronicle Milk's life, times, and assassination. Stone has been toying with the idea of directing the film but due to the gay activist community's furor is reevaluating that idea. A flier was recently faxed around Hollywood by Queer Nation, a direct-action group, promising "massive demonstrations" at this year's Academy Awards because of Stone's alleged homophobia in *JFK* and his involvement in *The Mayor of Castro Street*.

And although the flier abounds with misinformation, the activists did, indeed, spell Oliver Stone's name right.

Q: When does bad art deserve censure—not censorship?

A: I'm against artistic censorship in any form. Once you get into the "politically correct" way of doing things, you are in danger of destroying the concept of art. You're bordering on where the Russian socialists stood regarding their artists' freedom of expression. To be told you cannot portray anything gay, black, or Asian in a negative light is ridiculous. The filmmaker should have—and does have, I might add—the right to do it the way he wants.

Q: So you're saying that the gay community, in these times of employment discrimination, epidemic, and attacks on civil rights by state legislatures, should remain silent regarding something that is felt to be insensitive, gratuitous, and homophobic?

A: Are you referring to *JFK?*

Q: At this point I'm speaking in generalities.

A: As far as my movie goes, no one with a brain is going to walk out of *JFK* and think that gays are all president killers. The film is about who owns reality. Is it the press? The C.I.A.? Lee Harvey Oswald? To narrow this theme and to focus on these characters' homosexuality is to lose perspective.

Q: How do you respond to the accusations that *JFK* portrays gays in a homophobic manner?

A: The chief villains in the film are heterosexual. The finger is pointed at the power structure in Washington and its combination of C.I.A. and military intelligence people and/or military, who call the shots. I never said Clay Shaw was the mastermind of this conspiracy by any means. He's a fringe player who knows something about what is going on. I hardly think David Ferrie [Joe Pesci in *JFK*] was a mastermind either. The villains lie in Washington, not in New Orleans.

Q: But Shaw and Ferrie are on-screen a lot more than the Washingtonians. Do you understand that the gay community takes issue with this portrayal of homosexuals as deviants because of the dearth of images in films of gays who are not homicidal, psychotic, or both?

A: The characters of Shaw, Ferrie, and the composite character Willie O'Keefe were historically gay. You cannot be—at the same time—politically correct and a historical revisionist. They were gay, and they were involved in this conspiracy.

Q: A lot of gay people objected to the scene in the film depicting those three in drag. Shaw is shown in *JFK* painted gold from head to toe and sniffing amyl nitrate. Is there a historical basis for that scene?

A: Let me show you a picture. [He calls to an assistant outside of his private office and requests that two photographs be brought to him.] Here [pointing to the photos], there's Shaw, there's Ferrie. Both in wigs. The drag scene was important to the film because I had to make the point that Shaw was lying when he said he didn't know Ferrie. He obviously knew him. The point of that scene was to prove that Shaw perjured himself [at his subsequent trial] over and over on the witness stand.

Q: What does that photo really prove? I have a picture of myself with Madonna.

A: Many people said they knew each other. Raymond Broshears, David Logan, and Perry Russo, all gay friends of Ferrie's, testified [before the Warren Commission, which investigated the Kennedy assassination] to that fact. Russo's testimony is that which I gave to the Willie O'Keefe character. He said he went to a party with Ferrie and Shaw. At that party he listened while Shaw, Ferrie, and Lee Harvey Oswald talked about a triangulation of fire that would kill a president. He never changed his story in 28 years.

As far as the drag scene goes, we're sitting here looking at [Shaw and Ferrie] in these photographs in wigs. In terms of me showing Shaw painted gold, that came from an F.B.I. document from 1954 which said that Shaw was given to sadism and masochism in his homosexual activities, that he ran a gay club and presided over it with a whip in his hand, and that one year he painted himself gold at Mardi Gras.

Q: In pushing your point that all of these guys knew each other, aren't you verging on a stereotypical assumption—and a homophobic one—that all gay people know each other?

A: It's not about their being gay, it's about the connections that being gay makes. Jack Ruby may have been gay. I didn't get into that in the film, but several people in Texas told me that he was. He lived with a roommate for several years, George Senator, whom I met. Senator says he himself is straight but still leads "a bachelor existence." I believe Garrison. I believe all these guys were peripherally involved. Ferrie had something to do with this thing. He knew Oswald, Shaw, and Guy Banister—who was running Oswald. I have second and third sources on all of this.

Q: So you don't feel that *gay* is shorthand for villain in *JFK*?

A: No, I do not.

Q: Do you see that kind of homophobia taking place in other movies?

A: It may have been used that way in other films. I've never used it that way. I've never considered sex in a psychotic light. If [other directors] use it that way, they're probably making bad films, and hopefully people will take that into account.

I disagree with the controversy over *The Silence of the Lambs*. Maybe that killer was gay, maybe he was not. This whole line of thinking disturbs me because I think what we're really talking about is a form of censorship. A few years ago every killer on TV was a straight white male. It couldn't be a black man—blacks were sensitive about being portrayed as homicidal. That's happening now in films. If this kind of censorship takes hold, we'll have Dan Quayle doing all of the killings.

Q: People in New Orleans suggest that Garrison was on a personal vendetta to get Shaw because he was gay. In light of the jury's almost immediate acquittal of Shaw, what do you make of the personal vendetta theory? What about Kirkwood's book *American Grotesque*, which espouses this theory?

A: I met James Kirkwood before he died. It is very clear to me that he did not cover the trial with an open mind. He was a friend of Shaw's. Shaw was pictured by Kirkwood in *American Grotesque* as an innocent businessman. Shaw was the head of New Orleans's International Trade Mart and was thrown out of Italy for being on the Permadex board, a fascist organization that included a few of Mussolini's relatives. The organization was caught handling illegal funds in the assassination of Charles de Gaulle. Shaw was a serious espionage player, a suave, sophisticated international businessman with connections to the C.I.A..

Q: The judge in the case, Edward A. Haggerty Jr., told Kirkwood shortly after the trial that he thought Shaw was guilty. He was outraged, according to Kirkwood, that the prosecution didn't bring Shaw's sexuality directly into the court proceedings and ranted, "Queers know queers! They've got a clique better than the C.I.A. ..."

A: At that time in New Orleans, I bet most of the gay underground knew the others in the underground. As for *American Grotesque*, it was a good read but not even close to reality.

Q: You're upset because people are protesting *JFK*. Isn't the message behind the movie "speak up or shut up"?

A: Speaking up is a good thing when you're speaking up for the right reasons. I'm on the board of Hollywood Supports, which is trying to make people in Hollywood aware of homophobia but not to censor their views. If an artist is determined to portray homosexuals in a negative light, then he should have that right, regardless of what other people are saying.

Q: A lot of people in the activist community are saying that you shouldn't direct *The Mayor of Castro Street*. Some people in Queer Nation go so far as to say that the film should not be directed by anyone unless that person is gay.

A: It's wrong for them to say that if I wanted to, I shouldn't be able to direct the film because I'm straight.

Q: Will you direct the film?

A: No. I'm going to drop out at this point.

Q: Why?

A: Two reasons: the inescapable controversy that would result if I did direct it and the fact that I've just finished a political movie involving an assassination. [*The Mayor of Castro Street*] is very much along those same lines. I feel that many people would support me [if I did direct the film]. I know Randy Shilts does. But why should I feed the fires of hatred that already exist against me? Robin Williams will probably still star. It's not like I'm dropping out without helping the film. I've already helped.

It wasn't even going to be written at the point at which I came in. I only did it to help [producers] Craig Zadan and Neil Meron. I liked the story, and it seemed like they had their hearts riding on this. I got it done. Now we're on the last half of the journey. We'll get a good director, and we'll get it shot.

Q: Who?

A: I can't say.

Q: Someone at Warner Bros. told me that if you dropped out, Penny Marshall would step in.

A: I can't comment on that right now.

Q: You said you got involved because you felt you could help this movie get made. What is it about this film that interests you?

A: It's not only a story about gayness, it's a story about inner-city politics, about how rainbow coalitions are coming into their own. Also, the theme of Harvey's activism—his coming out—I find fascinating. The story should not, however, be whitewashed.

Q: Are you saying it might be, regardless of your participation?

A: Sure. Possibly. Warner Bros. owns the script.

Q: What elements do you think could or would be whitewashed?

A: There's an element of promiscuity in [Milk's] life that I find intriguing. I'd hate to see that Hollywoodized. Promiscuity was the fashion for many people in the late '60s and the early '70s. I'd hate to see all of that underrepresented by the film.

Q: Speaking of sex, have you ever had a homosexual experience?

A: Oh, God! [Laughs] Can you please just write "Oliver laughed"? I can't tell you that. I'll be in deep shit—

Q: With whom?

A: With the government. If I admit to that, then they'll really be on my ass! They're trying to nail me—well, I guess I've already done everything wrong in my life in their opinion.

Q: Then why would it matter?

A: [Laughs] Maybe you're right!

Q: You won't deny having had a homosexual experience.

A: I won't deny it.

Q: So you have had sex with a man.

A: I won't flatly deny that.

Q: I'd like to ask you about the details—

A: You mean which sailors? Which ports?

Q: We can start there. How significant—

A: That's all I'm going to say on this subject.

Q: I wonder if Queer Nation will change its tune after reading that you won't say no to homosexual sex?

A: They would just call me a closet fascist. They'd see me as the Clay Shaw of this generation. To be serious, I don't think they would care. Radicalism never thinks, it just destroys. They're a bunch of absolutists, their own worst enemies. Destroying everything around them. They live in a perpetual hell. They get reincarnated in worse and worse forms. Eventually, they'll become ineffective cynics, tired of their own absolutism.
All my life I've been a relativist. I think Harvey Milk is a good example of this. He lived with absolutists, with people who committed suicide, with people who couldn't get on with their lives. I think he was troubled by this absolutism that he saw around him in the gay community.

Q: So the absolutists have won. Their wish is that you not direct this film.

A: I'm tired of having my neck in the guillotine. These people are loud, vociferous; they don't give up. Radicalism in any society has, in my opinion, always been destructive. Left or right. It's ugly and self-destructive.

Q: You once considered yourself a radical.

A: Yeah, I was very radical when I was young. Some people still think I am radical. I'm not. I think that mainstream thinking goes farther in the long term. If you can subtly change mainstream thinking bit by bit, you'll go farther. That's what really gets things done.

Q: Queer Nation is neither mainstream nor subtle, but in this case it has, obviously, got something done. You claim you won't direct this movie because of their "loud, vociferous" protests.

A: Queer Nation is like a Nazi group. They work through intimidation and fear. They send hate mail. I'm not scared of them. But I had to ask myself, "Do I need this?"—especially since I don't think I'm bringing anything ultraspecial to the film if I do direct it. Also, I know that the gay community is extremely outspoken and everyone in it is a movie critic. I don't need that.

Q: People who work in Hollywood tell me that if this film doesn't make money, then there won't be another big-budget gay film made in this century.

A: That's probably true. *Making Love* with Harry Hamlin set gay-themed films back a number of years. It didn't live up to the hype. But with the way [*The Mayor of Castro Street*] is written, I think it's going to be a great movie.

Q: This interview is taking place while you're still weathering all sorts of attacks on *JFK*'s credibility as a docudrama. Has all of this criticism of you and of the film taken its toll on you personally?

A: Yes. I don't appreciate the press calling me a liar and having it said that I have no integrity and having it said that I am trying to destroy the youth of America through my filmmaking. The people who say these things are complete assholes and won't address the legitimate issues in *JFK*. There are 36 or 38 issues addressed by this film that have not been dealt with by the press. They're too busy saying, "Oliver Stone made all of this up."

Q: *The Advocate*'s film critic, David Ehrenstein, says you made up a lot of things.

A: He's another absolutist. That man is the worst. While he was writing his piece, he was trying to get a half-hour interview with me. Warner Bros. gave me his number because they said he had specific research questions for me. My chief researcher, Jane Rusconi, who did a lot of the specific work on Garrison, Shaw, etc., called Ehrenstein and introduced herself. At that point he announced, "I have no interest in talking to you. I want to talk to Oliver Stone." Jane explained that she was trying to facilitate that. Then he went into a tirade about how Warner Bros. was giving him a hard time about getting access to me. She repeated that she was trying to help get him get to me by figuring out exactly what it was he wanted to ask, and he said, "I have no interest in talking to you. It's too late, anyway. I've already written my piece." Then he hung up on her. Ehrenstein refused to talk to us—not the other way around. Maybe he didn't like her because she was a woman. I don't know.

Q: You were recently characterized by a newspaper as a sort of career homophobe. An article cited *Midnight Express* and *The Doors* as examples along with *JFK* of your insensitivity toward gays. Specifically, the writer charged you with deleting a homosexual love scene from your screenplay for *Midnight Express*.

A: This really pissed me off because it shows how ignorant the people who write about the film business really are about how a film gets made. I wrote *Midnight Express*. It was my first screenplay, and there was no way on earth that Columbia was going to let that scene stay in the script. Eventually, it was whittled away. There was no way they were going to let me do that in a mainstream film in 1977. It was not my decision. I wanted Billy to have homosexual action. [Director] Alan [Parker] suggested [homosexual action] in the film, with camera, but there was nothing concrete.

Q: Has the climate changed? Could you do that scene now?

A: It would be easy to do that kind of a scene today. Hollywood was homophobic then—and is now to some degree—but I think that's starting to change. I think a film like *The Mayor of Castro Street* will help things to change.

Q: The same article accused you of representing Andy Warhol in *The Doors* in a homophobic manner.

A: Bullshit. My portrayal of Warhol was not a homosexual put-down. By his own definition he was proud of being freakish. He hung out with drag queens. So what. These writers should be stopped. Talk about grasping at straws.

Q: There is concern that the current version of the script for *The Mayor of Castro Street* has no sex scenes involving Harvey Milk; that there are references to sex and promiscuity, but none of it is actually acted out for the camera. I know this script's not in its final form, but is this true?

A: I don't know. I don't know where the script stands on that point right now. But if that's true, that's a very good point to make. Those scenes should be in there.

Q: So you're saying that if you were consulted on this issue, you'd make sure those scenes were included and shot.

A: Yes. It might be a problem with Warner Bros., though.

Q: You just told me, referring to Midnight Express, that it would be no problem to shoot a homosexual love scene in today's Hollywood. Seconds later, you seem to think there is a problem.

A: Maybe you're right. Maybe there is still a problem. But I'll tell you one thing: That's an issue worth fighting for.

Reprinted by permission of the author.

MAY 13, 1992

THE NEW YORK TIMES

GATES ORDERS RELEASE OF SECRET CIA FILE ON OSWALD BEFORE '63

Special to The New York Times

WASHINGTON, May 12—Robert M. Gates, the Director of Central Intelligence, said today that he had ordered the release within days of a secret C.I.A. file on Lee Harvey Oswald's activities before the assassination of President John F. Kennedy in 1963.

Mr. Gates's announcement of the declassification of the 110-page file represented a first trickle in what could soon be a vast river of assassination documents to be made public soon. He testified on legislation to create a review board to speed the disclosure of the estimated one million documents on the case still in the Government's hands.

Mr. Gates announced the voluntary release of the Oswald material at a Senate hearing on the legislation, a Congressional effort to respond to public skepticism about the official accounts of the Kennedy assassination and revived interest in the matter spawned by the recent film *JFK*.

The movie, which challenged a central finding of a Presidential review commission convened after the killing, has been criticized by historians as distorting the facts. The commission concluded that Oswald acted alone when he shot Kennedy in a Dallas motorcade on Nov. 22,1963.

The material in the Oswald file relates to a shadowy period that has been the subject of decades of conjecture by historians and conspiracy theorists. During that period the former Marine Corps radar technician familiar with U-2 spy flights defected to the Soviet Union in 1959, redefected to the United States in 1962 and traveled to Mexico City in September 1963.

For Mr. Gates, the disclosure of the file seemed to represent an effort to align his agency on the side of full disclosure on a highly popular issue even though the C.l.A. has for years ferociously guarded even the most trivial secrets in its files.

The file, which was made available to The Associated Press today, consists of 33 documents, 11 of them originating in the C.l.A.

James Lesar, a lawyer who operates the Assassination Archive and Research Center in Washington, said that based on a cursory reading of the documents the material has been available to researchers. Many of the documents are F.B.I. memos sent to the C.l.A. and may be among those already released by the F.B.I. in response to Freedom of Information requests.

Mr. Gates and William S. Sessions, the Director of the Federal Bureau of Investigation, who also testified today before the Governmental Affairs Committee, embraced the goal of opening the records. But they warned that the powers the legislation would grant the review board encroached on executive branch prerogatives, like the authority to protect classified information.

THE NATION

A STONE'S THROW

Oliver Stone

Former Warren Commission assistant counsel Wesley J. Liebeler's defense of his résumé-building work is almost refreshing in its transparency ["Beat the Devil," March 9]. Abetted by Alexander Cockburn's total ignorance of the subject at hand, he improvises, freely associating sources and figures, and offers his opinion that the Warren Commission did a great job, except they got "the entrance woundsin the wrong place." They had the murder on film and some three dozen medical personne examined the body—but they never did pin down exactly where those wounds were. There goes the whole case: Without knowing where the entrance wounds are, there is absolutely no way to substantiate the lone-gunman thesis.

What we see in the interview is a merging of the far right and the far left for entirely different agendas. Liebeler's operating principle is fairly simple and human. Cover your ass. Cockburn's is philosophical. His dialectic view of history precludes the possibility of individual choice affecting the outcome of events— thus, the very thought that Kennedy might have betrayed his capitalist upbringing by halting the war in Vietnam is unbearable. As Cockburn puts it: "The effect of JFK is to make people think that America is a good country that produced a good President killed by bad elites." While that is exactly what I believe, it's a veritable nightmare for Cockburn, who clearly is convinced that a democratic country cannot be good, and could not elect a leader who wasn't merely another link in the inherently evil system.

The Nation joins in the fray with its marvelous illustration of the single bullet theory, a crude drawing swiped in toto from a January 19 article in New York Newsday. Poor Governor Connally is squatting in a mysterious hole (or perhaps on the floor of the limousine), a sitting duck for the überbullet heading downward into his armpit. That's an odd configuration, especially in light of the facts: (I) the extensive photographic record of the motorcade shows that Connally's seat was at the same approximate height as Kennedy's; and (2) if, in fact, the bullet did enter Kennedy's back and exit his throat as Liebeler et al. claim, the bullet would have had an upward trajectory upon leaving Kennedy. The Newsday-cum-Nation drawing turns the preposterous single-bullet path into a straight downward line through the two men—a lot more palatable, even believable, but showing something that never was. This is a tactic we usually ascribe to CBS and Time, and we expect The Nation to correct the record. Not sothis time out.

Instead, we get the Dan Rather school of journalism: It is because I say so. With what would be a good title for his memoirs, Cockburn shrugs off his factual errors in his original JFKcolumn: "I thought it was true when I wrote it." In journalism, in history, in criticism and in publishing, it is not enough to "think" something is true. Nor should it be necessary for the readers to call Cockburn on his errors; that is The Nation's job. It doesn't matter that Cockburn is a columnist with a considerable following and a penchant for provoking controversy. As a selling point, controversy helps, but please, don't misinform the public in the name of commerce.

The public is not stupid. As the polls show, a strong majority know the evidence does not support the fantasy that a lone nut shot and killed the President of the United States. Journalists (like Cockburn) and journals (like The Nation) should be our protection against official untruths. But in this unique instance, the media have bought wholesale the lies and distortions passed down from Washington. The Nation and Cockburn trivialize the event of November 22,1963, by dismissing it as nothing more momentous than an accident. That will not do. As the record shows, Mr. Cockburn, J.F.K. did not trip on Caroline's doll. He was murdered—and history changed—by parties still unknown.

Reprinted by permission of the author.

LOOSE BAZOOKA

John Newman

I have followed the current American debate over President Kennedy's Vietnam with keen interest. The Nation's chief contribution to this mushrooming controversy is the humorous pen of Alexander Cockburn. Because he knows little about this subject, however, Cockburn has distinguished himself by poking fun at serious scholars with witty feuilletonisms. While life would be boring if we could not laugh at ourselves, we must also recognize when it is time to stop joking around and get serious.

Several readers of The Nation have called on me to respond to Cockburn's attack on my book, JFK and Vietnam. They tell me Cockburn's otherwise good work has resulted in a certain following that will take his lead on this subject too. In other words, it would appear that we have in this case, to borrow an analogy from Victor Hugo, a loose cannon on the deck of the American left.

What is to be done? It is pointless to counter Cockburn with the ad hominem he inveighs against others. It is better to reason and gently persuade and raise the standard of debate to a more civilized and intellectually honest plane. It is in that spirit that I offer the following comments.

In my book, JFK and Vietnam, I discuss at length Kennedy's public comments that lend the impression he would not withdraw from Vietnam. I also deal with his private comments that lend the opposite impression. Since both sets of comments cannot be true, which set reflects Kennedy's genuine intent? Is there any hard evidence that can help us form a judgment about this? Indeed there is: the top-secret documentary record, especially Kennedy's withdrawal order itself and the records of those National Security Council (N.S.C.) meetings in which that decision was discussed and made.

There is no need (and certainly not the space) to repeat here the details of that record—The Nation's readers have had plenty of that. The crucial question is this: When J.F.K. set the withdrawal in motion, did he think South Vietnam was winning or losing on the battlefield?

The preponderance of evidence strongly suggests that by 1963 Kennedy knew the war was a lost cause. My book documents how the lie about war progress was constructed, the actions of those who blew the whistle inside the government and the top-secret memorandums—beginning in early 1963, from the C.I.A., the State Department and Kennedy's own N.S.C. staff—that directly impugned this lie about progress.

Given the state of the battlefield, Kennedy feared his withdrawal plan would harm his chances for re-election. This helps us understand why he hid his true intent from the public and why, when he ordered the withdrawal to begin, he included a provision to keep it a secret. Do I advance this argument, as Cockburn charges, "with a willful credulity akin to religious mania"? Cockburn's followers would do well to read and make up their own minds as to whether my theses are based on reason or hysteria.

I wonder if Cockburn's followers notice the inherent weakness in his argument. For someone who claims that the system always produces bad Presidents, Cockburn cuts a strange figure by believing so trustingly in J.F.K.'s public pronouncements on the Vietnam War. Does Cockburn believe everything Presidents say publicly about war policy—or just what Kennedy said on Vietnam?

When Cockburn canonizes Kennedy's public comments on Vietnam, he keeps interesting company—from the far right. Like two peas in a pod, neither Cockburn nor Col. Harry Summers questions the integrity of Kennedy's promises on Vietnam—Summers because he thinks Kennedy was inherently good, and Cockburn because he thinks he was inherently bad.

Colonel Summers charges that my work on J.F.K.'s withdrawal plans has "vilified Kennedy beyond the wildest dreams of his worst enemies." Summers thinks J.F.K.'s Vietnam promises were good, and idolizes Kennedy as a great "macho warrior" who never would have tolerated the loss of Vietnam. Cockburn, still in step with Summers, says "one can easily argue" that J.F.K., had he lived, would have escalated harder and quicker than L.B.J.

There is nothing easy about reconciling the contradictory and tragic record of J.F.K. and Vietnam. American myth and self-image are involved. Because I cast Kennedy neither as hero nor as villain, I have earned disdain from both sides of the political spectrum.

It is time to pay attention to the facts about the cornerstone years of the early

1960s, and time to stop worrying so much about what "effect" they might have. Too much attention to form instead of substance is stultifying— especially when the task before us is the reconstruction of a period in our history that has been suppressed and kept under lock and key. Cockburn should hit the books for a while; study the old documents and look at those newly declassified; maybe even interview some of the key participants while they are still alive.

Above all, Cockburn should discuss this subject with scholars of different persuasions. He should do so not to provide comic relief for Nation readers but to genuinely promote the search for truth. If we can transform the discussion in such a manner, I will be the first one listening.

Reprinted by permission of the author.

HUNKERED IN THE BUNKER

Philip Green

I find it very disturbing that The Nation has allowed itself to become a visible part of the anti-JFK campaign sweeping the media. The discussion about JFK is not a trivial event; it goes to the heart of American political consciousness and potential strategies for change. Over the years, as defenders of the Warren Commission have fought back against criticism with more and more arcane scientific tests piled onto a rickety structure of ever-diminishing credibility, they have established that it is not impossible (though it remains at best highly unlikely) for the lone-gunman hypothesis to withstand forensic doubts. What they have not done, because it cannot be done, is to show a persuasive chain of evidence supporting that hypothesis in the face of testimony from dozens of eyewitnesses to the contrary. Because of that circumstance, it has become crucial for anyone who thinks it important to arrive at an understanding of the assassination to focus on motive and milieu: If there was a conspiracy, then there ought to have been plausible grounds for a conspiracy, those grounds ought to be visible, and the real evidence demonstrating Oswald's involvement should fit into the conspiracy scenario without any difficulty.

However, attention has been drawn away from the real conspiracy scenario by one wonderfully bizarre scene in JFK in which it is suggested that Kennedy's (alleged) decision to withdraw from Vietnam led to high-level military involvement in the assassination plot. Oliver Stone, Peter Dale Scott and others have hunkered themselves more and more firmly into that probably indefensible bunker, into which a withering fire has been poured, by Alexander Cockburn and others. This entirely incidental debate, therefore, is in danger of obscuring the real demonstration (made more persuasively by Jim Garrison than anyone else, in his On the Trail of the Assassins) of a right-wing conspiracy to assassinate Kennedy.

I speak as one who protested against Kennedy's policies at the time of the Cuban missile crisis, who at the time of the test ban treaty gave a speech to a chapter of SANE in which I said that the test ban was not nearly as significant as the fact that in Vietnam the United States was following "the same fatal path as the French Fourth Republic " and who like most liberals and leftists of the time was furious at the pusillanimous way the Administration was handling its own civil rights bill. In other words, I absolutely shared the perception of Kennedy as a conservative cold warrior; so then did most of us on the left (not, obviously, Oliver Stone). However, what is not being understood today is that the left's view of Kennedy, even if it was a truthful view, in no way determined what the right thought of him. In fact, to see how easily right-wing conspiracy theory is compatible with a left structural analysis of the cold war liberal establishment, we can recall that when G. William Domhoff wrote The Higher Circles, he had to append a chapter in which he tried to distinguish his critique of that establishment from those of the radical right. That is, people on the right were convinced that men we thought of as conservatives were actually agents of the international Bolshevik conspiracy.

This was exactly the case with J.F.K., who at the time of his assassination was undoubtedly the most hated man in America. But he was hated by the right, not the left. There were no left-wing circles in which Oswald could have discussed assassination or found feelings that might have motivated it, but on the right it was easy! There was a price on J.F.K.'s head. From Miami to Dallas (the center of right-wing extremism), there was talk of getting rid of him, and I well remember that in Dallas there were classrooms where teachers led the students in cheers on the day he was killed.

Why? The Bay of Pigs, the nuclear test ban treaty and the civil rights bill. We can forget all those structural analyses about how the objective conditions of capitalism and imperialism really foredoomed the invasion and demanded those other initiatives. The fact is that from

(some of) the right's point of view, Kennedy was clearly at the very center of a conspiracy to take over the United States and deliver it to Russia. In short, he was a traitor. It doesn't matter if today we think that was nonsense; it doesn't matter if it was nonsense; thousands upon thousands of Americans believed it, and many of them were prepared to do something about it. (These are some of the same Americans who, years later, gave money to Oliver North because they thought the Russians were going to invade Texas through Nicaragua.) And that was exactly the conspiratorial milieu, so brilliantly depicted by Stone, in which Oswald moved when he was in New Orleans. And these were exactly the people with the resources and connections to provide all the emblemata of conspiracy that so many people saw in Dallas: fake Secret Service I.D.s, clean-cut "hobos" and the rest of it, not to mention Oswald's "legend" as a Communist and pro-Castro activist. Were there such people in the C.l.A. or F.B.I., whose help would have been essential? Does that question, in the era of James Jesus Angleton, even need to be asked? That is precisely where they were most likely to be found, most especially given that Kennedy had purged the leadership of the C.I.A. Nor is it necessary to posit (Stone doesn't) some overarching C.l.A./F.B.I./Mafia/military intelligence/anti-Castro institutional conspiracy, for there had been (and was to be again in the future) plenty of overlapping activity and cooperation among selected members of these organizations and groups, as in the continuing plot to assassinate Castro.

Indeed, in that milieu of right-wing anti-Communist (and racist) hysteria it is even possible that Kennedy was seen as soft on Vietnam, and that this perception did trigger participation in an assassination plot, or at least in covering it up. Many of these people were and still are capable of seeing the Devil's work everywhere, even in a single word; thus a rationalist, documentary examination of the putative grounds for their belief, the exact wording of NSAM 263 or 273 or whatever, outside its demonizing historical context, is completely beside the point.

Does any of this matter? Yes it does, very much so. Lenin once said that parliamentary government was "the best possible shell for capitalism." From this standpoint, democracy is just a sham, and it's foolish to make a big to-do over some alleged deviation from its conditions of legitimacy. I'd hardly want to deny that capitalism and imperialism are a large part of the truth of our democracy, and compromise it gravely. But they are not the whole truth, and it is not without its own unfolding meaning, its own dynamic. This is what Stone correctly understands. For many of us on the left, the elections of 1964, 1972 and 1980 were, each in its distinctive way, fatally compromised. The entire system, the entire contemporary historical period, therefore reeks of illegitimacy—exactly as Stone laments. Of course, some of the historical shift of the past thirty years is what "the people" have wanted, and some of it is what capital has demanded. But to blame "the people" or capitalism for all that befalls us is in either case a recipe for political paralysis. The people are not going to rebel against themselves, and they're apparently not yet ready to rebel against "capital" or exploitation or the logic of the market either. But an extraordinary number of people have already been moved by, and are responding to, Stone's revival of the assassination conspiracy. Therefore, it's not a self-delusion for us on the left to think that who killed Kennedy is important; making the case that Stone has tried to make may be one of the most useful things we can do for progressive political renewal.

LIEBELER REPLIES

Wesley J. Liebeler

Stone claims the illustration of the single bullet theory in Alexander Cockburn's interview of me was "swiped in toto from a January 19 article in New York Newsday." It comes from Volume VI (p. 54) of the House Assassinations Committee Hearings. If either Stone or his ghostwriters had looked there, they would know Connally was seated 8 centimeters lower than the President, whose upper body was leaning forward between 11 and 18 degrees, while the road sloped down 3 degrees. Estimates of the path of the bullet through Kennedy's body ranged from slightly upward to 4 degrees downward if he was sitting in a vertical position, which he was not. Given those parameters I look forward to Stone's drawing showing how "the bullet would have had an upward trajectory upon leaving Kennedy."

"The Newsday-cum-Nation drawing" is crude only in the sense Kennedy is shown sitting erect and the car level. But the House committee used the drawing only to illustrate the slope of the bullet trajectory, which (surprise!) led back to the upper southeast corner of the Texas Schoolbook Depository.

Stone also claims there is no way to prove the lone-gunman thesis, since the Warren Commission, absent access to the autopsy photographs and X-rays, erred in locating the entrance wounds. I will not defend this handling of the photographs and X-rays. After placing the wounds correctly, however, the House committee unanimously affirmed the commission's finding that the President was hit only by two bullets fired by Oswald from the rear.

Reprinted by permission of the author.

COCKBURN REPLIES

Alexander Cockburn

These letters, fraudulent in the case of Stone, flatulent in the case of Newman and Green, offer a fitting résumé of the intellectual and moral bankruptcy of the JFK sponsors and their claque, not the least of whose vices is their voracious consumption of valuable time and space. Much of their complaint has, after all, been addressed in an earlier exchange.

Stone's admonition to me not to "misinform the public in the name of commerce" is matchless effrontery. The film from which he stands to make millions is undoubtedly one of the most willfully error-riddled pieces of "historical reconstruction" in the history of cinema. Like all demagogues Stone is now a full-blown megalomaniac given to such sentiments (announced grandly at a Nation Institute symposium at Town Hall) that "Even when I'm wrong, I'm right." As his ludicrous mistake about the illustration I included in my Liebeler interview shows, he is wholly ignorant of the basic forensic, evidentiary and historical record, and is dependent on compliant "researchers" who tell him what he wants to hear. Any fact inhospitable to his preposterous überconspiracy is blandly denied. Example: In JFK, David Ferrie confesses to his involvement in the conspiracy. No such confession was made, as is clear even from Garrison's book. Aha, said Stone at the Town Hall event, the confession was made to one of Garrison's assistants. Ed Epstein, author of books on the Warren Commission and on Garrison, called this assistant, who said that Ferrie had done nothing of the sort and that the story was nonsense from start to finish. So far as historical scruple goes, Stone makes Cecil B. De Mille look like Braudel. One of the most squalid aspects of the whole affair is that Time-Warner plans to distribute "documentary materials" about the assassination to schoolchildren .

In tune with the fascist aesthetic of his movie, Stone now mounts the traditional fascist defense: He, like Kennedy, is victim of a gigantic conspiracy, and "the media have bought wholesale the lies and distortions passed down from Washington." Passed down by whom? Let's have precision here. In The Nation's case, exactly who pulled together myself and four other writers variously critical of Stone's version of history and "passed down" to us the necessary "lies and distortions"? It's one thing—not uncommon—to extract money from the public under false pretenses. It's another, á la Stone, to whine all the way to the bank.

But then whining has been a characteristic of Warren Commission critics down the years. Ever since the late 1960s they have successfully dominated debate, yet they still pretend that theirs is the persecuted and unpopular posture. I interviewed Liebeler because I think that the commission's conclusions, particularly in light of the 1978 House inquiry, are a good deal more plausible and soundly based than is commonly supposed. Most conspiracy mongers are either imbeciles or mountebanks, as I discovered when I did several months research, back in the early 1970s, on the murder of Robert Kennedy. In that case the "critics" couldn't even be bothered to find out which way R.F.K. was looking when he was shot. Absent this basic information, they invented another gunman in that crowded kitchen alley. What was striking in the wake of the Liebeler interview was readers' outrage that I had presumed to take a Warren Commission lawyer seriously. For this I was promptly labeled a Stalinist. (This latter term is being devalued with relentless speed. Before me is a letter savagely denouncing me as a Stalinist for my support of Jerry Brown.) But the commission staffers were conscientious people, of widely varied political opinion. They have been steadily libeled down the years, culminating in the oafish abuse by Stone, who espouses the most preposterous theory of all, aside from anything else requiring total suspension of disbelief, since not one among the several hundreds if not thousands party to this imagined conspiracy has ever surfaced, even on deathbed or in post mortem testimonial, to admit participating in the mighty plot.

Newman's letter is hot air from start to finish. I did him the courtesy of working my way carefully through his book, and offering—in my detailed reply published here on March 9— copious illustration of why he is a very bad historian who failed to prove his thesis and who indeed offered convincing evidence to prove the very opposite of his contention. There was nothing ad hominem in my remarks, just as there is nothing substantive in his defense. Indeed, his letter is a remarkable confession of defeat, relying upon slabs of pompous verbiage hauled painfully out of the dictionary. I kept waiting for the phrase "mere persiflage," but maybe Newman is saving that one up for the next time.

Green is the silliest of the lot. God help any youngster at Smith on the receiving end of this popcorn machine of self-regarding blather. What is it with the Five Colleges? Green and Michael Klare form a kind of toxic belt of data-free maundering stretching clear across I-91 from Northampton to Amherst, impeding all respectable intellectual traffic.

Like Stone, Green is ignorant of the record and furthermore declares that it doesn't matter anyway. Anyone who maintains, as he does, that Jim Garrison makes a persuasive case for "a right-wing conspiracy" should be confined to a lunatic asylum. Garrison was a berserk self-publicist with a penchant for locking up journalists who inconvenienced him—a trait that has earned him Stone's rapturous respect.

Notice how Green, like Stone, dismisses reality whenever its breath gets uncomfortably hot on his neck. All of a sudden "the exact wording" of "NSAM 263 or 273 or whatever[!] . . . is completely beside the point " So history doesn't matter at all, beyond what Green or Stone claims that history to be. Green covers himself here by saying that it's the right-wing nuts who care nothing for detail. But he's the one who deals only in the fake currency of mood, Zeitgeist and other impalpable categories.

"For many of us," Green writes, "the elections of 1964, 1972 and 1980 were . . . fatally compromised. The entire system, the entire contemporary historical period, therefore reeks of illegitimacy." Does he think that the fifties, when the A.C.L.U. refused to defend victims of McCarthyism, were somehow more "legitimate"? What was so illegitimate about the 1964 election, in which the proclaimed agendas of L.B.J. and Goldwater presented as clear a choice as any in our lifetime? And why is the election of 1960, which J.F.K. stole with the help of Mayor Daley of Chicago, somehow more legitimate than that of 1980?

Everything Green says is either wrong or irrelevant. His inference is that because the credibility of the Warren Commission is low, its critics must be right. This claim is endlessly popular: "Seventy percent of the American people now believe there was a conspiracy, the Warren Commission was wrong," etc., etc. According to a 1991 Gallup poll, 81 percent of Americans believe that the Bible is "the inspired word of God." Only 9 percent of Americans believe that man has developed over millions of years from less advanced life forms without divine intervention; 47 percent of Americans believe that God created man in essentially the present form all at one time within the past 10,000 years.

Kennedy, writes Green, "at the time of his assassination was undoubtedly the most hated man in America." As Presidents go, J.F.K. was always pretty well regarded. The Gallup poll taken in November 1963 gave him a 58 percent approval rating, up from his lowest ebb of 56 percent two months earlier. In the summer of 1960, Eisenhower had an all-time low approval rating of 49 percent. L.B.J.'s, in August 1968, stood at 35 percent. Carter bottomed out in July 1979 at 28 percent, and George Bush has dropped to 39 percent twice already this year. Of course, Green would say that the conspirators hated J.F.K. in a more violent and ultimately lethal way. More than Johnson was hated by foes of the Great

Society or, for that matter, of the war? Or Bush by some Jews? There is always someone around who will applaud a President's passing. (If a real conspiracy by the elites against a President is desired, look not at 1963 but at 1980. All the conspiracy mongering about the October Surprise throws a smokescreen in front of the obvious overt conspiracy by the militarists against Carter. As Gary Sick remarks at the start of his book, while clearly regarding it as only prolegomenon to the big stuff, military officers betrayed to the press the intended rescue attempts of the hostages. This was treason. On an almost hourly basis highlevel Pentagon officials transported secret documents to the Jack Anderson column and similarly favored sources, seeking to show how Carter was betraying the national interest by sapping America's strength. This was the true and successful coup d'état unfolding every day in the press.)

Green's letter is at least useful in that it musters in one place almost everything foolish said about JFK, as in "an extraordinary number of people have already been moved by, and are responding to, Stone's revival of the assassination conspiracy." This is the JFK-as-radical-catalyst thesis, for which no evidence exists. Assume that everything in JFK is true. Then what? How is this meant to be politically invigorating, except to those who accept the logic and rush down to Washington to assassinate Robert Gates and the Joint Chiefs of Staff? In political terms, apropos the effect of JFK, Chip Berlet hit the nail on the head when he quoted Wilhelm Reich's observation that "reactionary concepts plus revolutionary emotion result in Fascist mentality." Berlet has detailed how JFK has been used most productively by the far right, who naturally swarm like hummingbirds to a vision of the world so exactly in tune with their own. This is not to say that in material terms JFK has not been of great profit to its sponsors, such as Bill Schaap and Ellen Ray (new house in the Catskills), Jim Garrison (millions in royalties), Oliver Stone and indeed the producer of JFK, Arnon Milchan. Milchan, incidentally, was identified in one 1989 Israeli report as "probably [Israel's] largest arms dealer." A company he owned was once caught smuggling nuclear weapons fuses to Iraq. As part of a joint Israeli-South African government operation—"Muldergate"—he acted as launderer to money scheduled to quell liberal publications opposing apartheid.

From where I stand, one consequence of JFK has been a revival of anticommunism (the theme of a conference once organized by Schaap and Ray). After my interview with Liebeler of the Warren Commission, In These Times published a page-long article announcing that this interview was the equivalent of the Nazi-Soviet pact, with Liebeler as A.H. and myself as J.V.S. In the private entertainment at the Royalton Hotel after the Town Hall panel, Stone asked Christopher Hitchens why I was attacking JFK. An honest, forthright response would have been " Because you made a terrible movie." But instead Hitchens replied that it was because I was "an unreconstructed Stalinist." Now Hitchens and his wife, Carol Blue—the woman he describes in print with revolting coyness as "Carol Azul"— are writing movie scripts, so I can understand his chumminess with Stone, but In These Times? I called up Jim Weinstein, I.T.T.'s supremo, to say that if he was going to publish this kind of stuff, he might at least send me the $1,500 in back payments he owes me. Weinstein said he didn't know the article was in that week's paper, and would I accept $1,000 for the time being. And when I think of all the years I forbore out of pity for its parlous condition from abusing I.T.T. for publishing John Judis! Let me end by evoking the conspiracy mindset in full deshabille. Weinstein of course has an interest in defending JFK because it draws attention away from the Mafia, infuriated at J.F.K. for his aborting the Bay of Pigs, which would have given the Mob back its real estate in Havana. Weinstein's dad was just such a real estate investor. Need I say more?

Reprinted by permission of the author.

Historical Documents

JFK AND VIETNAM POLICY

JFK did not want a war in Vietnam. He said so privately to a number of his confidants — Kenny O'Donnell, Mike Mansfield, etc. —and also indicated it in a succession of directives signed over the course of his administration.

April 61 - JFK decides not to go into Laos. The Joint Chiefs wanted to invade and Lyndon Johnson supported them.

15 Nov. 61 - NSAM 111
Because the U.S. in effect is breaking the Geneva Accords and they are increasing the number of advisors and military personnel in Vietnam,

NSAM #111 is still a step forward in terms of overall escalation. However, the NSAM clearly states that is **advisors only, no combat troops.** JFK was adamant on this point - he told the Joint Chiefs that there was no way we could justify going into Vietnam while ignoring Cuba. The Joint Chiefs added that they still would like to go into Cuba, too.

4 April 62 - JFK signals intent to withdraw
A memo from J.K. Galbraith advises a policy change with respect to the Diem regime. JFK responds (we see this in a memo from Adm. Bagley's office to Gen. Maxwell Taylor's office) by saying that the U.S. involvement in South Vietnam **"should be reduced at the first favorable moment although it is recognized this may not be possible in the near future".**

13 April 62 - JCS responds
The Joint Chiefs are not amused. They respond to Galbraith's memo by saying that:

> **any reversal of U.S. policy could have disastrous effects, not only upon our relationship with South Vietnam but with the rest of our Asian and other allies as well.**

2 Oct 63 - White House Statement
Paragraph 3 of the statement concerns the withdrawal plan:

> **Secretary NcNamara and General Taylor reported their judgement that the major part of the U.S. military task can be completed by the end of 1965, although there may be a continuing requirement for a limited number of U.S. training personnel. They reported that by the end of this year, the U.S. program for training Vietnamese should have progressed to the point where 1,000 U.S. military personnel assigned to South Vietnam can be withdrawn.**

Of course, the statement is toothless: if things progress to some nebulous "point", we'll withdraw. The Joint Chiefs (among others) were upset by any public statement mentioning a possible withdrawal, and the language of the White House statement of 2 October is intentionally rather weak.

NSAM 263

NSAM 263 is dated 11 October 1963 but was decided on the same day as the White House statement. It actually *implemented* the withdrawal plan:

> **The President approved the military recommendations contained in Section I B (1-3) of the (McNamara-Taylor) report, but directed that no formal announcement be made of the implementation of plans to withdraw 1,000 U.S. military personnel by the end of 1963.**

The message is this: JFK is starting to withdraw, but he'd like to keep it quiet, perhaps fearing public outcry. NSAM 263, unlike the White House statement, was a "Top Secret" document, classified and unavailable to the public.

NSAM 273

The document comes out of the Honolulu conference, the upshoot of which was that the war situation was critical in the Delta region and escalation was on the agenda. McGeorge Bundy wrote a first draft either on his way back from Honolulu or immediately upon his return home. The draft, dated 21 November 63 and recently declassified, uses weaker language than the final version dated 26 November, probably because Bundy knew his current boss wasn't going to like it. But JFK did not leave Texas alive.

The final version, like the draft, is the first step in the policy reversal which led to the prolonged military activity in Vietnam. Paragraph 2 reads:

> **The objectives of the United States with respect to the withdrawal of U.S. military personnel remain as stated in the <u>White House statement of October 2, 1963</u>. (emphasis added)**

Rather than saying they **will implement** the 1,000 man withdrawal of NSAM 263, they go back to the "if things progress to a point" language of the White House statement.

Apparently, we never progressed to that "point". By the end of 1963 the withdrawal had occurred - on paper only, by rotating troops home in December. The total number of U.S. military personnel in Vietnam never dropped by 1,000 men. According to the Pentagon Papers:

In the last weeks of 1963, the U.S. government reassessed the progress of the counterinsurgency effort and the policy options. Plans for phased withdrawal of 1,000 U.S. advisers by end-63 went through the motions by concentrating rotations home in December and letting strength rebound in the subsequent two months. (Vol. II, p.303)

We don't know if JFK would have changed his plans for Vietnam. We do know that there was a change from his line of policy starting four days after his death and continuing until far too many people - American and Vietnamese - had suffered far too much.

There's a famous quote from Stanley Karnow's book on Vietnam. LBJ is at a Christmas party in 1963 with various government and military types. He says to a general, "Just get me elected and you can have your damn war.: So Johnson, the "Peace Candidate", gets elected, and we have a war.

J•F•K

JUNE 28. 1961

NATIONAL SECURITY ACTION MEMORANDUM NO. 55

TO: The Chairman, Joint Chiefs of Staff

SUBJECT: Relations of the Joint Chiefs of Staff to the President in
                         Cold War Operations

I wish to inform the Joint Chiefs of Staff as follows with regard to my views of their relations to me in Cold War Operations:

a. I regard the Joint Chiefs of Staff as my principal military advisor responsible both for initiating advice to me and for responding to requests for advice. I expect their advice to come to me direct and unfiltered.

b. The Joint Chiefs of Staff have a responsibility for the defense of the nation in the Cold War similar to that which they have in conventional hostilities. They should know the military and paramilitary forces and resources available to the Department of Defense, verify their readiness, report on their adequacy, and make appropriate recommendations for their expansion and improvement. I look to the Chiefs to contribute dynamic and imaginative leadership in contributing to the success of the military and paramilitary aspects of Cold War programs.

c. I expect the Joint Chiefs of Staff to present the military viewpoint in governmental councils in such a way as to assure that the military factors are clearly understood before decisions are reached. When only the Chairman or a single Chief is present, that officer must represent the Chiefs as a body, taking such preliminary and subsequent actions as may be necessary to assure that he does in fact represent the corporate judgement of the Joint Chiefs of Staff.

d. While I look to the Chiefs to present the military factor without reserve or hesitation, I regard them to be more than military men and expect their help in fitting military requirements into the over-all context of any situation, recognizing that the most difficult problem in Government is to combine all assets in a unifies, effective pattern.

cc. Secretary of Defense
General Taylor

JUNE 28, 1961

NATIONAL SECURITY ACTION MEMORANDUM NO. 56

TO: The Secretary of Defense

SUBJECT: Evaluation of Paramilitary Requirements

The President has approved the following paragraph:

> "It is important that we anticipate now our possible future
> requirements in the field of unconventional warfare and
> paramilitary operations. A first step would be to inventory the
> paramilitary assets we have in the United States Armed Forces,
> consider various areas in the world where the implementation
> of our policy may require indigenous paramilitary forces, and
> thus arrive at a determination of the goals which we should set
> in this field. Having determined the assets and the possible
> requirements, it would then become a matter of developing a
> plan to meet the deficit."

The President requests that the Secretary of Defense, in coordination with
the Department of state, and the CIA, make such an estimate of requirements
and recommend ways and means to meet these requirements.

McGeorge Bundy

cc: Secretary of State
Director, CIA
General Maxwell Taylor

J•F•K

OCTOBER 11, 1963

NATIONAL SECURITY ACTION MEMORANDUM NO. 263

TO: Secretary of State
                  Secretary of Defense
                  Chairman of the Joint Chiefs of Staff

SUBJECT: South Vietnam

At a meeting on October 5, 1963, the President considered the recommendations contained in the report of Secretary McNamara and General Taylor on their mission to South Vietnam.

The President approved the military recommendations contained in Section I B (1-3) of the report, but directed that no formal announcement be made of the implementation of plans to withdraw 1,000 U.S. military personnel by the end of 1963.

After discussion of the remaining recommendations of the report, the President approved the instruction to Ambassador Lodge which is set forth in State Department telegram No. 534 to Saigon.

McGeorge Bundy

Copy furnished:
Director of Central Intelligence
Administrator, Agency for International Development

11/21/63

DRAFT

TOP SECRET

NATIONAL SECURITY ACTION MEMORANDUM NO_____

The President has reviewed the discussions of South Vietnam which occurred in Honolulu, and has discussed the matter further with Ambassador Lodge. He directs that the following guidance be issued to all concerned:

1. It remains the central object of the United States in South Vietnam to assist the people and Government of that country to win their contest against the externally directed and supported Communist conspiracy. The test of all decisions and U.S. actions in this area should be the effectiveness of their contributions to this purpose.

2. The objectives of the United States with respect to the withdrawal of U.S. military personnel remain as stated in the White House statement of October 2, 1963.

3. It is a major interest of the United States Government that the present provisional government of South Vietnam should be assisted in consolidating itself in holding and developing increased public support. All U.S. officers should conduct themselves with this objective in view.

4. It is of the highest importance that the United States Government avoid either the appearance or the reality of public recrimination from one part of it against another, and the President expects that all senior officers of the Government will take energetic steps to insure that they and their subordinates go out of their way to maintain and to defend the unity of the United States Government both here and in the field.

More specifically, the President approves the following lines of action developed in the discussions of the Honolulu meeting of November 20. The office or offices of the Government to which central responsibility is assigned is indicated in each case.

5. We should concentrate our own efforts, and insofar as possible we should persuade the government of South Vietnam to concentrate its efforts, on the critical situation in the Mekong Delta. This concentration should include not only military but political, economic, social, educational and informational efforts. We should seek to turn the tide not only of battle but of belief, and we should seek to increase not only our control of land but the productivity of this area whenever the proceeds can be held for the advantage of anti-Communist forces.

(Action: The whole country team under the direct supervision of the Ambassador.)

6. Programs of military and economic assistance should be maintained at such levels that their magnitude and effectiveness in the eyes of the Vietnamese Government do not fall below the levels sustained by the United States in the time of the Diem Government. This does not exclude arrangements for economy on the MAP accounting for ammunition and any other readjustments which are possible as between MAP and other U.S. defense sources. Special attention should be given to the expansion of the import distribution and effective use of fertilizer for the Delta.

(Action: AID and DOD as appropriate.)

7. With respect to action against North Vietnam, there should be a detailed plan for the development of additional Government of Vietnam resources, especially for sea-going activity, and such planning should indicate the time and investment necessary to achieve a wholly new level of effectiveness in this field of action.

(Action: DOD and CIA)

8. With respect to Laos, a plan should be developed for military operations up to a line up to 50 kilometers inside Laos, together with political plans for minimizing the international hazards of such an enterprise.Since it is agreed that operational responsibility for such undertakings should pass from CAS to MACV, this plan should provide an alternative method of political liaison for such operations, since their timing and character can have an intimate relation to the fluctuating situation in Laos.

(Action: State, DOD and CIA.)

9. It was agreed in Honolulu that the situation in Cambodia is of the first importance for South Vietnam, and it is therefore urgent that we should lose no opportunity to exercise a favorable influence upon that country. In particular, measures should be undertaken to satisfy ourselves completely that recent charges from Cambodia are groundless, and we should put ourselves in a position to offer to the Cambodians a full opportunity to satisfy themselves on this same point.
(Action: State.)

10. In connection with paragraphs 7 and 8 above, it is desired that we should develop as strong and persuasive a case as possible to demonstrate to the world the degree to which the Viet Cong is controlled, sustained and supplied from Hanoi, through Laos and other channels. In short, we need a more contemporary version of the Jordan Report, as powerful and complete as possible.
(Action: Department of State with other agencies as necessary,.)

McGeorge Bundy

J•F•K

NOVEMBER 26, 1963

NATIONAL SECURITY ACTION MEMORANDUM NO. 273

TO: The Secretary of State
      The Secretary of Defense
      The Director of Central Intelligence
      The Administrator, AID
      The Director, USIA

The President has reviewed the discussions of South Vietnam which occurred in Honolulu, and has discussed the matter further with Ambassador Lodge. He directs that the following guidance be issued to all concerned:

1. It remains the central object of the United States in South Vietnam to assist the people and Government of that country to win their contest against the externally directed and supported Communist conspiracy. The test of all U.S. decisions and actions in this area should be the effectiveness of their contribution to this purpose.

2. The objectives of the United States with respect to the withdrawal of U.S. military personnel remain as stated in the White House statement of October 2, 1963.

3. It is a major interest of the United States Government that the present provisional government of South Vietnam should be assisted in consolidating itself and in holding and developing increased public support. All U.S. officers should conduct themselves with this objective in view.

4. The President expects that all senior officers of the Government will move energetically to insure the full unity of support for established U.S. policy in South Vietnam. Both in Washington and in the field, it is essential that the Government be unified. It is of particular importance that express or implied criticism of officers of other branches be scrupulously avoided in all contacts with the Vietnamese Government and with the press. More specifically, the President approves the following lines of action developed in the discussions of the Honolulu meeting of November 20. The offices of the Government to which central responsibility is assigned are indicated in each case.

5. We should concentrate our own efforts, and insofar as possible we should persuade the Government of South Vietnam to concentrate its efforts, on the critical situation in the Mekong Delta. This concentration should include not only military but political, economic, social, educational and informational effort. We should seek to turn the tide not only of battle but of belief, and we

should seek to increase not only the control of hamlets but the productivity of this area, especially where the proceeds can be held for the advantage of anti-Communist forces.
(Action: The whole country team under the direct supervision of the Ambassador.)

6. Programs of military and economic assistance should be maintained at such levels that their magnitude and effectiveness in the eyes of the Vietnamese Government do not fall below the levels sustained by the United States in the time of the Diem Government. This does not exclude arrangements for economy on the MAP account with respect to accounting for ammunition, or any other readjustments which are possible between MAP and other U.S. defense resources. Special attention should be given to the expansion of the import, distribution, and effective use of fertilizer for the Delta.
(Action: AID and DOD as appropriate.)

7. Planning should include different levels of possible increased activity, and in each instance there should be estimates of such factors as:

A. Resulting damage to North Vietnam;

B. The plausibility of denial;

C. Possible North Vietnamese retaliation;

D. Other international reaction.

Plans should be submitted promptly for approval by higher authority.
(Action: State, DOD, and CIA.)

8. With respect to Laos, a plan should be developed and submitted for approval by higher authority for military operations up to a line up to 50 kilometers inside Laos, together with political plans for minimizing the international hazards of such an enterprise. Since it is agreed that operational responsibility for such undertakings should pass from CAS to MACV, this plan should include a redefined method of political guidance for such operations, since their timing and character can have an intimate relation to the fluctuating situation in Laos.
(Action: State, DOD, and CIA.)

9. It was agreed in Honolulu that the situation in Cambodia is of the first importance for South Vietnam, and it is therefore urgent that we should lose no opportunity to exercise a favorable influence upon that country. In par-

ticular a plan should be developed using all available evidence and methods of persuasion for showing the Cambodians that the recent charges against us are groundless.
(Action: State.)

10. In connection with paragraphs 7 and 8 above, it is desired that we should develop as strong and persuasive a case as possible to demonstrate to the world the degree to which the Viet Cong is controlled, sustained and supplied from Hanoi, through Laos and other channels. In short, we need a more contemporary version of the Jordan Report, as powerful and complete as possible. (Action: Department of State with other agencies as necessary.

Mc George Bundy

cc: Mr. Bundy
   Mr. Forrestal
   Mr.Johnson
   NSC Files

JUNE 28, 1961

NATIONAL SECURITY ACTION MEMORANDUM NO. 57

TO: The Secretary of State
        The Secretary of Defense
        The Director, CIA

The President has approved the following recommendation:

The Special Group (5412 Committee) will perform the functions assigned in the recommendation to the Strategic Resources Group.

McGeorge Bundy

cc:General Maxwell D. Taylor

                    cc: Mrs. Lincoln
                            Mr. Smith
                            Mr. McG Bundy File

RESPONSIBILITY FOR PARAMILITARY OPERATIONS

      1. For the purpose of this study, a paramilitary operation is considered to be one which by its tactics and its requirements in military-type personnel, equipment and training approximates a conventional military operation. It may be undertaken in support of an existing government friendly to the U.S. or in support of a rebel group seeking to overthrow a government hostile to us. The U.S. may render assistance to such operations overtly, covertly or by a combination of both methods. In size these operations may vary from the infiltration of a squad of guerrillas to a military operation such as the Cuban invasion. The small operations will often fall completely within the normal capability of one agency; the large ones may affect State, Defense, CIA, USIA and possibly other departments and agencies.

      2. In order to conduct paramilitary operations with maximum effectiveness and flexibility within the context of the Cold War, it is recommended that current directives and procedures be modified to affect the following:

a. Any proposed paramilitary operation in the concept stage will be presented to the Strategic Resources Group for initial consideration and for approval as necessary by the President. thereafter, the SRG will assign primary responsibility for planning, for interdepartmental coordination and for execution to the Task Force, department or individual best qualified to carry forward the operation to success, and will indicate supporting responsibilities. Under this principle, the Department of Defense will normally receive responsibility for overt paramilitary operations. Where such an operation is to be wholly covert or disavowable, it may be assigned to CIA, provided that it is within the normal capabilities of the agency. Any large paramilitary operation wholly or partly covert which requires significant numbers of militarily trained personnel, amounts of military equipment which exceed normal CIA-controlled stocks and/or military experience of a kind and level peculiar to the Armed Services is properly the primary responsibility of the Department of Defense with the CIA in a supporting role.

GARRISON'S CLOSING STATEMENT

May it please the court. Gentlemen of the jury:

I know you're very tired. You've been very patient. This final day has been a long one, so I'll speak only a few minutes.

In his argument, Mr. Dymond posed one final issue which raises the question of what we do when the need for justice is confronted by power.

So, let me talk to you about the question of whether or not there was government fraud in this case—a question Mr. Dymond seems to want us to answer.

A government is a great deal like a human being. It's not necessarily all good, and it's not necessarily all bad. We live in a good country. I love it and you do, too. Nevertheless, the fact remains that we have a government which is not perfect.

There have been indications since November the 22nd of 1963—and that was not the last indication—that there is excessive power in some parts of our government. It is plain that the people have not received all of the truth about some of the things which have happened, about some of the assassinations which have occurred—and more particularly about the assassination of John Kennedy.

Going back to when we were children ... I think most of us—probably all of us in this courtroom—once thought that justice came into being of its own accord, that virtue was its own reward, that good would triumph over evil—in short, that justice occurred automatically. Later, when we found that this wasn't quite so, most of us still felt hopefully that at least justice occurred frequently of its own accord.

Today, I think that almost all of us would have to agree that there is really no machinery—not on this earth at least—which causes justice to occur automatically. Men have to make it occur.Individual human beings have to make it occur. Otherwise, it doesn't come into existence. This is not always easy. As a matter of fact, it's always hard, because justice presents a threat to power. In order to make justice come into being, you often have to fight power.

Mr. Dymond raised the question: Why don't we say it's all a fraud and charge the government with fraud, if this is the case? Let me be explicit, then, and make myself very clear on this point.

The government's handling of the investigation of John Kennedy's murder was a fraud. It was the greatest fraud in the history of our country. It probably was the greatest fraud ever perpetrated in the history of humankind.

That doesn't mean that we have to accept the continued existence of the kind of government which allows this to happen. We can do something about it. We're not forced either to leave this country or accept the authoritarianism that has developed—the authoritarianism that tells us that in the year 2039 we can see the evidence about what happened to John Kennedy.

Government does not consist only of secret police and domestic espionage operations and generals and admirals—government consists of people. It also consists of juries. And in cases of murder—whether the poorest individual or the most distinguished citizen in the land—should be looked at openly in a court of law, where juries can pass on them and not be hidden, not be buried like the body of the victim beneath concrete for countless years.

You men in recent weeks have heard witnesses that no one else in the world has heard. You've seen the Zapruder film. You've seen what happened to your President. I suggest to you that you know right now that, in that area at least, a fraud has been perpetrated.

That does not mean that our government is entirely bad; and I want to emphasize that. It does mean, however, that in recent years, through the development of excessive power because of the Cold War, forces have developed in our government over which there is no control and these forces have an authoritarian approach to justice—meaning, they will let you know what justice is.

Well, my reply to them is that we already know what justice is. It is the decision of the people passing on the evidence. It is the jury system. In the issue which is posed by the government's conduct in concealing the evidence in this case—in the issue of humanity as opposed to power—I have chosen humanity, and I will do it again without hesitation. I hope every one of you will do the same. I do this because I love my country and because I want to communicate to the government that we will not accept unexplained assassinations with the casual information that if we live seventy-five years longer, we might be given more evidence.

In this particular case, massive power was brought to bear to prevent justice from ever coming into this courtroom. The power to make authoritarian pronouncements, the power to manipulate the news media by the release of false information, the power to interfere with an honest inquiry and the power to provide an endless variety of experts to testify in behalf of that power, repeatedly was demonstrated in this case.

The American people have yet to see the Zapruder film. Why? The American people have yet to see and hear from the real witnesses to the assassination. Why? Because, today in America too much emphasis is given to secrecy, with regard to the assassination of our President, and not enough emphasis is given to the question of justice and to the question of humanity.

These dignified deceptions will not suffice. We have had enough of power without truth. We don't have to accept power without truth or else leave the country. I don't accept either of these two alternatives. I don't intend to leave the country and I don't intend to accept power without truth.

I intend to fight for the truth. I suggest that not only is this not un-American, but it is the most American thing we can do—because if truth does not endure, then our country will not endure.

In our country the worst of all crimes occurs when the government murders truth. If it can murder truth, it can murder freedom.If it can murder freedom it can murder your own sons—if they should dare to fight for freedom—and then it can announce that they were killed in an industrial accident, or shot by the "enemy" or God knows what.

In this case, finally, it has been possible to bring the truth about the assassination into a court of law—not before a commission composed of important and politically astute men, but before a jury of citizens.

Now, I suggest to you that yours is a hard duty, because in a sense what you're passing on is equivalent to a murder case. The difficult thing about passing on a murder case is that the victim is out of your sight and buried a long distance away, and all you can see is the defendant. It's very difficult to identify with someone you can't see, and sometimes it's hard not to identify to some extent with the defendant and his problems.

In that regard, every prosecutor who is at all humane is conscious of feeling sorry for the defendant in every case he prosecutes. But he is not free to forget the victim who lies buried out of sight. I suggest to you that, if you do your duty, you also are not free to forget the victim who is buried out of sight.

You know, Tennyson once said that "authority forgets a dying king." This was never more true than in the murder of John Kennedy. The strange and deceptive conduct of the government after his murder began while his body was still warm, and has continued for five years. You have even seen in this courtroom indications of interest of part of the government power structure in keeping the truth down, in keeping the grave closed.

We presented a number of eyewitnesses as well as an expert witness as well as the Zapruder film, to show that the fatal wound of the President came from the front. A plane landed from Washington and out stepped Dr. Finck for the defense, to counter the clear and apparent evidence of a shot from the front. I don't have to go into Dr. Finck's testimony in detail for you to show that it simply did not correspond to the facts. He admitted that he did not complete the autopsy because a general told him not to complete the autopsy.

In this conflict between power and justice—to put it that way—just where do you think Dr. Finck stands? A general who was not a pathologist, told him not to complete the autopsy, so he didn't complete it. This is not the way I want my country to be. When our President is killed he deserves the kind of autopsy that the ordinary citizen gets every day in the state of Louisiana. And the people deserve the facts about it. We can't have government power suddenly interjecting itself and preventing the truth from coming to the people.

Yet in this case, before the sun rose the next morning, power had moved into the situation and the truth was being concealed. And now, five years later in this courtroom the power of the government in concealing the truth is continuing in the same way.

We presented eyewitnesses who told you of the shots coming from the grassy knoll. A plane landed from Washington, and out came ballistics expert Frazier for the defense. Mr. Frazier's explanation of the sound of the shots coming from the front, which was heard by eyewitness after eyewitness, was that Lee Oswald created a sonic boom in his firing. Not only did Oswald break all of the world's records for marksmanship, but he broke the sound barrier as well.

I suggest to you, that if any of you have shot on a firing range—and most of you probably have in the service—you were shooting rifles in which the bullet traveled faster than the speed of sound. I ask you to recall if you ever heard a sonic boom. If you remember when you were on the firing line, and they would say, "Ready on the left; ready on the right; ready on the firing line; commence firing," you heard the shots coming from the firing line—to the left of you and to the right of you. If you had heard, as a result of Frazier's fictional sonic boom, firing coming at you from the pits, you would have had a reaction which you would still remember.

Mr. Frazier's sonic boom simply doesn't exist. It's a part of the fraud—a part of the continuing government fraud.

The best way to make this country the kind of country it's supposed to be is to communicate to the government that no matter how powerful it may be, we do not accept these frauds. We do not accept these false announcements. We do not accept the concealment of evidence with regard to the murder of President Kennedy.

Who is the most believable: A Richard Randolph Carr, seated here in a wheelchair and telling you what he saw and what he heard and how he was told to shut his mouth—or Mr. Frazier with his sonic booms?

Do we really have to actually reject Mr. Newman and Mrs. Newman and Mr. Carr and Roger Craig and the testimony of all those honest witnesses—reject all this and accept the fraudulent Warren Commission, or else leave the country?

I suggest to you that there are other alternatives. One of them has been put in practice in the last month in the State of Louisiana—and that is to bring out the truth in a proceeding where attorneys can cross-examine, where the defendant can be confronted by testimony against him, where the rules of evidence are applied and where a jury of citizens can pass on it—and where there is no government secrecy ... Above all, where you do not have evidence concealed for seventy-five years in the name of "national security."

All we have in this case are the facts—facts which show that the defendant participated in the conspiracy to kill the President and that the President was subsequently killed in an ambush.

The reply of the defense has been the same as the early reply of the government in the Warren Commission. It has been authority, authority, authority. The President's seal outside of each volume of the Warren Commission Report—made necessary because there is nothing inside these volumes ... men of high position and prestige sitting on a Board, and announcing the results to you, but not telling you what the evidence is, because the evidence has to be hidden for seventy-five years.

You heard in this courtroom in recent weeks, eyewitness after eyewitness after eyewitness and, above all, you saw one eyewitness which was indifferent to power—the Zapruder film. The lens of the camera is totally indifferent to power and it tells what happened as it saw it happen—and that is one of the reasons 200 million Americans have not seen the Zapruder film. They should have seen it many times. They should know exactly what happened. They all should know what you know now.

Why hasn't all of this come into being if there hasn't been government fraud? Of course there has been fraud by the government.

But I'm telling you now that I think we can do something about it. I think that there are still enough Americans left in this country to make it continue to be America. I think that we can still fight authoritarianism—the government's insistence on secrecy, government force used in counterattacks against an honest inquiry—and when we do that, we're not being un-American, we're being American. It isn't easy. You're sticking your neck out in a rather permanent way, but it has to be done because truth does not come into being automatically. Justice does not happen automatically. Individual men, like the members of my staff here, have to work and fight to make it happen—and individual men like you have to make justice come into being because otherwise it doesn't happen.

What I'm trying to tell you is that there are forces in America today, unfortunately, which are not in favor of the truth coming out about John Kennedy's assassination. As long as our government continues to be like this, as long as such forces can get away with such actions, then this is no longer the country in which we were born.

The murder of John Kennedy was probably the most terrible moment in the history of our country. Yet, circumstances have placed you in the position where not only have you seen the hidden evidence but you are actually going to have the opportunity to bring justice into the picture for the first time.

Now, you are here sitting in judgement on Clay Shaw. Yet you, as men, represent more than jurors in an ordinary case because of the victim in this case. You represent, in a sense, the hope of humanity against government power. You represent humanity, which yet may triumph over excessive government power— if you will cause it to be so, in the course of doing your duty in this case.

I suggest that you ask not what your country can do for you but what you can do for your country.

What can you do for your country? You can cause justice to happen for the first time in this matter. You can help make our country better by showing that this is still a government of the people. And if you do that, as long as you live, nothing will ever be more important.

CIA DOCUMENT #1035-960

RE: Concerning Criticism of the Warren Report

1. Our Concern. From the day of President Kennedy's assassination on, there has been speculation about the responsibility for his murder. Although this was stemmed for a time by the Warren Commission report, (which appeared at the end of September 1964), various writers have now had time to scan the Commission's published report and documents for new pretexts for questioning, and there has been a new wave of books and articles criticizing the Commission's findings. In most cases the critics have speculated as to the existence of some kind of conspiracy, and often they have implied that the Commission itself was involved. Presumably as a result of the increasing challenge to the Warren Commission's report, a public opinion poll recently indicated that 46% of the American public did not think that Oswald acted alone, while more than half of those polled thought that the Commission had left some questions unresolved. Doubtless polls abroad would show similar, or possibly more adverse results.

2. This trend of opinion is a matter of concern to the U.S. government, including our organization. The members of the Warren Commission were naturally chosen for their integrity, experience and prominence. They represented both major parties, and they and their staff were deliberately drawn from all sections of the country. Just because of the standing of the Commissioners, efforts to impugn their rectitude and wisdom tend to cast doubt on the whole leadership of American society. Moreover, there seems to be an increasing tendency to hint that President Johnson himself, as the one person who might be said to have benefited, was in some way responsible for the assassination. Innuendo of such seriousness affects not only the individual concerned, but also the whole reputation of the American government. Our organization itself is directly involved: among other facts, we contributed information to the investigation. Conspiracy theories have frequently thrown suspicion on our organization, for example by falsely alleging that Lee Harvey Oswald worked for us. The aim of this dispatch is to provide material countering and discrediting the claims of the conspiracy theorists, so as to inhibit the circulation of such claims in other countries. Background information is supplied in a classified section and in a number of unclassified attachments.

3. Action. We do not recommend that discussion of the assassination question be initiated where it is not already taking place. Where discussion is active [business] addresses are requested:

a. To discuss the publicity problem with [?] and friendly elite contacts (especially politicians and editors), pointing out that the Warren Commission made as thorough an investigation as humanly possible, that the charges of the critics are without serious foundation, and that further speculative discussion only plays into the hands of the opposition. Point out also that parts of the conspiracy talk appear to be deliberately generated by Communist propagandists. Urge them to use their influence to discourage unfounded and irresponsible speculation.

b. To employ propaganda assets to [negate] and refute the attacks of the critics. Book reviews and feature articles are particularly appropriate for this purpose. The unclassified attachments to this guidance should provide useful background material for passing to assets. Our ploy should point out, as applicable, that the critics are (I) wedded to theories adopted before the evidence was in, (II) politically interested, (III) financially interested, (IV) hasty and inaccurate in their research, or (V) infatuated with their own theories. In the course of discussions of the whole phenomenon of criticism, a useful strategy may be to single out Epstein's theory for attack, using the attached Fletcher [?] article and Spectator piece for background. (Although Mark Lane's book is much less convincing that Epstein's and comes off badly where confronted by knowledgeable critics, it is also much more difficult to answer as a whole, as one becomes lost in a morass of unrelated details.

4. In private to media discussions not directed at any particular writer, or in attacking publications which may be yet forthcoming, the following arguments should be useful:

a. No significant new evidence has emerged which the Commission did not consider. The assassination is sometimes compared (e.g., by Joachim Joesten and Bertrand Russell) with the Dreyfus case; however, unlike that case, the attacks on the Warren Commission have produced no new evidence, no new culprits have been convincingly identified, and there is no agreement among the critics. (A better parallel, though an imperfect one, might be with the Reichstag fire of 1933, which some competent historians (Fritz Tobias, A.J.P. Taylor, D.C. Watt) now believe was set by Van der Lubbe on his own initiative, without acting for either Nazis or Communists; the Nazis tried to pin the blame on the Communists, but the latter have been more successful in convincing the world that the Nazis were to blame.)

b. Critics usually overvalue particular items and ignore others. They tend to place more emphasis on the recollections of individual witnesses (which are less reliable and more divergent—and hence offer more hand-holds for criticism) and less on ballistics, autopsy, and photographic evidence. A close examination of the Commission's records will usually show that the conflicting eyewitness accounts are quoted out of context, or were discarded by the Commission for good and sufficient reason.

c. Conspiracy on the large scale often suggested would be impossible to conceal in the United States, esp. since informants could expect to receive large royalties, etc. Note that Robert Kennedy, Attorney General at the time and John F. Kennedy's brother, would be the last man to overlook or conceal any conspiracy. And as one reviewer pointed out, Congressman Gerald R. Ford would hardly have held his tongue for the sake of the Democratic administration, and Senator Russell would have had every political interest in exposing any misdeeds on the part of Chief Justice Warren. A conspirator moreover would hardly choose a location for a shooting where so much depended on conditions beyond his control: the route, the speed of the cars, the moving target, the risk that the assassin would be discovered. A group of wealthy conspirators could have arranged much more secure conditions.

d. Critics have often been enticed by a form of intellectual pride: they light on some theory and fall in love with it; they also scoff at the Commission because it did not always answer every question with a flat decision one way or the other. Actually, the make-up of the Commission and its staff was an excellent safeguard against over-commitment to any one theory, or against the illicit transformation of probabilities into certainties.

e. Oswald would not have been any sensible person's choice for a co-conspirator. He was a "loner," mixed up, of questionable reliability and an unknown quantity to any professional intelligence service.

f. As to charges that the Commission's report was a rush job, it emerged three months after the deadline originally set. But to the degree that the Commission tried to speed up its reporting, this was largely due to the pressure of irresponsible speculation already appearing, in some cases coming from the same critics who, refusing to admit their errors, are now putting out new criticisms.

g. Such vague accusations as that "more than ten people have died mysteriously" can always be explained in some natural way e.g.: the individuals concerned have for the most part died of natural causes; the Commission staff questioned 418 witnesses (the FBI interviewed far more people, conduction 25,000 interviews and reinterviews), and in such a large group, a certain number of deaths are to be expected. (When Penn Jones, one of the originators of the "ten mysterious deaths" line, appeared on television, it emerged that two of the deaths on his list were from heart attacks, one from cancer, one was from ahead-on collision on a bridge, and one occurred when a driver drifted into a bridge abutment.)

5. Where possible, counter speculation by encouraging reference to the Commission's Report itself. Open-minded foreign readers should still be impressed by the care, thoroughness, objectivity and speed with which the Commission worked. Reviewers of other books might be encouraged to add to their account the idea that, checking back with the report itself, they found it far superior to the work of its critics.

KEY FEATURES OF J.F.K. FILES RESOLUTION:

• Mandates a comprehensive review of all federal government records relating to the assassination of President John F. Kennedy, including the records of the Warren Commission, the House Assassinations Committee, the Church Committee, and all Executive branch agencies, including the C.I.A. and F.B.I.

• Establishes an impartial, independent 5-member Review Board appointed by the special federal court which appoints Independent Counsels with overall responsibility for conducting this review in accordance with the standards set forth in the Resolution.

• Requires that all federal records relating to the assassination of President Kennedy be made available to the Executive Director of the Review Board.

• To the extent the Executive Director of the Board and the Executive agency or congressional committee which originated an assassination record can agree that the record should be released pursuant to the standards in the Resolution, the record shall be automatically released to the public through the National Archives.

• Where the originating agency or committee raises objections to release of particular records pursuant to the standards set forth in the Resolution, or where there is a concern for individual privacy apparent in a record to be released, the Executive Director is required to refer the case to the Review Board for decision.

• The Review Board must evaluate each record referred. It may convene hearings, issue subpoenas, and make such consultations as may be necessary to arrive at a decision.

• The Resolution provides several general categories which might justify postponing the immediate disclosure of an assassination record, but provides that postponement will always be weighed against the public interest in disclosure of the record in question. These categories include the protection of current intelligence sources or methods, damage to current foreign relations, the preservation of guarantees of confidentiality made to witnesses, substantial invasions of personal privacy, and the disclosure of measures used by the Secret Service and other agencies to protect government officials.

• The Review Board is authorized to release portions of documents that are not affected by the originating agency or committee's objection, and to consider appropriate summaries or substitutions for information whose release would otherwise qualify for postponement, in the interest of the fullest disclosure.

• If the Review Board determines that release of a particular record should be postponed, it must assign a date or event after which such record should again be reviewed for release by the Archivist. Notice of the Board's decisions to postpone will be published in summary form.

• If the Review Board determines that a record should be disclosed, the Board's decision is final, except where the record was originated by an agency within the Executive Branch. In this case, should the President personally determine within 60 days that the Board's decision should be superceded, he may order that disclosure of the record concerned be postponed until a future date or event. The President is required to publish notice of his decisions in the Federal Register and to provide copies of the documents in question together with his reasons for postponing disclosure to the congressional committees charged with oversight of the Board.

• The Review Board is authorized to obtain detailees from Executive branch agencies necessary to enable it to accomplish its functions.

• The term of the Review Board is two years beginning from the date it is officially convened and operational. The Board may extend itself by majority vote for an additional year if needed to complete its work. Further extensions must be authorized by Congress.

102ND CONGRESS, 2ND SESSION

JOINT RESOLUTION:

To provide for the expeditious disclosure of records relevant to the assassination of President John F. Kennedy

Resolved by the Senate and House of Representatives of the United States of America in Congress assembled,

SECTION 1. SHORT TITLE.

This joint resolution may be cited as the "Assassination Materials Disclosure Act of 1992."

SEC.2. FINDINGS, DECLARATIONS, AND PURPOSE.

(a) FINDINGS AND DECLARATIONS.-The Congress finds and declares that-

(1) the legitimacy of any government in a free society depends on the consent of the people;

(2) the ability of a government in a free society to obtain the consent of the people is undermined to the degree that the people do not trust their government;

(3) the disclosure of records in the possession of the Government relevant to the assassination of President John F. Kennedy will contribute to the trust of the people in their government;

(4) the disclosure of records in the possession of the Government relevant to the assassination of President John F. Kennedy should proceed as expeditiously as practicable; and

(5) all records in the possession of the Government relevant to the assassination of President John F. Kennedy should be released to the public at the earliest opportunity, except where clear and convincing justification exists for postponing the disclosure of such records to a specified time or following a specified occurrence in the future.

(b) PURPOSE.- The purpose of this Joint Resolution is to secure the expeditious disclosure of records relevant to the assassination of President John F. Kennedy as soon as practicable consistent with the public-interest.

SEC. 3. DEFINITIONS.

In this Joint Resolution:

(1) "Archivist" means the Archivist of the United States.

(2) "Assassination material" means a record that relates in any manner or degree to the assassination of President John F. Kennedy, that was created or obtained by the House Committee, the Senate Committee, the Warren Commission, or an Executive agency or any other entity within the Executive branch of the Government, and that is in the custody of the House of Representatives, the Senate, the National Archives, or any other Executive agency, but does not include (A) material to the extent that it pertains to personnel matters or other administrative affairs of a congressional committee, the Warren Commission, or any entity within the Executive branch of the Government; or (B) the autopsy materials donated by the Kennedy family to the National Archives pursuant to a deed of gift regulating access to those materials, which are addressed in subsection 10(b) of this Joint Resolution.

(3) "Committee" means the House Committee or Senate Committee.

(4) "Executive agency" means an Executive agency as defined in subsection 552(f) of title 5, United States Code.

(5) "House Committee" means the Select Committee on Assassinations of the House of Representatives and the Permanent Select Committee on Intelligence of the House of Representatives acting under this Joint Resolution with respect to assassination materials in the custody of the House of Representatives.

(6) "National Archives" means the National Archives and Records Administration.

(7) "Originating body" means the Executive agency, commission, or congressional committee that created the particular record or obtained the particular record from a source other than another entity of the Government, or the custodian of records of that agency, commission, or committee for purposes of this Joint Resolution. For purposes of this Joint Resolution, (A) the custodian of records of the Select Committee on Assassinations of the House of Representatives is the Permanent Select Committee on Intelligence of the

House of Representatives; (B) the custodian of records of the Select Committee to Study Governmental Operations With Respect to Intelligence of the Senate; and (C) the custodian or records of the Warren Commission is the Archivist of the United States.

(8) "Record" includes a book, paper, map, photograph, machine readable material, computerized, digitized, or electronic information, regardless of the medium on which it is stored, or other documentary material, regardless of its physical form or characteristics.

(9) "Review Board" means the Assassination Material Review Board established under section 5.

(10) "Senate Committee" means the Select Committee to Study Governmental Operations with Respect to Intelligence of the Senate and the Select Committee on Intelligence of the Senate acting under this Joint Resolution with respect to assassination materials in the custody of the Senate.

(11) "Warren Commission" means the President's Commission on the Assassination of President John F. Kennedy.

SEC. 4. PUBLIC DISCLOSURE OF MATERIALS BY CONGRESS AND THE EXECUTIVE BRANCH.

(a) IN GENERAL.- Except for assassination material or particular information in assassination material the disclosure of which is postponed under section 8, all assassination materials shall be transferred to the National Archives and made available for inspection and copying by the general public as soon as practicable.

(b) FEES FOR COPYING.- The Archivist shall charge fees for copying and grant waivers of such fees pursuant to the standards established by section 552 of Title 5, United States Code.

(c) PRINTING AND DISSEMINATION OF ASSASSINATION MATERIALS.-

(1) The Archivist may provide copies of assassination materials of broad public interest to the Government Printing Office, which shall print copies for sale to the public.

(2) Assassination materials printed by the Government Printing Office pursuant to this subsection shall be placed in libraries throughout the United States that are Government depositories in accordance with the provisions of Chapter 19 of Title 44, United States Code.

SEC. 5. ASSASSINATION MATERIALS REVIEW BOARD.

(a) ESTABLISHMENT.- There is established as an independent agency a board to be known as the Assassination Materials Review Board.

(b) APPOINTMENT.-

(1) The division of the United States Court of Appeals for the District of Columbia Circuit established under section 49 of title 28, United States Code, shall, within 90 days of the date of enactment of this Joint Resolution, appoint, without regard to political affiliation, 5 distinguished and impartial private citizens, none of whom are presently employees of any branch of the Government and none of whom shall have had any previous involvement with any investigation or inquiry relating to the assassination of President John F. Kennedy, to serve as members of the Review Board.

(2) A vacancy on the Review Board shall be filled in the same manner as the original appointment was made under paragraph (1).

(3) The members of the Review Board shall be deemed to be inferior officers of the United States within the meaning of section 2 of article II of the Constitution.

(c) CHAIR.- The members of the Review Board shall elect 1 of its members as chair at its initial meeting.

(d) COMPENSATION OF MEMBERS.-

(1) A member of the Review Board shall be compensated at a rate equal to the daily equivalent of the annual rate of basic pay prescribed for level IV of the Executive Schedule under section 5315 of title 5, United States Code, for each day (including travel time) during which the member is engaged in the performance of the duties of the Review Board.

(2) A member of the Review Board shall be allowed reasonable travel expenses, including per diem in lieu of subsistence, at rates authorized for employees of agencies under subchapter I of chapter 57 of title 5, United States Code, while away from the member's home or regular place of business in the performance of services for the Review Board.

(e) STAFF.-

(1) The Review Board may, without regard to the civil service laws and regulations, appoint and terminate an Executive Director and such other additional personnel as are necessary to enable the Review Board to perform its duties. The individual appointed Executive Director shall be a person of integrity and impartiality who is not a present employee of any branch of the Government and has had no previous involvement with any investigation or inquiry relating to the assassination of President John F. Kennedy.

(2) The Review Board may fix the compensation of the executive director and other personnel without regard to the provisions of chapter 51 and subchapter III of chapter 53 of title 5, United States Code, relating to classification of positions and General Schedule pay rates, except that the rate of pay for the executive director and other personnel may not exceed the rate payable for level V of the Executive Schedule under section 5316 of that title.

(3) At the request of the Executive Director, Executive agencies, including the National Archives and other originating bodies within the Executive branch, shall detail to the Review Board such employees as may be necessary and appropriate to carry out the review required by this Joint Resolution. Any employee detailed to the Review Board for this purpose shall be detailed without reimbursement, and such detail shall be without interruption or loss of civil service status or privilege.

(4) The Review Board may procure temporary and intermittent services under section 3109(b) of title 5, United States Code, at rates for individuals that do not exceed the daily equivalent of the annual rate of basic pay prescribed for level V of the Executive Schedule under section 5316 of that title.

(f) INAPPLICABILITY OF CERTAIN LAWS.- The following laws shall not apply to the Review Board:

(1) Subchapter II of chapter 5 of title 5, United States Code.
(2) Chapter 7 of title 5, United States Code.
(3) Section 3105 and 3344 of title 5, United States Code.

(g) DUTIES.- The Review Board shall consider and render decisions on referrals by the Executive Director and appeals as provided in section 7 for a determination-

(1) whether a record constitutes assassination material subject to this Joint Resolution; and

(2) whether a record or particular information in a record qualifies for postponement of disclosure under this Joint Resolution.

(h) REMOVAL.-

(1) A member of the Review Board may be removed from office, other than by impeachment and conviction, only by the action of the President of the Attorney General acting on behalf of the President, and only for inefficiency, neglect of duty, malfeasance in office, physical disability, mental incapacity, or any other condition that substantially impairs the performance of the member's duties.

(2)(A) If a member of the Review Board is removed from office, the Attorney General shall promptly submit to the division of the court that appointed the members of the Review Board, the committee on the Judiciary of the Senate, and the Committee on the Judiciary of the House of Representatives a report specifying the facts found and the ultimate grounds for the removal. (B) The division of the court, the Committee on the Judiciary of the Senate, and the Committee on the Judiciary of the House of Representatives shall make available to the public a report submitted under subparagraph (A), except that the division of the court or either judiciary committee may, if necessary to protect the rights of a person named in the report or to prevent undue interference with any pending prosecution, postpone or refrain from publishing any or all of the report.

(3)(A) A member of the Review Board removed from office may obtain judicial review of the removal in a civil action commenced in the United States District Court, for the District of Columbia.(B) A member of the division of the court that appointed the members of the Review Board may not hear or determine a civil action or an appeal of a decision in a civil action brought under subparagraph (A). (C) The member may be reinstated or granted other appropriate relief by order of the court.

(i) OVERSIGHT.-

(1) The Committee _____ of the House of Representatives and the Select Committee on Intelligence of the Senate shall have continuing oversight jurisdiction with respect to the official conduct of the Review Board, to include access to any records held or created by the Review Board, and the Review Board shall have the duty to cooperate with the exercise of such oversight jurisdiction.

(2) The Review Board shall submit to the Congress such statements or reports on the activities of the Review Board as the Review Board considers to be appropriate in addition to the notifications required by subsection 8(g).

(j) SUPPORT SERVICES.- The Administrator of the General Services Administration shall provide administrative services for the Review Board on a reimbursable basis. The Archivist shall provide support services for the Review Board to include, as necessary, office space, clerical support, and personnel support, on a reimbursable basis.

(k) INTERPRETIVE REGULATIONS.- The Review Board may issue interpretive regulations.

(l) TERMINATION.-

(1) The Review Board and the terms of its members shall terminate within two years of the date upon which the Board is formally constituted pursuant to this Joint Resolution and begins operations. Provided that, if the Review Board has not completed its work pursuant to this Joint Resolution within such two-year period, it may, by majority vote, extend its term for an additional one-year period for such purpose. Any additional extension of the Review Board and the terms of its members shall be authorized by Congress.

(2) At least 30 days prior to the completion of its work, the Review Board shall provide written notice to the President and the Congress of its intention to terminate its operations at a specified date.

SEC. 6. GROUNDS FOR POSTPONEMENT OF DISCLOSURE.

Disclosure to the general public of assassination material or particular information in assassination material may be postponed if its release would —

(1) reveal —
    (A) an intelligence agent;
    (B) an intelligence source or method which is currently utilized, or reasonably expected to be utilized, by the United States Government; or
    (C) any other matter currently relating to the military defense, intelligence operations or conduct of foreign relations of the United States; and the threat to the military defense, intelligence operations or conduct of foreign relations of the United States posed by its disclosure is of such gravity that it outweighs any public interest in its disclosure;

(2) constitute an invasion of privacy of a living person, whether that person is identified in the material or not, and that invasion of privacy is so substantial that it outweighs any public interest in its disclosure.

(3) constitute a substantial and unjustified violation of an understanding of confidentiality, written or oral, between a Government agent and a witness or a foreign government; or

(4) disclose a security or protective procedure currently utilized, or reasonably expected to be utilized, by the Secret Service or other Government agency responsible for protecting Government officials, and that disclosure is so harmful that it outweighs any public interest in its disclosure.

SEC.7. REVIEW OF MATERIALS BY THE EXECUTIVE DIRECTOR

(a) RELEASE OF ALL ASSASSINATION MATERIALS TO TH EXECUTIVE DIRECTOR - . Each Executive agency, including the National Archives, shall make available to the Executive Director all assassination materials, as defined in section 3, in its possession, including but not limited to, in the case of the National Archives, the records of the Warren Commission, the House Committee, and the Senate Committee. Where the agency is uncertain if a record is assassination material, it shall make that record available to the Executive Director. The Executive Director shall have the authority and responsibility, where circumstances warrant, to inquire of any Executive agency as to the existence of further records that may be assassination materials beyond those made available by that agency, to obtain access to such records, and to recommend that the Review Board subpoena such records in the event of denial of such access.

(b) EXECUTIVE DIRECTOR RESPONSIBILITY- . The Executive Director shall have responsibility for reviewing all records that are made available by Executive agencies, including the National Archives, pursuant to subsection 7(a).

(c) CONSULTATION BY EXECUTIVE DIRECTOR -. The Executive Director may consult with the originating body for advice and information in reaching a decision with respect to the disclosure or nondisclosure of assassination materials.

(d) PRESUMPTION FOR RELEASE.- In the absence of clear and convincing evidence that an assassination material or particular information within an assassination material falls within the exemptions established in section 6 of this Joint Resolution, the Executive Director shall direct that the assassination material or particular information be released pursuant to subsection 7(e)(1).

(e) EXECUTIVE DIRECTOR DECISION — After review of each record, the Executive Director shall, as soon as practicable after the date of enactment of this Joint Resolution, either —

(1) notify the originating body or bodies that the record is assassination material that is appropriate for release in its entirety pursuant to the standards established in this Joint Resolution. In such event, the Executive Director shall transmit the record to the Archivist and the Archivist shall make the record available for inspection and appropriate copying by the public, unless within 30 calendar days of notification an originating body files a notice of appeal with the Review Board. PROVIDED that any record that, in the judgment of the Executive Director, arguably falls within subsection 6(2), shall automatically be referred to the Review Board pursuant to subsection 7 (e) (2) (D); or

(2) refer the record to the Review Board, accompanied by a written determination, indicating one of the following:

> (A) that, in the Executive Director's judgment, the record is not assassination material;
> (B) that, in the Executive Director's judgment, the record is assassination material that qualifies for postponement of disclo sure under Section 6 or contains particular information that qualifies for postponement of disclosure under Section 6;
> (C) that full Review Board investigation and/or Review Board judgment appears appropriate for a determination as to whether the record or particular information in the record qualifies for postponement of disclosure under sec. 6 and thus that this determination shall be vested in the Review Board rather than the Executive Director; or
> (D) that, in the Executive Director's judgment, the record arguably falls within subsection 6(2) and thus that the determi nation as to whether the record qualifies for postponement of disclosure shall be vested in the Review Board rather than the Executive Director.

SEC. 8. DETERMINATIONS BY THE REVIEW BOARD.

(a) APPEALS AND REFERRALS — The Review Board shall review and apply the standards for release set forth in this Joint Resolution to

(1) all records that are the subject of appeals pursuant to Sec. 7(e)(1); and

(2) all records referred to the Review Board by the Executive Director pursuant to Sec. 7(e)(2).

(b) PRESUMPTION FOR RELEASE.- In the absence of clear and convincing evidence that an assassination material or particular information within an assassination material falls within the exemptions established in section 6 of this Joint Resolution, the Board shall direct that the assassination material or particular information be released pursuant to subsection 8(h).

(c) POWERS.- The Review Board shall have authority to hold hearings, administer oaths, and subpoena witnesses and documents, and its subpoenas may be enforced in any appropriate Federal court by the Department of Justice acting pursuant to a lawful request of the Review Board.

(d) ADDITIONAL MATERIALS.- The Review Board shall have the authority to inquire of any Executive agency as to the existence of further records that may be assassination materials beyond those made available by that agency and to use its subpoena power in support of this authority.

(e) WITNESS IMMUNITY.- The Review Board shall be considered an agency of the United States for purposes of section 6001 of title 18, United States Code.

(f) REVIEW BOARD DETERMINATIONS — After review of each record, the Review Board shall determine whether such record is assassination material, and, if so, whether such assassination material, or particular information in the assassination material, qualifies for postponement of disclosure pursuant to section 6. Any reasonably segragable particular information in an assassination material shall be considered for release after deletion of information in that assassination material that qualifies for postponement of disclosure. Where an entire assassination material qualifies for postponement of disclosure pursuant to section 6, the Board may, after consultation with the originating body and if consistent with and to the extent consistent with section 6, create and prepare for release a summary of the assassination material in order to provide for the fullest disclosure feasible. When particular information in an assassination material qualifies for postponement of disclosure pursuant to section 6, the Board may, after consultation with the originating body and if consistent with and to the extent consistent with section 6, create and prepare for release appropriate substitutions for that information in order to provide for the fullest disclosure feasible.

(g) DECISIONS TO POSTPONE — Where the Board determines that a record is not assassination material, or that a record, or particular information in the record, qualifies for postponement of disclosure pursuant to section 6, the

Board shall transmit to the originating body written notice of such determination, together with a copy of the record at issue, and, if the originating body is an Executive agency, a copy of such notice and of the record shall be transmitted to the Committee _____ of the House of Representatives and the Select Committee on Intelligence of the Senate. Such notice shall contain a statement of the reason or reasons for the Board's decision. Any decision of the Board that a record is not assassination material, or that disclosure of a record or particular information in a record should be postponed pursuant to section 6, shall not be subject to judicial review.

(h) DECISIONS TO RELEASE

(1) NON-EXECUTIVE AGENCY MATERIAL — In the case of records for which the originating body is the Warren Commission, the House Committee, or the Senate Committee, where the Review Board determines that a record is assassination material, and that a record, particular information in a record, a summary of a record, or a substitution for particular information in a record is appropriate for release pursuant to this Joint Resolution, the Review Board shall transmit the record, particular information, summary, or substitution to the Archivist, and the Archivist shall make such record, particular information, summary, or substitution available for inspection and copying by the public. The Review Board's decision to release shall not be subject to review by the President or any other entity of the Government and shall not be subject to judicial review.

(2) EXECUTIVE AGENCY MATERIAL—In the case of records for which the originating body is an Executive agency, excluding the Warren Commission, where the Review Board determines that a record, particular information in a record, a summary of a record, or a substitution for particular information in a record is appropriate for release pursuant to this Joint Resolution, the Review Board shall transmit to the originating body written notice of its determination. In such event, the Review Board shall transmit the record, particular information, summary, or substitute to the Archivist, and the Archivist shall make such material available for inspection and appropriate copying by the public, unless, within 60 days of the date on which the Board has notified the originating body, the President has certified to the Review Board and the Archivist that the material qualifies for postponement of disclosure pursuant to section 6, in which case release of the material shall be postponed, and this decision shall not be subject to judicial review. The President shall not delegate this authority to any other official or entity.

(i) PRESIDENTIAL NOTICE TO CONGRESSIONAL COMMIT-TEES—Whenever the President makes a certification pursuant to subsection 8(h)(2), the President shall submit to the Committee _____ of the House of Representatives and the Select Committee on Intelligence of the Senate a written statement setting forth the reason or reasons for superseding the Board's determination and a complete copy of the material at issue.

(j) BOARD NOTICE TO PUBLIC—Every 60 days, beginning 60 days after the date on which the Review Board first postpones release of any assassination material pursuant to section 8(g), the Board shall make available for public inspection and copying a notice of all such postponements determined over the 60-day period, including a description of the size and nature of each assassination material concerned and the ground or grounds for postponement.

(k) PRESIDENTIAL NOTICE TO PUBLIC—In any case in which a determination of the Board to release assassination material is superseded by the President pursuant to this subsection, the President shall within 10 days publish in the Federal Register notice of such action, including a description of the size and nature of the assassination material concerned and the ground or grounds for postponement.

(l) IMMUNITY FROM SUIT.—No person shall have a cause of action against members, employees or detailees of the Review Board arising out of any action of failure to act with regard to assassination material under this Joint Resolution.

(m) RULES OF THE HOUSE OF REPRESENTATIVES AND SEN-ATE.—That portion of subsection 8(h)(1) that permits the Review Board to release materials for which the originating body is the House Committee of the Senate Committee without the concurrence or approval of any congressional body is enacted by the Congress—

(1) as an exercise of the rulemaking power of the House of Representatives and the Senate, respectively, and as such is deemed a part of the rules of each House, respectively, and such procedures supersede other rules only to the extent that they are inconsistent with such other rules; and

(2) with the full recognition of the constitutional right of either House to change the rules (so far as relating to the procedures of that House) at any time, in the same manner, and to the same extent as any other rule of that House.

SEC. 9—MARKING AND REVIEW OF MATERIALS THE DISCLO-SURE OF WHICH IS POSTPONED—

(a) MARKING—With respect to each assassination material or particular information in assassination material the disclosure of which is postponed pursuant to section 8, or for which only substitutions or summaries have been released to the public pursuant to subsection 8(h), the Review Board shall append to the material (i) all records of proceedings conducted pursuant to this Joint Resolution and relating to the material and (ii) a statement of the Review Board designating, based on a review of the proceedings and in conformity with the decisions reflected therein, a specified time at which or a specified occurrence following which the material may appropriately be reconsidered for release pursuant to the standards established in this Joint Resolution. The Review Board shall then transfer the material and appendices to the Archivist for placement in the Archives under seal.

(b) REVIEW.—The sealed assassination materials transferred by the Review Board pursuant to this section shall remain subject to the standards for release established by this Joint Resolution. It shall be the continuing duty of the Archivist to review the sealed assassination materials and the documents appended thereto pursuant to this section and to resubmit assassination materials to the Review Board, if it is still in existence, or to the originating body, or the Review Board has been abolished, whenever it appears to the Archivist that review may be appropriate.

SEC. 10. DISCLOSURE OF OTHER MATERIALS AND ADDITIONAL STUDY.

(a) MATERIALS UNDER SEAL OF COURT.-

(1) The Review Board may request the Department of Justice to petition, or through its own counsel petition, any court in the United States or abroad to release any information relevant to the assassination of President John F. Kennedy that is held under seal of the court.

(2) (A) The Review Board may request the Attorney General to petition, or through its own counsel petition, any court in the united States to release any information relevant to the assassination of President John F. Kennedy that is held under the injunction of secrecy of a grand jury. (B) A request for disclosure of assassination materials under this Joint Resolution shall be deemed to constitute a showing of particularized need under Rule 6 of the Federal Rules of Criminal Procedure.

(b) AUTOPSY MATERIALS — The Review Board shall, pursuant to the terms of the applicable deed of gift, seek access tot eh autopsy photographs and x-rays donated to the National Archives by the Kennedy family under the deed of gift. The Review Board shall, as soon as practicable, submit to the Committee _____ of the House and the Select Committee on Intelligence of the Senate a report on the status of these materials and on access to these materials by individuals consistent with the deed of gift.

(c) SENSE OF CONGRESS.- It is the sense of Congress that-

(1) The Attorney General should assist the Review Board in good faith to unseal any records that the Review Board determines to be relevant and held under seal by a court or under the injunction of secrecy of a grand jury;

(2) The Secretary of State should contact the government of the Republic of Russia and seek the disclosure of all records of the government of the former Soviet Union, including the records of the Komitet Gosudarstvennoy Bezopasnosti (KGB) and the Glavnoye Razvedyvatalnoye Upravleniye (GRU), relevant to the assassination of President Kennedy, and contact any other foreign government that may hold information relevant to the assassination of President Kennedy and seek disclosure of such information;

(3) all Executive agencies should cooperate in full with the Review Board to seek the disclosure of all information relevant to the assassination of President John F. Kennedy consistent with the public interest.

SEC. 11. RULES OF CONSTRUCTION.

(a) PRECEDENCE OVER OTHER LAW.- (1) Where this Joint Resolution requires release of a record, it shall take precedence over any other law, judicial decision construing such law, or common law doctrine that would otherwise prohibit such release.

(b) FREEDOM OF INFORMATION ACT.- Nothing in this Joint Resolution shall be construed to eliminate or limit any right to file requests with any Executive agency other than the Review Board or seek judicial review of the decisions of such agencies pursuant to section 552 of title 5, United States Code.

(c) EXISTING AUTHORITY.- Nothing in this Joint Resolution revokes or limits the existing authority of the President, any Executive agency, the Senate, or the House of Representatives, or any other entity of the Government to release records in its possession.

SEC. 12. TERMINATION OF EFFECT OF JOINT RESOLUTION.

The provisions of this Joint Resolution which pertain to the appointment and operation of the Review Board shall cease to be effective when the Review Board and the terms of its members have terminated pursuant to subsection 5(m). The remaining provisions of this Joint Resolution shall continue in effect until such time as the Archivist certifies to the President and the Congress that all assassination materials have been made available to the public in accordance with this Joint Resolution.

SEC. 13. AUTHORIZATION OF APPROPRIATIONS.

(a) IN GENERAL.- There are authorized to be appropriated such sums as are necessary to carry out this Joint Resolution, to remain available until expended.

(b) INTERIM FUNDING.- Until such time as funds are appropriated pursuant to subsection (a), the President may use such sums as are available for discretionary use to carry out this Joint Resolution.

SEC. 14. SEVERABILITY.

If any provision of this Joint Resolution or the application thereof to any person or circumstance is held invalid, the remainder of this Joint Resolution and the application of that provision to other persons not similarly situated or to other circumstances shall not be affected by the invalidation.

BIBLIOGRAPHY

Anson, Robert Sam. *"They've Killed the President!"*, New York: Bantam Books, 1975.

Ayers, Bradley Earl. *The War that Never Was*, New York: Bobbs-Merrill, 1976.

Blum, William. *The CIA: A Forgotten History*, London: Zed, 1986.

Blumenthal, Sid with Harvey Yazijian. *Government by Gunplay: Assassination Conspiracy Theories from Dallas to Today*, New York: Signet, 1976.

Bower, Tom. *The Paperclip Conspiracy*, New York: Little Brown, 1987.

Bremer, Milton. *The Garrison Case: A Study in the Abuse of Power*, New York: Potter, 1969.

Coates, James. *Armed and Dangerous*, New York: Hill and Wang, 1987.

Epstein, Edward J. *Counterplot*, New York: Viking, 1968.

————. *Inquest: The Warren Commission and the Establishment of Truth*, New York: Bantam Books, 1966.

————. *Legend: The Secret World of Lee Harvey Oswald*, New York: McGraw-Hill, 1978.

Evica, George Michael. *And We Are All Mortal*, Hartford: University of Hartford Press, 1978.

Feldman, Harold. *"Fifty-one Witnesses: The Grassy Knoll"*, Minority of One, March 1965.

Flammonde, Paris. *The Kennedy Conspiracy: an Uncommissioned Report on the Jim Garrison Investigation*, New York: Meridith, 1969.

Ford, Gerald R. with John Stiles, *Portrait of the Assassin*, New York: Simon & Schuster, 1965.

Garrison, Jim. *A Heritage of Stone*, New York: G.P. Putnam's Sons, 1970; Berkeley, 1972.

————. *On the Trail of the Assassins*, New York: Sheridan Square Press, 1988.

Groden, Robert J. and Harrison Edward Livingstone. *High Treason*, Baltimore: The Conservatory Press, 1989.

Hepburn, James (pseud.). *Farewell America*, Liechtenstein: Frontiers Publishing Co., 1968.

Hinckle, Warren and William W.Turner. *The Fish is Red*, New York: Harper & Row, 1981.

Hunt, Linda. *Secret Agenda*, New York: St. Martin's, 1991.

James, Rosemary, and Jack Wardlaw. *Plot or Politics?*, New Orleans: Pelican, 1967.

Jones, Penn. *The Continuing Inquiry and Forgive My Grief* (Vols. I-IV), Midlothian: The Midlothian Press, 1978.

Kantor, Seth. *Who Was Jack Ruby?*, New York: Everest House, 1978.

Karnow, Stanley. *Vietnam: A History*, New York: Viking, 1983.

Kirkwood, James. *American Grotesque: An Account of the Clay Shaw-Jim Garrison Affair in New Orleans*, New York: Simon & Schuster, 1970.

Kruger, Henrik. *The Great Heroin Coup: Drugs, Intelligence, & International Fascism*, Boston: South End Press, 1980.

Lane, Mark. *Rush to Judgment*, New York: Holt, Rinehart, & Winston, 1966.

———. *A Citizen's Dissent*, New York: Dell, 1975.

———. *Plausible Denial*, New York: Thunder's Mouth Press, 1991.

Lasby, Clarence. *Project Paperclip*, New York: Athanaeum, 1971.

Leek, Sybil, and Bert R. Sugar. *The Assassination Chain*, New York: Corwin Books, 1976.

Lifton, David S. *Best Evidence: Disguise and Deception in the Assassination of John F. Kennedy*, New York: Macmillan Publishing Co., 1980.

McMillan, Priscilla Johnson. *Marina and Lee*, New York: Harper & Row, 1978.

Manchester, William. *The Death of a President: November 20-25, 1963*, New York: Harper & Row, 1967; Popular Library, 1968.

Marchetti, Victor, and John Marks. *The CIA and the Cult of Intelligence*, New York: Alfred A. Knopf, 1974; Dell, 1975.

Marks, John. *The Search for the "Manchurian Candidate": The CIA and Mind Control*, New York: New York Times Books, 1979.

Marrs, Jim. *Crossfire: The Plot that Killed Kennedy*, New York: Carroll and Graf, 1989.

Martin, David C. *Wilderness of Mirrors*, New York: Harper and Row, 1980.

McCoy, Alfred M. *The Politics of Heroin: CIA Complicity in the Global Drug Trade*, New York: Lawrence Hill, 1991.

———, *The Politics of Heroin in Southeast Asia*, New York: Harper & Row, 1972.

Meagher, Sylvia. *Accessories After the Fact: The Warren Commission, the Authorities, and the Report*, New York: Bobbs-Merrill, 1967; Vintage, 1976.

Meagher, Sylvia and Gary Owens. *Master Index to the JFK Assassination Investigations*, Scarecrow Press, 1980.

Melanson, Philip, *Spy Saga: Lee Harvey Oswald and U.S Intelligence*, New York: Praeger, 1990.

Model, Peter, with Robert J. Groden. *JFK: The Case for Conspiracy*, New York: Manor Books, 1976.

Morrow, Robert D. *Betrayal: A Reconstruction of Certain Clandestine Events from the Bay of Pigs to the Assassination of John F. Kennedy*, Chicago: Henry Regnery Co., 1976.

———. *The Senator Must Die*, Los Angele: Roundtable, 1988.

Newman, John M. *JFK & Vietnam: Deception, Intrigue and the Struggle for Power*, New York: Warner Books, 1991.

Noyes, Peter. *Legacy of Doubt*, New York: Pinnacle Books, 1973.

Popkin, Richard H. *The Second Oswald*, New York: Avon Books, 1966.

Powers, Gary, with Curt Gentry. *Operation Overflight*, New York: Holt, Rinehart & Winston, 1970.

Prados, John. *Presidents's Secret Wars: CIA and Pentagon Covert Operations from WWII to Iranscam*, New York: Quill, 1986.

Prouty, Fletcher. *The Secret Team*, Englewood Cliffs, New Jersey: Prentice Hall, 1973.

Ranelagh, John. *The Agency: The Rise and Decline of the CIA*, New York: Simon & Schuster, 1986.

Rappleye, Charles and Ed Becker. *American Mafioso: The Johnny Roselli Story*, New York: Doubleday, 1991.

Report of the President's Commission on the Assassination of President John F. Kennedy, and twenty-six accompanying volumes of Hearings and Exhibits, 1964; published by U.S. Government Printing Office and also Doubleday, McGraw-Hill, Bantam, Popular Library, and Associated Press, 1964.

Report to the President by the Commission on CIA Activities Within the United States (Rockefeller Commission), U.S. Government Printing Office, 1975.

Schlesinger, Arthur. *A Thousand Days: John F. Kennedy in the White House*, Boston: Houghton Mifflin Co., 1965.

Scott, Peter Dale, with Paul Hoch and Russell Stetler. *The Assassinations: Dallas and Beyond: A Guide to Cover-ups and Investigations*, New York: Random House, Vintage Press, 1976.

Scott, Peter Dale, Paul L. Hoch, and Josiah Thompson. *Beyond Conspiracy*, Unpublished manuscript, 1979.

Scott, Peter Dale. *The Dallas Conspiracy*, Unpublished manuscript, 1971.

Shaw, J. Gary with Larry R. Harris. *Coverup*, Cleburne, TX, self-published, 1976

Simpson, Christopher. *Blowback*, New York: Weidenfield & Nicolson, 1988.

Summers, Anthony. *Conspiracy*, New York: McGraw-Hill Book Co., 1980.

The Third Decade, c/o Dr. Jerry Rose, SUNY-Fredonia College, Fredonia, NY 14063.

Thompson, Josiah. *Six Seconds in Dallas: A Microstudy of the Kennedy Assassination,* New York: Bernard Geis Associates, 1967; (rev.) Berkeley, 1976.

Torbitt, William (pseud.), *Nomenclature of an Assassination Cabal,*self-published, 1970.

U.S. House of Representatives, *Report of the Select Committee on Assassinations and twelve accompanying volumes of Hearings and Appendices,* U.S. Government Printing Office, 1979.

U.S. Sentate, Select Committee to Study Governmental Operations, with Respect to Intelligence Activities, *Alleged Assassination Plots Involving Foreign Leaders, Interim Report,* Washington, D.C.: U.S. Government Printing Office, 1975.

Weberman, A.J. and Michael Canfield. *Coup d'Etat in America,* New York: Third Press, 1975.

Weisberg, Harold. *Oswald in New Orleans: Case for Conspiracy with the CIA,* New York: Canyon Books, 1967.

———. *Post-Mortem,* Frederick, Maryland: self-published, 1975.

———. *Whitewash,* (Vols. I-IV), Hyattstown, Maryland: 1965, 1967, self-published; and (Vols. I & II) New York: Dell, 1966-1967.

INFORMATION ON SOURCES

Many of the books on the JFK assassination are out of print. The following book dealers specialize in political assassinations, covert operations and critiques of the mainstream media:

Aries Research/Tom Davis Books
P.O. Box 1107
Aptos, CA 95001-1107

Handy Book Exchange
1762 Avenue Road
Toronto, Ontario
CANADA M5M399
(416) 781-4139

Last Hurrah Book Shop
937 Memorial Avenue
Williamsport, PA 17701
(717) 327-9338

President's Box Books
P.O. Box 1255
Washington, DC 20012
(703) 998-7390

Prevailing Winds Research
P.O. Box 23511
Santa Barbara, CA 93121
(805) 566-8016

Periodicals:
The Third Decade: A Journal of Research on the John F. Kennedy Assassination
State University College
Fredonia, NY 14063

Echoes of Conspiracy
c/o Paul Hoch
1525 Acton Street
Berkeley, CA 94702

Backchannels
P.O. Box 9
Franklin Park, NJ 00823-0009

Covert Actiong Information Bulletin
1500 Massachusetts Avenue, NW
Suite 732
Washington, DC 20005

Lies of Our Times
145 West 4th Street
New York, NY 100012
(212) 254-1061

Extra! (A Publication of Fairness and Accuracy in Reporting)
130 W. 25th Street
New York, NY 10001
(212) 633-6700

Steamshovel Press
5927 Kingsbury
St. Louis, MO 63112

Unclassified (The newspaper of the Association of National Secuirty Alumni)
Suite 704
2001 S St., NW
Washington, DC 20009

Organizations:
Assassination Archives and Research Center
918 F St., NEW
Rm. 509
Washington, DC 20004
(202) 393-1917

Center for Defense Information
1500 Massachusetts Avenue, NW
Suite 500
Washington, DC 20036
(202) 797-0882

Association of National Security Alumni
Suite 704
2001 S St., NW
Washington, DC 20009
(202) 483-9222

WARNER BROS. Presents
In Association with LE STUDIO CANAL +, REGENCY ENTERPRISES and
ALCOR FILMS
An IXTLAN CORPORATION and an A. KITMAN HO Production
An OLIVER STONE Film
KEVIN COSTNER
"JFK"
KEVIN BACON
TOMMY LEE JONES
LAURIE METCALF
GARY OLDMAN
BEATA POZNIAK
MICHAEL ROOKER
JAY O. SANDERS
and SISSY SPACEK,
BRIAN DOYLE-MURRAY, GARY GRUBBS, WAYNE KNIGHT, JO
ANDERSON, VINCENT D'ONOFRIO, PRUITT TAYLOR VINCE
Casting by RISA BRAMON GARCIA and BILLY HOPKINS
and HEIDI LEVITT
Costume Designer MARLENE STEWART
Music by JOHN WILLIAMS
Co-Produced by CLAYTON WILLIAMS
Edited by JOE HUTSHING and PIETRO SCALIA
Production Designer VICTOR KEMPSTER
Director of Photography ROBERT RICHARDSON
Executive Producer ARNON MILCHAN
Based On The Books "ON THE TRAIL OF THE ASSASSINS"
by JIM GARRISON and "CROSSFIRE: THE PLOT
THAT KILLED KENNEDY" by JIM MARRS
Screenplay by OLIVER STONE & ZACHARY SKLAR
Produced by A. KITMAN HO and OLIVER STONE
Directed by OLIVER STONE

Associate Producer	JOSEPH REIDY
Production Manager	CLAYTON TOWNSEND
First Assistant Director	JOSEPH REIDY
Second Assistant Director	JOSEPH R. BURNS
Art Directors	DEREK R. HILL
	ALAN R. TOMKINS
Set Decorator	CRISPIAN SALLIS
Additional Editor	HANK CORWIN
Associate Editor	JULIE MONROE
Post Production Supervisor	BILL BROWN
Executive Music Producer	BUDD CARR
Comptroller	BARBARA-ANN STEIN
Production Coordinator	LEEANN STONEBREAKER
Production Sound Mixer	TOD A. MAITLAND, C.A.S.
Supervising Sound Editors	WYLIE STATEMAN
	MICHAEL D. WILHOIT
Recording Mixers	MICHAEL MINKLER
	GREGG LANDAKER

CAST
(In Order Of Appearance)

Rose Cheramie	SALLY KIRKLAND
Epileptic	ANTHONY RAMIREZ
Zapruder	RAY LePERE
John F. Kennedy—Double	STEVE REED
Jackie Kennedy—Double	JODI FARBER
Nellie Connally—Double	COLUMBIA DUBOSE
Gov. Connally—Double	RANDY MEANS
Jim Garrison	KEVIN COSTNER
Lou Ivon	JAY O. SANDERS
Plaza Witness #1	E.J. MORRIS
Plaza Witness #2	CHERYL PENLAND
Plaza Witness #3	JIM GOUGH
Angry Bar Patron	PERRY R. RUSSO
TV Newsman #1	MIKE LONGMAN
Guy Banister	ED ASNER
Jack Martin	JACK LEMMON
Bill Newman	VINCENT D'ONOFRIO
Lee Harvey Oswald	GARY OLDMAN
Liz Garrison	SISSY SPACEK
Mattie	PAT PERKINS
Jack Ruby	BRIAN DOYLE-MURRAY
Numa Bertel	WAYNE KNIGHT
Bill Broussard	MICHAEL ROOKER

Susie Cox	LAURIE METCALF
Al Oser	GARY GRUBBS
Marina Oswald	BEATA POZNIAK
L.B.J.	TOM HOWARD
L.B.J. voice	JOHN WILLIAM GALT
David Ferrie	JOE PESCI
FBI Spokesman	RON JACKSON
Senator Long	WALTER MATTHAU
Jasper Garrison	SEAN STONE
Virginia Garrison	AMY LONG
Snapper Garrison	SCOTT KRUEGER
Elizabeth Garrison	ALLISON PRATT DAVIS
Lee Bowers	PRUITT TAYLOR VINCE
Sgt. Harkness	RED MITCHELL
Hobo #1	RONALD von KLAUSSEN
Hobo #2	JOHN S. DAVIES
Hobo #3	MICHAEL OZAG
Carlos Bringuier	TONY PLANA
Clay Shaw	TOMMY LEE JONES
Leopoldo	TOMAS MILIAN
Angelo	RAUL ARANAS
Dean Andrews	JOHN CANDY
Prison Guard	JOHN C. MARTIN
Willie O'Keefe	KEVIN BACON
Maitre d'	HENRI ALCIATORE
George DeMohrenschildt	WILLEM OLTMANS
Janet Williams	GAIL CRONAUER
Bill Williams	GARY CARTER
Earlene Roberts	ROXIE M. FRNKA
J.C. Price	ZEKE MILLS
Sam Holland	JAMES N. HARRELL
Dodd	RAY REDD
Jean Hill	ELLEN McELDUFF
Mary Moorman	SALLY NYSTUEN
Julia Ann Mercer	JO ANDERSON
Mercer Interrogators	MARCO PERELLA
	EDWIN NEAL
FBI Agent #1 with Hill	SPAIN LOGUE
FBI Agent #2 with Hill	DARRYL COX
Hill Interrogator	T.J. KENNEDY
Stripper	CAROLINA McCULLOUGH
Earl Warren	JIM GARRISON
Mobster with Broussard	J.J. JOHNSTON
Bolton Ford Dealer	R BRUCE ELLIOTT

Man at Firing Range	BARRY CHAMBERS
Sylvia Odio	LINDA FLORES WADE
Will Fritz	WILLIAM LARSEN
TV Newsman #2	ALEC GIFFORD
French Reporter	ERIC A. VICINI
Russian Reporter	MICHAEL GURIEVSKY
British Reporter	CAROLINE CROSTHWAITE-EYRE
Garrison Receptionist	HELEN MILLER
Coroner	HAROLD HERTHUM
FBI Agent-Frank	WAYNE TIPPIT
X	DONALD SUTHERLAND
General Y	DALE DYE
Colonel Reich	NORMAN DAVIS
Man with Umbrella	ERROL McLENDON
General Lemnitzer	JOHN SEITZ
Board Room Men	BRUCE GELB
	JERRY DOUGLAS
	RYAN MacDONALD
	DUANE GREY
White House Men	GEORGE ROBERTSON
	BAXTER HARRIS
	ALEX RODZI RODINE
	SAM STONEBURNER
Officer Habighorst	ODIN K. LANGFORD
TV Newsman #3	BOB GUNTON
John Chancler	NATHAN SCOTT
Miguel Torres	JORGE FERNANDEZ
Irvin F. Dymond	ROY BARNITT
Bailiff	ALVIN SPICUZZA
Judge Haggerty	JOHN FINNEGAN
Vernon Bundy	WALTER BREAUX
James Teague	MICHAEL SKIPPER
FBI Receptionist	MELODEE BOWMAN
Dr. Peters	I.D. BRICKMAN
Dr. McClelland	JOSEPH NADELL
Dr. Humes	CHRIS ROBINSON
Colonel Finck	PETER MALONEY
Bethesda Doctor	CHRIS RENNA
Army General	DALTON DEARBORN
Admiral Kenney	MERLYN SEXTON
Pathologist #1	STEVE F. PRICE, JR.
Pathologist #2	TOM BULLOCK
Pathologist #3	RUARY O'CONNELL
FBI Agent at Autopsy	CHRISTOPHER KOSICIUKA

A Team Shooter	JOHN RENEAU
B Team Shooter	STANLEY WHITE
Fence Shooter	RICHARD RUTOWSKI
Prisoner Powell	BILL BOLENDER
Patrolman Joe Smith	LARRY MELTON
Carolyn Arnold	CAROL FARABEE
Bonnie Ray Williams.	WILLIE MINOR
Arnold Rowland	TED PENNEBAKER
Marion Baker	BILL PICKLE
Sandra Styles	MYKEL CHAVES
Tippit	PRICE CARSON
Tippit Shooter	GIL GLASGOW
Officer Poe	BOB ORWIG
Jury Foreman	LOYS BERGERON
Reporter	KRISTINA HARE
Stand-In for Mr. Costner	MARK THOMASON

CREW

Camera Operator	PHILIP PFEIFFER
First Assistant Camera	DONALD C. CARLSON
First Assistant-B Camera	ROBERT C. CARLSON
Second Assistant Camera	FAIRES KURIYAKIN ANDERSON
Second Assistant-B Camera	DAN TUREK
Loader	RICHARD SOBIN
Video Assist	MARTY KASSAB
Steadicam Operator	JAMES MURO
Still Photographer	SIDNEY BALDWIN
Additional Operators	MICHAEL McCLARY
	JERRY G. CALLAWAY
Boom Operator	TERENCE J. O'MARA
C.A.S. Utility Sound	DAVID ROBERTS
Sound Mixer-Dealey Plaza	BILL DALY
Video Playback	PETER J. VERRANDO
Technical Assistant to Mr. Stone	RICHARD RUTOWSKI
Script Supervisor	SUSAN MALERSTEIN
2nd Second Assistant Director	DEBORAH LUPARD
First Assistant Editor	F. PAUL BENZ
Second Assistant Editor	DEVON MILLER
Optical Supervisor	MILLER DRAKE
Assistant Editors	KATE CROSSLEY
	TATIANA S. RIEGEL
	MARIA SCHAAB
	GINA SILANO

Apprentice Editors	LOGAN BREIT
	CHRIS INNIS
Key Hairstylist	ELLE ELLIOTT
Hairstylists	BONNIE CLEVERING
	RON SCOTT
	MARTHA BERESFORD
	DEBORAH MILLS GUSMANO
Key Makeup	RON BERKELEY
Makeup	CRAIG BERKELEY
	WADE DAILY
	ELAINE THOMAS
	CASSANDRA SCOTT
Hair & Makeup for Ms. Spacek	KELVIN TRAHAN
Special Prosthetic Effects	FXSMITH INC.
Costume Supervisor	DAN BRONSON
Assistant Costume Designer	LISA LOVAAS
Costumers	FRAN ALLGOOD
	GAIL BIXBY
	JENNIFER DIXON
Stunt Coordinator	WEBSTER WHINERY
Key Grip	CHRIS CENTRELLA
Best Boy Grip	JEFF KLUTTZ
Dolly Grip	KEN DAVIS
Chief Lighting Technician	RAY PESCHKE
Assistant Chief Lighting Technician.	FRANK SCHEIDBACH
Rigging Gaffer	JOHN BROOK SHOEMAKER
Assistant Art Directors	MARGERY Z. GABRIELSON
	COLIN D. IRWIN
	MICHAEL RIZZO
Art Dept. Coordinator-Dallas	TANA BISHOP
Art Dept. Coordinator-New Orleans	KELLY CURLEY
Research Coordinator	JANE RUSCONI
Research Assistant	THOMAS HAYSLIP
Set Designer	MARY FINN
Graphics	CYNTHIA PATER
Set Dressing Lead-Dallas	PHIL SHIREY
Set Dressing Lead-New Orleans	FRANK HENDRICK, JR.
On-set Dressers	SCOTT ROSENSTOCK
	AMY SHAFF
Assistant Set Decorators	ALICE BAKER
	DAVIDSCHLESINGER
	GEORGE R. TOOMER, JR.

Swing Gang	LANCE CHEATHAM
	JIM WILLIAMS
	JEFF TAYLOR
	JASON PERLANDER
	ULYSSES FRED
Set Dressers	STEPHANIE EMERY
	MANDY BROU
	JAMIE MAHEU
	DAVID McGRATH
Property Master	J. GREY SMITH
Props	TOM WRIGHT
	BARBY KIRK
	TRAVIS WRIGHT
Music Editor	KEN WANNBERG
Assistant Music Editor	FABIENNE RAWLEY
Orchestrator	JOHN NEUFELD
ADR Supervisor	AVRAM D. GOLD
ADR Editors	MARY ANDREWS
	JERELYN HARDING
Foley Editors	SANDY BERMAN
	MEREDITH GOLD
	MARK PAPPAS
ADR Mixer	CHARLEEN RICHARDS
Foley Artists	DAN O'CONNELL
	ALICIA STEVENSON
Foley Mixer	GREG ORLOFF
Additional Audio	LON BENDER
	KIM WAUGH
	DAVID YOUNG
Sound Effects Editors	SCOTT MARTIN GERSHIN
	JAY RICHARDSON
	MARK LANZA
Dubbing Editor	KELLY OXFORD
Dialogue Editors	DAN RICH
	BOB NEWLAN
	RICHARD DWAN
	DAVID A. ARNOLD
	CHRISTOPHER ASSELLS
	MARK GORDON
	ALISON FISHER
	WILLY ALLEN
	HUGO WENG

Assistant Sound Editors	ROBERT BATHA
	ELIZABETH KENTON
	BOB BOWMAN
	LINDA YEANEY
	KURT COURTLAND
Apprentice Sound Editors	JOHN RICE
	JUDSON LEACH
Recordist	MARK "FRITO" LONG
Machine Operators	CHRIS MINKLER
	BOB HILE
Engineer	JOSEPH A. BRENNAN
Casting Associates	SUZANNE SMITH
	MARY VERNIEU
	JUEL BESTROP
	MELANIE TRAYLOR
Location Casting-Dallas	KRIS NICOLAU
Casting Assistant-Dallas	AMY LEVY LANCASTER
Location Casting-New Orleans	SANDRA DAWES
Casting Assistants-New Orleans	DAVE LEBLANC
	ROSE MARIE PUGLIA
Casting Assistant-New York	ANN GOULDER
Extras Casting-Dallas	KEVIN HOWARD
Asst. Prod. Coordinator-Dallas	STEVEN MCAFEE
Asst. Prod. Coordinator-New Orleans	MARGARET LANCASTER
Production Secretaries	LIAM FINN
	LORING SUMNER
L.A. Office Manager	ART TIZON
Location Auditor	MARGARET ANN McCOURT
Assistant Auditors	LISA D. KAUFMAN
	PETER McMANUS
	JERRI WHITEMAN
Naijo No Ko	ELIZABETH STONE
Assistant to Mr. Stone	KRISTINA HARE
Assistant to Mr. Ho	HAYDN REISS
Assistant to Mr. Costner	MOIRA McLAUGHLIN
Assistant to Mr. Milchan	SHAUNA BEAL
Location Managers-Dallas	JEFF FLACH
	PATRICIA ANNE DOHERTY
Location Manager-New Orleans	SARAH WHISTLER
Location Manager-Washington D.C.	PEGGY PRIDEMORE
Asst. Location Manager-Dallas	SANDRA PALACIOS-PLUGGE
Asst. Location Manager-New Orleans	GARY HUCKABAY
Site Coordinator-Dealey Plaza	CINDY NELSON
Unit Publicist	ROGER ARMSTRONG

Publicity	ANDREA JAFFE & ASSOCIATES
	M/S BILLINGS PUBLICITY, LTD.
Producers' Representative....................................	ARTHUR MANSON
Set Production Assistants....................................	TINA STAUFFER
	DANIEL BURNS
	JUAN ROS
	DAVE VENGHAUS
	JULIE HERRIN
Construction Coordinator....................................	RODNEY ARMANINO
Construction Foremen	LARRY LANGLEY
	JACK KOSTELNIK
Gang Bosses	DONALD E. KERNS
	BENNIE F. MILES, JR.
	JOHN PATTERSON
Construction Shop Manager	JEFF SULLIVAN
Lead Scenic Artist..	DALE HAUGO
Scenic Artist..	JOHN A. KELLY
Master Sign Writer-Dallas..................................	BRUCE KERNER
Stand-by Painter	BILL DARROW
Location Catering by......................................	GALA CATERING
Craft Service	KAYLA CHAILLOT
Mr. Oldman's Dialect Coach................................	TIMOTHY MONICH
Dialect Coaches	CARLA MEYER
	BROOKS BALDWIN
	ELENA BARANOVA
Production Physician	DR. CHRISTIAN RENNA
Technocrane Operator	SIMON JAYES
Transportation Coordinator.................................	ALVIN MILLIKEN, SR.
Transportation Captain	DAN DICKERSON
Transportation Captain-New Orleans..........................	WILLIAM B. BORGES
Picture Car Coordinator-New Orleans.........................	TUTT ESQUERRE
Negative Cutting	DONAH BASSETT
Color Timers	DALE CALDWELL
	DAVID ORR
Post Production Interns	SAAR KLEIN
	KURT A. SATERBAK
A.F.I. Intern..	KEITH SMITH
Sound Editing by	SOUNDELUX
Production Equipment provided by...........................	KEYLITE, PSI
Archival Sound Restoration by	POST SOUND CORP.
Color by	DUART FILM LABS
Answer Print Timing	DELUXE ®
Prints by	TECHNICOLOR ®

Titles & Opticals by ....PACIFIC TITLE

TECHNICAL ADVISORS:
NUMA V. BERTEL, JR., BOB BREALL, HOWARD K. DAVIS, DALE DYE, ROBERT GRODEN, ROY HARGRAVES, GERALD P. HEMMINGS, JR., LARRY HOWARD, DR. MARION JENKINS, RON LEWIS, DAVID LIFTON, JIM MARRS, JOHN NEWMAN, BEVERLY OLIVER, COL. L. FLETCHER PROUTY, ELLEN RAY, FRANK RUIZ, GUS RUSSO, PERRY RUSS, BOB SPIEGELMAN, JOHN R. STOCKWELL, CYRIL H. WECHT, M.D., J.D., STANLEY WHITE, TOM WILSON

PRODUCTION ASSISTANTS:
NICHOLAS IRWIN, DAN KARKOSKA, BRAD KELLER, TAMMY McGLYNN, BILL POAGUE, JOHN SEKULA, JOEY STEWART, CALVIN WIMMER, JOLETA BISHOP, MICHAEL JOHNSON, MELISSA JAMES, STEVE BRENNAN, DAVID NUELL JOHNSON, RON TOWERY, TRAVIS MANN, NICK SPETSIOTIS, MAX SALASSI, PATRICK PARRINO, ELSTON HOWARD, JONATHAN ABRAMS

ARCHIVAL FOOTAGE PROVIDED BY
Zapruder Film: "Copyright 1967" by LMH Company. All Rights Reserved. NBC News Archives; CBS News; UCLA Film and Television Archive; The Family of Orville O. Nix; Sherman Grindberg Film Libraries; Southern Methodist University through its Southwest Film/Video Archives; National Archives; Cartoon Clip Courtesy of Warner Bros. Inc.

SPECIAL THANKS TO
Manierre Dawson paintings loaned by Timothy A. Foley/Tilden-Foley Gallery, New Orleans, LA; National Park Service, National Capital Region and United States Park Police; Vintage radio and police equipment provided by Ken Scott Communications, St. Ignatius, Montana; Michael W. Proscia; Julie Shapiro, Travelcorps; University of North Texas; and the people of Dallas and New Orleans, Tim Morrison Principal Trumpet, (Boston Pops Orchestra) .

"DRUMMERS' SALUTE"
Arranged by D.G. McCroskie
Performed by The Royal Scots Dragoon Guards
Courtesy of Fiesta Records Co. Inc.

"TV JAM"
Written and Performed by Tom Hajdu and Andy Milburn
Courtesy of tomandandy music

"MUSKRAT RAMBLE"
Written by Edward Ory and Ray Gilbert
Performed by "Dr. Henry Levine's Barefoot Dixieland Philharmonic"
Courtesy of RCA Records Label of BMG Music

"FRANCIS BLUES"
Written and Performed by Sidney Bechet
Courtesy of Vogue Records

"SMALL DARK CLOUDS"
Written and Performed by Ed Tomney

"ON THE SUNNY SIDE OF THE STREET"
Written by Dorothy Fields and Jimmy McHugh
Performed by Sidney Bechet
Courtesy of da music/Black Lion

"SCRATCH MY HIDE"
"TRIBAL CONSCIOUSNESS"
"ODE TO BUCKWHEAT"
Written and Performed by Brent Lewis
From the recording: Earth Tribe Rhythms
Courtesy of Ikauma Records

"A STRANGER ON EARTH"
Written by Sid Feller and Rick Ward
Performed by Dinah Washington
Courtesy of Capitol Recordsby arrangement with CEMA Special Markets

"EL WATUSI"
Written and Performed by Ray Barretto
Courtesy of Tico Records/Sonido Inc.

"CUBANITO"
Written by Luis Pla
Performed by Valladares y Su Conjunto
Courtesy of Kubaney Publ. Corp.

"MY BUCKET'S GOT A HOLE IN IT"
Written by Clarence Williams
Performed by Jim Robinson
Courtesy of Atlantic Recording Corp.
by arrangement with Warner Special Products

"MAYBE SEPTEMBER"
Written by Percy Faith, Jay Livingston and Ray Evans
Performed by Tony Bennett
Courtesy of Columbia Records by arrangement with Sony Music Licensing

"TEQUILA"
Written by Chuck Rio
Produced by Barry Fasman

"CONCERTO No. 2 FOR HORN &
ORCHESTRA, K.417: I-ALLEGRO MAESTOSO"
Written by Wolfgang Amadeus Mozart
Performed by Dale Clevenger and the
Franz Liszt Chamber Orchestra, Janos Rolla, Leader
Courtesy of Sony Classical by arrangement with Sony Music Licensing

"KOKYO"
Written by Leonard Eto
Performed by Kodo
Courtesy of Sony Records by arrangement with Sony Music Licensing

Soundtrack Album on Elektra Records, Cassettes & CDs

Filmed in Panavision PANAVISION LOGO ®

DOLBY STEREO (SR) (logo)
In Selected Theatres

Approved #31561   (emblem)   (IATSE LABEL)
Motion Picture Association of America, Inc.

Filmed on location in New Orleans, Dallas and Washington D.C.

Distributed by Warner Bros. (logo) A Time Warner Company

**Michael Caine John Cleese
Eric Bentley John Houseman
Michael Chekhov John Patrick Shanley
Cicely Berry John Russell Brown
Jerry Sterner Steve Tesich
Harold Clurman Sonia Moore
Bruce Joel Rubin Jonathan Miller
Josef Svoboda Terry Jones
Stephen Sondheim Larry Gelbart**

TERMINATOR 2
Judgment Day
The Book of the Film

**An Illustrated Screenplay
by James Cameron
and William Wisher**
Introduction by James Cameron

*A landmark presentation of an action classic.
Special features include:*

Over 700 photos

Including 16 page of color

Plus

Altered and deleted scenes

The complete screenplay

The original storyboards

Over 100 detailed production notes

336 pages • ISBN: 1-55783-097-5

A HILL/OBST PRODUCTION FROM TRI-STAR PICTURES

THE FISHER KING
The Book of the Film
directed by Terry Gilliam

Screenplay written by
Richard LaGravenese

Terry Gilliam, the internationally acclaimed director of *Brazil* and *Time Bandits,* now investigates one man's attempt to redeem himself from a life of fatal cynicism through his unlikely alliance with a visionary street person.

The Applause Book of the Film includes

- The complete screenplay by Richard LaGravenese in professional screenwriter's format.

- Photographs from the film.

- Extensive interviews with Terry Gilliam and Robin Williams.

- An afterword by Richard LaGravenese detailing the writing and production history of the film.

- An annotated appendix of deleted and altered scenes, illustrating the evolution of the film.

Paper • ISBN: 1-55783-098-3

JACOB'S LADDER
by Bruce Joel Rubin
(the Oscar-winning writer of GHOST)

"Like *Ghost*, Rubin's mega-hit of last summer, *Jacob's Ladder* is a contemplation of life and death ... Rubin, the hottest new screenwriting talent ... in a personal essay, documents the emotional highs and lows that accompany the writer's existence in Hollywood ..."

—ALA BOOKLIST

"...The screenplay moves from the nightmarish to the visionary ... page for page, it is one of the very few screenplays I've read with the power to consistently raise hackles in broad daylight ... READ IT. IT'S EXTRAORDINARY." —AMERICAN FILM

"One of the most original and powerful screenplays to be seen in Hollywood in years ... One feels in the hands of a benevolent and sophisticated storyteller."

—CINEFANTASTIQUE

—HIGHLIGHTS—

- Jacob's Chronicle," Bruce Joel Rubin's book-length essay tracing the script's odyssey to the screen.
- The complete final shooting script in professional screenwriter's format
- Annotated appendix of deleted scenes
- Over 100 stills from the film

paper • ISBN: 1-55783-086-X

APPLAUSE
SCREENPLAY SERIES

LOSING THE
LIGHT

TERRY GILLIAM AND THE
MUNCHAUSEN ADVENTURE
BY ANDREW YULE

Heaven's Gate, by comparison, was a party in paradise. Some of cinema's most legendary artists–renowned for their work with Fellini, Godard, Fassbinder, and Herzog among others–would unwittingly unite to create the greatest financial disaster in movie history: *The Adventures of Baron Munchausen.* Andrew Yule, celebrated observer of Hollywood and author of *Fast Fade: David Puttnam and the Battle for Hollywood,* goes behind the scenes of Gilliam's epic. Yule unravels the contorted drama which saw the original budget of $23.5 million rocket to an astronomical $50 million–making it one of the most expensive features in history.

THE ACTOR AND THE TEXT
by Cicely Berry

As voice director of the Royal Shakespeare Company, Cicely Berry has worked with actors such as Jeremy Irons, Derek Jacobi, Jonathan Pryce, Sinead Cusack and Antony Sher. *The Actor and The Text* brings Ms. Berry's methods of applying vocal production skills within a text to the general public.

While this book focuses primarily on speaking Shakespeare, Ms. Berry also includes the speaking of some modern playwrights, such as Edward Bond.

As Ms. Berry describes her own volume in the introduction:

" … this book is not simply about making the voice sound more interesting. It is about getting inside the words we use …It is about making the language organic, so that the words act as a spur to the sound …"

paper•ISBN 1–155783–138–6

THE LIFE OF THE DRAMA
by Eric Bentley

" ... Eric Bentley's radical new look at the grammar of theater ... is a work of exceptional virtue, and readers who find more in it to disagree with than I do will still, I think, want to call it central, indispensable. ... The book justifies its title by being precisely about the ways in which life manifests itself in the theater. If you see any crucial interest in such topics as the death of Cordelia, Godot's non-arrival ... This is a book to be read and read again."

— Frank Kermode
THE NEW YORK REVIEW OF BOOKS

paper • ISBN: 1-55783-110-6

IN SEARCH OF THEATER

by

Eric Bentley

First published in 1953, *In Search of Theater* is widely regarded as the standard portrait of the European and American theater in the turbulent and seminal years following World War II. The book's influence contributed substantially to the rising reputations of such artists as Bertolt Brecht, Charles Champlin and Martha Graham.

"The most erudite and intelligent living writing on the theatre." —**Ronald Bryden**
THE NEW STATESMAN

"Certainly America's foremost theatre critic . . ." —**Irving Wardle**
THE TIMES

paper • ISBN: 1-55783-111-4

STANISLAVSKI REVEALED
by Sonia Moore

Other than Stanislavski's own published work, the most widely read interpretation of his techniques remains Sonia Moore's pioneering study, *The Stanislavski System*. Sonia Moore is on the frontier again now as she reveals the subtle tissue of ideas behind what Stanislavski regarded as his "major breakthrough," the Method of Physical Actions. Moore has devoted the last decade in her world-famous studio to an investigation of Stanislavski's final technique. The result is the first detailed discussion of Moore's own theory of psychophysical unity which she has based on her intensive practical meditation on Stanislavski's consummate conclusions about acting.

Demolishing the popular notion that his methods depend on private—self-centered—expression, Moore now reveals Stanislavski as the advocate of deliberate, controlled, conscious technique—internal and external at the same time—a technique that makes tremendous demands on actors but that rewards them with the priceless gift of creative life.

Stanislavski Revealed is a completely revised and updated re-assessment of Moore's classic book *Training an Actor*. In addition to detailed descriptions of the exercises she employs in her studio, she now extends Stanislavski's insights to enable playwrights and directors to benefit from his technique.

paper • ISBN: 1-55783-103-3

SHAKESPEARE'S PLAYS IN PERFORMANCE by John Russell Brown

In this volume, John Russell Brown snatches Shakespeare from the clutches of dusty academics and thrusts him centerstage where he belongs—in performance.

Brown's thorough analysis of the theatrical experience of Shakespeare forcibly demonstrates how the text is brought to life: awakened, colored, emphasized, and extended by actors and audiences, designers and directors.

"A knowledge of what precisely can and should happen when a play is performed is, for me, the essential first step towards an understanding of Shakespeare."
—*from the Introduction by John Russell Brown*

paper•ISBN 1-55783-136-X•$14.95

BEST AMERICAN SHORT PLAYS 1991-1992

Edited by Howard Stein and Glenn Young

This edition of Best American Short Plays includes a careful mixture of offerings from many prominent established playwrights, as well as up and coming younger playwrights. This collection of short plays truly celebrates the economy and style of the short play form. Doubtless, a must for any library!

Making Contact by Patricia Bosworth
Dreams of Home by Migdalia Cruz
A Way with Words by Frank D. Gilroy
Prelude and Liebestod by Terrence McNally
Success by Arthur Kopit
The Devil and Billy Markham by Shel Silverstein
The Last Yankee by Arthur Miller
Snails by Suzan-Lori Parks
Extensions by Murray Schisgal
Tone Clusters by Joyce Carol Oates
You Can't Trust the Male by Randy Noojin
Struck Dumb by Jean-Claude van Itallie
and Joseph Chaikin
The Open Meeting by A.R.Gurney

APPLAUSE

OTHER PEOPLE'S MONEY:
The Ultimate Seduction
by Jerry Sterner

"The best new play I've run across all season.
IT WOULD STAND OUT IN ANY YEAR."
—Douglas Watt ,DAILY NEWS

"Epic grandeur and intimate titillation
combined. **IT IS THE MOST
STIMULATING KIND OF
ENTERTAINMENT"**
—John Simon, NEW YORK MAGAZINE

"*Other People's Money* has a HEART OF
IRON which beats about the cannibalistic
nature of big business."
—Mel Gussow, THE NEW YORK TIMES

paper• ISBN 1-55783-061-4
cloth• ISBN 1-55783-062-2

THIRTEEN BY SHANLEY

The Collected Plays, Vol. 1
by John Patrick Shanley

The Oscar–Winning author of
Moonstruck

In this Applause edition of John Patrick Shanley's complete plays, ther reader will intercept one of America's major dramatists in all his many expressive incarnations and moods. His restless poetic spirit takes refuge in a whole array of forms; he impatiently prowls the aisles of comedy, melodrama, tragedy, and farce as he forges an alloy all his own. Fanciful, surreal, disturbing, no other playwright of his generation has so captivated the imagination of the serious American play-going public. In addition to Shanley's sustained longer work, this volume also offers the six short plays wich appear under the title *Welcome to the Moon*.

Applause presents Volume One of Mr. Shanley's complete work as the inaugural volume of its Contemporary Masters series.

ISBN: 1-55783-099-1 $27.95 doth $12.95 paper

SHAKESCENES
SHAKESPEARE FOR TWO
Edited with an Introduction
by John Russell Brown

Shakespeare's plays are not the preserve of "Shakespear-ean Actors" who specialize in a remote species of dramatic life. John Russell Brown offers guidance for those who have little or no experience with the formida-ble Bard in both the Introduction and Advice to Actors, and in the notes to each of the thirty-five scenes.

The scenes are presented in newly-edited texts, with notes which clarify meanings, topical references, puns, ambiguities, etc. Each scene has been chosen for its inde-pendent life requiring only the simplest of stage proper-ties and the barest of spaces. A brief description of char-acters and situation prefaces each scene, and is followed by a commentary which discusses its major acting chal-lenges and opportunities.

Shakescenes are for small classes and large workshops, and for individual study whenever two actors have the opportunity to work together.

From the Introduction:

"Of course, a way of speaking a character's lines meaningfully and clearly must be found, but that alone will not bring any play to life. Shakespeare did not write for talking heads ... Ac-tors need to be acutely present all the time; ... they are like boxers in a ring, who dare not lose concentration or the ability to perform at full power for fear of losing consciousness altogether."

paper • ISBN: 1-55783-049-5

ONE ON ONE

BEST MONOLOGUES FOR THE 90'S
Edited by Jack Temchin

You have finally met your match in Jack Temchin's new collection, **One on One**. Somewhere among the 150 monologues Temchin has recruited, a voice may beckon to you—strange and alluring—waiting for your own voice to give it presence on stage.

"The sadtruth about most monologue books,"says Temchin. "is that they don't give actors enough credit. I've compiled my book for serious actors with a passionate appetite for the unknown."

Among the selections:
Wendy Wasserstein THE SISTERS ROSENSWEIG
David Henry Hwang FACE VALUE
Tony Kushner ANGELS IN AMERICA
Alan Bennett TALKING HEADS
Neil Simon JAKE'S WOMEN
David Hirson LA BETE
Herb Gardner CONVERSATIONS
WITH MY FATHER
Ariel Dorfman DEATH AND THE MAIDEN
Alan Ayckborn A SMALL FAMILY BUSINESS
Robert Schenkkan THE KENTUCKY CYCLE

$7.95•paper
MEN: ISBN 1-55783-151-3•WOMEN: ISBN: 1-55783152-1

SOLILOQUY!
The Shakespeare Monologues
Edited by Michael Earley and Philippa Keil

At last, over 175 of Shakespeare's finest and most performable monologues taken from all 37 plays are here in two easy-to-use volumes (MEN and WOMEN). Selections travel the entire spectrum of the great dramatist's vision, from comedies and romances to tragedies, pathos and histories.

"Soliloquy is an excellent and comprehensive collection of Shakespeare's speeches. Not only are the monologues wide-ranging and varied, but they are superbly annotated. Each volume is prefaced by an informative and reassuring introduction, which explains the signals and signposts by which Shakespeare helps an actor on his journey through the text. It includes a very good explanation of blank verse, with excellent examples of irregularities which are specifically related to character and acting intentions. These two books are a must for any actor in search of a 'classical' audition piece."

ELIZABETH SMITH
Head of Voice & Speech
The Juilliard School

paper-MEN: ISBN 0-936839-78-3 • WOMEN: ISBN 0936839-79-1

MONOLOGUE WORKSHOP

From Search to Discovery
in Audition and Performance
by Jack Poggi

To those for whom the monologue has always been synonymous with terror, *The Monologue Workshop* will prove an indispensable ally. Jack Poggi's new book answers the long-felt need among actors for top-notch guidance in finding, rehearsing and performing monologues. For those who find themselves groping for speech just hours before their "big break," this book is their guide to salvation.

The Monologue Workshop supplies the tools to discover new pieces before they become over-familiar, excavate older material that has been neglected, and adapt material from non-dramatic sources (novels, short stories, letters, diaries, autobiographies, even newspaper columns). There are also chapters on writing original monologues and creating solo performances in the style of Lily Tomlin and Eric Bogosian.

Besides the wealth of practical advice he offers, Poggi transforms the monologue experience from a terrifying ordeal into an exhilarating opportunity. Jack Poggi, as many working actors will attest, is the actor's partner in a process they had always thought was without one.

paper•ISBN 1-55783-031-2

CLASSICAL TRAGEDY
GREEK AND ROMAN: Eight Plays

In Authoritative Modern Translations
Accompanied by Critical Essays

Edited by Robert W. Corrigan

AESCHYLUS	**PROMETHEUS BOUND** translated by David Grene **ORESTEIA** translated by Tony Harrison
SOPHOCLES	**ANTIGONE** translated by Dudley Fitts and Robert Fitzgerald **OEDIPUS THE KING** translated by Kenneth Cavander
EURIPIDES	**MEDEA** translated by Michael Townsend **THE BAKKHAI** translated by Robert Bagg
SENECA	**OEDIPUS** translated by David Anthony Turner **MEDEA** translated by Frederick Ahl

paper • ISBN: 1-55783-046-0

CLASSICAL COMEDY
GREEK AND ROMAN: Six Plays
Edited by Robert W. Corrigan

The only book of its kind: for the first time Greek and Roman masters of comedy meet in this extraordinary new forum devised and edited by a master scholar of comedy himself, Robert Corrigan. Corrigan has enlisted six superb translations to create an unmatched Olympiad of classical comedy.

ARISTOPHANES   **LYSISTRATA**
translated by Donald Sutherland
THE BIRDS
translated by Walter Kerr

MENANDER   **THE GROUCH**
translated by Sheila D'Atri

PLAUTUS   **THE MENAECHMI**
translated by Palmer Bovie
THE HAUNTED HOUSE
translated by Palmer Bovie

TERENCE   **THE SELF-TORMENTOR**
translated by Palmer Bovie

paper • ISBN: 0-936839-85-6

COMMEDIA IN PERFORMANCE SERIES

THE THREE CUCKOLDS
by Leon Katz
paper • ISBN: 0-936839-06-6

THE SON OF ARLECCHINO
by Leon Katz
paper • ISBN: 0-936839-07-4

CELESTINA
by Fernando do Rojas
Adapted by Eric Bentley
Translated by James Mabbe
paper • ISBN: 0-936839-01-5

MEDIEVAL AND TUDOR DRAMA

Twenty-four Plays
Edited and with introductions
by John Gassner

The rich tapestry of medieval belief, morality and manners shines through this comprehensive anthology of the twenty-four major plays that bridge the dramatic worlds of medieval and Tudor England. Here are the plays that paved the way to the Renaissance and Shakespeare. In John Gassner's extensively annotated collection, the plays regain their timeless appeal and display their truly international character and influence.

Medieval and Tudor Drama remains the indispensable chronicle of a dramatic heritage — the classical plays of Hrotsvitha, folk and ritual drama, the passion play, the great morality play *Everyman*, the Interlude, Tudor comedies *Ralph Roister Doister* and *Gammer Gurton's Needle*, and the most famous of Tudor tragedies *Gorboduc*. The texts have been modernized for today's readers and those composed in Latin have been translated into English.

paper • ISBN: 0-936839-84-8

ELIZABETHAN DRAMA
Eight Plays
Edited and with Introductions by
John Gassner and William Green

Boisterous and unrestrained like the age itself, the Elizabethan theatre has long defended its place at the apex of English dramatic history. Shakespeare was but the brightest star in this extraordinary galaxy of playwrights. Led by a group of young playwrights dubbed "the university wits," the Elizabethan popular stage was imbued with a dynamic force never since equalled. The stage boasted a rich and varied repertoire from courtly and romantic comedy to domestic and high tragedy, melodrama, farce, and histories. The Gassner-Green anthology revives the whole range of this universal stage, offering us the unbounded theatrical inventiveness of the age.

Arden of Feversham, **Anonymous**

The Spanish Tragedy, by **Thomas Kyd**

Friar Bacon and Friar Bungay, by **Robert Greene**

Doctor Faustus, by **Christopher Marlowe**

Edward II, by **Christopher Marlowe**

Everyman in His Humour, by **Ben Jonson**

The Shoemaker's Holiday, by **Thomas Dekker**

A Woman Killed with Kindness, by **Thomas Heywood**

paper • ISBN: 1-55783-028-2

LIFE IS A DREAM
and Other SPANISH Classics
Edited by Eric Bentley
Translated by Roy Campbell

LIFE IS A DREAM
by Calderon de la Barca

FUENTE OVEJUNA
by Lope de Vega

THE TRICKSTER OF SEVILLE
by Tirso de Molina

THE SIEGE OF NUMANTIA
by Miguel de Cervantes

paper • ISBN: 1-55783-006-1

ACTING IN RESTORATION COMEDY

Based on the BBC Master Class Series
By Simon Callow

The art of acting in Restoration Comedy, the buoyant, often bawdy romps which celebrated the reopening of the English theatres after Cromwell's dour reign, is the subject of Simon Callow's bold new investigation. There is cause again to celebrate as Callow, one of Britain's foremost actors, aims to restore the form to all its original voluptuous vigor. Callow shows the way to attain clarity and hilarity in some of the most delightful roles ever conceived for the theatre.

Simon Callow is the author of *Being an Actor* and *Charles Laughton: A Difficult Actor*. He has won critical acclaim for his performances in numerous productions including *Faust*, *The Relapse*, and *Titus Andronicus*.

paper • ISBN: 1-55783-119-X

THE ACTOR'S MOLIÈRE

A New Series of Translations for the Stage by

Albert Bermel

THE MISER and GEORGE DANDIN

ISBN: 0-936839-75-9

THE DOCTOR IN SPITE OF HIMSELF and THE BOURGEOIS GENTLEMAN

ISBN: 0-936839-77-5

SCAPIN and DON JUAN

ISBN: 0-936839-80-5

APPLAUSE

THE MISANTHROPE
AND OTHER FRENCH CLASSICS
Edited by Eric Bentley

"I would recommend Eric Bentley's collection to all who really care for theatre."

—Harold Clurman

THE MISANTHROPE
by Molière
English version by Richard Wilbur

PHAEDRA
by Racine
English version by Robert Lowell

THE CID
by Corneille
English version by James Schevill

FIGARO'S MARRIAGE
by Beaumarchais
English version by Jacques Barzun

paper • ISBN: 0-936839-19-8

ANTIGONE
by Bertolt Brecht
A Play
With selections from Brecht's Model Book
Translated by Judith Malina

Sophocles, Hölderlin, Brecht, Malina — four major figures in the world's theatre — they have all left their imprint on this remarkable dramatic text. Friedrich Hölderlin translated Sophocles into German, Brecht adapted Hölderlin, and now Judith Malina has rendered Brecht's version into a stunning English incarnation.

Brecht's *Antigone* is destined to be performed, read and discussed across the English-speaking world.

AVAILABLE FOR THE FIRST TIME IN ENGLISH

paper • ISBN: 0-936839-25-2

THE BRUTE

AND OTHER FARCES
By Anton Chekhov
Edited by Eric Bentley

"INDISPENSABLE!"
— Robert Brustein
Director, Loeb Drama Center
Harvard University

The blustering, stuttering eloquence of Chekhov's unlikely heroes has endured to shape the voice of contemporary theater. This volume presents seven minor masterpieces:

THE HARMFULNESS OF TOBACCO
SWAN SONG
A MARRIAGE PROPOSAL
THE CELEBRATION
A WEDDING
SUMMER IN THE COUNTRY
THE BRUTE

paper • ISBN: 1-55783-004-5

APPLAUSE